Macroeconomic theory and stabilization policy

This book is dedicated to my sister
Hens Buiter
in love and admiration

Macroeconomic theory and stabilization policy

Willem H. Buiter

University of Michigan Press
Ann Arbor

Published in the United States of America by
The University of Michigan Press

1992 1991 1990 1989 4 3 2 1

Library of Congress Cataloging in Publication Data applied for

ISBN 0-472-10138-2

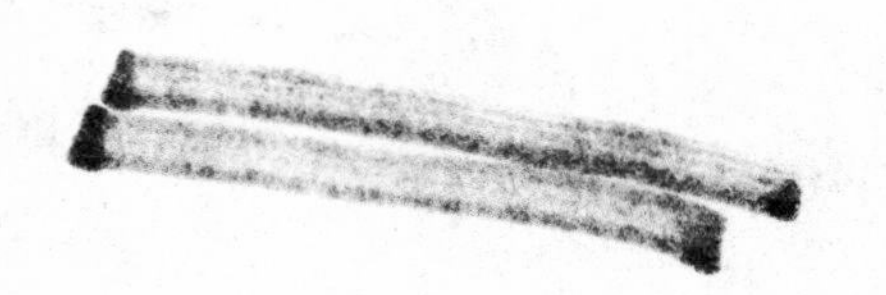

Typeset in Hong Kong
by Graphicraft Typesetters Ltd

Printed in Great Britain
by Biddles Ltd, Guildford and King's Lynn

Contents

Introduction
After the New Classical Macroeconomics

This volume is a collection of papers on macroeconomic theory that I wrote or co-authored and that were published between 1977 and 1988.

Most of the papers that are included can be viewed as a response to the methodological challenge, both theoretical and empirical, of the New Classical Macroeconomics (NCM). This introduction aims to take stock and to evaluate the contribution of the NCM to our understanding of macroeconomic phenomena and to the way in which economic research is conducted. In the hope of stimulating debate, key conclusions are stated bluntly, even provocatively, in the spirit of Lucas and Sargent [1979]. Part I contains some general reflections on the NCM. Part II puts the contributions to this volume in perspective.

I **Some reflections on the New Classical Macroeconomics**

The main innovative theoretical contributions of the creative wave that we now call the NCM (and a few key early empirical papers) were all published during the short period 1972–1978, many of them in the *Journal of Political Economy* and the *Journal of Monetary Economics*. Empirical testing of propositions suggested by the New Classical paradigm became a major growth industry in the late Seventies and is very much alive today. With the possible exception of the theoretical developments now referred to as Real Business Cycle (RBC) theory, the creative theoretical bolt of the NCM had been shot by 1979. Below I shall try to identify some reasons for this failure to maintain the early theoretical momentum.

While the application of any label is subject to both Type I and Type II errors, I believe that the core of the NCM can be summarized in the following list of characteristics.

(1) In New Classical models, private agents (households, consumers, portfolio holders, workers, firms) have *rational expectations* (RE). Their

subjective joint probability distribution functions over current and future endogenous and exogenous variables, conditional on the information at their disposal, are the same as the true objective conditional probability distribution functions, which characterize the models' equilibrium. Inferences of the present and anticipations of the future are 'model-consistent'. Private agents know[1] the true model of the economy (of which they are a (small) part).[2]

(2) The economy is represented by a sequential, competitive general equilibrium model. Competitive market clearing occurs instantaneously. The mechanism that achieves this coordination miracle is not part of the model. An 'auctioneer' is sometimes alluded to, but how he or she achieves market clearing in 'real time' is never made clear.

(3) Often, but by no means always, NCM dynamic competitive economies are Arrow-Debreu economies, i.e. economies with a complete set of state-contingent markets. Such economies can be interpreted as 'one-shot' economies in which all state-contingent prices are established once-and-for all at the initial market date.[3] (Debreu [1959], Arrow [1964])

(4) Within the class of Arrow-Debreu NCM models, a large subset is restricted to the case of a single representative agent.

(5) Information is often imperfect, but never 'asymmetric'. Agents may have incomplete information about current and past exogenous shocks perturbing the system or about current and past values of endogenous variables, such as prices. The parties to any given transaction do, however, have the same (and generally perfect) information about the characteristics of the commodity that is traded. Adverse selection and moral hazard issues therefore do not arise.

(6) In the more abstract models, private behaviour is derived from optimization subject to constraints. Consumers' objective functionals tend to be egoistic (defined over own consumption (including leisure) and sometimes over own real money balances as well). An important exception involving altruistic behaviour will be noted below. Constraints include parametric prices (static and intertemporal), budget constraints (including intertemporal solvency constraints), endowments, transactions technologies and information. Where firms are modelled, they maximize profits (in Arrow-Debreu economies), market value (in stock market economies) or expected profits. Constraints include parametric input and output prices, intertemporal prices, technology and information.

The large number of NCM models without explicit microfoundations based on constrained optimizing behaviour tend to be motivated as reasonable simple parables for more complex models derived from optimizing 'first principles'.

(7) Many NCM models have the 'Natural Rate' property: real equilibrium allocations are independent of fully perceived and/or anticipated changes in the nominal money stock. In its weakest form this amounts to

no more than the homogeneity postulate. Stronger versions include a range of (monetary) policy ineffectiveness or neutrality propositions that require much stronger conditions.

(8) While the behaviour of the policy authorities is often treated as exogenous, an important feature of a number of major contributions to the NCM literature is the derivation of the authorities' decision rules from 'first principles'.

The policymaker pursues her objectives constrained by the inevitable strategic or game-theoretic relationship between a 'large' public sector and the private competitive economy[4] and by the need to pursue a 'dynamically consistent' strategy over time. This 'new political economy' is a very rapidly expanding area of research.

When I date the key theoretical contributions of the NCM between 1972 and 1978, I do not mean to suggest that there were no important antecedents. Muth's seminal paper (Muth [1961]) which formalized the rational expectations hypothesis dates from 1961. While Milton Friedman never used the RE hypothesis, it is hard to visualize the NCM without his 1968 Presidential Address (Friedman [1968]). Lucas and Rapping's [1969] paper was a direct precursor of much subsequent theoretical and empirical work in the NCM tradition. The volume by Phelps *et al.* [1970] is a landmark in the quest for the microfoundations of macroeconomics. What may well be the most important New Classical model 'avant la lettre' of them all, Diamond's [1965] celebrated integration of the Samuelsonian overlapping generations [OLG] model and neoclassical growth theory, with its applications to key issues in debt management and public finance (see also Diamond [1970]) was published in 1965. (Diamond since then has of course gone on to rather different (and in my view even more challenging) things (e.g. Diamond [1982, 1988]).)

Nevertheless, the period 1972–1978 is when the New Classical methodology and policy prescriptions were developed fully in a limited number of key papers.

I can identify eighteen 'core' NCM papers. Six papers by Lucas: Lucas [1972a] 'Expectations and the neutrality of money'; Lucas [1972b] 'Econometric Testing of the Natural Rate Hypothesis'; Lucas [1973] 'Some international evidence on output-inflation trade-offs'; Lucas [1976] 'Econometric Policy Evaluation: A Critique'; Lucas [1977] 'Understanding business cycles' and Lucas [1978] 'Asset prices in an exchange economy'. A paper by Lucas and Prescott [1974] 'Equilibrium search and unemployment'. Two papers by Sargent: 'Rational Expectations, the Real Rate of Interest and the Natural Rate of Unemployment' [1973] and 'The observational equivalence of natural and unnatural rate theories of macroeconomics' [1976b]. Two papers by Sargent and Wallace: 'Rational expectations, the optimal monetary instrument and the optimal money supply rule' [1975] and 'Rational Expectations and the Theory of Economic Policy' [1976]. Four papers by Barro: 'Are government bonds net wealth?' [1974], 'Rational expectations and the role of monetary policy' [1976], 'Unanticipated money growth and unemployment in the United States' [1977a] and 'Long-term contracting, sticky prices and monetary policy' [1977b]. A paper by Kydland and Prescott [1977] 'Rules rather than discretion: the inconsistency of optimal plans', one by Hall [1978] 'Stochastic implications of the life-cycle permanent income hypothesis' and Prescott's review of Phelps' [1972] book *Inflation Policy and Unemployment Theory: The Cost-Benefit Approach to Monetary Planning*, 'Efficiency of the Natural Rate' (Prescott [1975]).

Hall's eclectic approach to economics precludes him from being classified as a New Classical Macroeconomist. The elegant and influential paper on consumption listed above is, however, a key New Classical paper both because it tested and appeared to find support for a representative agent version of the life-cycle or permanent income model and because of the nature of the test (which involved estimating a dynamic first-order condition or 'Euler equation'). This is now a major growth industry, especially in the area of financial economics, but also in other areas which have been approached with models of optimizing representative agents making intertemporal choices.

While there has been nothing in the 1980's to match this creative eruption, NCM methodology and doctrine has continued to grow in scope and range of theoretical and empirical applications. It has become part of the conventional wisdom for much of the profession and indeed the only wisdom in the Fresh-Water Belt of the USA. Intermediate textbooks presenting the NCM paradigm are available (e.g. Barro [1987]). More advanced texts with a high New Classical content such as Sargent [1987a] are on every graduate reading list. An advanced New Classical treatise (Sargent [1987b]) with an (extremely useful) how-to-do-it Supplement (Manuelli and Sargent [1987]) spreads both medium and message. Readers (Lucas and Sargent [1981]), collected essays (Barro [1981] and Lucas [1981]) and non-technical expositions (Lucas [1987]) now abound.

Like the 'Keynesian whale' attacked by Harry Johnson for its oppressive impact on macroeconomic thinking in England during the years following the Second World War, the New Classical Macroeconomics has acquired some of the negative attributes of a dominant paradigm: an uncritical acceptance by many of its adherents of key premises and assumptions; a dismissive and intolerant attitude towards criticism and alternative approaches; the appropriation for its own exclusive use of the label 'serious economics' etc. While, fortunately, some of the leading exponents of the NCM are open-minded, fair and self-critical, there is a threat of the New Classical whale promoting a form of intellectual censorship (or, worse, self-censorship), especially as it affects the younger and more vulnerable members of our profession.

The intellectual ascendancy of the NCM is rather surprising. Dissatisfaction in the early Seventies with the Neo-Keynesian conventional wisdom of the Fifties and Sixties can be explained partly by events external to the economics profession (the 'upward drift' of the Phillips curve; the rise and persistence of stagflation and the perceived failures of conventional demand management; the supply shocks etc.) and partly by the internal pressure of intellectual developments within macroeconomics where there was an intensifying search for 'deep structure' and microfoundations for aggregate economic relationships.

While conventional microeconomic analysis had been incorporated in bits and pieces of the Neo-Keynesian models (the life-cycle and permanent income hypothesis models of consumption; shoe-leather theories of the demand for money; term structure equations based on the expectations hypothesis; flexible accelerator models of investment rationalized through optimal capital accumulation in the presence of costs of adjustment etc.), these models were not grounded comprehensively in individual optimizing behaviour. Wage and price dynamics in particular were generated through some variant of the Phillips curve (sometimes augmented with a sluggishly moving 'core inflation' term), and expectation formation was typically modelled through 'mechanical' distributed lag mechanisms that were (implicitly) assumed to be independent of the stochastic processes (policy, external shocks etc.) driving the economy.

Dissatisfaction with the theoretical specification and forecasting performance of these Neo-Keynesian models is understandable; the emergence of the New Classical alternative, however, is surprising as the intellectual structure of the NCM is a house of cards more deficient and vulnerable than the Neo-Keynesian paradigm that preceded it, although the sources of its weakness are quite different. Consider, briefly, the key ingredients of the New Classical paradigm.

The need for microfoundations for aggregate economic analysis

It is difficult to find many expressions of disagreement with the proposition that aggregate economic relationships should be derived by explicit aggregation of the behaviour of the 'primitive' economic decision units (workers, portfolio holders, consumers (or households), firms etc.). While I am very sympathetic to the quest for microfoundations, the merits of the case are by no means self-evident. In physics, the behaviour of gaseous clouds is not approached via the aggregation of the behaviour of individual gas molecules. Mob behaviour is not in any obvious way expressible as the aggregation of the behaviour of individual yobbos. Also, why terminate the reductionist logic at the level of the individual human agent? Would it not be even more deeply structural to reduce human behaviour further to the behaviour of elementary particles and forces?

Even if methodological individualism is feasible and desirable in principle, the cost of collecting the panel data sets required for empirical implementation may be prohibitive. The possibility that in order to explain and predict aggregate behaviour it is sufficient (or even optimal) to postulate relationships directly at the level of the aggregates, without any reference to individual behaviour, optimizing or other, should be taken seriously. Keynes's [1936] consumption function appears to be motivated this way. The proof of the pudding here too is in the eating. I know of no convincing empirical test of the proposition that aggregate behaviour is always best explained and predicted through the aggregation of individual decision rules (see also Tobin [1978]).

Which microfoundations?

Even granted the desirability of some kind of microfoundations, we are left with a wide choice of competing paradigms. In the NCM, individual rationality is assumed to be the unifying principle and individual rationality is identified with the optimization of well-behaved objective functionals subject to constraints. Plausible alternatives such as the behaviourist approaches of Simon [1979], Cyert and March [1963], Winter [1964], Shiller [1984], Muellbauer [1986], Shefrin and Thaler [1987] etc. are ruled out. Alternative behavioural assumptions derived from psychology, social psychology, anthropology, sociology are not considered (see e.g. Tversky [1977], Tversky and Kahneman [1986]).

There are several problems with the strategy of deriving individual behaviour from individualistic constrained optimization. The first is that at its most general level the approach is vacuous: it does not rule out any kind of observable behaviour. If I am free (subject to mild consistent choice requirements such as transitivity) to choose the objective function and the constraints, any kind of individual behaviour can be rationalized. More than that, even when individual behaviour is generated by optimizing a standard egoistic utility function (defined over own consumption alone) subject to a standard budget constraint derived from given endowments and parametric prices, the resulting aggregate behaviour is essentially unrestricted.[5] As Townsend says:

> At some level general equilibrium theory is vacuous. For example, for pure exchange economies it is known that one can generate any aggregate excess demand function by a suitable specification of endowments and preferences. Related, unobserved shocks to preferences with arbitrary probability distributions can generate arbitrary patterns of cross household consumptions. So, if some version of an enlarged model always fits, to what extent does general equilibrium theory have content? (Townsend [1987b, p. 22])

In the same vein, Heckman and Macurdy argue, when discussing tests to verify the 'disequilibrium hypothesis' based on the observation that estimated labour-supply elasticities are too small and that wage variability is too small to account for observed movements in aggregate manhours:

> For the second type of test to be convincing, agreement is required on the 'correct' labor-supply theory, but there is no such current agreement and none is likely to emerge. Indeed, if a specific labor-supply model failed to predict aggregate fluctuations, it would likely be discarded. The infinite variety of 'plausible' alternative equilibrium models makes the equilibrium theory a tautology. Specific equilibrium models can be rejected. Equilibrium as a(n) hypothesis is irrefutable. (Heckman and Macurdy [1988, p. 256])

The second problem with the strategy of deriving individual behaviour from constrained optimization is that in almost all NCM contributions, the constraints are terribly ad-hoc and, in many cases, quite unbelievable. 'Ad-hoc' here is used in the negative sense of 'obtained by reverse deduction from the desired implications'. In its neutral meaning of 'for the particular end or purpose in hand and without consideration of wider application' or 'for this particular purpose' or 'special(ly)', any assumption or postulate is, by definition, ad-hoc. As Solow says, 'it doesn't matter that an assumption is ad-hoc; what matters is the hoc it's ad'. Since the assumption of behaviour derived from individual optimizing principles is, inevitably, 'ad-hoc', it is bemusing to find that the term 'ad-hoc' now often is used to label any behaviour not derived from constrained optimization.

Among the unacceptable assumptions found in most NCM analyses are the following: competitive behaviour by all agents in all markets; symmetric information for the parties involved in any transaction in any market; perfect financial markets; a topsy-turvy information structure, typically endowing agents with knowledge of the true structure of the model, while at the same time severely restricting their knowledge of current values of economy-wide economic variables.

Other constraints such as social norms, conventions, traditions, mores and rules that are likely to be important (see e.g. Akerlof [1984]) in labour markets or for saving behaviour (Japanese savings behaviour may not be easily rationalized without them) are ignored. While sub specie aeternitatis all these institutions are endogenous and may indeed at times change spectacularly and swiftly in response to changes in the environment, many of them are likely to be invariant under the kinds of policy changes or exogenous shocks studied by macroeconomists. They are certainly no more endogenous than the taste and technology parameters that are treated as the invariant 'deep structure' of the NCM.

In many monetary NCM models arbitrary transactions 'technologies' generate cash-in-advance constraints and thus a determinate demand for outside money. Even the term 'commitment technology' has been used to put a 'first-principles' veneer on the assumption that governments can credibly commit themselves. A similar criticism can be made of certain recent 'New Keynesian' optimizing explanations of nominal price stickiness. Sticky prices are generated as optimum outcomes by postulating a price-setting 'technology' with fixed or convex costs of changing prices. The point is that attaching the label 'technology' to an arbitrary assumption doesn't make it any less arbitrary.

Important constraints on data gathering and processing capacity, on computational capacity, ability to understand and to conceptualize are, however, ignored in virtually all optimizing models. Bounded rationality and the use of rules-of-thumb as an adaptation to lack of comprehension and ignorance are severely under-researched topics.

A good case can be made that behavioural rules derived from explicit optimization subject to constraints are implausible because such a derivation is complex and difficult (starting from the sheer computational complexity of deriving optimal decision rules).

As they are unable to solve anything other than rather trivial constrained optimization problems, rational economic agents experiment with simple rules-of-thumb. The rules-of-thumb that have survival value and are not obviously dominated by other rules whose outcomes are observable, are likely to be adhered to and imitated. Rules that lead to ruin or are clearly dominated by other rules of similar degrees of complexity that are currently being experimented with are abandoned. Quite new and distinct rules are developed when the economic environment changes drastically or as the results of (poorly understood) acts of individual or group creativity.

In a series of interesting recent papers, Akerlof and Yellen [1985a, b, 1988] have developed the notion that 'small' individual departures from full optimization may result in 'large' changes in aggregate equilibrium behaviour. Large individual departures from full optimization are likely to involve correspondingly larger changes in aggregate equilibrium behaviour.

The postulate of individual optimizing behaviour is sometimes defended with an appeal to 'as if' methodology. This, however, is not methodology at all but a verbal smokescreen which permits one to make an embarrassing assumption while maintaining that one does not really mean it. The use of the verbal smokescreen does not in any way affect the substantive role of the embarrassing assumption in generating conclusions.

Our inability (or severely limited ability) to conduct controlled experiments means that behavioural rules derived from the optimization of an implausible objective function subject to embarrassing constraints will be shielded against rejection by the battery of surrounding ancillary maintained hypotheses that have to be made before a model can be confronted with the data (time series, cross-section or panel) we have. Direct observation, introspection and common sense, as well as hundreds of empirical studies on market structure and consumer and firm behaviour, should, however, suffice to reject the NCM tool kit. For some reason this has not happened (yet). The most plausible explanation for this is the increasingly '*self-referential*' nature of much modern economic analysis (and by no means just the NCM). Models are judged and evaluated not in terms of their success in explaining or predicting real world behaviour, but in terms of their internal consistency and the extent to which their construction and design is true to some *a priori* set of rules and characteristics. Disciplines develop according to their own inner logic without reference to the economic reality that is (or should be) the ultimate object of the research.

Clearly, internal consistency is a necessary characteristic of any acceptable theory. That it is not sufficient is equally obvious. Internally consistent nonsense may be better than internally inconsistent nonsense, but it is still nonsense. The low power of conventional econometric methods in discriminating between rival economic theories means that we have been shielded by our very weakness against empirical embarrassment.

While my main objections to the particular application of the optimizing approach found in most NCM models relate to the *constraints*, I have some worries about the *objective functions* as well.

As regards the consumer (and ignoring the individual versus household issue), the standard specification of egoistic consumption machines is probably quite adequate for many purposes. There is a nagging worry about labour being a 'bad' (since leisure is a 'good'). Once I have a job, my well-being may well be increasing in the number of hours of leisure I have, yet losing my job may involve a loss of utility (even if there are no income consequences). The standard approach ignores the social dimension of work and its self-realization value; this puts question marks behind the conventional cost-benefit analysis of unemployment.

More interestingly, the introduction of even limited forms of altruism can have major qualitative consequences for our models. As shown by Barro [1974], with intergenerational caring and scope for private non-market transactions (bequests and child-to-parent gifts), debt neutrality may characterize some equilibria in OLG models while with egoistic utility functions there would always be an absence of debt neutrality. An especially spectacular set of conclusions (roughly that all government fiscal actions except variations in exhaustive public spending are neutral) are shown, by Bernheim and Bagwell [1988], to be implied by rather weak forms of interpersonal altruism.

While the objective of the firm in an Arrow-Debreu world is, quite naturally, the maximization of profits, with incomplete markets there is no obvious candidate. Maximizing the stock market value of the firm (e.g. Diamond [1967]), choosing a production plan that satisfies the criterion of Nash-Pareto Optimality for the stockholders (see for example

Drèze [1985]), or maximizing some utility function of the firm, defined exogenously over state-distributions of profits (e.g. Radner [1972]), have all been proposed. So also have more 'institutional' approaches allowing for (partial) delegation of authority by the owners (the stockholders) to an elected Board of Directors (Drèze [1985]).

Clearly, adopting an optimizing approach to the derivation of economic decision rules does not provide any safeguards against bad (even if internally consistent) economics. While I find constrained optimization a quite attractive starting point for the analysis of individual behaviour, it is as yet hard to come up with good reasons for this enthusiasm, other than the aesthetic pleasures that can be derived from the formal mathematical expression of these ideas.

The limited success (or the difficulty of establishing the degree of success) of models based on the individual optimizing approach in explaining, understanding and predicting real-world behaviour means, furthermore, that it would be very unwise to be dogmatic. Any economist should be eager to beg, steal or borrow any behavioural hypothesis (whether optimizing, satisficing, behaviouristic, rule-of-thumb, boundedly rational or systematically irrational) which can be used to characterize empirical regularities that are (or appear to be) invariant under interesting classes of exogenous shocks and policy interventions.

Competitive equilibrium models, Arrow-Debreu models and representative agent models

It is ironic that at the very time that microeconomic theory was abuzz with exciting new developments (the asymmetric information paradigm, principal-agent theories, monopolistic competition, oligopoly and game-theoretic approaches to rivalry between firms etc.), the NCM should have opted for a recycling of the conventional pre-Seventies competitive paradigm. That many NCM models are Arrow-Debreu complete contingent market models is even less understandable. The frequent specialization within the Arrow-Debreu class of NCM models to representative agent economies defies explanation other than in terms of analytical convenience and the self-referential way in which economic theorizing tends to be judged.

The Arrow-Debreu model is a landmark in the history of economic thought. It considers a very special case of an abstract, idealized competitive economy. Unfortunately, it is of no value (except the very limited didactic one of showing precisely what the real world is not like) as a tool for analyzing the real-world macroeconomic phenomena of business cycles, growth and development. It is an ingenious mental construct which does not capture, even as a first approximation, any of the essential properties of dynamic economic systems in which incomplete and asymmetric information, imperfect competition, externalities, increasing returns and other non-convexities are central to the functioning of market and non-market allocative mechanisms. To analyze business cycles, inflation, unemployment, growth and development using the representative agent version of the Arrow-Debreu complete contingent markets competitive equilibrium model is to enter a cul-de-sac inside a dead-end street.

Macroeconomic modelling should start from the self-evident and crucial facts of (1) incompleteness of markets, (2) non-competitive behaviour in most of the markets that do exist and (3) essential heterogeneity among economic agents.

There are several obvious reasons for the incompleteness of the market system. Like almost any social institution, markets (i.e. arrangements for bringing together potential buyers and sellers of a commodity) are costly to set up and operate. Fixed costs are likely to be important and it is often difficult or expensive to recover the cost of making and operating a market.

Asymmetric information is also a potential 'market killer' (see e.g. Arnott and Stiglitz [1987, 1988], Helpman and Laffont [1975]). Following Akerlof's famous market for 'lemons' paper (Akerlof [1970]), a veritable avalanche of theoretical papers has come forth, drawing out the consequences of asymmetric information and the resulting problems of adverse selection and moral hazard for the labour market (Solow [1979], Hart [1983], Shapiro and Stigliz [1983], Weiss and Stiglitz [1983], Katz [1986], Stiglitz [1985, 1986], Akerlof and Yellen [1986]), product markets (Stiglitz [1979], Maskin and Riley [1984]) and financial markets (including insurance markets) (Jaffee and Russell [1976], Townsend [1979], Stiglitz [1982], Rothschild and Stiglitz [1976], Wilson [1977], Weiss and Stiglitz [1981]). The implications of costly information gathering for the information-revealing properties of equilibrium prices were analyzed very simply and directly by Grossman and Stiglitz [1980]. An important application to the market for corporate control is Grossman and Hart [1980]. As is clear from the recent surveys of the asymmetric information paradigm (Katz [1986], Akerlof and Yellen [1986], Stiglitz [1985, 1987]), empirical testing lags well behind theoretical modelling, a condition shared with much of economics.

Unlike mainstream economics, formal game theory had continued to treat imperfect information seriously; much current research reflects a happy marriage between developments in non-cooperative game theory, bargaining theory and the 'lemons principle' (see e.g. Shavell [1979], Laffont and Maskin [1982], Rubinstein [1982], Roth and Murnighan [1982] and Sutton [1986]).

General equilibrium systems of imperfectly competitive markets present formidable technical difficulties. Progress is being made, however. See for example Hart [1982], Weitzman [1982], Rotemberg [1982, 1987],

Cooper and John [1985], Hall [1986] and Blanchard and Kiyotaki [1987]. The analytically tractable model of monopolistic competition due to Dixit and Stiglitz [1977] will undoubtedly continue to find its way into macroeconomic applications (e.g. Rotemberg [1987]).

Heterogeneity 'matters': the assumption of identical agents is a crucial simplification for virtually every issue in welfare economics and for most issues in positive economics. Let me illustrate with some examples of key areas in economics where the representative agent model is inappropriate.

(a) Any issue in open economy macroeconomics and international trade requires a heterogeneous agents model. One of the few robust empirical regularities in open economy macroeconomics is that the residents of a country (1) own the lion's share of the productive resources located in that country (both human and non-human capital) and (2) spend a larger share (on average and at the margin) of their total consumption on goods produced in that country (traded and non-traded) than do foreigners. Ignoring this and considering instead a pooling equilibrium in a global representative agent model as in Lucas [1982] or Stockman and Svensson [1987] means that the response of the system to both demand and supply shocks is seriously misrepresented because every aspect of the 'transfer problem' is ignored. Identical tastes means that an international transfer of wealth does not affect the terms of trade. Identical tastes plus pooling equilibrium means, for example, that a productivity shock in a country benefits domestic and foreign residents equally, as all own equal shares of each income-generating-asset.

The representative agent-pooling equilibrium is useful as a preliminary step towards an acceptable model for understanding the behaviour of terms of trade, trade balance, current account etc. only if the further step of introducing a heterogeneous agent model (incorporating the essential 'domestic bias' in private consumption and asset ownership) is indeed taken (see e.g. Buiter [1988d]).

(b) Any study of public debt management and deficit finance requires consumer heterogeneity if the analysis is not to prejudge the key issues. For example there can be absence of debt neutrality only if a change in the pattern over time of lump-sum taxes redistributes resources between heterogeneous private consumers, and thus changes their intertemporal choice sets (see Buiter [1988b]). The OLG model with its age heterogeneity (and often also life expectancy heterogeneity) provides the minimal structure required for the analysis of public debt and deficits.

(c) There can be no 'deep structural' theory of money in a representative agent model. The characteristics of the economic environment and of individual agents that make for a common medium of exchange are spatial or other (e.g. cultural) separation between potential traders, private information, limited communication, limited capacity for credible commitment, anonymity etc. Such characteristics are inconsistent with the existence of a representative agent. (See e.g. Prescott [1982], Wallace [1987], Lucas [1980], Townsend [1987a].)

Existing theories of money which are often set in a representative agent world merely *assume* the existence of a demand for money. For reasons that are not specified, non-interest-bearing fiat outside money is sometimes assumed to be wanted for its own sake (money in the direct utility function (Sidrauski [1967], or money in the production function (Fischer [1974])). Alternatively, a demand for non-interest-bearing outside money is generated through an arbitrary transactions 'technology' and by making money unobtainable on demand immediately and at each instant through an arbitrary sequencing of opening and closing times for credit and goods markets (cash-in-advance models such as Svensson [1985] or Lucas and Stokey [1983, 1987]). 'Legal restrictions' theories assume a binding and enforceable legal prohibition on the private provision of small denomination, payable-on-demand bearer bonds (e.g. Bryant and Wallace [1984]). This last approach has the virtue of reflecting a not uncommon real-world legal fact.

(d) The asymmetric information (or private information) paradigm with its revolutionary insights and implications both for the positive economics and for the welfare economics of competitive markets, non-competitive markets and non-market allocation mechanisms presupposes heterogeneity among agents.

(e) New theories of the business cycle that take finance seriously require heterogeneity (and private information). Balance sheet losses by debtors and corresponding gains by creditors do not 'wash out' because debtors and creditors respond differently (and not only because utility is strictly concave in wealth). This exciting new area of research, which promises to provide vital clues in our search to understand the trade cycle, presupposes heterogeneity. The whole notion of intermediation only makes sense in a model with heterogeneous agents (Bernanke [1983], Bernanke and Gertler [1987a,b], Gertler [1988]).

(f) Real business cycle models have had to abandon the representative agent assumption in order to account for labour market behaviour. Even the ex-ante homogeneous labour in Rogerson's [1988] model of indivisible labour and employment lotteries and insurance, becomes ex-post heterogeneous (see also Hansen and Sargent [1988]): Some people work and some people don't. In Rogerson's model, the utility levels are the same for employed and unemployed, and the actual employment and unemployment experience has no further consequences. Homogeneity therefore survives. More interesting forms of heterogeneity such as differential productivity (Cho and Rogerson [1988]), and skilled-unskilled (Kydland [1984]) are being considered.

(g) One of the interesting features of measured unemployment is its uneven incidence. While many workers have short spells of unemployment, most unemployment is accounted for by relatively few long spells. No representative agent model can begin to address this issue.

(h) Political economy (the positive theory of economic policy) requires the consideration of conflict between classes, interest groups etc.

One can go on. The set of positive economic issues that can be analyzed satisfactorily using representative agent models is small, probably of measure zero. Normative economics is inherently concerned with the effect of shocks and policies on the welfare of heterogeneous economic agents. Distributional issues by their very nature vanish in a representative agent universe. As a starting point (on grounds of analytical convenience) it is acceptable only if it is left behind very swiftly indeed.

Real Business Cycles

The most lively area of theoretical and empirical research in the NCM tradition today is RBC theory. That business cycle theory is back in fashion throughout the macroeconomics profession is clear from e.g. Gordon (ed.) [1986].

The 'thousand islands' or 'misperceptions' theories of the business cycle with monetary shocks as the main driving force (e.g. Lucas [1975, 1977]) lost favour among those sympathetic to the NCM paradigm because its *a priori* information restrictions were just not deemed reasonable. Ignorance about the current value of the money stock is not very convincing as the prime mover of the business cycle.

It has long been known that formally there are two reasonably straightforward ways of generating regular or persistent cyclical behaviour in (and covariation among) key economic variables. The first is through a stationary dynamic linear system driven by exogenous random shocks (Slutzky [1937]). The second is through non-linear deterministic dynamic systems (Kaldor [1940], Goodwin [1951, 1982] and many others) which generate 'endogenous' cycles, i.e. persistent, (undamped) cyclical behaviour, without being perturbed by repeated exogenous shocks. While these two known approaches suggest strongly that it should not be too hard to generate cyclical behaviour through stochastic non-linear dynamic systems, the formidable technical problems associated with the characterization of the solutions of such systems have not made this a popular choice. Where such non-linear stochastic dynamic systems arise (and they arise quite naturally in all but the simplest stochastic equilibrium models, including RBC models), the usual response is to linearize and hope for the best.

Starting with the contributions of Kydland and Prescott [1982] (foreshadowed in Kydland and Prescott [1980]) and of Long and Plosser [1983], RBC theory has developed in a few years to the point that there already are several surveys of the subject (e.g. Eichenbaum and Singleton

[1986], McCallum [1988] and also Lucas [1987]). Although the original RBC models were competitive, Arrow-Debreu complete contingent markets models with a representative consumer, the importance of dropping the representative agent assumption is being recognized gradually, for example (as noted already) in Cho and Rogerson [1988], Kydland [1984] and Rebelo [1987].

Non-competitive market structures and their role in the propagation of business cycles have been studied by Hall [1986, 1988]. His work also considers alternative impulses for the business cycle. Rather than restricting the shocks to the system to aggregate productivity shocks, he (like Lilien [1982]) emphasizes sectoral taste and productivity shocks.

One can expect the RBC approach to develop to include fiscal shocks (exhaustive spending, distortionary taxes and (for models without debt neutrality) public debt or non-distortionary taxes). A monetary misperceptions transmission channel and exogenous monetary shocks as an additional impulse can of course be tagged on to the existing RBC models without difficulty.

Further sources of lags and richer dynamics are found easily. Apart from the already familiar input-output lags and the inclusion of durable capital, convex costs of adjusting employment, hours, capital stock or capital utilization rates can generate very rich dynamics indeed.

I hope for an integration of 'impulse-driven' RBC methodology and its Slutzky approach to modelling business cycles with the endogenous or intrinsic business cycle literature associated in recent years with Benhabib, Day and Grandmont (Benhabib and Day [1981, 1982], Day [1982, 1983], Grandmont [1985, 1986]).

Recent work on 'sunspots' and cycles (Azariadis [1981], Azariadis and Guesnerie [1986], Chiappori and Guesnerie [1988], Woodford [1987], Farmer and Woodford [1986]) raises questions, both positive and normative, that must be addressed by any theory of the business cycle hoping to avoid the fate of the monetary misperceptions model. How do we test for *stationary* bubbles? What are the consequences of alternative policy rules in models driven, in part, by 'sunspots', etc.?

The RBC approach features linear or linearized dynamic systems driven by stochastic, exogenous 'intrinsic' or fundamental shocks. The endogenous business cycle approach starts from non-linear deterministic systems which can generate both periodic cycles and a-periodic 'chaotic' solutions that mimic stochastic behaviour without any exogenous shocks. The 'sunspots' literature augments the deterministic non-linear endogenous business cycle models with non-fundamental or 'extrinsic' stochastic shocks, and generates a richer set of endogenous fluctuations 'driven by states of mind rather than by states of the world' (Chiappori and Guesnerie [1986, p. 396]). The tantalizing possibility of an integrated approach including non-linear systems, fundamental exogenous shocks and non-fundamental extrinsic shocks should keep the mathematically gifted occupied for quite a while.

The exciting work on endogenous secular growth due to increasing returns to scale and externalities developed in Romer [1986, 1987a,b] (see also Lucas [1988]) would seem to be complementary in spirit, if not in mathematical technique, to the theory of endogenous cyclical fluctuations. King, Plosser and Rebelo [1988b] do incorporate the Romer-Lucas endogenous secular growth mechanism into a model of cyclical fluctuations. The stochastic model they analyze has a simple log-linear structure, however. This will not, of course, generate endogenous cycles if the stochastic shocks are stripped away. Replacing the representative agent specification of Romer and Lucas by the OLG specification typical of the optimizing endogenous fluctuations models would seem a logical next step.

Keynesian business cycle models relying on sticky nominal wages and prices still suffer from the embarrassment of the absence of any 'deep' theory of nominal stickiness (McCallum [1986]). The 'microfoundations of nominal inertia' surveyed by Rotemberg [1987] are no such thing. First, as was pointed out already one can hardly label 'deep structural' an explanation of nominal price stickiness which merely postulates real costs (fixed or strictly convex) of changing prices or which restricts the frequency of price adjustment arbitrarily. The 'menu costs' motivation is unconvincing and the other rationalizations involve stories of search, private information, uncertainty etc. that are not modelled explicitly and therefore difficult to judge.

More fundamentally, even if the 'cost of price adjustment' theory is correct, it only gives us a theory of *nominal* stickiness if prices are set in terms of money, i.e. if money is the numéraire. If some bundle of real goods were the numéraire and if the cost of changing prices applied to price changes in terms of this *real* numéraire, there would be no *nominal* stickiness. The unmotivated assumption that prices are set in money terms is therefore a crucial one. Until we have a theory of money, we are unlikely to see a theory of nominal inertia.

Since there is, at any rate in the major industrial countries, strong evidence of nominal inertia, the Keynesian 'descriptive' approach of characterizing the empirical regularities as accurately as possible without insisting on a prior 'deep structural' motivation is surely preferable to the NCM approach of ignoring these facts until a satisfactory deep structural explanation for them can be found.

The empirical testing of the RBC models thus far has suffered somewhat from three weaknesses.[6] The first is that the 'impulses' driving the system, (the exogenous productivity shocks), are unobserved. Assumptions are made about the variances and the serial correlation properties of these unobservable shocks, whose purpose is to permit the model to mimic as closely as possible the behaviour of selected time series statistics (certain variances and covariances) in the absence of any other shocks.

Second, except for the simplest models (e.g. Long and Plosser [1983] with full depreciation of capital in one period), the dynamics of the state variables in equilibrium is not characterized by a system of (log-) linear stochastic difference equations. Closed-form solutions typically cannot be found, but what one ends up with is obviously both non-linear and stochastic.

The 'testing' of the empirical content of these non-linear stochastic models is performed using linear approximations to the unknown non-linear stochastic system. While the details of the linearization procedures – which sometimes involve as many as four separate steps – differ (see e.g. King, Plosser and Rebelo [1988a,b], Christiano [1988], Hansen and Sargent [1988], Kydland and Prescott [1982, 1988]), they inevitably share the property that we have no idea how good or bad the final approximation is. In order to determine that, we should compare the solution of the final linear approximation with that of the original non-linear system and it is precisely because we cannot solve the non-linear stochastic system that the linear approximation has been opted for in the first place. An avid linearizer myself, I am very sympathetic with the plight of the RBC modellers. With what we know about non-linear deterministic systems, there is, unfortunately cause for concern. Third (or higher) order ordinary non-linear differential equations can exhibit chaotic behaviour. A first order (or higher) non-linear difference equation may exhibit various kinds of periodic solutions or chaotic behaviour (e.g. May and Oster [1976], Benhabib and Day [1981, 1982], Day [1983], van der Ploeg [1986], Grandmont [1985]). Linear approximations to such systems would not be very informative.

Third, rather than subjecting the (linearized) models to conventional econometric time series tests, a method of verification (or falsification) is often adopted (pioneered by Kydland and Prescott) which can perhaps best be described as 'selective positivism'. A selection or subset of the implications of the model, with 'calibrated' rather than estimated values for the key structural parameters, is confronted with the facts. Typically the statistics of interest include the contemporaneous variances and covariances of output, consumption, investment, capital stock, wages, hours worked and, recently, inventory investment (Christiano [1988]). While the models have equally direct predictions concerning the real interest rate, these tend not to be tested. Less attention is paid to the serial correlation properties of the variables of interest and even less to their cross-serial correlation properties. Since a model is only as good as *all* of its implications, it is to be hoped that the 'selective stylized facts' approach to empirical verification will make place for a more robust and comprehensive confrontation of models and data.

Conclusion

When I make the points, elaborated here, about incomplete markets, imperfect competition, heterogeneous agents and non-Walrasian equilibrium to my New Classical friends, they often concur 'in principle'. Yes, the world we live in and try to understand does indeed possess these crucial characteristics that render the conventional competitive model (and *a fortiori* the Arrow-Debreu complete contingent markets version and $(a\ fortiori)^2$ its representative agent special case)) an inadequate and misleading parable for positive and normative analysis. The justification sometimes given for continuing to play the NCM game is that we do not know how to build and solve models that incorporate these crucial features, while we do know how to construct, solve and manipulate NCM models.

This response is not unlike that of a man who, having been invited to participate in a game of tennis, arrives on court not with a tennis racket but with a set of golf clubs. To the comment 'the game is tennis, not golf' he replies 'I know that, but I don't know how to play tennis. However, I play a mean round of golf.' He would do better to borrow a tennis racket and make the best of a bad job, rather than insisting on playing with his seven iron, or worse, insisting that, despite the presence of net and lines and the absence of greens and fairways, the game really is golf.

II **The Papers in this Volume**

Theoretical aspects of the policy ineffectiveness proposition

The first part of this volume deals with theoretical aspects of the policy ineffectiveness proposition, the Lucas critique and the time-inconsistency of optimal plans.

It is unfortunate that the important insights of model-consistent expectations and the Lucas critique for all of economics were obscured initially by bundling them with an analysis of the role of monetary policy in NCM models. The policy ineffectiveness propositions can often be shown to be wrong or irrelevant (i.e. applicable only in economic models that omit some key feature(s) of the real world whose inclusion would invalidate the proposition). The notion that government actions affect private expectations and that the 'reduced form' relationship between private behaviour and policy instruments can therefore depend on the characteristics of the policy rule is clearly correct in principle, although its empirical significance will have to be established from case to case.

Policy ineffectiveness Much of the policy ineffectiveness literature focuses on the so-called Lucas supply function given in equation (1a), taken, with minor modifications, from Lucas [1973].

$$y_t(z) = \alpha[p_t(z) - E[p_t \mid \Omega_t(z)]] + v_t(z) + \lambda y_{t-1}(z)$$
$$\alpha > 0; \mid \lambda \mid < 1 \tag{1a}$$

$y_t(z)$ is supply in period t in local market z, $p_t(z)$ the price of output in local market z in period t, p_t the general price level at time t (an average of all local prices), $v_t(z)$ a white noise supply shock, $E(p_T \mid \Omega_t(z))$ the expectation of p_T conditional on information available at time t in local market z, $\Omega_t(z)$. Persistence is introduced (for the sake of data description) through an ad-hoc lagged dependent variable (rationalized, say, through costs of adjusting the volume of output). Trends (stochastic or deterministic) are ignored for simplicity.

The 'microfoundations' of (la) are somewhat awkward. It is not the supply function of Lucas [1972a] 'Expectations and the neutrality of money' paper. In the endowment economy of that paper, there is only one store of value (fiat outside money) and one intertemporal relative price, (1 plus) the rate of inflation. A certainty-equivalent linear approximation to this supply function (similar to the one found in Lucas [1972b]) is given in (2).

$$y_t(z) = \alpha[p_t(z) - E[p_{t+1} \mid \Omega_t(z)]] + v_t(z) + \lambda y_{t-1}(z) \tag{2}$$

Equation (2) (plus a(n) (inessential) wealth effect and without the (inessential) lagged dependent variable) is used in Barro [1976]. When non-interest-bearing money is the only store of value, the expected rate of inflation is the negative of the real rate of interest. Intertemporal substitution arguments suggest that a higher expected real interest rate raises current labour supply.

When the asset menu is extended to allow for interest-bearing assets with a one-period nominal interest rate i_t, the intertemporal substitution hypothesis suggests the certainty equivalent linear approximation to the supply function given in (3), where r_t is the one-period real rate of interest.

$$y_t(z) = \alpha E(r_t \mid \Omega_t(z)) + v_t(z) + \lambda y_{t-1}(z)$$
$$1 + r_t \equiv [1 + i_t] \frac{p_t(z)}{p_{t+1}} \tag{3}$$

If the real wage can vary, the intertemporal substitution hypothesis may involve the comparison of the current (local) real wage $w_t(z)$ and the discounted present value of the future real wage, as given in (4)

$$y_t(z) = \alpha\left[E\left[\frac{w_{t+1}}{1 + r_t} \middle| \Omega_t(z)\right] - w_t(z)\right] + v_t(z) + \lambda y_{t-1}(z) \tag{4}$$

The misperceptions supply function (1a) and the separated islands parable that motivates it are awkward because, unlike equations (2), (3) and (4), the local price and the average price refer to the same date (the present). It isn't clear that this represents an actual market opportunity to anyone. It is possible to tell a story about working in one place (market, island) only but shopping everywhere in the same period (e.g. a working spouse and a shopping spouse making up a single consumption unit). Milton Friedman's [1968] story of a competitive economy in which the demand for labour is a decreasing function of the real product wage (money wage deflated by *own* product price, which is known to employers) and the supply of labour is an increasing function of the real consumption wage (money wage deflated by CPI, which is known only imperfectly to shoppers-workers) also generates a supply function like (1a).

Finally, an equation similar to (1a) can be rationalized along the lines of Phelps and Taylor [1977] or Fischer [1977], who assume that the money wage in period t is set, unconditionally, in some earlier period $t-i$, $i \geqslant 1$. If the wage is set at the level that would clear the labour market in period t (assuming no unexpected shocks between $t-i$ and t) and if ex-post employment is determined unilaterally by competitive firms equating real wage and marginal product, then a surprise supply function like equation (1b) emerges.[7]

$$y_t = \alpha[p_t - E\,[p_t \mid \Omega_{t-i}] + v_t + \lambda y_{t-1} \qquad i \geqslant 1 \tag{1b}$$

Barro [1977b, 1979b] has of course questioned the rationality of such a non-contingent nominal contracting procedure and his arguments are quite convincing except for the fact that such contracts actually appear to be quite common. His criticism applies with equal force to more sophisticated contracting schemes such as the ones in Taylor [1979, 1980].

I shall focus on the supply functions (1a) or (1b) and (2).

At its most basic level policy effectiveness exists if different realizations of some policy instrument imply different realizations of some endogenous variable of interest. I now consider the outside nominal money stock m_t as the instrument and real output or employment (y_t) as the endogenous variable of interest. For simplicity in what follows all variables other than interest rates are in natural logarithms.

In stochastic models, the policy effectiveness question can be phrased in terms of the influence of policy on the conditional and unconditional moments of the joint probability density function of some set of variables of interest. In the log-linear models I am concentrating on here, the influence of policy on the conditional and unconditional mean and variance of real output is what matters.

It is clear that with a supply function such as (2), (or its non-linear, non-certainty equivalent version implicit in Lucas [1972a]), the fact that monetary policy can determine the inflation rate and thus the intertemporal terms of trade even in the non-stochastic version of the model means that systematic monetary policy can influence real output. In the stochastic version, different known monetary feedback rules will generate different conditional and unconditional first and second moments of real output.

To filter out these so-called Tobin or Mundell effects of different anticipated inflation rates, the criterion for policy effectiveness was rephrased by Barro [1976] in terms of the monetary authority's ability to influence the gap between actual output (employment etc.) and its 'full information' value. Full information here means complete knowledge of current and past realizations of economy-wide shocks as well as of relevant information in the local market.

Consider equation (1b) with i period in advance contracts and, for simplicity, $\lambda = 0$.

$$y_t = \alpha[p_t - E[p_t \mid \Omega_{t-i}] + v_t \qquad i \geqslant 1 \tag{5}$$

As became clear from the papers by Turnovsky [1980] and Weiss [1980], it is impossible to say anything about policy effectiveness involving the second moment of y until we know the rest of the model.

Let the policy rule for the (logarithm) of the nominal money stock be

$$m_t = f(I_{t-j}, t) \qquad j \geqslant 0 \tag{6}$$

I_{t-j} is the government's information set in period $t-j$. It is trivial to show policy effectiveness when the government has an information advantage over the private sector ($I_{t-j} \supset \Omega_{t-j}$), or if the government can respond more swiftly to news ($I_{t-j} = \Omega_{t-j}$ but m_t responds to Ω_{t-j} and private behaviour in period t responds to Ω_{t-i} where $j < i$), even if that news is available equally to the private sector. Consider therefore only the case where the information set available to the private sector in any period is at least equal to that available to the public sector ($I_{t-j} \subseteq \Omega_{t-j}$) and the lags in the government feedback rule, j, are at least as long as the private 'inside lag' i.

Take a standard IS-LM completion of the simple macro model

$$y_t = -\beta[i_t - E[(p_{t+1} - p_t) \mid \Omega_t]] + \varepsilon_t \qquad \beta > 0 \tag{7}$$

$$m_t - p_t = -\gamma i_t + \delta y_t + \eta_t \qquad \gamma, \delta > 0 \tag{8}$$

ε_t and η_t are white noise disturbances

Consider the case of one-period contracts in equation (5), i.e. $i = 1$. Through the non-predetermined intertemporal substitution term $E[[p_{t+1} - p_t] \mid \Omega_t]$ in equation (7), the current price level, p_t, will be a function of all future values of the money stock anticipated at time t. Through the one-period contract in equation (5) together with (7) and (8), p_t will also be a function of the expectations of future money stocks formed at time $t-1$. As shown in Turnovsky [1980], this *revision-of-expectations channel* permits a policy maker to do anything he or she wants to the conditional or unconditional second moments of real output, using deterministic feedback rules relating m_t to information arbitrarily far back in the past. Sargent [1973] had this structure, but Sargent and Wallace [1975] no longer did, as the information set conditioning private information in the financial and goods markets became the same as the information set conditioning the price surprise in the supply function, i.e. (7) was replaced by

$$y_t = -\beta[i_t - E[[p_{t+1} - p_t] \mid \Omega_{t-1}]] + \varepsilon_t. \tag{7'}$$

This result is reviewed in Buiter [1981 (in this bundle)]. The intuition is that even if m_t is a function of Ω_{t-3000} (which is obviously known at time $t-1$ by the private sector), m_{t+3000} will be a function of Ω_t which will not be fully known at time $t-1$. Current expectations of this future m_{t+3000} will influence the current price, p_t, in a way not reflected in contracts drawn up at time $t-1$ if there is a non-predetermined forward-looking intertemporal substitution term (see Buiter [1982] (in this bundle)) somewhere in the model which affects p_t.

Buiter [1980a (in this bundle)] illustrates how certain kinds of nominal inertia can give monetary policy a handle on the first moment of output as well as on its variance. McCallum [1977, 1979] showed that price-level stickiness was not sufficient for policy effectiveness (in terms of first or second moments).

Moving to the 'thousand islands' or 'misperceptions' model of Lucas [1972a] (which actually has only two islands), Barro [1976] and others, Marini [1985] showed that in any model which has (a) signal extraction by private agents with incomplete current information and (b) a non-predetermined intertemporal substitution term somewhere in the model which affects current local prices, the following holds. Policy feedback rules relating the current money stock to information known currently to the private sector can completely eliminate the gap between actual and full information output. The monetary authority has an informational disadvantage *vis-à-vis* the private sector in the sense that it never has any 'local' information. Furthermore, the economy-wide information to which the current money stock responds can be arbitrarily far in the past and may contain less recent aggregate information than that contained in the information set $\Omega_t(z)$ used currently by private agents.

Buiter [1988c] (chapter 5 in this volume) restates this result of Marini and generalizes it slightly to the case of a government that doesn't control its instrument perfectly but can respond today to its past errors.

Chapter 5 also points out some common misperceptions concerning the implications of recent developments in efficiency wage theory and imperfect competition in product markets (a) for the role of demand in determining output and employment and (b) for the role of demand management.

Efficiency wage theory provides microfoundations for the existence of non-Walrasian equilibria in the labour market, including equilibria with quantity rationing. It does not by itself create a role for demand. Efficiency wage theory in the labour market and imperfect competition in the goods market also do not create a role for demand if all firms are conventional fully optimizing monopolistic competitors and if there is a unique value of the marginal revenue product for each level of firm output and aggregate output. We may get an equilibrium with persistent (and socially inefficient) unemployment, but these models generate unique and aggregate-demand invariant equilibrium values for output, employment and the real wage.

Akerlof and Yellen ([1985a,b], [1988]) broke out of this box by postulating (individually) small departures from full optimizing behaviour by a number of firms (see also Jones and Stock [1987]). Van Ees [1987] and I achieve a similar result for fully maximising firms by introducing a kinked demand curve for output and thus a discontinuity in the marginal revenue curve of the representative firm. These two approaches leave real demand free as a potential influence on equilibrium employment and output. It still doesn't follow however, that policy can influence real demand. Akerlof and Yellen achieve this by assuming that their departure from fully optimizing behaviour takes the form of some firms keeping *money* wages and prices consistent. If it had instead taken the form of keeping *relative* wages and prices constant, monetary policy still wouldn't have been able to influence real demand, output and employment. In the kinked demand curve model there is full optimization and one indeterminate nominal variable. The real wage is fixed, real output lies between an upper and a lower bound. Any combination of money wage and price level that puts real demand between these bounds is an equilibrium. Where the nominal anchor comes from is not explained within the model.

Whatever the merits of these models, the point that the existence of non-Walrasian, quantity-constrained, suboptimal equilibria does not automatically imply a role for real demand, let alone for demand management, must be robust. So is the fact that efficiency wages, imperfect competition, hysteresis etc, do not contribute anything to the understanding of *nominal inertia*. Nominal inertia is, despite McCallum's counterexamples, the most likely feature of the economy capable of creating a role for demand management[8], but it is not explained in any of these models.

Rational expectations, the Lucas critique and Sims' Critique of the Lucas Critique

In Buiter [1980a] I wrote:

'Private sector behaviour is influenced in many ways by expectations of future variables. If changes in government behaviour change these expectations, models that ignore such links from government behaviour via private expectations to private behaviour are likely to forecast poorly and to lead to misleading conclusions being drawn from policy simulations. This conclusion does not require Muth-rational expectations *per se*, only some direct effect of government behaviour on private expectations. The assumption of Muth-rational expectations provides the additional hypothesis that the link between private sector expectations and government behaviour comes through the private sector's knowledge of the true structure of the model, including the parameters that describe government behaviour'. [Buiter 1980a, pp. 35–6]

It is by now probably too late to purge the economic vocabulary of the use of the term 'rational expectations' (or even to insert the qualifier 'Muth-rational') when what is meant is the coincidence of subjective and objective conditional distribution functions of current and future endogenous and exogenous variables. Standard neoclassical usage would reserve the label 'rational expectations' for the outcome of an expected utility maximising decision process in which the costs of acquiring, processing and evaluating additional information are balanced against the anticipated benefits from further refinement of the forecast. Formal models of 'rational learning' are, unfortunately, wrought with conceptual problems and technical difficulty. (See, for example, Cyert and De Groot [1974], Bray [1982, 1983], Bray and Kreps [1987], Woodford [1987] and Marcet and Sargent [1988]). Until we have operational theories of rational learning, we will probably have to live with the embarrassment of 'rational expectations'.

A simple example of the Lucas critique is given in Buiter [1983b] (an excerpt from which is included in this volume) and reproduced in equation (9) below

$$y_t = Ay_{t-1} + BE(y_t \mid \Omega_{t-1}) + Cx_t + u_t \tag{9}$$

Ω_{t-1} includes the true structure of the model and all values of y and x in period $t-1$ and earlier. u_t is white noise.

If $I - B$ is of full rank, equation (9) implies the semi-reduced form

$$\begin{aligned} y_t = [1 - B]^{-1} Ay_{t-1} + [1 - B]^{-1} Cx_t \\ - B[I - B]^{-1}C[x_t - E(x_t \mid \Omega_{t-1})] + u_t \end{aligned} \tag{10}$$

Let the policy rule governing x during the sample be

$$x_t = \varepsilon_t \text{ where } \varepsilon_t \text{ is white noise.} \tag{11a}$$

An econometrician who, unlike the private agents inhabiting the model, is ignorant of the true structure estimates the reduced form

$$\hat{y}_t = \pi_1 y_{t-1} + \pi_2 x_t \tag{12}$$

Estimates of π_1 and π_2 using OLS will be biased but consistent and asymptotically efficient estimates of $[I - B]^{-1} A$ and C respectively.[9] Assuming a sufficiently large sample size the estimated model would be

$$y_t = [1 - B]^{-1} Ay_{t-1} + Cx_t + u_t \tag{13a}$$

Believing he had captured the invariant structure of the economy with equation (13a), our econometrician now uses it to simulate the economy's behaviour under the feedback rule

$$x_t = Gy_{t-1} + \varepsilon_t, \qquad G \neq 0 \tag{11b}$$

Based on (13a) he would expect the model to behave according to

$$y_t = [[1 - B]^{-1}A + CG]y_{t-1} + C\varepsilon_t + u_t \tag{14a}$$

In fact, from (10), it behaves according to

$$y_t = [1 - B]^{-1}(A + CG)y_{t-1} + C\varepsilon_t + u_t \tag{14b}$$

Only if B is the zero matrix (expectations play no role) will policy simulations based on (14a) not be misleading. Running the reduced form regression (12) when the sample consists of x_t generated by (11b) instead of (11a) would yield (13b) instead of (13a)

$$y_t = [[I - B]^{-1} A + B[I - B]^{-1}CG]y_{t-1} + Cx_t + u_t \tag{13b}$$

Note that it is not, in this example, the coefficient on the policy instrument that is altered by the change in policy regime, but the coefficient on the lagged dependent variable.

This example of the Lucas critique (Lucas [1976]) can be used to illustrate an interesting and valid critique by Sims [1982, 1987] of the Lucas critique. Elaborating and extending some important insights in Sargent and Wallace [1976], Sims pointed out that the *difference* between (13a) and (13b) (or (14a) and (14b)) cannot be interpreted as the *change* in the stochastic process governing y that would occur 'in real time' if the authorities were to *change* the policy rule at some time $t = t_1$ from (11a) to (11b). This identification of *differences* between system behaviour under different rules governing x with *changes* in system behaviour when the policy rule is changed at some point in time is valid only under very restrictive conditions.

(1) Trivially, when there are no (model-consistent) expectations in the structure of the model, (i.e. when $B = 0$ in our example) and no dynamics (no lagged y in our example and no lagged y or x in general). In static systems without model-consistent expectations, the comparison of two 'parallel universes', each identical in all respects except for the policy rule, is the same as the analysis of a change in the policy rule in a given universe at a point in time. Without model-consistent expectations but with a non-trivial dynamic structure (and assuming the system is stationary under the old and under the new policy rule), 'parallel universe counterfactuals' are the same as 'change in real time experiments' only in the long run, after the influence of initial conditions (lagged values of y and x) established under the old regime has vanished.

(2) When the change in policy regime at time t_1 is unanticipated, immediate and permanent and there are no dynamics in the model. When there is a non-trivial dynamic structure (lagged y's or x's in the system governing y) even this won't do. The original Lucas critique not only requires one to assume that before and after the change in the policy rule (or the change in the values of the parameters characterizing the policy rule) private agents have complete subjective certainty about the policy rule (or about the values of the parameters); if the model is dynamic, it is assumed to behave, after the policy rule change, as if the new policy rule had been in effect all along, which is inconsistent. The Lucas critique therefore requires more than certainty-equivalent private sector perceptions or anticipations of the policy rule parameters and martingale-like processes for the policy rule parameters. Once the new parameter values are in effect the system is assumed to behave as if they always have been and always will be in effect.

The 'Lucas experiments' therefore describe a-historical, 'parallel universes' counterfactuals, not 'real time' changes in policy parameters.

Sims [1982, 1987], along with Sargent and Wallace [1976] is interested in 'real time' policy regime changes. He therefore proposes to model the parameters of the policy rule (G in equation (11b) and perhaps the variance of ε_t) as realizations of a 'higher order' stochastic process, the policy regime distribution function, $G_t = F(\theta)$, where θ is the (truly) deep invariant structure, summarized as a vector of parameters.

Private agents are assumed to have subjective distribution functions characterizing their beliefs concerning future realizations of G_t. With rational expectations, the conditional subjective distribution function $\hat{F}(\theta \mid \Omega_t)$ is the same as the conditional objective distribution function $F(\theta \mid \Omega_t)$.

The effect of a *change* in the policy rule (now the effect of a realization or drawing G_t different from G_{t-1}) will depend on the effect of this realization on expectations of future realizations of G_{t+i} $i \geqslant 1$. Analyzing the consequences of a change in regime in 'real time' therefore involves ceasing to interpret the policy rule 'parameters' as parameters and treating them as random variables instead.

How different will the historical analysis of policy regime changes be from the a-historical counterfactual?

First, looking forward, a random walk view of the key policy parameters may well be a reasonable approximation. While not the same as the complete subjective certainty (or known, constant parameters) implicit in the a-historical counterfactual, it may well be an acceptable 'first pass'.

Second, the assumption implicit in the a-historical counterfactual that the new (strictly the alternative) regime has always been in effect, will not be too misleading if the influence of the old regime realizations wears off quickly, i.e. if there is little 'persistence' in the model.

Third, the policy parameter changes of interest are often infrequent. They may indeed not have occurred at all during the sample period. Parameter constancy (strictly speaking repeated identical realizations of the policy rule random variables) during the sample does not, of course, imply that the (perhaps slight) subjective probability of a change does not influence behaviour during the sample (*vide* the *Peso Problem* analysed by Blanco and Garber [1986]).

If the subjective probability of a different realization of the policy rule random variable in the future is very small, if conditional on a change having occurred, the probability of subsequent change is again very small and if a change, when it occurs, is large, then the a-historical Lucas counterfactual may not be a bad approximation to the historical change experiment.

Changes in the parameters describing policy regimes tend to have the following properties. (a) They are not observed directly but must be inferred from the time series behaviour of policy instrument realizations. (b) They are infrequent relative to the sample size. (c) They are 'large' when they do occur. (d) They often cannot be predicted at all on the basis of conventional macroeconomic time series but may be partly predictable on the basis of wider social, political and economic indicators that are categorical or at best ordinal rather than cardinal in nature.

The stochastic process representing the behaviour of policy regime parameters are therefore unlikely to be suitable candidates for modeling as conventional linear time series processes with Gaussian or other nice disturbances. Poisson processes have some, but not all, of the desired characteristics.

The notion that private agents (act as if they) have (ever) higher order (rational) conditional subjective distribution functions concerning everything that might conceivably happen is also quite farfetched. Rational expectations only make sense (if ever) when there is a reasonable empirical basis for these subjective probability laws. In the real world, certain policy changes do come 'out of the blue', i.e. were not part of the 'event space' at all.

Sims's critique of the Lucas critique is correct in principle. How to handle major, infrequent policy regime changes in practice is still an open question.

Policy (in)effectiveness and a-theoretical econometrics

It is now widely recognised that a-theoretical econometrics (unrestricted VAR models and their applications in Granger-causality tests, exogeneity tests innovation accounting, impulse response analysis etc) is uninformative for policy evaluation and for determining presence or absence of policy effectiveness[10]. While potentially useful for sample data description these methods do not permit the identification of the key structural parameters that are required for policy analysis. Given sufficient *a priori* restrictions it may become possible to identify and estimate the structural parameters of interest, but that of course is true for all (dynamic) simultaneous equations methods (for models with or without rational expectations). To be useful, a-theoretical econometrics must cease to be a-theoretical.

The key references on Granger-causality are Granger [1969, 1980] and Sims [1972, 1977]. A useful survey is Geweke [1984]. VARs, innovation accounting, impulse responses and the use of 'unrestricted[11]' VARs for policy evaluation were pioneered in Sims [1980a,b, 1982, 1987]. The connections between Granger-(non)causality, the many different kinds of statistical exogeneity, predeterminedness etc and the concepts of effectiveness of policy instruments, ability to influence and control etc have been discussed many times (e.g. Hsiao [1979], Jacobs, Leamer and Ward [1979], Schwert [1979], Zellner [1979] and Engle, Hendry and Richard [1983]). Gordon and King [1982] brought out clearly the (often incredible) *a priori* restrictions required if the orthogonalized VAR innovations are to be treated as exogenous variables. This point was expanded in Blanchard and Watson [1986] and Bernanke [1985] (see also Sargent [1984]).[12] The definitive critique of a-theoretical econometrics, summarizing most of the arguments in a non-technical manner is Cooley and Leroy [1985].

The simple 2-equation dynamic simultaneous equation model (augmented with a few rational expectations frills) given in equations (15) and (16) below can be used to illustrate how the latest attempts to get around Koopmans' strictures against measurement without theory have come unstuck and how the latest versions of 'post hoc ergo propter hoc' (Tobin [1970]) did, inevitably, suffer the fate of their predecessors.

$$\begin{aligned} y_t = {} & \alpha_0 y_{t-1} + \alpha_1 E[y_{t+1} \mid \Omega_{t-1}] + \alpha_2 x_t + \alpha_3[x_t - E[x_t \mid \Omega_{t-1}]] \\ & + \alpha_4 x_{t-1} + \alpha_5[x_{t-1} - E[x_{t-1} \mid \Omega_{t-2}]] + u_t^y \end{aligned} \tag{15}$$

$$x_t = \beta_1 y_{t-1} + \beta_2 y_t + \beta_3[y_t - E[y_t \mid \Omega_{t-1}]] + \beta_4 x_{t-1} + u_t^x \tag{16}$$

y is some endogenous economic variable, x is the policy instrument, u_t^y and u_t^x are exogenous white noise 'structural' disturbances. In addition to being normally, identically and independently distributed with zero means and variances σ_y^2 and σ_x^2 respectively, they are also assumed to be contemporaneously independent. The α_i and β_i are constants. y and x are jointly covariance-stationary. The private sector (whose behaviour is given by equation (15)) and the public sector (whose decision rule is given by equation (16)) have (for simplicity) the same information set Ω_t conditioning expectations formed in period t. (Different private and public information sets would not alter the main message). Ω_t contains the true model and all current and past values of y and x.

The policy rule has lagged feedback components ($\beta_1 y_{t-1}$ and $\beta_4 x_{t-1}$), an instantaneous feedback component such as an automatic fiscal stabilizer ($\beta_2 y_t$) and permits a different response to anticipated and unanticipated realizations of y (through the term $\beta_3[y_t - E[y_t | \Omega_{t-1}]]$. There may be a 'trembling hand' disturbance term in the policy rule ($\sigma_x^2 > 0$).

Since simultaneity is inherent in most economic equilibrium concepts, equations (15) and (16) can be expected to have a 'full' simultaneous structure: $\alpha_2 \neq 0$ and $\beta_2 \neq 0$ (and also in general, $\alpha_3 \neq 0$ and $\beta_3 \neq 0$).

The dynamic reduced form of the model of equations (15) and (16) is given in equation (17) below

$$\begin{bmatrix} y_t \\ x_t \end{bmatrix} = \begin{bmatrix} \pi_{11} & \pi_{12} \\ \pi_{21} & \pi_{22} \end{bmatrix} \begin{bmatrix} y_{t-1} \\ x_{t-1} \end{bmatrix} + \begin{bmatrix} \eta_t^y \\ \eta_t^x \end{bmatrix} \tag{17}$$

π_{11} and π_{12} are obtained by solving equations (18*a*, *b*). For the system to be economically sensible, the solutions to (18*a*, *b*) should of course for real[13].

$$\pi_{11} = \frac{\alpha_0 + \alpha_2\beta_1 + \alpha_1 \left(\pi_{11}^2 + \pi_{12}(\beta_1 + \beta_2\pi_{11})\right)}{1 - \alpha_2\beta_2} \qquad (18a)^{14}$$

$$\cdot_{12} = \frac{\alpha_4 + \alpha_2\beta_4 + \alpha_1(\pi_{11}\pi_{12} + \pi_{12}(\beta_4 + \beta_2\pi_{12})^1)}{1 - \alpha_2\beta_2} \tag{18b}$$

also:

$$\pi_{21} = \beta_1 + \beta_2\pi_{11} \tag{18c}$$

$$\pi_{22} = \beta_4 + \beta_2\pi_{12}. \tag{18d}$$

The 'reduced form' disturbances are white noise if $\alpha_5 = 0$, MA1 processes if $\alpha_5 \neq 0$.

$$\eta_t^y = \frac{1}{k} u_t^y + \frac{(\alpha_2 + \alpha_3)}{k} u_t^x + \frac{\alpha_5(\beta_2 + \beta_3)}{k[1 - \alpha_2\beta_2]} u_{t-1}^y + \frac{\alpha_5}{[1 - \alpha_2\beta_2]k} u_{t-1}^x \tag{19a}$$

$$\eta_t^x = \frac{\beta_2 + \beta_3}{k} u_t^y + \frac{1}{k} u_t^x + \frac{\beta_2\alpha_5(\beta_2 + \beta_3)}{[1 - \alpha_2\beta_2]k} u_{t-1}^y + \frac{\beta_2\alpha_5}{[1 - \alpha_2\beta_2]k} u_{t-1}^x \tag{19b}$$

where

$$k = 1 - (\alpha_2 + \alpha_3)(\beta_2 + \beta_3) \tag{19c}$$

When there are no expectations of future y in the private sector equation (15) ($\alpha_1 = 0$), the π_{ij} simplify to:

$$\pi_{11} = \frac{\alpha_0 + \alpha_2\beta_1}{1 - \alpha_2\beta_2} \tag{19a'}$$

$$\pi_{12} = \frac{\alpha_4 + \alpha_2\beta_4}{1 - \alpha_2\beta_2} \tag{19b'}$$

$$\pi_{21} = \frac{\beta_1 + \alpha_0\beta_2}{1 - \alpha_2\beta_2} \tag{19c'}$$

$$\pi_{22} = \frac{\beta_4 + \alpha_4\beta_2}{1 - \alpha_2\beta_2} \tag{19d'}$$

Policy effectiveness of x with respect to y is present when α_2, α_3, α_4 and α_5 are not all equal to zero. Policy effectiveness is determined by the structural parameters of the y equation (15). It has nothing to do with equation (16), which describes the actual process governing the instrument x in the sample. Policy effectiveness is present when different realizations ('drawings') of x imply, *cet. par.*, different realizations for current or future y. The effect of x on y may differ depending on whether and when the realization of x is anticipated and, in models which (unlike equation (15)) do not exhibit certainty equivalence, on the degree of subjective confidence with which these expectations are held. In dynamic models, when there are lagged policy effects, either direct (α_4 and α_5 in equation (15)) or indirect (through lagged dependent variables (when $\alpha_0 \neq 0$ in equation (16)), the effects on y of anticipated or unanticipated changes in x will be distributed over time and can be characterized through impact, cumulative and steady state multipliers. The latter two will be functions of all the α_i, $i = 0, \ldots, 5$.

Instead of looking at the effect of different realizations of x_t on the realizations of y_{t+i}, $i \geqslant 0$, we could summarize this information by considering the effect of different realizations of x_t (or of different rules for generating x_t) on the moments of the conditional and unconditional distribution functions of y_{t+i}.

It is important to realize that 'policy effectiveness' does not concern the actual behaviour of policy over the sample. What we are interested in is 'potential' effectiveness, when the x process is effectively unconstrained. In the case of exhaustive public spending e.g., x would only be required, in each period, to be non-negative and, in a closed economy, no larger than GDP. The nominal money stock would be required to be non-negative and bounded from above. Whether or not x Granger-causes y in the sample, whether it is predetermined or strictly exogenous is irrelevant for policy effectiveness. It may of course be rather easier to establish the presence or absence of policy effectiveness on the basis of time series observations if we know *a priori* that x happens to be governed by a process under which it Granger-causes x, or is predetermined or strictly exogenous.

The precise characterization of the way in which x can affect y is obtained from the 'semi-reduced form' given in equation (20) where y_t is expressed as a function of its own past value and of past, present and anticipated future values of x.[16]

$$
\begin{aligned}
y_t = {} & \pi_1 y_{t-1} + u_t^y + \frac{\alpha_4}{1-\alpha_1\pi_1}x_{t-1} + \frac{\alpha_5}{1-\alpha_1\pi_1}\left[x_{t-1} - E\left[x_{t-1} \mid \Omega_{t-2}\right]\right] \\
& + \frac{1}{1-\alpha_1\pi_1}\left[\alpha_2 + \frac{\alpha_1\alpha_4}{1-\alpha_1\pi_1}\right]x_t \\
& + \left[\alpha_3 - \frac{\alpha_1}{1-\alpha_1\pi_1}\left[\pi_1\alpha_2 + \frac{\alpha_4}{1-\alpha_1\pi_1}\right]\right]\left[x_t - E\left[x_t \mid \Omega_{t-1}\right]\right] \\
& + \left[\frac{1}{1-\alpha_1\pi_1}\right]\left[\alpha_2 + \frac{\alpha_1\alpha_4}{1-\alpha_1\pi_1}\right]\sum_{i=1}^{\infty}\left[\frac{\alpha_1}{1-\alpha_1\pi_1}\right]^i E\left[x_{t+i} \mid \Omega_{t-1}\right]
\end{aligned} \tag{20}
$$

where

$$\pi_1 = \alpha_0 + \alpha_1\pi_1^2, \qquad |\pi_1| < 1 \tag{21a}$$

and

$$\left|\frac{\alpha_1}{1-\alpha_1\pi_1}\right| < 1 \tag{21b}$$

Cet. par. the 'multiplier' of an anticipated change in x_t on y_t is $\frac{1}{1-\alpha_1\pi_1}\left[\alpha_2 + \frac{\alpha_1\alpha_4}{1-\alpha_1\pi_1}\right]$. When there are no expectations of future y in equation (15) ($\alpha_1 = 0$) this simplifies to α_2. The multiplier of an unanticipated change in x_t on y_t is $\alpha_2 + \alpha_3$. The multiplier of an anticipated change in x_{t-1} on y_t is $\frac{\alpha_4}{1-\alpha_1\pi_1}$ ($= \alpha_4$ if $\alpha_1 = 0$), while the multiplier of an unanticipated change in x_{t-1} on y_t is $\frac{\alpha_4+\alpha_5}{1-\alpha_1\pi_1}$ ($= \alpha_4 + \alpha_5$ if $\alpha_1 = 0$).

The *cet. par.* clause of the previous paragraph included the expectations of future x formed at time $t-1$. If we are restricted to a particular rule for x, such as the one given in equation (16), anticipated or unanticipated changes in x_t may well be associated with offsetting or reinforcing changes in $E(x_{t+i} \mid \Omega_{t-1})$, $i \geqslant 1$. This may complicate the identification of the key α_i parameters from time series data. It is, however, only the α_i, $i = 0, \ldots, 5$ that are relevant for policy evaluation and design.

What do Granger-causality tests tell us about policy effectiveness? First, if neither anticipated nor unanticipated changes in x_t affect y_t (if $\alpha_2 = \alpha_3 = \alpha_4 = \alpha_5 = 0$), then x_t will not Granger-cause y_t. In real-world applications of Granger-causality tests, a policy instrument x may appear to Granger-cause a variable y despite the absence of policy effectiveness (anticipated and unanticipated) because x is correlated with some omitted variable, z, say, which Granger-causes y. In the idealized example under consideration, this is ruled out.

Second, x can Granger-cause y even if only lagged *unanticipated* changes in x affect y (i.e. if $\alpha_2 = \alpha_3 = \alpha_4 = 0$ but $\alpha_5 \neq 0$). This was pointed out in Sargent [1976a]. The reason is obvious from equations (15) and (16). In addition to $\alpha_2 = \alpha_3 = \alpha_4 = 0$, assume also, for simplicity, that $\beta_2 = \beta_3 = 0$. In that case $x_{t-1} - E(x_{t-1} \mid \Omega_{t-2}) = u^x_{t-1} \cdot u^x_{t-1}$ is imperfectly predictable from y_{t-i}, $i \geqslant 1$ but can be inferred exactly using x_{t-i} and y_{t-i}, $i \geqslant 1$. x has incremental predictive power over y or 'Granger-causes' y even though the conditional and unconditional expectations of y are independent of the rule governing x.

From now on we set $\alpha_5 = 0$ in equation (15). Equation (17) now has white noise disturbances η^y_t and η^x_t and is the VAR representation of the model of equations (15) and (16). x fails to Granger-cause y if $\pi_{12} = 0$, assuming that the variance-covariance matrix of the reduced form disturbances Σ is non-singular.

$$\Sigma \equiv \begin{bmatrix} \Sigma_{yy} & \Sigma_{yx} \\ \Sigma_{yx} & \Sigma_{xx} \end{bmatrix} \tag{22}$$

$$\Sigma_{yy} = \frac{1}{k^2}\,[\sigma^2_y + [\alpha_2 + \alpha_3]^2\sigma^2_x] \tag{23a}$$

$$\Sigma_{xx} = \frac{1}{k^2}\,[[\beta_2 + \beta_3]^2\sigma^2_y + \sigma^2_x] \tag{23b}$$

$$\Sigma_{yx} = \frac{1}{k^2}\,[[\beta_2 + \beta_3]\,\sigma^2_y + (\alpha_2 + \alpha_3)\sigma^2_x] \tag{23c}$$

Third, while $\alpha_2 = \alpha_4 = 0$ (anticipated current and past values of x don't affect y) implies $\pi_{12} = 0$, $\pi_{12} = 0$ is consistent with $\alpha_2 \neq 0$ if $\alpha_4 = \beta_4 = 0$. Granger-causality tests will fail to pick up contemporaneous effects of x_t on y_t if lagged x do not enter the structural equations for y and x. Note that the hands of the controller can be shaky ($\sigma^2_x > 0$) (see Buiter [1981] included in this volume) without this affecting the result.

Fourth, if the policy rule is non-stochastic ($\sigma^2_x = 0$), x will fail to Granger-cause y. (This implies that Σ is singular).

If the policy rule is derived from standard optimizing behaviour (excluding randomized strategies), the instrument will be a non-stochastic (strictly deterministic) function of the authorities' information set. x will (since y_t is assumed to belong to the information set Ω_t) therefore fail to Granger-cause y. It is of course possible to endow private and public agents with different information sets, most plausibly with each sector having an informational advantage (at least temporarily) vis a vis the other for some set of variables. All variables could be measured with error, (by the private agents, the government and the econometrician) implying the need for Kalman filtering etc. Granger (non)-causality may correctly flag policy (in)effectiveness for certain informational structures. Unless the correctness of the informational assumptions can be verified independently or can be asserted to be plausible *a priori*, we must still conclude that Granger-causality tests are uninformative about policy (in)effectiveness.

The message in the innovations. Consider the estimation of (17), with $\alpha_5 = 0$, under ideal circumstances. First, the right 'universe' is known *a priori.* y and x and only y and x are known to belong in the VAR. The maximal lag lengths (1) are known *a priori*. Second, there are no restrictions on sample size, so all parameters can be estimated with ideal precision. Unrestricted estimation yields seven parameters, the four π_{ij}, i, $j = 1, 2$, given in (18a, b, c, d) and the three independent components of the variance-covariance matrix of the reduced from disturbances, Σ, given in (22) and (23a, b, c).

The reduced form innovations will typically be contemporaneously correlated ($\Sigma_{yx} \neq 0$). Sims diagonalizes the reduced form error covariance matrix and uses the transformed residuals in innovation accounting exercises, impulse response analyses and policy analyses. In the context of our simple model these approaches aim to evaluate the contribution of shocks to x to the total variance of y. As was pointed out by Sachs [1982] and Gordon and King [1982], it is only correct to interpret the impulse response functions thus obtained as capturing the effect of an exogenous shock (or 'intervention') in x on y, if x is predetermined, i.e. if $\beta_2 + \beta_3 = 0$. The alternative causal ordering of the innovations, assuming the y innovation to be causally prior, is equivalent to the assumption that y is predetermined ($\alpha_2 + \alpha_3 = 0$). In general simultaneous systems neither assumption is credible. The VAR innovations both are linear combinations of the two structural innovations. Few interesting economic structures are recursive.

As Cooley and Leroy point out [1985], even if Σ is diagonal, we cannot automatically assume that x and y are both predetermined. $\Sigma_{yx} = 0$ is consistent with $\beta_2 + \beta_3 \neq 0$ and $\alpha_2 + \alpha_3 \neq 0$ as long as

$$(\beta_2 + \beta_3)\sigma_{\bar{y}}^2 = -(\alpha_2 + \alpha_3)\sigma_{\bar{x}}^2 \text{ (see (23c)).}$$

Since the *a priori* predeterminedness assumptions necessary for the validity of the treatment of orthogonalized VAR innovations as exogenous shocks will typically be implausible or even incredible, innovation accounting, impulse response analysis etc. are uninformative for policy evaluation and design.

In Buiter [1983c] in this volume, this same issue appears in a discussion of Barro's tests of the effects of anticipated and unanticipated money growth on output, unemployment etc. (e.g. Barro [1977a, 1978]). Interpreting y as output and x as monetary growth, it is obvious that the contemporaneous effect of unanticipated money growth on output, $\alpha_2 + \alpha_3$, is identified only if the prior restriction is imposed that unanticipated output doesn't affect money growth ($\beta_2 + \beta_3 = 0$).

Barro's *a priori* restriction that permitted the identification of the effect of anticipated current money growth on output (α_2 in our model), involved the exclusion of a fiscal variable from the output equation. While I consider this exclusion restriction to be extremely implausible, it is clear that without an *a priori* restriction of this kind, nothing can be said about the effects of anticipated policy on output (in our model, α_2 will e.g. be identified if we impose the prior restriction that $\alpha_0 = 0$, since in that case $\alpha_2 = \pi_{11}/\pi_{21}$).

To sum up: a-theoretical econometrics fails as a method for policy evaluation for the old, familiar reason the it cannot resolve the identification problems inherent in simultaneous equation systems. This is true for dynamic models with or without rational expectations. (In the former, the distinction between anticipated and unanticipated policy actions exacerbates the usual identification problem.)

The meaning both of the coefficients on the lagged dependent variables (the raw material of Granger-causality tests) and of the variance-covariance matrix of the contemporaneous VAR disturbances (the raw material of innovation accounting etc) cannot be ascertained without prior information. As regards the lag coefficients, a variable x can Granger-cause a variable y because there is a 'strong structural' ordering from x to y (anticipated x influences y) or because, although there is only a 'weak structural' ordering from x to y (only unanticipated x influences y), x anticipates, forecasts and helps predict y for the reasons discussed in Sargent [1976a]. This can occur even without omitted variables problems, which might provide another reason for Granger-causality from x to y without either anticipated or unanticipated x influencing y. x can fail to Granger-cause y even though anticipated and/or unanticipated x influences y.

As regards the variance-covariance matrix of the VAR disturbances, the construction of exogenous disturbances requires the (generally incredible) prior assumption of a recursive structure for the endogenous variables. The damage is therefore indeed done by the old familiar simultaneity problem.

Cooley and Leroy's concluding comment on the contribution of unrestricted VAR models is very much to the point:

'Assuming that VAR models are interpreted as non-structural, the only conclusions that can properly be generated from them are those which are invariant across observationally equivalent versions of the same model. This excludes any kind of causal[17] statement since, as we have stressed, different but observationally equivalent versions of a given model have different causal interpretations. Now there exist important applications of VAR models that in fact have this invariance property. Forecasts, being constructed directly from the reduced form, will be invariant across observationally equivalent versions of a given model. The same is true of Granger causality. Therefore theories which have implications for the outcome of causality tests[18] ... can be tested using the methods of a-theoretical macroeconometrics. Finally, VAR models can be used to determine the existence of Granger-causal orderings even in the absence of any theoretical reason to expect them, the idea being that theorists will regard the outcome of such exercises as stylized facts requiring subsequent explanation in terms of structural models'. (Cooley and Leroy [1985, p. 306]; notes added by author.)

Rules vs discretion

Buiter [1980a], Buiter [1981] and Buiter [1986] (in this bundle) contain some short references to the issue of the time inconsistency of optimal plans. The seminal paper by Kydland and Prescott [1977] on this issue has spawned a large and growing theoretical literature. Key references are Prescott [1977], Fischer [1980], Barro and Gordon [1983], Barro [1986], Bachus and Driffill [1985], Lucas and Stokey [1983], Persson and Svensson [1984], Rogoff [1985], Alesina [1987] and Rogoff and Sibert [1988]. The importance of Schelling's *The Strategy of Conflict* [1960] for the current research on pre-commitment, credibility, sequential rationality, dynamic non-cooperative game theory, bargaining theory etc. has not been recognized sufficiently. Recognition of the similarity between Kydland and Prescott's analysis of time-consistency and the concepts of sequential equilibrium and subgame perfect equilibrium in the theory of repeated games (Kreps and Wilson [1982]) has created opportunities for productive interdisciplinary exchange.

My 'contribution' was to re-emphasize the obvious point that the 'rule' or 'constitution' that may have to be imposed or legislated (or which emerges in some other ad-hoc manner) to overcome the problem of precommitment and credibility in a non-cooperative sequential game, should be a 'flexible', 'conditional' or 'contingent' rule or constitution. It should permit the instruments of policy to respond (in a known and observable manner) to observable 'news' about developments in the exogenous variables that form the environment of the game. Unconditional, non-contingent, open-loop or fixed rules (e.g. k-percent rules) are always suboptimal (except in those uninteresting cases where there is no exogenous state uncertainty or instruments don't have any effect on economic variables of interest).

Any optimal (or merely sensible) constitution should also leave room for 'discretion'. Not 'discretion' in its post-time consistency sense of ability to cheat or to renege on previous commitments, but discretion in the sense of the assignment of a 'residual' authority to act in response to unforeseen and/or unspecified contingencies. Exogenous events will occur in the future that cannot be conceived of today, i.e. that do not belong to the current (subjective) event space. In addition, those future contingencies that do belong to the current event space may be too numerous to be mapped, without unreasonable expenditure of time and other resources, into a grand contingent policy response function. The constitution should delegate to the policy maker the authority to deal with all contingencies not explicitly covered or allowed for in the conditional policy rule or 'contract'. Discretion in this sense as the right to the 'residual' authority to decide on issues not covered by explicit rules or contracts is therefore inevitable and indeed desirable.

I don't think the new 'positive' theories of economic policy (mainly concerning monetary policy but also some dealing with fiscal policy (Barro [1979a]) have brought us much closer, as yet, to an understanding of what determines the conduct of economic policy. The games that are analysed bear as yet little resemblance to the 'true game'. The real-world objectives and constraints of policy makers (electoral system, party-political organization, ideological concerns, class structure, interest groups, information, administrative bureaucracy, resources etc) are still too far from these assumed in the formal models for the latter to give us useful parables, but there is hope that this may change. (See, for example, Alesina and Tabellini [1988], Canzoneri and Henderson [1987], Persson [1988].

At this stage, rather than attempting to determine what policies would be time-consistent given an arbitrary set of policy maker objective functions and constraints, I would give priority to the 'normative' approach of determining the optimal policy (for some reasonable consensus objective function) ignoring the time consistency constraints (i.e. assuming complete ability to precommit) and without attempting to model the political processes constraining economic policy choices. Having derived the optimal policy, I would then turn towards the design of institutions that might support the optimum as a time-consistent outcome. Sometimes repetition and reputation can achieve that by themselves. Often, I fear, more serious social engineering may be required.

Wage and price dynamics

Chapter 8 in this volume (Buiter and Jewitt [1981]) is a 'sensitivity analysis' of Taylor's model of staggered, overlapping nominal wage contracts (Taylor [1979, 1980]). Taylor's model can be viewed as a relative money wage (RMW) model. The N-period nominal contract wage set in period t by contracting firms and unions depends on the nominal contract wages set (or expected to be set) by other firms and unions that will be in effect during the life of the contract negotiated at time t. Our alternative relative real wage (RRW) model instead views the N-period nominal contract wage negotiated in period t as a function of the *real* wages achieved or expected to be achieved by other wage bargainers with whose contract periods there is some degree of overlap.

The implications of this change in assumption for the 'univariate final forms' of the wage and price processes are quite marked. With N-period contracts, the RMW model yields an $(N-1)^{\text{th}}$ order stochastic difference equation (with a random disturbance term) for the contract wage and an ARIMA $(N-1, N-1)$ process for the general price level. The RRW model yields a $2N-2$ order stochastic difference equation for the contract wage and an ARIMA $(2N-2, 2N-2)$ process for the general price level. With the RMW model, the coefficients on lagged contract wages in the contract wage equation always have a common sign. The lag coefficients in the RRW model will generally have mixed signs. It is also shown that Taylor's RMW model is observationally equivalent to a real wage model without relative wage effects, i.e. one in which the nominal contract wage in period t is set to achieve a given real wage over the life of the contract, without any reference to other contract wages.

Chapter 9, Buiter and Miller [1985] looks at the output or unemployment cost of achieving a permanent reduction in the rate of inflation under a variety of assumptions about the nature of the wage-price process. A 'sacrifice ratio' (Gordon [1973]) of zero can be achieved with credibility alone in neoclassical flex-price models. Models with *price level inertia* such as the ones developed by Mussa [1981] and Calvo [1982] require credibility plus a once-off 'level jump' in the nominal money stock, if the demand for money is interest-sensitive and the nominal interest rate declines with the rate of inflation. Models with *price level* and *inflation inertia* require credibility, a nominal money jump plus some other means of melting core inflation such as changes in (indirect) taxes or a 'deus-ex-machina' like incomes policy. In general a positive sacrifice ratio may not be avoidable.

In an open economy, the sacrifice ratio need not be reduced by the use of an 'up-front' sharp appreciation of the exchange rate, if the long-run real exchange rate is independent of the rate of inflation. In a 'hysteretic' model of the natural rate with adaptive 'core inflation' the sacrifice ratio becomes infinite, just as in the old 'unaugmented' Phillips curve models. The reason is that the natural rate adjusts (gradually) towards the actual unemployment rate, thus destroying gradually the anti-inflationary effect of higher unemployment.

The problems of time-inconsistency of anti-inflationary strategies in models with forward-looking wage contracts is addressed both in Buiter and Miller [1985] and in Buiter [1986], chapters 9 and 10 in this volume.

Debt neutrality and financial crowding out

Barro's celebrated 1974 paper on debt neutrality (Barro [1974]) stimulated a new wave of theoretical and empirical work on the subject. Of the four contributions included in Part 4 of this volume, the one most directly inspired by Barro's analysis is Buiter [1980b, Chapter 11]. It considers the consequences of introducing intergenerational caring along the lines suggested by Barro, into Diamond's [1965] two-period OLG model with a neoclassical production function. I had a rather less successful earlier stab at the same problem (Buiter [1979]). It was the work of Jeffrey Carmichael [1979], then a PhD student of mine at Princeton, that showed the correct way ahead (see also Carmichael [1982]). Using the additive specification suggested by Barro, the utility function of a member of generation t who cares directly about his descendant(s) is given by

$$W_t = u(c_t^1, c_t^2) + (1 + \delta)^{-1} W_{t+1} \tag{24}$$

c_t^1 is consumption while young of a member of generation t; c_t^2 is the consumption while old, $u(.,\ .)$ is the egoistic lifetime utility function, assumed to have all the usual nice properties. W_{t+1} is the utility of a representative descendant (born in period $t+1$). The weight attached to the representative descendant's total utility, W_{t+1}, is $(1+\delta)^{-1}$. Carmichael and I assume $\delta > 0$, i.e. altruism is limited and children's welfare is discounted. If the chain of descendants is never expected to end, $\delta > 0$ is of course necessary for the forward looking infinite sum implied by (24) to converge. The discount factor $(1+\delta)^{-1}$ can be reinterpreted to incorporate a 'the more the merrier' view of the utility derived from one's children. Let $1 + \delta \equiv \dfrac{(1 + \delta')}{1 + n}$. The number of children is $1 + n \geqslant 0$ and δ' is the true generational discount rate.

The other one-sided form of intergenerational caring involves direct concern for one's immediate ancestors only, as in (25)

$$W_t = u(c_t^1\ c_t^2) + (1 + \rho)^{-1} W_{t-1} \tag{25}$$

Again Carmichael and I assume $\rho > 0$, i.e. parental utility is discounted. We assume this because we believe this to be intrinsically plausible and because, if the ancestral chain stretches back infinitely far into the past, the infinite sum in (25) only converges if $\rho > 0$. Burbridge [1983] objected to this, in part (if I interpret him correctly) because it involves *discounting* utility that was enjoyed earlier, rather than compounding it. I view time preference as quite distinct from generational discounting (see Buiter and Carmichael [1984], in this volume). $\rho > 0$ has the interesting property that any steady state (without productivity growth) in which the child-to-parent gift motive is operative will be dynamically inefficient (the interest rate is below the growth rate). Since the model does not have infinite-lived agents or private institutions to take advantage of the potentially profitable Ponzi game implied by such a configuration of interest rate and growth rate, I consider this to be an acceptable equilibrium.

The case of two-sided intergenerational caring is not dealt with satisfactorily in my 1980 paper. The correct resolution of this case had to wait for Kimball's elegant treatment (Kimball [1987]). (See also Buiter [1988b].)

Buiter [1983a] is a non-technical survey of some of the issues involved in the debt neutrality debate. It also reviews the issues of government solvency, the consistency of fiscal, financial and monetary plans, the sustainability of public sector deficits and the eventual monetization of deficits. While the distinction between current and capital expenditures is considered, the composition and content of public spending is not emphasized sufficiently (see e.g. Barro [1981b]).

Buiter [1988a], Chapter 14 in this volume, analyses the necessary and sufficient conditions for debt neutrality in Blanchard's elegant OLG model (Blanchard [1984, 1985]), based on Yaari's work on uncertain lifetimes (Yaari [1965]). It appeared from Blanchard's work that in an OLG model with a common, constant probability of death, a positive probability of death drove a wedge between the government's rate of discount and the private sector's risk-of-death adjusted discount rate. This then accounted for absence of debt neutrality. Weil [1985] showed that even with infinite individual horizons (i.e. a zero probability of death), a positive birth rate was sufficient for absence of debt neutrality (always assuming no (operative) intergenerational caring). My analysis shows that in the Blanchard model, a positive birth rate is *necessary* and *sufficient* for absence of debt neutrality. The probability of death is not relevant. In Blanchard's model population was constant, so birth and death rates were equal. When the two are disentangled, it is clear that the birth rate does all the work: when everybody has the same life expectancy (finite or infinite), postponing lump-sum taxes on human capital income only makes those currently alive better off if there are 'new-entrants' whose human capital can bear (part of) the burden of the postponed taxes.

Odds 'n ends

The last two chapters in this volume do not fit neatly into any category. Chapter 15 (Buiter and Lorie [1977]), written with Henri Lorie while we both spent a year at the LSE in 1976–77, analyses the behaviour of output, employment, real wage and general price level in what used to be viewed as the textbook neo-Keynesian aggregate demand-aggregate supply model. The familiar IS-LM model is supplemented with a production function making output an increasing function of employment with diminishing marginal productivity of labour. Competitive labour demand equates real wage and marginal product of labour. The supply of labour is an increasing function of the real wage. The price level is freely flexible but the money wage is predetermined. The money wage is fixed at a point in time both when labour supply exceeds demand and when labour demand exceeds supply. The 'principle of voluntary exchange' applies (i.e. the short side rules). For levels of the real wage below the Walrasian market-clearing one, the labour supply function therefore governs employment and employment and output are increasing functions of the real wage.

An augmented wage-Phillips curve governs the adjustment of money wages over time. Core inflation is modelled adaptively (including the special case of exogenous core inflation or static inflation expectations) or as a rational (forward-looking) inflation expectations process. The model can generate pro-cyclical variations of the real wage (when the labour supply function binds) as well as output and employment levels that fall below the Walrasian full employment levels in response to expansionary demand shocks.

Finally, chapter 16 (Buiter [1980c]) considers some of the conceptual and technical issues involved in going from discrete period models to models in which the unit period goes to zero. A key point is that the 'time structure' of asset demand functions (and expectation functions) involves (at least) 4 'time dimensions'. (1) The date, t_0, at which plans are made, demands are formulated or expectations are formed. (2) The market date to which these plans, demands (or expectations) refer, $t_1 \geqslant t_0$. (3) The maturity of the forward contract to be concluded in that market, $t_2 - t_1 \geqslant 0$. (4) The length of the interval between successive market openings ($t_3 - t_1 \geqslant 0$).

When previous authors took the limit as the length of 'the' unit interval went to zero, it often wasn't very clear which of the various unit intervals was being manipulated. A common implicit assumption was $t_1 = t_0$ and $t_2 - t_1 = t_3 - t_1 = \Delta$ say. The usual limiting process as $\Delta \rightarrow 0$ therefore involved simultaneously taking the maturity of the forward contract and the interval between successive market dates to zero.

The distinction between end-of-period and beginning-of-period asset market equilibrium specifications introduced by Foley [1975], foreshadowed in May [1970] and Chand [1973] and elaborated in Buiter and Woglom [1977], Turnovsky [1977] and Turnovsky and Burmeister [1977], has recently become relevant again through the popularity of cash-in-advance models which have a discrete time structure with a beginning-of-period asset market equilibrium specification. The consequences of mixing up beginning- and end-of-period specifications can be seen in Kuska [1978] who argued that equality between the demand for and supply of money implied that the overall balance of payments had to be in equilibrium. It is of course precisely balance of payments deficits and surpluses and the associated losses and gains of international reserves which, given domestic credit expansion, permit money demand and money supply in an open economy to be brought into equilibrium (see Buiter and Eaton [1981]).

III Conclusion

Macroeconomics appears to be redirecting itself slowly from its recent self-referential preoccupation with a certain kind of abstract elegance to the rather messier, much harder but also ultimately much more rewarding task of modelling the essential features of an awkward economic reality.

Certain of the developments associated with the NCM will be of lasting value in the (no doubt never-ending) quest for a better understanding of real-world economic systems. First among these is the emphasis on the importance of modelling expectation formation as another activity of purposeful economic agents. Whether the strong-form rational expectations hypothesis will survive as the leading operational expression of reasonable expectation formation is an open question. As yet there are no obvious alternative candidates. The recognition of the problem of the time-inconsistency of optimal plans and the representation of economic policy making as a non-co-operative leader–follower game are also contributions that will last.

The preoccupation of the NCM with Walrasian competitive equilibrium models is likely to prove a diversion or even a step backwards on the road to a better understanding of real-world economic phenomena. The complete state-contingent markets, Arrow-Debreu paradigm is clearly not a useful starting point for further investigation of real-world economic questions. The focus on representative agent models within the Arrow-Debreu class can only be explained by the self-referential nature of New-Classical discourse already referred to, i.e. its tendency to use only its own methodology, tools and criteria to evaluate and criticise the products it creates.

The OLG model is a much more likely survivor, both because it introduces, inevitably, some heterogeneity among consumers and because it does not fit comfortably into the 'one-shot' interpretation of the Arrow-Debreu models (an interpretation that ends their usefulness for studying issues in economic dynamics).

The (slow) development of general equilibrium models with imperfect competition in labour and product markets bodes well for the future. The application of the insights of the asymmetric information paradigm to labour, product and financial markets will no doubt continue to bring us closer to an understanding of the world we live in.

I am quite convinced that a better understanding of labour market behaviour, consumption behaviour and portfolio allocation will require us to abandon our view of the 'primitive' economic unit as an optimizing egoistic consumption machine, constrained only by endowments, prices and exogenous search technologies and information sets. The spirit of inquiry that springs from Okun's book (Okun [1981]) or from Akerlof's book (Akerlof [1984]) is therefore, to me, of greater significance as an indicator of the shape of things to come than any contribution of the NCM.

We shall probably have to learn (or even develop) new mathematical tools (non-linear stochastic ordinary and partial differential equations, non-linear stochastic difference equations, catastrophe theory, complexity theory, fuzzy sets and what not), which is bad news for those who, like me, are already straining to hang on.

In addition, a much greater knowledge of institutions and of economic history will be required and a willingness to take on board insights from other disciplines ranging from cybernetics and biology to (social) psychology, sociology, political science, and anthropology. It may be that the superman-or-woman (or the super-team) capable of keeping all these balls in the air doesn't exist and is unlikely to emerge in the near future. In that case all one can do is to plod on as best one may. It is, however, surely better to work towards imperfect (or even downright poor) abstractions of an awkward reality than to create elegant constructs that are orthogonal to what we know of the real world.

Notes

1 Sometimes an 'act "as if"' caveat is appended. This does not change the substance of the RE assumption.
2 Lucas [1987, p. 13, fn. 4] objects to this characterization, for reasons that are not clear to me.
3 In its most abstract representation, the Arrow-Debreu model dispenses with RE. Preferences defined over contingent state commodities reflect time preference, attitudes towards risk, interactions between states and consumption as well as subjective probability beliefs.
4 Sometimes, as in Barro and Gordon [1983], the government plays against a 'large' private agent, such as a union.
5 Except for the aggregate excess demand function satisfying Walras's Law, continuity and homogeneity.
6 I am ignoring the problems of the closed economy framework that has been used almost universally to analyze US data. It is unfortunate that even in the 1980's the potentially empirically relevant fact of the openness of the US economy is not universally recognized.
7 In (1b) there is a single labour market.
8 Note that even if the pricing policies of individual firms exhibit nominal inertia, aggregate price behaviour may be smooth and money may be neutral. Caplin and Spulber [1987] show this for an economy in which firms follow (s, S) pricing rules.
9 Note that, under (11a) $x_t - E(x_t \mid \Omega_{t-1}) = x_t$.
10 The structural interpretation of 'error-correction' mechanisms is subject to many of the same criticisms, see e.g. Campbell and Shiller [1988].
11 The choice of variables to be included in (and excluded from) the VAR is of course a key prior restriction that cannot be avoided. Degrees of freedom problems also create the need for a-priori restrictions on the maximum number of lags. In the example discussed below, neither problem arises. The variables are also assumed to be covariance stationary.

12 An extensive discussion of identification in linear rational expectations models can be found in Pesaran [1987]. (An early classic on the subject is Sargent [1976b]). Like most of the traditional identification literature, it is cast in terms of the identification of all the parameters in an equation or system of equations. The parameters of interest in an economic investigation are often a subset of the (structural) parameters in an equation or system of equations (not infrequently just a single parameter). It would be more useful to have identification conditions for individual parameters or subsets of the parameters.
13 The system in (17) is assumed to be stationary.
14 We assume $1 \neq \alpha_2\beta_2$.
15 We assume $1 \neq (\alpha_2 + \alpha_3)(\beta_2 + \beta_3)$.
16 We choose the 'minimal-state' (no-bubbles) solution, assuming that (21a) has one stable and one unstable root.
17 'Causal' is used here in the sense of 'concerning causal (or recursive) orderings'. The status of variables (in linear models) as predetermined or strictly exogenous cannot be inferred from the data. (x is predetermined in the model of equations (15) and (16) if $\beta_2 + \beta_3 = 0$. It is predetermined and strictly exogenous if $\beta_2 + \beta_3 = 0$ and $\beta_1 = 0$).
18 Cooley and Leroy mention certain restricted versions of the efficient asset markets model; the failure of optimally determined policy instruments in LQG models to Granger-cause any variables in the information set of the policy maker; certain restricted versions of the natural rate hypothesis; Hall's version of the life-cycle – permanent income hypothesis and certain market equilibrium models with noisy price measurement.

References

Akerlof, G. (1970), 'The Market for "Lemons": Quality Uncertainty and the Market Mechanism', *Quarterly Journal of Economics*, 84, August, pp. 488–500.

—— (1984), *An Economic Theorist's Book of Tales*, Cambridge University Press, Cambridge.

—— and Yellen, J. (1985a), 'A Near Rational Model of the Business Cycle, with Wage and Price Inertia', *Quarterly Journal of Economics*, August, pp. 823–38.

—— and —— (1985b), 'Can small deviations from rationality make significant differences to economic equilibria?', *American Economic Review*, 75, September, pp. 708–20.

—— and —— (1986), *Efficiency Wage Models of the Labor Market*, Cambridge University Press, Cambridge.

—— and —— (1988), 'How large are the losses from rule-of-thumb behaviour in models of the business cycle?', mimeo, May.

Alesina, A. (1987), 'Macroeconomic policy in a two-party system as a repeated game', *Quarterly Journal of Economics*.

—— and Tabellini, G. (1988), 'Credibility and Politics', *European Economic Review*, 32, pp. 542–50.

Arnott, R. and Stiglitz, J. (1987), 'Equilibrium in Competitive Insurance Markets with Moral Hazard', mimeo.

—— and —— (1988), 'The Basic Analytics of Moral Hazard', *NBER Working Paper*, No. 2484, January.

Arrow, K. (1964), 'The Role of Securities in the Optimal Allocation of Risk Bearing', *Review of Economic Studies*, 31, pp. 91–6.

Azariadis, C. (1981), 'Self-fulfilling Prophecies', *Journal of Economic Theory*, 25, pp. 380–96.
—— and Guesnerie, R. (1986), 'Sunspots and Cycles', *Review of Economic Studies*, 53, pp. 787–806.
Backus, D. and Driffill, J. (1985), 'Inflation and Reputation', *American Economics Review*, 75, June, pp. 530–38.
Barro, R. (1974), 'Are Government Bonds Net Wealth?', *Journal of Political Economy*, 82, November–December, pp. 1095–117.
—— (1976), 'Rational Expectations and the Role of Monetary Policy', *Journal of Monetary Economics*, 2 January, pp. 1–32.
—— (1977a), 'Unanticipated Money Growth and Unemployment in the United States', *American Economic Review*, 67, March pp. 101–15.
—— (1977b), 'Long-term Contracting, Sticky Prices and Monetary Policy', *Journal of Monetary Economics*, 3, pp. 305–16.
—— (1978), 'Unanticipated Money, Output and the Price Level in the United States', *Journal of Political Economy*', 86, August, pp. 549–81.
—— (1979a), 'On the Determination of the Public Debt', *Journal of Political Economy*, 87, Pt. 1, October, pp. 940–71.
—— (1979b), 'Second Thoughts on Keynesian Economics', *American Economic Review*, Papers and Proceedings, 69, May, pp. 54–9.
—— (1981a), *Money, Expectations and Business Cycles, Essays in Macroeconomics*, Academic Press, New York.
—— (1981b), 'Output Effects of Government Purchases', *Journal of Political Economy*, 89, December, pp. 1086–121.
—— (1986), 'Recent Developments in the Theory of Rules versus Discretion', *Economic Journal*, 96, Supplement, pp. 23–37.
—— (1987), *Macroeconomics*, 2nd ed., Wiley, New York.
—— and Gordon, D. (1983), 'A Positive Theory of Monetary Policy in a Natural Rate World', *Journal of Political Economy*, 91, August, pp. 589–610.
Benhabib, J. and Day, R. (1981), 'Rational Choice and Erratic Behaviour', *Review of Economic Studies*, 48, pp. 459–71.
—— and —— (1982), 'A Characterization of Erratic Dynamics in the Overlapping Generations Model', *Journal of Economic Dynamics and Control*, 4, pp. 37–55.
Bernanke, B. (1983), 'Non-Monetary Effects of the Financial Crisis in the Propagation of the Great Depression', *American Economic Review*, 73, June, pp. 257–76.
—— (1985), 'Alternative Explanations of the Money-Income Correlation', *Carnegie-Rochester Conference on Public Policy*, ed. K. Brunner and A. H. Weltman.
—— and Gertler, M. (1987a), 'Banking and Macroeconomic Equilibrium', in W. A. Barnett and K. J. Singleton (eds.), *New Approaches to Monetary Economics*, Cambridge University Press, Cambridge, pp. 89–111.
—— and —— (1987b), 'Financial Fragility and Economic Performance', *NBER Working Paper*, No. 2138, July.
Bernheim, B. and Bagwell, K. (1988), 'Is Everything Neutral?' *Journal of Political Economy*, 96, April, pp. 308–38.
Blanchard, O. (1984), 'Current and Anticipated Deficits, Interest Rates and Economic Activity', *European Economic Review*, 25, pp. 7–27.
—— (1985), 'Debt, Deficits and Finite Horizons', *Journal of Political Economy*, 93, April, pp. 223–47.
—— and Kiyotaki, N. (1987), 'Monopolistic Competition and the Effects of Aggregate Demand', *American Economic Review*, 77, September, pp. 647–66.

—— and Watson, M. (1986), 'Are Business Cycles All Alike?', in R. J. Gordon (ed.), *The American Business Cycle*, University of Chicago Press, Chicago, pp. 123–56.
Blanco, H. and Garber, P. (1986), 'Recurrent Devaluation and Speculative Attacks on the Mexican Peso', *Journal of Political Economy*, 94, No. 4, February, pp. 148–66.
Bray, M. (1982), 'Learning, Estimation and the Stability of Rational Expectations', *Journal of Economic Theory*, 26, pp. 318–39.
—— (1983), 'Convergence to Rational Expectations Equilibrium', in R. Frydman and E. S. Phelps (eds.), *Individual Forecasting and Aggregate Outcomes*, Cambridge University Press, Cambridge.
—— and Kreps, D. (1987), 'Rational Learning and Rational Expectations', in G. R. Feiwel (ed.), *Arrow and the Ascent of Modern Economic Theory*, NYU Press, New York.
Bryant, J. and Wallace, N. (1984), 'A Price Discrimination Analysis of Monetary Policy', *Review of Economic Studies*, Vol. 51, April, pp. 279–88.
Buiter, W. (1979), 'Government Finance in an Overlapping Generations Model with Gifts and Bequests', in G. M. von Fürstenberg (ed.), *Social Security vs. Private Saving*, Ballinger.
—— (1980a), 'The Macroeconomics of Dr. Pangloss: A Critical Survey of the New Classical Macroeconomics', *Economic Journal*, 90, March, pp. 34–50.
—— (1980b), '"Crowding Out" of private capital formation by government borrowing in the presence of intergenerational gifts and bequests', *Greek Economic Review*, Vol. 2, No. 2, August, pp. 111–42.
—— (1980c), 'Walras' Law and All That: Budget Constraints and Balance Sheet Constraints in Period Models and Continuous Time Models', *International Economic Review*, 21, No. 4, February, pp. 1–16.
—— (1981), 'The superiority of Contingent Rules over Fixed Rules in Models with Rational Expectations', *Economic Journal*, 91, September, pp. 647–70.
—— (1982), 'Predetermined and non-predetermined variables in rational expectations models', *Economics Letters*, 10, pp. 49–54.
—— (1983a), 'The Theory of Optimum Deficits and Debt', in *The Economics of Large Government Deficits*. Federal Reserve Bank of Boston Conference Series, No. 27, pp. 46–69.
—— (1983b), 'Expectations and Control Theory', *Economie Appliquée*, Vol. 36, No. 1, pp. 129–56.
—— (1983c), 'Real Effects of Anticipated and Unanticipated Money: Some Problems of Estimation and Hypothesis Testing', *Journal of Monetary Economics*, 11, pp. 207–24.
—— (1984), 'Granger Causality and Policy Effectiveness', *Economica*, 51, May 1984, pp. 151–62.
—— (1986), 'Policy Evaluation and Design for Continuous Time Linear Rational Expectations Models; Some Recent Developments', in M. H. Peston and R. E. Quandt (eds.), *Prices, Competition and Equilibrium*, Philip Allen, Barnes & Noble Books, Oxford, pp. 84–108.
—— (1988a), 'Death, Birth, Productivity Growth and Debt Neutrality', *Economic Journal*, 98, June, pp. 279–93.
—— (1988b), 'Debt Neutrality, Redistribution and Consumer Heterogeneity: a Survey and some Extensions', *NBER Working Paper*, No. 2578, May.
—— (1988c), 'The Right Combination of Demand and Supply Policies: The Case for a Two-Handed Approach', in H. Müller-Groeling (ed.), *Macro- and Micro-Policies for More Growth and Employment*, Kiel Institute of World Economics.

—— (1988d), *Budgetary Policy, International and Intertemporal Trade in the Global Economy*, to be published by North-Holland, Amsterdam.
—— and Carmichael, J. (1984), 'Government Debt: Comment', *American Economic Review*, 74, pp. 762–5.
—— and Eaton, J. (1981), 'Keynesian Balance of Payments Models: Comment', *American Economic Review*, 71, September, pp. 784–95.
—— and Jewitt, I. (1981), 'Staggered Wage Setting With Real Wage Relativities: Variations on a Theme of Taylor', *The Manchester School*, Vol. 49, September, pp. 211–28.
—— and Lorie, H. (1977), 'Some Unfamiliar Properties of a Familiar Macroeconomic Model', *Economic Journal*, 87, December, pp. 743–54.
—— and Miller, M. (1985), 'Costs and Benefits of an Anti-Inflationary Policy: Questions and Issues', in V. Argy and J. Nevile (eds.), *Inflation and Unemployment: Theory, Experience and Policy Making*, George Allen & Unwin, London, pp. 11–38.
—— and Woglom, G. (1977), 'On Two Specifications of Asset Equilibrium in Macroeconomic Models: A Note', *Journal of Political Economy*, 85, April, pp. 395–400.
Burbidge, J. (1983), 'Government Debt in an overlapping Generations Model with Bequests and Gifts', *American Economic Review*, 73, March, pp. 222–7.
Calvo, G. (1982), 'Staggered Contracts and Exchange Rate Policy', Columbia University Discussion Paper Series, No. 129, New York.
Campbell, J. Y. and Shiller, R. J. (1988), 'Interpreting Cointegrated Models', *NBER Working Paper*, No. 2568, April.
Canzoneri, M. and Henderson, D. (1987), 'Is sovereign policy making bad?', *Carnegie-Rochester Conference Series on Public Policy*, North-Holland, Amsterdam.
Caplin, A. and Spulber, D. (1987), 'Menu Costs and the Neutrality of Money', *Quarterly Journal of Economics*, 102, Issue 4, November, pp. 703–25.
Carmichael, J. (1979), 'The Role of Government Financial Policy in Economic Growth', unpublished PhD Thesis, Princeton University.
—— (1982), 'On Barro's Theorem of Debt Neutrality: The Irrelevance of Net Wealth', *American Economic Review*, 72, March, pp. 202–13.
Chand, S. (1973), 'Period Analysis and Continuous Analysis in Patinkin's Macroeconomic Model – A Critical Note', *Journal of Economic Theory*, 6, October, pp. 520–24.
Chiappori, P. and Guesnerie, R. (1988), 'Endogenous Fluctuations under Rational Expectations', *European Economic Review*, 32, pp. 389–97.
Cho, J-O. and Rogerson, R. (1988), 'Family Labour Supply and Aggregate Fluctuations', *Journal of Monetary Economics*, 21, March–May, pp. 233–46.
Christiano, L. (1988), 'Why does inventory investment fluctuate so much?', *Journal of Monetary Economics*, 21, March–May, pp. 247–80.
Cooley, T. and Leroy, S. (1985), 'A-theoretical Macroeconometrics: A Critique', *Journal of Monetary Economics*, 16, No. 3, November, pp. 283–308.
Cooper, R. and John, A. (1985), 'Co-ordination Failures in Keynesian Models', Cowles Foundation mimeo.
Cyert, R. and De Groot, M. (1974), 'Rational Expectations and Bayesian Analysis', *Journal of Political Economy*, 82, pp. 521–36.
—— and March, J. (1963), *A Behavioural Theory of the Firm*, Prentice Hall, Englewood Cliffs.
Day, R. (1982), 'Irregular Growth Cycles', *American Economic Review*, 72, pp. 406–14.
—— (1983), 'The Emergence of Chaos from Classical Economic Growth', *Quar-*

terly Journal of Economics, 98, pp. 201–13.
Debreu, G. (1959), *Theory of Value*, Yale University Press, New Haven, Connecticut.
Diamond, P. (1965), 'National Debt in a Neo-Classical Growth Model', *American Economics Review*, 55, December, pp. 1126–50.
—— (1967), 'The Role of a Stock Market in a General Equilibrium Model with Technological Uncertainty', *American Economic Review*, 57, pp. 759–76.
—— (1970), 'Incidence of an Interest Income Tax', *Journal of Economic Theory*, 2, pp. 211–24.
—— (1982), 'Aggregate Demand Management in Search Equilibrium', *Journal of Political Economy*, 90, pp. 881–94.
—— (1988), 'Credit in Search Equilibrium', in Meir Kohn and Sho-Chieh Tsiang, *Finance Constraints, Expectations, and Macroeconomics*, pp. 36–53, Oxford University Press, Oxford.
Dixit, A. and Stiglitz, J. (1977), 'Monopolistic Competition and Optimum Product Diversity', *American Economic Review*, 67, pp. 297–308.
Drèze, J. (1985), 'Uncertainty and the Firm in General Equilibrium Theory', *Economic Journal*, 95, Supplement, pp. 1–20.
Drifill, J. (1988), 'Macroeconomic Policy Games with Incomplete Information: A Survey', *European Economic Review*, 32, pp. 533–41.
Ees, H. van (1987), 'An explanation of unemployment through an integration of the efficiency wage theory and the kinked demand curve approach', mimeo, University of Groningen (revised), October.
Eichenbaum, M. and Singleton, K. (1986), 'Do equilibrium real business cycle theories explain post-war US business cycles?', in S. Fischer (ed.), *NBER Macroeconomics Annual 1986*, MIT Press, Cambridge, pp. 91–134.
Engle, R., Hendry, D. and Richard, J. (1983), 'Exogeneity', *Econometrica*, 51, pp. 277–304.
Farmer, R. and Woodford, M. (1986), 'Self-fulfilling prophecies and the business cycle', CARESS Discussion Paper.
Fischer, S. (1974), 'Money and the Production Function', *Economic Inquiry*, 12, December, pp. 517–33.
—— (1977), 'Long-term Contracts, Rational Expectations and the Optimal Money Supply Rule', *Journal of Political Economy*, 85, pp. 191–206.
—— (1980), 'Dynamic Inconsistency, Co-operation, and the Benevolent Dissembling Government', *Journal of Economic Dynamics and Control*, 2, pp. 93–107.
Foley, D. (1975), 'On Two Specifications of Asset Equilibrium in Macroeconomic Models', *Journal of Political Economy*, 83, April, pp. 305–24.
Friedman, M. (1968), 'The Role of Monetary Policy', *American Economic Review*, 58(1), March, pp. 1–17.
Gertler, M. (1988), 'Financial Structure and Aggregate Economic Activity: An Overview', *NBER Working Paper*, No. 2559, April.
Geweke, J. (1984), 'Inference and Causality in Economic Time Series Models', Ch. 9 in Z. Griliches and M. Intriligator (eds.), *Handbook of Econometrics*, Vol. 2, North-Holland, Amsterdam, pp. 1101–44.
Goodwin, R. (1951), 'The Non-linear Accelerator and the Persistence of Business Cycles', *Econometrica*, 19, pp. 1–17.
—— (1982), Essay in Economic Dynamics', Macmillan, New York.
Gordon, R. (1973), 'The Welfare Costs of Higher Unemployment', *Brookings Papers on Economic Activity*, 1, pp. 133–205.
—— (ed.) (1986), *The American Business Cycle*, University of Chicago Press, Chicago.

—— and King, S. (1982), 'The Output Cost of Disinflation in Traditional and Vector Autoregressive Models', *Brookings Papers on Economic Activity*, 1, pp. 205–42.

Grandmont, J. (1985), 'On Endogenous Competitive Business Cycles', *Econometrica*, 53, pp. 995–1045.

—— (1986), 'Stabilizing Competitive Business Cycles', *Journal of Economic Theory*, 40, pp. 57–76.

Granger, C. (1969), 'Investigating Causal Relations by Econometric Models and Cross-spectral Methods', *Econometrica*, 37, July, pp. 424–38.

—— (1980), 'Testing for Causality: A Personal Viewpoint', *Journal of Economic Dynamics and Control*, 2, pp. 329–52.

Grossman, S. and Hart, O. (1980), 'Take-over bids, the free rider problem and the theory of the corporation', *Bell Journal of Economics*, 11, pp. 42–64.

—— and Stiglitz, J. (1980), 'On the Impossibility of Informationally Efficient Markets', *American Economics Review*, 70, June, pp. 393–408.

Hall, R. (1978), 'Stochastic Implications of the Life-Cycle Permanent Income Hypothesis: Theory and Evidence', *Journal of Political Economy*, 86, December, pp. 971–87.

—— (1986), 'Market Structure and Macroeconomic Fluctuations', *Brookings Papers on Economic Activity*, 2, pp. 283–322.

—— (1988), 'A Non-Competitive, Equilibrium Model of Fluctuations', *NBER Working Paper*, No. 2576, May.

Hansen, G. and Sargent, T. (1988), 'Straight Time and Overtime in Equilibrium', *Journal of Monetary Economics*, March–May, pp. 281–308.

Hart, O. (1982), 'A Model of Imperfect Competition with Keynesian Features', *Quarterly Journal of Economics*, 97, February, pp. 109–38.

—— (1983), 'Optimal Labour Contracts under Asymmetric Information: An Introduction', *Review of Economic Studies*, pp. 3–35.

Heckman, J. and Macurdy, T. (1988), 'Empirical Tests of Labour-market Equilibrium: An Evaluation', *Carnegie-Rochester Conference Series on Public Policy*, Vol. 28, Spring 1988, *Stabilization Policies and Labour Markets*, pp. 231–58.

Helpman, E. and Laffont, J. (1975), 'On Moral Hazard in General Equilibrium', *Journal of Economic Theory*, 10, pp. 8–23.

Hsiao, C. (1979), 'Causality Tests in Econometrics', *Journal of Economic Dynamics and Control*, 1, pp. 321–46.

Jacobs, R., Leamer, E. and Ward, M. (1979), 'Difficulties with Testing for Causation', *Economic Enquiry*, 17, pp. 247–79.

Jaffee, D. and Russell, T. (1976), 'Imperfect Information and Credit Rationing', *Quarterly Journal of Economics*, 90, pp. 651–66.

Jones, S. and Stock, J. (1987), 'Demand Disturbances and Aggregate Fluctuations: The Implications of Near Rationality', *Economic Journal*, 97, March, pp. 49–64.

Kaldor, N. (1940), 'A Model of the Trade Cycle', *Economic Journal*, 50, pp. 78–92.

Katz, L. (1986), 'Efficiency Wage Theories: A Partial Evaluation' in S. Fischer (ed.), *NBER Macroeconomics Annual 1986*, MIT Press, Cambridge, Mass., pp. 235–76.

Keynes, J. M. (1936), *The General Theory of Employment, Interest and Money*, Macmillan, London.

Kimball, M. (1987), 'Making Sense of Two-sided Altruism', *Journal of Monetary Economics*, 20, September, pp. 301–26.

King, R., Plosser, C. and Robelo, S. (1988a), 'Production, Growth and Business

Cycles: I. The Basic Neoclassical Model', *Journal of Monetary Economics*, 21, March–May, pp. 195–232.
——, —— and —— (1988b), 'Production, Growth and Business Cycles: II. New Directions', *Journal of Monetary Economics*, 21, March–May, pp. 309–42.
Kreps, D. and Wilson, R. (1982), 'Reputation and Imperfect Information', *Journal of Economic Theory*, 27, August, pp. 253–79.
Kuska, E. (1978), 'On the almost total inadequacy of Keynesian balance-of-payments theory', *American Economic Review*, 68, September, pp. 659–70.
Kydland, F. (1984), 'Labour Force Heterogeneity and the Business Cycle', *Carnegie-Rochester Conference Series on Public Policy*, 21, pp. 173–208.
—— and Prescott, E. (1977), 'Rules rather than Discretion: the Inconsistency of Optimal Plans', *Journal of Political Economy*, Vol. 85, June, pp. 473–91.
—— and —— (1980), 'A Competitive Theory of Fluctuations and the Feasability and Desirability of Stabilization Policy', in S. Fischer, (ed.), *Rational Expectations and Economic Policy*, University of Chicago Press, Chicago, pp. 169–87.
—— and —— (1982), 'Time to build and aggregate fluctuations', *Econometrica*, 50, 1345–70.
Kydland F. E. and Prescott, E. C. (1988), 'The workweek of capital and its cyclical implications', *Journal of Monetary Economics*, 21, March–May, pp. 309–42.
Laffont, J-J. and Maskin, E. (1982), 'The Theory of Incentives: An Overview', in W. Hildenbrand (ed.), *Advances in Economic Theory*, Cambridge University Press, Cambridge.
Lilien, D. M. (1982), 'Sectoral shifts and cyclical unemployment', *Journal of Political Economy*, 90, August, pp. 777–93.
Long, J. B. and Plosser, C. I. (1983), 'Real Business Cycles', *Journal of Political Economy*, 91, February, pp. 39–69.
Lucas, R. E. (1972a), 'Expectations and the neutrality of money', *Journal of Economic Theory*, 4, April, pp. 103–24.
—— (1972b), 'Econometric Testing of the Natural Rate Hypothesis' in O. Eckstein (ed.), *The Econometrics of Price Determination*, Board of Governors of the Federal Reserve System and Social Science Research Council.
—— (1973), 'Some International Evidence on Output-Inflation Tradeoffs', *American Economic Review*, 63, pp. 326–34.
—— (1975), 'An Equilibrium Model of the Business Cycle', *Journal of Political Economy*, 83, December, pp. 1113–44.
—— (1976), 'Econometric Policy Evaluation: A Critique' in *The Phillips curve and Labour Markets*, K. Brunner and A. H. Meltzer (eds.), North-Holland, Amsterdam.
—— (1977), 'Understanding Business Cycles', *Journal of Monetary Economics*, Supplement (Carnegie-Rochester Conference Series, Vol. 5).
—— (1978), 'Asset prices in an exchange economy', *Econometrica*, 46, pp. 1429–45.
—— (1980), 'Equilibrium in a pure currency economy', *Economic Inquiry*, 18, pp. 203–20.
—— (1981), *Studies in Business Cycle theory*, Basil Blackwell, Oxford.
—— (1982), 'Interest Rates and Currency Prices in a Two-Country World', *Journal of Monetary Economics*, Vol. 10, No. 3, November, pp. 335–60.
—— (1987), *Models of Business Cycles*, Basil Blackwell, Oxford.
—— (1988), 'On the mechanics of economic development', *Journal of Monetary Economics*, 22, July, pp. 3–42.
—— and Prescott, E. C. (1974), 'Equilibrium Search and Unemployment', *Journal of Economic Theory*, 7, January, pp. 188–209.

—— and Rapping, L. A. (1969), 'Real Wages, Employment and Inflation', *Journal of Political Economy*, 77, October, pp. 721–54.

—— and Sargent, T. J. (1979), 'After Keynesian Macroeconomics', *Federal Reserve Bank of Minnesota Quarterly Review*, 23, pp. 1–16.

—— and —— (eds.) (1981), *Rational Expectations and Econometric Practice*, George Allen & Unwin, London.

—— and Stokey, N. L. (1983), 'Optimal fiscal and monetary policy in an economy without capital', *Journal of Monetary Economics*, 12 (1), pp. 55–93.

—— and —— (1987), 'Money and Interest in a Cash-in-advance economy', *Econometrica*, 55, May, pp. 491–513.

McCallum, B. T. (1977), 'Price-level stickiness and the feasibility of monetary stabilization policy with rational expectations', *Journal of Political Economy*, 85.

—— (1979), 'The current state of the policy-ineffectiveness debate', *American Economic Review*, Papers and Proceedings, Vol. 69, No. 2.

—— (1986), 'On "real" and "sticky price" theories of the business cycle', *Journal of Money, Credit and Banking*, November, pp. 397–414.

—— (1988), 'Real Business Cycle Models', *NBER Working Paper*, No. 2480, January.

Manuelli, R. E. and Sargent, T. J. (1987), *Exercises in Dynamic Economic Theory*, Harvard University Press, Cambridge, Mass.

Marcet, A. and Sargent, T. J. (1982), 'Least Squares Learning and the Dynamics of Hyperinflation', Mimeo, March.

Marini, G. (1985), 'Intertemporal substitution and the role of monetary policy', *Economic Journal*, 95, pp. 87–100.

Maskin, E. and Riley, J. (1984), 'Monopoly with Incomplete Information', *Rand Journal of Economics*, 15, pp. 171–96.

May, J. (1970), 'Period Analysis and Continuous Analysis in Patinkin's Macroeconomic Model', *Journal of Economic Theory*, 2, March, pp. 1–9.

May, R. M. and Oster, G. T. (1976), 'Bifurcations and dynamic complexity in simple ecological models', *The American Naturalist*, 110, No. 974, pp. 573–99.

Muellbauer, J. (1986), 'Habits, rationality and myopia in the life-cycle consumption function', Centre for Economic Policy Research Discussion Paper, No. 112, June.

Mussa, M. (1981), 'Sticky prices and disequilibrium adjustment in a rational model of the inflationary process', *American Economic Review*, 71, December, pp. 1020–27.

Muth, J. F. (1961), 'Rational Expectations and the Theory of Price Movements', *Econometrica*, Vol. 29, July, pp. 315–35.

Okun, A. M. (1981), *Prices and Quantities: A Macroeconomic Analysis*, Brookings, Washington DC.

Persson, T. (1988), 'Credibility of Macroeconomic Policy: An Introduction and a Broad Survey', *European Economic Review*, 32, pp. 519–32.

—— and Svensson, L. E. O. (1984), 'Time-consistent fiscal policy and government cash-flow', *Journal of Monetary Economics*, 14 (3), pp. 365–74.

Pesaran, M. H. (1987), *The limits to rational expectations*, Basil Blackwell, Oxford.

Phelps, E. S. *et al.* (1970), *Microeconomic Foundations of Employment and Inflation theory*, W. W. Norton, New York.

—— (1972), *Inflation Policy and Unemployment Theory: the Cost-Benefit Approach to Monetary Planning*, W. W. Norton, New York.

—— and Taylor, J. B. (1977), 'Stabilizing powers of monetary policy under rational expectations', *Journal of Political Economy*, 85, pp. 163–89.

Ploeg, F. van der (1986), 'Rational Expectations, Risk and Chaos in Financial Markets', *Economic Journal*, Supplement, 96, pp. 151–62.
Prescott, E. C. (1975), 'Efficiency of the Natural Rate', *Journal of Political Economy*, 83, December, pp. 1229–36.
—— (1977), 'Should control theory be used for economic stabilization?' in K. Brunner and A. H. Meltzer (eds.), *Optimal Policy, Control Theory and Technological Exports*, Carnegie-Rochester series on Public Policy, Vol. 7, pp. 13–38.
—— (1982), 'Money as a means of payment', University of Minnesota Working Paper.
Radner, R. (1972), 'Existence of equilibrium of plans, prices and price expectations in a sequence of markets', *Econometrica*, Vol. 40, pp. 289–303.
Rebelo, S. (1987), 'Tractable heterogeneity and near steady state dynamics', unpublished, University of Rochester, New York.
Rogerson, R. (1988), 'Indivisible labour, lotteries and equilibrium', forthcoming, *Journal of Monetary Economics*.
Rogoff, K. (1985), 'Can international monetary policy co-operation be counterproductive?', *Journal of International Economics*, 18, February, pp. 199–217.
—— and Sibert, A. (1988), 'Elections and macroeconomic policy cycles', *Review of Economic Studies*, 55, pp. 1–16.
Romer, P. M. (1986), 'Increasing Returns and Long-run Growth', *Journal of Political Economy*, 94, pp. 1002–1037.
—— (1987a), 'Increasing returns, specialization and external economies: growth as described by Allyn Young', Centre for Economic Research Working Paper No. 64, University of Rochester.
—— (1987b), 'Crazy explanations for the productivity slowdown', in S. Fischer (ed.), *NBER Macroeconomics Manual*, 1987, pp. 163–202.
Rotemberg, J. J. (1982), 'Monopolistic Price Adjustment and Aggregate Output', *Review of Economic Studies*, 49, pp. 517–31.
—— (1987), 'The New Keynesian Microfoundations', in S. Fischer ed. *NBER Macroeconomic Annual*, MIT Press, Cambridge, Mass., pp. 69–104.
Roth, A. and Murnighan, J. (1982), 'The Role of Information in Bargaining: An Experiment Study', *Econometrica*, 50, pp. 1123–42.
Rothschild, M. and Stiglitz, J. E. (1976), 'Equilibrium in competitive insurance markets: an essay on the economics of imperfect information', *Quarterly Journal of Economics*, 90, November, pp. 629–49.
Rubinstein, A. (1982), 'Perfect Equilibria in a Bargaining Model', *Econometrica*, 50, pp. 97–110.
Sachs, J. (1982), 'Comments on Simms', *Brookings Papers on Economic Activity*, 82, 1, pp. 157–62.
Sargent, T. J. (1973), 'Rational Expectations, the Real Rate of Interest and the Natural Rate of Unemployment', *Brookings Papers on Economic Activity*, 2, Washington DC, pp. 429–72.
—— (1976a), 'A Classical Macroeconometric Model of the United States', *Journal of Political Economy*, 84, No. 2.
—— (1976b), 'The observational equivalence of natural and unnatural rate theories of macroeconomics', *Journal of Political Economy*, 84, June, pp. 631–40.
—— (1984), 'Vector Autoregressions, Expectations, and Advice', *American Economic Review*, 74, pp. 408–15.
—— (1987a), *Macroeconomic Theory*, 2nd ed., Academic Press, Orlando, Fla.
—— (1987b), *Dynamic Macroeconomic Theory*, Harvard University Press, Cambridge, Mass.

—— and Wallace, N., (1975), 'Rational Expectations, the Optimal Monetary Instrument and the Optimal Money Supply Rule', *Journal of Political Economy*, Vol. 83, pp. 241–54.
—— and —— (1976), 'Rational Expectations and the Theory of Economic Policy', *Monetary Economics*, 84 (2), April, pp. 207–37.
Schelling, T. C. (1960), *The Strategy of Conflict*, Harvard University Press.
Schwert, G. W. (1979), 'Tests of causality. The message in the innovations' in K. Brunner and A. H. Meltzer (eds.), *Three Aspects of Policy and Policy Making: Knowledge, Data and Institutions*, North-Holland, Amsterdam, pp. 55–96.
Shapiro, C. and Stiglitz, J. F. (1983), 'Equilibrium unemployment as a worker discipline device', *American Economic Review*, 73, June, pp. 433–45.
Shavell, S. (1979), 'Risk sharing and incentives in the principal and agent relationship', *The Bell Journal of Economics*, 10, pp. 55–73.
Shefrin, H. M. and Thaler, R. H. (1987), 'The Behavioural Life-Cycle Hypothesis', forthcoming *Economic Inquiry*.
Schiller, R. (1984), 'Stock Prices and Social Dynamics', *Brookings Papers on Economic Activity*, 2, pp. 457–98.
Sidrauski, M. (1967), 'Rational Choice and Patterns of Growth in a Monetary Economy', *American Economic Review*, 57 (2), 534–44.
Simon, H. A. (1979), 'Rational decision making in business organizations', *American Economic Review*, 69, pp. 493–513.
Sims, C. A. (1972), 'Money, income and causality', *American Economic Review*, 62, pp. 540–52.
—— (1977), 'Exogeneity and causal ordering in macro-economic models', in C. A. Sims (ed.) *New methods of business cycle research*, Federal Reserve Bank of Minneapolis.
—— (1980a), 'Macroeconomics and Reality', *Econometrica*, 48, pp. 1–47.
—— (1980b), 'Comparison of interwar and postwar business cycles: Monetarism Reconsidered', *American Economic Review*, 70, pp. 250–59.
—— (1982), 'Policy Analysis with Econometric Models', *Brookings Papers on Economic Activity*, pp. 107–52.
—— (1987), 'A rational expectations framework for short-run policy analysis', in W. A. Barrett and K. J. Singleton (eds.), *New Approaches to Monetary Economics*, Cambridge University Press, Cambridge, pp. 293–308.
Slutsky, E. (1937), 'The summation of random causes as the source of cyclic processes', *Econometrica*, 5, pp. 105–46.
Solow, R. (1979), 'Another possible source of wage stickiness', *Journal of Macroeconomics*, 1, pp. 79–82.
Stiglitz, J. E. (1979), 'Equilibrium in Product Markets with Imperfect Information', *American Economic Review*, 69, May, pp. 339–45.
—— (1982), 'Information and the capital market', in *Financial Economics: Essays in Honor of Paul Cootner*, W. F. Sharp and C. Cootner (eds.), Prentice Hall, Englewood Cliffs, N.J. pp. 118–58.
—— (1985), 'Information and Economic Analysis: A Perspective', *Economic Journal*, Supplement, Vol. 95, pp. 21–41.
—— (1986), 'Theories of Wage Rigidity' in J. L. Butkiewicz, K. J. Koford and J. B. Miller (eds.), *Keynes' Economic Legacy*, Praeger, pp. 153–206.
—— (1987), 'The causes and consequences of the dependence of quality on price', *The Journal of Economic Literature*, 25, pp. 1–48.
Stockman, A. and Svensson, L. (1987), 'Capital flows, investment and exchange rates', *Journal of Monetary Economics*, 19, No. 2, March, pp. 171–20.
Sutton, John (1986), 'Noncooperative Bargaining Theory: An Introduction', *Re-*

view of Economic Studies, 53, pp. 709–24.
Svensson, L. E. O. (1985), 'Money and Asset Prices in a Cash-in-Advance Economy', *Journal of Political Economy*, 93, pp. 919–44.
Taylor, J. B. (1979), 'Staggered Wage Setting in a Macro Model', *American Economic Review*, Papers and Proceedings, 69, pp. 108–13.
—— (1980), 'Aggregate Dynamics and Staggered Contracts', *Journal of Political Economy*, 88, pp. 1–23.
Tobin, J. (1970), 'Money and Income: Post Hoc Ergo Propter Hoc?', *Quarterly Journal of Economics*, 84, May, pp. 301–17.
—— (1978), *Asset Accumulation and Economic Activity*, University of Chicago Press, Chicago.
Townsend, R. M. (1979), 'Optimal Contracts and Competitive Markets with Costly State Verification', *Journal of Economic Theory*, 21, pp. 265–93.
—— (1987a), 'Asset Return Anomalies in a Monetary Economy', *Journal of Economic Theory*.
—— (1987b), 'Models as Economies', *Economic Journal*, 98, Supplement, pp. 1–24.
Turnovsky, S. J. (1977), 'On the formulation of continuous time macro-economic models with asset accumulation', *International Economic Review*, 18, February, pp. 1–27.
—— and Burmeister, E. (1977), 'Perfect foresight expectational consistency and macroeconomic equilibrium', *Journal of Political Economy*, 85, April, pp. 379–93.
—— (1980), 'The choice of monetary instruments under alternative forms of price expectations', *Manchester School*, March, pp. 39–62.
Tversky, A. (1977), 'Features of similarity', *Psychological Review*, 84, 1977, pp. 327–52.
—— and Kahneman, D. (1986), 'Rational choice and the framing of decisions', *Journal of Business*, 59, October, pp. S251–S278.
Wallace, N. (1987), 'A suggestion for oversimplifying the theory of money', *Economic Journal*, 98, Supplement, pp. 25–36.
Weil, P. (1985), *Essays on the Valuation of Unbacked Assets*, Harvard University PhD Thesis, May.
Weiss, A. and Stiglitz, J. E. (1981), 'Credit Rationing in Markets with Imperfect Information', *American Economic Review*, 71, June, pp. 393–410.
—— and —— (1983), 'Incentive effects of terminations: applications to the credit and labour markets', *American Economic Review*, 73, December, pp. 912–27.
Weiss, L. (1980), 'The role for active monetary policy in a rational expectations model', *Journal of Political Economy*, 88, April, pp. 221–3.
Weitzman, M. L. (1982), 'Increasing Returns and the Foundations of Unemployment theory', *Economic Journal*, 92, pp. 727–40.
Wilson, C. A. (1977), 'A model of insurance markets with incomplete information', *Journal of Economic Theory*, 16, December, pp. 167–207.
Winter, S. (1964), 'Economic "natural selection" and the theory of the firm', *Yale Economic Essays*, Spring, pp. 224–72.
Woodford, M. (1987), 'Learning to believe in sunspots', Mimeo, University of Chicago, Graduate School of Business, 1987.
Yaari, M. (1965), 'Uncertain Lifetime, Life Insurance and the Theory of the Consumer', *Review of Economic Studies*, 32, April, pp. 137–50.
Zellner, A. (1979), 'Causality and Econometrics' in K. Brunner and A. H. Meltzer (eds.), *Three Aspects of Policy and Policy Making: Knowledge, Data and Institutions*, North-Holland, Amsterdam.

Part 1

Theoretical aspects of the policy ineffectiveness proposition

Chapter 1

The macroeconomics of Dr Pangloss: a critical survey of the New Classical Macroeconomics

Pangloss: 'Tis demonstrated ... that things cannot be otherwise; for, since, everything is made for an end, everything is necessarily for the best end'

(Voltaire 1949, p. 230).

Candide: 'If this is the best of all possible worlds, what are the others?'

(Voltaire 1949, p. 241).

The short-run and long-run effects of monetary and fiscal policy continue to be the subject of considerable research activity and lively debate. For a while in the early and mid-70's Panglossian theorising dominated the stage. Activist monetary and fiscal policies were argued to have, at best, no effects on real economic variables; at worst they could be responsible for a net increase in economic instability. During the last two or three years, however, the professional consesus seems to have shifted again towards a more balanced view of the scope for fiscal and monetary policy in influencing cyclical fluctuations – stabilisation policy – and in co-determining the nature of the long-run trend growth path of the economic system.

A more precise statement of the 'policy neutrality' (Tobin and Buiter [1980]) view is that deterministic policy rules can have no effect on the joint probability distribution functions of real economic variables, but that stochastic policy behaviour can increase the variability of real variables relative to their full information values. The formal analysis supporting this view is invariably conducted in terms of monetary policy alone. Conclusions often tend to be phrased in terms of stabilisation policy in general (McCallum [1977]). The important practical policy implication is that attempts to stabilise the real economy through (monetary) feedback rules will at best have no real effects, but may very well lead to outcomes inferior to those resulting from the application of a simple, easily understood fixed rule such as a constant growth rate of the nominal money stock. Various aspects of the policy neutrality view can be found in Lucas [1972a,b, 1975, 1976], Sargent and Wallace [1975, 1976], Barro [1976a] and McCallum [1977, 1978]. The theoretical foundations of this view are the two pillars of Muth-rational expectations and the 'Phelps-Friedman-Lucas-instantaneous-natural rate or only-wage-and-price-surprises-matter' supply function. (Phelps *et al.* [1970], Friedman [1968], Lucas [1972b], Lucas and Rapping [1969]). For brevity this supply function will be referred to as the 'surprise' supply function. In the first section of this paper I evaluate the implications of Muth-rational expectations for macroeconomic and macroeconometric modelling. The foundations and implications of the 'surprise' supply function are scrutinised in Section II. While most of the points emphasised in this paper have been made before, there has not been any attempt to focus them into a broad and consistent critique of the new classical macroeconomics. The purpose of this paper is to provide such a survey and synthesis.

I Rational expectations

In accordance with normal usage in economics, the term rational (or optimal) expectations ought to be reserved for forecasts generated by a rational, expected utility maximising decision process in which the costs of acquiring, processing and evaluating additional information are balanced against the anticipated benefits from further refinement of the forecast. The rational expectations concept introduced by Muth [1961] and first applied to macroeconomics by Lucas [1972a,b] and by Sargent and Wallace [1975, 1976] goes well beyond that of a 'Bayesian' predictor derived from explicit optimising behaviour (Turnovsky [1969]; Cyert and DeGroot [1974]). Muth hypothesised that the mean expectation of firms with respect to some phenomenon, say price, was equal to the prediction that would be made by the relevant (and correct!) economic theory. Future variables anticipated at time *t* are 'true mathematical expectations of the future variables conditional on all variables in the model which are known to the public at time *t*' (Shiller [1978, p. 3]).[2] To emphasise the fact that such expectations have not been generated by an explicit, rational cost-benefit calculus I shall henceforth refer to them as Muth-rational expectations.

Dependence of structural parameters on policy rules

The Muth-rational expectations literature and Lucas in particular have made a significant and lasting contribution to the theory of economic policy and the construction of policy-oriented econometric models. The basic insight is the possibility of non-invariance of private sector structural behavioural relationships when public sector behavioural relationships are altered. Private sector behaviour is influenced in many ways by expectations of future variables. If changes in government behaviour change these expectations, models that ignore such links from government behaviour via private expectations to private behaviour are likely to forecast poorly and to lead to misleading conclusions being drawn from policy simulations. This conclusion does not require Muth-rational expectations *per se*, only some direct effect of government behaviour on private expectations. The assumption of Muth-rational expectations provides the additional hypothesis that the link between private sector expectations and government behaviour comes through the private sector's knowledge of the true structure of the model, including the parameters that describe government behaviour. Thus the main implication of the Muth-rational expectations hypothesis for macro-modelling is the necessity of solving simultaneously for the currently anticipated value of a variable and its future value calculated from the model. When this has been done, the model – which now incorporates the Muth-rational expectations assumption (i.e. the response of the private sector to current and anticipated future policy actions) and thus respects the 'principle of policy-dependent structural parameters' – can be used for policy simulation in the standard manner. See, for example, Chow [1978] and Buiter [1979]. The computational requirements of a full Muth-rational expectations equilibrium calculation may be formidable, especially for non-linear models, but there are no special conceptual problems involved.

Inconsistency of optimal plans

Interesting and important issues arise in Muth-rational models when policy optimisation rather than policy simulation is considered. Standard stochastic dynamic programming approaches to the derivation of optimal policies may be inappropriate when the model takes on the features of a dynamic game[3] (Kydland [1975, 1977]). Private agents optimise with reference to private objective functions and the government attempts to optimise a social welfare function. The assumption of Muth-rational expectations (or its deterministic counterpart: perfect foresight) implies that all agents know each other's aims and anticipate each other's actions. This may lead to what Kydland and Prescott [1977] have called the inconsistency of optimal plans.

The Principle of Optimality of Dynamic Programming states that 'An optimal policy has the property that, whatever the initial state and decision (i.e. control) are, the remaining decisions must constitute an optimal policy with regard to the state resulting from the first decision' (Bellman [1957]). This permits the derivation of the fundamental recurrency relation of dynamic programming and the closed-loop optimal feedback controls familiar from, e.g. linear-quadratic regulator problems (Chow [1975]). Such policies will be optimal in a 'game against nature' but not in a game between (two) rational, optimising agents such as the private and public sectors, each one of which is endowed with Muth-rational expectations as regards the behavioural strategies of the other. Traditional optimal control techniques fail to take account of the impact of future policy measures on current events through the changes in current behaviour induced by anticipation of these future policy measures.

Paraphrasing Prescott [1977], we can define a consistent policy or plan as a sequence of rules, one for each period, which specifies policy actions contingent on the state of the world in that period. Each such rule has the property of being optimal given the subsequent elements in the sequence. In dynamic games between optimising agents endowed with rational expectations, it can happen that the optimal plan in subsequent periods is not the continuation of the first-period optimal plan over the remainder of the planning period: the optimal plan is not consistent. A two-period flood disaster control example can illustrate this.

There are two states of the world, good and bad, in period 2. In the bad state a major flood occurs; in the good state there is no flood. The true state will not be known until the beginning of period 2. In period 1 the government can try to discourage people from living in the potential flood disaster zones by promising not to send any relief in period 2, should a disaster occur. If, at the beginning of period 2, people have ignored the warning given in period 1 and have settled in the potential disaster area, it may be optimal – since bygones are bygones – for the government to break its promise of period 1 and to send relief if the bad state occurs. Rational private economic agents will anticipate such behaviour and will be more inclined to settle in the potential disaster area.

The implication of examples such as this, however, is not that policy optimisation is impossible in rational expectations models. Instead, as Taylor [1977, p. 94] points out, 'any optimisation technique used for macroeconomic stabilisation should be able to incorporate the endogeneity of expectations'. It has been demonstrated in a number of papers (Taylor [1976], Buiter [1979]) that by restricting the search for optimal policies to a particular class of functions (e.g. linear feedback) characterised by some set of parameters, restricted consistent optimal policy rules can be derived. In the flood disaster example, we could, for example, constrain the set of solutions by insisting that the government cannot renege on its period 1 promises. A constrained optimal policy rule can then be derived quite easily. By suitably restricting the class of policy rules over which the government can optimise, it will in general be possible to write current decisions as functions only of current and past variables, even when both public and private agents 'forecast efficiently conditional on their information sets' (Brunner and Meltzer [1977, p. 5]). As another example, a constant growth rate for a monetary aggregate, M, is a very special case of a linear feedback rule ($\Delta \ln M_t = \Delta M_{t-1}$). It would be of considerable interest to investigate, for a given macromodel, whether, and under what circumstances, the constant growth rate rule is the optimal linear feedback rule. It is quite possible that the optimal linear feedback rule will be dominated be some non-linear policy rule, but current methods do not permit us to derive the optimal unrestricted, non-linear policy rule. Many important unresolved problems remain, including the formulation of an appropriate dynamic game-theoretic equilibrium concept in a Prescott-Kydland-type model (see Leitman and Wan [1978]). The influence of anticipated or unanticipated policy on real economic outcomes and consequently the potential for beneficial or detrimental policy actions is not an issue here.[4]

How good an assumption are Muth-rational expectations? Unfortunately the hypothesis is seldom tested in isolation. Instead composite hypotheses tend to be tested: natural rate *cum* Muth-rational expectations, term structure *cum* Muth-rational expectations, international interest parity *cum* Muth-rational expectations, etc. The hypothesis appears to be in danger of being consistent with any conceivable body of empirical evidence, because the assumption of optimal use of the available information cannot be tested independently of an assumption about the available information set.[5] In empirical applications, Muth-rational expectations are best linear unbiased predictors, conditional on some information set. By suitable redefinition of the information set conditioning the forecast, any pattern of serial correlation in the endogenous variables of a model can be rationalised as consistent with Muth-rational expectations. By becoming irrefutable, the hypothesis would cease to belong to the realm of scientific (i.e. positive or empirical) theory, as defined by Popper [1959], although it would not lose its heuristic value.

Muth-rational expectations are best not viewed as a positive theory of how expectations are actually formed. The issue of how economic agents acquire their knowledge of the true structure of the economy, which they use in making their rational forecasts is not addressed by the theory. The appeal of Muth-rational expectations is that any expectations scheme that is not Muth-rational will be consistently wrong, in the sense of yielding systematic expectational errors. Sensible economic agents will ultimately abandon such a scheme (see, for example, Minford [1978]). Very little is known, unfortunately, about the learning process by which unsatisfactory forecasting schemes are revised. Convergence to a Muth-rational expectations mechanism cannot be postulated as self-evident or inevitable (Taylor [1975]; DeCanio [1979]). It seems reasonable to view strict Muth-rational expectations as an acceptable representation of private (and public) agents' forecasting behaviour only in the tranquility of a long-run steady-state equilibrium. It is in the evaluation of the scope for short-run stabilisation policy, however, that Muth-rational expectations – combined with the hypothesis that government policy can only affect the real variables of the economic system by influencing the price or wage forecast errors of private economic agents – have had their most powerful and challenging implications.

II The 'surprise' supply function

When the hypothesis (1) that only price or wage surprises cause the economy to diverge from the exogenous 'natural rate of unemployment' or the 'natural level of output' is combined with the Muth-rational expectations assumption (2) that the government cannot introduce systematic surprises into the economy when the deterministic part of government behaviour is included in the information set conditioning private forecasts, the conclusion (3) that deterministic policy rules cannot affect the probability density functions of the real side of the economy emerges inexorably: How plausible a construct is the 'surprise' supply function? Both theoretical considerations and empirical evidence suggest overwhelmingly that anticipated and unanticipated changes in monetary and fiscal policy will have real effects, short run and long run. I shall emphasise the theoretical objections to the 'surprise' supply function in what follows.

Real effects of anticipated fiscal and monetary policy in frictionless, market-clearing models

It is trivial to show that fully anticipated changes in fiscal policy will have real effects. From the standard microeconomics of the utility maximising household, changes in tax rates will alter labour supply and saving behaviour (Fair [1978, 1979]). The theory of the firm tells us of the effects of the payroll tax on labour demand and of the influence of investment tax credits, depreciation allowances, etc. on capital formation. In the classical full employment model, the short-run effects of an increase in exhaustive public spending on private consumption and capital formation and the long-run effects on productive capacity and real output are well-known. The importance of direct complementarity or substitutability between various components of private and public spending has been analysed in Buiter [1975, 1977] and Tobin and Buiter [1980]. Such real effects occur even in perfect foresight models, whether or not the state of the economy is characterised at each instant by a frictionless, market-clearing competitive Walrasian temporary equilibrium. Clearly fiscal policy is 'non-neutral' even in the most classical of economic systems.

Retaining for the moment the temporary Walrasian equilibrium assumption, we can also establish the non-neutrality of monetary policy. First consider 'superneutrality' – invariance of real variables under different proportional rates of growth of the nominal stock of money. Different fully anticipated proportional rates of growth of the nominal money supply are associated with different proportional rates of inflation. This will alter the composition of output in the short run and the level of output in the long run. The mechanism is that changes in the rate of inflation alter the real rate of return on money balances whose nominal rate of return is fixed at zero.[6] This changes equilibrium portfolio composition and alters the rate of capital formation in the short run and the capital-labour ratio in the long run. In simple 2 asset (money-capital) models, higher rates of monetary expansion tend to be associated with higher steady-state capital-labour ratios, but this result does not automatically generalise to models with richer asset menus.

Carrying the argument one step further, we ignore real capital formation so that no real effects of fully anticipated monetary policy can operate through that channel. Fully anticipated once-and-for-all changes in the quantity of money will still have real effects if non-monetary nominally denominated claims on the public sector (bonds) are held by the private sector and if these bonds enter as arguments into private sector behavioural relationships. Traditionally, this issue has been characterised by the question 'Are government bonds net wealth' (Barro [1974]), but it is not at all necessary for the effect of public sector debt on private behaviour to take the form of a wealth effect. Liquidity effects or portfolio composition effects could also be the source of non-neutrality of public interest-bearing debt. Debt neutrality in its simplest form is due to the cancellation of private sector holdings of public debt as a component of private net worth by the present discounted value of future taxes 'required' to service this debt. It is a precondition both for the neutrality of *level* changes in the quantity of money and for the absence of effects on aggregate demand from a shift between tax financing and borrowing.

The theoretical underpinnings of the debt neutrality theorem (Barro [1974, 1976b, 1978]) have been scrutinised by Buiter [1980] and Tobin and Buiter [1980]. They conclude that the debt neutrality theorem is a theoretical curiosum. Beyond the near-certainty of non-neutrality, there is a strong presumption about the direction of the effect of substitution of borrowing for tax financing. In the short run it is likely to absorb saving; in a world with Keynesian unemployment of resources, this can stimulate effective demand and increase output and employment. In the long run, it is likely to crowd out real capital. An open market purchase of bonds is likely to be expansionary (or inflationary) in the short run. Its long-run effect is very sensitive to assumptions about relative asset substitutabilities and about the policy rules that govern the behaviour of the various components of the government budget constraint (Currie [1978], Tobin and Buiter [1980]).

Real effects of fiscal and monetary policy in non-Walrasian equilibrium models

Even if one were to ignore all the previously mentioned channels of real effects of fully anticipated monetary and fiscal policy, abandoning the continuous Walrasian equilibrium assumption can generate real effects of fully anticipated monetary and fiscal policy. Two examples will be presented.

For a very simple and familiar case, consider an economy in which money wage and money price level are fixed, either indefinitely because of wage and price controls or temporarily because of multi-period contracts. Such an economy could be in the Keynesian general excess supply configuration of the Barro–Grossman disequilibrium model (Barro and Grossman [1971]). Fully anticipated changes in the quantity of money (or in the level of public spending) will have the familiar fixed price level *IS–LM* effects. The fixed price assumption is perhaps somewhat unsatisfactory, but no more so than the *ad hoc* assumption of instantaneous and continuous competitive equilibrium applied so routinely to labour and commodity markets by economists of the 'New Classical School'; the Walrasian auctioneer is no substitute for a theory of price determination and exchange.

One approach to the micro-foundations of price and wage stickiness and of non-market clearing equilibria can be found in the exciting recent work on equilibrium in markets with imperfect and costly information associated with Akerlof [1970], Stiglitz [1979], Salop [1978], Wilson [1979] and others. This work demonstrates how socially inefficient quantity-constrained (rationing) equilibria with sticky prices can be generated by privately rational optimising behaviour. It therefore invalidates the often heard criticism that the non-Walrasian equilibrium models are ad-hoc in the sense of depicting situations in which not all feasible trades that are to the perceived mutual advantage of the exchanging parties have been exhausted (Barro [1979, p. 56]).

Relatively little empirical work has been aimed at testing the Walrasian equilibrium hypothesis for labour and commodity markets. Rosen and Quandt [1978] test for the existence of equilibrium or disequilibrium in the aggregate U.S. labour market and find that the data reject the hypothesis that the labour market is in continuous equilibrium. Fair indirectly tested the disequilibrium hypothesis by including a 'disequilibrium variable' representing a binding constraint in the loan market and in the labour market in his econometric model of the U.S. economy. This variable was found to be significant (Fair [1979]). As the authors of those studies are the first to point out, these conclusions are highly tentative and provisional. When combined with the (at any rate to this author) overwhelming casual empirical evidence as to the existence and persistence of disequilibrium in factor and product markets, there would seem to be a strong prima facie case for the practical relevance of the disequilibrium macroeconomics literature.

A rather more interesting but still very simple disequilibrium price adjustment mechanism is the following. Let p^* denote the log of the equilibrium price level, p the log of the actual price level and $\hat{p}_{t,t+1}$ the log of the price level expected, at time t, to prevail at time $t + 1$. Y_t is actual output and $\bar{Y}_t$ full employment or capacity output. We postulate the equilibrium price equation:

$$p_t^* = \alpha(Y_t - \bar{Y}_t) + \hat{p}_{t-1,t} \qquad (\alpha > 0). \tag{1}$$

The actual price level adjusts sluggishly to the equilibrium price level according to:

$$\Delta p_t \equiv p_t - p_{t-1} = \beta(p_t^* - p_{t-1}) \qquad (0 \leq \beta \leq 1). \tag{2}$$

This specification is not implausible in an economic system without a clear underlying inflationary or deflationary trend. With such a trend, the partial adjustment price mechanism should incorporate first or higher order differences of p^*.[7] Combining the equilibrium price equation and the partial adjustment, disequilibrium price mechanism we obtain:

$$\Delta p_t = \alpha\beta(Y_t - \bar{Y}_t) + \beta(\hat{p}_{t-1,t} - p_{t-1}). \tag{3}$$

If there are no stochastic elements, Muth-rational expectations are equivalent to perfect foresight: $\hat{p}_{t-1,t} = p_t$. Equation (3) suggests that even perfect foresight implies $Y_t \equiv \bar{Y}_t$ only if $\beta = 1$, i.e. only if the adjustment of actual price to equilibrium price is immediate. Only for the limiting case of the disequilibrium model in which it is equivalent to an equilibrium model, does the Muth-rational expectations assumption constrain the economy to be at the natural level of output. Disequilibrium specifications (or non-Walrasian equilibrium specifications) thus permit one to avoid the conclusion so often derived from models incorporating the 'surprise' supply function construct, that actual output differs from its natural level (or that the rate of unemployment differs from the natural rate) if and only if there are price or wage forecast errors. Fischer [1977], Phelps and Taylor [1977], and Taylor [1978] have constructed quite plausible simple models with multi-period wage contracts or price setting in advance of the period in which the price will apply. This causes the information set available at the time of the current money supply decision to be richer than the information set available at the time that the current wage or price was decided on. Public and private agents have the same *information set* at any point in time, but only the public agent is free to change his controls in response to new information; the private agent is contractually committed by the past. Public and private agents do not have the same *opportunity sets*. It may not be feasible for private economic agents to react to a fully anticipated change in public sector policy in such a way as to undo all real effects of this change. Even if it is feasible, full neutralisation may not be optimal. Deterministic monetary (and fiscal) feed-back rules can then affect the probability distributions of real output and employment, even with rational expectations. (See also Baily

[1978]). A lot of work remains to be done to show rigorously how such multi-period contracts can be generated as the (game-theoretic?) equilibrium outcomes of realistic labour market and product market strategies pursued by workers, unions and firms. It is tempting, and very simple, to turn the multi-period private contracts into contingent forward contracts that are isomorphic to the sequence of contracts that would be concluded were markets to re-open continuously. If our aim is to model the economic system as it is rather than as we would like it to be, this temptation is to be resisted.

In equations (1) and (2) both Y_t *and* p_t are endogenous variables. To identify the exact scope for monetary and fiscal policy, it is necessary to obtain the reduced form equation for Y_t. To complete the model we add a demand side and a very simple stochastic structure. Output is equal to real effective demand, A.

$$Y_t = A_t. \tag{4}$$

Effective demand is an increasing function of the real stock of money balances and of real exhaustive public spending, G. m is the log of the nominal stock of money. ε_t^d is a random demand disturbance.

$$A_t = \gamma(m_t - p_t) + \delta G_t + \varepsilon_t^d \qquad (\gamma > 0,\ \delta > 0). \tag{5}$$

Full employment output is a constant plus a random supply disturbance:

$$\bar{Y}_t = \bar{Y} + \varepsilon_t^s. \tag{6}$$

$\bar{Y}$ can be interpreted as the full information level of capacity output. The Muth-rational expectation of the price level, $\hat{p}_{t-1,t}$, is $E(p_t \mid \phi_{t-1})$ where ϕ_{t-1} denotes the information set available at $t-1$ and E is the mathematical expectation operator. If the disturbances are mutually serially independently and identically distributed random variables with zero means, if economic agents know the structure of the model and if they observe p_{t-1} at time $t-1$, the Muth-rational expectation of the price level is easily found to be:

$$E(p_t \mid \phi_{t-1}) = \frac{\alpha\beta\gamma}{1-\beta+\alpha\beta\gamma}E(m_t \mid \phi_{t-1}) + \frac{\alpha\beta\delta}{1-\beta+\alpha\beta\gamma}E(G_t \mid \phi_{t-1}) - \frac{\alpha\beta}{1-\beta+\alpha\beta\gamma}\bar{Y} + \frac{(1-\beta)}{1-\beta+\alpha\beta\gamma}p_{t-1}. \tag{7}$$

With $\beta = 1$ this reduces to:

$$E(p_t \mid \phi_{t-1}) = E(m_t \mid \phi_{t-1}) + \frac{\delta}{\gamma}E(G_t \mid \phi_{t-1}) - \frac{1}{\gamma}\bar{Y}. \tag{7'}$$

The reduced form of real output is given by

$$Y_t = \frac{\gamma}{1+\alpha\beta\gamma} m_t - \frac{\alpha\beta^2\gamma^2}{(1+\alpha\beta\gamma)(1-\beta+\alpha\beta\gamma)} E(m_t \mid \phi_{t-1}) + \frac{\delta}{1+\alpha\beta\gamma} G_t$$
$$- \frac{\alpha\beta^2\gamma\delta}{(1+\alpha\beta\gamma)(1-\beta+\alpha\beta\gamma)} E(G_t \mid \phi_{t-1}) + \frac{\alpha\beta\gamma\bar{Y}}{1-\beta+\alpha\beta\gamma}$$
$$- \frac{(1-\beta)\gamma}{1-\beta+\alpha\beta\gamma} p_{t-1} + \frac{1}{1+\alpha\beta\gamma} \varepsilon_t^d + \frac{\alpha\beta\gamma}{1+\alpha\beta\gamma} \varepsilon_t^s. \tag{8}$$

If the policies pursued by the authorities are known exactly by the private sector, $E(m_t \mid \phi_{t-1}) = m_t$ and $E(G_t \mid \phi_{t-1}) = G_t$. In that case (8) simplifies to:

$$Y_t = \frac{\gamma(1-\beta)}{1-\beta+\alpha\beta\gamma} m_t + \frac{\delta(1-\beta)}{1-\beta+\alpha\beta\gamma} G_t + \frac{\alpha\beta\gamma}{1-\beta+\alpha\beta\gamma} \bar{Y}$$
$$- \frac{\gamma(1-\beta)}{1-\beta+\alpha\beta\gamma} p_{t-1} + \frac{1}{1+\alpha\beta\gamma} \varepsilon_t^d + \frac{\alpha\beta\gamma}{1+\alpha\beta\gamma} \varepsilon_t^s. \tag{8'}$$

If $\beta = 1$ this reduces to:

$$Y_t = \bar{Y} + \frac{1}{1+\alpha\gamma} \varepsilon_t^d + \frac{\alpha\gamma}{1+\alpha\gamma} \varepsilon_t^s. \tag{8''}$$

If the policies pursued by the authorities have a stochastic component, $E(m_t \mid \phi_{t-1}) = e_{t-1,t}^m + m_t$ and $E(G_t \mid \phi_{t-1}) = e_{t-1,t}^G + G_t$. Here $e_{t-1,t}^m$ and $e_{t-1,t}^G$ are forecast errors orthogonal to (independent of) the private information set ϕ_{t-1}. If we assume that the private sector information set ϕ_t is identical to the public sector information set ψ_t, the private forecast errors $e_{t-1,t}^m$ and $e_{t-1,t}^G$ do not constitute channels through which the authorities can exercise *systematic* influence on private sector behaviour. If the authorities are aware of their own systematic policy behaviour, i.e. if the deterministic part of the policy rule belongs to ψ_t, it will also belong to ϕ_t.[8] The authorities are able to influence the probability distribution of output by randomizing their behaviour and thereby introducing additional noise into the system. They are ill-advised to do so, however. Random policy behaviour will never be consistent with minimising the variance of real output around its full information value. Thus, if the public sector has no informational advantage over the private sector, equations (8′) and (8″) are sufficiently general for the analysis of the scope for systematic stabilisation policy.

When the Walrasian equilibrium condition ($\beta = 1$) is imposed, we see from (8″) that real output is not affected by deterministic monetary and fiscal policies. This, however, is on the assumption that $\bar{Y}$ is independent of such policies. The earlier discussion of the effects of fully anticipated fiscal and monetary policy on capacity output in market-clearing models led to the conclusion that $\bar{Y}$ *will* be affected by anticipated (and unanticipated) fiscal and monetary policies because of the effects of such policies on labour supply, portfolio allocation and capital formation.[9]

Equation (8′) shows that even without making $\bar{Y}$ dependent on the parameters of fiscal and monetary policy, real output can be influenced by known, activist policy rules if $\beta < 1$. Inertia in the adjustment of actual price to equilibrium price provides scope for fully anticipated changes in m_t and G_t to render Y_t systematically different from $\bar{Y}$.

McCallum [1978] has argued recently that price level stickness by itself is not always sufficient to invalidate the proposition that deterministic stabilisation policy cannot affect the probability distributions of real variables. It is indeed possible to disguise a classical market-clearing sheep in non-Walrasian wolf's clothing.[10] In McCallum's model the behaviour of real output is governed ultimately by a second order stochastic difference equation in real output. Policy can only affect the behaviour of output via a one-period price forecast error: $p_t - \hat{p}_{t|t-1}$. With rational expectations policy is automatically emasculated. I would therefore argue that more weight should be attached to the conclusion reached in this section: it is very simple to construct quite plausible models with sluggish wage or price adjustment that do leave scope for real effects of deterministic monetary and fiscal policy.[11] The example developed in equations (1) to (6) suffices to establish this.

The desirability of feasible intervention

The previous sections established that in virtually all economically interesting models there will be real consequences of monetary and fiscal policy – anticipated and unanticipated. This makes the cost–benefit analysis of feasible policy intervention the focus of the practical economist's concern.

It might be argued that in the absence of obvious externalities, the policy authorities are incapable of improving on *laisser-faire:* policy intervention in optimal private arrangements will have real consequences that are welfare-decreasing.[12] While economists – in their less guarded moments–frequently advance variants on this argument,[13] it has no sound foundation as a generally valid proposition, either in economic theory or in careful empirical observation. The efficiency and Pareto-Optimality of a decentralised economy have been established only within the narrow and rather artifical confines of the Arrow–Debreu general competitive equilibrium model. Once one moves beyond this 'one-shot' – i.e. non-sequential – economy with its complete set of contingent forward markets and its absence of externalities and inconvenient non-convexities, there is no presumption that decentralised (including competitive) outcomes will be Pareto–Optimal, efficient, or even just superior to the outcomes generated by alternative feasible mechanisms involving different kinds and degrees of policy intervention. In the absence of such a general presumption of superiority, 'unaided' decentralised, competitive outcomes should be compared on a case-by-case basis with outcomes under policy intervention.

The burden of proof does not lie automatically with the proponents of policy intervention. A few examples will illustrate how various departures from the Arrow-Debreu model create the potential for inefficiency resulting from privately optimal arrangements and for welfare-improving policy intervention.

In the overlapping generations model of Diamond [1965] there is no complete set of forward markets: those currently alive cannot enter into binding contracts with the unborn. A savings externality results: the privately optimal demand for real capital as a store of value may generate a suboptimal availability of capital as a factor of production. A high propensity to save may result in a steady-state capital–labour ratio in excess of the golden rule capital–labour ratio. This socially inefficient 'unaided' competitive outcome can be remedied by the government issuing bonds to substitute for real capital as a store of value.

The absence of a complete set of contingent forward markets and the existence of imperfect – often asymmetric – and costly information may result in inefficient, non market-clearing equilibria (Salop [1978, 1979]; Stiglitz [1979]; Wilson [1979]). The welfare implications of different kinds of monetary, fiscal and regulatory policies in an economy characterised by such markets are still *terra incognita*. While it may be true that in the presence of ignorance caution is the wisest course of action, it is not obvious that caution corresponds to *laisser-faire*.

The assumption of competitive behaviour is inappropriate in many markets. When market participants act as monopolistic competitors or as oligopolists, the appropriate equilibrium concept may well be that of a non-co-operative game. Privately rational game-theoretic equilibria can be sub-optimal; the prisoner's dilemma is the simplest (although probably not very relevant economically) example. Nash–Cournot equilibria do not in general lie on the contract curve. Again little can be said at a very general level about the welfare enhancing or reducing effects of monetary, fiscal and other policy intervention in an economy where market participants are not atomistic competitors. This provides neither an argument for, nor against such intervention. It does provide a strong argument for further research on the non-Walrasian, non-competitive paradigm.

III Conclusion

Muth-rational expectations are a useful addition to the small collection of simple and tractable hypotheses about expectation formation in the macro-economist's toolkit. The assumption that economic agents use the true model to make their (unbiased) forecasts suggests that Muth-rational expectations are likely to be most appropriate when the analysis is restricted to the tranquility of a long-run steady state. The positive economic question as to how economic agents form forecasts when they do not know the true underlying economic model still remains to be answered (see DeCanio [1979] and Friedman [1979]).

The dependence of the structural parameters of economic and econometric models on the policy rules followed by the authorities in Muth-rational expectations models is an important theoretical insight. Its *practical* importance for policy evaluation exercises using econometric models still remains to be established on a case-by-case basis.

Optimal control theory can be used – with care – in Muth-rational expectations models once the endogeneity of expectations has been allowed for in the specification of these models. The distinction between a game against nature and a game between optimising players endowed with foresight is extremely important and has implications well beyond the current debate. Once we cease to model private agents as playing a game against nature – the competitive market – standard optimisation techniques are no longer applicable *within* the private sector.

The weakness of the theoretical foundations of the 'surprise' supply function, according to which alternative anticipated fiscal and monetary policy rules will not generate different outcomes for real economic variables, can be exposed in four propositions.

Proposition 1
The behaviour of real economic variables is not in general[14] invariant under alternative fully anticipated trajectories of fiscal policy instruments such as government spending and tax rates, even in classical, frictionless models.

Proposition 2
The behaviour of real economic variables is not in general invariant under alternative fully anticipated proportional rates of growth of the nominal money stock, even in classical, frictionless models.

Proposition 3
The behaviour of real economic variables is not in general invariant under alternative, fully anticipated levels of the nominal money stock – i.e. money is not neutral – even in classical, frictionless models.

Propositions 1–3 rely on the effects of fiscal and monetary policy on labour supply, saving and investment behaviour and portfolio composition. Even if, for the sake of argument, the standard microeconomic and portfolio-theoretic considerations underlying Propositions 1–3 are dismissed, policy-neutrality can be invalidated because of Proposition 4.

Proposition 4
Non-Walrasian equilibria with quantity rationing and inertia in the adjustment processes of wages and prices can cause real economic variables to

track different time paths when alternative, fully anticipated fiscal or monetary policies are followed. Fiscal and monetary policy changes, anticipated or unanticipated, can alter real effective demand, output and employment even if the notional supply of and demand for labour, the real interest rate and the composition of private sector portfolios are not affected.

Now that Sargent [1976] has convincingly argued the 'observational equivalence of natural and unnatural (sic) rate theories of macroeconomics', the evidence concerning the relevance of the Walrasian and the non-Walrasian equilibrium models will have to come either from the comparison of sample periods during which different policy rules were in effect or from the detailed study of price, wage and quantity adjustments in individual markets.

There is no reasonable case that deterministic monetary and fiscal policy rules cannot alter the cyclical fluctuations of the economic system or the nature of its trend growth path. Whether 'stabilisation policy' has in fact been stabilising or destabilising is a separate empirical issue – one that will be extremely difficult to settle with any degree of confidence. The recognition that monetary and fiscal policy give the government a handle on the real economy implies the existence of scope for both beneficial and detrimental policy behaviour. There is no presumption at all that a government that sits on its hands and determines the behaviour of its instruments by the simplest possible fixed rules is guaranteed to bring about the best of all possible worlds.

Notes

Originally published in the *Economic Journal*, 90, March 1980, pp. 34–50.

1 I would like to thank, without implicating, the following for comments on an earlier draft of the paper: Jonathan Eaton, Ray Fair, Robert Hall, Peter Kenen, Finn Kydland, Richard Lipsey, Michael Parkin, Douglas Purvis and Harvey Rosen. I have also benefited from audience feedback at seminars in Southampton University and Queen's University. John Flemming's comments stimulated the section on 'The desirability of feasible intervention.'

2 This definition of Muth-rational expectations has been extended in a natural manner by Lucas and Prescott [1974]. They define rational expectations by the condition that the subjective probability distribution of future economic variables held at time t coincides with the actual, objective conditional distribution based on the information assumed to be available at time t.

3 The game will probably not be a *symmetric* game. There are many 'small' private sector agents facing a 'large' public sector. It is probably better to model the public sector as the dominant player and the private sector as the non-dominant player. An asymmetric equilibrium concept such as a Stackelberg equilibrium suggests itself.

4 It should be noted that Kydland and Prescott's proposition about the time-inconsistency of (unrestricted) optimal plans is also applicable to games involving only private economic agents. The same fundamental problems arise within the private sector, e.g. when oligopolistic interdependence of firms is combined with rational expectations. Another example can be drawn from the optimal labour market contracts literature (see, e.g. Grossman [1978]). Multi-period employer–worker contingent contracts involving elements of risk-sharing have the property that 'although both parties can improve their expected outcomes by making the arrangement, one of the parties usually will find that his actual outcome would be better if he were not bound by the arrangement' (Grossman [1978, p. 666]). In such states of nature reneging on the contract would be optimal. Thus optimal labour-market contracts can be 'inconsistent'. In response to this, institutions tend to be created that restrict the opportunities for private agents to re-optimise as time passes and new states of nature are realised. Legal enforcement of long-term contracts after the present value of continuing to honour the contract becomes negative for one of the parties, is an example. It would seem unreasonable to argue that because optimisation is thus restricted, the whole notion of utility maximisation and market value maximisation is a useless one and should be replaced by the study of the operating characteristics of various fixed rules of thumb. Yet this is exactly what Prescott appears to insist should be done in dynamic games with rational expectations involving the public and private sectors.

5 It should be noted that 'available' is not an economic category. The information set can presumably be expanded by the expenditure of additional resources.

6 The only kind of model that exhibits super-neutrality obtains this result by incorporating real money balances as an argument in the direct utility function of (infinitely lived) households. A constant total real rate of return on money balances can be made up of any combination of the explicit return (due to changes in the general price level) and the implicit marginal utility yield from holding money balances (Sidrauski, [1967]). No proper transactions role for money balances is included. A comprehensive analysis of the real consequences of alternative monetary growth rates can be found in Carmichael [1979]. In this important original study the store of value and transactions roles of money balances are incorporated in an overlapping generations model.

7 Such a 'multi-geared price adjustment equation' can be constructed in a manner analogous to John Flemming's 'multi-geared adaptive expectations hypothesis' (Flemming, [1976]). The price adjustment mechanism of equation (2) would be optimal if the cost of departing from the equilibrium price and cost of adjusting towards the equilibrium price were both quadratic.

8 It should be clear that, if the government has an informational advantage over the private sector ($\psi_t \supset \phi_t$), e.g. because of differential access to or capacity to utilise certain kinds of information, monetary (and fiscal) policy can have real effects even when the continuous Walrasian equilibrium assumption is maintained (Barro, [1976a]).

9 These effects could be incorporated in the model of equations (1), (2), (4), (5) and (6) in the following way. Add a labour market. The supply of labour depends (*inter alia*) on the after-tax real wage. The notional demand for labour depends on marginal wage and non-wage labour costs and on the capital stock. $\bar{Y}$ is now the full information level of output that would be produced if the labour market were to clear with the given stock of capital. Equation (5) is decomposed into an effective demand (*IS*) equation and a monetary equilibrium (*LM*) equation. Real capital formation depends on the *real* interest rate. The demand for real money balances depends on the nominal interest rate. Private sector net worth, which is an argument in all household sector behavioural relationships (including labour supply) depends on private sector holdings of interest-bearing public debt.

10 This has been familiar since the early days of the expectations-augmented wage-Phillips curve. What *prima-facie* looks like a disequilibrium labour market adjustment mechanism is transformed into an instaneous natural rate model once Muth-rational expectations are added. w denotes the log of the money wage rate, u the actual unemployment rate, u^* the natural unemployment rate and II the rate of growth of labour productivity. Combining a disequilibrium wage adjustment equation with a mark-up price equation (or with the real wage equals marginal product of labour condition) we obtain a 'surprise' supply function model of deviations of the actual from the natural rate of unemployment.

$$w_t - w_{t-1} = \Pi_t + \eta(u - u^*) + \hat{p}_{t-1,t} - p_{t-1} \; (\eta < 0) \text{ and}$$
$$p_t - p_{t-1} = w_t - w_{t-1} - \Pi_t$$

imply $p_t = \eta(u - u^*) + \hat{p}_{t-1,t}$.

11 In the wage-price model of the previous footnote, inertia can be built into the labour market adjustment equation or into the price adjustment equation as in equations (1) and (2). This would restore the scope for activist policy.

12 The role of policy is restricted to lump-sum redistribution of 'initial' endowments or property rights.

13 See, for example, Prescott [1975], Barro [1979], Kahn [1979].

14 Here and in what follows 'in general' is shorthand for 'except in very special conditions that are not likely to be of practical interest'.

References

Akerlof, G. A. (1970), 'The market for "lemons": qualitative uncertainty and the market mechanism.' *Quarterly Journal of Economics*, Vol. 84 (August), pp. 488–500.

Baily, Martin N. (1978), 'Stabilization policy and private economic behavior.' *Brookings Papers on Economic Activity*, No. 1, pp. 11–50.

Barro, Robert J. (1974), 'Are government bonds net wealth.' *Journal of Political Economy* (November–December) Vol. 82 (b), pp. 1095–117.

—— (1976a), 'Rational expectations and the role of monetary policy.' *Journal of Monetary Economics*, Vol. 2 (1) (January), pp. 1095–117.

—— (1976b), 'Reply to Feldstein and Buchanan.' *Journal of Political Economy*, Vol. 84 (2) (April), pp. 343–9.

—— (1978), *The Impact of Social Security on Private Saving, Evidence from the U.S. Time Series*. With a Reply by Martin S. Feldstein, Washington, D.C.: American Enterprise Institute, Studies in Social Security and Retirement Policies.

—— (1979), 'Second thoughts on Keynesian economics.' *American Economic Review*, Papers and Proceedings, Vol. 69 (May), pp. 54–9.

—— and Grossman, Herschel (1971), A general disequilibrium model of income and employment. *American Economic Review* Vol. 61 (1) (March), pp. 82–93.

Bellman, Richard (1957), *Dynamic Programming*. Princeton, New Jersey: Princeton University Press.

Brunner, Karl and Meltzer, Allen H. (1977), 'Optimal policies, control theory and technology exports.' In *Optimal Policies, Control Theory and Technology Exports* (ed. K. Brunner and A. H. Meltzer). Carnegie-Rochester Conference Series on Public Policy, Vol. 7, pp. 1–11.

Buiter, Willem H. (1975), 'Temporary equilibrium and long-run equilibrium.' Yale Ph.D. thesis (December). New York: Garland.

—— (1977), 'Crowding out and the effectiveness of fiscal policy.' *Journal of Public Economics*, Vol. 7 (3) (June), pp. 309–28.

—— (1979), 'Optimal foreign exchange market intervention with rational expectations', *Trade and Payments Adjustment under Flexible Exchange Rates* (ed. J. Martin and A. Smith). London: Macmillan.

—— (1980), 'Government finance in an overlapping generations model with gifts and bequests.' Forthcoming in *Social Security versus Private Saving in Post-industrial Democracies* (ed. G. von Furstenberg).

Carmichael, Jeffrey (1979), 'The role of government financial policy in economic growth.' Unpublished Ph.D. thesis, Princeton University.

Chow, Gregory C. (1975), *Analysis and Control of Dynamic Economic Systems*, New York: John Wiley.

—— (1978), 'Econometric policy evaluation and optimization under rational expectations.' Paper given at the NBER Stochastic Control Conference, Austin, Texas (May).

Currie, David (1978), 'Macroeconomic policy and the government financing requirement: a survey of recent developments.' In *Studies in Contemporary Economic Analysis*, Vol. 1 (ed. Michael Artis and R. Nobay). London: Croom-Helm.

Cyert, Richard M. and DeGroot, Morris H. (1974), 'Rational expectations and Bayesian analysis.' *Journal of Political Economy*, Vol. 82, pp. 521–36.

DeCanio, Stephen (1979), 'Rational expectations and learning from experience.' *Quarterly Journal of Economics* (February) pp. 47–57.

Diamond, Peter A. (1965), 'National debt in a neo-classical growth model.' *American Economics Review*, Vol. 55 (December), pp. 1126–50.

Fair, Ray (1978), 'A criticism of one class of macroeconomic models with rational expectations.' *Journal of Money, Credit and Banking*, Vol. 10 (4) (November), pp. 411–17.

—— (1979), 'On modeling the effects of government policies.' *American Economic Review*, Papers and Proceedings, Vol. 69 (2) (May), pp. 86–91.

Fischer, Stanley (1977), 'Long-term contracts, rational expectations and the optimal money supply rule.' *Journal of Political Economy*, Vol. 85 (1) (February), pp. 191–206.

Flemming, John (1976), *Inflation*. Oxford: Oxford University Press.

Friedman, Benjamin M. (1979), 'Optimal expectations and the extreme information assumptions of "rational expectations" macromodels.' *Journal of Monetary Economics*, Vol. 5 (January), pp. 23–41.

Friedman, Milton (1968), 'The role of monetary policy.' *American Economic Review*, Vol. 58 (1) (March), pp. 1–17.

Grossman, Herschel I. (1978), 'Risk shifting, layoffs, and seniority.' *Journal of Monetary Economics*, Vol. 4 (November), pp. 661–86.

Kahn, Alfred E. (1979), 'Applications of economics to an imperfect world.' *American Economic Review*, Papers and Proceedings (May) pp. 1–13.

Kydland, Finn E. (1975), 'Noncooperative and dominant player solutions in discrete dynamic games. *International Economic Review*, Vol. 16, pp. 321–35.

—— (1977), 'Equilibrium solutions in dynamic dominant player models.' *Journal of Economic Theory* Vol. 6, (August).

—— and Prescott, Edward C. (1977), 'Rules rather than discretion: the inconsistency of optimal plans.' *Journal of Political Economy*, Vol. 85 (3) (June), pp. 473–91.

Leitman, George and Wan, Henry (1978), 'Anticyclical policy, rational expectations and demand management under uncertainty.' Paper presented at the NBER Stochastic Control Conference, Austin, Texas (May).

Lucas, Robert E. (1972a), 'Expectations and the neutrality of money.' *Journal of Economic Theory*, Vol. 4 (April), pp. 103–24.

—— (1972b), 'Econometric testing of the natural rate hypothesis.' In *The Eco-*

nometrics of Price Determination (ed. O. Eckstein), a conference sponsored by the Board of Governors of the Federal Reserve System and Social Science Research Council.
—— (1975), 'An equilibrium model of the business cycle.' *Journal of Political Economy*, Vol. 83 (December) pp. 1113–44.
—— (1976), 'Econometric policy evaluation: a critique.' In *The Philips Curve and Labor Markets* (ed.) Karl Brunner and Allan H. Meltzer). Amsterdam: North Holland.
—— and Prescott, E. G. (1979), 'Investment under uncertainty.' *Econometrica*, Vol. 39 (September), pp. 659–82.
—— and Rapping, L. A. (1969), 'Real wages, employment and inflation.' *Journal of Political Economy* Vol. 77 (October), pp. 721–54.
McCallum, Bennett T. (1977), 'Price-level stickiness and the feasibility of monetary stabilization policy with rational expectations.' *Journal of Political Economy*, Vol. 85 (3) (June), pp. 627–34.
—— (1978), 'Price level adjustments and the rational expectations approach to macroeconomic stabilization policy.' *Journal of Money, Credit and Banking*, Vol. 10 (4) (November).
Minford, Patrick (1978), *Substitution Effects, Speculation and Exchange Rate Stability*. North Holland: Amsterdam.
Muth, John F. (1961), 'Rational expectations and the theory of price movements.' *Econometrica*, Vol. 29 (July), pp. 315–35.
Phelps, Edmund S. *et al.* (1970), *Microeconomic Foundations of Employment and Inflation Theory*. New York: W. W. Norton.
—— and Taylor, John B. (1977), 'Stabilizing powers of monetary policy under rational expectations.' *Journal of Political Economy*, Vol. 85 (1) (February), pp. 163–90.
Popper, Karl (1959), *The Logic of Scientific Discovery*. London: Oxford University Press.
Prescott, Edward C. (1975), 'Efficiency of the natural rate,' *Journal of Political Economy*, Vol. 83, (December), pp. 1229–36.
—— (1977), 'Should control theory be used for economic stabilization?' in Karl Brunner and Allen H. Meltzer (eds.) *Optimal Policies, Control Theory and Technological Exports*. Carnegie-Rochester Conference series on Public Policy, Vol. 7, pp. 13–38. Amsterdam: North Holland.
Rosen, Harvey S. and Quandt, Richard E. (1978), 'Estimation of a disequilibrium aggregate labor market,' *Review of Economics and Statistics*, Vol. 60 (August), pp. 371–5.
Salop, S. (1978), 'Parables of information transmission,' in *The Effect of Information on Consumer and Market Behaviour*, (ed. A. Mitchell). Chicago.
—— (1979), 'A model of the natural rate of unemployment.' *American Economic Review*, Vol. 69 (March), pp. 117–25.
Sargent, T. J. (1976), 'The observational equivalence of natural and unnatural rate theories of macro-economics.' *Journal of Political Economy*, Vol. 84 (June), pp. 631–40.
—— and Wallace, Neil (1975), 'Rational expectations, the optimal monetary instrument and the optimal money supply rule.' *Journal of Political Economy*, Vol. 83 (2) (April), pp. 241–54.
—— (1976), 'Rational expectations and the theory of economic policy.' *Journal of Monetary Economics*, Vol. 84 (2) (April), pp. 207–37.
Shiller, Robert J. (1978), 'Rational expectations and the dynamic structure of macroeconomic models: a critical review.' *Journal of Monetary Economics*, Vol. 4 (January), pp. 1–44.

Sidrauski, Miguel (1967), 'Rational choice and patterns of growth in a monetary economy.' *American Economic Review*, Vol. 57 (2) (May), pp. 534–44.

Stiglitz, J. E. (1979), 'Equilibrium in product markets with imperfect information.' *American Economic Review*, Papers and Proceedings, Vol. 69 (March), pp. 339–45.

Taylor, John B. (1975), 'Monetary policy during a transition to rational expectations.' *Journal of Political Economy*, Vol. 83 (October), pp. 1009–21.

—— (1976), 'Estimation and control of a macroeconomic model with rational expectations.' Working paper, Columbia University.

—— (1977), 'Control theory and economic stabilization: a comment on the Kalchbrenner and Tinsley and Prescott Papers.' In *Optimal Policies, Control Theory and Technology Exports* (ed. K. Brunner and A. H. Meltzer), Carnegie-Rochester Conference Series on Public Policy, Vol. 7, pp. 93–8.

—— (1978), 'Aggregate dynamics and staggered contracts.' Paper given at the NBER Workshop on Control and Economics, Austin, Texas, May.

Tobin, James and Buiter, Willem (1980), 'Fiscal and monetary policies, capital formation and economic activity.' Forthcoming in *The Government and Capital Formation* (ed. George von Furstenberg).

Turnovsky, Stephen J. (1969), 'A Bayesian approach to the theory of expectations.' *Journal of Economic Theory*, Vol. 1 (August), pp. 220–7.

Voltaire (1949), *Candide*. In *The Portable Voltaire* (ed. Ben Ray Redman). New York: Viking Press.

Wilson, Charles A. (1979), 'Equilibrium and adverse selection.' *American Economic Review*, Papers and Proceedings, Vol. 69 (March), pp. 313–7.

Chapter 2

The superiority of contingent rules over fixed rules in models with rational expectations[1]

This paper analyses an old controversy in macroeconomic theory and policy: 'rules versus discretion' or, more accurately, *fixed* rules (rules without feedback or open-loop rules) versus *flexible* rules (contingent rules, conditional rules, rules with feedback or closed-loop rules). With open-loop policies the actual current and future values of the policy instruments are specified at the beginning of the policy maker's planning period. The time paths of the policy instruments are therefore functions only of the information available at the beginning of the planning period; they are to be implemented without regard to any new information that may accrue as time passes. Milton Friedman's advocacy of a fixed growth rate for some monetary aggregate is probably the best-known example of a (very simple) open-loop rule.[2] Formally, let x_t denote the value of the instrument vector in period t, I_t the information set available to the policy maker at the beginning of period t, when x_t is chosen. $t = 1$ is the beginning of the planning period and $t = T > 1$ the end. A plan or rule consists of a choice, at $t = 1$, of a set of functions f_t, $t = 1, \ldots, T$ or $\{f_t\}$ relating the x_t, $t = 1, \ldots, T$ to some information set. Open-loop policies or fixed rules are defined by:

$$x_t = f_t(I_1) \qquad (t = 1, \ldots, T). \tag{1}$$

Contingent policies or flexible rules specify the values of the policy variables in current and future periods as functions g_t, $t = 1, \ldots, T$, or $\{g_t\}$, known at $t = 1$, of the information that will be available when these instrument values will actually have to be assigned (i.e. I_t for x_t),[3] but may not yet be available at the beginning of the planning period when the rule $\{g_t\}$ is chosen. Thus future policy instrument values are known functions of observations yet to be made. In an uncertain world, this means that instrument values in periods $\tau > 1$ can respond to the observation of realisations of random variables between periods 1 and τ. Closed-loop policies or contingent rules are therefore defined by:

$$x_t = g_t(I_t) \qquad (t = 1, \ldots, T). \tag{2}$$

Note again that the g_t are chosen at $t = 1$ for the entire planning period. There is no serious disagreement that policy should be determined by rules, i.e. by functions known at $t = 1$, rather than by arbitrary, unpredictable actions 'on the spur of the moment'. There is no consensus on the desirability of fixed rules *vis-á-vis* contingent rules.

The standard theory of optimisation in stochastic dynamic models appears to yield the unambiguous conclusion that in an uncertain world the optimal contingent rule will always dominate the optimal fixed rule. This is most easily demonstrated using the familiar linear-quadratic stochastic dynamic programming problem studied, e.g. in Chow [1975]. A quadratic loss function (3) is minimised subject to the constraints of a stochastic linear model (4).

$$\min_{\{x_t\}} E_1\left[\frac{1}{2}\sum_{t=1}^{T}(y_t - a_t)'K_t(y_t - a_t)\right] \tag{3}$$

subject to

$$y_t = A_t y_{t-1} + C_t x_t + b_t + u_t,^1$$
$$y_0 = \bar{y}_0. \tag{4}$$

y_t is the state vector, $\bar{y}_0$ the initial state. x_t is a vector of control instruments, b_t is a vector of exogenous variables. u_t is a vector of stochastic disturbances which has a zero mean and a constant contemporaneous variance-covariance matrix and is serially uncorrelated. E_1 is the expectation operator, conditional on the information available at the beginning of period 1, a_t is a vector of target values of the state vector and K_t a non-negative definite weighting matrix penalising deviations of the state variables from their target values. a_t, K_t, A_t, C_t and b_t are known vectors or matrices.

If the information at the beginning of a period, τ, includes the model (the a_t, K_t, A_t, C_t and b_t matrices for $t = 1, \ldots, T$) and the past values of y_t and x_t (and therefore of u_t) but not the current, period τ, value of y_t or u_t, the optimal closed-loop policy rule takes the following time-varying linear feedback form: (see Chow [1975])[4]

$$x_t = G_t y_{t-1} + g_t, \tag{5a}$$

$$G_t = (C_t'H_tC_t)^{-1}C_t'H_tA_t, \tag{5b}$$

$$g_t = -(C_t'H_tC_t)^{-1}C_t'(H_tb_t - h_t), \tag{5c}$$

$$H_{t-1} = K_{t-1} + A_t'H_t(A_t + C_tG_t), \qquad (t = 1, \ldots, T-1), \tag{5d}$$

$$h_{t-1} = K_{t-1}a_{t-1} - A_t'[H_t(b_t + C_tg_t) - h_t], \qquad (t = 1, \ldots, T-1), \tag{5e}$$

$$H_T = K_T, \tag{5f}$$

$$h_T = K_Ta_T. \tag{5g}$$

For future reference a short digression on the standard solution technique for this class of stochastic dynamic models is required. The optimal feedback policy is derived using stochastic dynamic programming. According to Bellman's Principle of Optimality, 'An optimal policy has the property that, whatever the initial state and decision (i.e. control) are, the remaining decisions must constitute an optimal policy with regard to the state resulting from the first decision' (Bellman, 1957). This means that the optimal instrument choice for period t, x_t^*, $t = 1, \ldots, T$, can be obtained as the solution of the one-period optimisation problem:

$$\min_{x_t} W_t = E_t\left[\frac{1}{2}(y_t - a_t)'K_t(y_t - a_t)\right] + W_{t+1}^*, \qquad (6)$$

where $W_{t+1}^* = \min W_{t+1}$ subject to (4).

Thus the problem for the last period, T, is solved first, and the best policy x_T is chosen for the last period, contingent on any initial condition y_{T-1}. Next the two-period problem is solved for the last two periods by choosing the optimal x_{T-1}, contingent on the initial condition y_{T-2} and allowing for the fact that next period x_T will be chosen optimally, given y_{T-1}. Next the three period problem for the last three periods is solved, etc. It should be noted that the T-period problem is solved backward in time, one step at a time, thus taking advantage of the 'time-structure' of the model. At each step, only one unknown policy vector x_t is determined as a function of the initial state y_{t-1}. The policy instruments in period t are a known (as of $t = 1$) function of all the information available in period t, represented in this case by y_{t-1}. The value of y_{t-1} is partly determined by the random disturbance u_{t-1}, which is observed (or inferred) when x_t is chosen but not in any earlier period. The optimal closed-loop policy which permits a flexible response to new information as it becomes available, therefore dominates any open-loop policy: the expected loss under the optimal closed-loop policy is smaller than the expected loss under the optimal open-loop policy (Chow [1975]). This result appeals to commonsense: it should always be possible to do better if one can respond to unforeseen events and other new information than if such a response is ruled out. Only in the uninteresting special case of a model without uncertainty will the optimal closed-loop policy and the optimal open-loop policy be equivalent, i.e. generate equal values for the loss function.

This proposition that the optimal closed-loop rule dominates any fixed rule, including the optimal fixed rule, is robust. It holds for non-linear models and for more general objective functions. The model parameters A_t, C_t and b_t may be random variables (see Chow [1975]). Generalisations of (5a)–(5g) exist for the case in which y_{t-1} is not observable at the beginning of period t when x_t is chosen, due to measurement lags, and for the case in which y_t is never measured perfectly, no matter how often the estimate is revised.[15] The superiority of the optimal closed-loop rule over the optimal open-loop rule also holds when it takes time to decide upon and physically realise a control action and when not every policy instrument can be adjusted each period – the case of 'intermittent' controls (Deissenberg [1979a]). Finally, the dominance of the optimal flexible rule carries over to the case in which more information is available when x_t is chosen. The solution given in (5a)–(5g) assumed that neither y_t nor u_t had been observed when x_t was set. If instead a possibly imprecise and partial observation ζ_t on y_t is available at time t when x_t is chosen, in addition to full and accurate information on lagged values of y_t, (5a)–(5g) generalises to an optimal, time-varying linear feedback rule that makes x_t a function not only of y_{t-1} but also of ζ_t.[6]

The proposition that optimal contingent rules are superior to optimal fixed rules is analytically robust and appeals to commonsense: contingent rules permit new information to be taken into account when the actual course of the policy instruments is selected. Fixed rules do not permit any response to new information – the policy maker is 'locked in'. In view of this happy marriage of analytical rigour and intuition, how can respected economists argue in favour of fixed rules over flexible rules? Four grounds for such a view are analysed in the next four sections of the paper. The first is Friedman's 'long and variable lags' argument. It predates the New Classical Macroeconomics. The second concerns a possible trade-off between flexibility and simplicity in the design of policy rules. The last two are based on quite distinct aspects of the rational expectations or New Classical Macroeconomics revolution. One derives from the assumption that only unanticipated stabilisation policy will have real effects. The second is based on the 'inconsistency of optimal plans', the proposition due to Kydland and Prescott [1977] that, even when anticipated policies have real effects, feedback rules derived from dynamic programming (called 'consistent' policies by Kydland and Prescott) will be suboptimal in models in which the current state is a function of rational expectations of future states.

I Long and variable lags and the not-so-competent or not-so-well-intentioned government

Unlike the New Classical Macroeconomics School, Milton Friedman does not reject in principle the proposition that even anticipated monetary, fiscal and financial policies can have important real effects, in the short run and possibly even in the long run. However, these effects come with lags that are often long and always variable and uncertain.[7] In such an uncertain environment, the derivation of the best contingent rule becomes a difficult task, even for a well-informed, competent and well-intentioned policy maker. By itself, uncertainty about the magnitude and timing of the response of target variables to instruments in no way affects the dominance of the optimal feedback rule over any fixed rule. Random A_t, C_t and b_t matrices in (4) increase the magnitude of the minimum expected value of the loss function in (3) relative to the case where there is no uncertainty about the parameters of the model, but the principle that it is always optimal to make full use of all available information remains valid. Friedman's preference for fixed rules over flexible rules can therefore not be derived from uncertainty about model specification *per se*. It requires the further assumption that, unconstrained by fixed rules, the government either pursues the wrong objectives or pursues the right objectives in the wrong manner, because of inferior information or incompetent use of available information in the design of feedback rules. It is important to note that it is only the *optimal* contingent rule that is necessarily superior to any fixed rule, given an agreed upon objective function or loss function, not *any* contingent rule.

Even if the public and the private sector have the same objective functions, there certainty exist contingent rules that are a lot worse than any fixed rule. Misdirected 'stabilization policy' can be destabilising, as was first formally demonstrated by Phillips [1957, 1964]. The converse of the proposition is that if monetary, fiscal and financial policies have important effects on the real economy and if the magnitude and timing of these effects is uncertain, then the adoption of fixed rules (and even of the optimal fixed rule) may lead to very unfavourable outcomes, quite possibly worse than would result from the adoption of some less-than-ideal, sub-optimal flexible rule. To reach Friedman's conclusion that a fixed monetary rule should be adopted, it is necessary to assume not only that the government would not adopt the optimal feedback rule but that it would choose from among all sub-optimal feedback rules, one that would be dominated by a simple fixed rule.

Instead of the inefficient pursuit of the right objectives, the efficient pursuit of the wrong objectives by the government could be the reason for advocating fixed rules. If short-run political and electoral expediency takes precedence over the pursuit of economic welfare, it may be preferable to constrain the policy options of the authorities by committing them to simple fixed rules, if necessary by law or even, in the United States, by constitutional amendment.

To summarise, uncertainty about the timing and magnitude of the response of the economy to policy changes does not negate the validity of the general proposition that the optimal contingent rule dominates the optimal fixed rule. Whether the optimal contingent rule will be adopted does of course depend on the ability and integrity of those responsible for the conduct of economic policy. Friedman's advocacy of a fixed rule for the money supply cannot be derived from 'long and variable lags'. Instead it should be viewed as the expression of a very practical concern about the wisdom of leaving powerful instruments with uncertain effects in the hands of persons or agencies with limited ability and sometimes dubious motives. Even if this concern is valid, a fixed monetary rule may well be destabilising in a world that is subject to a variety of internal and external disturbances. If anticipated money matters for the real economy, a fixed monetary rule is not necessarily a safe rule. Such a rule would make sense only if there are no significant sources of disturbances elsewhere in the system and if the exogenous variables follow smooth growth paths.

II **The trade-off between flexibility and simplicity**

The optimal contingent rule stated in (5a)–(5g) shows that the values of the policy instruments in period t are a complicated function of the entire state vector. If there are constraints on the ability of the private sector to understand and predict government behaviour, the complex contingent rule that emerges as optimal when such constraints are ignored may well turn out to be far from optimal in practice. The predictability of government behaviour may be impaired and the credibility of its policies undermined (see e.g. Minford [1980]). Against this, it should be noted that very simple fixed rules may well be subject to equally severe credibility problems. There are likely to be contingencies under which any fixed rule is bound to be discarded. For example, an unanticipated doubling of world oil prices is likely to be associated with some relaxation of the money supply target. If the direction and magnitude of the policy response to such an unanticipated shock have not been announced in advance in the form of a conditional rule, the credibility of the open-loop policy is undermined and uncertainty about future policy enhanced (see Artis [1980] and Buiter [1980d]). It is possible, in principle, to strike a balance between conditionality and simplicity by selecting the optimal contingent rule among a restricted class of simple feedback rules. Since every fixed rule is always a special case of any contingent rule, however simple, it will be possible to identify the circumstances, if any, under which the optimal open-loop rule will be no worse than the restricted optimal contingent rule. Unless any form of conditionality, however, simple, introduces policy instrument uncertainty that is not present when fixed rules are adopted, the optimal open-loop rule can never dominate even a very restricted optimal contingent rule.

III **Only unanticipated stabilisation policy has real effects**

The third argument in favour of fixed rules or, more generally in favour of simple rules is based on the proposition that stabilisation policy is irrelevant for the behaviour of the real economy to the extent that it is anticipated or perceived by private agents. This view can be illustrated with the 'semi-reduced form model' of equation (7), made familiar through the work of Barro [1977, 1978a]. y_t denotes a vector of real economic variables, x_t a vector of stabilisation policy instruments, z_t a vector of exogenous and predetermined variables possibly including other non-stabilisation policy instruments and u_t a white noise disturbance vector. Equations such as (7) are called 'semi-reduced forms' because instrument expectations which are potentially endogenous still appear on the right-hand side, $\hat{x}_{t_1|t_0}$ denotes the value of x in period t_1 as anticipated in period t_0.

$$y_t = A_1 z_t + \sum_{i=0}^{T_1} B_i\,(x_{t-i} - \hat{x}_{t-i|t-i}) + \sum_{i=0}^{T_1} C_i x_{t-i} + u_t. \tag{7}$$

The effect of an anticipated or more precisely, contemporaneously perceived increase in x_{t-i} on y_t is given by

$$\frac{\partial y_t}{\partial x_{t-i}} + \frac{\partial y_t}{\partial \hat{x}_{t-i|t-i}} = C_i. \tag{8a}$$

The effect of an unanticipated or contemporaneously unperceived increase in x_{t-i} on y_t is given by

$$\frac{\partial y_t}{\partial x_{t-i}} = B_i + C_i. \tag{8b}$$

The New Classical Macroeconomics School asserts that for some set of stabilisation policy instruments, x_t, all the C_i matrices are zero: anticipated stabilisation policy has no effect on the joint probability density functions of real variables. If this view is correct, the government can influence real economic activity only by making the actual behaviour of its stabilisation instruments different from what the private sector anticipates or infers them to be, i.e. only by 'fooling' the private sector. Since changes in real economic behaviour brought about only through faulty perceptions of the actual policies pursued by the authorities are unlikely to be welfare-increasing,[8] the implications of the restriction that $C_i = 0$ for the conduct of policy appear self-evident: the only contribution that government can make to minimising variations in real economic activity is to minimise uncertainty about its own behaviour, i.e. to maximise the predictability of its own actions. Any known rule, fixed or contingent, will be 'neutral'. The demands made on the information gathering and processing resources of the private sector and on private sector forecasting and inference ability are likely to be minimised if the simplest possible fixed rule is adopted: a simple fixed rule is more easily incorporated in private information sets than a complex contingent rule. Even in a model like (7), deterministic monetary policy rules can have real effects if the authorities have an informational advantage over the private sector. As this issue is treated clearly elsewhere (e.g. Barro [1976]) no further attention need be paid to it here.

The conclusion that if only unanticipated policy affects real variables, known deterministic policy feedback rules are without real effects is not robust. There are two generalisations of (7) for which known contingent policy rules are effective by influencing the monetary prediction or forecast errors. They are given below.

Expectations of policy instrument values in a given period conditioned at different dates and the speed of policy response

Assume for the sake of argument that in (7), $C_i = 0$ for all i. If the policy forecast error term includes forecast errors for current and lagged x based on forecasts made currently or in the past (say for forecast horizons $j = 0, 1, \ldots, S_1$), equation (7) becomes

$$y_t = A_1 z_t + \sum_{i=0}^{T_1} \sum_{j=0}^{S_1} B_{ij} \, (x_{t-i} - \hat{x}_{t-i|t-i-j}) + u_t. \qquad (7')$$

If expectations are rational

$$\hat{x}_{t_1|t_0} = E(x_{t_1} \mid I_{t_0}), \qquad (9)$$

E is the mathematical expectation operator and I_τ the information set at $t = \tau$ conditioning the expectation.

The following proposition is now easily established.

Proposition 1. Provided at least some private actions affecting y_t depend on private forecasts of x_{t-i} that are based on earlier, and therefore less complete information than the information used by the policy authorities in setting x_{t-i}, known contingent rules will affect the probability density function of y_t even if $C_i = 0$ for all i.

This proposition is due to Fischer [1977] and to Phelps and Taylor [1977]. Note that both public and private agents can have the same *information set* in any given period (I_t in period t, I_{t-1} in period $t - 1$, etc.). If, however, the lag with which some private agents react to new information is longer than the lag with which the policy authorities can adjust at least one of their instruments, or if the authorities can write and enforce contingent forward contracts (the contingent policy rules) that the private sector either cannot duplicate or does not find in its perceived best interest to duplicate, then these known contingent policy rules will influence real outcomes. The crucial assumption is the existence of a difference in private and public *opportunity sets* (see Woglom [1979]; Buiter [1980a,c,e]; McCallum and Whitaker [1979].[9] Multi-period private nominal wage or price contracts that are not made contingent on the information that will become available over the life of the contract but are a function only of the information at the initial contract date,[10] combined with monetary policy rules that make the money supply in any given period a known function of the full information set available to public and private agents in that period, provide the best-known examples of deterministic monetary feedback rules with real effects (see Fischer [1977]; Phelps and Taylor [1977], Taylor [1979, 1980], Buiter and Jewitt [1980]). A simple example that closely follows Fischer [1977] is given below.

$$a_t = y_t, \tag{10}$$

$$a_t = \alpha_1 y_t + \alpha_2 (m_t - p_t) + u_t^a \qquad (\alpha_1, \alpha_2 > 0), \tag{11}$$

$$w_t - p_t = -\beta l_t^d + u_t^l \qquad (\beta > 0), \tag{12}$$

$$l_t^s = \gamma(w_t - p_t) \qquad (\gamma > 0), \tag{13}$$

$$l_t = l_t^d, \tag{14}$$

$$y_t = \delta l_t \qquad (1 > \delta > 0). \tag{15}$$

All variables are in logarithms. (10) states that aggregate demand a equals aggregate supply y. Aggregate demand depends on real output and real money balances, $m-p$; m is the nominal money stock, p the price level; u^a is a demand disturbance (11). Demand for labour, l^d, is determined by equating the marginal product of labour to the real wage. w_t is the money wage rate. The marginal product of labour has a random component, u_t^l (12). The supply of labour depends on the real wage (13). Actual employment is equal to the demand for labour (14).[11] The production function is given in (15). u_t^a and u_t^l are white noise disturbances.

If the labour market is characterised by an instantaneously flexible money wage $l_t^d = l_t^s$ and the equilibrium money wage is given by:

$$w_t = p_t + \frac{u_t^l}{1 + \beta\gamma} \tag{16}$$

Now assume that the money wage for period t has to be predetermined in period $t-1$, i.e. that it has to be chosen in a non-contingent, open-loop manner. We assume it is chosen in such a way that the expected (as of $t-1$) excess demand or supply in the labour market is zero, i.e. w_t is given by:

$$w_t = E\left(p_t + \frac{u_t^l}{1 + \beta\gamma} \mid I_{t-1}\right) = \hat{p}_{t|t-1}. \tag{16'}$$

From (15), (14), (12) and (16′) it then follows that

$$y_t = \delta\beta^{-1}(p_t - \hat{p}_{t|t-1}) + \delta\beta^{-1}u_t^l. \tag{17}$$

This is one possible derivation of the Sargent–Wallace [1975] supply function, although not the one they prefer. From (10) and (11) we obtain:

$$y_t = (1 - \alpha_1)^{-1}\alpha_2 m_t - (1 - \alpha_1)^{-1}\alpha_2 p_t + (1 - \alpha_1)^{-1}u_t^a. \tag{18}$$

Equating (17) and (18), solving for p_t and taking expectations as of $t-1$[12] we get:

$$p_t - \hat{p}_{t|t-1} = \frac{(1-\alpha_1)^{-1}\alpha_2}{(1-\alpha_1)^{-1}\alpha_2 + \delta\beta^{-1}}(m_t - \hat{m}_{t|t-1}) + \frac{(1-\alpha_1)^{-1}}{(1-\alpha_1)^{-1}\alpha_2 + \delta\beta^{-1}} u_t^a$$
$$- \frac{\delta\beta^{-1}}{[(1-\alpha_1)^{-1}\alpha_2 + \delta\beta^{-1}]} u_t^l,$$
$$y_t = \frac{\delta\beta^{-1}(1-\alpha_1)^{-1}\alpha_2}{(1-\alpha_1)^{-1}\alpha_2 + \delta\beta^{-1}}(m_t - \hat{m}_{t|t-1}) + \frac{\delta\beta^{-1}(1-\alpha_1)^{-1}}{(1-\alpha_1)^{-1}\alpha_2 + \delta\beta^{-1}} u_t^a$$
$$+ \frac{\delta\beta^{-1}(1-\alpha_1)^{-1}\alpha_2}{(1-\alpha_1)^{-1}\alpha_2 + \delta\beta^{-1}} u_t^l. \quad (19)$$

If m_t is set in open-loop fashion, or if m_t is some linear function of I_{t-1}, the information set available to both public and private agents when w_t was set, then $m_t = \hat{m}_{t|t-1}$. If, however, m_t can be set as a known (in period $t-1$) function of I_t, then such a contingent rule will affect the probability density function of y_t. Consider, for example, the following instantaneous feedback rule:

$$m_t = \pi_a u_t^a + \pi_l u_t^l. \quad (20)$$

It is easily seen that y_t can be stabilised perfectly by choosing π_a and π_l such that

$$\pi_a = \alpha_2^{-1}, \quad (21a)$$

and

$$\pi_l = -1. \quad (21b)$$

If the money wage had to be set two periods in advance, monetary feedback rules relating the current money supply either to the current information set or to last period's information set will affect the behaviour of real output. If m_t were to be a deterministic linear function of I_{t-2} (or of I_{t-i}, $i > 2$) no effect on real output is obtained in this model. It will be shown next that in a slightly different model monetary policy effectiveness can be present even if the public sector cannot respond faster to new information than the private sector, or indeed even if the reverse is the case.

Policy effectiveness through revisions in forecasts of future instrument values

Consider the following very simple macroeconomic model of a small open economy with perfect capital mobility and a freely floating exchange rate:

$$m_t - p_t = \alpha_1 y_t - \alpha_2 r_t + u_t^m \qquad (\alpha_1, \alpha_2 > 0), \quad (22)$$

$$y_t = \beta(p_t - \hat{p}_{t|t-1}) + u_t^y \qquad (\beta > 0), \quad (23)$$

$$r_t = r_t^* + \hat{e}_{t+1|t} - e_t, \quad (24)$$

$$p_t = e_t + p_t^*. \quad (25)$$

All variables except for interest rates are in logarithms. (22) is a standard LM curve. r_t is the domestic nominal interest rate, u_t^m a monetary disturbance. (23) is a Sargent–Wallace supply function. u_t^y is a supply disturbance. (24) states that the domestic interest rate equals the exogenous world interest rate, r^*, plus the expected proportional rate of depreciation of the exchange rate e. (This assumes perfect capital mobility and risk neutrality.) Note that the future exchange rate expectation linking r_t with r_t^* is conditioned at time t. This reflects the assumption that financial markets clear each period and that the portfolio allocation decisions for period t can be made instantaneously on the basis of the information available in that period. This stands in contrast to the labour market where the period t money wage has to be decided on (in an open-loop manner) in period $t-1$. The 'law of one price' holds instantaneously and equates the domestic price level to the exogenous world price level, p_t^* plus the exchange rate. To save on algebra we set $p_t^* = r_t^* = 0$ for all t.

From the earlier discussion it is clear that if m_t could be made a function of I_t, then such an instantaneous policy response function would alter the behaviour of y_t, since y_t depends on private forecasts of p_t (and therefore of m_t) made in period $t-1$ on the basis of I_{t-1}. In this example, however, y_t can be influenced by a monetary feedback rule even if m_t is made a function of I_{t-1} or more generally of I_{t-i}, $i \geqslant 1$. The reason is that p_t (and therefore $p_t - \hat{p}_{t|t-1}$ and y_t) depends, through the LM curve, the interest parity condition and the law of one price, on expectations of future price levels (and future money supplies) formed in period t. If m_t is a known linear function of I_{t-1}, $m_t = f(I_{t-1})$ say, current period information cannot influence m_t. Such information can influence $m_{t+1} = f(I_t)$, however. In models such as (22)–(25), therefore, which incorporate expectations of future endogenous variables conditioned at different dates ($\hat{p}_{t|t-1}$ and $\hat{e}_{t+1|t}$) monetary feedback rules can affect real output via (changes in) anticipations of *future* money supplies (Turnovsky [1980]; Weiss [1980]; Buiter [1980c,e,f]; Buiter and Eaton [1980]).

Assuming stability, the model of equations (22)–(25) can be solved for $p_t - \hat{p}_{t|t-1}$ and thus for y_t. This yields.

$$\begin{aligned} y_t = {} & \frac{\beta}{1 + \alpha_1\beta + \alpha_2}(m_t - \hat{m}_{t|t-1}) \\ & + \frac{\beta\alpha_2}{(1 + \alpha_1\beta + \alpha_2)(1 + \alpha_2)} \sum_{i=0}^{\infty}\left(\frac{\alpha_2}{1 + \alpha_2}\right)^i (\hat{m}_{t+1+i|t} - \hat{m}_{t+1+i|t-1}) \\ & - \frac{\beta u_t^m - (1 + \alpha_2)u_t^y}{1 + \alpha_1\beta + \alpha_2} \end{aligned} \tag{26}$$

Real output and the price forecast error $p_t - \hat{p}_{t|t-1}$ depend on the revision, between $t-1$ and t, in the forecast of the money supply in period t and in all future periods. To see the stabilisation role of lagged monetary feedback rules, consider the policy rule of (27) which makes the current money stock a function of all past random disturbances

$$m_t = \sum_{i=1}^{\infty}(\pi_{y,i}u^y_{t-i} + \pi_{m,i}u^m_{t-i}). \tag{27}$$

Taking expectations of current and future m conditional on I_t and on I_{t-1} using (27) and substituting the resulting expressions in (26) we get:

$$\begin{aligned} y_t = {} & \frac{\beta\alpha_2}{(1 + \alpha_1\beta + \alpha_2)(1 + \alpha_2)} \sum_{i=0}^{\infty}\left(\frac{\alpha_2}{1 + \alpha_2}\right)^i (\pi_{y,1+i}\, u^y_t + \pi_{m,1+i}\, u^m_t) \\ & - \frac{\beta u^m_t - (1 + \alpha_2)u^y_t}{1 - \alpha_1\beta + \alpha_2}. \end{aligned} \tag{28}$$

It is possible to stabilise output perfectly by choosing the $\pi_{y,i}$ and $\pi_{m,i}$ such that:

$$1 + \alpha_2 + \frac{\beta\alpha_2}{1 + \alpha_2} \sum_{i=0}^{\infty}\left(\frac{\alpha_2}{1 + \alpha_2}\right)^i \pi_{y,1+i} = 0, \tag{29a}$$

and

$$- \beta + \frac{\beta\alpha_2}{1 + \alpha_2} \sum_{i=0}^{\infty}\left(\frac{\alpha_2}{1 + \alpha_2}\right)^i \pi_{m,1+i} = 0.\text{[13]} \tag{29b}$$

E.g. output can be stabilised perfectly by responding, in period t, only to u^y_{t-1} and u^m_{t-1}. This involves setting $\pi_{y,1+i} = \pi_{m,1+i} = 0$ $(i \geq 1)$ and

$$\pi_{y,1} = -\frac{(1 + \alpha_2)^2}{\beta\alpha_2} \tag{30a}$$

$$\pi_{m,1} = \frac{1 + \alpha_2}{\alpha_2} \tag{30b}$$

Alternatively, perfect stabilisation of output could be achieved by responding, in period t, only to u^y_{t-2} and u^m_{t-2} or to even earlier random disturbances or by responding to some or all of the past disturbances according to (29a) or (29b). Even if the government is at an informational *disadvantage vis-á-vis* the private sector, in the sense that it receives information on realisations of u^m_t and u^y_t later than private agents do, a known feedback rule using its inferior information will influence private sector behaviour.[14] This is achieved by the government committing itself, in advance, to respond in a known manner to the random disturbances in some future period. In the example given here, it is irrelevant when the government responds to the disturbances. An equivalent effect on real output can be achieved via instantaneous response, lagged response or some mixture of the two. This suggests the following proposition.

Proposition 2. If in the 'semi-reduced form' real variables depend on revisions in private sector forecasts of future instrument values, known deterministic feedback rules will affect real behaviour. Such revisions in future policy instrument forecasts will enter the semi-reduced form of the model if expectations of future endogenous variables conditioned at different dates are present in the structural equations of the model.

This suggests that equations like (7′) should be augmented with a term like

$$\sum_{k=1}^{R_1} \sum_{i=-T_3}^{T_2} \sum_{j=0}^{S_2} d_{ijk}\, \hat{x}_{t+i|t-j} - \hat{x}_{t+i|t-j-k}$$

Anticipated future policy. In equations such as (7), which have been the starting point for empirical work in this area, only anticipated current and past instrument values enter as arguments. When the role of monetary policy is being investigated, however, there are good theoretical reasons for believing that real variables will be functions of anticipated *future* monetary growth. This is illustrated with the simple money, capital and growth model of equations (31)–(35). It is taken from Lucas [1975], which in turn is a development of Tobin [1965]. (See also Fischer [1979].)

$$k_{t+1} = \alpha_1 r_{Kt} - \alpha_2 r_{Mt} + \alpha_3 k_t \qquad (\alpha_1, \alpha_2, \alpha_3 > 0),$$
$$(\alpha_1 > \alpha_2, \alpha_3 < 1), \tag{31}$$

$$m_{t+1} - p_t = -\beta_1 r_{Kt} + \beta_2 r_{Mt} + \beta_3 k_t \qquad (\beta_1, \beta_2, \beta_3 > 0),$$
$$(\beta_2 > \beta_1, \beta_3 < 1), \tag{32}$$

$$r_{Kt} = -\delta_1 k_{t+1} \qquad \delta_1 > 0, \tag{33}$$

$$r_{Mt} = p_t - p_{t+1}, \tag{34}$$

$$m_{t+1} - m_t = \mu_t. \tag{35}$$

For notational simplicity all constants are omitted. Variables other than rates of return are in logarithms. The constant labour force, which is always fully employed, is scaled to unity. k_t is the capital stock, r_{Kt} the real rate of return on capital and r_{Mt} the real rate of return on non-interest-bearing money. There is no uncertainty, so rational expectations amount to perfect foresight. (31) and (32) state that the desired (and actual) end-of-periods stocks of capital and real money balances depend on the real rates of return on the two assets and on the initial capital stock. The rate of return on capital equals the marginal product of capital (33). The rate of return on money is minus the (expected) rate of inflation. Let $m_t = \ln M_t$, μ_t is the proportional rate of growth of the money supply in period t: $M_{t+1} = (1 + \mu_t) M_t$. Therefore $m_{t+1} \approx \mu_t + m_t$.

To find a rational expectations solution for (31)–(35), try a solution for k_t and p_t of the following form:

$$k_{t+1} = \pi_{11}k_t + \pi_{12}m_t + \sum_{i=0}^{\infty}\Psi_{k,i}\mu_{t+i}, \tag{36a}$$

$$p_t = \pi_{21}k_t + \pi_{22}m_t + \sum_{i=0}^{\infty}\Psi_{p,i}\mu_{t+i}. \tag{36b}$$

Substituting (33), (34) and (35) into (31) and (32), using (36a) and (36b) and rearranging, we obtain another set of equations of the same form as (36a) and (36b). Equating coefficients between these two sets of equations we obtain the following solutions for the π_{ij}, $\Psi_{k,i}$ and $\Psi_{p,i}$.

$$\pi_{11} = -\alpha_1\delta_1\pi_{11} - \alpha_2\pi_{21}(1 - \pi_{11}) + \alpha_3, \tag{37a}$$

$$\pi_{12} = 0, \tag{37b}$$

$$-\pi_{21} = \beta_1\delta_1\pi_{11} + \beta_2\pi_{21}(1 - \pi_{11}) + \beta_3, \tag{37c}$$

$$\pi_{22} = 1, \tag{37d}$$

$$\Psi_{k,0} = (1 + \alpha_1\delta_1 - \alpha_2\pi_{21})^{-1}\alpha_2(1 - \Psi_{p,0}), \tag{38a}$$

$$\Psi_{k,i} = (1 + \alpha_1\delta_1 - \alpha_2\pi_{21})^{-1}\alpha_2(\Psi_{p,i-1} - \Psi_{p,i}) \qquad (i > 0), \tag{38b}$$

$$\Psi_{p,0} = (1 + \beta_2)^{-1}[1 + \beta_2 - (\beta_1\delta_1 - \beta_2\pi_{21})\Psi_{k,0}], \tag{38c}$$

$$\Psi_{p,i} = (1 + \beta_2)^{-1}[\beta_2\Psi_{p,i-1} - (\beta_1\delta_1 - \beta_2\pi_{21})\Psi_{k,i}] \qquad (i > 0). \tag{38d}$$

Equations (37a) and (37c) define two solutions for π_{11} and π_{21}. It can be shown (Lucas [1975]) that the stable solution is characterised by:

$$\frac{\alpha_3}{1 + \alpha_1\delta_1} < \pi_{11} < 1, \tag{39a}$$

$$\pi_{21} < 0. \tag{39b}$$

Since $\pi_{12} = 0$ and $\pi_{22} = 1$, money is neutral in this model. An increase in m_t, the level of the money stock, leads to an equal proportional increase in p_t and leaves k_{t+1} unaffected.[15] Money is not, however, super-neutral. Different current and future rates of growth of the money stock, i.e. different μ_{t+i}, $i \geqslant 0$, will be associated with different paths for the capital stock. Money will only be super neutral if $\Psi_{k,j} = 0$, for all j. From (38a) and (38b) it is apparent that if $\alpha_2 = 0$, i.e. if the demand for capital is independent of the real rate of return on money, then all values of $\Psi_{k,i}$ will be zero. If $\alpha_2 \neq 0$, $\Psi_{k,0} = 0$ only if $\Psi_{p,0} = 1$: an increase in the current period rate of monetary growth (μ_t) by one percentage point raises the current price level by one percent. If $\Psi_{k,0}{=}0$, $\Psi_{k,1}{=}0$ only if $\Psi_{p,1} = \Psi_{p,0} = 1$ (38b). This, however, is possible only if $\beta_2 = +\infty$ (38d), i.e. if the demand for real money balances is infinitely elastic with respect to the rate of return on money. This forces the price level to be constant over time, regardless of the behaviour of future rates of monetary growth.

If $\Psi_{k,i}$ is to be equal to zero for all other i as well, it now follows that all other $\Psi_{p,i}$ will equal unity. From (36b) it is then clear that for any constant positive value of μ_t, the current price level will be infinite!

Ruling out the two special cases $\alpha_2 = 0$ and $\beta_2 = +\infty$, the path of the capital stock will therefore not be invariant under alternative fully perceived fixed rules for the future rates of growth of the money supply. Different anticipated future rates of monetary growth will be associated with different anticipated inflation rates. The portfolio allocation between money and real capital will not be invariant to this 'inflation tax'. In particular, the steady-state capital stock (found by setting $k_t = k_{t+1}$, $m_t - p_t = m_{t+1} - p_{t+1}$ and $\mu_t = \mu$ in (31)–(35) is given by

$$k = (1 + \alpha_1\delta_1 - \alpha_3)^{-1}\alpha_2\mu. \tag{40}$$

The long-run capital stock is an increasing function of the rate of monetary growth if $\alpha_2 > 0$. For completeness, the following well-known monetary policy effectiveness proposition can now be stated.

Proposition 3. If the expected rate of inflation affects the portfolio choice between money and real assets, alternative open-loop policies for future monetary growth will have real effects.

This monetary policy effectiveness result is very different from those stated in propositions (1) and (2). The first two propositions (policy response interval shorter than private forecast horizon and revisions in policy instrument forecasts) rely on contingent policy rules influencing private forecast errors. Such policies are *stabilisation* policies that influence deviations of real variables from their full information or equilibrium levels. In the absence of uncertainty there would be no role for them. Proposition 3 relies on the *structural* or *allocative* role of monetary policy. 'Effectiveness' here refers to the ability to influence the equilibrium values of real variables, not to the capacity to influence deviations from these equilibrium values. Here effectiveness holds for fixed rules as for contingent rules and is not dependent on the presence of uncertainty. In a stochastic model of capital, money and growth, monetary policy can play both a stabilisation role and an allocative role.

The potential importance of anticipated future instrument values suggests that equation (7) or (7′) should have added to it a term such as

$$\sum_{i=0}^{T_4} \sum_{j=0}^{S_3} e_{ij}\, \hat{x}_{t+i|t-j}.$$

While it is hard to assess the empirical significance of the inflation tax argument, Feldstein [1979] has argued – it is not quite clear how seriously – that the dead-weight loss associated with a higher rate of inflation in the United States may well be infinite! It should be possible to discover the presence of such effects in empirical work.

The implications of the results of this Section for the fixed vs. flexible rules debate are straightforward. Unless policy instruments affect real behaviour only via contemporaneous inference errors, i.e. only via terms such as $x_\tau - \hat{x}_{\tau|\tau}$, deterministic feedback rules will have real effects. If anticipated past or future instrument values have real effects, alternative open-loop rules too will alter real behaviour. In models with uncertainty, the optimal fixed rule will never dominate the optimal flexible rule.

Anticipated policies without real effects: an empty box? Are there policy instruments for which a plausible theoretical case can be made that they have no effects to the extent that they are anticipated? The discussion in this Section has so far been entirely in terms of monetary policy. There is only one other policy action for which neutrality has been argued on theoretical grounds. This is the substitution of government borrowing for lump-sum taxation, keeping constant the size and composition of the government's real spending programme. All other fiscal policy changes, on the spending side and on the revenue side, are likely to have real effects even in classical market-clearing models because they alter the constraints faced by private agents in a way that cannot be neutralised by utility maximising and profit maximising private actions. When such policy changes are anticipated their effects are in general different from what they are when they come as a surprise. The degree of confidence with which these expectations are held will also matter for the outcome, as will the length of the interval between the 'announcement' of a previously unanticipated policy change and its subsequent implementation. Finally, the extent to which the policy change is expected to be permanent or transitory will make a difference. It is, however, very difficult to come up with interesting models in which the solution trajectories of all real variables are invariant under alternative fully anticipated paths for the fiscal policy instruments (see e.g. Buiter [1977, 1979a, 1980c,d]), Fair [1978]).

This leaves only the two 'stabilisation' instruments, monetary policy and changing the borrowing-taxation mix, as candidates for the 'neutral when anticipated' category. The case for debt neutrality was restated elegantly by Barro [1974]. His conclusion that if (1) private agents rationally foresee the future tax obligations 'required' to service current government borrowing and (2) private agents are linked to later and earlier generations via an operative voluntary intergenerational chain of gifts or bequests, then government borrowing (or unfunded social security retirement programmes) will not affect the real trajectories of consumption and capital formation, has since been shown not to be robust (Buiter [1979b, 1980b], Buiter and Tobin [1979], Tobin and Buiter [1980], Carmichael [1979]). A presumption exists that the substitution of borrowing for lump-sum taxation will crowd out private saving in the short run and reduce the capital-labour ratio in the long run.

Empirical work on measuring the degree of (non)-neutrality of public sector debt has so far been inconclusive. Feldstein [1974] found a very strong negative effect of social security wealth on private saving, which was lowered by as much as one third. Barro [1978b] found no significant effect. Using Barro's data Feldstein [1978] again reported a significant depressing effect of social security wealth on private saving. The value of this work hinges crucially on the construction of the social security wealth variable. In essence, estimates of social security wealth have been obtained by extrapolating current or past payment/benefit ratios over the remaining life span of the economically active population. This is one more area of research where use of the rational expectations hypothesis could be very fruitful, as it is the present value of *anticipated* future payments and benefits that is the crucial explanatory variable.

The case against monetary superneutrality has already been argued. It is important to note that debt neutrality is a logical prerequisite for neutrality of the *level* of the money stock. If government bonds are net wealth (or more accurately, if the real value of government interest-bearing debt enters as an argument in some private sector behavioural relationship(s)), an equal proportional increase in the stock of money and in all money prices will not be neutral if nominally denominated, fixed price interest-bearing government debt is held by the private sector.

Even if no strong theoretical case can be made for monetary neutrality and superneutrality, the empirical magnitudes of the non-neutralities could still be insignificant. Elsewhere (Buiter [1980f]) I have discussed some of the problems associated with the empirical work inspired by Barro [1977, 1978a] (see also Barro and Rush [1980], Attfield *et al.* [1979a,b]), which attempts to evaluate the real effects of unanticipated and anticipated monetary growth using equations such as (7). One problem is the omission from (7) of private sector forecast horizons of different lengths, of revisions in forecasts of future instrument values and of anticipations of future monetary growth. Another problem is that the effect of unanticipated money on output (or unemployment) is identified only if the implausible a *priori* constraint is imposed that money does not respond to unanticipated output (or unemployment). No empirical resolution of these issues is as yet available.

IV **The time inconsistency of optimal plans**

The fourth argument in favour of fixed rules takes aim at the application of traditional optimal control techniques based on dynamic programming to the derivation of optimal economic policies in models with optimising agents endowed with rational expectations, in which the current state depends on expectations of future states and therefore on expectations of future disturbances, exogenous variables and policy choices. We saw in the introduction that traditional optimal control techniques such as stochastic dynamic programming lead to optimal policy rules that in models with uncertainty must be expressed in feedback or closed-loop form. Kydland and Prescott [1977] have shown that policies derived by dynamic programming, which they call 'time consistent' policies,[16] may be suboptimal in models with optimising agents endowed with rational expectations of the future, because such time consistent policies fail to allow for the effect of anticipated future instrument values on current and past states. The optimal policy in such models, they argue, is a time-inconsistent rule. Given the inappropriateness of dynamic programming methods the search for a good policy rule should be limited to a comparison (analytically or by simulation methods) of alternative policy rules in order to select the one with the most attractive operating characteristics (see also Prescott [1977]). Kydland and Prescott's proposition is quite distinct from the New Classical proposition that only unanticipated stabilisation policy can have real effects. It applies with full force only if anticipated future values of policy instruments affect real variables.

Traditional dynamic programming techniques do not allow for the impact of future policy measures on the current state through changes in current and past behaviour induced by anticipation of these future policy measures. This does not matter for *causal* or backward-looking models, such as the one given in equation (4). Here the current state is, in the structural model, a function only of the past state and the current values of the 'forcing variables', that is the policy instruments, the exogenous variables and the disturbance term. It matters greatly in *non-causal* or forward-looking models, such as the one given in equation (41) in which, in the structural model, the current state depends on the anticipated future state(s) as well as, possibly, on the past state and the current values of the forcing variables.

$$y_t = A_t y_{t-1} + C_t x_t + b_t + u_t + D_t E(y_{t+1}|I_t). \tag{41}$$

By repeated substitution for $E(y_{\tau+1}|I_\tau)$, equation (41) can be solved for y_t as a function of y_{t-1} and of the current and anticipated future values of the instruments, the exogenous variables and the disturbances. The application of dynamic programming, which takes y_{t-1} as given when the optimal value of x_t is chosen, runs into trouble here because y_{t-1} depends on expectations, formed in period $t-1$, of x_t, x_{t+1}, etc.

The analysis of this section shows that while Kydland and Prescott's rejection of dynamic programming methods in non-causal models is correct, the optimal (time-inconsistent) policy will, in models with uncertainty, still be a contingent, closed-loop rule. Time-inconsistency creates two problems, one for economists and one for economic policy makers. The problem facing economists is that a particular method or technique of optimisation in dynamic models – one which has proven very useful in the natural sciences and in engineering – is inappropriate in the social sciences when expectations of the future affect current outcomes. New optimisation techniques for non-causal models must be developed (see e.g. Chow, [1980]).

Even if these technical problems are overcome and the optimal time-inconsistent rule has been computed, as in the simple example of this section, the problem of pursuing or implementing time-inconsistent policies remains. Since, almost by definition, rational, non-cooperative behaviour in sequential models is time-consistent behaviour, how can the policy maker constrain himself to pursue optimal but time-inconsistent policies and how can he convince private agents that this is what he will do? No solution is offered here to the problem of adopting and executing time-inconsistent optimal plans. We do, however, establish that the rule or 'constitution' representing the optimal time-inconsistent policy will be a contingent rule or a flexible constitution. In non-causal models with uncertainty the optimal fixed rule will be both time-inconsistent and dominated by the optimal (time-inconsistent) feedback rule. E.g. in the previous section, the lagged feedback rules that perfectly stabilise real output by influencing revisions in expectations of future money supplies are time-inconsistent: past anticipations of the current money supply affect past output; this, of course, is a bygone when the current period arrives and a value is assigned to the current money stock.

A simple stochastic model with time-inconsistency. The model of equations (42)–(44) is a stochastic, linear-quadratic version of the two-period model of Kydland and Prescott [1977]

$$W = E[k_1(y_1 - a_1)^2 + k_2(y_2 - a_2)^2 + k_3(x_1 - a_3)^2 | I_1] \quad (k_1, k_2, k_3 > 0), \tag{42}$$

$$y_t = \alpha y_{t-1} + \gamma x_t + \delta E(x_{t+1} | I_t) + u_t \qquad (t = 1, 2;\ \alpha, \gamma, \delta \neq 0), \tag{43}$$

$$y_0 = 0, \tag{44a}$$

$$x_3 = 0, \tag{44b}$$

(42) is the objective function the policy maker aims to minimise. y_t is the state variable, x_t the policy instrument and u_t a white noise random disturbance. An initial condition for y_0 and a terminal condition for x_3 are given in (44a,b). The constraint faced by the policy maker is the simple model of (43). One interpretation of (43) is as follows. Let real output, y_t, depend on the expected real rate of return and, because of adjustment costs, on lagged output. If money is the only asset, the expected real rate of return is minus the expected rate of inflation. The supply function is therefore:

$$y_t = \mu_1 y_{t-1} - \mu_2[p_t - E(p_{t+1} | I_t)] + \varepsilon_t.$$

ε_t is a white-noise random disturbance term, μ_1, $\mu_2 > 0$. If the country is small in the world commodity market and instantaneous purchasing-power parity (PPP) prevails, we have

$$p_t = e_t + p_t^*,$$

e_t is the logarithm of the exchange rate, p_t^* the logarithm of the world price level which is assumed to behave like a white noise disturbance term. The exchange rate is the policy instrument. Substituting the PPP relationship into the supply function we get

$$y_t = \mu_1 y_{t-1} - \mu_2 e_t + \mu_2 E(e_{t+1}|I_t) + \varepsilon_t - \mu_2 p_t^*.$$

This corresponds to (43) with $\mu_1 = \alpha$, $\mu_2 = \delta = -\gamma$; $\varepsilon_t - \mu_2 p_t^* = u_t$.

More generally, we can interpret a model like (43) as representing the optimising behaviour of the private sector, which takes as given the behaviour of the policy maker, represented by x_t and $E(x_{t+1}|I_t)$. We assume that I_t, the information set conditioning expectations formed in period t, contains the model, including any deterministic policy rule, y_{t-1} and x_t but not y_t or u_t. x_t also has to be set before y_t and u_t are observed. Private agents have rational expectations about future policy behaviour but are 'Stackelberg followers'. By taking x_t and $E(x_{t+1}|I_t)$ as given they do not allow, when selecting the optimal values of their private controls, for any response of the policy maker to their choices. Private optimising behaviour is subsumed in the constant parameters α, γ, δ. The policy maker is the 'Stackelberg leader'. When selecting his optimal course of action he allows for the private sector's response to his choice of intruments, as represented in equation (43). This representation of public-private sector interaction as an asymmetric leader-follower non-cooperative game is quite common (see e.g. Fischer [1980]). Note that it is possible (but not necessary) for the (explicit) public sector objective function (42) to be the same as the (implicit) private sector objective function.

The model of (43) is non-causal: the current state, y_t, depends on an anticipated future instrument value. This suggests that time-consistent policies derived by dynamic programming will be sub-optimal. The time-consistent value of x_2 will be chosen to minimise $E[k_2(y_2 - a_2)^2 | I_2]$, taking as given y_1 (and x_1). While there is no doubt that y_1 will be a bygone once period 2 has arrived, y_1 is, from (43) a function of $E(x_2 | I_1)$. Therefore, to choose the time-consistent value for x_2 on the assumption that y_1 is unaffected by the choice of x_2 will in general be sub-optimal.

It is also clear that any open-loop rule for x_t is likely to be suboptimal. When x_2 is set in period 2, u_1 is known. u_1 is unknown, however, at the beginning of period 1, when any rule, fixed or flexible, for x_1 has to be announced. A contingent rule permits a known response of x_2 to the as yet unknown realisation of the random variable u_1. A fixed rule permits no such response and will therefore be suboptimal.

The optimal (but time-inconsistent) rule both permits a response of x_2 to the new information u_1 and allows for the dependence of y_1 on $E(x_2 | I_1)$. It is derived as follows. Substitute the constraints (43)–(44a,b) into the objective function (42). This yields

$$\begin{aligned} W = E\{&k_1[\gamma x_1 + \delta E(x_2 | I_1) + u_1 - a_1]^2 \\ &+ k_2[\alpha\gamma x_1 + \alpha\delta E(x_2 | I_1) + \gamma x_2 \\ &+ \alpha u_1 + u_2 - a_2]^2 + k_3(x_1 - a_3)^2 | I_1\}. \end{aligned} \tag{45}$$

Restricting ourselves to linear policy rules, the difference between x_2 and $E(x_2 | I_1)$ will be a linear function of the new information that has accrued between periods 1 and 2. This new information consists of u_1. Therefore

$$x_2 = E(x_2 | I_1) + \pi u_1, \tag{46}$$

π is a linear policy response function, to be chosen by the policy maker. Substituting (46) into (45) we get:

$$\begin{aligned} W = E\{&k_1[\gamma x_1 + \delta E(x_2 | I_1) + u_1 - a_1]^2 \\ &+ k_2(\alpha\gamma x_1 + (\alpha\delta + \gamma)E(x_2 | I_1) \\ &+ (\alpha + \gamma\pi)\, u_1 + u_2 - a_2]^2 + k_3(x_1 - a_3)^2 | I_1\}, \end{aligned} \tag{47}$$

(47) is now minimised with respect to x_1, $E(x_2 | I_1)$ and π. This yields optimal values x_1^*, $E(x_2 | I_1)^*$ and π^* given by

$$x_1^* = \frac{\gamma^2[a_1(\alpha\delta + \gamma) - a_2\delta]k_1k_2 + a_3\delta^2 k_1k_3 + a_3(\alpha\delta + \gamma)^2 k_2k_3}{\gamma^4 k_1k_2 + \delta^2 k_1k_3 + (\alpha\delta + \gamma)^2 k_2k_3}, \tag{48a}$$

$$E(x_2 | I_1)^* = \frac{\gamma^3(a_2 - \alpha a_1)k_1k_2 + \delta(a_1 - \alpha a_3)k_1k_3 + (\alpha\delta + \gamma)(a_2 - \alpha\gamma a_3)k_2k_3}{\gamma^4 k_1k_2 + \delta^2 k_1k_3 + (\alpha\delta + \gamma)^2 k_2k_3}, \tag{48b}$$

$$\pi^* = -\alpha\gamma^{-1}. \tag{48c}$$

The optimal (time-inconsistent) feedback rule given in (48a–c) can be contrasted with the optimal (time-inconsistent) open-loop rule. For any non-stochastic fixed rule, $x_2 = E(x_2 | I_1)$. The optimal open-loop rule, $\bar{x}_1$, $\bar{x}_2$ is therefore given by:

$$\bar{x}_1 = x_1^*, \tag{49a}$$

$$\bar{x}_2 = E(x_2 | I_1)^*. \tag{49b}$$

The optimal feedback rule can now be seen to consist of two parts, the optimal open-loop rule plus a (linear) response to the disturbance or 'innovation'. The response coefficient $\pi^* = -\alpha\gamma^{-1}$ is chosen so as to neutralise the effect of u_1 on y_2 exactly. By substituting the optimal instrument values (48a–c) or (49a,b) into the objective function (45) we can evaluate the expected loss under the feedback and the open-loop policies. Let W^* be the expected loss under the optimal feedback policy and $\bar{W}$ the expected loss under the optimal open-loop policy. σ_u^2 is the variance of u_t, $t = 1, 2$. It follows by inspection that

$$\bar{W} - W^* = k_2\alpha^2\sigma_u^2 > 0. \tag{50}$$

Thus, provided there is uncertainty ($\sigma_u^2 > 0$), provided u_1 affects y_2 ($\alpha \neq 0$) and provided y_2 enters the objective function ($k_2 > 0$), the optimal feedback policy dominates the optimal open-loop policy. If there is no uncertainty, as in the two-period example of Kydland and Prescott [1977], the two policies are equivalent.

The optimal time-inconsistent feedback rule not only dominates the optimal time-inconsistent fixed rule. It is also superior to the time-consistent policy derived by stochastic dynamic programming. The ranking of the time-consistent policy and the optimal fixed rule is ambiguous, however. The time-consistent solution for x_2 and x_1 is derived by first selecting the value of x_2 that minimises $E[k_2(y_2 - a_2)^2 \mid I_2]$, taking as given the value of y_1. Since $y_2 = \alpha y_1 + \gamma x_2 + u_2$, the time-consistent solution for x_2 is given by

$$\tilde{x}_2 = (a_2 - \alpha y_1)\gamma^{-1}. \tag{51a}$$

This implies that $E(y_2 - a_2 \mid I_2) = E(y_2 - a_2 \mid I_1) = 0$. The time-consistent value of x_1 is then derived by choosing the value of x_1 that minimises (42), assuming that in period 2, x_2 will be set according to (51*a*). The solution for x_1 is:

$$\tilde{x}_1 = \frac{[(\alpha\delta + \gamma)a_1 - \delta a_2]\gamma^2 k_1 + (\alpha\delta + \gamma)^2 a_3 k_3}{k_1\gamma^4 + k_3(\alpha\delta + \gamma)^2}. \tag{51b}$$

The time-consistent solution for x_1 and x_2 in (51a,b) differs from the optimal time-inconsistent feedback rule in (48a–c) and will therefore be inferior to it.[17] We can compare the expected loss under the optimal open-loop rule, $\bar{W}$, and under the time-consistent policy, $\widetilde{W}$, by substituting (49a,b), respectively (51a,b) into the objective function (45), noting that

$$E(\tilde{x}_2 \mid I_1) = (a_2 - \alpha\gamma\tilde{x}_1)(\alpha\delta + \gamma)^{-1}$$

and

$$\begin{aligned}\tilde{x}_2 &= a_2\gamma^{-1} - \alpha\tilde{x}_1 - \alpha\gamma^{-1}\delta E(\tilde{x}_2 \mid I_1) - \alpha\gamma^{-1}u_1 \\ &= (a_2 - \alpha\gamma\tilde{x}_1)(\alpha\delta + \gamma)^{-1} - \alpha\gamma^{-1}u_1.\end{aligned}$$

The algebra is simplified if we set $a_1 = a_2 = 0$. After rearranging terms we get:

$$\bar{W} - \tilde{W}_u = k_1\left\{\left[\frac{a_3\gamma^2(\alpha\delta + \gamma)k_2k_3}{\gamma^4k_1k_2 + \delta^2k_1k_3 + (\alpha\delta + \gamma)^2k_2k_3}\right]^2 - \left[\frac{a_3\gamma^2(\alpha\delta + \gamma)k_2k_3}{\gamma^4k_1k_2 + (\alpha\delta + \gamma)^2k_2k_3}\right]^2\right\}$$
$$+ k_2\left[\frac{a_3\delta\gamma^2k_1k_3}{\gamma^4k_1k_2 + \delta^2k_1k_3 + (\alpha\delta + \gamma)^2k_2k_3}\right]^2$$
$$+ k_3\left\{\left[\frac{a_3\gamma^4k_1k_2}{\gamma^4k_1k_2 + \delta k_1k_3 + (\alpha\delta + \gamma)^2k_2k_3}\right]^2 - \left[\frac{a_3\gamma^4k_1k_2}{\gamma^4k_1k_2 + (\alpha\delta + \gamma)^2k_2k_3}\right]^2\right\}$$
$$+ k_2\alpha^2\sigma_u^2 \tag{52}$$

Because of the last term, $k_2\alpha^2\sigma_u^2$, it is clear that if there is sufficient uncertainty in the model (i.e. for sufficiently large σ_u^2) the expected loss under the time-consistent policy will be less than under the optimal open-loop rule. It is easily checked[18] that the first three terms on the right-hand side of (52) measure the difference between the expected loss under the optimal open-loop rule and under the time-consistent policy for the case in which there is no uncertainty. Since without uncertainty the optimal open-loop rule is the globally optimal policy, the sum of the first three terms on the right-hand side of (52) is negative. This explains the ambiguity in the ranking of the optimal open-loop rule and the time-consistent policy in the case where there is uncertainty. The optimal open-loop rule is superior to the time-consistent policy insofar as it allows for the dependence of y_t on the anticipated future value of x_{t+1}. The time-consistent policy inappropriately treats y_t as given when the rule for x_{t+1} is chosen. The time-consistent policy on the other hand, being a feedback rule, permits a response of the instrument to new information. No open-loop rule permits such a response. The ranking of the two policies depends therefore on the numerical values of the parameters of the model and the objective function. The optimal time-inconsistent feedback rule dominates both the optimal open-loop rule and the time-consistent rule because it both allows for the dependence of the state on anticipated future instrument values and permits a response of the instruments to new information.

V Conclusions

The single most important conclusion is that the case for conditionality in the design of policy rules has not been weakened by the 'rational expectations revolution'. This conclusion is uncontroversial for those policy instruments that are generally recognised as having real effects whether anticipated or unanticipated. Most fiscal instruments fall into this category. Even if there exist 'pure stabilisation' instruments – monetary policy and changes in the (lump-sum) taxation-borrowing mix – that are neutral when anticipated, known contingent rules may still affect real outcomes. This will be the case if feedback rules alter private forecast errors or influence revisions in private forecasts of future endogenous variables.

Time-inconsistency of optimal plans in non-causal models does not affect the superiority of conditional rules over open-loop rules.

The case against conditionality can therefore only be based on one or both of the following assumptions. First, that any form of conditionality in policy design introduces uncertainty about current and future policy instrument values that is absent under fixed rules. Second, that unconstrained by fixed rules, the authorities either pursue the wrong objectives or pursue the right objectives in an inept manner.

Notes

Originally published in the *Economic Journal*, 91, Sept. 1981, pp. 647–70.

1 The research reported here is part of the NBER's research in International Studies. Any opinions expressed are those of the author and not those of the National Bureau of Economic Research.

This paper grew out of seminars given at the International Monetary Fund, the University of Manchester, the University of Warwick, the University of Bristol, the London School of Economics and Essex University. I have benefited from the comments and insights of George von Furstenberg, Mohsin Khan, Arturo Brillenbourg, Marcus Miller, Douglas Purvis, C. R. Birchenhall, David Demery and David Webb. None of these is in any way responsible for the analysis or its conclusions.

2 In general, open-loop policies only require all present and future instrument values to be known at the beginning of the planning period. These known values need not, however, be constant.

3 I assume for simplicity that there are no 'delayed controls', i.e. x_t does not have to be chosen before t because it takes time to decide upon and realise a control action x_t. This assumption can be relaxed without altering any of the conclusions of this paper. See e.g. Deissenberg [1979b].

4 Any finite order vector autoregressive process in y_t with a random disturbance vector following any finite order ARIMA process can be rewritten in the first-order format given in (4). The state vector could also depend on a distributed lag in x_t; lagged x_t will in that case be included in the state vector y_t in (4). See Chow [1975].

5 See Deissenberg [1979b]. With measurement lags and imperfect state measurement, y_{t-1} in (5a) is replaced with its minimum variance prediction, given the information available at t. Kalman filtering is the standard technique for obtaining an estimate of y_{t-1} in the case in which some stochastic linear function of y_{t-1}, $\xi_{t-1} = Dy_{t-1} + \varepsilon_{t-1}$ is observed when x_t is chosen rather than the true state y_{t-1}: (ε_t is a white noise random disturbance vector). See Chow [1975] and Deissenberg [1979b].

6 In essence, the optimal feedback rule specified x_t as a function of the best estimate, at t, of y_t. If neither y_t nor u_t are observable at t, $E(y_t \mid I_t) = A_t y_{t-1} +$

$C_t x_t + b_t$. Assume some random function of y_t, $\xi_t = Dy_t + e_t$ is observable when x_t is chosen, in addition to exact information on y_{t-1}. D is a known matrix and e_t a white noise disturbance vector. Then

$$E(y_t | I_t) = (I - MD)(A_t y_{t-1} + C_t x_t + b_t) + M\zeta_t,$$
$$M = (\Sigma_{uu}D' + \Sigma_{ue})(D\Sigma_{uu}D' + \Sigma_{ee} + D\Sigma_{ue} + \Sigma_{ue}D')^{-1},$$
$$\Sigma_{uu} = E(u_t u_t'); \Sigma_{ee} = E(e_t e_t'); \Sigma_{ue} = E(u_t e_t').$$

7 Friedman made this point mainly with reference to monetary policy. See Friedman [1968].
8 This intuitively obvious statement is made more precise in Barro [1976]. In his model, policy 'surprises' increase the variances of real variables relative to their 'full information' variances, i.e. their variances when the only uncertainty is irreducible, exogenous uncertainty. This will reduce welfare. Phelps [1978] considers optimal inflation policy in a model with adaptive inflation expectations. In such a model it is possible to trade off more employment today for more inflation tomorrow. Given a high enough discount rate, such a policy, which operates by fooling private agents into believing that the rate of inflation is less than it actually is, may appear to be optimal. This conclusion is somewhat suspect, as no costs are attached to the misinformation engineered by the monetary authorities.
9 I offer no theory to explain this asymmetry in public and private opportunity sets; the argument solely concerns the consequences of such asymmetries, should they exist. Problems of moral hazard and adverse selection are probably behind the failure of many contingent forward markets to exist. The government's ability to tax (to exact unrequited transfers of wealth and income) and to declare some of its liabilities legal tender, and the associated difference in default risk between public and private sector bonds are likely to be sufficient to generate asymmetries in opportunity sets.
10 That is, *open-loop*, non-indexed, multi-period nominal wage and price contracts.
11 Using the perhaps more acceptable specification of the employment equation $l_t = \min(l_t^d, l_t^s)$ adds complexity without affecting the main conclusion.
12 We assume that the information set in period t includes all current and past observations of endogenous variables, policy instruments and random disturbances as well as the true structure of the model.
13 Alternatively, the authorities could choose to eliminate the price forecast error $p_t - \hat{p}_{t|t-1}$ completely, thus equating output to its *ex post* 'natural' level, u_t^y.
14 The delayed response of policy need not be due to an information disadvantage. It could also reflect a slower response by policy-makers to new information than by private agents due to 'inside' policy lags.
15 This neutrality result has two interpretations. (1) The comparison of two solution trajectories for all time with identical μ_t for all t but with the *level* of the money supply path higher by a constant fraction (in each period) for one of the paths. (2) The result of an unanticipated and immediately implemented once-and-for-all increase in the money supply, with the same percentage growth rates of money being maintained after the unanticipated money stock increase.
16 A sequence of policy actions is time consistent if, for each time period, the policy action in that period maximises the objective function, taking as given all previous policy actions and private agents' decisions and that all future policy actions will be similarly determined. (Kydland and Prescott [1977, p. 475].) This is Bellman's principle of optimality (Bellman [1957]).
17 Note that if $k_3 = 0$, i.e. if no costs are attached to the policy instrument in period 1, the time-consistent policy is optimal in this simple example.
18 By setting $u_1 = u_2 \equiv 0$.

References

Artis, M. (1980), 'Memorandum on monetary policy.' In House of Commons Treasury and Civil Service Committee, *Memoranda on Monetary Policy*, Vol. 11. HMSO.

Attfield, C. L. F., Demery, D. and Duck, N. W. (1979a), 'Unanticipated monetary growth, output and the price level. U.K. 1946–77.' University of Bristol Discussion Paper. (July).

——, —— and —— (1979b), 'A quarterly model of unanticipated monetary growth and output in the U.K. 1963–1978.' University of Bristol Discussion Paper. (September).

Barro, R. J. (1974), 'Are government bonds net wealth?' *Journal of Political Economy*, Vol. 82 (November–December), pp. 1095–117.

—— (1976), 'Rational expectations and the role of monetary policy.' *Journal of Monetary Economics*, Vol. 2 (January), pp. 1095–117.

—— (1977), 'Unanticipated money growth and unemployment in the United States.' *American Economic Review*, Vol. 67 (March), pp. 101–15.

—— (1978a), 'Unanticipated money, output and the price level in the United States.' *Journal of Political Economy*, Vol. 86 (August), pp. 549–80.

—— (1978b), *The Impact of Social Security on Private Saving. Evidence from the U.S. Time Series*. Washington, D.C.: A.E.I.

—— and Rush, M. (1980), 'Unanticipated money and economic activity.' In *Rational Expectations and Economic Policy* (ed. S. Fischer). Chicago: University of Chicago Press.

Bellman, R. (1957), *Dynamic Programming*. Princeton, N.J.: Princeton University Press.

Buiter, W. H. (1977), 'Crowding out and the effectiveness of fiscal policy.' *Journal of Public Economics*, Vol. 7 (June), pp. 309–28.

—— (1979a), *Temporary and Long-Run Equilibrium*. New York: Garland.

—— (1979b), 'Government finance in an overlapping generations model with gifts and bequests.' In *Social Security versus Private Saving* (ed. G. M. von Furstenberg). Ballinger.

—— (1980a), 'The macroeconomics of Dr Pangloss. A critical survey of the New Classical Macroeconomics.' *Economic Journal*, Vol. 90 (March), pp. 34–50.

—— (1980b), '"Crowding out" of private capital formation by government borrowing in the presence of intergenerational gifts and bequests.' *Greek Economic Review* (August).

—— (1980c), 'Monetary, financial and fiscal policies under rational expectations'. *IMF Staff Papers* (December).

—— (1980d), 'The design of economic policy: its uses and limitations.' In *Monetarism: Traditions, Debate and Policy* (ed. A. Courakis). Macmillan. (Forthcoming).

—— (1980e), 'The role of economic policy after the New Classical Macroeconomics.' In *Contemporary Economic Analysis* (ed. D. Currie and D. A. Peel), Vol. IV. Croom-Helm. (Forthcoming).

—— (1980f), 'Real effects of anticipated and unanticipated money. Some problems of estimation and hypothesis testing.' Unpublished.

—— and Eaton, J. (1980), 'Policy decentralisation and exchange rate management in interdependent economies.' NBER Working Paper No. 531 (August).

—— and Jewitt, I. (1980), 'Staggered wage setting without money illusion. Variations on a theme of Taylor.' NBER Working Paper No. 545 (September).

—— and Tobin, J. (1979), 'Debt neutrality. A brief review of doctrine and evidence.' In *Social Security versus Private Saving* (ed. G. M. von Furstenberg). Ballinger.

Carmichael, J. (1979), The Role of Government Policy in Economic Growth. Unpublished Ph.D, Thesis, Princeton University.

Chow, G. C. (1975), *Analysis and Control of Dynamic Economic Systems*. New York: John Wiley.

—— (1980), 'Econometric policy evaluation and optimisation under rational expectations.' *Journal of Economic Dynamics and Control*, Vol. 2 (February), pp. 47–60.

Deissenberg, C. (1979a), 'Optimal control of linear econometric models with intermittent controls.' Fakultät für Wirtschafts-Wissenschaften und Statistik, Universität Konstanz, Working paper, serie A, No. 127 (June).

—— (1979b), 'Optimal stabilisation policy with delayed controls and imperfect state measurement.' Fakultät für Wirtschafts-Wissenschaften und Statistik, Universität Konstanz, Working Paper, serie A, No. 133 (November).

Fair, R. (1978), 'A criticism of one class of macroeconomic models with rational expectations.' *Journal of Money, Credit and Banking*, Vol. 10 (November), pp. 411–7.

Feldstein, M. (1974), 'Social security, induced retirement and aggregate capital accumulation.' *Journal of Political Economy*, Vol. 82 (September-October), pp. 905–26.

—— (1978), 'Reply.' In *The Impact of Social Security on Private Saving, Evidence from the U.S. Time Series'* (by R. J. Barro), pp. 37–47. Washington, D.C.: A.E.I.

—— (1979), 'The welfare cost of permanent inflation and optimal short-run economic policy.' *Journal of Political Economy*, Vol. 87 (August), pp. 749–68.

Fischer, S. (1977), 'Long-term contracts, rational expectations and the optimal money supply rule.' *Journal of Political Economy*, Vol. 85 (February), pp. 191–206.

—— (1979), 'Capital accumulation on the transition path in a monetary optimising model.' *Econometrica*, Vol. 47 (November), pp. 1433–40.

—— (1980), 'Dynamic inconsistency, cooperation and the benevolent dissembling government.' *Journal of Economic Dynamics and Control*, Vol. 2 (February), pp. 93–107.

Friedman, M. (1968), 'The role of monetary policy.' *American Economic Review*, Vol. 58 (March), pp. 1–17.

Kydland, F. E. and Prescott, E. C. (1977), 'Rules rather than discretion: the inconsistency of optimal plans.' *Journal of Political Economy*, Vol. 85 (June), pp. 473–91.

Lucas, R. E. (1975), 'An equilibrium model of the business cycle.' *Journal of Political Economy*, Vol. 83 (December), pp. 1113–44.

McCallum, B. T. and Whitaker, J. K. (1979), 'The effectiveness of fiscal feedback rules and automatic stabilisers under rational expectations.' *Journal of Monetary Economics*, Vol. 5 (April), pp. 171–86.

Minford, P. (1980), 'Memorandum on monetary policy.' In House of Commons Treasury and Civil Service Committee, *Memoranda on Monetary Policy*, Vol. I. HMSO.

Phelps, E. S. (1972), *Inflation Policy and Unemployment Theory: The Cost-Benefit Approach to Monetary Planning*. New York: W. W. Norton.

—— and Taylor, J. B. (1977), 'Stabilising of powers of monetary policy under rational expectations.' *Journal of Political Economy*, Vol. 85 (February), pp. 163–90.

Phillips, A. W. (1957), 'Stabilisation policy and the time-form of lagged responses.' Economic Journal, Vol. 67, No. 266 (June), pp. 265–77.
—— (1964), 'Stabilisation policy in a closed economy.' *Economic Journal*, Vol. 64 (June), pp. 290–323
Prescott, E. C. (1977), 'Should control theory be used for economic stabilisation?' In *Optimal Policies, Control Theory and Technological Exports* (ed. K. Brunner and A. H. Meltzer), *Carnegie-Rochester Conference series on Public Policy*, Vol. 7, Amsterdam: North Holland, pp. 13–38.
Sargent, T. J. and Wallace, N. (1975), 'Rational expectations, the optimal monetary instrument and the optimal money supply rule.' *Journal of Political Economy*, Vol. 83 (April), pp. 241–54.
Taylor, J. B. (1979), 'Staggered wage setting in a macro model.' *American Economic Review*, Papers and Proceedings, Vol. 69 (May), 108–13.
—— (1980), 'Aggregate dynamics and staggered contracts.' *Journal of Political Economy*, Vol. 88 (February), pp. 1–23.
Tobin, J. (1965), 'Money and economic growth.' *Econometrica*, Vol. 33 (October), pp. 671–84.
—— and Buiter, W. H. (1980), 'Fiscal and monetary policies, capital formation and economic activity.' In *The Government and Capital Formation* (ed. G. M. von Furstenberg). Ballinger.
Turnovsky, S. J. (1980), 'The choice of monetary instruments under alternative forms of price expectations.' *Manchester School* (March), pp. 39–62.
Weiss, L. (1980), 'The role for active monetary policy in a rational expectations model.' *Journal of Political Economy*, Vol. 88 (April), pp. 221–23.
Woglom, G. (1979), 'Rational expectations and monetary policy in a simple macroeconomic model.' *Quarterly Journal of Economics*, Vol. 93 (February), pp. 91–105.

Chapter 3

Predetermined and non-predetermined variables in rational expectations models

The distinction between predetermined and non-predetermined variables is an extremely important one in rational expectations models. In a recent paper Blanchard and Kahn [1980] proposed the following definition. (For any variable Z_t, ${}_{t-i}Z_{t+j} \equiv E(Z_{t+j}|\Omega_{t-i})$, where E denotes the mathematical expectation operator and Ω_t the information set at t conditioning expectations formed at t.) 'A predetermined variable $[X_{t+1}]$ is a function only of variables known at time t, that is of variables in Ω_t, so that $X_{t+1} = {}_tX_{t+1}$ whatever the realization of the variables in Ω_{t+1}. A non-predetermined variable P_{t+1} can be a function of any variable in Ω_{t+1}, so that we can conclude that $P_{t+1} = {}_tP_{t+1}$ only if the realizations of all variables in Ω_{t+1} are equal to their expectations conditional on Ω_t.' (Blanchard and Kahn [1980, p. 1305].)

For concreteness, consider the linear first-order system of Blanchard and Kahn:

$$\begin{bmatrix} X_{t+1} \\ {}_tP_{t+1} \end{bmatrix} = A\begin{bmatrix} X_t \\ P_t \end{bmatrix} + \gamma Z_t = \begin{bmatrix} A_{11} & A_{12} \\ A_{21} & A_{22} \end{bmatrix}\begin{bmatrix} X_t \\ P_t \end{bmatrix} + \begin{bmatrix} \gamma_1 \\ \gamma_2 \end{bmatrix} Z_t, \qquad (1)$$

$$X_{t_0} = X_0,$$

$$\begin{bmatrix} X_t \\ P_t \end{bmatrix} \text{ is the state vector,}$$

Z_t the vector of exogenous or forcing variables, X_t is an n-vector, P_t an m-vector and Z_t a k-vector,

$\begin{bmatrix} A_{11} & A_{12} \\ A_{21} & A_{22} \end{bmatrix}$ represents a partitioning of A conformable with X and P,

γ_1 is the first n rows of γ and γ_2 the last m rows.

If A is of full rank, $n + m$ linearly independent boundary conditions for the state variables are required to obtain a unique solution. For the predetermined variables, X, these boundary conditions take the form of n initial values at $t = t_0$, say, determined by the past history of the system. At a point in time, t, the predetermined variables X_t cannot respond to changes in expectations formed at t, due to new information becoming available at t, about the future behaviour of the endogenous or exogenous variables.

For the m non-predetermined variables, the boundary conditions do not take the form of historically given initial values. Instead they typically take the form of the transversality or terminal condition that the homogeneous part of the equation system,

$$\begin{bmatrix} X_{t+1} \\ {}_tP_{t+1} \end{bmatrix} = A \begin{bmatrix} X_t \\ P_t \end{bmatrix} \tag{2}$$

converges to zero as $t \to \infty$ from any X_0.

If characteristic equation of A has n stable (modulus < 1) roots and m unstable (modulus > 1) roots, this convergence condition provides the 'missing' m independent boundary conditions required for a unique solution (Blanchard and Kahn [1980]). P_t represents in economic applications such 'forward-looking' variables as asset prices determined in efficient auction markets dominated by arbitrageurs and speculators endowed with forward-looking rational expectations. X_t represents such 'backward-looking' variables as the physical capital stock and, in some Keynesian models, temporarily fixed money wages or prices.

It seems self-evident that Blanchard and Kahn's definition of a predetermined variable is far too restrictive to capture the economic meaning of the concept. It is also unnecessarily restrictive for the validity of the solution method for (1) that they present. Consider, e.g., the naive scalar autoregressive model in (3). ε is a white noise disturbance term,

$$y_{t+1} = \alpha y_t + \varepsilon_{t+1}. \tag{3}$$

Clearly $y_{t+1} = \alpha y_t + \varepsilon_{t+1} \neq E(y_{t+1} \mid \Omega_t) = \alpha y_t$. y_{t+1} doesn't have to be perfectly predictable on the basis of information available at time t, for it to be a predetermined variable in the economic sense or for Blanchard and Kahn's solution method to be applicable. Equation (3) is the special case of (1) with $A_{11} = \alpha$, $A_{12} = A_{21} = A_{22} = 0$, $\gamma_1 = 1$, $\gamma_2 = 0$ and $Z_t = \varepsilon_{t+1}$. Its 'final form' solution, given the initial condition $y_{t-t_0} = y_0$ is

$$y_t = \alpha^{t_0} y_0 + \sum_{i=0}^{t_0-1} \alpha^i \varepsilon_{t-i}. \tag{4}$$

In equation (1) we can permit current-dated exogenous variables and random disturbances to affect X_t without this requiring any significant alteration in the solution method. Replace (1) by (1′),[1]

$$\begin{bmatrix} X_{t+1} \\ {}_tP_{t+1} \end{bmatrix} = A \begin{bmatrix} X_t \\ P_t \end{bmatrix} + \gamma Z_{t+1}. \tag{1'}$$

The reduced form solution is, using the notation of Blanchard and Kahn,

$$P_t = -C_{22}^{-1}C_{21}X_t - C_{22}^{-1}\sum_{i=0}^{\infty} J_2^{-i-1}[C_{21}\gamma_1 + C_{22}\gamma_2]_t Z_{t+i+1},$$

$$X_t = X_0 \qquad \text{for } t = 0,$$

$$X_t = B_{11}J_1B_{11}^{-1}X_{t-1} + \gamma_1 Z_t - [B_{11}J_1C_{12} + B_{12}J_2C_{22}]C_{22}^{-1}$$

$$\times \sum_{i=0}^{\infty} J_2^{-i-1}[C_{21}\gamma_1 + C_{22}\gamma_2]_{t-1}Z_{t+i}^{i} \qquad \text{for } t > 0,$$

where[2]

$$A = C^{-1}JC,$$

$$J = \begin{bmatrix} J_1 & 0 \\ 0 & J_2 \end{bmatrix}, \; C = \begin{bmatrix} C_{11} & C_{12} \\ C_{21} & C_{22} \end{bmatrix}, \; C^{-1} = \begin{bmatrix} B_{11} & B_{12} \\ B_{21} & B_{22} \end{bmatrix}.$$

In a recent paper Chow (1981) proposed the following less restrictive definition of a predetermined variable: X_t is predetermined i.f.f. $X_t \equiv E(X_t \mid \Omega_t)$. This definition too leads to a characterization that may contradict economic sense and may not fit into the solution method proposed by Blanchard and Kahn. Consider the following model where ε_t again represents white noise:

$$y_t = \beta E(y_{t+1}|\Omega_t) + \delta Z_t + \varepsilon_t. \tag{5}$$

Assume that Ω_t includes the true structure of the model and complete contemporaneous information on the endogenous (y) and exogenous (Z) variables. This implies that $y_t = E(y_t|\Omega_t)$, yet the natural economic interpretation of y is that of a forward-looking, non-predetermined variable. Assuming that $\lim_{n\to\infty}\beta^n E(y_{t+n}|\Omega_t) = 0$ and that the infinite sum on the right-hand side of (6) exists, the forward-looking solution for (5) is

$$y_t = \delta Z_t + \varepsilon_t + \delta \sum_{i=1}^{\infty} \beta^i E(Z_{t+i}|\Omega_t). \tag{6}$$

y_t is a non-predetermined variable because it is a function of expectations formed at time t: it can 'jump' in response to 'news'.

Apart from classifying certain non-predetermined variables as predetermined, Chow's proposed definition also classifies certain predetermined, variables as non-predetermined. Consider again equation (3). Whether or not $E(y_{t+1}|\Omega_{t+1}) = y_{t+1}$ depends on the information set. If agents don't observe y_{t+1} exactly until period $t + 2$ and observe in period $t + 1$ some noisy function of y_{t+1}, say $\zeta_{t+1} = \mu y_{t+1} + w_{t+1}$, they are faced with a signal extraction problem. Let $E(w_t) = E(\varepsilon_t) = 0$, $E(w_t^2) \equiv \sigma_w^2$, $E(\varepsilon_t^2) \equiv \sigma_\varepsilon^2$, $E(\varepsilon_t w_t) = \sigma_{\varepsilon w}$ for all t and $E(\varepsilon_t w_s) = 0$ for all t and s, $s \neq t$,

$$E(y_t|\Omega_t) = E(y_t|y_{t-1}, \zeta_t) = \alpha y_{t-1} + \frac{\mu\sigma_\varepsilon^2 + \sigma_{\varepsilon w}}{\mu^2\sigma_\varepsilon^2 + \sigma_w^2 + 2\mu\sigma_{\varepsilon w}}(\mu\varepsilon_t + w_t)$$
$$\neq y_t = \alpha y_{t-1} + \varepsilon_t. \tag{7}$$

Yet y is still a predetermined variable: y_t is not a function of expectations, formed at t, of future endogenous and/or exogenous variables.

It will be clear from this discussion what the proposed alternative definition of a predetermined and non-predetermined variable is.

Definition. X_t is predetermined i.f.f. X_t is not a function of expectations, formed at t, of future endogenous and/or exogenous variables.

P_t is non-predetermined i.f.f. P_t is a function of expectations, formed at t, of future endogenous and/or exogenous variables.

Note that this fits the general solution method proposed by Blanchard and Kahn for their model. Their final form solution for X_t depends on expectations of future exogenous variables formed in period $t - 1$ and before. The final form solution for P_t depends on expectations of future exogenous variables formed in period t and before.

Consider the following three examples:

$$y_t = \alpha y_{t-1} + \beta E(y_t|\Omega_{t-1}) + \gamma Z_t + \varepsilon_t, \tag{8a}$$

$$y_t = \alpha y_{t-1} + \beta E(y_{t+1}|\Omega_t) + \gamma Z_t + \varepsilon_t, \tag{8b}$$

$$y_t = \alpha y_{t-1} + \beta E(y_{t+1}|\Omega_{t-1}) + \gamma Z_t + \varepsilon_t. \tag{8c}$$

Assume Ω_t includes the correct structure of the model and all current and past values of the exogenous and endogenous variables. According to our definition, y in (8a) is a predetermined variable. (Note that (8a) cannot be put in Blanchard and Kahn's 'first order' form.) In equation (8b), which fits Blanchard and Kahn's format, y_t is non-predetermined. y_t in equation (8c) is predetermined in spite of the presence of forward-looking expectations. It is not a function of *current* anticipations of future events and does not respond to current 'new'. Equation (9) shows that (8c) can be written in the modified Blanchard and Kahn format given in equation (1′).

$$\begin{bmatrix} y_{t+1} \\ E(y_{t+2}|\Omega_t) \end{bmatrix} = \begin{bmatrix} 0 & 1 \\ -\beta^{-1}\alpha & \beta^{-1} \end{bmatrix} \begin{bmatrix} y_t \\ y_{t+1} \end{bmatrix} + \begin{bmatrix} 0 & 0 \\ -\beta^{-1}\gamma & -\beta^{-1} \end{bmatrix} \begin{bmatrix} Z_{t+1} \\ \varepsilon_{t+1} \end{bmatrix}. \tag{9}$$

Conclusion

The current values of non-predetermined variables, unlike predetermined variables, are functions of current anticipations of future values of endogenous and/or exogenous variables. This property is crucial both for the mathematical derivation of solution algorithms for rational expectations models and for their economic interpretation.

Notes

Originally published in *Economics Letters*, 10, 1982, pp. 49–54.

1 For this to make economic sense, the components of γ_2 corresponding to values of the forcing variables in period $t + 1$ should be zero: P_t cannot be a function of actual future realizations of Z, only of anticipated future realizations.
2 J_1 is the $n \times n$ diagonal matrix whose diagonal elements are the n stable characteristic roots of A; J_2 is the $m \times m$ diagonal matrix whose diagonal elements are the unstable characteristic roots of A. C is the matrix whose columns are the right-characteristic vectors of A. A is assumed to be diagonalizable.

References

Blanchard, O. and C. Kahn (1980), 'The solution of linear difference models under rational expectations', *Econometrica*, 48, July, 1305–11.
Chow, G. (1981), 'Solution and estimation of simultaneous equations under rational expectations', *Econometric Research Program Research memo*. No. 291, October (Princeton University, Princeton, NJ).

Chapter 4

Expectations and control theory

Rational expectations, the Lucas Critique and the ineffectiveness of anticipated policy

In principle, most economists would consider an extension of the assumption of optimizing behaviour to expectations formation (forecasting or prediction) by private agents to be a step forward from the past practice of postulating mechanical, *ad hoc* forecasting rules that tended to generate *systematic* forecast errors. The term 'rational expectations' does not, however, refer to forecasts generated by an explicit rational, expected utility maximizing decision process in which the costs of acquiring, processing and evaluating further information are balanced against the benefits anticipated from further informational investments. Rational expectations in the sense of Muth [1961], applied to macroeconomics first by Lucas [1972a,b] postulates that the subjective joint probability distribution function of future variables held by economic agents at time t coincides with the actual, objective conditional distribution function based on the information assumed to be available at time t. Since most work involving rational anticipations only considers first moments, future variables anticipated at time t are 'true mathematical expectations of future variables conditional on all variables in the model which are known to the public at time t' (Shiller [1978, p. 3]).

The strengths of the rational expectations hypothesis are first the weakness of the alternative hypotheses (*ad hoc* adaptive, regressive or extrapolative expectations etc., which relate anticipated future values in a mechanical way to past observables) and second the comparative ease of empirical implementation, at any rate in linear models. While one might in principle prefer a 'Bayesian' predictor derived from explicit optimizing behaviour, practical problems of implementing this in all but the most trivial models rule this out.

One major weakness of the hypothesis is that the issue of how economic agents acquire their knowledge of the true structure of the economy, which is used in making the 'rational' forecasts is not addressed by the theory. Any expectations scheme that is not rational in the sense of Muth will be consistently wrong in the sense of yielding systematic expectational errors. Sensible economic agents will ultimately abandon such a scheme. The learning and revision processes by which inadequate forecasting schemes are revised or abandoned are not spelled out. Convergence of such a learning process to a Muth-rational expectation mechanism is certainly not self-evident or inevitable.

Moreover, while in the rational expectations literature it is always clear what the correct model of the economy is (it is the author's own model) – there is no consensus in practice on the way in which the economy works. The meaning of rational expectations is unclear in a world where some economists adhere to the Cambridge Economic Policy Group's view that the economic system is characterized by persistent and even cumulative disequilibrium, others take the 'Liverpool' view that the economy is a very quickly equilibrating and self-correcting mechanism and yet others believe that neither of the previous two views is correct.

Nevertheless, the rational expectations literature and Lucas in particular have made a significant and lasting contribution to the theory of economic policy and the construction of policy-oriented econometric models. The postulate that anticipations of future values of variables should be formed in a way that is consistent with the stochastic processes actually generating these variables, given the information available to the forecasting agent, is revolutionizing the specification and estimation of macroeconometric models.

Private sector behaviour is influenced in many ways by expectations of futures variables (including government instruments). If changes in government behaviour alter these expectations, models that ignore such links from government behaviour via private expectations to private behaviour are likely to forecast poorly and to lead to misleading conclusions being drawn from policy simulations. This conclusion of course does not require Muth-rational expectations *per se*, only some direct effect of government behaviour on private sector expectations. Muth-rational expectations provides the additional hypothesis that the link between private sector expectations and government behaviour comes through the private sector's knowledge of the true structure of the model, including the parameters of the stochastic process that characterizes government behaviour. The main practical implication of the Lucas critique, which states that private sector behavioural relationships will, since they reflect private expectation formation, not be invariant under perceived changes in public sector behavioural relationships, is therefore obvious. One should solve *simultaneously* for the currently anticipated value of a variable and its future value calculated from the model, which in turn is a function of these anticipations. Once this is done, the model incorporates the rational expectations assumption, including the response of the private sector to current and anticipated future policy actions, and respects the 'principle of policy-dependent structural parameters'. It can now be used for policy simulation in the standard manner.

A simple example will illustrate the force of the Lucas critique.

$$y_t = Ay_{t-1} + B\hat{y}_{t|t-1} + Cx_t + u_t \tag{1}$$

With rational expectations, $\hat{y}_{t|t-1} = E(y_t|I_{t-1})$. The information set includes the true structure of the model and all current and past values of y_t and x_t. u_t is again a zero mean i.i.d. disturbance vector. Taking expectations of (1) conditional on I_{t-1} and substituting the resulting solution for $y_{t|t-1}$ into (1) we obtain

$$y_t = [I - B]^{-1} Ay_{t-1} + Cx_t + B[I - B]^{-1}C\, E(x_t|I_{t-1}) + u_t \tag{2}$$

or

$$y_t = [I - B]^{-1} Ay_{t-1} + C(x_t - E(x_t|I_{t-1})) + [I - B]^{-1}C\, E(x_t|I_{t-1}) + u_t \tag{2'}$$

Consider an econometrician who, unlike the private agents inhabiting our little model, is ignorant of the true structure of the economy and wishes to estimate it for use in policy evaluation. Assume that over the sample period the policy instrument vector, x_t, has followed a white noise stochastic process, $x_t = \varepsilon_t$ where ε_t is a zero mean i.i.d. normal disturbance term. If our econometrician uses OLS to regress y_t on y_{t-1} and x_t he will obtain

$$y_t = \hat{M}_1 y_{t-1} + \hat{M}_2 x_t + \eta_t \tag{3}$$

where M_1 and M_2 are biased but consistent and asymptotically efficient estimates of $[I - B]^{-1}$ A and C respectively. If the sample size were sufficiently large, the estimated model would be

$$y_t = [I - B]^{-1} Ay_{t-1} + Cx_t + \eta_t{}^1 \tag{4}$$

If our econometrician believed that he had identified and estimated the invariant structure of the economy with equation (4), he would use it for policy simulation. Assume he wishes to investigate the model's behaviour under the feedback rule $x_t = Gy_{t-1}$.

Based on (4) he would expect the model to behave according to

$$y_t = ([I - B]^{-1} A + CG)y_{t-1} + \eta_t \tag{5}$$

In fact, from (2) it behaves according to:

$$y_t = [I - B]^{-1} (A + CG)y_{t-1} + u_t \tag{5'}$$

Only if B is the zero matrix (i.e. only if expectations play no role) will the policy simulations based on (4) not yield nonsensical results. This is an example of the trap that the Lucas critique (Lucas [1976]) warns us against. It has contributed to the 'sanitizing' of a large number of spurious econometric relationships and to the explanation of certain kinds of apparent parameter instability in important econometric relationships. Interesting examples are the apparent instability of the unemployment-inflation trade-off or Phillips curve and shifts in the cyclical relationship between output and productivity.

It is clear that M_2 in (3) does not represent an estimate of the invariant structural relationship between y_t and x_t: the relationship between y_t and x_t estimated from the sample is not invariant under changes in the stochastic processes governing the exogenous variables (including the policy instruments). The invariant structure is represented by the A, B and C matrices on (1) (or by $[I - B]^{-1} A$, C and $B[I - B]^{-1} C$ in equation (2) and by the stochastic properties of the disturbance vector u_t. For policy simulation and optimal control, it is necessary that the invariant structure be identified and estimated. This may be very difficult in practice as many different models may be observationally equivalent if only a single 'regime' for the exogenous variables is represented in the sample. E.g. if x_t is white noise, the model of (1) is observationally equivalent to the structural model

$$y_t = D_1 y_{t-1} + D_2 x_t + u_t. \tag{6}$$

If the sample contains two subperiods with different stochastic processes for x_t, the estimates of D_1 and D_2 would be the same for the two subsamples[2] if (6) were the true model, while the corresponding reduced form equation of the model given in (1) would differ between the two subsamples.

There is a second aspect of the Lucas critique, which involves an even more fundamental criticism of standard macroeconomic modelling practice. Again, however, it does not imply a denial of the scope, in principle, for using optimal control methods in macroeconomic policy design. This second Lucas critique argues that even the coefficient matrices A, B and C in 'first generation' rational expectations models such as (1) are unlikely to be truly structural. These 'parameters' are likely not to be invariant under (perceived) changes in the stochastic processes governing the inputs into the system. The point can be illustrated with a simple model due to Muth (1961) of equilibrium in a single market for a storable commodity.

$$C_t = -\beta p_t + u_t^d \qquad \beta > 0 \tag{7a}$$

$$S_t = \alpha(\hat{p}_{t+1|t} - p_t) \qquad \alpha > 0 \tag{7b}$$

$$Y_t = \gamma \hat{p}_{t|t-1} + \delta x_t + u_t^y \qquad \gamma > 0 \tag{7c}$$

$$Y_t = C_t + S_t - S_{t-1} \tag{7d}$$

Consumption demand, C_t depends negatively on price, p_t and on a disturbance term u_t^d. The stock of inventories to be carried over into period $t + 1$, S_t, is increasing function of the expected rate of change of the price. Production Y_t is subject to a one period lag and depends therefore on last period's expectation of the current price. It also depends on some policy instrument, x_t, and on a supply disturbance u_t^y. Equation (7d) states that supply equals demand. The two disturbances are both white noise. Assuming that expectations are rational, it is easily checked, using the method of undetermined coefficients that the solution for the equilibrium price is of the form given in (8)

$$p_t = \pi_1 p_{t-1} + \pi_2 x_t + \pi_3(u_t^y - u_t^d) + \sum_{i=1}^{\infty} \Omega_i \; E(x_{t+i}|I_t) + \sum_{i=1}^{\infty} \varepsilon_i E(x_{t-1+i}|I_{t-1}) \tag{8}$$

The first Lucas critique warns us that different stochastic processes for the x_t will lead to different dynamic reduced form relationships between p_t and current and past observables. The second Lucas critique warns that it may be inappropriate even to take the α, β, γ, and δ coefficients as parameters invariant under changes in policy regime and changes in the stochastic processes governing the other forcing variables. The point can be illustrated by deriving α, the responsiveness of inventory demand to the expected change in the price, from optimal speculative behaviour.

Consider a risk averse speculator who maximizes the expected utility from inventory speculation profits $Z_t \equiv (p_{t+1} - p_t)S_t$. His utility function u has the properties $u' > 0$ and $u'' < 0$. He chooses S_t to maximize $E[u(Z_t)|I_t]$. Taking a second order approximation of $E(u)$ at the expected value of profits we obtain

$$E(u(Z_t|I_t)) \approx u([E(p_{t+1}|I_t) - p_t]S_t) + \frac{1}{2} u''([E(p_{t+1}|I_t) - p_t]S_t)E[(p_{t+1} - E(p_{t+1}|I_t))^2|I_t]S_t$$

Assuming that $u''' = 0$ the first-order condition for an interior maximum yields the inventory demand function:

$$S_t = -\frac{u'}{u''\sigma^2(p_{t+1}|I_t)} \; [E(p_{t+1} \,|\, I_t) - p_t] \tag{9}$$

$\sigma^2(p_{t+1}|I_t)$ is the conditional variance of the future price level, i.e.

$$\sigma^2(p_{t+1}|I_t) \equiv E[(p_{t+1} - E(p_{t+1}|I_t))^2|I_t].$$

Comparing (7b) with (9) we note that

$$\alpha = \frac{-u'}{u''\sigma^2(p_{t+1}|I_t)}$$

While

$$-\frac{u'}{u''}$$

(the reciprocal of the coefficient of absolute risk aversion) can be treated as a parameter, i.e. as part of the invariant structure. $\sigma^2(p_{t+1} \mid I_t)$ is clearly a function of the policy regime and of the stochastic behaviour of the forcing variables in general. Estimating the model on the assumption that α is a parameter and treating it as such for policy simulation or optimization will lead to potentially serious errors.

This second Lucas critique is really a criticism of bad economic theory and bad econometrics. Starting from the proper microeconomic foundations (whether optimizing, satisficing or behavioural), an invariant structure exists and is, in principle, a proper subject for optimal control. The identification and estimation of this invariant structure will of course in practice often be an extremely complicated task.

An unfortunate and largely accidental by-product of the 'rational expectations revolution' has been the resurgence of the view that there is no role for active stabilization policies. Rationally anticipated stabilization policies, such as monetary policy based on feedback rules, have been argued not to have any effect on the joint density functions of real economic variables such as output, unemployment and competitiveness. To minimize the uncertainty about the conduct of policy, monetary and budgetary policies should therefore be governed by fixed, unconditional or non-contingent rules, i.e. rules that do not permit instrument responses to new information about the state of the world. In terms of the model of equation (1), it is assumed that for the set of real state variables y_t and for some set of stabilization policy instruments x_t, we have $[I - B]^{-1}C = 0$, so that (2′) reduces to:

$$y_t = [I - B]^{-1}Ay_{t-1} + C[x_t - E(x_t \mid I_{t-1})] + u_t \qquad (2'')$$

Since in (2″) only unanticipated policy actions have real effects, uncertainty about y_t is minimized by minimizing the uncertainty surrounding x_t. The demands made on the forecasting abilities of private agents are minimized if the simplest possible open-loop rule for x_t is adopted.

Note that it is not the rational expectations assumption *per se* that emasculates policy. It is the combination of the rational expectations assumption and the further assumption about the structure of the economy that only unanticipated stabilization policy matters for real variables. I have argued elsewhere (Buiter [1980a,b,c,d, 1981]) that the set of policy instruments that will not have real effects if the policy rule is known, is empty. The effects of policy actions will certainly differ according to whether they are anticipated or unanticipated, according to the extent to which they are perceived as transitory or permanent and according to the degree of confidence with which these expectations are held. The standard argument that optimal contingent or conditional rules dominate unconditional rules is not affected by the incorporation of rational expectations in non-trivial economic models.

Notes

Originally published as section 3b of 'Expectations and Control Theory', *Economie Appliquée*, 36, 1983, pp. 129–56.

1 η_t is a normal, zero mean, i.d.d. disturbance term with the same variance as u_t.
2 Ignoring sampling variance.

References

Buiter, W. H. (1980a), 'The Macroeconomics of Dr Pangloss: A Critical Survey of the New Classical Macroeconomics', *Economic Journal*, 90, March, pp. 34–50.

—— (1980b), 'Crowding out of Private Capital Formation by Government Borrowing in the presence of Intergenerational Gifts and Bequests', *Greek Economic Review*, 2, August, pp. 111–42.

—— (1980c), 'Monetary, Fiscal and Financial Policies under Rational Expectations', *IMF Staff Papers*, December, pp. 795–813.

—— (1980d), 'The Role of Economic Policy after the New Classical Macroeconomics', in D. Currie, R. Nobay and D. Peel (eds.), *Macroeconomic Analysis*, Croom Helm, London.

—— (1981), 'The Superiority of Contingent Rules over Fixed Rules in Models with Rational Expectations, *Economic Journal*, 91, Sept., pp. 617–46.

Lucas, R. E. (1972a), 'Expectations and the Neutrality of Money', *Journal of Economic Theory*, 4, April, pp. 103–24.

—— (1972b), 'Econometric Testing of the Natural Rate Hypothesis', in O. Ekstein (ed.), *The Econometrics of Price Determination*, a conference sponsored by the Board of Governors of the Federal Reserve System and the Social Research Council.

—— (1976), 'Econometric Policy Evaluation: A Critique', in *The Philips Curve and Labour Markets*, ed. K. Brunner and A. H. Meltzer, North Holland, Amsterdam.

Muth, J. (1961), 'Rational Expectations and the Theory of Price Movements', *Econometrica*, 29, July, pp. 315–35.

Shiller, R. J. (1978), 'Rational Expectations and the Dynamic Structure of Macroeconomic Models: A Critical Review', *Journal of Monetary Economics*, 4, January, pp. 1–44.

Chapter 5

The right combination of demand and supply policies: the case for a two-handed approach[1]

I Introduction

The title of this paper was chosen *for* me, *not by* me. Its ring of open-mindedness, evenhandedness and balance all but compels an author to parade as a man of the extreme centre, a fanatical moderate in analysis and policy prescription. I identify with such characterization only reluctantly.

My uneasiness with the title of this chapter is, however, due to something more fundamental than an innate inability to try and please both sides of an argument. The usefulness of the very concepts of 'demand-side' and 'supply-side' should be questioned for a number of reasons.

Firstly, even where in individual markets demand and supply can be distinguished conceptually (i.e. in traditional competitive analysis), the uses of these concepts are at times confused and confusing. The demand for labour is part of the aggregate supply side. The supply side of credit is part of aggregate demand. However, in working capital models of production (or in any model involving input-output lags) interest rates and/or the availability of credit affect aggregate supply (see for example, Blinder [1987]). In any model with endogenous capital formation, financial market conditions affect aggregate supply in the long run.

Secondly, every non-trivial policy action (monetary, fiscal, financial, regulatory, incomes-policy, etc.) influences both aggregate demand and aggregate supply (whenever these concepts are well-defined). We therefore cannot speak of demand policies and supply policies but only of the demand effects and the supply effects of given policies, which will always have both kinds of effects.

Thirdly, and most fundamentally, modern theoretical developments which are only just entering the stage of being the subject of systematic econometric testing, suggest that demand and supply may not even conceptually be separated. The best-known of these developments are those concerning efficiency wages and those related to hysteresis or path-dependence.

While I believe it to be important and even essential for progress in our understanding of how mature industrial economies work and how to improve their performance, to escape from the clutches of an intellectually moribund conventional competitive analysis, I cannot offer an integrated, coherent alternative 'Weltanschauung'[2]. I shall however list a few of the many promising developments that may become the bricks and mortar of the economics of the twenty-first century. Enough has been achieved already to suggest the need for major changes in our view of how modern mixed economies work and in our appreciation of the scope for and limits to what policy can achieve.

If the demand-side versus supply-side dichotomy is no longer very useful, the distinction between *stabilization policy* and *structural* or *allocative* policy may still have some limited taxonomic usefulness. Stabilization policy aims to influence (and, one hopes, to minimize) deviations of the actual equilibrium (in general a non-Walrasian and possibly a quantity-constrained, rationing equilibrium), which will in general not be (constrained) Pareto-efficient, from the (constrained) Pareto-efficient equilibrium. In the context of the aggregate labour market, stabilization policy aims at deviations of actual employment from full employment or from a (presumed stabilization policy-invariant) 'natural' level of employment. As regards aggregate output, stabilization policy is concerned with the gap between actual output and its full employment capacity value or some other appropriate notion of the 'natural' level of output. Sometimes stabilization policy is defined more broadly to include the stability of the internal and external values of the currency and the achievement of 'sustainable' financial deficits and surpluses for the public and private sectors (and by implication for the external sector).

Structural or allocative policy aims to influence the nature of (constrained) Pareto-efficient equilibria in labour, product and financial markets. In the labour market, such policies aim to influence the (presumed stabilization policy-invariant) natural rate of unemployment. In the aggregate product market, it seeks to modify the capacity or full-employment level of output.

The dichotomy is not neat but can be helpful in focussing policy debate. It is again true, however, that any nontrivial monetary, financial, fiscal, regulatory, and such like policy action will almost always have both allocative and stabilization consequences (see Buiter [1983]).

The plan of this paper is as follows. In section II I review the role of stabilization policy in New Classical macroeconomic models. I reproduce a result of Marini [1985] that in all New Classical models which have (i) signal extraction and (ii) a non-predetermined intertemporal speculation term (somewhere in the model), monetary policy (and by direct extension fiscal policy) is very effective as a stabilization instrument in the sense that it can eliminate entirely the gap between actual and 'full information' output or employment even when the policy authority is no better (or even less) informed than the private sector.

In section III, the efficiency wage hypothesis and the hysteresis or path-dependence hypothesis are shown to blur or eliminate entirely the distinction between the demand and supply side. The far-reaching implications for policy are sketched briefly. Section IV sums up and touches briefly on some other important policy issues that could not be addressed in the body of the paper for reasons of space. It also contains some forthright policy recommendations aimed at challenging prevalent Euro-pessimistic complacency.

II The role of stabilization policy in New Classical Macroeconomic models

New Classical Macroeconomic models are sequential competitive equilibrium models where market participants have symmetric information and (Muth)-rational expectations. This discussion relates only to the monetary variant of the New Classical School, associated with the names of Lucas, Sargent, Wallace and Barro. It ignores the real business cycle models developed by Kydland and Prescott [1982], Long and Plosser [1983] and others.

Since markets clear continuously, with equilibrium prices determined by the equality of competitive supply and demand, stabilization policy in New Classical models has a much more restricted meaning than in Keynesian or neo-Keynesian models.

Because of incomplete (albeit symmetric) information, markets may clear at the 'wrong' prices and quantities: actual prices and quantities may differ from what they would be under full current or contemporaneous information. Policy rules might therefore influence (and indeed eliminate) the gap between the actual competitive equilibrium and the 'full information' competitive equilibrium.

On reading recent contributions to this literature, the conclusion is inescapable that Marini's [1985] powerful and general result about policy effectiveness in New Classical macromodels has not yet permeated a large part of the professional economic awareness. I shall therefore reproduce it very briefly, using Marini's example of Barro's [1976] well-known model.

Leaving out some unimportant intercept terms, Barro's model is given in equations (1)–(7). Equation (8) is a generalization of his policy rule. The (self-explanatory) notation is as in Barro [1976].[3]

$$y_t^s(z) = \alpha_s(P_t(z) - E(P_{t+1} \mid \Omega_t(z))) - \beta_s(M_t + E(\Delta M_{t+1} \mid \Omega_t(z)) - E(P_{t+1} \mid \Omega_t(z))) + u_t^s + \varepsilon_t^s(z) \quad (1)$$

$$y_t^d(z) = -\alpha_d(P_t(z) - E(P_{t+1} \mid \Omega_t(z))) + \beta_d(M_t + E(\Delta M_{t+1} \mid \Omega_t(z)) - E(P_{t+1} \mid \Omega_t(z))) + u_t^d + \varepsilon_t^d(z) \quad (2)$$

$$y_t^s(z) = y_t^d(z) = y_t(z) \qquad \text{for all } z, t \quad (3)$$

$$\alpha \equiv \alpha_d + \alpha_s \quad (4a)$$

$$\beta \equiv \beta_d + \beta_s \quad (4b)$$

$$\varepsilon_t(z) \equiv \varepsilon_t^d(z) - \varepsilon_t^s(z) \quad (4c)$$

$$u_t \equiv u_t^d - u_t^s \quad (4d)$$

$$P_t \equiv \frac{1}{N}\left(\sum_z P_t(z)\right) \quad (4e)$$

$$y_t \equiv \sum_z y_t(z) \quad (4f)$$

$$\sum_z \varepsilon_t(z) = 0 \quad (5)$$

$$u_t = u_{t-1} + v_t \quad (6)$$

$$E(\varepsilon_t, v_t, m_t) = 0 \quad (7a)$$

$$E\left[\begin{pmatrix} \varepsilon_t \\ v_t \\ m_t \end{pmatrix} (\varepsilon_s v_s m_s)\right] = O; \qquad t \neq s$$

$$= \begin{bmatrix} \sigma_\varepsilon^2 & 0 & 0 \\ 0 & \sigma_v^2 & 0 \\ 0 & 0 & \sigma_m^2 \end{bmatrix}^i ; \quad t = s \quad (7b)$$

$$\Delta M_t \equiv M_t - M_{t-1} = m_t + \sum_{j=1}^{\infty} \gamma_j v_{t-j} + \sum_{j=1}^{\infty} \delta_j m_{t-j} \quad (8)$$

E is the mathematical expectation operator and $\Omega_t(z)$ the information set conditioning expectations formed at time t in local market z. N is the (large) number of local markets. $\Omega_t(z)$ contains the model (equations (1)–(8)), lagged values of all exogenous and endogenous aggregate variables, $\{P_{t-1}, P_{t-2}, \ldots; M_{t-1}, M_{t-2}, \ldots; v_{t-1}, v_{t-2}, \ldots; m_{t-1}, m_{t-2}, \ldots\}$ and $P_t(z)$, the current local price. It does not contain $\varepsilon_t(z)$, v_t, m_t, M_t or P_t · v_t is the aggregate real shock, $\varepsilon_t(z)$ the local real shock and m_t the monetary shock. Note that the policy feedback rule contains a response to past (white noise) monetary shocks, m_{t-j}. The past shocks are all white noise and are in the information set of the private sector.

The actual solution values $P_t(z)$, P_t and y_t will, in general, be different from the full-information solution values $P_t^*(z)$, P_t^* and y_t^*. These are the solution values that would prevail if there were full contemporaneous information; i.e., with information set $\Omega_t = \Omega_t(z)\ U\{m_t, M_t, \varepsilon_t(z), v_t, P_t\}$. Using, for example, the method of undetermined coefficients, it is easily checked that the difference between the actual intertemporal substitution term $P_t(z) - E(P_{t+1} \mid \Omega_t(z))$ and the 'full-information' intertemporal substitution term $P_t^*(z) - E(P_{t+1}^* \mid \Omega_t)$ can be written as[4]:

$$D_t \equiv P_t(z) - E(P_{t+1} \mid \Omega_t(z)) - [P_t^*(z) - E(P_{t+1}^* \mid \Omega_t)]$$
$$= \frac{\beta}{\alpha}[m_t - E(m_t \mid \Omega_t(z))] + \frac{1}{\alpha}[v_t - E(v_t \mid \Omega_t(z))]$$
$$- \frac{\beta}{\alpha}\sum_{i=1}^{\infty}\left[\left(\frac{\alpha-\beta}{\alpha}\right)\right]^{i-1}[E(\Delta M_{t+1+i} \mid \Omega_t(z)) - E(\Delta M_{t+1+i}^* \mid \Omega_t)] \quad (9)$$

D_t therefore depends on the 'inference errors' concerning the current monetary shock $(m_t - E(m_t \mid \Omega_t(z)))$ and the current aggregate shock $(v_t - E(v_t \mid \Omega_t(z)))$, and on the difference between current estimates of future monetary growth based on actual information and estimates based on full current information:

$$E(\Delta M_{t+1+i} \mid \Omega_t(z)) - E(\Delta M_{t+1+i}^* \mid \Omega_t); \qquad i = 1, 2, \ldots$$

Note that, through some idiosyncrasy of the (ad-hoc) model, only monetary growth estimates for period $t+2$ and beyond (i.e., not for periods $t+1$) matter. This is the source of Barro's erroneous generalization (Barro [1976, p. 20]) from his policy rule $\Delta M_t = m_t + \gamma_1 v_{t-1}$, a special case of our general rule. For the general rule, (9) becomes:

$$D_t = \frac{\beta}{\alpha}\left(1 + \sum_{i=1}^{\infty}[(\alpha - \beta)/\alpha]^{i-1}\delta_{i+1}\right)(m_t - E(m_t \mid \Omega_t(z)))$$
$$+ \frac{1}{\alpha}\left(1 + \beta\sum_{i=1}^{\infty}[(\alpha - \beta)/\alpha]^{i-1}\gamma_{i+1}\right)(v_t - E(v_t \mid \Omega_t(z))) \quad (9')$$

The δ_{i+1} and γ_{i+1} are policy-choice parameters. Clearly we can set $D_t \equiv 0$ by choosing any values of δ_{i+1} and γ_{i+1} such that $1 + \Sigma_{i=1}^{\infty}[(\alpha - \beta)/\alpha]^{i-1}\delta_{i+1} = 0$ and $1 + \beta\,\Sigma_{i=1}^{\infty}[(\alpha - \beta)/\alpha]^{i-1}\gamma_{i+1} = 0$[5].

With $D_t \equiv 0$, it follows immediately that actual output y_t is also equal full-information output y_t^*. Three points should be noted.

Firstly, Barro's rule $\Delta M_t = m_t + \gamma_1 v_{t-1}$ is indeed ineffective. While he deserves credit for having found the only lagged feedback rule to yield ineffectiveness, that result clearly lacks any generality. Feeding back in a deterministic manner (i.e., with known δ_{i+1} and γ_{i+1}) from aggregate information arbitrarily far in the past, monetary policy can eliminate the gap between actual and full-information output. Note also that both the conditional and unconditional variances of output can be set at any value, including zero.

Secondly, this perfect stabilization can be achieved even when the monetary authorities have an informational disadvantage vis-à-vis the private sector, in the sense that the authorities could, in period t, use only information older than the most recent information available to the private sector. For example, with $\Delta M_t = m_t + \gamma_{375} v_{t-375} + \delta_{375} m_{t-375}$, the authorities can achieve $D_t \equiv 0$, provided $1 + [(\alpha-\beta)/\alpha]^{373}\delta_{375} = 1 + \beta[(\alpha-\beta)/\alpha]^{373}\gamma_{375} = 0$. This contradicts King [1983].

Thirdly, it doesn't matter if the monetary authority randomizes its policy ($\sigma_m^2 > 0$), as long as it responds appropriately to one or more past monetary shocks (through the δ_j) so as to undo the effects of its own unpredictability!

Intuitively, what makes for effectiveness, is that the lagged feedback rules act like contingent forward contracts by the policy authority, which complete the incomplete set of contingent private markets implicit in this model. Private agents at time t are (implicitly) prevented from making future actions contingent on the future revelation of the as yet unknown realizations of m_t and v_t. The policy maker, through its lagged rule, can do this, because the presence of a (nonpredetermined) intertemporal substitution term means that current endogenous variables are functions of current expectations of all future values of the policy instrument(s). Through the lagged feedback rule, these *future* instrument values can be made functions of the (currently unknown) *current* realizations of the exogenous variables. By adopting such a rule and, with rational expectations, by being known to be doing so, the policy maker can change the information content of the currently observed local price and indeed make it fully revealing. In the ad-hoc models of Barro [1976, 1980, 1981] and others, the reason for this asymmetry in private and public opportunity sets isn't clear. In optimizing models, a finite-horizon OLG structure might explain the asymmetry (e.g. Lucas [1972]).

It is easily checked (but left as an exercise for the reader) that policy effectiveness remains if we replace the intertemporal substitution term in the supply and demand functions (1) and (2) by a real interest rate term such as $i_t + (P_t(z) - E(P_{t+1}|\Omega_t(z))$ where i_t is the nominal interest rate. (We must of course ensure that if i_t belongs to $\Omega_t(z)$, say because it is set in an economy-wide capital market, a signal extraction problem remains. This will require adding another independent source of noise to the system.) Replacing the intertemporal substitution term in the supply function by a 'surprise' term such as $P_t(z) - E(P_t|\Omega_t(z))$ also does not affect Marini's policy effectiveness result. Only if there is no signal extraction problem, either because P_t is known or because there is no current (period t) information in $\Omega_t(z)$ will there be policy ineffectiveness. Sargent and Wallace [1975] fall into this category with a model that can be summarized as follows:

$$y_t = \alpha(P_t - E(P_t|\Omega_{t-1})) + u_t^y \quad \text{(Aggregate supply)}$$
$$y_t = -\beta(i_t - E((P_{t+1} - P_t)|\Omega_{t-1}))) + u_t^d \quad \text{(IS)}$$
$$M_t - P_t = -\lambda i_t + ky_t + u_t^m \quad \text{(LM)}$$

Here u_t^y, u_t^d and u_t^m are white noise and Ω_{t-1} contains the model and aggregate information dated period $t-1$ and earlier. The intertemporal substitution term is predetermined and there is no policy effectiveness. Policy effectiveness is restored if, as in Sargent [1973] the term $E((P_{t+1} - P_t)|\Omega_{t-1})$ in the IS curve is replaced by $E((P_{t+1} - P_t)|\Omega_t)$. This makes the intertemporal substitution term nonpredetermined. Marini's result can be summarized as follows:

Proposition: Signal extraction + (non-pretermined) intertemporal substitution (somewhere in the model) → policy effectiveness

Marini's result about stabilization-policy effectiveness in New Classical macromodels is important from the perspective of the intellectual developments in our discipline. It corrected a pervasive logical error in a wide range of policy analyses. I do not consider it equally important for practical policy design, because the object of New Classical stabilization policy (the gap between symmetric actual and full-information equilibria) is, practically, a side-show. If markets do indeed clear in traditional competitive fashion, stabilization policy based on signal extraction problems is a second-order affair. With efficient competitive markets (conditional on the symmetric information held by the private agents), the gains in welfare to be gained by informing private agents more promptly of the current value of the aggregate money stock (or by pursuing feedback policies that have the same effect) are bound to be trivial. This literature also has the information problem exactly backwards; private agents are assumed to know (or to act as if they know) the true structure of the model (the values of all the parameters of the model; the behavioral parameters of the government included) but to be badly informed about the current realization of the money stock. In practice the money stock can be known very quickly and at very little cost, while neither the private agents nor the policy authorities have much of a clue about the true structure of the model.

To have non-trivial scope for stabilization policy, the actual equilibrium must be a non-Walrasian one. Marini's policy effectiveness result has very little to do, therefore, with Keynesian or neo-Keynesian stabilization policy concerns, which are motivated (even if only informally) by non-Walrasian equilibria.

One point of practical importance brought out by Marini's analysis is the distinction between *asymmetries in information sets* between the public and the private sector and *asymmetries in opportunity sets*, as a source of policy effectiveness. Even with equal or inferior public sector information, policy effectiveness will emerge because there are things the authorities can and will do that the private sector cannot do or chooses not to do. The power to tax and to regulate, the monopoly of legal tender and the longevity of the *institutions* of government (even if not of individual administrations) are some of the obvious 'deep' sources of such asymmetries between public and private opportunity sets.

Finally, as shown by Marini [1985], it is easily checked for Barro's model and similar ones, that the feedback rules that influence (and possibly eliminate) the gap between the actual and the full-information equilibrium also affect the full-information equilibrium itself. Stabilization policy and structural or allocative policy in this model are inextricably intertwined.

III The dependence of demand on supply (and vice-versa): efficiency wages and hysteresis

To conduct one's analysis and to specify one's policy recommendations in items of demand and supply betrays old-fashioned competitive thinking. The crucial issue is whether this represents a robust, felicitous shortcut or a misleading or indeed dangerous focus on a rather uninteresting special case.

It may no longer be correct that the way to make a good economist is to teach a parrot the two words 'supply' and 'demand'. This possibility is apparent even in conventional non-competitive analysis where we teach our first-year students that there is no monopolist's supply schedule. Recent developments have undermined the primacy of the law of supply and demand from at least two different perspectives. The *efficiency wage hypothesis* with its new asymmetric information microfoundations destroys the conventional distinction between demand and supply even in competitive markets. It has implications for labour markets, insurance markets, credit markets and heterogeneous product markets in general. The '*hysteresis*' or '*path-dependence*' hypothesis, based on human capital or insider-outsider microfoundations suggests that today's actual unemployment rate may be tomorrow's 'natural' unemployment rate. It destroys the distinction between aggregate demand and aggregate supply outside the very short run. I now turn to these two developments in turn.

Efficiency wages and the death of the law of demand and supply

In a conventional competitive market, equilibrium price and quantity are determined by the intersection of competitive demand and supply schedules derived from the utility maximizing behavior of price-taking households and the profit maximizing behavior of price-taking firms. Both parties to a transaction have identical (symmetric) information.

In order not to be unnecessarily awkward, it will be assumed in what follows that the (uncompensated) competitive demand schedule is downward-sloping, that the competitive supply schedule is upward-sloping and that a unique equilibrium exists.

Consider, for example, the familiar competitive aggregate labour market. The representative firm, i, maximizes profits π_i:

$$\pi_i = PY_i - W(1 + \tau_p)L_i \tag{10}$$

P is the parametric price of output, W the parametric money wage paid to workers, τ_p the proportional payroll tax rate, Y_i output (and sales) of firm i and L_i the employment of homogeneous labour by firm i. The production function is given by

$$Y_i = f(Q_iL_i); \qquad f' > 0; f'' < 0; Q_i > 0 \tag{11}$$

Q_i is the quality, efficiency or productivity of labor, assumed to be exogenous to the firm. Taking P, W, τ_p and Q_i as given, the firm optimally chooses its level of employment L_i^d according to

$$Q_if'(Q_iL_i^d) = W/P(1 + \tau_p) \tag{12}$$

Competitive supply of homogenous labour is assumed to be an increasing function of the after-tax real wage, $w(1 - \tau_w)$, where τ_w is the proportional labour income tax rate and $w = W/P$.

$$L_i^s = s(w(1 - \tau_w)); \qquad s' > 0 \tag{13}$$

Competitive equilibrium prevails when

$$L_i^d = L_i^s = L_i \tag{14}$$

Policy analysis in this simple static model is the comparative static analysis of the effects of changes in the two tax rates on the equilibrium real wage and level of employment. This amounts to determining the 'reduced form multipliers', i.e., the partial derivatives of equations (15) and (16) below, which are obtained by solving equations (12), (13), and (14) for w and L.

$$w = h(Q_i; \tau_p, \tau_w); \qquad h_{Q_i} > 0; h_{\tau_p} < 0; h_{\tau_w} > 0. \tag{15}$$

$$L = j(Q_i; \tau_p, \tau_w); \qquad j_{Q_i} > 0; j_{\tau_p} < 0; j_{\tau_w} < 0 \tag{16}$$

This comparative static analysis can always, often in an illuminating way, be decomposed in terms of the shifts in the demand schedule and/or the supply schedule, drawn in $w - L$ space, as one or more parameters change. Figure 1 shows as an example the effect of a higher payroll tax rate on real wages and employment.

This analysis can be fancied up considerably, e.g., by introducing labor adjustment costs, many factors of production and rational expectations.

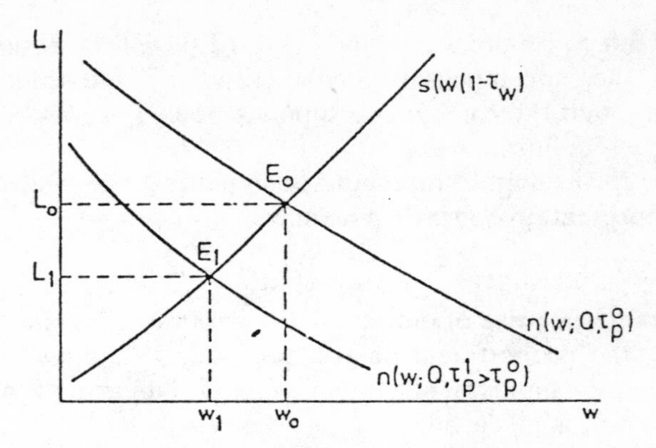

Figure 1: The effect of a higher payroll tax rate in a conventional competitive labour market

Comparative statics become comparative dynamics. The actual and anticipated nature of the policy changes becomes important (when were changes first anticipated? How permanent, transitory or reversible are they perceived to be? How confidently are these expectations held and so on?). But this is not important for our purposes. What matters here is that demand functions and demand shocks are conceptually and (subject to the standard identification caveats) also operationally distinct from supply functions and supply shocks. The intersection of the two schedules determines the Walrasian, competitive, market-clearing price and quantity.

This picture changes dramatically when efficiency-wage considerations are permitted. In the context of our simple example this means that labor is no longer viewed as homogeneous. Different workers have different levels of productivity or efficiency, but employers cannot (perfectly) discriminate between workers of different qualities. The average quality (or efficiency level) of the workforce is, however, an increasing function of the real wage (other versions make it an increasing function of the firm's wage relative to the wage of its competitors). The literature suggests a whole range of possible mechanisms for this positive dependence of Q_i on w (for recent surveys see Katz [1986] and Stiglitz [1987]). Most of those that are relevant to a mature industrial economy rely on asymmetric information between workers and employers and resulting adverse selection or moral hazard problems. In the adverse selection model of Weiss [1980], for example, employers do not know the quality of the individual worker and a worker's reservation wage is an increasing function of his/her quality (a more efficient worker is also better at painting his/her home). In other models with imperfect monitoring of workers by employers and consequent incentives to shirk, a higher wage increases the worker's opportunity cost of being found shirking. Other models rely on labour turnover costs or on morale effects.

For the efficiency wage hypothesis to bite, Q_i should be an increasing function of w_i and there should be initially a region of 'increasing returns' in which a higher wage induces a more than proportionate increase in labour quality. η denotes the elasticity of quality with respect to the real wage, i.e., $\eta \equiv \partial Q_i/\partial w_i \cdot w_i/Q_i$. For simplicity, I assume that for any given value of the parameter vector θ, which contains all exogenous factors and policy instruments affecting the price-quality relationship, there exists a unique $\bar{w}_i(\theta)$ such that for all $w_i \leqq \bar{w}_i$ we have $\eta > 1$ and for all $w_i > \bar{w}_i$ we have $\eta < 1$. Thus

$$Q_i = Q(w_i, \theta); \quad Q_{w_i} > 0; \quad \eta(w_i, \theta) \gtrless 1 \Leftrightarrow w_i \lessgtr \bar{w}_i \qquad (17)$$

It is easy to generate reasonable models with this property (see, Stiglitz [1987] and the references contained therein).

The representative firm now maximizes (10) with respect to L_i and W_i, subject to both (11) and (17). For the moment, the 'availability constraint', i.e., the ability of the firm to obtain the labour it demands, is ignored. The first-order conditions can be written as in (12) and (18).

$$\eta(w_i, \theta) = 1 \quad \text{or} \quad w_i = \bar{w}_i(\theta) \qquad (18)$$

$\bar{w}_i$ is called the efficiency wage. It minimizes the cost of employing an effective (quality-adjusted) unit of labour w_i/Q_i. The quantity of labour demanded $\tilde{L}_i^d$ is solved from

$$Q(\bar{w}_i(\theta), \theta)\, f'(Q(\bar{w}_i(\theta), \theta)\, \tilde{L}_i^d = \bar{w}_i(\theta)(1 + \tau_p) \qquad (19)$$

The availability constraint for the firm (often called the individual rationality constraint) is that V, the utility of the representative worker selling to the firm an amount of labour L_i of quality Q at a wage w_i should be at least as high as the utility obtainable in the next best alternative use V^*, that is to say

$$V(w_i, L_i, Q(w_i, \theta), \theta') \geqq V^*(\theta'') \qquad (20)$$

θ' and θ'' are vectors of parameters. Reasonable restrictions on V would be $V_{w_i} > 0$, $V_{L_i} < 0$, $V_Q < 0$. When (20) holds with equality we can solve for the labor supply schedule

$$\tilde{L}_i^s = \tilde{s}(w_i, Q(w_i, \theta), \theta', V^*(\theta'')); \qquad \tilde{s}_{w_i} > 0; \ \tilde{s}_Q < 0, \ \tilde{s}_{V^*} < 0 \qquad (21)$$

Note that it is possible (though not necessary) that at the efficiency wage $w_i = \bar{w}_i(\theta)$, $\tilde{L}_i^d < \tilde{L}_i^s$. The firm's optimizing demand for labour can be met without the constraint (20) being binding. If at the efficiency wage there is excess supply of labour, there is no 'disequilibrium' downward pressure on wages. Labour costs per efficiency unit of labour are minimized at a real wage in excess of the market-clearing wage. Note also that the demand function and the quantity of labour demanded by the firm $\tilde{L}_i^d$ are crucially dependent on supply parameters. Q is part of the 'supply side' of the labour market. We can see this clearly by considering the case where θ contains the wage income tax rate, i.e., by assuming, in the spirit of the model of Weiss [1980], that average quality depends on the after-tax wage Q = $Q(w_i(1 - \tau_w))$. In that case, the efficiency wage increases and the quantity of labour demanded decreases as the tax on labour income increases. A supply-side parameter shifts labour demand! The old language clearly is less than helpful here.

The possibility (*not* the inevitability) of quantity-constrained, rationing equilibria and other non-Walrasian equilibria is complemented by comparative statics that may be very different form those of traditional symmetric information competitive analysis. Apart from explaining real wage rigidity in the face of persistent (equilibrium!) excess supply, these models can generate, in rationing equilibria, quantity responses with multiplier properties in response to exogenous shocks, with little or no (or even perverse) adjustment in the real wage.

It can similarly explain persistent excess demand in credit markets and the 'non-Walrasian' response of credit and interest rates to changes in monetary and fiscal policy. It cannot, however, motivate any form of *nominal* rigidity in wages, prices or interest rates. 'Rigid' real wages and real interest rates can be equilibrium outcomes in the efficiency wage universe. Nominal inertia of any kind still awaits another explanation.

When the efficiency wage model of the labour market is combined with imperfect competition in the product market, the scope for demand management becomes more transparent. I first summarize an interesting model of Akerlof and Yellen [1985]. Blanchard and Kiyotaki [1985] and Ball and Romer [1987] are in the same spirit as Akerlof and Yellen. They rationalize nominal inertia through the rather arbitrary device of assigning a lumpy cost to nominal price adjustment. The availability constraint is assumed non-binding. Let there be $N > 1$ firms selling similar but non-identical products. Each firm i faces the following demand curve for its product (1):[6]

$$y_i^d = (Y/N)\,(P_i/P)^{-\varepsilon}; \qquad \varepsilon > 1 \tag{22}$$

Y is aggregate demand and P the general price level, defined as the geometric mean of the P_i

$$P = \left[\prod_{j=1}^{N} P_j\right]^{1/N} \tag{23}$$

Each firm has the identical production function $Y_i = f(Q(W_i/P)L_i)$ and maximizes profits $\pi_i = P_iY_i - W_iL_i$ by optimally choosing W_i and P_i, taking as given P and Y. The first-order conditions are:

$$\eta(W_i/P) = [Q'(W_i/P)/Q(W_i/P)]\ (W_i/P) = 1 \tag{24}$$

$$Q(W_i/P)\ f'(Q(W_i/P)L_i)\left(1 - \frac{1}{\varepsilon}\right) = W_i/P \tag{25}$$

Equation (24) reproduces the fixed efficiency wage. In a symmetric equilibrium, $P_i = P$ and $W_i = W$ for all i. The real wage and aggregate employment are therefore given by:

$$\eta(w) = 1 \tag{26a}$$

$$Q(w)f'\left(Q(w)\ \frac{L}{N}\right)\left(1 - \frac{1}{\varepsilon}\right) = w \tag{26b}$$

$$L \leqq L^* \tag{26c}$$

L^* is the aggregate supply of (physical) units of labour, assumed to be independent of the real wage for simplicity.

Akerlof-Yellen 'Near-Rationality' As in Akerlof and Yellen [1985], aggregate demand is given by the constant velocity quantity equation (27), the production function is Cobb-Douglas as in (28) and Q_i takes the form given in (29).

$$Y = M/P \tag{27}$$

$$Y_i = (Q_iL_i)^\alpha; \qquad 0 < \alpha < 1 \tag{28}$$

$$Q(w_i) = -a + bw_i^\gamma; \qquad 0 < \gamma < 1;\ a > 0;\ b > 0 \tag{29}$$

It follows that, for an initial money stock M_o, the general price level P_o is given by equations (30) and (31) where w_o is the initial (real) efficiency wage.

$$P_o = kM_o \tag{30}$$

$$k = (\varepsilon w_o/\alpha(\varepsilon - 1)Q(w_o))^{\alpha/1-\alpha} \tag{31}$$

Equations (26)–(31) characterize a full, long-run, optimizing equilibrium in which all firms are Bertrand maximizers. Assume that, at this long-run equilibrium, a perturbation in the form of an increase in the nominal money stock from M_o to $M_o(1 + \nu)$ leads to a short-run optimizing response by only a fraction $1 - \beta$ of the total number of firms. The remaining fraction of firms β keeps its money wage and nominal output price unchanged. For small shocks, this suboptimal behavior is *near-rational*, in the sense that the profit loss resulting from the suboptimal behavior is an order of magnitude smaller than the shock. The reason for the second-order nature of the profit loss is that the imperfectly competitive firm's profit function is differentiable in its two controls: own price and own wage. As regards own price, this follows immediately from the monopolistically competitive Bertrand behavior. As regards own wage, the efficiency wage hypothesis does the work. In other words, at a full, long-run equilibrium, a failure optimally to adjust the own price and wage has no first-order effect on profits because the envelope theorem strikes for the individual firm.

The effect of the nominal money shock on real demand and employment, however, has the same order of magnitude as the shock.

Let the superscript n denote variables pertaining to near-maximizing firms and the superscript m variables pertaining to maximizing firms. It is easily shown (Akerlof and Yellen [1985]) that

$$P^n = P_o \tag{32a}$$

$$P^m = P_o(1 + \nu)^{\lambda} \tag{32b}$$

$$P = P_o(1 + \nu)^{(1-\beta)\lambda} \tag{32c}$$

$$w^n = w_o(1 + \nu)^{-(1-\beta)\lambda} \tag{32d}$$

$$w^m = w_o \tag{32e}$$

Where

$$\lambda = (1 - \alpha)\alpha^{-1}[\beta(\varepsilon\alpha^{-1} - \varepsilon + 1) + (1 - \beta)(1 - \alpha)\alpha^{-1}]^{-1}; \quad 0 < \lambda \leqq 1 \tag{33}$$

The near-maximizing firms increase their demand for labour because the relative price of their output has declined and because real money balances have increased. Their reduction in profits as a result of their failure to optimize fully in response to the shock is simply the difference between the profit of a fully optimizing firm Π^m and that of a near-optimizing firm Π^n. Some arithmetic shows that

$$\left.\frac{d(\Pi^m - \Pi^n)}{d\nu}\right|_{\nu=0} = 0 \tag{34}$$

The response of aggregate employment is given by

$$\left.\frac{d(N/N_0)}{d\nu}\right|_{\nu=o} = \frac{1}{\alpha}(1 - (1 - \beta)\lambda) + \beta(1 - \beta)\lambda \tag{35}$$

Only when $\beta = 0$ (which implies $\lambda = 1$) is the employment effect zero. For $\beta > 0$ there is a first-order employment effect.

A kinked demand curve[7] With the demand function (22), the price elasticity $-\varepsilon$ is independent of aggregate demand. In general, however, the price elasticity will depend both on Y and on P_i/P, that is

$$\varepsilon = \varepsilon(Y, P_i/P) \tag{36}$$

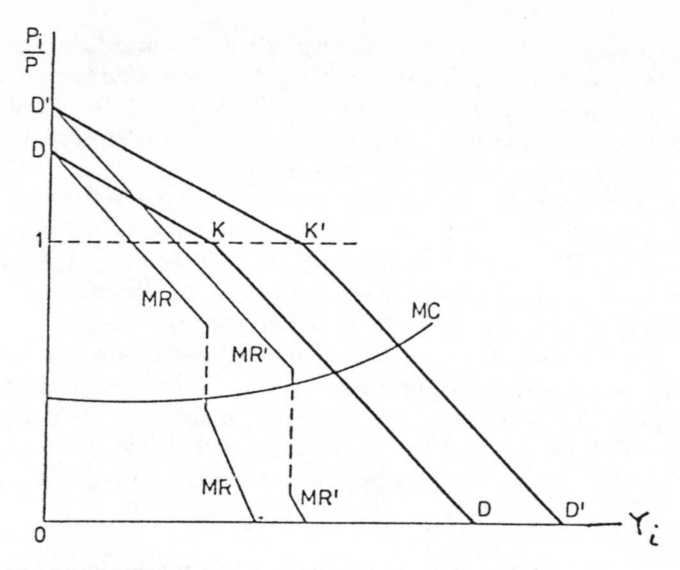

Figure 2: The kinked demand curve and aggregate demand

In a fully optimizing symmetric equilibrium, $P_i = P$ and real aggregate demand will have a positive (negative) effect on the employment of an individual firm if ε_Y is positive (negative). Note however, that since aggregate demand, Y, must equal aggregate supply, the equilibrium conditions will still generate unique equilibrium values for L and Y as long as there is a unique value of ε for any given Y (and for any given P_i/P). This is obvious from equations (37) and (38) below.

$$Q(w)f'\left(Q(w)\frac{L}{N}\right)\left(1 - \frac{1}{\varepsilon(Y, 1)}\right) = w \tag{37}$$

$$Y = Nf\left(Q(w)\frac{L}{N}\right) \tag{38}$$

An interesting model that permits one to escape from this box (effectively by making equation (37) nonbinding for a range of Y values) is the piecewise-linear kinked demand curve given in (39) and shown in Figure 2.

$$Y_i^d = \min\left(\frac{1}{N}Y - \alpha\left(\frac{P_i}{P} - 1\right), \frac{1}{N}Y - \beta\left(\frac{P_i}{P} - 1\right)\right); \qquad \alpha > \beta > 0 \tag{39}$$

The greater responsiveness of sales to increases in P_i relative to P compared to decreases can be rationalized using search-theoretic 'shopping models'. An increase in P_i relative to P discourages potential new customers that visit the firm in the same way that a decrease $P_i - P$ attracts potential new customers. An increase in $P_i - P$ in addition causes the existing clientele of the firm to leave in order to search for a lower price elsewhere. A reduction in $P_i - P$ does not have a corresponding sales-boosting effect on the firm's current customers.

In Figure 2, an increase in real aggregate demand shifts the demand schedule from DKD to D′K′D′. The firm's marginal cost curve is given by $MC((W_i/P), Y_i) = (W_i/P). [1/(Q(W_i/P)f'(Q(W_i/P)L_i))]$ where L_i is, given Q, an increasing function of Y_i through the production function given in (11) or (28). Figure 2 shows where the upward-sloping marginal cost-curve MC intersects the marginal revenue correspondences MR and MR′ of both demand curves in their vertical segments. A higher level of real aggregate demand in this case generates a higher level of supply and employment. Each firm sets $P_i = P$ (even before the assumption of a symmetric equilibrium is imposed). 'At the kink', output demanded and supplied is therefore given by $Y_i = Y_i^d = \frac{1}{N}Y$.

The real wage, output and employment are therefore given as functions of real aggregate demand by:

$$\eta(w) = 1 \tag{40}$$

$$f\left(Q(w)\frac{L}{N}\right) = \frac{Y}{N} \tag{41}$$

A symmetric equilibrium exists in this model for real demand values in the range $\underline{Y} \leqq Y \leqq \bar{Y}$. $\underline{Y}$ is the level of real demand for which marginal cost (MC) equals $-\beta^{-1}(Y/N) + 1$, the lowest value of marginal revenue 'at the kink'. $\bar{Y}$ is the level of real demand for which MC equals $-\alpha^{-1}(Y/N) + 1$, the highest value of marginal revenue 'at the kink'. Note that at the kink, $MC(Y_i) = MC(Y/N)$. $\bar{Y}$ can be below the level of output corresponding to full employment of the labor force.

An ad-hoc model of real demand and nominal prices Can the authorities influence real aggregate demand and if so, can they do this systematically or only through policy surprises? Consider the following standard ad-hoc model of aggregate demand and of the determination of nominal prices and wages. M is the nominal money stock, B the stock of government bonds, G exhaustive public spending, T taxes net of transfers. The aggregate demand schedule is given in equation (42). Two alternative nominal wage-price blocks are given. The first, represented in equations (44), (47), and (48), has a sticky general price level and a flexible money wage. The second, represented in equations (45), (46), (47), and (48), has a sticky money wage and a flexible general price level. Following McCallum [1980] P_t^* is the general price level that would prevail at full employment,

W_t^* the money wage that would prevail at full employment and w^* is the labor market-clearing real wage.

$$Y = y(G, T, M/P, B/P); \qquad y_G > 0;\ y_T \leqq 0;\ y_m > 0;\ y_b \geqq 0 \quad (42)$$

$$w \equiv W/P \quad (43)$$

$$P_t = \delta P_t^* + (1 - \delta)P_{t-1}; \qquad 0 \leqq \delta \leqq 1; \quad \text{or} \quad (44)$$

$$W_t^* = w_t^* P_t^* \quad \text{and} \quad (45)$$

$$W_t = \delta' W_t^* + (1 - \delta')W_{t-1}; \qquad 0 \leqq \delta' \leq 1 \quad (46)$$

where P_t^* is defined by:

$$Y^* = y(G_t, T_t, M_t/P_t^*, B_t/P_t^*) \quad (47)$$

$$Y^* = f[Q(w^*)L^*] \quad (48)$$

With the addition of the government budget identity given in (49), where i is the nominal interest rate, we now have a sample of a wider class of dynamic macromodels with the potential for persistent equilibrium unemployment.

$$(\Delta M + \Delta B)\ P^{-1} \equiv G + i(B/P) - T \quad (49)$$

The scope for demand management to influence Y is transitory in these models unless there is complete nominal rigidity, i.e., $\delta = 0$ in the version with equation (44) or $\delta' = 0$ in the version with equations (45) and (46). I consider an exogenously given money wage or nominal price level to be quite acceptable in a model such as this. There seems to be no good reason for the money wage (nominal price level) to be driven towards the full employment equilibrium money wage (nominal price level) when that full employment equilibrium need never be reached. The further analysis of the determination of the exogenous nominal anchor by history, convention, habit or accident is beyond the scope of this paper. What matters for our purposes is that there are no obvious disequilibrium forces within the model, no perceived free lunches, that will tend to move the nominal anchor from any arbitrarily-assigned value.

This model and many like it suggest that aggregate demand expansion can expand employment without the need for a reduction in real wages (or more generally in real marginal labour costs). The conventional competitive model rules out this possibility. If, as I believe, the imperfect competition-efficiency wage model is a better parable for Europe today than the conventional competitive parable or other real wage-constrained employment parables, the case against a demand stimulus is weakened considerably. The authorities must of course be able to influence real aggregate demand. In a monetary model, this ability hinges on the behaviour of money wages and prices, something about which the real efficiency wage-imperfect competition model has nothing to say.

Hysteresis and the footloose NAIRU

Hysteresis is a property of dynamic systems. If it is present, the steady-state or long-run equilibrium position of the system will not be a function only of the long-run values of the exogenous variables but also of the initial condition of the state variables and of the values assumed by the exogenous variables outside the steady state. Hysteretic or path-dependent systems are therefore 'historical' systems: how you get there determines where you get to. In discrete time linear systems for predetermined variables hysteresis is present when there are one or more unit roots in the characteristic equation of the state matrix.[8]

Hysteresis in the natural rate of unemployment is present when today's natural rate of unemployment is a function of past actual unemployment rates. Consider, for example, the simple first-order partial adjustment mechanism used in Buiter and Gersovitz [1981], Hargreaves-Heap [1980] and Buiter and Miller [1985]. u is the actual unemployment rate and u^* the natural rate:

$$u_t^* = \alpha u_{t-1}^* + (1 - \alpha)u_{t-1}; \qquad 0 \leqq \alpha \leqq 1; 0 \leqq u_o \leqq 1 \qquad (50)$$

Equation (50) specifies the natural rate as moving average of past actual unemployment rates with geometrically declining weights, since

$$u_t^* = (1 - \alpha) \sum_{i=0}^{\infty} \alpha^i \, u_{t-1-i} \qquad (51)$$

The idea of hysteresis in the natural rate is not a new one (Phelps [1972]; Tobin [1980]). The two most popular economic mechanisms for generating hysteresis are the 'human capital' hypothesis and the 'insider-outsider' hypothesis. According to the human capital hypothesis the experience of unemployment destroys the human capital of the unemployed by having a negative effect both on their attitudes towards working (the 'culture of unemployment and dependence' and so on) and on their aptitudes (skills, knowledge and so on) for work.

The effective labour supply represented by a given number of unemployed workers therefore declines over time with the duration of the unemployment spell. Empirical evidence that the long-term unemployed do not have any explanatory power in Phillips-curve type equations when the shorter-term unemployed are also included as an argument (see, for example Layard, Nickell [1986]) is consistent with this view. Insider-outsider theory[9] attributes very different influences on the firm's wage bargain to those currently employed (the 'insiders') and to the unemployed, both previous employees of the firm and new job candidates (the 'outsiders'). In the limit, the unemployed are disenfranchised completely and the wage bargain is conducted solely in the interests of the firm and those currently employed. A range of explanations of varying degrees of plausibility is offered for the inability of the outsiders to undercut the insiders either by offering to work for less than the insiders in the existing firm or by seeking employment in new firms that might be able to undercut the insider-controlled firm. In this model too, the unemployed are, gradually or immediately, effectively excluded from the bargaining process in the labour market.

As it stands, equation (50) is clearly too strong. The notion that the natural rate can be anywhere between zero and one hundred percent is most implausible. The concept of *local* hysteresis, as opposed to the *global* hysteresis of equation (50), would be much more acceptable. The kinked demand curve model just analyzed has such local hysteresis properties.

Equation (50) suggests that, by keeping u at any given level for long enough, the natural rate u^* can be made to approach that level and reach it (asymptotically). Physical capital formation theories of prolonged and persistent unemployment do not quite generate that very strong property (e.g., Modigliani *et al.* [1986]). These theories suggest that the kinds of shocks that produce unemployment also produce low physical capital formation. Either because of real wage rigidity and real wage-constrained employment or because of strong physical complementarity and limited substitutability between physical capital and labour (fixed coefficients are the extreme example), employment will fall or rise with the physical capital stock. Declining rates of capital formation will therefore have a long-lasting effect on unemployment. Unless there is hysteresis in the capital stock itself, however, this mechanism will not generate hysteresis in unemployment. The roots may be close to but will not be equal to unity. For practical purposes, it may of course not matter very much whether we have unit roots or merely roots close to unity, hysteresis or near-hysteresis. If the natural rate returns to its invariant long-run equilibrium level only very slowly after being perturbed by a movement in the actual rate, the economy will exhibit near-hysteretic behaviour for long periods of time.

To obtain the implications of hysteresis for the existence of an unemployment-inflation trade-off, we must consider the remainder of the wage-price mechanism. I will short-cut most of this mechanism and consider the simple augmented price Phillips curve given in (52). P is the logarithm of the price level, π the augmentation term and $\Delta P_t \equiv P_t - P_{t-1}$.

$$\Delta P_{t+1} = -\beta(u_t - u_t^*) + \pi_{t+1}; \qquad \beta > 0 \tag{52}$$

Equations (50) and (52) imply that

$$u_t^* = u_{t-1}^* + (1 - \alpha)\beta^{-1} (\pi_t - \Delta P_t) \tag{53a}$$

$$u_t = u_{t-1} - \beta^{-1} (\Delta P_{t+1} - \pi_{t+1}) - \alpha\beta^{-1} (\Delta P_t - \pi_t) \tag{53b}$$

It should be noted that, hysteresis or not, the old debate about the presence and nature of nominal inertia or stickiness in wage and price formation and about the backward-looking or forward-looking nature of the augmentation term π is still relevant if we are to evaluate policy options (compare, for example, Taylor [1980], Buiter, Jewitt [1981], Buiter, Miller [1985]). In other words, equation (50) tells us that, depending on the behaviour of the actual unemployment rate, the natural rate can assume any value. The remainder of the wage-price mechanism (i.e., equations such as (52) and (53a) or (53b)) determines whether actual unemployment (or real demand) can be influenced systematically through policy or only through policy surprises. Blanchard and Summers [1986] perhaps surprisingly, choose what translates into a 'surprise supply function' specification of π_{t+1}, i.e., in their model

$$\pi_{t+1} = E_t(P_{t+1} - P_t) \tag{54a}$$

where E_t is the expectation operator conditional on information in period t. If only unanticipated inflation can drive a wedge between the natural and the actual rate, the natural rate becomes a random walk, since $\pi_t - \Delta P_t = E_{t-1}(P_t) - P_t$ which is white noise when expectations are rational. The change in the actual unemployment rate will be an MA1 process. With (54a), only *unanticipated* expansionary (contractionary) shocks can lower (increase) the natural rate. Bad luck (OPEC) or bad management (unexpected contractionary fiscal or monetary policy) caused the rise in unemployment in the 1970's. Only good luck or expansionary policy surprises will get it back down.

Neither the theoretical nor the empirical foundations of the 'surprise supply function' are terribly robust, however. With some inertia in the inflation process, anticipated, systematic policy too can drive the natural and actual unemployment rate to more desirable levels. Buiter and Miller [1985] consider the familiar partly backward-looking adaptive process for core inflation π, given in (54b).

$$\pi_{t+1} = \gamma\pi_t + (1 - \gamma)E_t\Delta P_{t+1}; \qquad 0 \leqq \gamma \leqq 1 \tag{54b}$$

With this specification we have

$$u_t^* = u_{t-1}^* + (1-\alpha)\beta^{-1}[E_{t-1}(\Delta P_t) - \Delta P_t] - (1-\alpha)\beta^{-1}\gamma(E_{t-1}\Delta P_t - \pi_{t-1})$$

Systematic policy keeping expected (and actual) inflation ahead of core inflation will lower the natural rate. With rational expectations and any constant rate of inflation, actual unemployment will, in the long run, equal the natural rate. The 'long run' Phillips curve is vertical but it can be located at any unemployment rate. Similar results can be derived using staggered, overlapping nominal contracting models as in Taylor [1980],

Buiter and Jewitt [1981] or Buiter and Miller [1985]. Nominal inertia of the kind considered by McCallum [1978, 1980] does not permit systematic policy to influence the mean level of unemployment or real demand.

With hysteresis, the case for a boost to demand in current economic conditions is irresistible. With core inflation given by (54b) and $\gamma > 0$, the sacrifice ratio is infinite; i.e., the cumulative undiscounted unemployment cost of achieving a one percentage point sustained and sustainable reduction in the rate of inflation is infinite. That also means that the permanent inflation cost of achieving any lasting reduction in unemployment is zero. In the 'surprise supply function' case, we can only hope that the authorities will succeed in surprising us. Even in economies that are merely near-hysteretic, the case for expansionary demand policy is overwhelming. We would be as far removed as we could possibly be from the prevailing Euro-pessimist perception that the supply side constrains everything.

I believe that the case for the existence of a high degree of hysteresis in Europe is strong enough and that the European unemployment situation is desperate enough for us to 'have to go' at a significant (supply-side-friendly) boost to aggregate demand. The risk exists that the situation has been diagnosed wrongly, but it is dwarfed by the cost of not seizing the opportunity that may be there.

IV **Conclusion**

Unemployment in Europe is very high and shows no signs of coming down significantly in the next few years. Under current policies, the growth of real demand is barely sufficient to keep pace with the trend growth rate of productive potential, leaving the existing reservoir of unused and underutilized labor power untouched. Three kinds of responses to this situation are possible. The first response (or nonresponse) is to accept the situation, if not as a God-given punishment for our past sins, in any case as beyond the scope of the existing policy instruments and/or beyond the existing capacities and institutions for formulating and implementing policy. This, by revealed preference, seems to be the approach of many European governments, including those of the United Kingdom, West Germany, France, Belgium and the Netherlands.

The second response blames policy-induced 'supply-side' failures for much of the deterioration of the employment situation and recommends 'supply-side' measures to remedy the situation. Among the past policy measures that are in the dock are the following: socalled employment protection policies that raise the cost of hiring and firing; policies providing rights, privileges and immunities for organized labor; minimum wage laws; laws and regulations limiting relative wage flexibility; laws and regulations limiting regional, occupational and industrial mobility of labor; taxes that raise the nonwage component of marginal labor costs, such as employers' social security contributions; high marginal income tax rates on wage income; high marginal benefit rates for the unemployed and lax administration of eligibility requirements for unemployment benefits and medical disability payments. Growth of the public sector in any of its dimensions ('exhaustive' public spending, employment, total spending, total revenue, scope of regulatory interventions in the market sector, public sector production of marketable commodities, and so forth) is viewed as synonymous with waste and inefficiency. In the short run, such expansion of public sector activity may appear to improve the employment picture (in terms of simple 'body count'), but ultimately the 'real' jobs that finance and sustain these unproductive public sector activities will suffer, the 'wealth-creating' sector will shrink and with it, in due course, the public sector activities and employment it can no longer support.

Large public sector deficits, probably causally connected with the growing scope of public sector activities (because of a tendency for the political mechanism to try and avoid paying with current taxes for current outlays) are either monetized; causing high inflation, or financed by borrowing, thus 'crowding out' interest-sensitive private spending. Both the inflation tax and borrowing are viewed as inimical to private capital formation, which further weakens the supply side.

The policy prescription following from this diagnosis is self-evident; reverse all these developments to the maximum possible extent. This explanation is at best incomplete and exaggerated and at worst simply wrong. While many intelligent 'supply-side' measures can and should be implemented to improve both efficiency and equity in the European economies, a good case can be made that adverse policy-induced supply-side developments did not cause the bulk of the deterioration of the European employment performance, and that 'supply-side' measures will not be sufficient or even necessary, if the hysteresis view is valid, to remove much of the existing labor slack.

Much of the increase in European unemployment since the mid-1970s can reasonably be attributed to the two massive adverse supply shocks of OPEC I and II and to the deliberate global demand deflation, never reversed in Europe, of the early 1980s. With the recent decline in the real price of oil and related energy products, the adverse supply shocks are being reversed. It will take years for this to take its full effect, however, because the scrapping of productive capacity and low rates of capital formation following OPEC I and II have resulted in a secularly low path of the physical capital stock.

This suggests the need for the third response: a significant, sustained supply-side-friendly, co-ordinated expansion of aggregate demand through monetary and fiscal stimuli. Both the efficiency wage view and the Blanchard-Summers version of the insider-outsider model suggest that an expansion of demand can result in a sustainable increase in employment and production without significant upward pressure on real wages, and without permanently higher inflation. The near-hysteretic behavior of the unemployment rate in Europe indeed suggests that any adverse inflationary consequences of a demand stimulus will be temporary, while the output and employment effects will be lasting. The parallel with the rapid non-inflationary recovery of employment and output in Britain and other European countries in the late 1930s, under the impetus of rearmament spending, comes to mind.

Even if it were agreed that a boost to demand could solve many of the European problems, it would not automatically follow that the authorities could actually engineer such a stimulus.[10] I will consider briefly the following obstacles to expansionary monetary and fiscal policy. As regards monetary policy, firstly the absence of *nominal inertia* and secondly the threat of inflation. As regards fiscal policy, the threats of financial crowding out and of government insolvency. As regards both, the threats of adverse exchange rate or current account consequences. The issue of government *credibility* will be seen to be central in determining the ability of the government to stimulate aggregate demand. In what follows, I shall concentrate on anticipated or perceived government policy since, except in the hysteresis-cum-'surprise'-supply-function view of the world (given in equations (50), (52), and (54)), unanticipated or unperceived policy actions are unlikely to be welfare-increasing, even if they were feasible in a systematic manner.

As stated in Section II, the effectiveness of anticipated or perceived policy requires either superior public sector information or a public sector opportunity set that is superior to the private sector's opportunity set in at least one dimension. While some of those responsible for the design and implementation of economic policy may have a (temporary) information advantage over at least some private sector agents, – for example as regards the behavior of the monetary aggregates, international reserves and – most importantly – as regards the future intentions of the policy authorities, it would seem unwise to base the case for stabilization policy on that slim foundation. *Pace* Fischer's 'benevolent dissembling government' (Fischer, 1980) it is hard to see how in practice a government could do better as a rule than by divulging both its privileged information and its future intentions[11].

The existence of a public sector opportunity set which in some ways dominates that of the private sector is very plausible indeed. The proximate reason for stabilization policy effectiveness is the government's superior access to the capital markets. Governments can borrow on terms not generally available to private agents (at any rate in the main industrial countries). This is reflected both in lower required rates of return on government debt compared with private debt of the same maturity, currency denomination and so on, and in the ability of governments to continue borrowing when private agents encounter credit rationing. The fundamental reason for this public sector financial clout is that the government's collateral consists of the maximal stream of current and future resources it can appropriate through taxation and seigniorage. (The binding constraints that define the maximum tax revenue are likely to be political rather than narrowly economic or administrative in character.) The government's monopoly of the power to exact legitimate unrequited transfers of purchasing power both at a point in time and over time may also account for the private sector's willingness to hold noninterest-bearing nominal government debt (high-powered money). In addition, restrictions on what constitutes legal tender and reserve requirements may generate a private sector demand for base money. The absence of perfect private sector substitutes for base money, for whatever reasons, creates the tax base for the seigniorage tax.

The asymmetry between public and private opportunity sets in financial markets is sometimes formalized by attributing finite horizons (in OLG models without operative intergenerational gift and bequest motives) or uncertain lifetimes to households, while governments are treated as having effectively infinite lifetimes[12]. Note that it is not the lifetime of individual administrations that matters here, but the lifetime of the institution of government. More precisely what matters is that successive governments are expected to assume the debt they inherit from their predecessors or, as in the case of balanced-budget intergenerational redistributions, that they are expected to implement the schemes initiated by their predecessors. The implication is that debt neutrality is absent: given the exhaustive spending program, the substitution of current borrowing for current lump-sum taxes by a solvent government will not leave the path of private consumption unchanged. The substitution of seigniorage revenue for either explicit lump-sum taxes or borrowing will also in general have real effects[13]. Given these basic considerations, I now turn to the main instruments of stabilization policy.

As a revenue-raiser, seigniorage is now of very limited actual and potential importance in most industrial countries[14]. For monetary policy to be an effective stabilization instrument, other channels of influence must therefore be present.

Ignoring as empirically unimportant the ability of the authorities to influence the inflation rate and through it the real interest rate (via the Tobin effect) even in an economy with flexible money wages and prices, and ignoring for the same reason the ability of systematic monetary feedback rules to influence the variance of real output and employment even in flexprice 'surprise' supply models (see section II in this paper and Buiter [1981]), monetary policy can only be an effective instrument for aggregate demand management if there is some form of nominal inertia or stickiness: money wages and/or prices must be predetermined[15]. Recent empirical evidence suggesting that the degree of nominal inertia is low in Europe (in contrast to the US) (see, for example, Bruno and Sachs [1985]) would therefore put into question the ability of monetary policy in Europe to be an important instrument of demand expansion. The empirical evidence on this issue is, however, by no means clear-cut[16], and as long as there is some nominal inertia, monetary policy can play a supporting role in a co-ordinated expansion of demand.

The monetary expansion required for a demand stimulus is of the nature of a once-off increase in the *level* of the path of the nominal money stock, not a sustained increase in the *rate of growth* of the nominal money stock. In due course such a level shift will only raise the level of the price path without any long-run effect on the inflation rate. In 'real time', the process of moving from a lower to a higher price-level path will in practice involve a *temporary* increase in the inflation rate[17]. With imperfect information, non-rational expectations or mechanical indexation procedures, this temporary increase in the inflation rate may trigger a wage-price spiral that will prolong the bout of higher inflation. Provided the money stock is not permitted to respond endogenously to this further inflationary twist, the process will be damped and the long-run rate of inflation will not be affected.

Convincing the private players in the labour markets, the product markets and the financial markets that the increase in the money stock they are witnessing is a once-off level shift rather than the first step in a repeated process of ever-increasing monetary injections, requires a credible government[18], i.e., a government with a strong, proven record of anti-inflationary preferences and actions. The three conservative administrations in London, Bonn and Paris have such credibility as do the Japanese and, to a lesser extent, the US governments. For most of the important players, the desirable monetary policy is actually likely to be time-consistent.

Even in the absence of debt neutrality, fiscal policy may fail to stimulate aggregate demand because of complete financial crowding-out. A variable velocity of circulation of money and/or accommodating monetary policy will prevent full crowding-out (in the presence of idle real resources) unless current fiscal expansion creates expectations of continued future expansion leading to an ever-increasing debt burden and, ultimately, the threat of *de jure* or *de facto* partial or complete repudiation of the public debt. Again the *credibility* of the temporary nature of the fiscal stimulus and the limited increase in the debt-GNP ratio it entails is crucial for the success of expansionary fiscal measures. If the financial markets panic, complete crowding-out is likely[19].

The current conservative administrations in the larger OECD countries

Table 1 *General government financial deficit as a percentage of nominal GNP/GDP*

	1984	*1985*	*1986*
US	2.8	3.3	3.5
Japan	2.1	0.8	1.1
West Germany	1.9	1.1	1.2
France	2.7	2.9	2.9
UK	3.9	2.9	2.7
Italy	11.7	12.6	11.6
Canada	6.6	7.0	5.5
Total smaller OECD countries	4.1	4.0	3.4

Source: OECD *Economic Outlook*, 43, June 1988, table R13.

Table 2 *Net debt of general government as a percentage of GNP/GDP*

	1974	*1981*	*1982*	*1983*	*1984*	*1985*	*1986*
US	22.0	18.8	21.4	24.0	25.1	26.8	28.8
UK	54.9	47.2	46.4	47.1	48.5	46.9	46.9
Italy	49.2	66.8	73.4	80.6	87.8	96.3	99.2
France	8.8	9.9	11.3	13.4	15.2	16.7	18.5
West Germany	−4.7	17.4	19.8	21.4	21.7	22.1	22.2
Japan	−5.4	20.7	23.2	26.2	26.9	26.5	26.2

Source: OECD *Economic Outlook*, 41, June 1987, table 15.

(with the exception of Italy) are uniquely well-placed to provide a credible temporary fiscal stimulus. Their reputations for fiscal prudence again make the right policy time-consistent. Table 1 gives the general government financial balances for some of the OECD countries.

Combined with the public debt figures of Table 2, these figures suggest that, with the exception of Italy, the debt-deficit situation in the major European countries is well under control. Even the much-maligned US budgetary deficit is much less dramatic than has been suggested. With the US General Government public debt at 30 percent of GNP and a modest 8 per cent growth of nominal GNP, the public sector deficit could be almost 2.4 per cent of GNP without this adding to the debt-GNP ratio. The actual US general government deficit of 3.5 percent of GNP in 1986 is only one percentage point of GDP higher than the deficit that would stabilize the (low) debt-GDP ratio. A US fiscal correction is required in due course, but there is no need to be panicked into one right now.

A fiscal stimulus in an economy with idle resources need not 'crowd out' private investment even if interest rates rise. The positive response of investment to the higher future profits stream permitted by higher demand will mitigate and may even overcome the negative effect of higher interest rates. Such a positive response is even more likely if the composition of the fiscal stimulus is investment and supply-side-friendly.

This implies such actions as temporary investment tax credits and temporary investment subsidies. Reductions in marginal payroll tax rates should also be part of the package as would be increases in public sector investment in Europe's crumbling infrastructure. The stimulus should be modulated across countries to take account of their differing budgetary and debt conditions. On average for Europe, a modest proposal would be a three or four-year boost equal to 2 percent of GDP per year, with sufficient monetary accommodation to prevent a significant increase in short nominal interest rates or an appreciation of the ECU against the US dollar and the yen.

In an open economy with a fixed exchange rate, part of any expansion of demand will 'leak' abroad through increased demand for imports. With a floating exchange rate and a high degree of capital mobility, a fiscal expansion will be partly or even completely crowded-out by an appreciation of the currency. Even if an accommodating monetary policy succeeds in keeping the nominal exchange rate constant, the problem of a worsening current account still exists. This calls for a co-ordinated expansion, involving at least the major European economies and preferably also Japan. The US should ensure that any attempt to restore its fiscal equilibrium does not lead to a recession (see, for example, Blanchard *et al.* [1986]). This would be an interesting first challenge for the new chairman of the Federal Reserve Board.

With a modicum of common sense and a bit of luck this kind of co-ordinated, supply-side-friendly, temporary expansion, differentiated by country according to its internal and external circumstances will contribute to the resolution of the European unemployment problem and the restoration of its prosperity. Under present circumstances, 'two-handed' rules out 'tight-fisted'.

Notes

Originally published in Giersch, H. (ed.) (1988), *Macro and Micro Policies for More Growth and Employment*, Kiel Institute of World Economics, pp. 305–45.

1 This chapter was written while I was an academic visitor at the University of Groningen during May and June 1987. I would like to thank Klaus-Werner Schatz, Christian Seidl, Alan Blinder and Bennett McCallum for helpful comments on the first version of this chapter.

2 I include in this quasi-competitive fix-price analysis of Barro, Grossman [1971], Malinvaud [1977] and the French School. The occasional replacement of competitive agents by a conventional monopolist does not represent a great gain in insight either.

3 The occurrence of M_t in the local demand and supply functions, even though it does not belong to the information set at time t, if there are monetary disturbances, is rather awkward.

4 Bubble solutions are ruled out and $\left|\dfrac{\alpha - \beta}{\alpha}\right| < 1.$

5 Since Barro's model does not exhibit superneutrality of money, even different constant and known proportional rates of growth of money will alter both the actual and the full-information equilibrium. Models with 'suprise' supply functions will not have this property.

6 ϵ could be a function of N.

7 Hans van Ees [1987] independently developed the idea of combining the efficiency wage hypothesis in the labour market and the kinked demand curve in the product market in order to create scope for a potential influence of aggregate demand on employment. His paper contains a much more elaborate and thorough development of these ideas.

8 For non-predetermined variables a unit root indicates quite the opposite of persistence; the unit root for consumption generated by certain life cycle models and the unit root for stock prices generated by certain efficient asset pricing models are examples. David Begg has, on many occasions, emphasised the different interpretation of unit roots for backward-looking and forward-looking variables.

9 Compare, for example, Gregory [1982, 1983, 1986], Lindbeck and Snower [1984, 1986a,b,c], Solow 1985 and Blanchard and Sumners [1986]. For some empirical tests of the insider-outsider hypothesis see Blanchflower, Oswald and Garrett [1988].

10 It is noteworthy that a demand stimulus from abroad (or from a boom in private domestic capital formation) is often welcomed (or even sought) by some of the most ardent opponents of a public sector-led expansion of demand: the source of the demand stimulus determines its desirability.

11 Note that in the 'thousand islands' literature, the private sector is assumed to possess local information ($P_t(z)$) that the authorities do not possess. It is clearly realistic to assume that private agents have superior firm-specific information.

12 As shown in Buiter [1988], finite or uncertain lifetimes are not sufficient for absence of debt neutrality in OLG models without operative intergenerational gift and bequest motives. A positive birth rate is sufficient.

13 Distortionary taxes will introduce a further reason for absence of debt neutrality.

14 Note that seigniorage is defined as $(\Delta H)/P$, where H is the high-powered money stock. Unanticipated changes in the price level will of course reduce the real value of the government's nominally-denominated debt and thus provide another source of revenue.

15 McCallum [1977, 1980] shows that while this is necessary, it is not sufficient for policy effectiveness.

16 The theoretical foundations of nominal stickiness are unfortunately virtually non-existent.

17 With a flexible price level, there could be a once-off discrete jump in the price-level path.

18 The central bank is, for our purposes, part of the government.

19 For a more extended discussion, see Buiter [1985].

Bibliography

Akerlof, G. A., 'The Market for 'Lemons': Qualitative Uncertainty and the Market Mechanism'. *The Quarterly Journal of Economics*, Vol. 24, 1970, pp. 488–500.

——, J. Yellen, 'A Near Rational Model of the Business Cycle, with Wage and Price Inertia'. *The Quarterly Journal of Economics*, Vol. 100, 1985, pp. 823–38.

Ball, L., D. Romer, 'Are Prices Too Sticky?' NBER Working Papers, 2171, Cambridge, Mass., February 1987.

Barro, R. J., 'Rational Expectations and the Role of Monetary Policy'. *Journal of Monetary Economics*, Vol. 2, 1976, pp. 1–32.

——, 'A Capital Market in an Equilibrium Business Cycle Model'. *Econometrica*, Vol. 48, 1980, pp. 1393–417.

——, 'Intertemporal Substitution and the Business Cycle', Carnegie-Rochester Conference Series on Public Policy, 14, 1981, pp. 237–68.

——, H. I. Grossman, 'A General Disequilibrium Model of Income and Employment'. *The American Economic Review*, Vol. 61, 1971, pp. 82–93.

Blanchard, O., 'Debt, Deficits and Finite Horizons'. *Journal of Political Economy*, Vol. 93, 1985, pp. 223–47.

——, R. Dornbusch, R. Layard (eds.), *Restoring Europe's Prosperity*. Cambridge, Mass., 1986.

——, L. H., Summers 'Hysteresis and the European Unemployment Problem'. In S. Fischer (ed.), *NBER Macroeconomics Annual 1986*. Cambridge, Mass., 1986, pp. 15–78.

——, N. Kiyotaki, 'Monopolistic Competition, Aggregate Demand Externalities, and Real Effects of Nominal Money'. NBER Working Papers, 1770, December 1985.

Blanchflower, D. G., A. J. Oswald and M. D. Garrett, 'Insider power in wage determination', mimeo, LSE, London, June 1988.

Blinder, Alan, 'Credit-Rationing and Effective Supply Failures'. *The Economic Journal*, Vol. 97, 1987, pp. 327–52.

Bruno, M. J. Sachs, *The Economics of Worldwide Stagflation*. New Haven, Conn., 1985.

Buiter, W. H., 'The Superiority of Contingent Rules over Fixed Rules in Models with Rational Expectations'. *The Economic Journal*, Vol. 91, 1981, pp. 647–70.

——, 'Allocative and Stabilization Aspects of Budgetary and Financial Policy'. Centre for Economic Policy Research Working Papers, 2, January, 1983.

——, 'A Guide to Public Sector Debt and Deficits'. Economic Policy, Vol. 1, 1985, pp. 13–60.

——, 'Death, birth, productivity growth and debt neutrality,' *Economic Journal*, Vol. 98, No. 391, June 1988, pp. 279–93.

Buiter, W. H., Gersovitz, 'Issues in Controllability and the Theory of Economic Policy'. *Journal of Public Economics*, Vol. 88, 1981, pp. 33–43.

——, I. Jewitt, 'Staggered Wage Setting with Real Wage Relativities: Variations on a Theme of Taylor'. The Manchester School of Economic and Social Studies, Vol. 49, 1981, pp. 221–8.

——, M. H. Miller, 'Costs and Benefits of Anti-Inflationary Policy: Questions and Issues'. In V. Argy, J. Nevile (eds.), *Inflation and Unemployment: Theory, Experience and Policy Making*. London, 1985, pp. 11–38.

Ees, van, H., 'An explanation of unemployment through an integration of the efficiency wage theory and the kinked demand curve approach'. Mimeo, University of Groningen, October 1987 (revised).

Fischer, S, 'Dynamic Inconsistency, Cooperation and the Benevolent Dissembling Government'. *Journal of Economic Dynamics and Control*, Vol. 2, 1980, pp. 93–107.

Gregory, R. G., 'Work and Welfare in the Years ahead'. *Australian Economic Papers*, Vol. 21, 1982, pp. 219–43.

——, The Slide into Mass Unemployment; Labour Market Theories, Facts and Policies. The Academy of Social Science, Annual lectures, Australia, 1983.

——, 'Wages Policy and Unemployment in Australia'. *Economica*, Vol. 53, 1986, Supplement.

Hargreaves-Heap, S. P., 'Choosing the Wrong Natural Rate, Accelerating Inflation or Decelerating Unemployment and Growth'. The Economic Journal, Vol. 90, 1980, pp. 611–20.

Katz, L. F., 'Efficiency Wage Theories: A Partial Evaluation'. In S. Fischer (ed.), *NBER Macroeconomics Annual 1986*. Cambridge M. A. 1986, pp. 235–276.

King, R. G. 'Interest Rates, Aggregate Information and Monetary Policy'. *Journal of Monetary Economics*, Vol. 12, 1983, pp. 199–234.

Kydland, F. and E. Prescott, 'Time to Build and Aggregate Fluctuations' *Econometrica*, Vol. 50, pp. 1345–70.

Layard, R. S. Nickell, 'Unemployment in Britain'. *Economica*, Vol. 53, 1986, Supplement, pp. S121–170.

Lindbeck, A. D., Snower, 'Labor Turnover, Insider Morale and Involuntary Unemployment'. Institute for International Economic Studies, Seminar Papers, 310, Stockholm 1984.

——, —— (1986a), Wage Rigidity, Union Activity and Unemployment'. In W, Beckerman (ed.), Wage Rigidity and Unemployment. Duckworth, Oxford. 1986, pp. 97–125.

——, —— (1986b), 'Explanations of Unemployment'. Oxford Review of Economic Policy, Vol. 1, 1986, pp. 34–59.

——, ——, 'Wage Setting, Unemployment and Insider-Outsider Relationships'. *American Economic Review*, 76, May 1986c, pp. 235–9.

Long, J., C. Plosser, 'Real Business Cycles', *Journal of Political Economy*, 91, 1983, pp. 1345–70.

Lucas, R. E., 'Expectations and the Neutrality of Money'. Journal of Economic Theory, Vol. 4, 1972, pp. 103–24.

Malinvaud, E., The Theory of Unemployment Reconsidered. Oxford 1977.

Mccallum, B. The Current State of the Policy Ineffectiveness Debate, Economic Review, Vol. 60, no. 2, May 1978, pp. 240–5.

——, 'Rational Expectations and Macroeconomic Stabilization Policy: An Overview'. *Journal of Money, Credit and Banking*, Vol. 12, 1980, pp. 716–746.

Marini, G., 'Intertemporal Substitution and the Role of Monetary Policy'. *The Economic Journal*, Vol. 95, 1985, pp. 87–100.

——, 'Employment Fluctuations and Demand Management'. Economica, Vol. 53, 1986, pp. 209–218.

Modigliani, F. *et al.*, Reducing Unemployment in Europe: The Role of Capital Formation. CEPS Papers, 28, Brussels 1986.

Organization for Economic Co-operation and Development (OECD), Economic Outlook, June 1987 and June 1988, Paris.

Phelps, E., Inflation Policy and Unemployment Theory. New York 1972.

Sargent, T. J., 'Rational Expectations, the Real Rate of Interest, and the Natural Rate of Unemployment'. Brookings Papers on Economic Activity, 2, Washington DC, 1973, pp. 429–72.

——, N. Wallace, 'Rational Expectations, the Optimal Monetary Instrument, and the Optimal Money Supply Rule'. *Journal of Political Economy*, Vol. 83, 1975, pp. 241–54.

Solow, R. 'Insiders and Outsiders in Wage Determination', *Scandinanian Journal of Economics*, Vol. 87, 1985, pp. 411–28.

Stiglitz, Joseph 'The Causes and Consequences of the Dependence of Quality on Price'. *The Journal of Economic Literature*, Vol. 25, 1987, pp. 1–48.

Taylor, J. B., 'Aggregate Dynamics and Staggered Contracts'. *Journal of Political Economy*, Vol. 88, 1980, pp. 1–23.
Tobin, J., 'Stabilization Policy Ten Years After'. *Brookings Papers on Economic Activity*, Vol. 1, 1980, pp. 19–71.
Weiss, A., 'Job Queues and Layoffs in Labor Markets with Flexible Wages.' *Journal of Political Economy*, Vol. 88, 1980, pp. 526–38.

Part 2

Econometric tests for policy (in)effectiveness

Chapter 6

Real effects of anticipated and unanticipated money: some problems of estimation and hypothesis testing

I Introduction

This paper addresses two issues that arise in the estimation of models of the real effects of anticipated and unanticipated changes in the money supply and in tests of hypotheses in such models. It is motivated by Barro's seminal empirical work on the role of anticipated and unanticipated monetary growth (Barro [1978, 1979], Barro and Rush [1980]; see also Gordon [1979], Attfield, Demery and Duck [1981,b]). The first issue concerns an identification problem. The observational equivalence is established of models in which a real variable (say, output) is a function of unanticipated money growth and models in which money growth is a function of unanticipated output, e.g., via a policy reaction function or through a response of the private banking system. Identification of the effects of current unanticipated (or unperceived) monetary growth on real output is possible only if the *a priori* restriction is imposed that monetary growth does not depend on current unanticipated (or unperceived) output. The restriction that there be no effects of unanticipated output on money growth is quite distinct from the restriction(s) required for the identification of the effects of anticipated money on output (see, e.g., Barro [1978, 1979]).

The second issue remains even if reliable time series on anticipated and unanticipated monetary growth are somehow available. It concerns the ways in which anticipated and unanticipated monetary growth can enter a 'semi-reduced form'[1] equation for output or any other real variable. Barro's specification of the output equation includes only current and lagged actual monetary growth and a distributed lag on unperceived contemporaneous monetary growth.[2] The literature suggests at least three further channels through which money affects real output. (1) Past and present anticipated *future* monetary growth. (2) Past and present revisions in forecasts of monetary growth. (3) A more general specification of unanticipated money, with expectations of monetary growth in a given period conditioned at various preceding dates – a Fischer [1977]-type hypothesis.

If anticipated future monetary growth affects real output, alternative fixed (open-loop) monetary growth paths will be associated with different paths for real output. If one of the other two channels is operative, alternative flexible (closed-loop) money supply rules or feedback rules will be associated with different distribution functions for real output. Omission of the first channel may lead to biased estimates of the output effects of past anticipated monetary growth. The other two channels are likely to be very difficult to identify. The issue of the observational equivalence of natural and unnatural (*sic*) rate theories of macroeconomics was first addressed by Sargent [1976]. McCallum [1979] showed that there were circumstances in which Sargent's general observational equivalence proposition did not rule out the construction of tests capable of discriminating between classical and Keynesian hypotheses. Barro [1979] provides a penetrating discussion of the observational equivalence problem and of the kinds of *apriori* information (generally cross-equation overidentifying restrictions on the reduced form parameters) required for testing classical against Keynesian hypotheses. This paper confirms the conclusion reached by Sargent [1976] and others that a change, during the sample period or the forecasting interval, in the stochastic process governing the policy variables will often be required in order to establish the presence or absence of a role for stabilization policy.

II The identification of the effects of anticipated and unanticipated monetary growth on output

Monetary growth independent of anticipated and unanticipated output

A simplified version of Barro's model of the effect of anticipated and unanticipated money on output is given in equations (1), (2) and (3),

$$Y_t = a_1 X_t + b_1(\dot{m}_t - \dot{m}_{t|t}) + c_1 \dot{m}_t + u_{1t}, \tag{1}$$

$$\dot{m}_t = a_2 X_t + u_{2t}, \tag{2}$$

$$\Sigma = E((u_{1t}, u_{2t})'(u_{1t}, u_{2t})) = \begin{bmatrix} \sigma^2_{u_1} & 0 \\ 0 & \sigma^2_{u_2} \end{bmatrix}. \tag{3}$$

Y is real output, X a vector of regressors and $\dot{m}$ the actual rate of growth of money.

u_1 and u_2 are serially uncorrelated normally distributed random variables with means zero and constant variances. They are also assumed to be contemporaneously independent – a necessary condition for the identification of the effect of unanticipated monetary growth. The X variables may be stochastic but are distributed independently of the current and future values of the vector of disturbances $u_t = (u_{1t}, u_{2t})'$, in the sense that $\text{cov}(u_t, X_{t-s}) = 0$ for all t and all $s \geqq 0$. Thus X_t cannot include current endogenous variables but may include lagged endogenous variables (predetermined variables) as well as exogenous variables. Lagged actual and anticipated monetary growth rates will always be entered as separate arguments in the equations although they constitute proper regressors according to our definition. Thus X_t could include such variables as *FEDV*[3] and *MIL*[4] and *MINW*[5] in the original Barro papers. Agents forming expectations are assumed to know the true structure of the model (a_1, a_2, b_1, c_1 and Σ in the current example). X_t is also assumed to be known when expectations of $\dot{m}_t$ are formed in period t but Y_t, $\dot{m}_t$, u_{1t} and u_{2t}, are unobserved until period $t + 1$. $\hat{\dot{m}}_{t|\tau}$ is the rate of growth of money in period t, anticipated in period τ. $\dot{m}_t - \hat{\dot{m}}_{t|t}$ is therefore the currently unperceived part of current period monetary growth. Equation (1) is the output equation; (2) describes the money supply process. For simplicity only the current innovation in the money supply process and current actual monetary growth are assumed to be arguments in the output equation.[6]

The assumption of rational expectations means that equations (1), (2) and (3) are known to private agents when they infer the growth of the money supply. u_{1t}, u_{2t}, Y_t and $\dot{m}_t$ are assumed unknown when the current expectations of money supply growth is formed. Thus, assuming that anticipations are mathematical expectations conditional on the available information set, I_t, which consists of the model and X_t we have

$$m_{t|t} = E(\dot{m}_t \mid I_t) = a_2 X_t. \tag{4}$$

The reduced form of the model of (1), (2) and (3) is

$$Y_t = \beta_1 X_t + v_{1t}, \tag{5}$$

$$\dot{m}_t = \beta_2 X_t + v_{2t}, \tag{6}$$

$$\beta_1 = a_1 + c_1 a_2, \tag{7}$$

$$\beta_2 = a_2, \tag{8}$$

$$v_{1t} = (b_1 + c_1)u_{2t} + u_{1t}, \tag{9a}$$

$$v_{2t} = u_{2t}, \tag{9b}$$

$$\begin{aligned} \Omega_1 &= E((v_{1t}, v_{2t})'(v_{1t}, v_{2t})) \\ &= \begin{bmatrix} \sigma^2_{v_1} & \sigma_{v_1 v_2} \\ \sigma_{v_1 v_2} & \sigma^2_{v_2} \end{bmatrix} = \begin{bmatrix} (b_1 + c_1)^2 \sigma^2_{u_2} + \sigma^2_{u_1} & (b_1 + c_1)\sigma^2_{u_2} \\ (b_1 + c_1)\sigma^2_{u_2} & \sigma^2_{u_2} \end{bmatrix}. \end{aligned} \tag{9c}$$

The effect of anticipated money on output, $\partial y_t / \partial \dot{m}_t + \partial y_t / \partial \hat{\dot{m}}_{t|t}$, is given by c_1, the effect of unanticipated money on output, $\partial y_t / \partial \hat{\dot{m}}_{t|t}$, by $b_1 + c_1$. The effect of unanticipated money can be obtained from Ω_1, the variance–covariance matrix of the reduced form disturbances: $b_1 + c_1 =$

$\sigma_{v_1v_2}/\sigma_{v_2}^2$.[7] Note that this requires independence of the structural disturbances u_{1t} and u_{2t}. To identify the effect of anticipated money, however, further *a priori* restrictions are required. Since we can obtain consistent and asymptotically efficient estimates of $\beta_1 = a_1 + c_1a_2$ and $\beta_2 = a_2$, an exclusion restriction permitting the identification of c_1 is that $a_1 = 0$. Barro's exclusion restriction that government purchases do not affect real output falls in this category (Barro [1979]).[8]

Monetary growth dependent on anticipated and unanticipated output
The structure of equations (1), (2) and (3) is observationally equivalent to the model of equations (10), (11) and (3),

$$Y_t = a_1X_t + u_{1t}, \tag{10}$$

$$\dot{m}_t = a_2X_t + b_2(Y_t - \hat{Y}_{t|t}) + c_2Y_t + u_{2t}. \tag{11}$$

Neither anticipated nor unanticipated money affect output but monetary growth responds both to anticipated and unanticipated output. Such a money supply response could reflect either the behaviour of the authorities through a monetary policy reaction function or the response of the private banking system to changes in the demand for money due to anticipated and unanticipated changes in income and associated changes in interest rates. A positive value of $b_2 + c_2$ or of c_2 can be interpreted as 'leaning with the wind' by the monetary authorities: with an unchanged monetary policy stance an (unanticipated) increase in output would tend to raise interest rates. The money supply expands to counteract this. Negative values of $b_2 + c_2$ or of c_2 could indicate a policy of 'leaning against the wind'. Note that $\hat{Y}_{t|t} \equiv E(Y_t \mid I_t) = a_1X_t$. The reduced form of (10), (11) and (3) is

$$Y_t = \alpha_1X_t + \eta_{1t}, \tag{12}$$

$$\dot{m}_t = \alpha_2X_t + \eta_{2t}, \tag{13}$$

$$\alpha_1 = a_1, \tag{14a}$$

$$\alpha_2 = a_2 + c_2a_1, \tag{14b}$$

$$\eta_{1t} = u_{1t}, \tag{14c}$$

$$\eta_{2t} = (b_2 + c_2)u_{1t} + u_{2t}, \tag{14d}$$

$$\Omega_2 = E((\eta_{1t}, \eta_{2t})'(\eta_{1t}, \eta_{2t}))$$
$$= \begin{bmatrix} \sigma_{\eta_1}^2 & \sigma_{\eta_1\eta_2} \\ \sigma_{\eta_1\eta_2} & \sigma_{\eta_2}^2 \end{bmatrix} = \begin{bmatrix} \sigma_{u_1}^2 & (b_2 + c_2)\sigma_{u_1}^2 \\ (b_2 + c_2)^2\sigma_{u_1}^2 & (b_2 + c_2)^2\sigma_{u_1}^2 + \sigma_{u_2}^2 \end{bmatrix}. \tag{14e}$$

The model of (1), (2) and (3) is observationally equivalent to the model of (10), (11) and (3): their reduced forms cannot be distinguished (compare (5)–(9) with (12)–(14)) and will yield identical likelihood functions for the endogenous variables.

For the model of (10), (11) and (13) the effect of unanticipated output on money growth is identified *via* Ω_2 as $b_2 + c_2 = \sigma_{\eta_1\eta_2}/\sigma^2_{\eta_1}$. The effect of anticipated output on money can then be identified from α_1 and α_2 if, e.g., an exclusion restriction is imposed on one of the elements of a_2. If the true model is given by (10) and (11) but the econometrician mistakenly believes the true model to be (1) and (2), what is thought to be an estimate of $b_1 + c_1$, using the estimated variance-covariance matrix of the reduced form $\hat{\sigma}_{\eta_1\eta_2}/\hat{\sigma}^2_{\eta_2}$, is neither that nor an estimate of $b_2 + c_2$, which would be given by $\hat{\sigma}_{\eta_1\eta_2}/\hat{\sigma}^2_{\eta_1}$.

Observational equivalence in a more general model

Consider the general model that permits, in principle, dependence of output on both anticipated and unanticipated money and dependence of monetary growth on both anticipated and unanticipated output,

$$Y_t = a_1X_t + b_1(\dot{m}_t - \hat{\dot{m}}_{t|t}) + c_1\dot{m}_t + u_{1t}, \tag{1}$$

$$\dot{m}_t = a_2X_t + b_2(Y_t - \hat{Y}_{t|t}) + c_2Y_t + u_{2t}. \tag{11}$$

The disturbance terms are again as in (3).

With rational expectations the reduced form of this model is given by

$$Y_t = \delta_1X_t + \Psi_{1t}, \tag{15}$$

$$\dot{m}_t = \delta_2X_t + \Psi_{2t}, \tag{16}$$

$$\delta_1 = (a_1 + c_1a_2)/(1 - c_1c_2), \tag{17a}$$

$$\delta_2 = (a_2 + c_2a_1)/(1 - c_1c_2), \tag{17b}$$

$$\Psi_{1t} = [1 - (b_1 + c_1)(b_2 + c_2)]^{-1}\,[u_{1t} + (b_1 + c_1)u_{2t}], \tag{17c}$$

$$\Psi_{2t} = [1 - (b_1 + c_1)(b_2 + c_2)]^{-1}[(b_2 + c_2)u_{1t} + u_{2t}], \tag{17d}$$

$$\begin{aligned}\Omega_3 &= E((\Psi_{1t}, \Psi_{2t})'(\Psi_{1t}, \Psi_{2t}))\\ &= \begin{bmatrix}\sigma_{\Psi_1^2} & \sigma_{\Psi_1\Psi_2}\\ \sigma_{\Psi_1\Psi_2} & \sigma_{\Psi_2^2}\end{bmatrix} = [1 - (b_2 + c_1)(b_1 + c_2))^{-2}\\ &\times \begin{bmatrix}\sigma^2_{u_1} + (b_1 + c_1)^2\sigma^2_{u_2} & (b_2 + c_2)\sigma^2_{u_1} + (b_1 + c_1)\sigma^2_{u_2}\\ (b_2 + c_2)\sigma^2_{u_1} + (b_1 + c_1)\sigma^2_{u_2} & (b_2 + c_2)^2\sigma^2_{u_1} + \sigma^2_{u_2}\end{bmatrix}.\end{aligned} \tag{17e}$$

The general structural model of equations (1), (11) and (3) in which both unanticipated and anticipated money affect real output ($b_1 + c_1 \neq 0$ and $c_1 \neq 0$ respectively) is observationally equivalent to a large set of sub-models with widely differing implications for the conduct of monetary policy. While these sub-models are special cases of the general structural model they are not nested either in each other or in the general model. The most interesting cases are the following:

(a) Only anticipated money affects real output ($c_1 \neq 0$ and $b_1 + c_1 = 0$).
(b) Anticipated money has the same effect on output as unanticipated money ($c_1 = b_1 + c_1$ or $b_1 = 0$).
(c) Only unanticipated money affects real output ($c_1 = 0$ and $b_1 + c_1 \neq 0$).
(d) Neither anticipated nor unanticipated money affect real output ($b_1 = c_1 = 0$).

For simplicity and without loss of generality for the observational equivalence propositions, we assume in what follows that X_t (and therefore a_1 and a_2) is a scalar. If both anticipated and unanticipated output can affect money ($c_2 \neq 0$, $b_2 + c_2 \neq 0$, a model in which both anticipated and unanticipated money can have (possibly distinct) effects on output ($c_1 \neq 0$, $b_1 + c_1 \neq 0$) is observationally equivalent to a model in which only anticipated money affects output ($c_1 \neq 0$; $b_1 + c_1 = 0$) and to a model in which anticipated and unanticipated money have the same effect on output ($b_1 = 0$). A model in which only anticipated money affects output ($c_1 \neq 0$, $b_1 + c_1 = 0$) is observationally equivalent to a model in which neither anticipated nor unanticipated money have real effects ($b_1 = c_1 = 0$).

A priori knowledge of the value of a_1 is in some cases sufficient to discriminate between, on the one hand, 'Both anticipated and unanticipated money matter' ($c_1 \neq 0$, $b_1 + c_1 \neq 0$) or 'Only anticipated money matters' ($c_1 \neq 0$, $b_1 + c_1 = 0$) and, on the other hand, 'Only unanticipated money matters' ($c_1 = 0$, $b_1 + c_1 \neq 0$) or 'Neither anticipated nor unanticipated money matter' ($b_1 = c_1 = 0$). If the hypothesis $\delta_1 = a_1$ is consistent with the data, either $a_1 = -a_2/c_2$ or $c_1 = 0$. If $c_1 = 0$, anticipated money does not affect real output. If $a_1 = -a_2/c_2$, $\delta_2 = 0$, a hypothesis that can be tested. Thus if δ_1 is not significantly different from a_1 and δ_2 is significantly different from zero, $c_1 = 0$ is accepted. Even if this hypothesis is accepted, we cannot further discriminate between the hypothesis that only unanticipated money affects real output ($c_1 = 0$, $b_1 + c_1 \neq 0$) and the hypothesis that neither anticipated nor unanticipated money affect real output ($b_1 = c_1 = 0$) unless we impose the *a priori* constraint that anticipated output does not affect monetary growth ($b_2 + c_2 = 0$). Given that further restriction the variance-covariance matrix of the reduced form disturbances (17e), will be a diagonal matrix if $b_1 + c_1 = 0$.

Thus, starting from the general model of eqs. (1), (11) and (3) we can identify both the effect of anticipated money on output (c_1) and the effect of anticipated output on money (c_2) if we have two independent restrictions on the reduced form coefficients δ_1 and δ_2. To identify just c_1, the exclusion restriction $a_1 = 0$ is sufficient. This is of course the standard identification problem, familiar from partial equilibrium demand and supply analysis, when one does not encounter the additional problem of innovations from one process entering as arguments into another process. If innovations in either process can enter as an argument in the other, the identification problem is compounded. Evidence other than the time series properties of $\dot{m}_t$, Y_t and X_t is required to establish the validity of the restriction that there is no effect of unanticipated output on monetary growth, a restriction required for the identification of the effect of unanticipated money on output.

Lagged money and output innovations

In empirical applications the output equation given in (1) has been modified to include current and lagged anticipated and unanticipated money as arguments. The rationale for this is inertia in the real output process due to costs of adjustment (capital stock, inventories, quasi-fixed labour etc.), or to lags in the perception of new information (see, e.g., Lucas [1975]).[9] Note that in the presence of such real costs of adjustment the anticipated real rate of return on money balances, which is a function of the anticipated component of the money supply process, should affect the probability density function of real output. The empirical importance of this 'inflation tax' argument would be reflected in the coefficients on current and lagged anticipated future monetary growth. (See section III below.) Monetary growth can also, in principle, be a function of current and lagged anticipated and unanticipated output. The monetary reaction function can incorporate *measurement* or *perception* lags (the time interval between the occurrence of an event and its observation) and *realisation* lags (the time needed to decide upon and realise a control action) (see Deissenberg [1979]). Eqs. (18) and (19) are a generalisation of (1) and (11), with output a function of a T-period distributed lag on anticipated and unanticipated money and money a function of a T-period distributed lag on anticipated and unanticipated output. It is assumed that the maximal lag is known *a priori*,

$$Y_t = a_1 X_t + \sum_{i=0}^{T} b_{1,i}(\dot{m}_{t-i} - \hat{\dot{m}}_{t-i|t-i}) + \sum_{i=0}^{T} c_{1,i}\, \dot{m}_{t-i} + u_{1t}, \tag{18}$$

$$\dot{m}_t = a_2 X_t + \sum_{i=0}^{T} b_{2,i}(Y_{t-i} - \hat{Y}_{t-i|t-i}) + \sum_{t=0}^{T} c_{2,i} Y_{t-i} + u_{2t}. \tag{19}$$

u_{1t} and u_{2t} are as before.

The presence of the distributed lag terms does alter the conditions for identification. A general discussion, including a detailed analysis of the case where $T = 1$ is given in Buiter [1980b]. The main result is that when output is a function of lagged as well as current anticipated and unanticipated monetary growth, the identification of the effect of current anticipated monetary growth is 'easier' than when only current anticipated and unanticipated monetary growth are included as arguments in the output equation. The identification of the effect of current money growth innovations, however, is 'more difficult' than before. It still requires the *a priori* restriction that current unanticipated output does not affect monetary growth, but this is no longer sufficient for identification. When $T = 1$, the simplest sufficient condition appears to be that current unanticipated output does not affect monetary growth and that anticipated and unanticipated lagged output have the same effect on monetary growth.

Underlying the analysis of the conditions for identification of the effects of anticipated and unanticipated monetary growth, is the assumption that the maximal orders of the distributed lags are known *a priori*. If anticipated and unanticipated money and output enter their respective equations with distributed lags of unknown order, or if the u_{it} are not white noise but instead follow a general ARIMA process, identifying and estimating the response of output to money growth and tests of the relevant hypotheses become much more difficult. The maximal orders of the distributed lags must be inferred from the data and the lagged endogenous variables are less informative from the point of view of identification (see Sims [1980] and Wallis [1980]).

The identification of the output effects of unanticipated monetary growth is essential for the empirical confirmation of the new monetary theories of the business cycle (see, e.g., Lucas [1977]). These theories require both that anticipated monetary growth has no effect on deviations of actual from capacity output and that monetary innovations account for a significant fraction of the variance of real output. Failure to identify the output effects of unanticipated money would make the new monetary theories of the business cycle untestable.

III Anticipated and unanticipated money in the output equation and the role of monetary policy

In this section of the paper I show that even if an effect of unanticipated output on monetary growth can be ruled out *a priori*, there remain a number of serious problems with the interpretation of the results obtained by Barro *et al.*, especially as regards their implications for the role of monetary policy. The central issue is the observational equivalence between models for which the density function of real output is invariant under alternative deterministic (and known) feedback rules for the money stock and models for which this invariance property does not hold.

The output equation (18) used by Barro *et al.* is a restrictive special case which omits at least three potentially important transmission mechanisms for monetary policy. Various not implausible structural macromodels will yield 'semi-reduced form' output equations that include anticipated and unanticipated money in a number of ways not included in equation (18). A more general output equation is given in (20),

$$
\begin{aligned}
Y_t = a_1 X_t &+ \sum_{i=0}^{T_1} \sum_{j=0}^{S_1} b_{ij}[\dot{m}_{t-1} - E(\dot{m}_{t-i} \mid I_{t-i-j})] + \sum_{i=0}^{T_1} c_i \dot{m}_{t-i} \\
&+ \sum_{k=1}^{Q} \sum_{i=0}^{T_2} \sum_{j=0}^{S_2} d_{ijk}[E(\dot{m}_{t-j+i} \mid I_{t-j}) - E(\dot{m}_{t-j+i} \mid I_{t-j-k})] \\
&+ \sum_{i=0}^{T_3} \sum_{j=0}^{S_3} e_{ij} E(\dot{m}_{t-j+i} \mid I_{t-j}) + u_{1t}. \qquad (20)
\end{aligned}
$$

Anticipated future monetary growth
Anticipated future inflation and therefore anticipated future monetary growth will affect the density function of real output in equilibrium models if output is a function of the real stock of capital and money is not superneutral (Tobin [1965] and Fischer [1979]). This 'Tobin effect' affects actual output and capacity output equally. It therefore concerns the structural or allocative role of monetary policy rather than its stabilization role. There are two ways of allowing for such an effect in empirical work. One is to keep actual output as the dependent variable and include a term like $\sum_{i=0}^{T_3} \sum_{j=0}^{S_3} e_{ij} E(\dot{m}_{t-j+i} | I_{t-j})$ on the right-hand side. The other is to respecify the output equation with the difference between actual and capacity output as the dependent variable. In that case the measure of capacity output should be constructed in such a way as to allow for the possible presence of a Tobin effect. Existing empirical work (e.g., Barro [1978], Barro and Rush [1980]) which has actual output as the dependent variable and allows for changes in capacity output merely by including a time trend among the regressors precludes the consideration of the Tobin effect. The question of the direction and magnitude of the bias imparted to estimates of b_{ij} and c_i by the omission of anticipated future monetary growth as an explanatory variable if $e_{ij} \neq 0$ for some i and j is an 'omitted variables' problem. (See, e.g., Maddala [1979, pp. 155–157] and Schmidt [1976, pp. 39–40].) It depends both on the magnitudes of the e_{ij} and on the correlation between past anticipated and unanticipated monetary growth and future anticipated monetary growth. In the quarterly model of Barro and Rush [1980], monetary growth depends (among other things) on its own past values at lags one through six. The matrix of regression coefficients from the 'auxiliary' regression of anticipated future monetary growth on past monetary growth is therefore unlikely to be the zero matrix.

A distributed lag on forecast horizons
In all empirical work except for Fischer [1980], unanticipated monetary growth is represented by a distributed lag on unperceived contemporaneous monetary growth.[10] In (20) this is generalized to prediction errors

from forecasts of $\dot{m}_{t-i}$, $i = 0, 1, \ldots, T_1$, made at the beginning of period $t - i$ and in earlier periods

$$t - i - j,\ j = 1, 2, \ldots, S_1 \quad \text{or} \quad \sum_{i=0}^{T_1} \sum_{j=0}^{S_1} b_{ij}(\dot{m}_{t-i} - E(\dot{m}_{t-1} \mid I_{t-i-j})).$$

Such a reduced form could emerge if the money wage in period t had to be set in open-loop or unconditional fashion in a period before t (see, e.g., Fischer [1977], Phelps and Taylor [1977], Taylor [1979]).

With a simple example I will show that models in which $b_{ij} \neq 0$ for some $j > 0$ ('Phelps-Fischer-Taylor' or P.F.T. models) can under certain conditions be observationally equivalent to models in which $b_{ij} = 0, j \neq 0$ ('Barro models'). This can be so, regardless of whether $c_i = 0, i = 1, \ldots, T_1$, that is regardless of whether or not past anticipated monetary growth affects output. This issue is of some interest because if $b_{ij} > 0$ for some $j > 0$, the second moment of the density function of real output will not be invariant under changes in the deterministic components of monetary feedback rules.

In the example $T_1 = 0$ and $S_1 = 1$; G_t denotes real public spending.

$$\begin{aligned} Y_t = a_{11}G_t + b_{00}(\dot{m}_t - \dot{m}_{t|t}) + b_{01}(\hat{\dot{m}}_t - \hat{\dot{m}}_{t|t-1}) \\ + c_0\dot{m}_t + c_1\dot{m}_{t-1} + u_{1t}, \end{aligned} \tag{21}$$

$$\dot{m}_t = a_{21}G_t + a_{22}\dot{m}_{t-1} + u_{2t}. \tag{22}$$

Equation (21) is a P.F.T. equation. The reduced form equations of this model are given by (22) and (23)

$$\begin{aligned} Y_t = {} & (a_{11} + c_0a_{21})G_t + (c_0a_{22} + c_1)\dot{m}_{t-1} + u_{1t} + (c_0 + b_{00} + b_{01})u_{2t} \\ & + b_{01}a_{22}u_{2t-1} + b_{00}a_{21}(G_t - \hat{G}_{t|t}) + b_{01}a_{22}a_{21}(G_{t-1} - \hat{G}_{t-1|t-1}) \\ & + b_{01}a_{21}(G_t - \hat{G}_{t|t-1}). \end{aligned} \tag{23}$$

Now consider a Barro version of equation (20) with $T_1 = 1$ and $S_1 = 0$,

$$\begin{aligned} Y_t = {} & a_{11}G_t + b_{00}(\dot{m}_t - \hat{\dot{m}}_{t|t}) \\ & + b_{10}(\dot{m}_{t-1} - \hat{\dot{m}}_{t-1|t-1}) + c_0\dot{m}_t + c_1\dot{m}_{t-1} + u_{1t}. \end{aligned} \tag{24}$$

The reduced form equation for output under the Barro hypothesis is, using (22)

$$\begin{aligned} Y_t = {} & (a_{11} + c_0a_{21})G_t + (c_0a_{22} + c_1)\dot{m}_{t-1} + u_{1t} + (c_0 + b_{00})u_{2t} \\ & + b_{10}u_{2t-1} + b_{00}a_{21}(G_t - \hat{G}_{t|t}) + b_{10}a_{21}(G_{t-1} - \hat{G}_{t-1|t-1}). \end{aligned} \tag{25}$$

One problem with a money growth equation such as (22) is that by permitting $\dot{m}_t$ to respond to the current value of the fiscal variable, G_t, the authorities are given an informational advantage over the private sector, unless $G_t = \hat{G}_{t|t}$. A role for stabilization policy then emerges even in the Barro model as can be seen by noting that in equation (25) the coefficients on $G_t - \hat{G}_{t|t}$ and $G_{t-1} - \hat{G}_{t-1|t-1}$ are functions of the policy parameter a_{21}. To avoid this problem, I shall assume that for all t, $G_t \equiv \hat{G}_{t|t}$. Almost identical conclusions emerge if it is assumed that $G_t \neq \hat{G}_{t|t}$ but G_{t-1} or $\hat{G}_{t|t}$ is substituted for G_t in (22).

Leaving aside comparisons of alternative policy regimes (specifically a change in a_{22}), we can hope to discriminate between the P.F.T. equation (21) with $b_{10} = 0$ and $b_{01} \neq 0$ and the Barro equation (24) with $b_{10} \neq 0$ and $b_{01} = 0$ only through the presence of the term $G_t - \hat{G}_{t|t-1}$ in (23), the reduced form P.F.T. equation. Consider the assumption made by Fischer [1980, p. 235]: 'Finally, the exogenous variables *FEDV*, *MIL* and *MINW* were assumed known with perfect foresight'. With $G_t = \hat{G}_{t|t-1}$ (and $G_\tau = \hat{G}_{\tau|\tau}$) (23) and (25) are observationally equivalent.

Note that the Barro-type exclusion restriction $a_{11} = 0$, which permits the identification of c_0 and c_1, is not sufficient for distinguishing between P.F.T. and Barro models. While the $a_{11} = 0$ restriction is necessary for the identification of the effects of *past* anticipated monetary growth, it is neither necessary nor sufficient to resolve the observational equivalence of a distributed lag on 'contemporaneous' forecast errors ($b_{10} \neq 0$ and $b_{01} = 0$ in our examples and forecast errors from forecasts of monetary growth in a given period, made contemporaneously and at various earlier dates ($b_{10} = 0$ and $b_{01} \neq 0$ in our example). This can be seen immediately by setting $a_{11} = 0$ in (23) and (25). Indeed, even if one were to accept the further hypothesis that anticipated monetary growth does not affect output ($c_0 = c_1 = 0$) the problem of observational equivalence of the Barro and P.F.T. models remains. This can be seen by setting $a_{11} = c_0 = c_1 = 0$ in (23) and (25), which yields (again assuming that $G_\tau = \hat{G}_{\tau|\tau}$),

$$Y_t = u_{1t} + (b_{00} + b_{01})u_{2t} + b_{01}a_{22}u_{2t-1} + b_{01}a_{21}(G_t - \hat{G}_{t|t-1}), \quad (23')$$

$$Y_t = u_{1t} + b_{00}u_{2t} + b_{10}u_{2t-1} \quad (25')$$

With $G_t = \hat{G}_{t|t-1}$ equations (23′) and (25′) are observationally equivalent. Yet in (23′) the distribution function of Y_t depends on a known parameter of the monetary feedback rule, a_{22}, while in (25′) the deterministic part of the monetary rule is irrelevant for the behaviour of real output. The only way to discriminate between (23′) and (25′) is along the lines suggested by Sargent [1976]. If a change in the monetary regime (a different value of a_{22}) is known to have occurred at some specific point in time, (25′) would be invariant under such a change while (23′) would be affected.

The foregoing argument does not mean that it is never possible to discriminate between Barro and P.F.T. models in a given policy regime. It does mean that discrimination between the two models requires restrictions on the stochastic processes governing the regressors (other than $\dot{m}_{t-i}$) in the money growth equation – G_t in our example. If G_t can be predicted exactly on the basis of information available at the beginning of period $t-1$, as we assumed in our example, observational equivalence is inescapable. More generally, $G_t - \hat{G}_{t|t-1} = \varepsilon_t$ where ε_t, the public spending forecast error, has the property that $E(\varepsilon_t \mid I_{t-1}) = 0$. Equation (23′) becomes (23″) while equation (25′) remains unchanged,

$$Y_t = u_{1t} + (b_{00} + b_{01})u_{2t} + b_{01}a_{22}u_{2t-1} + b_{01}a_{21}\varepsilon_t. \qquad (23'')$$

Note that $a_{21} \neq 0$ is a necessary condition for discriminating between Barro and P.F.T. models. $a_{11} = 0$ is neither necessary nor sufficient.

Let ε_t be given by

$$\varepsilon_t = \pi_1 u_{1t} + \pi_2 u_{2t} + \pi_3 u_{2t-1} + \pi_4 \xi_t.$$

where $E(\xi_t \mid u_{1t}, u_{2t}, u_{2t-1}) = 0$ and π_i $i = 1, \ldots, 4$, are constants. Remember that u_{2t-1} does not belong to I_{t-1}. Equation (23″) now becomes

$$\begin{aligned} Y_t = {} & (1 + b_{01}a_{21}\pi_1)u_{1t} + (b_{00} + b_{01}(1 + a_{21}\pi_2))u_{2t} \\ & + b_{01}(a_{22} + a_{21}\pi_3)u_{2t-1} + b_{01}a_{21}\pi_4\xi_t. \end{aligned} \qquad (23''')$$

If the public spending forecast error ε_t can be written as an exact linear combination of u_{1t}, u_{2t} and u_{2t-1}, i.e., if $\pi_4 = 0$, equations (25) and (23″) will be observationally equivalent. If $\pi_4 \neq 0$ (and $a_{21} \neq 0$) finding a non-zero coefficient on $G_t - \hat{G}_{t|t-1}$ in the reduced form output equation permits the rejection of the Barro hypothesis.

A final problem that arises in tests of the P.F.T. model against the Barro model relates to the output effects of public spending. Even if one is willing to grant Barro's exclusion restriction that anticipated (or actual) public spending (*FEDV*) does not belong in the 'structural' output equations (21) and (24), i.e., that $a_{11} = 0$, unanticipated public spending (or deviations of *FEDV* from normal) may well belong in the structure. If $G_t - \hat{G}_{t|t-1}$ enters the structural equations (21) and (24) *directly*, we can no longer identify its *indirect* presence through $\dot{m}_t - \hat{\dot{m}}_{t|t-1}$ in the reduced form of (21).

Revisions in forecasts of future money supplies

The third transmission mechanism of monetary policy that is omitted in the work of Barro *et al.* is represented by the term

$$\sum_{k=1}^{Q} \sum_{i=0}^{T_2} \sum_{j=0}^{S_2} d_{ijk}[E(\dot{m}_{t-j+i} \mid I_{t-j}) - E(\dot{m}_{t-j+i} \mid I_{t-j-k})]$$

in (20). Current output may be a function of *revisions* in forecasts of future monetary growth rates (or of future levels of the money stock).[11] If such a transmission channel is present, alternative deterministic monetary feedback rules relating the current money stock to information available arbitrarily far in the past will alter the stochastic process governing real variables. (See, e.g., Turnovsky [1980], Weiss [1980], McCallum [1980], Buiter [1980a, 1981a,b], Buiter and Eaton [1980]). In this subsection I show that models in which this transmission mechanism is present are observationally equivalent to models from which it is absent. Note that this issue is quite distinct from the presence or absence of effects of past or future anticipated monetary growth on real variables. I shall therefore make the point using a model in which past anticipated monetary growth has no effect on real output and in which Barro's exclusion restriction – fiscal variables do not effect output – holds.

The model consists of equations (26) and (27)

$$Y_t = \beta(p_t - \hat{p}_{t|t-1}) + u_t^y, \qquad \beta > 0, \tag{26}$$

$$m_t - p_t = \alpha_1 y_t - \alpha_2(\hat{p}_{t+1|t} - p_t) + u_t^m, \qquad \alpha_1, \alpha_2 > 0. \tag{27}$$

Equation (26) is a Sargent–Wallace supply function, equation (27) a Cagan-style money demand function. p_t is the log of the general price level. u_t^y and u_t^m are white noise disturbance terms. The model contains the two ingredients necessary for the forecast revision mechanism to be operative: (1) current output is a function of expectations of a future endogenous variable ($p_{t+1|t}$), and (2) current output is a function of expectations conditioned at different points in time ($\hat{p}_{t|t-1}$ and $\hat{p}_{t+1|t}$). The information set I_t conditioning forecasts made in period t is assumed to contain the true model and all current and past endogenous variables, exogenous variables and random disturbances.

Assuming stability we can obtain the following expression for real output (see Buiter [1980a]):

$$\begin{aligned} y_t = {} & \frac{\beta}{1 + \alpha_1\beta + \alpha_2}[m_t - \hat{m}_{t|t-1}] + \frac{\beta\alpha_2}{(1 + \alpha_1\beta + \alpha_2)(1 + \alpha_2)} \\ & \times \sum_{i=0}^{\infty}\left(\frac{\alpha_2}{1 + \alpha_2}\right)^i (\hat{m}_{t+1+i|t} - \hat{m}_{t+1+i|t-1}) \\ & + \frac{1}{1 + \alpha_1\beta + \alpha_2}((1 + \alpha_2)u_t^y - \beta u_t^m). \end{aligned} \tag{28}$$

Thus, current output is a function of $m_t - \hat{m}_{t|t-1}$ and of the revision, between periods $t - 1$ and t, in the forecasts for all future money supplies.[12]

If we replace $\hat{p}_{t+1|t}$ by $\hat{p}_{t+1|t-1}$ in equation (27), we lose the feature of the model that current output is a function of expectations conditioned on information available at different points in time. The corresponding output equation is

$$\begin{aligned} y_t = {} & \frac{\beta}{1 + \alpha_1\beta + \alpha_2}(m_t - \hat{m}_{t|t-1}) \\ & + \frac{1}{1 + \alpha_1\beta + \alpha_2}((1 + \alpha_2)u_t^y - \beta u_t^m). \end{aligned} \tag{29}$$

In (28) deterministic monetary feedback rules $m_t = f(I_{t-i})$, $i \geqq 0$, i.e., both *instantaneous* and *lagged* feedback rules will affect the density function of output. In (29) only *instantaneous* monetary feedback rules or automatic stabilizers $m_t = f(I_t)$ will affect the density function of output. Yet it is quite easily appreciated that (28) and (29) are observationally equivalent. Both $m_t - \hat{m}_{t|t-1}$ and all terms such as $\hat{m}_{t+1+i|t} - \hat{m}_{t+1+i|t-1}$ are functions only of the 'news' accruing between periods $t - 1$ and t. This 'news' consists of u_t^y and u_t^m and the innovation in the money supply process.

Let m_t be governed by any indeterministic covariance–stationary stochastic process. It may be one element in a vector of jointly indeterministic covariance–stationary random variables. It will have the moving average representation

$$m_t = d(L)\varepsilon_t,$$

$$d(L) = \sum_{j=0}^{\infty} d_j L^j, \tag{30}$$

where L is the lag operator, $Lx_t \equiv x_{t-1}$ and without loss of generality, $d_0 = 1$. $\{\varepsilon_t\}$ is the sequence of one-step ahead linear least squares forecasting errors (innovations) in predicting m_t as a function of all past information I_{t-1}, i.e., $\varepsilon_t \equiv m_t - E(m_t \mid I_{t-1})$. I_{t-1} includes m_{t-i}, $i > 1$ and the values, at date $t - 1$ and before, of all other variables that may Granger-cause m. Note that ε_t need not be contemporaneously independent of u_t^y and u_t^m. From (30)

$$m_t - \hat{m}_{t|t-1} = \varepsilon_t, \quad \text{and} \tag{31a}$$

$$\hat{m}_{t+1+i/t} - \hat{m}_{t+1+i/t-1} = d_{i+1}\varepsilon_t. \tag{31b}$$

Substituting (31a) and (31b) into (28) and (29) yields

$$y_t = \frac{\beta}{1 + \alpha_1\beta + \alpha_2}\left[1 + \sum_{i=0}^{\infty}\left(\frac{\alpha_2}{1 + \alpha_2}\right)^{i+1} d_{i+1}\right]\varepsilon_t + \frac{1}{1 + \alpha_1\beta + \alpha_2}((1 + \alpha_2)u_t^y - \beta u_t^m), \tag{28'}$$

$$y_t = \frac{\beta}{1 + \alpha_1\beta + \alpha_2}\varepsilon_t + \frac{1}{1 + \alpha_1\beta + \alpha_2}((1 + \alpha_2)u_t^y - \beta u_t^m). \tag{29'}$$

(28′) and (29′) are 'almost always' observationally equivalent.[13] This result holds for any covariance-stationary process for m_t. Specifically, it will hold for a process in the spirit of Barro such as $m_t = \mu_1 G_t + \mu_2 m_{t-1} + \eta_t$ where G_t is (an element in) a covariance-stationary (vector) process and η_t is white noise. The two classes of models can be distinguished only if a change in the stochastic process governing m_t (i.e., in the d_i) is known to have occurred during the sample or prediction interval.

IV Conclusion

The main conclusions are stated in the introduction. In future empirical work on the real effects of anticipated and unanticipated money the specification and estimation of the money supply process will require even greater attention. The crucial issue of whether unanticipated output affects monetary growth will have to be resolved. Since most empirical work uses monetary aggregates that are wider than the monetary base, the interpretation of the money supply process as a policy reaction function seems overly simple. It may be necessary to model the behaviour of the private banking sector whose liabilities constitute most of M_1, M_2 or M_3. Another surprising (or even worrying) feature of past empirical work on the money supply process is that no structural break has been reported in that process at the time of the demise of the Bretton Woods adjustable peg exchange rate regime.

As regards the output equation, a firm distinction needs to be made between the proposition that anticipated (current and past) money has no real effects ($c_i = 0$ for all i) and the proposition that deterministic monetary feedback rules have no real effects and cannot be used for stabilization purposes. Known contingent monetary rules can influence monetary forecast errors (Fischer [1977]) and revisions in money supply forecasts (Turnovsky [1980], Weiss [1980]). This may give monetary policy a handle on the real economy. Serious identification problems make the empirical resolution of these issues doubtful.

Finally, changes in anticipated future monetary growth rates will, by altering the anticipated real rate of return on money *vis-à-vis* real assets, alter the composition and (in the long run) the magnitude of 'full information' real output. The importance of this monetary transmission channel can in principle be empirically evaluated in a Barro-type framework.

The empirical work on anticipated and unanticipated money has not so far brought us much closer to an assessment of the stabilization and structural (or allocative) roles of monetary policy.

Notes

Originally published in *Journal of Monetary Economics*, 11, 1983, pp. 207–24.

1 Semi-reduced form because endogenous expectations still appear on the right-hand side.
2 Or, in empirical applications, a distributed lag on one period ahead forecast errors for monetary growth.
3 Real Federal expenditure relative to normal.
4 The military personnel/conscription variable.
5 The minimum wage variable.
6 Barro includes a distributed lag function on actual and unanticipated monetary growth in (1), i.e., (1) is replaced by

$$Y_t = a_1 X_t + \sum_{i=0}^{T} b_{1,i} (\dot{m}_{t-i} - \dot{m}_{t-i|t-i}) + \sum_{i=0}^{T} c_{1,i} \dot{m}_{t-i} + u_{1t}. \quad (1')$$

It is true that even a model in which only unanticipated money has real effects, these effects can be distributed over time, e.g., because the monetary surprises are 'built into' changes in the capital stock or in inventories. If such were the case and if neither the lagged capital stock nor lagged inventories are included as arguments in the reduced form equation for output, this equation should include an infinite distributed lag on past monetary innovations, not a finite order lag as in Barro.

7 Consistent and asymptotically efficient estimates of β_1, β_2 and $b_1 + c_1$ can be obtained by estimating (5) and (6) with an unrestricted variance-covariance matrix of the reduced from disturbances.

8 It is of course not necessary that the entire vector a_1 equal zero. Let X_t be an N-component vector $X_t = [X_{1t}, \ldots, X_{it}, \ldots, X_{Nt}]'$ and let $a_1 = [a_{11}, \ldots, a_{1i}, \ldots, a_{1N}]$ and $a_2 = [a_{21}, \ldots, a_{2i}, \ldots, a_{2N}]$. Given estimates of $\beta_1 = [a_{11} + c_1 a_{21}, \ldots, a_{1i} + c_1 a_{2i}, \ldots, a_{1N} + c_1 a_{2N}]$ and $\beta_2 = [a_{21}, \ldots, a_{2i}, \ldots, a_{2N}]$, c_1 is identified provided $a_{ij} = 0$ for some $j = 1, \ldots, N$.

9 But see note 6 for a brief discussion of a problem associated with this specification.

10 In practice this is approximated by prediction errors from forecasts, made at the beginning of the unit period of analysis, of monetary growth during that period. The forecasting equations typically have been estimated using observations from the entire sample period, i.e., including data generated in periods beyond the date at which the forecasts are made.

11 The change from growth rates to levels of the money stock is of no consequence for the point we aim to establish.

12 Again we have shifted from rates of changes of m to levels of m.

13 Exceptions would be such as the following: (a) the d_i are chosen in such a way as to make the first term of the right-hand side of (28′) identically equal to zero and ε_t is not an exact linear combination of u_t^y and u_t^m. (b) ε_t is an exact linear combination of u_t^y and u_t^m and the d_i are chosen so as to make the entire right-hand side of (28′) equal to zero.

References

Attfield, C. L. F., D. Demery and N. W. Duck (1981a), Unanticipated monetary growth, output and the price level: U.K. 1946–77, *European Economic Review*, 16, 367–85.

—— (1981b). A quarterly model of unanticipated monetary growth and output in the UK 1963–78, *Journal of Monetary Economics*, 8, November, 331–50.

Barro. R. J. (1977), Unanticipated money growth and unemployment in the United States, *American Economic Review*, 67, March, 101–115.

—— (1978), Unanticipated money, output and the price level in the United States, *Journal of Political Economy*, 86, August, 549–81.

—— (1979), The equilibrium approach to business cycles, November, unpublished.

—— and M. Rush (1980), Unanticipated money and economic activity, in S. Fischer, ed., *Rational expectations and economic policy*, University of Chicago Press, Chicago, IL, 23–73.

Buiter, W. H. (1980a), Monetary, financial and fiscal policies under rational expectations, *IMF Staff Papers 27*, December, 785–813.

—— (1980b), Real effects of anticipated and unanticipated money: Some problems of estimation and hypothesis testing, NBER working paper No. 601, December.
—— (1981a), The role of economic policy after the new classical macroeconomics, in D. Currie, R. Nobay and D. Peel, (eds.), *Macroeconomic analysis* (Croom Helm, London) 233–85.
—— (1981b), The superiority of contingent rules over fixed rules in models with rational expectations, *Economic Journal*, 91, September 647–670.
—— and Jonathan Eaton (1980), Policy decentralization and exchange rate management in interdependent economies, NBER working paper No. 531, August.
Deissenberg, C. (1979), Optimal stabilisation policy with delayed controls and imperfect state measurements, Fakultät für Wirtschafts-wissenschaften und Statistik, Universität Konstanz, Working paper, Series A, No. 133, November.
Fischer, S. (1977), Long-term contracts, rational expectations and the optimal money supply rule, *Journal of Political Economy*, 85, February, 191–206.
—— (1979), Capital accumulation on the transition path in a monetary optimizing model, *Econometrica*, 47, November, 1433–40.
—— (1980), On activist monetary policy with rational expectations, in: S. Fischer, ed., *Rational expectations and economic policy*, University of Chicago Press, Chicago, IL, 211–47.
Gordon, R. J. (1979), New evidence that fully anticipated monetary changes influence real output after all, NBER working paper No. 361, June.
Lucas, R. E. (1975), An equilibrium model of the business cycle, *Journal of Political Economy*, 83, December, 1113–44.
—— (1977), Understanding business cycles, *Journal of Monetary Economics*, Supplement, Carnegie-Rochester Conference Series, Vol. 5.
Maddala, G. S. (1979), *Econometrics* McGraw-Hill, New York.
McCallum, B. T. (1979), On the observational inequivalence of classical and Keynesian models, *Journal of Political Economy*, 87, April, 393–402.
—— (1980), Rational expectations and macroeconomic stabilization policy, *Journal of Money Credit and Banking*, Part 2, November, 716–46.
Phelps, E. S. and J. B. Taylor (1977), Stabilising powers of monetary policy under rational expectations, *Journal of Political Economy*, 84, June, 631–40.
Sargent, T. J. (1976), 'The observational equivalence of natural and unnatural rate theories of macroeconomics', *Journal of Political Economy*, 84, June, 631–40.
Schmidt, P. (1976), *Econometrics*, Marcel Dekker, New York.
Sims, C. A. (1980), Macroeconomics and reality, *Econometria*, 48, January, 1–48.
Taylor, J. B. (1979), Staggered wage setting in a macro model, *American Economic Review*, 69, Papers and Proceedings, May, 108–113.
Tobin, J. (1965), Money and economic growth, *Econometrica*, 33, October, 671–84.
Turnovsky S. J. (1980), The choice of monetary instruments under alternative forms of price expectations, Manchester School, March, 39–62.
Wallis, K. F. (1980), Econometric implications of the rational expectations hypothesis, *Econometrica*, 48, January, 49–73.
Weiss, L. (1980), The role for active monetary policy in a rational expectations model, *Journal of Political Economy*, 88, April, 221–33.

Chapter 7

Granger-causality and policy effectiveness

I Introduction

It is generally recognized that, if a set of monetary and fiscal policy variables Granger-cause[1] real economic variables, this does not imply that alternative deterministic rules for determining the values of these policy instruments will alter the joint density function of the real variables.[2] It has, however, also been asserted that (letting X denote a (suitably restricted) vector of 'real' economic aggregates, g a list of monetary and fiscal policy variables and E the mathematical expectation operator), 'a model *in general* will have classical policy implications if it satisfies

$$E(X_t \mid X_{t-1}, X_{t-2}, \ldots; g_{t-1}, g_{t-2}, \ldots) = E(X_t \mid X_{t-1}, X_{t-2}, \ldots)$$

so that as a block the aggregate real variables X are statistically exogenous with respect to (not caused by, in Granger's sense) the variables in g.' (Sargent [1976a, p. 221], my italics). Cuddington [1980, p. 539] also argues that

> various classical policy implications emerge from models in which the conditional expectations of all real variables are invariant with respect to government policy instruments. This is equivalent to the statistical hypothesis that the simultaneously determined variables of the economic model are jointly exogenous with respect to all policy variables.

Classical policy implications here means independence of the conditional means of real economic variables of the feedback rules for the monetary and fiscal policy variables, or more loosely that 'government manipulations of monetary and fiscal policy variables have no predictable effects on unemployment, output or the interest rate and hence are useless for pursuing counter-cyclical policy' (Sargent [1976a, p. 208]). In other papers (e.g. Sargent, [1976b]), Sargent gives a correct diagnosis of the lack of any necessary connection between Granger-causality and policy effectiveness or neutrality.

In Sargent [1976a] it is also recognized that 'it is possible to concoct nonclassical systems that will mimic the classical characteristics that my tests look for' [p. 222] and an example of such a system is given. The comment about this example that, 'while the tests might be fooled by such a structure, that structure itself seems unlikely to me' (Sargent, [1976a, p. 223]) reinforces the earlier statement that models in which monetary and fiscal policy variables fail to Granger-cause real economic aggregates will *in general* have classical policy implications.

In this paper it is shown that Granger-causality is unnecessary for policy effectiveness, insufficiency having been established already by Sargent. Warnings about the pitfalls in Granger-causality tests are contained in a number of papers, notably Jacobs, Leamer and Ward [1979], Sims [1977] and Zellner [1979]. This paper goes beyond these earlier contributions by demonstrating that no inferences about policy ineffectiveness can be drawn from the results of Granger-causality tests. It can be viewed as an investigation of the statement by Sims that 'The fact that policy variables are always in one sense causally prior to the other variables in a model is sometimes assumed to make it likely that they are causally prior (i.e. exogenous) in data used for estimation' (Sims [1979, pp. 105–106]).[3] It therefore addresses an issue very similar to the one that concerned Tobin in his paper 'Money and Income: *Post Hoc Ergo Propter Hoc*?' (Tobin, [1970]), and can indeed be viewed as a stochastic, rational expectations extension of Tobin's analysis.

Most of the statistical literature on Granger-causality has dealt with the relationship between Granger-causality and econometric exogeneity – independence of the regressors and the current and future values of the disturbances (predeterminedness), or independence of the regressors and current, past and future values of the disturbances (strict exogeneity). For example, Sims [1972] has shown that failure of y to Granger-cause x is a necessary, but not a sufficient, condition for x to be strictly exogenous. This is not what this chapter is concerned with. Indeed, a very similar paper could have been written on the absence of any systematic relationship between (strict) econometric exogeneity and policy effectiveness.

Section I deals with the case of an optimizing controller and a fairly general linear model which permits forward-looking rational expectations. Whether the controller pursues an optimal (possibly time-inconsistent) or a time-consistent (possibly non-optimal) policy, the instruments do not Granger-cause the endogenous variables while the endogenous variables, in general, do Granger-cause the policy instruments. The instruments fail to Granger-cause the endogenous variables even though changing the policy rule may alter any of the conditional and asymptotic moments of the joint distribution function of the endogenous variables.

Section II considers the policy effectiveness information content of Granger-causality tests for two important kinds of *ad hoc* policy rules:

automatic stabilizers or instantaneous feedback rules, and *ad hoc* lagged feedback rules.

For important classes of policy rules, Granger-causality tests fail to reveal whether or not 'the conditional expectations of all real variables are invariant with respect to government policy instruments'. If the value of a vector of current endogenous variables is a function of the (expected) current or lagged instruments, and if the (expected) instruments are functions of current or lagged values of the endogenous variables, then the instruments will not Granger-cause the endogenous variables even though changing the policy rule will alter the dependence of the endogenous variables on their own lagged values and on the exogenous variables.

A fortiori, Granger-causality tests tend to be uninformative about the invariance of the second or higher moments of the distributions of real variables with respect to policy instruments. Stabilization policy tends to be concerned primarily with the second moments of such variables as output, employment and inflation.[4] The importance of these straightforward propositions lies in the fact that many interesting policy rules have the property that the instruments are functions (often exact, i.e. non-stochastic) of current and lagged values of the endogenous variables.

Before establishing the second half of the two-way non-implication between Granger-causality and policy effectiveness, formal definitions are given of Granger-causality and 'structural invariance'.

In a linear Gaussian setting, a vector of random variables x fails to Granger-cause another vector y if, in a least squares regression of y on its own past values and on past values of x, the regression coefficients on past values of x are all equal to (insignificantly different from) zero.

To permit consideration of the more general definition of Granger-causality proposed, e.g. in Granger [1980], the causality concept just referred to will be called causality *in mean*. Formally:

$$\text{For any vector } x_t \text{, let } X^t \equiv \{x_s,\ s < t\}.$$

Definition 1. x_t is said to Granger-cause y_t in mean if

$$E(y_t \mid Y^t, X^t) \not\equiv E(y_t \mid Y^t).$$

x_t fails to Granger-cause y_t in mean if (Granger [1980, p. 337])

$$E(y_t \mid Y^t, X^t) \equiv E(y_t \mid Y^t).$$

A stronger form of Granger-causality refers to the entire conditional distribution of random variables instead of merely their conditional means. For any vector x let $\tilde{F}(x_t \mid z_t)$ denote the conditional distribution function of x_t given z_t.

Definition 2. x_t is said to Granger-cause y_t if

$$\tilde{F}(y_t \mid Y^t, X^t) \not\equiv \tilde{F}(y_t \mid Y^t).$$

x_t fails to Granger-cause y_t if (Granger [1980] pp. 336–337)

$$\tilde{F}(y_t \mid Y^t, X^t) \equiv \tilde{F}(y_t \mid Y^t).$$

The concept of invariance or structural invariance, which is the relevant one for the issue of policy effectiveness, is defined in Buiter [1982].

Definition 3. y_t is said to be structurally invariant *in mean* with respect to x_t if changes in the deterministic components of the stochastic process governing x_t do not alter the mean of y_t.[5]

A stronger invariance property is:

Definition 4. y_t is said to be structurally invariant *in distribution* with respect to x_t if changes in the deterministic components of the stochastic process governing x_t do not alter the distribution of y_t.

Note that our concept of ineffectiveness, neutrality or structural invariance relates to a restricted class of changes in the distribution function of the policy instruments. This definition essentially restricts the distribution changes to changes in the deterministic coefficients of the linear feedback rules characterizing the behaviour of the policy instruments. Such alterations in the distribution function of the policy instruments as changes in the variance-covariance matrix of the innovations in the policy instrument processes are ruled out; they would virtually always affect the second and higher movements of the distribution function of real economic variables, but have little bearing on the policy effectiveness debate.

II Granger-causality and policy effectiveness with an optimizing controller

As has already been recognized by Sims [1972], policy instruments must always fail to Granger-cause target variables, whether nominal or real, if the controller is optimizing a quadratic objective functional subject to the constraints of a linear model. Sims referred to the case where the information lag in the control process is no more than one period. This result remains valid in rational expectations models. Consider the linear-quadratic optimal control problem of equations (1) and (2):

$$\min_{\{x_t\}} E\left\{\sum_{t=1}^{T}(y_t - a_t)'K_t(y_t - a_t) \mid \Omega_1\right\} \tag{1}$$

subject to

$$y_t = A_1 y_{t-1} + B_1 E(y_{t+1} \mid \Omega_{t-1}) + B_2 E(y_t \mid \Omega_{t-1}) + C_1 x_t + \bar{b}_t + u_t \tag{2}$$

where y_t is a vector of state, target or endogenous variables, a_t is a vector of desired values for y_t and K_t is a symmetric positive semi-definite matrix; x_t is a vector of instruments, $\bar{b}_t$ a vector of exogenous variables, and u_t a white noise disturbance vector with $E(u_t u_t') = \Sigma_u$; A_1, B_1, B_2 and

C_1 are constant matrices. The information set Ω_τ conditioning expectations formed in period τ contains the true structures of the models, and $y_{\tau-i}$, $x_{\tau-i}$, $\bar{b}_{\tau-i}$, $i \geq 0$.[6]

By taking expectations of both sides of (2) conditional on Ω_{t-1}, we can eliminate $E(y_t | \Omega_{t-1})$. Equation (2) becomes

$$y_t = Ay_{t-1} + BE(y_{t+1} | \Omega_{t-1}) + CE(x_t | \Omega_{t-1}) + E(b_t | \Omega_{t-1}) + \eta_t \quad (3)$$

where

$$A = (I - B_2)^{-1}A_1, \qquad B = (I - B_2)^{-1}B_1, \qquad C = (I - B_2)^{-1}C_1 \quad (4a)$$
$$b_t = (I - B_2)^{-1}\bar{b}_t$$

and

$$\eta_t = C_1\{x_t - E(x_t | \Omega_{t-1})\} + \{\bar{b}_t - E(\bar{b}_t | \Omega_{t-1})\} + u_t. \quad (4b)$$

Note that η_t will also be white noise. Assume b_t is non-stochastic.

Taking $E(y_{t+1} | \Omega_{t-1})$ in (3) as given when x_t is set in period t, we can apply dynamic programming as in Chow (1980) to find the *time-consistent* feedback control rule:

$$x_t = G_{1t}E(y_{t+1} | \Omega_{t-1}) + G_{2t}y_{t-1} + g_t. \quad (5)$$

where G_{1t}, G_{2t} and g_t are non-stochastic functions of A, B, C and $\{b_\tau, a_\tau, K_\tau; \tau \geq t\}$. Note that (5) implies that $x_t = E(x_t | \Omega_{t-1})$.

If $a_t = a$, $K_t = \text{k}$ and $b_t = b$ for all t, then, under conditions given in Chow [1975, pp. 170–172], G_{1t}, G_{2t} and g_t may become time-invariant as $T \to \infty$.[7] The behaviour of the covariance-stationary system is governed by

$$y_t = R_1E(y_{t+1} | \Omega_{t-1}) + R_2y_{t-1} + r + \eta_t \quad (6)$$

where $R_1 = B + CG_1$, $R_2 = A + CG_2$, and $r = b + Cg$.

If (6) is covariance-stationary there exists a representation

$$y_t = Qy_{t-1} + q + \eta_t \quad (7)$$

where the roots of Q all have modulus less than one and

$$Q = (I - R_1Q)^{-1}R_2$$
$$q = \{I - R_1(Q + I)\}^{-1}r.$$

Since $E(y_{t+1} | \Omega_{t-1}) = Q^2y_{t-1} + (Q + I)q$, the behaviour of the instrument vector x under optimal control is governed by

$$x_t = (G_1Q^2 + G_2)y_{t-1} + G_1(Q + I)q + g. \quad (8)$$

Since x_t is an exact (non-stochastic) function of y_{t-1}, it is clear that $\tilde{F}(y_t | Y^t) \equiv \tilde{F}(y_t | Y^t, X^t)$: when the controller behaves in a time-consistent manner, the instruments will never Granger-cause the state variables. The state variables will, however, in general Granger-cause the instruments, since

$$E(x_t \mid X^t) = (G_1Q^2 + G_2)Qy_{t-2} + [G_1\{Q(Q + I) + I\} + G_2]q + g$$

and

$$E(x_t \mid X^t, Y^t) = (G_1Q^2 + G_2)Qy_{t-2} + [G_1\{Q(Q + I) + I\} + G_2]q + g + (G_1Q^2 + G_2)\eta_{t-1} = x_t.$$

Thus, unless $G_1Q^2 + G_2 = 0$, the state variables, y, Granger-cause the instruments, x.

If, instead of pursuing *time-consistent* policies, the authorities pursue optimal but possibly time-inconsistent policies, Granger-causality tests continue to be uninformative as regards the presence or absence of policy effectiveness. When optimal policies are pursued, the controller does not take $E(y_{t+1} \mid \Omega_{t-1})$ as given when choosing x_t, but allows for the effect of x_t on $E(y_{t+I} \mid \Omega_{t-1})$ through the effect of x_t on $E(x_t \mid \Omega_{t-1})$ (see Buiter [1981a,b; 1983b]). As in the case of *time-consistent* policies, the optimal policy will be a non-stochastic linear feedback rule:

$$x_t = F_t y_{t-1} + f_t.$$

If the system can be made covariance-stationary by using such a rule (virtually a necessary condition for econometric estimation and hypothesis testing), the instruments will be governed by

$$x_t = Fy_{t-1} + f. \tag{9}$$

Combining (9) and (3) with $b_t = b$, we get

$$y_t = (A + CF)y_{t-1} + BE(y_{t+1} \mid \Omega_{t-1}) + Cf + b + \eta_t.$$

If this is covariance-stationary there exists a representation

$$y_t = \bar{Q}y_{t-1} + \bar{q} + \eta_t \tag{10}$$

with

$$\bar{Q} = (I - B\bar{Q})^{-1}(A + CF) \tag{11a}$$

$$\bar{q} = \{I - B(\bar{Q} + I)\}^{-1}(Cf + b) \tag{11b}$$

Again, x_t will not Granger-cause y_t in mean or in distribution while, in general, y_t will Granger-cause x_t.

Whether we consider (7) and (8) or (9) and (10), the Granger-causality tests reveal nothing about policy effectiveness. It can be shown for the model of equations (2) or (3) that, unless $C = O$, the expected instruments x_t will affect the expectation of y_t. Consider again the model of equation (2) or (3) with, for simplicity, $b_t = b$ for all t. Solving for y_t as a function of current and anticipated future values of x_t, we obtain

$$y_t = \Pi_1 y_{t-1} + \Pi_2 b + \sum_{i=0}^{\infty} \Lambda_i E(x_{t+i} \mid \Omega_{t-1}) + C_1\{x_t - E(x_t \mid \Omega_{t-1})\} + u_t \tag{12}$$

where

$$\Pi_1 = A + B\Pi_1^2 \tag{13a}$$

$$\Pi_2 = B(\Pi_1 + I)\Pi_2 + I \tag{13b}$$

$$\Lambda_0 = C + B\Pi_1\Lambda_0 \tag{13c}$$

$$\Lambda_i = B(\Pi_1\Lambda_i + \Lambda_{i-1}), \qquad i \geq 1. \tag{13d}$$

Provided $C \neq O$, i.e. provided $(I - B_2)^{-1}C_1 \neq O$, anticipated current and future values of x will affect both the conditional first moment of y, $E(y_t \mid \Omega_{t-1})$, and the asymptotic or unconditional first moment.

'Policy ineffectiveness' emerges only if $C = O$. If in addition $C_1 \neq 0$ we are in a world where anticipated policy actions do not affect any moment of the distribution function of y_t but unanticipated policy actions can affect the second and higher moments of this distribution.

Except in some non-co-operative games in which randomized strategies may be optimal, rational expected utility-maximizing or expected loss-minimizing policy-makers will always set x_t (time-consistently or optimally) as a non-stochastic function of the information available at the time the instrument values have to be assigned. In our set-up y_{t-1} is a sufficient statistic for all relevant information available to the policy-maker (assuming knowledge of the structure of the model and of $\bar{b}$ or b).

Note that, if there is a longer information lag in the control process, the results of this section remain valid. Assume, for example that when the controller chooses x_t he knows only y_{t-2} (as well as equation (2) or (3)). For simplicity let $\bar{b}_t = \bar{b}$. A time-invariant optimal or time-consistent policy rule will now take the form

$$x_t = \tilde{F}y_{t-2} + \tilde{f} \tag{14}$$

where $\tilde{F}$ and $\tilde{f}$ are non-stochastic.

Substituting (14) into (2) or (3), the behaviour of the system under optimal or time-consistent control will be governed by an equation of the form

$$y_t = \Pi_1 y_{t-1} + \Pi_2 y_{t-2} + \Pi_3(C_1 f + \bar{b}) + u_t \tag{15}$$

where

$$\Pi_1 = (I - B_2)^{-1}\{A_1 + B_1(\Pi_1^2 + \Pi_2)\},$$

$$\Pi_2 = (I - B_2)^{-1}(C_1 F + B_1\Pi_1\Pi_2)$$

and

$$\Pi_3 = (I - B_2)^{-1}\{I + B_1(\Pi_1 + I)\Pi_3\}.$$

Clearly, x will fail to Granger-cause y in mean and distribution while y, in general, Granger-causes x.

III Granger-causality and policy effectiveness with ad hoc policy rules

Two kinds of *ad hoc* policy rules will be considered. The first is the instantaneous feedback rule or automatic stabilizer; the second, the lagged feedback rule.

Granger-causality and automatic stabilizers

Granger-causality tests convey no information about the presence or absence of policy effectiveness for a set of instruments if during the sample period the instruments have been used as *automatic stabilizers*, that is, if they were governed by an instantaneous feedback rule relating the current values of the policy instruments to *current* endogenous variables. The discussion of automatic stabilizers is usually restricted to fiscal policy: 'features of the tax structure that make tax liabilities respond automatically to current economic conditions' (McCallum and Whitaker, [1979, p. 172]). McCallum and Whitaker [1979] rationalize the stabilizing potential of automatic stabilizers through the *decentralized* setting of the control variables that they permit. Aggregative information on GDP and the general price level is assumed to be available only with a lag. Transfer payments such as unemployment benefits are, however, paid out according to fixed rules on a decentralized basis, when claims are made by the individual unemployed workers. This permits an immediate response to changing economic conditions without any need to wait for aggregate output and unemployment data to become available. There are many problems associated with this interpretation. One is that, with efficient capital markets, the *timing* of the unemployment benefits would be of no concern. Any rule for delayed payments of the benefits that leaves the real present value of these benefits unchanged would have the same effect on behaviour. Unspecified capital market imperfections must therefore play a role if automatic stabilizers have a stabilizing potential that is not present with feedback rules, which make current policy instrument values functions only of lagged information. As a satisfactory treatment of these issues would require a full paper in its own right, I shall say no more about them here.

If automatic decentralized fiscal stabilizers exist, so, in principle, do monetary stabilizers. Those in charge of the local unemployment registers could be instructed to perform an open-market purchase of government bonds of a given amount for every worker joining the unemployment register, and an open-market sale for every notified vacancy.[8]

Consider the general rational expectations model of equation (2) or (3)) with $\bar{b}_t = \bar{b}$ for simplicity. The simultaneous feedback rule is given by

$$x_t = Ry_t + \varepsilon_t$$

ε_t represents an *ad hoc* random element in the policy rule. It is a white noise disturbance vector with $E(\varepsilon_t \varepsilon_t') = \Sigma_\varepsilon$.
With this automatic stabilizer the reduced form solution for y_t is.

$$y_t = \Pi_1 y_{t-1} + \Pi_2 \bar{b} + \Pi_3(u_t + C_1 \varepsilon_t) \tag{16a}$$

with

$$\Pi_1 = (I - C_1 R)^{-1}\{A_1 + (B_1 \Pi_1 + B_2)\Pi_1\} \tag{16b}$$

$$\Pi_2 = (I - C_1 R)^{-1}\{B_1(\Pi_1 + I)\Pi_2 + B_2 \Pi_2 + I\} \tag{16c}$$

$$\Pi_3 = (I - C_1 R)^{-1}. \tag{16d}$$

Clearly, the instruments do not Granger-cause endogenous variables (in mean or in distribution): $\tilde{F}(y_t \mid Y^t) \equiv \tilde{F}(y_t \mid Y^t, X^t)$. If $\Sigma_\varepsilon = 0$, i.e. if the automatic stabilizer is non-stochastic, y_t also fails to Granger-cause x_t; the endogenous variables and the instruments are merely linear transformations of each other. If $\Sigma_\varepsilon \neq 0$, y_t will, in general, Granger-cause x_t. For example,

$$E(x_t \mid X^t, Y^t) = R\Pi_1 y_{t-1} + R\Pi_2 \bar{b} \not\equiv E(x_t \mid X^t).$$

Note that the conditional and unconditonal second moments of y will be functions of the parameters of the automatic stabilizer rule R, if $C_1 \neq 0$. The conditional and unconditional first moments of y will be functions of R provided $\partial\Pi_1/\partial R$ and $\partial\Pi_2/\partial R$ are not both equal to zero. Changing the nature of the policy rule to, e.g. a fixed, open-loop rule or to a lagged feedback rule will in general alter the first and higher moments of y. Regardless of its capacity for influencing the distribution function of y, x will fail to Granger-cause y if during the sample period it has been used as an automatic stabilizer.

Granger-causality and ad hoc *lagged feedback rules*
It is obvious that any *ad hoc* non-stochastic lagged feedback rule

$$x_t = \sum_{i=1}^{N} R_i y_{t-i} + r_t$$

where r_t is the non-stochastic, open-loop, component of the policy rule, will, when applied to the model of equations (2) or (3), result in the policy instruments failing to Granger-cause the endogenous variables 'in distribution'. Depending on the precise structure of the model, changes in the R_i may affect any of the conditional or asymptotic moments of y_t and changes in the non-stochastic open-loop component r_t may affect the conditional or asymptotic first moments.

Consider instead the stochastic lagged feedback rule:

$$x_t = Ry_{t-1} + \varepsilon_t \tag{17}$$

where ε_t is the vector of innovations in the stochastic process governing the instruments. ε_t is assumed to be orthogonal to Ω_{t-1}. Substituting (17) into (2) with $\bar{b}_t = \bar{b}$, and eliminating $E(y_t | \Omega_{t-1})$, we obtain

$$y_t = (I - B_2)^{-1}(A_1 + C_1R)y_{t-1} + (I - B_2)^{-1}B_1E(y_{t+1} | \Omega_{t-1}) + (I - B_2)^{-1}\bar{b} + C_1\varepsilon_t + u_t.$$

Provided the system is covariance-stationary, it will have a first-order representation.

$$y_t = \Pi_1 y_{t-1} + \Pi_2 \bar{b} + C_1\varepsilon_t + u_t. \tag{18}$$

Π_1 and Π_2 are constant matrices to be determined, e.g. through the method of undetermined coefficients.

Note that x will again fail to Granger-cause y (in mean and in distribution) while y will Granger-cause x. This result stands if (17) is replaced by the more general process

$$x_t = \sum_{i=1}^{N} R_i y_{t-1} + \varepsilon_t.$$

Finally, consider the class of rational expectations models in which anticipated policy has no effect on the first moments of real variables while their second moments are functions of the parameters of the instrument feedback rules. Such stabilization policy effectiveness comes about through anticipations of future policy actions, which change the informational content of observed endogenous variables such as prices, etc. (Turnovsky [1980]; Weiss [1980]; Buiter [1980, 1981a,b, 1983a,b]; King [1982]).

In such models, the semi-reduced form for the endogenous variables (after substituting out current and past expectations of future endogenous variables) has the following form, using the notation of equation (2):

$$y_t = \Pi_1 y_{t-1} + \Pi_2 \bar{b} + \Pi_3 u_t + \Lambda_0\{x_t - E(x_t | \Omega_{t-1})\} + \sum_{t=1}^{\infty} \Lambda_i\{E(x_{t+i} | \Omega_t) - E(x_{t+i} | \Omega_{t-1})\}. \tag{19}$$

The current value of y is a function of the revision, between periods $t - 1$ and t, in the expectations of all future values of the instruments.

Let the instrument vector x_t be governed by any feedback rule such as

$$x_t = \sum_{i=1}^{M} F_i y_{t-i} + \sum_{i=1}^{M} G_i x_{t-1} + \varepsilon_t \tag{20}$$

where ε_t is a white noise disturbance vector. From (20), $x_t - E(x_t | \Omega_{t-1}) = \varepsilon_t$. $E(x_{t+i} | \Omega_t) - E(x_{t+i} | \Omega_{t-1})$ for $i > 1$ can only be a function of the new information (the news) that accrued between periods $t - 1$ and t, that is, of u_t and ε_t. We can therefore write the last term of the right-hand side of (19) as $K_1 u_t + K_2 \varepsilon_t$ where K_1 and K_2 are functions of the policy parameters F_i and G_i. Rewrite (19) as

$$y_t = \Pi_1 y_{t-1} + \Pi_2 \bar{b} + (\Pi_3 + K_1)u_t + (\Lambda_0 + K_2)\varepsilon_t. \quad (21)$$

The potential scope for stabilization policy in these models is apparent now. In certain models (Buiter, 1980, 1981b, 1983a) it is possible to choose the policy parameters in such a way that $\Pi_3 = -K_1$ and $\Lambda_0 = -K_2$; all randomness in y_t can be eliminated. More generally, the conditional and asymptotic second moments of y will be functions of the parameters of the feedback rule. It is, however, clear from (20) and (21) that x does not Granger-cause y in mean or in distribution. Specifically

$$E(y_t \mid Y^t) = \Pi_1 y_{t-1} + \Pi_2 \bar{b} = E(y_t \mid Y^t, X^t)$$

$$\begin{aligned} &E[\{y_t - E(y_t \mid Y^t)\}\{y_t - E(y_t \mid Y^t)\}' \mid Y^t] \\ &\quad = (\Pi_3 + \Omega_1)\Sigma_u(\Pi_3 + \Omega_1)' + (\Lambda_0 + \Omega_2)\Sigma_\varepsilon(\Lambda_0 + \Omega_2)' \\ &\quad = E[\{y_t - E(y_t \mid Y^t, X^t)\}\{y_t - E(y_t \mid Y^t, X^t)\}' \mid Y^t, X^t].^9 \end{aligned}$$

IV Conclusion

The purpose of this chapter has been to reject the notion that any inferences about policy effectiveness, structural invariance or the ability of instruments to influence endogenous variables in a systematic way can be drawn from the results of Granger-causality tests. It is not necessary to 'concoct' unlikely structures in order to support the proposition that there is two way non-implication between Granger non-causality and structural invariance. Just as Sargent [1976a, p. 222] cautioned against the Type I error of inferring non-invariance from Granger-causality, so this paper warns against the Type II error of inferring structural invariance from Granger non-causality.

It is not difficult to come up with examples in which failure of instruments to Granger-cause endogenous variables coincides with ineffectiveness of the instruments with respect to the endogenous variables. Such findings are, however, merely accidental, like bagging the vicar at a grouse-shoot. Granger-causality tests are tests of 'incremental predictive content' (Schwert [1979]). They are one among a number of statistical exogeneity tests (see Engle, Hendry and Richard [1983]) and play an important role in the estimation and testing of data-coherent econometric models. They are not informative as to the presence or absence of structural invariance in general and policy effectiveness in particular. Tests for policy effectiveness require the presence of changes in the generating process of the policy instruments, either in the sample or in the forecast periods, in order to ascertain whether such changes are associated with changes in the distribution functions of the endogenous variables under consideration.

Notes

Originally published in *Economica*, 51, 1984, pp. 151–62.

1 One set of variables, x, is said to Granger-cause another set, y, if adding past values of x in a regression equation for predicting y, which already includes all past values of y as regressors, improves the predictive power of the equation in the sense that it reduces the mean squared forecast error (e.g. Hsaio [1979]). A more formal definition is given below.

2 An example of Sargent [1976a, p. 222] suffices to make this point. Let V_t be the unemployment rate and m_t the logarithm of the nominal money stock

$$V_t = \lambda V_{t-1} + \beta_0\{m_t - E(m_t \mid I_{t-1})\} + \beta_1\{m_{t-1} - E(m_{t-1} \mid I_{t-2})\} + u_t$$

$$m_t = \sum_{i=1}^{n} \delta_i m_{t-i} + \varepsilon_t.$$

where ε_t and u_t are Gaussian random disturbances, E is the expectation operator and I_t the information set in period t conditioning expectations formed in period t. It is easily seen that

$$E(V_t \mid V_{t-1}, V_{t-2}, \ldots; m_{t-1}, m_{t-2}, \ldots) = \lambda V_{t-1} + \beta(m_{t-1} - \sum_{i=1}^{n} \delta_i m_{t-1-i}).$$

Therefore, m helps predict, or Granger-causes, V. However, deterministic feedback rules making m_t a linear function of I_{t-i}, $i > 0$, cannot affect the density function of V_t. Note that, if it is possible to relate m_t to I_t, such *instantaneous* feedback rules will affect the density function of V_t (see Section III).

3 Sims does not endorse the view he refers to.

4 An earlier version of this paper (Buiter [1982]) analyses the effect of monetary feedback rules on the second moment of output in a number of small rational expectations models and the inability of Granger-causality tests to detect such effects.

5 This can apply either to the conditional mean or to the unconditional, asymptotic, mean.

6 It is assumed that when x_t is set, the controller knows y_{t-1} and b_t but not u_t or y_t. Generalizations giving the controller more information do not alter the conclusions.

7 Even if G_{1t} and G_{2t} are time-invariant but g_t changes over time in response to variations in b_t, the system under control may remain covariance-stationary. If the system cannot be made covariance-stationary, most of our statistical and econometric techniques become inapplicable.

8 I owe this idea to John Flemming.

9 $\Sigma_u = E(u_t u_t')$; $\Sigma_\varepsilon = E(\varepsilon_t \varepsilon_t')$; for simplicity u and ε are assumed to be contemporaneously uncorrelated.

References

Buiter, W. H. (1980), Monetary, financial and fiscal policies under rational expectations. *IMF Staff Papers*, 27, 785–813.

—— (1981a), The role of economic policy after the 'New Classical Macroeconomics. In D. Currie and D. A. Peel (eds.), *Contemporary Economic Analysis*, Vol. IV. London: Croom-Helm.

—— (1981b), The superiority of contingent rules over fixed rules in models with rational expectations. *Economic Journal*, 91, 647–70.

—— (1982), Granger-causality and stabilization policy. Centre for Labour Economics, Discussion Paper No. 128, mimeo.

—— (1983a), Real effects of anticipated and unanticipated monetary growth: some problems of estimation and hypothesis testing. *Journal of Monetary Economics*, 11, 207–24.

—— (1983b), Expectations and control theory. *Economie Appliquée*, 36, 129–56.

Chow, G. C. (1975), *Analysis and Control of Dynamic Economic Systems*. New York: John Wiley.

—— (1980), Econometric policy evaluation and optimization under rational expectations. *Journal of Economic Dynamics and Control*, 2, 47–59.

Cuddington, J. T. (1980), Simultaneous-equations tests of the natural rate and other classical hypotheses. *Journal of Political Economy*, 88, 539–47.

Engle, R. F., Hendry, D. F. and Richard, J. F. (1983), Exogeneity. *Econometrica*, 51, 277–304.

Granger, C. W. J. (1980), Testing for causality: a personal viewpoint. *Journal of Economic Dynamics and Control*, 2, 329–52.

Hsiao, C. (1979), Causality tests in econometrics. *Journal of Economic Dynamics and Control*, 1, 321–46.

Jacobs, R. L., Leamer, E. E. and Ward, M. P. (1979), Difficulties with Testing for Causation. *Economic Inquiry*, 17, 401–13.

King, R. G. (1982), Monetary policy and the information content of prices. *Journal of Political Economy*, 90, 247–79.

McCallum, B. T. and Whitaker, J. K. (1979), The effectiveness of fiscal feedback rules and automatic stabilizers under rational expectations. *Journal of Monetary Economics*, 5, 171–86.

Sargent, T. J. (1976a), A classical macroeconomic model for the United States. *Journal of Political Economy*, 84, 207–37.

—— (1976b), The observational equivalence of natural and unnatural rate theories of macroeconomics. *Journal of Political Economy*, 84, 631–40.

Schwert, G. W. (1979), Tests of causality. The message in the innovations. In K. Brunner and A. H. Meltzer (eds.), *Three Aspects of Policy and Policy Making: Knowledge, Data and Institutions*. Amsterdam: North-Holland, 55–96.

Sims, C. A. (1972), Money, income and causality. *American Economic Review*, 62, 540–42.

—— (1977), Exogeneity and causal ordering in macroeconomic models. In C. A. Sims (ed.), *New Methods in Business Cycle Research*. Minneapolis: Federal Reserve Bank of Minneapolis.

—— (1979), A comment on the papers by Zellner and Schwert. In K. Brunner and A. H. Meltzer (eds.), *Three Aspects of Policy and Policy Making: Knowledge, Data and Institutions*. Amsterdam: North-Holland.

Tobin, J. (1970), Money and income: *post hoc ergo propter hoc*? *Quarterly Journal of Economics*, 84, 301–17.

Turnovsky, S. J. (1980), The choice of monetary instruments under alternative forms of price expectations. *Manchester School*, 48, 39–62.

Weiss L. (1980), The role for active monetary policy in a rational expectations model. *Journal of Political Economy*, 88, 221–33.

Zellner, A. (1979), Causality and econometrics. In K. Brunner and A. H. Meltzer (eds.), *Three Aspects of Policy and Policy Making: Knowledge, Data and Institutions*. Amsterdam: North-Holland.

Part 3

Wage and price dynamics

Chapter 8

Staggered wage setting with real wage relativities: variations on a theme of Taylor

Written with Ian Jewitt

I Introduction

In a number of influential recent papers, Taylor [1979a,b; 1980a,b] has analysed the behaviour of an economy characterized by staggered overlapping wage contracts and rational expectations. His model has the 'Keynesian' feature that the second moment of the distribution function of real output is not invariant under changes in the deterministic (and known) components of monetary policy rules. The reason for this is the inertia in the money wage process induced by the staggered multi-period contracts and the assumption that the wage payments due in any given period under the contract are not 'indexed', that is not made contingent on the actually realized values of such nominal variables as the general price level. We retain the crucial assumption of multi-period (staggered) non-contingent contracts but wish to examine the consequences of altering Taylor's assumption that wage bargainers are influenced by relative money wages rather than relative real wages. In Taylor's model money wage contracts are negotiated without reference to past, current and expected future prices. Our suggested modification that wage bargainers are influenced by relative real wages, which we consider somewhat more plausible, has some interesting implications for the empirical estimation of models with staggered wage contracts (see especially Taylor [1980b]).

Section II presents our general N-period overlapping staggered real wage model or relative real wage model (RRW) and contrasts it with Taylor's relative money wage model (RMW). One can distinguish three influences on the contract wage. These are the average price level expected to prevail over the contract, demand effects and the response of bargainers to relative (real or nominal) wages. Taylor's model contains the demand effect and the relative nominal wage effect. Section III analyses staggered real and money wage contracts without relative wage effects. One conclusion is that Taylor's RMW model is observationally equivalent to a staggered real wage model without relative wage effects. Section IV considers some empirical implications of the RRW model.

II A comparison of the general solution of Taylor's relative money wage model and the relative real wage model

Taylor's RMW model is presented in equations (1)–(4)

$$x_t = \sum_{s=1}^{N-1} d_{-s}\, x_{t-s} + \sum_{s=1}^{N-1} d_s\, \hat{x}_{t-1|t+s} + \frac{\gamma}{N} \sum_{s=0}^{N-1} \hat{y}_{t-1|t+s} + \varepsilon_t; \qquad \gamma > 0 \tag{1}$$

$$y_t + p_t = m_t + v_t \tag{2}$$

$$p_t = \frac{1}{N} \sum_{i=0}^{N-1} x_{t-i} \tag{3}$$

$$m_t = (1 - \beta)p_t \tag{4}$$

The logarithm of the money contract wage negotiated in period t is denoted by x_t. Wage contracts last N periods. A constant fraction $\frac{1}{N}$ of all firms and all workers settle in any given period. The contract wage is constant over the duration of the contract. We shall assume in this section, along with Taylor [1980a], that the weights on future and past contract wages are symmetric, linearly declining in s and sum to unity, i.e.

$$d_s = d_{-s} = b_s = [N(N-1)]^{-1}(N - s) \qquad s = 1, \ldots, N-1 \tag{5}$$

y_t, the log of real output, is also a measure of excess demand in the labour market, since the level of full employment output is assumed to be constant throughout. p_t and m_t are the logs of the price level and the nominal money stock respectively. The terms ε_t and v_t are white noise disturbances with zero means and a constant contemporaneous variance-covariance matrix. For any variable, z, say, $\hat{z}_{t-1|t+s}$ is the mathematical expectation of z_{t+s} conditional on the information available in period $t-1$. Equation (2) is a very simple aggregate demand equation.[1] Equation (3) specifies the current price level, p_t, as a proportional mark-up on the average of the contract wages in effect during period t. Equation (4) is an instantaneous monetary policy response function.[2]

In Taylor's own words, the two key assumptions of the RMW model are '(1) wage contracts are staggered, that is, not all wage decisions in the economy are made at the same time, and (2) when making wage decisions, firms (and unions) look at the wage rates which are set at other firms and which will be in effect during their contract period' (Taylor [1980a, p. 2]).

It is important to note that the second assumption refers to current multi-period *money* wage contract decisions that are made with reference to all other *money* wage contracts that will be in effect during the periods covered by the current contract. While currently contracting firms and unions may well be interested in their wages relative to those of firms and unions contracting at earlier and later dates, rational behaviour would seem to require that the relative real values of these contracts and not the relative money wages *per se* should be the proper focus of concern. It can therefore be argued that Taylor's RMW model does not isolate the implications of having multi-period non-contingent (i.e., open-loop) money wage contracts[3] from those of having a form of money illusion.

The RRW model modifies the wage setting process in the following way. The contract money wage of firms and unions settling in period t, x_t, is set to achieve a given expected (target) real wage over the duration of the contract. This expected target real wage depends on expected average excess demand during the contract interval and on the real wages that are expected to be achieved by other firms and unions whose contracts overlap with the period t contract. With N-period contracts, the current contract money wage is therefore directly dependent on current expectations of the price level during the current and the following N-1 periods. Indirectly, because of the dependence of the current contract wage on the expected real value of the contract wages with which it overlaps, the current contract wage will depend on current expectations of the price level during the next 2N-2 periods.

In general there are three kinds of arguments in the structural equation for the current contract wage. First, the price expectation effect, which reflects the influence of the average price level expected over the life of the contract. This effect is absent in the RMW model. Second, the relative wage effect, which can be in terms of either real or money wages. Finally, the demand effect, which represents the influence of the average level of excess demand in the labour market expected over the life of the contract.

Formally, the RRW model retains equations (2)–(5) but replaces (1) by

$$x_t - \frac{1}{N}\sum_{s=0}^{N-1}\hat{p}_{t-1|t+s} = \sum_{s=1}^{N-1} d_{-s}\left(x_{t-s} - \frac{1}{N}\sum_{j=0}^{N-1}\hat{p}_{t-1|t-s+j}\right) + \sum_{s=1}^{N-1} d_s\left(\hat{x}_{t-1|t+s} - \frac{1}{N}\sum_{j=0}^{N-1}\hat{p}_{t-1|t+s+j}\right) + \frac{\gamma}{N}\sum_{s=0}^{N-1}\hat{y}_{t-1|t+s} + \varepsilon_t \qquad (6)$$

Note that in (6) we specify the expected real contract wage represented by the money contract wage that is expected to be negotiated in period

Table 1 Real wage perceptions of firms and unions contracting during period t in the RRW model (solid rectangles) and the RMW model (dashed rectangles).

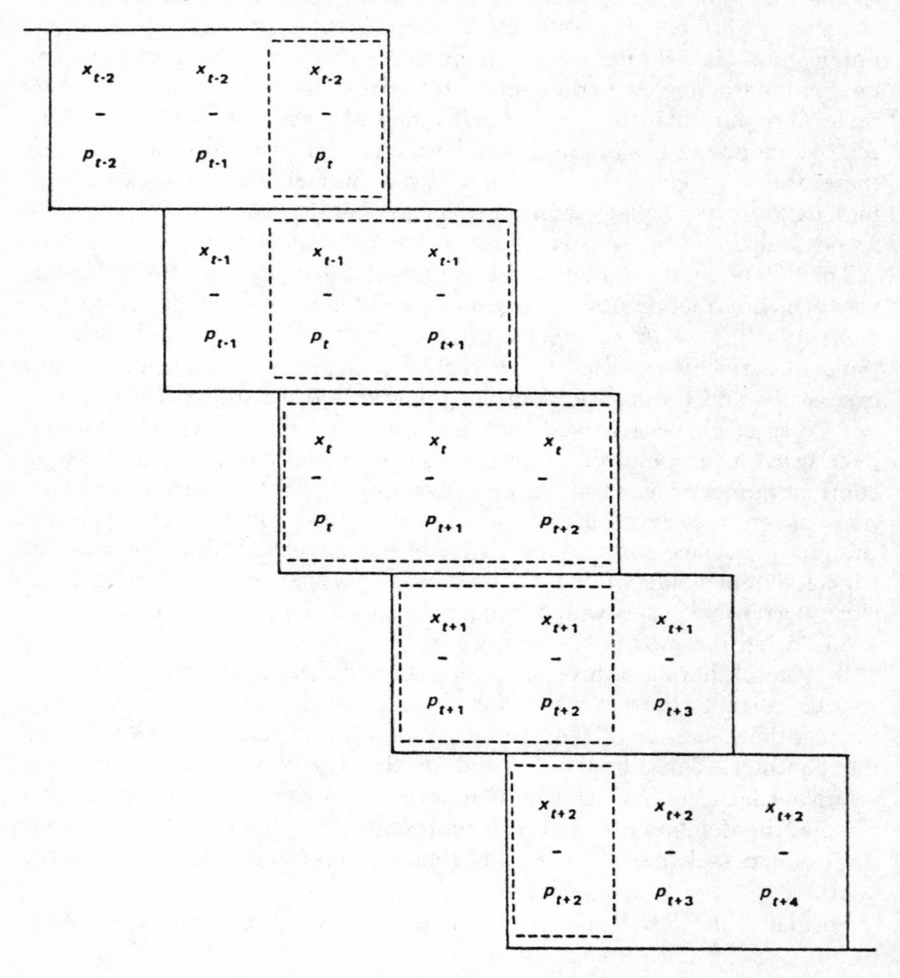

$t + s$ by $\hat{x}_{t-1|t+s} - \frac{1}{N}\sum_{j=0}^{N-1} \hat{p}_{t-1|t+s+j}$. This is the expectation of the average real wage negotiated by firms and unions contracting in period $t + s$ over the entire duration of that contract, i.e., from period $t + s$ to period $t + s + N - 1$. One interpretation of the Taylor RMW model is that firms and unions negotiate not on the basis of the actual and expected values of contracts established by other firms and unions but on the basis only of those real wages earned by other workers whilst the currently negotiated contract is in force. According to this interpretation, (6) should be replaced by

$$x_t - \frac{1}{N}\sum_{s=0}^{N-1} \hat{p}_{t-1|t+s} = \sum_{s=1}^{N-1} d_{-s}\left(x_{t-s} - \frac{1}{N-s}\sum_{j=s}^{N-1} \hat{p}_{t-1|t-s+j}\right)$$
$$+ \sum_{s=1}^{N-1} d_s\left(\hat{x}_{t-1|t+s} - \frac{1}{N-s}\sum_{j=0}^{N-1-s} \hat{p}_{t-1|t+s+j}\right)$$
$$+ \frac{\gamma}{N}\sum_{s=0}^{N-1} \hat{y}_{t-1|t+s} + \varepsilon_t \quad (7)$$

The two possible interpretations of relative real wages are illustrated in Table 1. In the model of equation (6) firms and unions contracting in period t interpret the real value of the contract formed in period $t+2$ as $\hat{x}_{t-1|t+2} - \frac{1}{3}(\hat{p}_{t-1|t+2} + \hat{p}_{t-1|t+3} + \hat{p}_{t-1|t+4})$. The model of (7), on the other hand, would substitute $\hat{x}_{t-1|t+2} - \hat{p}_{t-1|t+2}$ for this expression. It can be shown (and is apparent from Table 1) that

$$\frac{1}{N}\sum_{s=0}^{N-1} \hat{p}_{t-1|t+s} = \sum_{s=1}^{N-1} b_s(N-s)^{-1}\sum_{j=s}^{N-1} \hat{p}_{t-1|t-s+j}$$
$$+ \sum_{s=1}^{N-1} b_s(N-s)^{-1}\sum_{j=0}^{N-1-s} \hat{p}_{t-1|t+s+j}\text{[4]} \quad (8)$$

Therefore, if (5) holds, equation (7) is identically equal to equation (1), the relative money wage equation of the RMW model.

Taylor argues that firms and unions negotiating the current contract wage look at the contract wages which are set at other firms and will be in effect during their contract period. If overlapping contract wages matter because of what they imply for the real standards of living achieved by other workers and the real wage costs paid by other firms, the RRW model is clearly the appropriate one.

The solution method for the RRW model is similar to that for the RMW model (see Taylor [1980a]), although the algebra is somewhat more involved. From (3) we see that $\hat{p}_{t-1|t+k} = \frac{1}{N}\sum_{i=0}^{N-1} \hat{x}_{t-1|t+k+i}$ and from (2), (3) and (4) that $\hat{y}_{t-1|t+s} = -\frac{\beta}{N}\sum_{i=0}^{N-1} \hat{x}_{t-1|t+s-i}$. Substitute these two expressions into (6) to obtain:

$$x_t - \frac{1}{N^2}\sum_{j=0}^{N-1}\sum_{i=0}^{N-1} \hat{x}_{t-1|t+j-i} = \sum_{s=1}^{N-1} b_s\left(x_{t-s} - \frac{1}{N^2}\sum_{j=0}^{N-1}\sum_{i=0}^{N-1} \hat{x}_{t-1|t-s+j-i}\right)$$
$$+ \sum_{s=1}^{N-1} b_s\left(\hat{x}_{t-1|t+s} - \frac{1}{N^2}\sum_{j=0}^{N-1}\sum_{i=0}^{N-1} \hat{x}_{t-1|t+s+j-i}\right)$$
$$- \frac{\gamma\beta}{N^2}\sum_{s=0}^{N-1}\sum_{i=0}^{N-1} \hat{x}_{t-1|t+s-i} + \varepsilon_t \quad (9)$$

Taking expectations of (9) as of $t - 1$ and rearranging yields:

$$\hat{x}_{t-1|t} = \sum_{s=1}^{N-1} b_s \hat{x}_{t-1|t-s} + \sum_{s=1}^{N-1} b_s \hat{x}_{t-1|t+s} + \frac{(1 - \gamma\beta)}{N^2} \sum_{s=0}^{N-1} \sum_{i=0}^{N-1} \hat{x}_{t-1|t+s-i}$$
$$- \frac{1}{N^2} \sum_{s=1}^{N-1} b_s \sum_{j=0}^{N-1} \sum_{i=0}^{N-1} \hat{x}_{t-1|t-s+j-i} - \frac{1}{N^2} \sum_{s=1}^{N-1} b_s \sum_{j=0}^{N-1} \sum_{i=0}^{N-1} \hat{x}_{t-1|t+s+j-i} \tag{10}$$

Like Taylor we use the following identity:

$$\frac{1}{N^2} \sum_{s=0}^{N-1} \sum_{i=0}^{N-1} \hat{x}_{t-1|t+s-i} \equiv \left(\frac{N-1}{N}\right) \sum_{s=1}^{N-1} b_s \hat{x}_{t-1|t-s} + \left(\frac{N-1}{N}\right) \sum_{s=1}^{N-1} b_s \hat{x}_{t-1|t+s} \tag{11}$$

Equation (10) becomes:

$$\hat{x}_{t-1|t}\left(1 - \left(\frac{1-\beta\gamma}{N}\right)\right) = \left[1 + (1-\beta\gamma)\left(\frac{N-1}{N}\right) - \frac{1}{N}\right] \sum_{s=1}^{N-1} b_s \hat{x}_{t-1|t-s}$$
$$+ \left[1 + (1-\beta\gamma)\left(\frac{N-1}{N}\right) - \frac{1}{N}\right] \sum_{s=1}^{N-1} b_s \hat{x}_{t-1|t+s}$$
$$- \left(\frac{N-1}{N}\right) \sum_{s=1}^{N-1} \sum_{j=1}^{N-1} b_s b_j \hat{x}_{t-1|t-s+j}$$
$$- \left(\frac{N-1}{N}\right) \sum_{s=1}^{N-1} \sum_{j=1}^{N-1} b_s b_j \hat{x}_{t-1|t+s-j}$$
$$- \left(\frac{N-1}{N}\right) \sum_{s=1}^{N-1} \sum_{j=1}^{N-1} b_s b_j \hat{x}_{t-1|t-s-j}$$
$$- \left(\frac{N-1}{N}\right) \sum_{s=1}^{N-1} \sum_{j=1}^{N-1} b_s b_j \hat{x}_{t-1|t+s+j} \tag{12}$$

Equation (12) can be written as:

$$\sum_{s=1}^{2N-2} B_{-s} \hat{x}_{t-1|t-s} + B_0 \hat{x}_{t-1|t} + \sum_{s=1}^{2N-2} B_s \hat{x}_{t-1|t+s} = 0 \tag{13}$$

where, as we show in the appendix, the B_i are given by:

$$B_0 = (3N^2 - N - 1 + 3N\beta\gamma)/3N^2 \tag{14a}$$

$$B_s = B_{-s} = -\frac{N-1}{N}\left((2-\beta\gamma)b_s - \sum_{i=1}^{N-1-s} b_i\, b_{s+i} - \sum_{i=1}^{s-1} b_i\, b_{s-i}\right), \quad s = 1, \ldots, N-1 \tag{14b}$$

$$B_s = B_{-s} = \frac{N-1}{N}\left(\sum_{i=s-N+1}^{N-1} b_i\, b_{s-i}\right) \qquad s = N, \ldots, 2N-2 \tag{14c}$$

Using well-known formulae, the summations in (14b) and (14c) yield third-order polynomials in s. When the summations run from a larger to a smaller number in (14b) we take the terms to vanish.

The following points are worth noting. First, B_0 is always positive for positive $\beta\gamma$. This can be contrasted with Taylor's model. Second, in (14c) B_s is always positive and independent of $\beta\gamma$. Third, in (14b) B_s is a function of $\beta\gamma$; since the terms in the summation signs are all non-negative these B_s will all change sign for some sufficient large value of $\beta\gamma$, which will in general be different for different s.

Equation (13) can now be solved using the method presented in Taylor [1980a]. Let $L^s x_t \equiv x_{t-s}$ and define the polynomial $B(L) = \sum_{s=-(2N-2)}^{2N-2} B_s L^s$, where B_0 and $B_s = B_{-s}$, $s = 1, 2, \ldots, 2N-2$, are as in (14a–c). Equation (13) can now be rewritten as:

$$B(L)\hat{x}_{t-1|t} = 0 \tag{15}$$

Because of its symmetry $B(L)$ can be factored as in (16):

$$B(L) = \lambda A(L)\, A(L^{-1}) \tag{16}$$

where λ is a normalization constant and $A(L)$ is a polynomial of order $2N-2$

$$A(L) = \sum_{s=0}^{2N-2} \alpha_s L^s \tag{17}$$

with $\alpha_0 = 1$.

A unique rational expectations solution to (15) is obtained by choosing the polynomial $A(L)$ that corresponds to the unstable roots of $B(L)$. With this choice of $A(L)$ we can divide (15) by $\lambda A(L^{-1})$. This yields:

$$A(L)\hat{x}_{t-1|t} = 0 \tag{18}$$

A rational expectations reduced form stochastic difference equation for x_t, the contract wage, is therefore given by:

$$A(L)x_t = \varepsilon_t \tag{19}$$

The α_i, $i = 0, \ldots, 2N-2$ are obtained by solving the $2N-1$ equations

$$B_s = \lambda \sum_{u=0}^{2N-2-s} \alpha_u \alpha_{u+s} \qquad s = 0, 1, 2, \ldots, 2N-2. \tag{20}$$

It is instructive to compare the behaviour of our RRW model with that of Taylor's RMW model, for identical values of all parameters, including contract length. This will serve to bring out the separate contributions of money illusion and 'nominal inertia' due to overlapping, staggered non-contingent money wage contracts.

The reduced form solution for the contract wage in the N-period RRW model (equations (14a–c), (19) and (20)) differs dramatically from the corresponding solution to Taylor's RMW model. The analogue to (13) in the RMW model is:

$$\sum_{s=1}^{N-1} \bar{B}_{-s}\, \hat{x}_{t-1|t-s} + \bar{B}_0\, \hat{x}_{t-1|t} + \sum_{s=1}^{N-1} \bar{B}_s\, \hat{x}_{t-1|t+s} = 0 \tag{21}$$

where

$$\bar{B}_0 = \frac{-(N + \beta\gamma)}{N - (N - 1)\beta\gamma} \tag{22a}$$

$$\bar{B}_s = \bar{B}_{-s} = b_s, \qquad s = 1, \ldots, N - 1 \tag{22b}$$

Using the same approach as in equations (15)–(20), we get:

$$\bar{A}(L)x_t = \varepsilon_t \tag{23}$$

Here $\bar{A}(L)$ is an $N - 1$ degree polynomial.

$$\bar{A}(L) = \sum_{s=0}^{N-1} \bar{\alpha}_s L^s \tag{24}$$

The $\bar{\alpha}_s$, $s = 1, \ldots, N - 1$ are found by solving the N equations

$$\bar{B}_s = \lambda \sum_{u=0}^{N-1-s} \bar{\alpha}_u \bar{\alpha}_{u+s} \qquad s = 0, 1, 2, \ldots, N - 1 \tag{25}$$

where the $\bar{B}_s$, are defined in (22a,b).

Thus with N-period contracts, the RRW model yields a $2N$-2 order stochastic difference equation in the contract wage while Taylor's RMW model yields an $N - 1$ order stochastic difference equation in the contract wage. In Taylor's RMW model as $\beta\gamma$ increases, the coefficients on all lagged values of the contract wage decline monotonically to -1. The coefficients change sign together at $\beta\gamma = N/N - 1$.[5] This change of sign is due to two effects working in opposite directions. If $\beta\gamma$ is low then a higher value of x_t will be associated with higher money wage settlements in all subsequent periods, through the relative (money) wage effect. If policy is more restrictive, $\beta\gamma > N/N - 1$, the demand effect dominates the relative wage effect and a higher value of x_t leads through expectations of monetary contraction and consequent excess supply of labour to lower wage settlements in subsequent periods. The above pattern can be contrasted with the RRW model. In this model the coefficients on lagged contract wages x_{t-s} tend to -1 as $\beta\gamma \to +\infty$ for $1 \leqslant s \leqslant N - 1$ and to 0 for $M \leqslant s \leqslant 2N - 2$.[6] We expect the coefficients on $x_{t-2N+2}, \ldots, x_{t-N}$ to be negative for all finite positive values of $\beta\gamma$[7] and the coefficients on $x_{t-N+1}, \ldots, x_{t-1}$ to be positive for small values of $\beta\gamma$. Table 2 shows how the lag weights vary with $\beta\gamma$ for $N = 2, 3$ in the RMW model and for $N = 2$ in the RRW model.

Table 2 Examples of the contract wage equation in the RMW and RRW models

The RMW model, N = 2										
$\beta\gamma$ =	0	.1	.2	.3	.4	.5	.6	1.0	2.0	$+\infty$
$-\bar{\alpha}_1$ =	1.0	.64	.52	.44	.38	.33	.29	.17	0	−1
The RMW model, N = 3										
$-\bar{\alpha}_1$ =	.73	.46	.38	.31	.27	.23	.19	.09	−.07	−1
$-\bar{\alpha}_2$ =	.27	.19	.16	.14	.11	.10	.09	.04	−.03	−1
The RRW model, N = 2										
$-\alpha_1$ =	2	.81	.63	.52	.44	.38	.33	.19	0	−1
$-\alpha_2$ =	−1	−.27	−.21	−.18	−.16	−.15	−.13	−.11	−.07	0
Money wage model without relative wage effects, N = 2										
$-\alpha_1$ =	0	−.024	−.046	−.065	−.084	−.101	−.116	−.172	−.537	−1
Money wage model without relative wage effects, N = 3										
$-\alpha_1$ =	0	−.022	−.041	−.058	−.077	−.092	−.106	−.159	−.533	−1
$-\alpha_2$ =	0	−.011	−.021	−.030	−.040	−.048	−.056	−.086	−.363	−1

III Staggered wage contracts without relative wage effects

In this section we examine the money and real wage models when Taylor's second key assumption is removed. That is, when the bargaining process does not take into account relative wages. This corresponds to the special case of the wage equations in (1) and (6) when $d_s = d_{-s} = 0$. It enables us to separate the consequences of having relative wage effects from those having staggered, overlapping contracts *per se*.

The contract determination equation in the money wage model becomes

$$x_t = \frac{\gamma}{N} \sum_{s=0}^{N-1} \hat{y}_{t-1|t+s} + \varepsilon_t \tag{26}$$

Substituting in for expected demand and taking expectations of both sides gives

$$\hat{x}_{t-1|t} = -\frac{\beta\gamma}{N} \sum_{s=0}^{N-1} \hat{p}_{t-1|\,t+s} \tag{27}$$

Substituting for expected prices and using (11) we get

$$-\frac{\hat{x}_{t-1|t}}{\beta\gamma} = \frac{N-1}{N} \sum_{s=1}^{N-1} b_s\, \hat{x}_{t-1|t-s} + \frac{\hat{x}_{t-1|t}}{N} + \frac{N-1}{N} \sum_{s=1}^{N-1} b_s\, \hat{x}_{t-1|t+s}$$

or rearranging

$$-\left(\frac{N+\beta\gamma}{\beta\gamma(N-1)}\right)\hat{x}_{t-1|t} = \sum_{s=1}^{N-1} b_s\, \hat{x}_{t-1|t-s} + \sum_{s=1}^{N-1} b_s\, \hat{x}_{t-1|t+s} \tag{28}$$

We can solve equation (28) exactly as before. Table 2 presents the lag weights on the resulting stochastic difference equation for $N = 2, 3$ and various values of $\beta\gamma$.

In the money wage model without relative wage effects, less accommodating policy (that is, larger values of $\beta\gamma$) *increases* the dependence of current wages on past wages, as reflected in the larger absolute values of the (negative) lag coefficients. The behaviour of Taylor's RMW model is similar to that of the money wage model without relative wage effects, when the demand effect dominates, that is for large values of $\beta\gamma$. For small values of $\beta\gamma$ the relative wage effect dominates the demand effect in Taylor's model and the dependence of current wages on past wages *diminishes* as $\beta\gamma$ increases from zero to $N(N-1)^{-1}$. This behaviour can be seen clearly in Table 2.

In the real wage model we can similarly disentangle the demand effect from the relative real wage effect and the price expectation effect. In equation (6) we set $d_s = d_{-s} = 0$, which gives

$$x_t - \frac{1}{N}\sum_{s=0}^{N-1} \hat{p}_{t-1|t+s} = \frac{\gamma}{N}\sum_{s=0}^{N-1} \hat{y}_{t-1|t+s} + \varepsilon_t. \tag{29}$$

Substituting for expected demand we have

$$x_t - \frac{1}{N}\sum_{s=0}^{N-1} \hat{p}_{t-1|t+s} = -\frac{\beta\gamma}{N}\sum_{s=0}^{N-1} \hat{p}_{t-1|t+s} + \varepsilon_t. \tag{30}$$

Now substituting money wages for prices and taking expectations of both sides gives

$$\hat{x}_{t-1|t} = \frac{1-\beta\gamma}{N^2}\sum_{s=0}^{N-1}\sum_{i=0}^{N-1} \hat{x}_{t-1|t+s-i},$$

which upon applying (11) and rearranging gives

$$\frac{N+(N-1)^{-1}N\beta\gamma}{N-N\beta\gamma}\,\hat{x}_{t-1|t} = \sum_{s=1}^{N-1} b_s\,\hat{x}_{t-1|t-s} + \sum_{s=1}^{N-1} b_s\,\hat{x}_{t-1|t+s} \tag{31}$$

Comparing this with the equivalent expression in the RMW model (21, 22a, 22b) we can see that the equations are identical when $\beta\gamma$ in this model takes a value $(N-1)N^{-1}$ times that in the RMW model. This means that policy is $N(N-1)^{-1}$ times more effective in this model than it is in the RMW model, but that otherwise they are identical.

The only way to distinguish empirically between the money wage model with relative wage effects and the real wage model without relative wage effects is by knowing $\beta\gamma$ and N *a priori*. Otherwise the two methods are observationally equivalent.

It has already been shown (Phelps and Taylor [1977]; Fischer [1977]) that in order to obtain the conclusion that known monetary policy rules affect real output, it is sufficient to have multi-period non-contingent money wage (or price) contracts. It is neither essential to have relative wage effects nor for contracts to be staggered. Different policy rules will have different effects whenever the money stock can be made to respond to new information before private agents can revize wage contracts. To include such features as relative wage effects and staggered contracts may of course be desirable for its own sake because it captures an essential feature of reality.

IV **Some empirical implications of the relative real wage model**

With the aggregate demand equation (2), the price equation (3) and the policy reaction function as our maintained hypothesis, the RRW model and the RMW model have some directly testable implications even if the contract wage cannot be observed. From the price level equation (3) we see that, if $N = 2$, the price equation of the RMW model is the ARIMA (1, 1) process

$$p_t = -\bar{\alpha}_1 p_{t-1} + \tfrac{1}{2}\varepsilon_t + \tfrac{1}{2}\varepsilon_{t-1} \quad \text{with } -1 \leqslant -\bar{\alpha}_1 \leqslant 1. \tag{32a}$$

With $N = 2$, the price equation of the RRW model is the ARIMA (2, 2) process

$$p_t = -\alpha_1 p_{t-1} - \alpha_2 p_{t-2} + \tfrac{1}{3}\varepsilon_t + \tfrac{1}{3}\varepsilon_{t-1} + \tfrac{1}{3}\varepsilon_{t-2} \quad \text{with } -1 \leqslant -\alpha_1 \leqslant 2 \text{ and } -1 \leqslant -\alpha_2 \leqslant 0. \tag{32b}$$

The price equation for the RMW model with $N = 3$ is also an ARIMA (2, 2) process:

$$p_t = -\bar{\alpha}_1 p_{t-1} - \bar{\alpha}_2 p_{t-2} + \tfrac{1}{3}\varepsilon_t + \tfrac{1}{3}\varepsilon_{t-1} + \tfrac{1}{3}\varepsilon_{t-2}$$
$$\text{with } .732 \geqslant -\bar{\alpha}_1 \geqslant -1;\ .268 \geqslant -\bar{\alpha}_2 \geqslant -1;\ |\bar{\alpha}_1| > |\bar{\alpha}_2|.$$
$$\text{sign}(-\bar{\alpha}_1) = \text{sign}(-\bar{\alpha}_2). \tag{32c}$$

Given *a priori* knowledge of N, we can test the RRW hypothesis that the price data follow an ARIMA ($2N - 2$, $2N - 2$) process against the RMW hypothesis test that the price data follow an ARIMA ($N - 1$, $N - 1$) process. It is much less straightforward to include in these tests the inequality constraints on the α_i and $\bar{\alpha}_i$ coefficients shown for $N = 2$ in (32b) and (32c). Alternatively, without prior knowledge of N, we can select the best-fitting ARIMA (i, i) process ($i \geqslant 1$) for the price data. If $i = 1$ and the other restrictions of (32a) are not rejected by the data, the RMW model is consistent with the data and the RRW model is not. If $i > 1$, non-nested hypothesis tests are in general required to discriminate between the RRW and the RMW model on the basis of inequality constraints such as those given in (32b) and (32c). However, finding a positive coefficient for the longest lag on p_t is always inconsistent with the RRW model and finding coefficients with different signs is always inconsistent with the RMW model. Taylor, in his empirical work on the RMW model (see specifically Taylor [1980b], but also Taylor [1979b]) estimates the $N = 2$ version of the model using annual data, which yields the ARIMA (1, 1) process of equation (32a). This equation could never have been generated by the RRW model which always yields at least an ARIMA (2, 2) process for the general price level. In the most direct test of the RMW model (Taylor [1980b]) with $N = 2$, it is found necessary to let the random disturbances ε_t and v_t follow a first order MA process. It is, in principle, always undesirable to have to attribute systematic explanatory power to the disturbance terms of a model. In this case, however, one might go further and argue that equation (32a) with an MA (1) process for ε_t may well be a misspecification that should be tested against (32b), the RRW model with $N = 2$, or against (32c), the RMW model with $N = 3$, both with *i.i.d.* ε_t. However, the RMW model with $N = 3$ is implausible on *a priori* grounds as three year contracts are not found in most of the countries in Taylor's sample.

A problem with such a test, as with other tests of the RMW or RRW hypotheses, is that reduced form equations such as (32a, b and c) reflect not only a particular model of wage and price determination but also the remaining equations of the model such as the rudimentary aggregate demand equation (2) and the simple instantaneous policy feedback rule (4). If these relations were respecified to include, say, lagged output, wage or price terms, the order of the autoregression in p found in equations (32a, b and c) would inevitably be altered. There may well be observational equivalence of reduced forms for a model embodying either the RMW or the RRW hypotheses if the specification of other equations in the model is altered even in quite minor and not implausible ways.[8] If the maintained hypothesis of equations (2) and (4) is deemed unacceptably restrictive, time-series analyses using aggregate data will never permit a conclusive test of the various wage hypotheses against each other.

V Conclusion

The RRW model we developed as an alternative to Taylor's RMW model differs from the latter in one important respect. Taylor's RMW model views the money wage decision of firms and unions contracting in a given period as influenced by the *money* wage rates set (or expected to be set) by other firms and unions that will be in effect during their own contract period. The RRW model views current wage bargainers as attempting to achieve a real wage target over the life of their contract that is influenced by the real wages achieved or expected to be achieved by those other wage bargainers with whose contract periods there is some degree of overlap.

Quite significant differences in behaviour are exhibited in otherwise identical RRW and RMW models. With N-period contracts, the RRW model yields a $2N$-2 order stochastic difference equation for the contract wage and an ARIMA ($2N$-2, $2N$-2) process for the general price level. The corresponding RMW model yields an N-1 order stochastic difference equation for the contract wage and an ARIMA (N-1, N-1) process for the general price level. With the RMW model the coefficients on lagged contract wages in the contract wage equation always have a common sign and decline both in the order of the lag and with the degree of non-accommodation of monetary policy. The lag coefficients in the RRW model will generally have mixed signs. It was also shown that Taylor's RMW model is observationally equivalent to a real wage model without relative wage effects.

What is perhaps the major qualitative conclusion of Taylor's RMW model is not affected, however. This is that rational expectations combined with nominal inertia due, e.g., to overlapping, staggered, non-contingent money wage contracts, leave scope for known contingent monetary policy rules to influence such real variables as the variance of output.

Appendix

In this appendix we show that equation (13), with the B_j as given in (14a,b,c), is equivalent to equation (12). Except for rearrangement we only have to determine the coefficients of $\hat{x}_{t-1|t+r}$, $\hat{x}_{t-1|t-r}$, for $r = 0, \ldots, 2N - 2$, in the bilinear forms on the right-hand side of equation (12). There are four such bilinear forms but by symmetry we need only consider two cases. The problem, then, is to find K_r and M_r such that (A1) and (A2) hold:

$$\left(\sum_{s=1}^{N-1}\sum_{j=1}^{N-1} b_s b_j \hat{x}_{t-1|t-s+j} + \sum_{s=1}^{N-1}\sum_{j=1}^{N-1} b_s b_j \hat{x}_{t-1|t+s-j} =\right) \tag{A1}$$

$$2\sum_{s=1}^{N-1}\sum_{j=1}^{N-1} b_s b_j \hat{x}_{t-1|t-s+j} = \sum_{r=1}^{N-2} K_r \hat{x}_{t-1|t+r} + K_o \hat{x}_{t-1|t} + \sum_{r=1}^{N-2} K_r \hat{x}_{t-1|t-r}$$

$$\sum_{s=1}^{N-1}\sum_{j=1}^{N-1} b_s b_j \hat{x}_{t-1|t+s+j} = \sum_{r=2}^{2N-2} M_r \hat{x}_{t-1|t+r}. \tag{A2}$$

Consider (A1) first. In this equation we have

$$j = s + r \tag{A3}$$

The fact that j takes values only between 1 and $N - 1$ means that, for $r \geqslant 0$, s is constrained to taking the values between 1 and $N - 1 - r$. For each s in this domain we have a corresponding j (given by (A3)) and a value for $b_j b_s$; the sum of all these (multiplied by 2) is the coefficient of $\hat{x}_{t-1|t+r}$. Hence

$$K_{-r} = K_r = \sum_{i=1}^{N-1-r} b_i b_{r+i}, \qquad r = 0, \ldots, N-2 \tag{A4}$$

Because of the linearity of b_k in k we can easily carry out the summation in (A4). Substituting in for b_i and b_{r+i} (A4) becomes:

$$K_{-r} = K_r = \sum_{i=1}^{N-1-r} \frac{(N-i)(N-r-i)}{[N(N-1)]^2}$$

$$= \sum_{i=1}^{N-1-r} \frac{N(N-r) - (2N-r)i + i^2}{[N(N-1)]^2} \tag{A4'}$$

Now using the following identities:

$$\sum_{i=1}^{N-1-r} N(N-r) = (N-1-r)N(N-r)$$

$$\sum_{i=1}^{N-1-r} (r-2N)i = \tfrac{1}{2}(N-1-r)(N-r)(r-2N)$$

$$\sum_{i=1}^{N-1-r} i^2 = \tfrac{1}{6}(N-1-r)(N-r)(2N-2r-1)$$

we have

$$K_{-r} = K_r = \frac{(N-1-r)(N-r)(2N+r-1)}{6[N(N-1)]^2} \qquad r = 0, \ldots, N-2. \tag{A5}$$

And in particular

$$K_0 = \frac{2N-1}{6N(N-1)} \tag{A6}$$

Now we deal with (A2). Proceeding as before, M_r is the sum of the series $b_s b_j$ for which

$$s + j = r, \tag{A7}$$

and both s and j lie between 1 and $N - 1$. Hence,

$$1 \leqslant j \leqslant N-1 \qquad \text{and}$$
$$1 \leqslant s = r - j \leqslant N - 1 \Rightarrow r - N + 1 \leqslant j \leqslant r - 1$$

The upper and lower bounds on j depend on the value of r. There are two cases

$2 \leqslant r \leqslant N - 1$, in which case j lies between 1 and $r - 1$ (I)

$2N - 2 \geqslant r \geqslant N$, in which case j lies between $r - N + 1$ and $N - 1$ (II)

Therefore,

$$M_{-r} = M_r = \sum_{j=1}^{r-1} b_j b_{r-j} \qquad r = 2, \ldots, N - 1 \tag{A8}$$

$$M_{-r} = M_r = \sum_{j=r-N+1}^{N-1} b_j b_{r-j} \qquad r = N, \ldots, 2N - 2 \tag{A9}$$

We can now write equation (12) as

$$\frac{N-1}{N} \sum_{s=N}^{2N-2} M_{-s}\hat{x}_{t-1|t-s} - \frac{N-1}{N} \sum_{s=1}^{N-1} ((2 - \beta\gamma)b_s + K_{-s} + M_{-s})\hat{x}_{t-1|t-s}$$

$$+ \left(1 - \frac{(1 - \beta\gamma)}{N} + \frac{N-1}{N} K_0\right)\hat{x}_{t-1|t}$$

$$- \frac{N-1}{N} \sum_{s=1}^{N-1} \left(((2 - \beta\gamma)b_s + K_s + M_s)\hat{x}_{t-1|t+s}\right.$$

$$+ \frac{N-1}{N} \sum_{s=N}^{2N-2} M_s \hat{x}_{t-1|t+s} = 0 \tag{A10}$$

Notes

Originally published in *The Manchester School*, 49, 1981, pp. 211–28.

1 The simplest interpretation of (2) is that of the quantity theory equation of exchange with the (logarithm of the) income velocity of circulation represented by a white noise disturbance term v_t.

2 In Taylor's RMW model, as in the RRW model specified below, output would be affected by lagged monetary feedback as well (e.g., $m_t = \delta p_{t-1}$). Unless the policy rule is 'symmetric in time' (e.g., $m_t = \delta p_{t-1} + (1 - \beta)p_t + \delta p_{t-1|t+1}$) the simple algebraic structure of the RMW model and the RRW model is lost because the polynomial equation in the expected contract wage is no longer symmetric.

3 The non-contingent nature of these contracts means that the N-period wage contract negotiated in period t does not make the wages paid under the contract in periods $t+1, \ldots, t+N-1$ contingent on information (on future contract wages, future prices and future excess demands) that may become available during the life of the contract. If a multi-period contract made the money wages paid over the life of the contract contingent on future information, it would be equivalent to a sequence of single-period contracts.

4 Substituting for b_s in equation (8) gives

$$(N-1)\sum_{s=0}^{N-1} \hat{p}_{t-1|t+s} = \sum_{s=1}^{N-1}\left(\sum_{j=s}^{N-1} \hat{p}_{t-1|t-s+j} + \sum_{j=0}^{N-1-s} \hat{p}_{t-1|t+s+j}\right)$$

Noticing that

$$\sum_{j=s}^{N-1} \hat{p}_{t-1|t-s+j} = \sum_{j=0}^{N-1-s} \hat{p}_{t-1|t+j}$$

$$\sum_{j=0}^{N-1-s} \hat{p}_{t-1|t+s+j} = \sum_{j=s}^{N-1} \hat{p}_{t-1|t+j}$$

and

$$\sum_{s=1}^{N-1}\sum_{j=0}^{N-1-s} \hat{p}_{t-1|t+j} = \sum_{s=0}^{N-2} (N-1-s)\hat{p}_{t-1|t+s}$$

$$\sum_{s=1}^{N-1}\sum_{j=s}^{N-1} \hat{p}_{t-1|t+j} = \sum_{s=1}^{N-1} s\hat{p}_{t-1|t+s}$$

the identity is easily established.

5 From (22a) $\bar{B}_0$ goes to infinity as $\beta\gamma$ goes to $\frac{N}{N-1}$. Dividing (21) by $\bar{B}_0$ and taking the limit as $\beta\gamma \to \frac{N}{N-1}$ yields $\hat{x}_{t-1|t} = 0$. Therefore $x_t = \varepsilon_t$ is a solution. Again from (22a) $\bar{B}_0$ goes to $(N-1)^{-1}$ as $\beta\gamma$ goes to $+\infty$. By direct substitution it can be checked that $a_s = 1$, $s = 1, \ldots, N-1$, satisfies (25). (Note that $\lambda = [(N-1)N]^{-1}$.)

6 From equations (14a,b,c) we get $\lim_{\beta\gamma\to\infty} \left(\frac{B_s}{B_0}\right) = \frac{N-s}{N}$ for $1 \leq s \leq N-1$ and $\lim_{\beta\gamma\to\infty} \left(\frac{B_s}{B_0}\right) = 0$ for $N \leq s \leq 2N-2$. Dividing (20) by B_0 we get

$$\frac{B_s}{B_0} = \frac{\sum_{u=0}^{2N-2-s} \alpha_u\alpha_{u+s}}{\sum_{i=0}^{2N-2} \alpha_i^2}, \quad s = 1, \ldots, 2N-2.$$

Taking the limit as $\beta\gamma \to \infty$ this reduces to

$$\frac{N-s}{N} = \frac{\sum_{u=0}^{2N-2-s} \alpha_u\alpha_{u+s}}{\sum_{i=0}^{2N-2} \alpha_i^2}, \quad s = 1, \ldots, N-1$$

$$0 = \frac{\sum_{u=0}^{2N-2-s} \alpha_u\alpha_{u+s}}{\sum_{i=0}^{2N-2} \alpha_i^2}, \quad s = N, \ldots, 2N-2.$$

These two sets of equations are satisfied by

$$\alpha_i = \begin{cases} 1, & i = 1, \ldots, N-1 \\ 0 & i = N, \ldots, 2N-2 \end{cases}$$

7 It is obvious that the coefficient on $\hat{x}_{t-2N+2}$ is always negative for finite positive $\beta\gamma$.

8 We would like to thank an anonymous referee for bringing this to our attention.

References

Fischer, S. (1977), 'Long-term Contracts, Rational Expectations, and the Optimal Money Supply Rule', *Journal of Political Economy*, Vol. 85, No. 1, 1977, pp. 191–206.

Phelps, E. S. and Taylor, J. B. (1977), 'Stabilizing Powers of Monetary Policy under Rational Expectations', *Journal of Political Economy*, Vol. 85, No. 1, 1977, pp. 163–90.

Taylor, J. B. (1979a), 'Staggered Wage Setting in a Macro Model', *American Economic Review*, Vol. 69, No. 2, pp. 108–13.

—— (1979b), 'Estimation and Control of a Macroeconomic Model with Rational Expectations', *Econometrica*, Vol. 47, No. 5, pp. 1267–86.

—— (1980a), 'Aggregate Dynamics and Staggered Contracts', *Journal of Political Economy*, Vol. 88, No. 1, pp. 1–23.

—— (1980b), 'Output and Price Stability', *Journal of Economic Dynamics and Control*, Vol. 2, No. 1, pp. 109–32.

Chapter 9

Costs and benefits of an anti-inflationary policy: questions and issues

Written with Marcus H. Miller

I Introduction

Unlike many contributions to this subject, this chapter has the virtue that at any rate its title (which was chosen by the organizers of the conference) makes sense. As Hall [1981, p. 432] states, 'Inflation is an outcome of economic processes, not an exogenous causal influence'. At the level of the economy as a whole, it is therefore a nonsense to refer, as is often done, to the costs of inflation or to the benefits from lower inflation. Since inflation is endogenous, the benefits or costs of lower inflation can be discussed sensibly only by specifying the changes in exogenous variables and parameters (policy actions or rules, external events, etc.) that bring about and sustain the lower rate of inflation. Partial equilibrium or single-structural-equation 'costs of inflation' analyses are void of policy implications.

As regards the benefits from policies to achieve a sustained reduction in the rate of inflation, we shall be brief, because we have nothing much to add to the received wisdom on the topic.[1] First consider a non-stochastic economy. We shall assume that a permanent reduction in the proportional rate of growth of the nominal stock of money is a necessary condition for a permanent reduction in the rate of inflation. Unless debt neutrality prevails or government interest-bearing debt is index linked, the reduction in the growth rate of the nominal money stock will have to be matched by an equal reduction in the growth rate of the stock of government bonds in order to achieve sustained reduction in the rate of inflation.

It is important to appreciate that it is the same institutional feature of the economy that causes costs to be associated both with policies that cause inflation and with policies to reduce inflation. That feature is the existence of nominal contracts that are not perfectly price-level contingent or inflation contingent. The reasons for the existence of such contracts have to do with the advantages of using money in the first place – the benefits from using a common numeraire, standard of deferred payment, medium of exchange and means of payment. They are either too obvious or too deep to be considered in this paper. Bringing down inflation is costly because of the existence of non-contingent money wage and price contracts. In a deterministic setting, imperfect and incomplete indexation of prices and rates of return is the main reason for welfare costs to be associated with policies that cause inflation. The only other cost is the 'relabeling cost', i.e. the cost of changing prices more frequently, which can be generalized to the cost of the disruption of well-established methods of transacting business (Carlton [1982, p. 139]).

The best-known cost of non-indexation is the loss of consumer surplus suffered when the demand for real money balances declines as (and to the extent that) the nominal interest rate rises in response to an increase in the (expected) rate of inflation. With the nominal rate of return on money balances assumed fixed (typically at zero), the nominal interest rate represents the opportunity cost of holding money. Partial equilibrium approaches take the real interest rate as given and have the nominal interest rate rising one for one with an increase in the (expected) inflation rate. This represents a tax on the holding of money balances. If the demand for money is interest sensitive and money is produced costlessly, this will impose a dead-weight loss of consumer surplus given by the trapezoidal area under the (compensated) money demand function between the low inflation and high inflation quantities of money demanded.[2] General equilibrium approaches treat the real interest rate as endogenous and not necessarily invariant to the policy changes that cause the higher rate of inflation. In a multi-period setting, the entire sequence of discounted instantaneous (or single-period) trapezoidal utility losses must be considered (Feldstein [1979]).

Non-indexation or incomplete indexation extend in practice well beyond the rate of return on high-powered money balances, and affect private contracts as well as tax laws and regulations. Extensive work on the subject has been done by Fischer and Modigliani [1978], and Fischer [1981b].

When comparing a situation of low inflation with one of high inflation, the lower level of welfare (presumably) enjoyed in the latter can be attributed either to the policy that brings about the higher inflation (i.e. higher monetary growth) or to the failure to implement policies that permit a partial or complete adaptation to the higher inflation. If indexation is cheap, let alone costless, dead-weight losses, incurred because of a combination of inflation and incomplete indexation, can be attributed with as much justice to the failure to implement policies to adapt to inflation as to the policies that cause the inflation. This holds for any undesired distributional consequences of policies that cause inflation as much as for the inefficiencies that they entail.

Turning to a stochastic world, a vast literature has sprouted in recent years on the costs of variable or uncertain inflation and on the links between expected inflation and the variability or uncertainty of the price level, the rate of inflation or relative prices.[3] Even in deterministic models it is possible, if not all prices can be adjusted costlessly and continuously, to establish a causal link between the (anticipated) mean inflation rate and the (anticipated) variability of relative prices. The costs of such anticipated variability can be evaluated using conventional deterministic welfare economic tools. In what follows only unanticipated or currently unperceived variability, i.e. inflation or relative price uncertainty, will be considered. Causal chains have been proposed that run from high (expected) inflation rates through to relative price uncertainty, suggesting that inflation may raise the noise-to-signal ratio for relative price movements, thus impairing the allocative efficiency of the price mechanism.

Since the expected rate of inflation, its variance and the variance of relative prices are all jointly endogenous in any reasonable macroeconomic model, it is very hard to understand what the 'costs of inflation uncertainty' literature is trying to say. It is certainly interesting to study the time-series behavior of mean inflation, of inflation variability and uncertainty and of relative price variability and uncertainty (see, for example, Fischer [1981a]). By regressing any one of these on any subset of the remaining ones, one cannot hope to extract a structurally invariant relationship. The statement 'high expected inflation causes highly uncertain inflation' makes no sense. The statement 'certain policies or events that cause the first moment of the distribution function of inflation to increase also tend to raise its second moment' does make sense. For example, if higher mean monetary growth is associated with increasingly unpredictable monetary growth, both the higher mean inflation and the increasing unpredictability of inflation can be attributed to monetary policy.

Perhaps the argument is that there is a structurally invariant relationship between mean monetary growth and the unpredictability of monetary growth for a monetary aggregate with the following two properties. First, it is the relevant causal one in the inflation process and, second, the parameters of its distribution function can be chosen by the authorities only subject to some constraints, e.g. the authorities cannot control monetary growth exactly, but they can choose the first two moments of its distribution function, subject to the contraint that mean and variance are positively related. Since it is likely to be welfare-reducing for the authorities to throw more extraneous noise into the system, a further argument for lower mean money growth exists if the variance of the innovation in the money stock process is an increasing function of the expected rate of monetary growth. Unless this is the case, finding a positive pattern of covariation between mean inflation and relative price uncertainty carries no implications for monetary policy.

Note that none of this provides an argument for maximizing the predictability of future monetary growth rates but only for minimizing the variance of the innovation in the money stock process. Consider, for example, the monetary growth rule $m_{t+1} - m_t = \alpha_t + u^m_{t+1}$, where m_t is the logarithm of the nominal money stock, u^m_t is the random, unpredictable, component in the money growth process, i.e. $E_t u^m_{t+1} = 0$, while α_t is the predictable component, i.e. $E_t \alpha_t = \alpha_t$. Let $\sigma^2_{m,t} \equiv E_t(u^m_{t+1})^2$; the inflation uncertainty hypothesis can be represented by

$$\frac{\partial \sigma^2_{m,t}}{\partial |\alpha_t|} > 0.$$

α_t itself could be a non-stochastic known function of current and past realizations of random variables, i.e. it could be governed by a non-stochastic feedback rule. While such rules tend to make $m_{t+2} - m_{t+1}$, say, less predictable, in period t and earlier, than a non-stochastic open loop path for money growth, such feedback rules may well help diminish the uncertainty that matters. Examples are changes in the information content of observed market prices induced by monetary feedback rules (Turnovsky [1980]; Weiss [1981]; Buiter [1980, 1981]).

From the proposition that governments should not throw extraneous random noise into the economic system by randomizing their monetary policy rules, it also does not follow that minimizing uncertainty about future inflation or future relative prices is sensible policy. For example, by freezing all relative prices through legislative fiat, their predictability is maximized but any shocks to demand or supply will have to be absorbed through rationing and other disequilibrium mechanisms. Random shocks to the system will, in general, be absorbed by unexpected changes in prices and in quantities produced, sold and consumed and by unexpected changes in the values of policy instruments such as the money supply, which are set according to some contingent or conditional rule. By removing the elements of conditionality in the monetary rule to enhance the predictability of the future money stock path, shocks will have to be absorbed in some other way. Only detailed analysis of fully specified models can determine what kind of monetary rule maximizes expected utility.

A final argument for policies consistent with low or zero inflation is that price-level stability (zero inflation) is the only stable equilibrium. Positive inflation inevitably entails rising rates of inflation. (The symmetric argument for negative inflation rates is not made; there have been hyper-inflations but no hyper-deflations.)

The political economy of inflationary monetary growth creating pressures for higher and more inflationary rates of monetary growth has never been spelled out satisfactorily. The historical experience of most OECD countries would seem to contradict it. If any inflation carried in itself the seeds of a hyper-inflation (with some non-negligible probability), the case for striving for price-level constancy would of course be strengthened considerably.

II The cost of policies to achieve a permanent reduction in inflation

In this section we shall consider the familiar Okun-style output costs of securing a lasting reduction in the rate of inflation. There are well-known objections to taking the cumulative net output loss (perhaps discounted) associated with an anti-inflationary policy as a measure of its costs. It ignores the benefits of additional output produced at home by the unemployed and not recorded in GNP, as well as the marginal valuation of their leisure and search time. We shall proceed regardless for two reasons. First, it has been argued (see e.g. Gordon, [1973]) that if one attempts a conventional triangle approach grounded in applied welfare economics, the answers do not come out all that differently from the crude Okun's gap measure. Second, it is hard to take seriously an approach that cannot differentiate between an employed worker taking a vacation and a worker becoming unemployed. Conventional microeconomic analysis models utility as increasing in leisure (i.e. leisure is a 'good thing') and thereby confines labour to the category of 'bads'. Overwhelming empirical evidence on the importance of work (i.e. of being employed, of having a job) for most people's well-being, happiness and even sanity has not made much of a dent in the 'extended holiday' approach to unemployment.

Formally, it is quite easy to combine the 'leisure as a good thing' and 'work as a good thing' approaches. Consider the state-dependent utility function $v(..)$ given below, where c is a vector of goods and services other than leisure, L is the endowment of time and l is hours spent working. θ is an indicator variable that takes on values $\theta = 1$ if employed and $\theta = 0$ if unemployed.

$$U = v(c, L - l, \theta).$$

The utility function is well-behaved in consumption and leisure (strictly increasing and quasi-concave). The benefit from being employed is represented by the assumption that, for any given $c = \bar{c}$ and $l = \bar{l}$ we have

$$v(\bar{c}, L - \bar{l}, 1) > v(\bar{c}, L - \bar{l}, 0).^4$$

Depending on what further properties one attributes to the utility function[5] and on the budget constraints when employed and unemployed, one could still have people choosing voluntary unemployment.

In this chapter, only conventional output gap costs will be considered. Even if they have no clear welfare significance, it would still be worthwhile from a positive economics viewpoint to know their magnitude.

Bringing down inflation with a policy-invariant natural rate
In this subsection we consider models that have the long-run natural rate property: the same level of real output (rate of unemployment) is consistent with any steady-state and fully anticipated rate of inflation. While output and unemployment can differ from their natural levels outside the steady state, these natural levels themselves are taken to be constant. For this class of models we shall show that *price-level inertia* is not sufficient to generate output costs of policies to bring down inflation. For there to be such costs, inertia should attach to the *rate of change* of the price level. A number of 'Keynesian' models – e.g. Buiter and Miller's [1981, 1982] variant of Dornbusch's [1976] overshooting model, Calvo's [1982a,b,c] continuous-time version of Taylor's [1980] staggered overlapping money wage contract model,[6] Mussa's [1981] sticky price model and Obstfeld and Rogoff's [1982] version of a price adjustment rule of Barro and Grossman [1976] – all have the property that, in principle, inflation can be reduced or eliminated costlessly. Well-designed and credible monetary and fiscal policy can make these economic systems mimic the real behavior of a completely flexible money wage and price economy.

After considering these models, we analyze the cost of bringing down inflation in models with sluggish core inflation. These costs, and the properties of desirable anti-inflationary policies, turn out to depend crucially on the relative importance of backward-looking ('long-term contracts') versus forward-looking ('expectations') determinants of current inflation.

Closed economy models
This subsection deals with closed economy models. Much of the analysis requires consideration only of the wage-price block. Where a complete, if rudimentary, macroeconomic model is required, the following standard loglinear *IS–LM* model will be used.

$$m - p = -\lambda r + ky \qquad \lambda \geqslant 0;\ k \geqslant 0 \tag{1}$$

$$y(t) = -\gamma[r(t) - \dot{p}(t, t)] + \varepsilon[m(t) - p(t)] + \eta f(t) \qquad \gamma > 0;\ \varepsilon \geqslant 0;\ \eta \geqslant 0. \tag{2}$$

where m is the nominal stock of money balances, p the general price level, r the short nominal interest rate, y real output and f a measure of fiscal impact on aggregate demand. All variables except r are measured in logarithms. For any variable x, $\dot{x}(t)$ denotes its time derivative, i.e.

$$\dot{x}(t) \equiv \lim_{h \to 0}\left(\frac{x(t + h) - x(t)}{h}\right).$$

$x(s, t)$ denotes the value of x expected, at time t, to prevail at times s. We assume $x(s, t) = x(s)$, $x \leqslant t$. The expected instantaneous rate of change of x is denoted

$$\dot{x}(t, t) \equiv \lim_{\substack{h \to 0 \\ h > 0}} \left(\frac{x(t + h, t) - x(t, t)}{h} \right).$$

The unexpected change in x is denoted by

$$\frac{\partial}{\partial t} x(s, t) = \lim_{\substack{h \to 0 \\ h > 0}} \left(\frac{x(s, t) - x(s, t - h)}{h} \right).$$

Costless disinflation with price flexibility

Let capacity output or the natural level of output be denoted $\bar{y}$. This is treated as exogenous and constant. The benchmark case for costless disinflation is represented by the flexible price-level model, which complements (1) and (2) with the assumption of continuous full-capacity utilization:

$$y = \bar{y}. \tag{3}$$

For simplicity, it is assumed here and in what follows that the initial position of the economy is one of full stationary equilibrium with a high constant rate of monetary growth $\bar{\mu}$. All models considered will have the classical property that the steady-state rate of inflation equals the steady-state rate of growth of money.[7]

It is easily checked that, regardless of what the initial rate of inflation happens to be, an unanticipated, immediately implemented and permanent fixing of the rate of monetary growth $\dot{m}(t) \equiv \mu(t)$ at $\bar{\bar{\mu}}$ will immediately and permanently set the rate of inflation at $\bar{\bar{\mu}}$ if expectations are rational. If the *IS* curve is vertical ($\gamma = 0$) and there is a real balance effect ($\varepsilon \neq 0$), this follows trivially from the stronger proposition that real money balances are determined uniquely by $\bar{y}$ and f. If neither γ nor λ equals zero, the behavior of expected real money balances is governed by

$$\dot{l}(t, t) = (\lambda^{-1} + \gamma^{-1})l(t) + \mu(t) - (\gamma^{-1} + \lambda^{-1}k)\bar{y} + \gamma^{-1}\,\eta f(t)$$

where

$$l(t) \equiv m(t) - p(t).$$

Since $\lambda^{-1} + \gamma^{-1}\varepsilon$ is positive, there is, for a given information set, a unique continuous convergent solution given by

$$l(t) = \left(\frac{\lambda + k\gamma}{\gamma + \lambda\varepsilon} \right) \bar{y} - \int_t^{\infty} e^{(\lambda^{-1} + \gamma^{-1}\varepsilon)(t-s)} [\gamma^{-1}\eta f(s, t) + \mu(s, t)]\, ds.$$

When both f and μ are expected to remain constant at $\bar{f}$ and $\bar{\bar{\mu}}$ respectively for all future time, this simplifies to

$$l(t) = \left(\frac{\lambda + k\gamma}{\gamma + \lambda\varepsilon} \right) \bar{y} - \frac{\eta\lambda}{\gamma + \lambda\varepsilon} \bar{f} - \frac{\gamma\lambda}{\gamma + \lambda\varepsilon} \bar{\bar{\mu}} \tag{4}$$

Thus, while the level of the real stock of money balances will, in general, be a function of the rate of monetary growth (even across steady states) through the effect of anticipated money growth on the expected rate of inflation and thus on the nominal interest rate, the adjustment of the real stock of money balances to a new rate of growth of the nominal money stock will be instantaneous. The price level will jump discontinuously if required to satisfy (4). After that, the rate of inflation equals the new constant rate of money growth.

The general solution for the expected rate of inflation for constant $\bar{y}$ and $\bar{f}$ is:

$$\dot{p}(t, t) = (\lambda^{-1} + \gamma^{-1}\varepsilon) \int_t^{\infty} e^{(\lambda^{-1}+\gamma^{-1}\varepsilon)(t-s)}\mu(s, t)\, ds.$$

$$= \bar{\bar{\mu}} \text{ if } \mu(s, t) = \bar{\bar{\mu}} \qquad \text{for } s \geqslant t. \tag{5}$$

The actual rate of inflation – the sum of anticipated and unanticipated inflation – is given by

$$\dot{p}(t) = \int_t^{\infty} e^{(\lambda^{-1}+\gamma^{-1}\varepsilon)(t-s)} \left[(\lambda^{-1} + \gamma^{-1}\varepsilon)\mu(s, t) + \frac{\partial}{\partial t}\mu(s, t)\right] ds.^{8} \tag{6}$$

Note that in this model the *credibility* of current announcements of future policy is both necessary and sufficient for a sustained reduction in inflation to any level. Although, by construction, there never are any output costs of bringing down inflation, a desired reduction in inflation may not be achievable, regardless of the actual past and current path of monetary growth, simply because expectations concerning future monetary growth are sufficiently pessimistic. Inflation, and policies to combat inflation, are exclusively forward-looking. We shall return to this credibility issue when we discuss the fiscal preconditions for a sustained deceleration of monetary growth below.

Costless disinflation with price-level inertia

The following four sluggish price-adjustment mechanisms permit, in principle, costless and instantaneous sustained reductions in the rate of inflation:

$$\dot{p}(t) = \Psi[y(t) - \bar{y}] + \mu^{+}(t) \qquad \Psi > 0 \text{ (Dornbusch)} \tag{7}$$

$$\dot{p}(t) = \Psi[y(t) - \bar{y}] + \bar{\dot{p}}(t) \qquad \text{(Barro-Grossman)} \tag{8}$$

$$\dot{p}(t) = \Psi[y(t) - \bar{y}] + \dot{\bar{p}}(t) \qquad \text{(Mussa)} \tag{9}$$

$$\dot{p}(t) = \delta[v(t) - p(t)] \qquad \delta > 0 \text{ (Calvo)} \tag{10a}$$

$$\dot{v}(t, t) = \delta\{v(t) - p(t) - \Psi[y(t) - \bar{y}]\}. \tag{10b}$$

In all four cases the price level, p, is treated as predetermined: it cannot move discontinuously in response to current changes in expectations about the future. Also in all four cases, the rate of change of the price level is an increasing function of excess demand pressure, measured as the excess of the level of current output (which is viewed as demand-determined) over the natural level of output. In equations (7), (8) and (9) it is only current excess demand that, given 'core' inflation, affects current inflation. In Calvo's model both current and anticipated future excess demand affect current inflation. Equations (7), (8) and (9) differ only in the augmentation term, or core inflation – the rate of inflation when there is no excess demand or supply. In equation (7), core inflation is identified with the right-hand-side derivative of the money stock path:

$$\mu^{+}_{(t)} \equiv \lim_{\substack{h \to 0 \\ h > 0}} \frac{m(t+h) - m(t)}{h}.$$

In equation (8), core inflation is given by $\dot{\tilde{p}}$, which is the right-hand-side derivative of the equilibrium price path that would be generated if the price level were fully flexible. This is, of course, the rate of inflation calculated in equation (5). Mussa's equation (9), as developed by Obstfeld and Rogoff [1982], specifies core inflation as the right-hand-side derivative of the price path $\bar{p}(t)$ that would clear the output market (set $y(t) = \bar{y}$) given the actual (and in general non-Walrasian equilibrium) values of the other endogenous variables, $p(t)$, $\dot{p}(t, t)$ and $r(t)$. $\bar{p}(t)$ is therefore defined by:

$$\bar{y} = -\gamma[r(t) - \dot{p}(t, t)] + \varepsilon[m(t) - \bar{p}(t)] + \eta f(t).$$

In the spirit of Taylor, Calvo specifies the current contract price, $v(t)$, as a forward-looking moving average with exponentially declining weights of the future expected general price level $p(t)$ and future expected excess demand:

$$v(t) = \delta \int_{t}^{\infty} \{p(s, t) + \Psi[y(s, t) - \bar{y}]\} e^{-\delta(s-t)} \, ds + e^{\delta t} \lim_{\tau \to \infty} [e^{-\delta \tau} v(\tau, t)]. \tag{11a}$$

Note that the current contract price $v(t)$ is non-predetermined. The general price level, which is predetermined, is a backward-looking, exponentially declining moving average of past contract prices:

$$p(t) = \delta \int_{t_0}^{t} v(s) e^{-\delta(t-s)} \, ds + e^{-\delta(t-t_0)} p(t_0). \tag{11b}$$

In a full employment, stationary equilibrium $\dot{v}(t, t) = \dot{v}(t) = \dot{p}(t)$. A positive (zero, negative) steady-state rate of inflation requires a current contract price, $v(t)$, above (equal to, below) the current general price level, $p(t)$.

It will be apparent that all four mechanisms in equations (7)–(10) have flexible core inflation. It would appear that simply reducing monetary growth to $\bar{\mu}$, say, and keeping it there would be sufficient to reduce inflation in (7) without output costs. In equations (8), (9) and (10a,b), the further proviso of credibility of current announcements of future reductions in monetary growth has to be added.

The reason that this is not quite correct is that a *ceteris paribus* reduction in money growth would in general affect the money market and output market. To effect a permanent reduction in inflation at full employment other policy parameters will have to be changed when monetary growth is reduced. Steady-state output $y = \bar{y}$ is, from (4), sustained by monetary and fiscal policy as follows:

$$y(t) = \bar{y} = \frac{\eta\lambda}{\lambda + k\gamma}\bar{f} + \frac{\gamma\lambda}{\lambda + k\gamma}\bar{\bar{\mu}} + \left(\frac{\gamma + \lambda\varepsilon}{\lambda + k\gamma}\right)[m(t) - p(t)].$$

The long-run effect of a reduction in money growth is to reduce inflation one-for-one, reduce the nominal interest rate (but less than one-for-one if there is a real balance effect[9]) and thus raise the demand for real money balances. In the classical flex-price model, the real money balances required to effect an instantaneous transition to low inflation at full employment comes about through a discontinuous jump down in the price level. With a predetermined price level, the required increase in real money balances can instead be achieved by a discrete, discontinuous increase in the level of the nominal money stock at the same time, t, that its rate of change is reduced permanently. The required money jump is given by:

$$\mathrm{d}m(t) = \frac{-\gamma\lambda}{\gamma + \lambda\varepsilon}\, d\bar{\bar{\mu}}.^{10} \tag{12a}$$

Alternatively, expansionary fiscal policy could accompany the reduction in money growth in such a way as to leave the nominal interest rate unchanged. The required fiscal expansion is given by

$$\mathrm{d}\bar{f} = \frac{-\gamma}{\eta}\,\mathrm{d}\bar{\bar{\mu}}. \tag{12b}$$

This fiscal action relies on the direct aggregate demand effect of increased public spending or lower taxes. We shall show below how cost- and price-reducing indirect tax cuts could be used as a substitute for an increase in the nominal money stock as a means for achieving an increase in real money balances at a given before-tax price level.

It can be checked easily that, provided the money stock is raised according to (12a) or a fiscal stimulus is provided according to (12b) when monetary growth is lowered to $\bar{\bar{\mu}}$, the rate of inflation will settle immediately and permanently at $\bar{\bar{\mu}}$ while output remains equal to $\bar{y}$ throughout.[11]

For Calvo's model the existence of costless disinflation policies may not be quite as transparent as for the other three. First note that, treating $y - \bar{y}$ as exogenous, both roots of the dynamic system (10a,b) are zero. Following Buiter [1983c], the convergent solutions for v and p are given by:

$$p(t) = p(t_0) + \delta \int_{t_0}^{t} K(s)\mathrm{d}s + \delta^2\Psi \int_{t_0}^{t}\int_{s}^{\infty} [y(\tau, s) - \bar{y}]\mathrm{d}\tau\mathrm{d}s \qquad (13a)$$

$$v(t) = p(t) + K(t) + \Psi\delta \int_{t}^{\infty} [y(\tau, t) - \bar{y}]\mathrm{d}\tau. \qquad (13b)$$

K is a parameter to be determined from the terminal boundary condition. A natural transversatility condition to determine K (and one consistent with (11a)) is

$$K(t) = \lim_{\tau\to\infty} [v(\tau, t) - p(\tau, t)] = \lim_{\tau\to\infty} \frac{\dot{v}(\tau, t)}{\delta} = \lim_{\tau\to\infty} \frac{\dot{p}(\tau, t)}{\delta} \qquad (13c)$$

It is easily seen from equations (1) and (2) that, along any (anticipated) full employment path ($y(\tau, t) = \bar{y}$) with a constant expected rate of money growth $\bar{\bar{\mu}}$ and a constant expected value of f, it must be true that $K(t) = \bar{\bar{\mu}}/\delta$. Thus, as $\bar{\bar{\mu}}$ is lowered from $\bar{\mu}$ to $\bar{\bar{\mu}}$ and m is increased once and for all to maintain full employment, v will drop discontinuously by $(\bar{\mu} - \bar{\bar{\mu}})/\delta$ and inflation is reduced costlessly and permanently. The dependence of the current price level on a 'two-sided' moving average of output expectations will re-emerge in a slightly modified form when inflation inertia is added to price-level inertia.

If monetary or fiscal policy actions to maintain full employment when the monetary growth rate is reduced are ruled out, the increased demand for real money balances resulting from a successful anti-inflationary policy can be satisfied only by a lowering of the price-level path relative to the nominal money stock path. This will involve unemployment and excess capacity in all four sticky price-level models. For example, in the Dornbusch variant,

$$\int_{t_0}^{t} (y(s) - \bar{y})\mathrm{d}s = \Psi^{-1}[l(t_0) - l(t)].$$

By the time the economy settles down to a new stationary equilibrium and a new, higher, stationary stock of real money balances after a reduction in μ, the undiscounted cumulative net output loss will be

$$\int_{t_0}^{\infty} [y(s) - \bar{y}]\mathrm{d}s = \Psi^{-1} \frac{\gamma\lambda}{\gamma + \lambda\varepsilon}(\bar{\bar{\mu}} - \bar{\mu}).$$

The net output cost of reducing steady-state inflation decreases as the short-run Phillips curve steepens and the interest sensitivity of money demand decreases.

These costs of bringing down the price *level* will be different for the four price-adjustment mechanisms considered in this subsection. They are not considered any further here because of space constraints. The methods of the next subsection, which deals with inflation inertia, can be brought to bear on the problem of price-level inertia with obvious modifications.

Inflation inertia
The simplest way of introducing inflation inertia is by postulating a backward-looking adaptive process for core inflation, π, as in (14a,b).

$$\dot{p} = \Psi(y - \bar{y}) + \pi \tag{14a}$$

$$\dot{\pi} = \xi(\dot{p} - \pi) \qquad \xi > 0. \tag{14b}$$

Both the price level, p, and core inflation, π, are predetermined. It is now no longer possible to avoid paying the output or unemployment cost of bringing down inflation merely by manipulating aggregate demand as in the previous subsection. In the model of equations (14a,b), a sustained reduction in inflation requires a reduction in core inflation. Since

$$\pi(t) = \pi(t_0) + \xi\Psi\int_{t_0}^{t}[y(s) - y]\mathrm{d}s,$$

the undiscounted cumulative net output cost of bringing down inflation permanently is given by

$$\int_{t_0}^{\infty}(y(s) - \bar{y})\mathrm{d}s = \frac{\pi(\infty) - \pi(t_0)}{\xi\Psi} \tag{15}$$

It is a decreasing function of the slope of the short-run Phillips curve and an increasing function of the mean lag of the backward-looking core inflation process $1/\xi$. This loss measure cannot be altered by changing the timing or the intensity of the anti-inflationary package. Given ξ, ϕ and the desired reduction in steady-state inflation, the net output cost is a constant. (See e.g. Miller [1979]; Buiter and Miller [1982, 1983].)

Clearly, with discounting, policy makers will not be indifferent between different trajectories with the same net output cost. We shall not address these issues as they are both well understood (see e.g. Phelps [1972], and Hall [1976]) and comparatively unimportant: characterizing efficient policies (and inefficient policies!) would seem to be more useful than searching for an optimal policy.

The major drawback of the model of core inflation in equation (14b) is the complete irrelevance for current core inflation of current and/or past anticipations of future economic events. To remedy this (14b) is replaced by (15a,b). Core inflation, π, is a backward-looking exponentially declining moving average of past 'contract inflation', q, while q is a forward-looking moving average of future expected inflation.

$$\pi(t) = \pi(t_0)e^{-\xi_1(t-t_0)} + \xi_1\int_{t_0}^{t} q(s)e^{-\xi_1(t-s)}\mathrm{d}s \qquad \xi_1 > 0 \tag{15a}$$

$$q(t) = \xi_2\int_{t}^{\infty} \dot{p}(\tau, t)e^{-\xi_2(\tau-t)}\mathrm{d}\tau.^{12} \tag{15b}$$

By differentiating (15a,b) and using (14a) we obtain the two-equation system:

$$\dot{\pi}(t) = -\xi_1[\pi(t) - q(t)] \tag{16a}$$

$$\dot{q}(t, t) = -\xi_2[\pi(t) - q(t)] - \xi_2\Psi[y(t) - \bar{y}]. \tag{16b}$$

Comparing this with Calvo's model in equation (10a,b) two differences stand out. First, equations (16a,b) have 'slipped a derivative' compared to (10a,b). Inertia now attaches both to the level and to the first derivative of the price-level path. Second, the mean lags of the backward-looking core inflation process, ξ_1^{-1}, and of the forward-looking contract inflation process, ξ_2^{-1}, are permitted to be different from each other.

Treating the output gap $y - \bar{y}$ as exogenous, the convergent solutions for $\pi(t)$ and $q(t)$ are found to be:[13]

$$\pi(t) = \pi(t_0) + \xi_1\xi_2\Psi\int_{t_0}^{t}\int_{s}^{\infty} e^{(\xi_2-\xi_1)(s-\tau)}[y(\tau, s) - \bar{y}]\,\mathrm{d}\tau\,\mathrm{d}s \tag{17a}$$

$$q(t) = \pi(t) + \xi_2\Psi\int_{t}^{\infty} e^{(\xi_2-\xi_1)(t-s)}[y(s, t) - \bar{y}]\,\mathrm{d}s. \tag{17b}$$

For convergence it is assumed that $\xi_2 \geqslant \xi_1$: current contract inflation adjusts more quickly than core inflation, or the mean lag of the contract inflation process is no longer than that of the core inflation process.

Equation (17b) shows that 'current contract inflation', $q(t)$, can be brought down discontinuously by announcing, at t, a credible path of future recession. Core inflation, $\pi(t)$, is a function of the expectations, formed at each instant in the past, of the entire future path of the output gap. It can come down (gradually) only in response to credible announcements that policies to generate a recession will be pursued in the future.

To get a better appreciation of the cost of bringing down inflation in this model, we now consider an example of a specific path for expected output. The initial position at t_0 is one of current and expected future full employment with actual, core and current contract inflation all equal to each other. At t_0, output is unexpectedly lowered to $y(t_0) < \bar{y}$. The output gap is then expected to decay exponentially at a rate γ so that

$$y(\tau, t) - \bar{y} = [y(t_0) - \bar{y}]e^{-\gamma(\tau-t_0)} \qquad \tau \geqslant t_0 \cdot \gamma > 0. \tag{18}$$

Substituting (18) into (17a,b) yields

$$\pi(t) = \pi(t_0) + \frac{\xi_1\xi_2\Psi}{(\gamma + \xi_2 - \xi_1)\gamma}[y(t_0) - \bar{y}][1 - e^{-\gamma(t-t_0)}] \quad (19a)$$

$$q(t) = \pi(t) + \frac{\xi_2\Psi}{\gamma + \xi_2 - \xi_1}[y(t_0) - \bar{y}]e^{-\gamma(t-t_0)}. \quad (19b)$$

The long-run effect on core inflation of this policy is, from (19a).

$$\pi(\infty) - \pi(t_0) = \frac{\xi_1\xi_2\Psi}{\gamma + \xi_2 - \xi_1}[y(t_0) - \bar{y}] = \dot{p}(\infty) - \dot{p}(t_0^-) = q(\infty) - q(t_0^-).^{14} \quad (20a)$$

The undiscounted cumulative net output loss incurred for this reduction in inflation is

$$\int_{t_0}^{\infty}(y(t) - \bar{y})\,\mathrm{d}t = \frac{y(t_0) - \bar{y}}{\gamma} \quad (20b)$$

Consider the special case where $\gamma = \xi_1$ (the mean lag of the output process equals the mean lag of the core inflation process). In this case the impact of the current and expected future recession is to reduce actual inflation and current contract inflation immediately to their new long-run equilibrium levels:

$$\dot{p}(t) = q(t) = \pi(t_0) + \Psi[y(t_0) - \bar{y}], \qquad t \geqslant t_0.$$

Core inflation only approaches its long-run equilibrium value gradually according to

$$\pi(t) = \pi(t_0) + \Psi[y(t_0) - \bar{y}][1 - e^{-\gamma(t-t_0)}].$$

In this case, actual inflation and current contract inflation have been eliminated immediately and permanently, but the output cost is still to come. This would be obvious to an observer who can measure core inflation, which has yet to be brought down. It will be shown below that there are policies that reduce both actual and core inflation to any desired level before any of the output costs have actually been incurred. This raises the problem of time inconsistency and credibility of policy.

'Gradualism' versus 'cold turkey'

It can be seen from (19b) and (20a) that if γ is larger (smaller) that ξ_1, current contract inflation will on impact fall below (stay above) its new long-run equilibrium level. This might suggest that a short, sharp recession would, by changing current contract inflation promptly, be a more effective means of bringing down core inflation than a longer and milder recession. In fact, the opposite is the case. From (20a,b) it follows that, holding constant the cumulative net output loss $[y(t_0) - \bar{y}]/\gamma$, a deeper initial recession (a smaller value of $y(t_0)$) followed by a faster recovery (a larger value of γ) would produce a smaller reduction in steady-state inflation. The reason is, from (17a), that later expected output gaps, although discounted as regards their effect on $\pi(t)$, are also counted again and again (in fact continuously) on the interval $t_0 - t$.

In the presence of inflation inertia that is due to contractual or other institutional arrangements rather than to sluggish expectation adjustments, there are 'diminishing returns' to cold turkey deflation and gradualism is preferable. Only if a short, sharp shock can break down the nominal inertia, i.e. if the adjustment equations (15a,b) or (16a,b) are not structurally invariant to certain dramatic changes in the policy regime, is there a case for anti-inflationary heroics.

Time inconsistency and the timing of anti-inflationary benefits and output costs

It has already been shown that it is possible, through credible policy announcements, to bring down actual and current contract inflation immediately – before the output losses (whose expectation generated this reduction in inflation) have been incurred. It will be apparent from equations (17a,b) that it is also possible, if policy announcements are credible, to bring down core inflation gradually (i.e. over any finite time interval) to any desired level before any of the output costs have been incurred. Consider, for example, a policy that, starting at t_0, keeps output at its capacity level $\bar{y}$ until $\bar{t} > t_0$, at $\bar{\bar{y}}$ from $\bar{t}$ till $\bar{\bar{t}} > \bar{t}$ and again at $\bar{y}$ after $\bar{\bar{t}}$.

$$y(\tau, s) = \begin{cases} \bar{y};\ t_0 < \tau \leq \bar{t} \\ \bar{\bar{y}};\ \bar{t} < \tau \leq \bar{\bar{t}} \\ \bar{y};\ \tau > \bar{\bar{t}}. \end{cases} \tag{21}$$

It follows that

$$\pi(\bar{t}) = \pi(t_0) + \frac{\xi_1 \xi_2 \Psi}{(\xi_2 - \xi_1)^2}[1 - e^{-(\xi_2 - \xi_1)(\bar{t} - t_0)} - e^{-(\xi_2 - \xi_1)(\bar{\bar{t}} - \bar{t})} + e^{-(\xi_2 - \xi_1)(\bar{\bar{t}} - t_0)}](\bar{\bar{y}} - \bar{y}).$$

A recession strategy announced (and made credible) at $t = t_0$ that permits a reduction in core inflation at $t = \bar{t}$ to $\bar{\pi}(\bar{t})$, say, is therefore given by (21) with $\bar{\bar{y}}$ defined by

$$\bar{\bar{y}} - \bar{y} = \frac{[\bar{\pi}(\bar{t}) - \pi(t_0)](\xi_2 - \xi_1)^2}{\xi_1 \xi_2 \Psi [1 - e^{-(\xi_2 - \xi_1)(\bar{t} - t_0)} - e^{-(\xi_2 - \xi_1)(\bar{\bar{t}} - \bar{t})} + e^{-(\xi_2 - \xi_1)(\bar{\bar{t}} - t_0)}]} \tag{22}$$

As expected, the announced future recession is deeper the larger the reduction in core inflation, $\bar{\pi}(\bar{t}) - \pi(t_0)$, that is required.

Having achieved the desired reduction in core inflation at $t = \bar{t}$ without actually having suffered any output costs as yet, the temptation to renege on the earlier commitment to create a recession between $\bar{t}$ and $\bar{\bar{t}}$ would be hard to resist.

The argument that the recession must take place in order to validate and confirm the expectations held between $t = t_0$ and $t = \bar{t}$ and thus to preserve or invest in credibility for future policy announcements is unlikely to prove a political winner. Why have a recession when core inflation has already subsided? A policy maker treating bygones as bygones will, at $t = \bar{t}$ and beyond, keep output at its capacity level.

What this suggests is that any optimal policy will be time-inconsistent (Kydland and Prescott [1977]; Buiter [1981, 1983b]) if it has the property that some output costs still have to be incurred (if previous expectations are to be validated) after the inflation objectives have been achieved. Unless credible precommitment is possible, such policy announcements will not be believed by the private sector.

Time-consistent policies must be characterized by a better matching of the time profiles of costs and benefits: if a credible strategy cannot have the costs following the benefits, the recession will have to be brought forward in time. If a speedy reduction in inflation is sought, a deep, short recession will be the only credible strategy. It has already been shown that 'short, sharp shocks' of this kind are likely to be inefficient.

The model under consideration has implications not only for policy design but also for policy evaluation. Consider again the general expressions (17a,b). Conventional cost measures focus on output or unemployment costs incurred up to the time that a given reduction in core inflation has been achieved. When forward-looking expectations and inflation inertia play a role (as they do in this model), some, most or all of the costs attributable to the reduction in core inflation may be incurred after the anti-inflationary objective has been achieved.

Higher-order inertia

It is not difficult to visualize economic systems in which not only the price level and the core rate of inflation but also the rate of change of core inflation adjusts sluggishly. Attributing inertia to higher derivatives of the price and wage process is the continuous-time analogue to increasing the number of periods for which nominal contracts hold in discrete time models. For example, by slipping another derivative in the model of equations (14a and 16a, b) we obtain:

$$\ddot{\pi}(t) = \xi_1[\dot{q}(t) - \dot{\pi}(t)]$$

$$\ddot{q}(t, t) = \xi_2[\dot{q}(t) - \dot{\pi}(t) - \Psi(y(t) - \bar{y})]$$

$$\dot{p}(t) = \Psi[y(t) - \bar{y}] + \dot{\pi}(t).$$

With nominal inertia in the price level, core inflation and the rate of change of core inflation, the output costs of bringing down steady-state inflation will be high indeed.[15]

Some open-economy considerations and the sensible use of fiscal policy in a disinflationary program

In an open economy, appreciation of the exchange rate might seem to offer a mechanism for bringing down inflation more rapidly or at less cost than in a closed economy or an economy on a fixed exchange rate.

This will be considered in an open-economy extension of the model with backward-looking core inflation given in (14a,b). Possible direct cost and price effects of direct and indirect taxes are also introduced here. They can be applied to all closed-economy models in an obvious way. The economy is a price taker in the world market for its imports, whose world price is p^*, and in international financial markets. The country has some market power in the market for its exportable. Perfect capital mobility and international asset substitutability are assumed. The model is given in equations (23–29), where r^* is the foreign nominal interest rate, w denotes domestic costs, i.e. labor costs per unit of output or even the GDP deflator at factor cost; p is the consumer price index; e is the price of foreign exchange, g is exhaustive public spending; τ_i is the rate of indirect taxation; and τ_d is the income tax rate. All coefficients are positive.

$$\frac{d}{dt}[w(t) - \beta\tau_d(t)] = \Psi(y - \bar{y}) + \pi(t) \qquad 0 \leq \beta \leq 1 \tag{23}$$

$$p(t) = \tau_i(t) + \alpha w(t) + (1 - \alpha)[p^*(t) + e(t)] \qquad 0 < \alpha < 1 \tag{24}$$

$$\dot{\pi} = \xi[\dot{p} - \pi(t)] \tag{25}$$

$$\begin{aligned} y(t) = -\gamma[r(t) - \dot{p}(t, t)] + \delta[e(t) + p^*(t) - p(t)] \\ + \varepsilon[m(t) - p(t)] + \eta_1 g(t) - \eta_2[\tau_i(t) + \tau_d(t)] \end{aligned} \tag{26}$$

$$m(t) - p(t) = ky(t) - \lambda r(t) \tag{27}$$

$$\dot{e}(t, t) = r(t) - r^*(t) \tag{28}$$

$$c \equiv e + p^* - w \tag{29a}$$

$$l \equiv m - w. \tag{29b}$$

The model is similar to the one considered in Buiter and Miller [1982, 1983]. Note that taxes have both aggregate demand effects (equation (26)) and direct cost effects (equations (23) and (24)). Only a fraction β of an increase in income tax rates is translated into higher wage settlements (equation (23)). One interpretation of (23) is that it is the (adjusted) after-tax money wage, $w - \beta\tau_d$, that is predetermined or sticky rather than the before-tax wage, w. Note that the consumer price index (CPI) can move discontinuously, even if w is predetermined, through changes in indirect tax rates and in the exchange rate. The latter influences the CPI through the share of imports in final consumption $1 - \alpha$.

From equations (23)–(25) and (29b) it follows that

$$\begin{aligned} \pi(t) - \pi(t_0) = \xi\Psi\int_{t_0}^{t}[y(s) - \bar{y}]\,ds + \xi(1 - \alpha)[c(t) - c(t_0)] \\ + \xi[\tau_i(t) - \tau_i(t_0)] + \xi\beta[\tau_d(t) - \tau_d(t_0)] \end{aligned} \tag{30a}$$

or

$$\int_{t_0}^{t} [y(s) - \bar{y}]\, ds = \frac{\pi(t) - \pi(t_0)}{\xi\Psi} - \frac{(1-\alpha)}{\Psi}[c(t) - c(t_0)] - \left[\frac{\tau_i(t) - \tau_i(t_0) + \beta(\tau_d(t) - \tau_d^{(t_0)}}{\Psi}\right]. \tag{30b}$$

The familiar closed-economy output costs given in equation (15) are found back is the first term on the right-hand side of (30b). They can be reduced by an appreciation of the real exchange rate, c, by a cut in indirect taxes and, if $\beta \neq 0$, by a cut in direct taxes.

A balanced budget cut in indirect taxes matched by an increase in direct taxes helps reduce the output cost of disinflation only if direct tax increases do not raise before-tax wage settlements one-for-one.

Consider the steady state of the model:

$$l = \tau_i + (1-\alpha)c - \lambda(r^* - \dot{p}^* + \mu) + k\bar{y} \tag{31}$$

$$\bar{y} = -\gamma(r^* - \dot{p}^*) + (\delta\alpha - \varepsilon(1-\alpha))c + \varepsilon l - \varepsilon\tau_i + \eta_1 g - \eta_2(\tau_i + \tau_d) \tag{32}$$

$$\dot{p} = \pi = \mu = \dot{p}^* + \dot{e} \tag{33}$$

Across steady states, a reduction in monetary growth lowers actual and core inflation one-for-one. It will have no effect on competitiveness if there is no real balance effect ($\varepsilon = 0$). If there is a real balance effect, the increased stock of real balances associated with a lower rate of monetary growth will require a loss of competitiveness to maintain equilibrium in the output market if $(\delta + \varepsilon)\alpha > \varepsilon$. Assuming that there is no long-run effect on competitiveness from a reduction in the rate of inflation, any favorable short-run or impact effects on the price level, the rate of inflation and the core rate of inflation from an initial appreciation of the exchange rate will not lower the undiscounted cumulative net output cost of securing a sustained reduction in core inflation. Buiter and Miller [1982, 1983] show that, on impact, a reduction in monetary growth will be associated with a discrete, jump appreciation of the nominal exchange rate (a step down in e and c). If e jumps down, so, from (24), does p and so, from (25), does π. Core inflation jumps on impact but the apparent reduction in output cost that entails is nullified by the net depreciation of the real exchange rate that will be required during the remainder of the adjustment process to restore competitiveness. Only if the short, sharp shock of a sudden revaluation breaks down the inertia captured in (23) and (25) will it help reduce the output cost of bringing down inflation.

In principle, by using indirect and, if $\beta \neq 0$, direct tax cuts to melt core inflation instantaneously, a costless and immediate transition to a sustained lower rate of inflation is possible. The higher stock of real money balances demanded in a low-inflation equilibrium can be provided either by engineering a step increase in the level of the nominal money stock at the same time that its growth rate is reduced or by cutting taxes. Indirect tax cuts will do the job and so will direct tax cuts, if $\beta \neq 0$ and if it is the after-tax money wage rather than the before-tax money wage that is predetermined. If step adjustments in m are ruled out, immediate attainment of the new long-run equilibrium values of $m - p$ and π while maintaining full employment will, in general, require use of all three fiscal instruments, g, τ_i and τ_d.

Finally, in the context of this model, incomes policy can be seen as the ability to 'override' the core inflation adjustment equation (25). An extreme version would permit the authorities to pick a new starting value for π. The model clearly is not rich enough to suggest reasons why such policies have a habit of breaking down.

Hysteresis[16] *in the natural rate*

One of the most striking macroeconomic coincidences of the last fifteen years has been the way in which estimates of the natural rate of unemployment have moved up, along with the actual rate of unemployment. In this subsection we consider the implications of the hypothesis that this co-movement represents a causal influence running from current and past actual unemployment to the current natural unemployment rate. Letting $-y$ stand for the actual unemployment rate and $-\bar{y}$ for the natural rate, we postulate that

$$\bar{y}(t) = \bar{y}(t_0)e^{-\theta_2(t-t_0)} + \theta_2 \int_{t_0}^{t} y(s)\, e^{-\theta_2(t-s)}\, ds + \theta_1 \int_{t_0}^{t} e^{-\theta_2(t-s)}\dot{R}(s)\, ds \quad (35)$$

or

$$\dot{\bar{y}}(t) = \theta_2[y(t) - \bar{y}(t)] + \theta_1\dot{R}(t), \qquad \theta_2 \geqslant 0. \quad (35')$$

$R(t)$ stands for whatever structural factors or policies may affect the natural rate (union power, unemployment benefits, minimum wage, etc.). The second term on the right-hand side of (35) and the first term on the right-hand side of (35′) represent the hypothesis that unemployment destroys human capital by having a negative effect both on attitudes towards working and on the aptitude for work. The idea is an old one. Recent formalizations can be found in Buiter and Gersovitz [1981], Hargreaves Heap [1980], Gregory [1982, 1983] and Gregory and Smith [1983]. Clearly, as written in (35) the hypothesis is too strong, since no bounds are set on the natural rate in the long run: by selecting an appropriate path for unemployment, the natural rate can be steered to any level. Such global hysteresis is implausible. Over some finite range of unemployment rates, the hypothesis may, however, have merit. Equation (35) should be viewed as the log-linear approximation in the relevant range of unemployment rates to a model with local hysteresis. While the long-run or stationary Phillips curve is vertical, it can be made vertical at any point within that range.

To keep the exposition brief, the simple sluggish core inflation model of equations (14a, b) is added to (35). It is, of course, still true that

$$\pi(t) = \pi(t_0) + \xi\Psi\int_{t_0}^{t}[y(s) - \bar{y}(s)]\,\mathrm{d}s.$$

Since the natural rate no longer is invariant under the disinflation process, deviations from the natural rate cease to be a useful measure of cost. In the absence of tax cuts or incomes policy, core inflation can only be lowered by raising the actual unemployment rate above the natural rate. This, however, will, by (35′), begin to raise the natural rate, thus reducing gradually the disinflationary effect of any given increase in the actual rate. Formally, since

$$\bar{y}(t) = \bar{y}(t_0) + \theta_1[R(t) - R(t_0)] + \theta_2\int_{t_0}^{t}[y(s) - \bar{y}(s)]\,\mathrm{d}s,$$

it follows, using (35), that, if structural factors affecting the actual rate remain unchanged (i.e. if $\dot{R}(t) = 0$),

$$\int_{t_0}^{t}[y(s) - \bar{y}(s)]\,\mathrm{d}s = \int_{t_0}^{t}[y(s) - \bar{y}(t_0)]e^{-\theta_2(t-s)}\,\mathrm{d}s.$$

The disinflationary effect of any given increase in unemployment above its initial value will decay exponentially over time as the natural rate catches up with the actual rate.

In the hysteresis model a *permanent* increase in the rate of unemployment $-\Delta y$ will buy only a finite long-run reduction in the rate of inflation $-\Delta\pi = (\xi\Psi/\theta_2)(-\Delta y)$. With an exogenous natural rate, that same steady-state reduction in inflation can be achieved by having the same constant increase in unemployment for only a finite period of time.

The simple hysteresis model outlined here has much the same implications for the inflation-unemployment process as does entering the rate of change of output (unemployment) rather than its level as an argument in the Phillips curve. The simplest version of this model is

$$\dot{p} = \phi\dot{y} + \pi \tag{36}$$

$$\dot{\pi} = \xi(\dot{p} - \pi). \tag{14b}$$

The solution for core inflation is:

$$\pi(t) = \pi(t_0) + \xi\phi[y(t) - y(t_0)], \tag{37a}$$

while current inflation is given by

$$\dot{p}(t) = \phi\dot{y}(t) + \phi\xi[y(t) - y(t_0)] + \pi(t_0). \tag{37b}$$

The striking implication of this model is that all anti-inflationary gains from a contractionary policy are completely reversed if the economy is permitted to recover. As Tobin [1980, p. 61] says,

It is possible that there is no NAIRU, no natural rate, except one that floats with actual history. It is just possible that the direction the economy is moving in is at least as important for acceleration and deceleration as its level. These possibilities should give policy makers pause as they embark on yet another application of the orthodox demand management cure for inflation.

Note that equation (37b) is consistent with some of the early work on Phillips curves, which argued that both the level and the rate of change of unemployment could be significant in inflation equations but ignored endogenous core inflation (e.g. Phillips [1958], and Lipsey [1960]).

This similarity between the hysteresis model and the model of equations (36) and (14b) is especially striking when we consider the effect, in the hysteresis model, of a constant path $y(s) = \bar{\bar{y}}$ for $t_0 < s \leqslant t$. This yields the following expression for core inflation:

$$\pi(t) = \pi(t_0) + \frac{\xi\phi}{\theta_2}[\bar{\bar{y}} - \bar{y}(t_0)][1 - e^{-\theta_2(t-t_0)}].$$

As t goes to infinity, this approaches

$$\lim_{T\to\infty}\pi(t) = \pi(t_0) + \frac{\xi\phi}{\theta_2}[\bar{\bar{y}} - \bar{y}(t_0)].$$

Asymptotically, the hysteresis model too has complete reversibility of inflationary gains achieved through contractionary policy.

Although the economic mechanisms involved are very different, the output, or unemployment, costs of achieving a permanent reduction in inflation are similar for the hysteresis model and the 'unaugmented', pre-Phelps and Friedman, Phillips curve. With the $\dot{p} = \phi(y - \bar{y}) + \pi$ specification, an exogenous natural rate $\bar{y}$ and no adjustment, however gradual, of core inflation π towards actual inflation, the 'sacrifice ratio' – the cumulative, undiscounted net output or unemployment cost (expressed as a percentage) divided by the steady-state reduction in the inflation rate – is infinite. The same specification with an exogenous natural rate but gradual convergence of core inflation to actual inflation yields a positive but finite sacrifice ratio, whose exact magnitude depends on the details of the core inflation adjustment mechanism. The assumption of instantaneous adjustment of core inflation through rational perception and anticipation of credible policy actions produces a sacrifice ratio of zero. The hysteresis model with gradually adjusting core inflation again yields an infinite sacrifice ratio. Not because, as with the old Phillips curve, core inflation never adjusts but because the natural rate adjusts gradually towards the actual unemployment rate. The case for any policy action(s) that can 'override' the core inflation adjustment equations is therefore even stronger if the hysteresis hypothesis has anything to recommend it.

Credibility and the consistency of monetary and fiscal policy
All models considered in this chapter have the property that a sustained reduction in the rate of inflation requires a long-run reduction in the rate of monetary growth. While the exact nature of the relevant monetary aggregate is not apparent from these models, it seems reasonable to assume that a long-run sustained reduction in the rate of growth of any monetary aggregate presupposes corresponding reduction in the growth rate of the monetary base. If this is the case, a necessary condition for the credibility of a policy to reduce steady-state inflation is the consistency of the long-run monetary objectives with the government's fiscal program.

We can get some sense of the 'eventual monetization' implied by the government's fiscal program by considering the government's comprehensive balance sheet (see Buiter [1983c], given in (38)).

$$N(t) \equiv p_k(t)K(t) + p_R(t)R(t) + T(t) + \Pi(t) - \frac{M(t)}{p(t)} - \frac{B(t)}{p(t)} - \frac{p_c(t)C(t)}{p(t)}, \tag{38}$$

where N is real government net worth, K the public sector capital stock, p_k the present value of the future returns to a unit of public sector capital, R the number of shares of public sector natural resource property rights, p_R the price of a share in these property rights, T the present value of future taxes net of transfers, Π the capital value of the government's note issue monopoly, M the nominal stock of high-powered money, B the stock of nominally denominated short bonds, C the number of consols paying a coupon of £1, p_c the price of a consol, and p the general price level.

Let δ_k be the capital rental rate, δ_R the return on a share of public sector natural resource property rights, g government consumption, τ current taxes net of transfers, i the short nominal interest rate and r the short real rate. Then, assuming that $r(t) = i(t) - [\dot{p}(t, t)/p(t)]$,

$$p_k(t) = \int_t^{\infty} \delta_k(s, t) \exp[-\int_t^s r(u, s)\, du]\, ds \tag{39a}$$

$$p_R(t) = \int_t^{\infty} \delta_R(s, t) \exp[-\int_t^s r(u, s)\, du]\, ds. \tag{39b}$$

$$T(t) = \int_t^{\infty} \tau(s, t) \exp[-\int_t^s r(u, s)\, du]\, ds \tag{39c}$$

$$\Pi(t) = \frac{1}{p(t)}\int_t^\infty i(s, t)M(s, t) \exp[-\int_t^s i(u, s) \, du] \, ds$$

$$= \int_t^\infty i(s, t)\frac{M(s, t)}{p(s, t)} \exp[-\int_t^s r(u, t) \, du] \, ds \tag{39d}$$

$$p_c(t) = \int_t^\infty \exp[-\int_t^s i(u, s) \, du] \, ds. \tag{39e}$$

Note that the capital value of the note issue monopoly, Π, is given by the discounted future income derived from the assets that are (and will be) held to 'back' the note circulation. Equalization of expected rates of return is assumed.

Since the present value of future planned public consumption cannot exceed public sector net worth (a constraint we shall assume to hold with strict equality), we have

$$G(t) = N(t), \tag{40}$$

where

$$G(t) = \int_t^\infty g(s, t) \exp[-\int_t^s r(u, t) \, du] \, ds. \tag{40'}$$

Let

$$S(T) \equiv \Pi(t) - \frac{M(t)}{p(t)}$$

Integrating by parts, it is found that $S(t)$ is the present value of future seigniorage, i.e.

$$S(t) \equiv \frac{1}{p(t)}\int_t^\infty \dot{M}(s, t) \exp[-\int_t^s i(u, t) \, du] \, ds$$

$$\equiv \int_t^\infty \frac{\dot{M}(s, t)}{M(s, t)} \frac{M(s, t)}{p(s, t)} \exp[-\int_t^s r(u, t) \, du] \, ds. \tag{41}$$

Treating $S(t)$ as the residual item, (40) and (38) tell us the amount of revenue to be raised through seigniorage (in present-value terms), given the present value of the government's consumption program and the government's tangible and intangible non-monetary assets and liabilities, i.e.

$$S(t) = G(t) - \left[p_k(t)K(t) + p_R(t)R(t) + T(t) - \left(\frac{B(t) + p_c(t)C(t)}{p(t)}\right)\right]. \tag{42}$$

Let y denote trend output and n its rate of growth. A real (index-linked) consol will have a coupon yield $\bar{R}$ if the instantaneous real rate of return is $r - n$, where $\bar{R}$ is given by

$$\bar{R}(t) = \left\{ \int_t^\infty e^{-\int_t^s (r(u,\, t) - n)\mathrm{d}u} \mathrm{d}s \right\}^{-1}$$

We can solve (42) for a constant proportional rate of monetary growth $\dot{M}/M$ and a constant trend income velocity of circulation $V \equiv py/M$ to yield

$$\frac{\dot{M}}{M} = V\bar{R}(t) \left[\frac{G(t) - T(t)}{y(t)} - \frac{p_K(t)K(t) + p_R(t)R(t)}{y(t)} + \frac{\mathrm{B}(t) + p_c(t)C(t)}{p(t)y(t)} \right] \quad (43)$$

If (and only if) the public sector consumption and tax programs together with its other non-monetary assets and liabilities, imply a high value of $\dot{M}/M$, then a fiscal correction is a necessary condition for achieving credibility for an anti-inflationary policy. Note that in full steady-state equilibrium, (43) becomes the familiar expression

$$\frac{\dot{M}}{M} = V\left[\frac{g - \tau}{y} - (r - n)\left(\frac{p_k K + p_R R}{y} - \frac{B + p_c C}{py} \right) \right].$$

Eventual monetary growth is governed in steady state by the trend public sector current account (or consumption account) deficit, with debt service evaluated at the real interest rate net of the natural rate of growth. This deficit measure can differ dramatically from the conventionally measured public sector financial deficit (PSBR), which is often and erroneously taken as a guide to eventual monetization.

III Conclusion

One conclusion that emerges strongly from this chapter is the importance of fiscal policy in securing a lasting reduction in inflation at least cost. First, the long-run reduction in monetary growth that is necessary for a sustained reduction in inflation is credible only if it is consistent with the government's spending and tax programs and its outstanding non-monetary assets and liabilities. Second, indirect tax cuts (and, under certain conditions, direct tax cuts) can be used in ways first suggested by Okun [1978] to secure a painless melting away of core inflation. Tax cuts or a once-and-for-all increase in the level of the nominal money stock path must also be used in order to provide the higher stock of real money balances demanded when the inflation rate is lower at a given price level rather than through a further downward shift in the price-level path.

A final comment suggested by the analysis of the chapter relates to the apparent contrast between the findings of R. J. Gordon, who has documented many historical episodes during which bringing down inflation appears to have been costly (Gordon [1982]), and T. S. Sargent, who finds that the ends of four hyper-inflations in the post-World War I era were achieved without dramatic output losses (Sargent [1982]). These findings can be reconciled by arguing that, during hyper-inflations, inflation inertia (if not price-level inertia) disappears. All the advantages of longer-term non-contingent nominal contracts are overriden by the need to revise prices almost continuously. During hyper-inflations (at any rate in their final phases) the inflation process is characterized by models like the ones in equations (8), (9) and (10a,b) or even by the purely classical flexible price model.

If there is no inflation inertia but still some price-level inertia, optimal anti-inflationary policy has the following features. First, a credible announcement of current and future reductions in monetary growth. This was provided by fiscal reform and currency reform plus the general realization that something had to be done and was going to be done to stop the hyper-inflations. Second, a once-and-for-all increase in the level of the nominal money stock to raise the stock of real money balances without any need to lower the price-level path. The real world counterpart to this was the very large increases in the nominal money stocks in the periods following the sudden ending of the hyper-inflations (Sargent [1982]). Such money stock jumps make no sense in a flexible price model[17] but may be called for in models with price-level inertia.

Gordon [1982] considered episodes of moderate inflation. Long-term non-contingent nominal contracts are adopted because they permit economic agents to economize on frequent, costly renegotiations, on the search and information costs of first identifying all possible relevant contingencies and then monitoring them and on the costs of enforcing complicated conditional contract clauses. Continuously variable and perfectly flexible prices or fully contingent contracts are costly and undesirable when the costs from changing prices frequently outweigh the benefits. In moderate inflations, long-term nominal contracts are still viewed as viable and desirable by private agents. Such changes in the length of these contracts and in other relevant characteristics as one would expect to occur when the trend rate of inflation changes are likely to be second-order for the range of inflation rates experienced in most OECD countries since World War II. With the unconditional long-term nominal contract structure intact, even fully credible announcements of future reductions in monetary growth will not remove the need for a period of (expected) output losses and unemployment if inflation is to be brought down.

Notes

Originally published in A. Argy and J. Nevile, (eds.) (1985), *Inflation and Unemployment: Theory, Experience and Policy Making*, London, George Allen & Unwin.

1 An elegant statement and extension of the traditional theory of the welfare costs of inflation is Fischer [1981b].
2 This assumes that lump-sum taxes are available to the government. If higher monetary growth and the associated higher inflation increase the real value of new money issues (if the elasticity of demand for real money balances with respect to the interest rate is less than unity), the same real public spending program can be financed with lower explicit taxes. If these taxes are distortionary, the usual welfare loss measure overstates the true cost.
3 The most careful and informative work in this area has been done by Fischer [1981a,b; 1982]. See also Taylor [1981].
4 $v(\bar{c}, L - l, 1) > v(\bar{c}, L, 0)$ for any l $(0 \leqslant l \leqslant L)$ would mean that, even without any pecuniary advantage of employment over unemployment, people would choose to be employed. It is a much stronger condition than the one given in the text.
5 Separability, i.e. $v(c, L - l, \theta) = v[u(c, L - l), \theta]$, would be convenient analytically.
6 See also Buiter and Jewitt [1981].
7 The natural rate of growth is assumed equal to zero.
8 Actual and expected $\bar{y}$ and $\bar{f}$ are again held constant.
9 In the long run,

$$r = \left(\frac{-1 + \lambda^{-1}k\lambda\varepsilon}{\gamma + \lambda\varepsilon}\right)\bar{y} + \frac{\eta}{\gamma + \lambda\varepsilon}\bar{f} + \frac{\gamma}{\gamma + \lambda\varepsilon}\bar{\bar{\mu}}.$$

10 When both γ and ε are equal to zero, a reduction in monetary growth and inflation leaves the nominal interest rate unaffected and costless disinflation is automatic.
11 Note that, since m and f are manipulated to keep output at its full employment level, the Barro-Grossman equation (8) and the Mussa equation (9) coincide.
12 It is assumed that there is no long-run trend in the rate of inflation.
13 Note that the characteristic roots of the homogeneous system (16a,b) are 0 and $\xi_2 - \xi_1$.
14 For any variable x, let $x(t^-) \equiv \lim_{\substack{h \to 0 \\ h > 0}} x(t - h)$.
15 This is very similar in spirit to John Flemming's suggestion in Flemming [1976].
16 Hysteresis is the property of dynamic systems that the stationary equilibrium is a function of the initial conditions and/or the transition trajectory towards the steady state. In systems of linear differential equations with constant coefficients such as $Dx = Ax + Bz$, hysteresis is present when A has one or more zero eigenvalues.
17 Except for government revenue reasons. We owe this point to Bob Flood.

References

Barro, R. J. and Grossman, H. I. (1976), *Money, Employment and Inflation.* Cambridge, Cambridge University Press.

Buiter, W. H. (1980), 'Monetary, financial and fiscal policy under rational expectations', *IMF Staff Papers*, 27, December, 758–813.

—— (1981), 'The superiority of contingent rules over fixed rules in models with rational expectations', *Economic Journal*, 91, September, 647–70.

—— (1983a), 'The measurement of public sector deficits and its implications for policy evaluation and design', *IMF Staff Papers*, 30 (2), June, 306–49.

—— (1983b), 'Optimal and time-consistent policies in continuous time rational expectations models', LSE Econometrics Program, *Discussion Paper No. A 39*, June.
—— (1983c), 'Saddlepoint problems in continuous time rational expectations models: a general method and some macroeconomic examples', revised, March, *Econometrica*, 52 (3), May 1984, 665–80.
—— and Gersovitz, M. (1981), 'Issues in controllability and the theory of economic policy', *Journal of Public Economics*, 15, February, 33–43.
—— and Jewitt, I. (1981), 'Staggered wage setting with real wage relativities: variations of a theme of Taylor', *Manchester School of Economic and Social Studies*, 49 (3), September, 211–28.
—— and Miller, M. (1981), Monetary policy and international competitiveness', *Oxford Economic Papers*, 33, July, Supplement, 143–74.
—— and Miller, M. (1982), 'Real exchange rate overshooting and the output cost of bringing down inflation', *European Economic Review*, 18, May/June, 85–123.
—— and Miller, M. (1983), 'Real exchange rate overshooting and the output cost of bringing down inflation; some further results', in J. Frenkel (ed.), *Exchange Rates and International Macroeconomics*, Chicago, Ill., University of Chicago Press.
Calvo, G. A. (1982a), 'Staggered contracts and exchange rate policy', *Discussion Paper Series No. 129*, New York, Columbia University.
—— (1982b), 'Staggered contracts in a utility-maximizing framework', *Discussion Paper Series No. 130*, New York, Columbia University.
—— (1982c), 'Real exchange rate dynamics with fixed nominal parities: on the economics of overshooting and interest-rate management with rational price setting', *Discussion Paper Series No. 162*, New York, Columbia University.
Carlton, D. W. (1982), 'The disruptive effect of inflation on the organization of markets', in R. E. Hall (ed.), *Inflation: Causes and Effects*, Chicago, Ill., University of Chicago Press, 139–152.
Dornbusch, R. (1976), 'Expectations and exchange rate dynamics', *Journal of Political Economy*, 84, December, 1161–76.
Feldstein, M. S. (1979), 'The welfare cost of permanent inflation and optimal short-run economic policy', *Journal of Political Economy*, 87 (4), August, 749–68.
Fischer, S. (1981a), 'Relative shocks, relative price variability and inflation', *Brookings Papers on Economic Activity*, 2, 381–431.
—— (1981b), 'Towards an understanding of the costs of inflation: II', in K. Brunner and A. H. Meltzer (eds.), *The Costs and Consequences of Inflation*, Carnegie-Rochester Conference Series on Public Policy, 15, Amsterdam, North-Holland, 5–42.
—— (1982), 'Relative price variability and inflation in the United States and Germany', *European Economic Review*, 18, May/June, 171–96.
—— and Modigliani, F. (1978), 'Towards an understanding of the real effects and costs of inflation', *Weltwirtschaftliches Archiv*, 114, 810–33.
Flemming, J. (1976), *Inflation*, London, Oxford University Press.
Gordon, R. J. (1973), 'The welfare costs of higher unemployment', *Brookings Papers on Economic Activity*, 1, 133–205.
—— (1982), 'Why stopping inflation may be costly: evidence for fourteen historical episodes', in R. E. Hall (ed.), *Inflation, Causes and Effects*, Chicago, Ill., University of Chicago Press, 11–40.
Gregory, R. G. (1982), 'Work and welfare in the years ahead', *Australian Economic Papers*, 21, December, 219–43.

—— (1983), 'The slide into mass unemployment; labour market theories, facts and policies', *Annual Lectures*, The Academy of the Social Sciences, Australia.
—— and Smith, R. E. (1983), 'Unemployment, inflation and job creation policies in Australia', unpublished.
Hall, R. E. (1976), 'The Phillips curve and macroeconomic policy', in K. Brunner and A. H. Meltzer (eds.), *The Phillips Curve and Labor Markets*, Carnegie-Rochester Conference Series on Public Policy, 1, Amsterdam, North-Holland, 127–48.
—— (1981), 'Comment' on S. Fischer, 'Relative shocks, relative price variability, and inflation', *Brookings Papers on Economic Activity*, 2, 432–4.
Hargreaves Heap, S. P. (1980), 'Choosing the wrong "natural" rate: accelerating inflation or decelerating employment and growth', *Economic Journal*, 90, September, 611–20.
Kydland, F. and Prescott, E. (1977), 'Rules rather than discretion: the time-inconsistency of optimal plans', *Journal of Political Economy*, 85 (3), June, 473–91.
Lipsey, R. G. (1960), 'The relationship between unemployment and the rate of change of money wages in the United Kingdom, 1862–1957: A further analysis', *Economica*, 27 (105), February, 1–31.
Miller, M. (1979), 'The unemployment cost of changing steady state inflation', mimeo, University of Warwick.
Mussa, M. (1981), 'Sticky prices and disequilibrium adjustment in a rational model of the inflationary process', *American Economic Review*, 71, December, 1020–27.
Obstfeld, M. and Rogoff, K. (1982), 'Exchange rate dynamics with sluggish prices under alternative price-adjustment rules', unpublished May.
Okun, A. (1978), 'Efficient disinflationary policies', *American Economic Review*, 68, May, 348–52.
Phelps, E. S. (1972), *Inflation Policy and Unemployment Theory: The Cost Benefits Approach to Monetary Planning*, New York, Norton.
Phillips, A. W. (1958), 'The relation between unemployment and the rate of change of money wage rates in the United Kingdom, 1861–1957', *Economica*, 25 (100), November, 283–99.
Sargan, J. D. (1980), 'A model of wage-price inflation', *Review of Economic Studies*, 47, January, 97–112.
Sargent, T. S. (1982), 'The ends of four big inflations', in R. E. Hall (ed.), *Inflation, Causes and Effects*, Chicago, Ill., University of Chicago Press, 41–97.
Taylor, J. B. (1980), 'Aggregate dynamics and staggered contracts', *Journal of Political Economy*, 88 (1), February, 1–23.
—— (1981), 'On the relation between the variability of inflation and the average inflation rate', in K. Brunner and A. H. Meltzer (eds.), *The Costs and Consequences of Inflation*, Carnegie-Rochester Conference Series on Public Policy, 15, Amsterdam, North-Holland, 57–68.
Tobin, J. (1980), 'Stabilization policy ten years after', *Brookings Paper on Economic Activity*, 1, 19–71.
Turnovsky, S. J. (1980), 'The choice of monetary instruments under alternative forms of price expectations', *Manchester School of Economic and Social Studies*, 48 (1), March, 39–62.
Weiss, L. (1980), 'The role for active monetary policy in a rational expectations model', *Journal of Political Economy*, 88 (2), April, 221–33.

Chapter 10

Policy evaluation and design for continuous time linear rational expectations models: some recent developments

I Introduction

The first systematic introduction to economic dynamics came for me, as for many of my contemporaries, through William Baumol's lucid and 'user-friendly' book *Economic Dynamics* (Baumol [1970]).[1] It seems appropriate, therefore, to survey, in this volume honouring William Baumol's contributions to economics, some of the recent developments in modelling dynamic macroeconomic systems. All these developments bear the hallmark of the rational expectations revolution which has swept macroeconomics and international finance since the early seventies. Only models represented by systems of first order linear differential equations with constant coefficients are considered. The reason for limiting the discussion to linear systems will be obvious to those who have attempted to analyse even very simple non-linear rational expectations models. The restriction to continuous time systems reflects the existence of many excellent survey articles on general discrete time systems (e.g. Whiteman [1983], Blanchard [1983], and McCallum [1983]). Continuous time rational expectations models, by contrast, appear extensively in the literature in one, two or occasionally three dimensions, but have not been the subject of systematic surveys to anything like the same extent. (Exceptions are Dixit [1980], Buiter [1981a, 1982], and Currie and Levine [1982].)

Section II of the paper summarises the continuous time analogue of the discrete time solution method of Blanchard and Kahn [1980], as developed in Buiter [1982]. Section III considers some problems that are associated (or may appear to be associated) with this solution method. Section IV contains the solution to the general linear-quadratic optimal control problem in continuous time rational expectations models. It builds on work by Calvo [1978], Driffill [1982], Miller and Salmon [1982, 1983] and Buiter [1983].

Both optimal (but in general time-inconsistent) and time-consistent (but in general sub-optimal) solutions are derived in a uniform framework. A numerical example, involving optimal and time-consistent anti-inflationary policy design in a contract model (using an algorithm developed by Austin and Buiter [1982]), serves as an illustration of the general approach in Section V.

II Solving continuous time linear rational expectations models

Consider the continuous time linear rational expectations model given in (1):

$$\begin{bmatrix} \dot{x}(t) \\ E_t\dot{y}(t) \end{bmatrix} = A\begin{bmatrix} x(t) \\ y(t) \end{bmatrix} + Bz(t) \tag{1}$$

with boundary conditions

$$F_1x(t_0) + F_2y(t_0) = f$$

$$F_1 \text{ is } n_1 \times n_1 \text{ and of full rank.} \tag{2a}$$

$$\text{The solution is restricted to lie on the stable manifold.} \tag{2b}$$

x is an n_1 vector of predetermined state variables, y an $n - n_1$ vector of non-predetermined state variables, and z a k-vector of exogenous or forcing variables. A, B, F_1 and F_2 are known constant matrices; f is a known vector of constants. E is the expectation operator and $\Omega(t)$ the information set conditioning expectations formed at time t. For any vector w, $E_tw(s) \equiv E[w(s) \mid \Omega(t)]$ and $\dot{w}(t) \equiv \lim_{s \downarrow t}\left(\frac{w(s) - w(t)}{s - t}\right)$. The information set $\Omega(t)$ contains all current and past values of x, y and z and the true structure of the model given in (1) and (2a,b). Formally, we assume:

$$E_tw(s) = w(s) \qquad s \leqslant t \tag{A1}$$

$$\Omega(t) \supseteq \Omega(s) \qquad t > s \tag{A2}$$

We shall make use of the 'law of iterated projections', i.e.:

$$E[E(w(s) \mid \Omega(t_0)) \mid \Omega(t_1)] = \begin{cases} E[w(s) \mid \Omega(t_1)] & t_1 \leqslant t_0 \\ E[w(s) \mid \Omega(t_0)] & t_0 \leqslant t_1 \end{cases} \tag{3}$$

Assumption (A1) combines 'perfect hindsight' ($s < t$) and 'weak consistency' ($s = t$)(see Turnovsky and Burmeister [1977]). Assumption (A2) means that memory does not decay. Condition (3) is a basic property of conditional expectations, if (A2) holds.

For ordinary n-dimensional first-order linear differential equation systems, a unique solution exists if there are n linearly independent boundary conditions.[2] For the n_1 predetermined variables x, the boundary conditions take the form of n_1 linear restrictions at the initial date t_0. For many applications these linear restrictions will take the form of n_1 initial values, i.e.:

$$x(t_0) = \bar{x}(t_0) \tag{2a'}$$

In Buiter and Miller [1982, 1983a] a more general form of the boundary conditions for the predetermined variables such as (2a) was necessary.

The meaning of the boundary condition (2b) will become apparent below. A sufficient condition for ruling out the explosive growth of the expectation, held at time t, of future values of z, is that $E_t z(s)$ is a bounded function of s on $(t, +\infty)$ and continuous almost everywhere.

The solution for x and y is restricted to be a continuous function of time when there is no change in current expectations of future values of the forcing variables, i.e. $x(t)$ and $y(t)$ are continuous functions of t as long as $E_t z(s)$, $s > t$, does not vary with t. This rules out anticipated future discrete jumps in y.[3] The economic rationale for this restriction appears sound: an infinite instantaneous rate of capital gain cannot be anticipated in models with reasonably rich opportunities for intertemporal arbitrage and speculation.

There is no formal recognition of uncertainty in the model. The expectations are to be interpreted as single-valued or point expectations, i.e. expectations held with complete subjective certainty. It will be clear, however, that the results obtained for (1) are applicable to the stochastic linear differential equation system given in (4), provided there are no measurement errors in the observation of the state vector $[x, y]^T$.[4]

$$\begin{bmatrix} dx(t) \\ E_t dy(t) \end{bmatrix} = A \begin{bmatrix} x(t)dt \\ y(t)dt \end{bmatrix} + Bz(t)dt + dv \tag{4}$$

The continuous time vector process $v(t)$ is a stationary zero mean stochastic process with independent increments. Examples are Wiener processes (or Brownian motion), the Poisson (or jump) process and mixed Poisson and Brownian processes. $z(t)$ is a strictly deterministic function of time. Because of the linearity of (4), certainty equivalence applies and the solutions for the deterministic case are directly transferable (with suitable redefinition of the integrals as stochastic integrals) to the stochastic system given in (4). The same applies to the optimal decision rules for the linear-quadratic control problem analysed in Section 4. If the state vector is measured with error, e.g. if the information set consists of current and past observations on:

$$\Psi(t) = H \begin{bmatrix} x(t) \\ y(t) \end{bmatrix} + \varepsilon(t)$$

where H is an $m \times n$ known matrix and $\varepsilon(t)$ is a stationary zero mean stochastic process with independent increments and independent of

$[x, y]^T$, then the solution of (4) involves optimal (e.g. Kalman) filtering (see e.g. Bryson and Ho [1975]). For reasons of space this case is not considered further.

Returning to the model of equations (1) and (2a,b) we assume:

A can be diagonalised by a similarity transformation (A3)

A has n distinct eigenvalues (A4)

A has n_1 eigenvalues with non-positive real parts (stable roots) and $n - n_1$ eigenvalues with positive real parts (unstable roots) (A5)

Necessary and sufficient for (A3) is that A should have n linearly independent eigenvectors. (A4) is sufficient for (A3) and saves us the notational bother of having to give the general solution for the case of repeated eigenvalues. The example in Section III shows that no problems of principle are involved. There exists a straightforward Jordan canonical form generalisation of the method of this section to the case where A cannot be diagonalised by a similarity transformation.

Assumption (A5) states that there are as many stable roots as predetermined variables and as many unstable roots as non-predetermined variables. Section III contains an example with one predetermined variable, one non-predetermined variable and two zero roots. The solution method of this section is nevertheless applicable.

Given (A3)–(A5) we can write:

$$A = V^{-1}\Lambda V \tag{5}$$

or

$$VAV^{-1} = \Lambda$$

V is an $n \times n$ matrix whose rows are linearly independent left eigenvectors of A. Λ is a diagonal matrix whose diagonal elements are the eigenvalues of A. A, B, V, V^{-1} and Λ are partitioned conformably with x and y as in (6).

$$A = \begin{bmatrix} A_{11} & A_{12} \\ A_{21} & A_{22} \end{bmatrix}; \; B = \begin{bmatrix} B_1 \\ B_2 \end{bmatrix}; \; V = \begin{bmatrix} V_{11} & V_{12} \\ V_{21} & V_{22} \end{bmatrix}; \; V^{-1} \equiv W = \begin{bmatrix} W_{11} & W_{12} \\ W_{21} & W_{22} \end{bmatrix}$$

$$\Lambda = \begin{bmatrix} \Lambda_1 & 0 \\ 0 & \Lambda_2 \end{bmatrix} \tag{6}$$

Λ_1 is an $n_1 \times n_1$ diagonal matrix containing the stable roots of A and Λ_2 an $(n - n_1) \times (n - n_1)$ diagonal matrix containing the unstable roots of A.

We also define:

$$\begin{bmatrix} p \\ q \end{bmatrix} = V\begin{bmatrix} x \\ y \end{bmatrix} \text{ or } \begin{bmatrix} x \\ y \end{bmatrix} = W\begin{bmatrix} p \\ q \end{bmatrix} \tag{7}$$

p is an n_1 vector and q an $n - n_1$ vector.

Taking expectations conditional on E_t on both sides of (4) and using (5), (6) and (7), we obtain:

$$E_t\dot{q}(t) = \Lambda_2 E_t q(t) + DE_t z(t) \tag{8}$$

where

$$D \equiv V_{21}B_1 + V_{22}B_2 \tag{9}$$

From the law of iterated projections given in (3) it follows that, for $t \leqslant s$:

$$E_t\dot{q}(s) = \Lambda_2 E_t q(s) + DE_t z(s)$$

Treating this as a differential equation in s, conditional on E_t, we can write the solution for $E_t q(s)$ in 'forward-looking' form as:

$$E_t q(s) = [\exp\Lambda_2 s]K_2 - \int_s^\infty [\exp\Lambda_2(s - \tau)]DE_t z(\tau)d\tau \qquad s \geqslant t \tag{10}$$

K_2 is an $n - n_1$ vector of arbitrary constants. Since Λ_2 contains unstable roots only, boundary condition (2b), that the solution should be convergent, compels us to choose K_2 as follows:

$$K_2 = 0 \tag{2b$'$}$$

Given (2b′) we evaluate (10) at $t = s$. From the weak consistency assumption (A1) it then follows that:

$$q(t) = -\int_t^\infty [\exp\Lambda_2(t - \tau)]DE_t z(\tau)d\tau \tag{10$'$}$$

From equations (6) and (7) we know that $q = V_{21}x + V_{22}y$. If V_{22} is invertible, the solution for the non-predetermined variables can therefore be written as:

$$y(t) = -V_{22}^{-1}V_{21}x(t) - V_{22}^{-1}\int_t^\infty [\exp\Lambda_2(t - \tau)]DE_t z(\tau)d\tau \tag{11}$$

An equivalent expression, provided W_{11} has an inverse, is:

$$y(t) = W_{21}W_{11}^{-1}x(t) - V_{22}^{-1}\int_t^\infty [\exp\Lambda_2(t - \tau)]DE_t z(\tau)d\tau \tag{11$'$}$$

Substituting (11) or (11′) into the equations of motion for $\dot{x}$ given in (1) and choosing the backward-looking solution for $x(t)$ we find that the predetermined variables are given by (12) or (12′):

$$x(t) = W_{11}[\exp\Lambda_1(t - t_0)]\, W_{11}^{-1}x(t_0) + \int_{t_0}^{t} W_{11}[\exp\Lambda_1(t - s)]\, W_{11}^{-1}B_1 z(s)ds$$

$$- \int_{t_0}^{t} W_{11}[\exp\Lambda_1(t - s)]W_{11}^{-1}A_{12}V_{22}^{-1}\int_{s}^{\infty} [\exp\Lambda_2(s - \tau)]DE_s z(\tau)d\tau ds$$

$$x(t) = W_{11}[\exp\Lambda_1(t - t_0)]W_{11}^{-1}x(t_0) + \int_{t_0}^{t} W_{11}[\exp\Lambda_1(t - s)]W_{11}^{-1}B_1 z(s)ds$$

$$- \int_{t_0}^{t} W_{11}[\exp\Lambda_1(t - s)]\, [\Lambda_1 V_{12}V_{22}^{-1} + W_{11}^{-1}W_{12}\Lambda_2]$$

$$\times \int_{s}^{\infty} [\exp\Lambda_2(s - \tau)]DE_s z(\tau)d\tau ds \qquad (12')$$

Boundary condition (2a) can be written as:

$$x(t_0) = -F_1^{-1}F_2 y(t_0) + F_1^{-1}f \qquad (13)$$

The initial value for x at $t = t_0$ is solved for from (13) and (11) or (11′) with y evaluated at $t = t_0$.

Thus the non-predetermined variables can be expressed as a function of the current predetermined variables and of current expectations of future values of the forcing variables. The predetermined variables at time t depend in a non-explosive manner on their initial values at t_0, on the *actual* values of the forcing variables between t_0 and t and on the expectations, formed at each instant between t_0 and t, of the future values of the forcing variables.

It is clear that, if the process governing the forcing variables z can be expressed by a system of simultaneous first order linear differential equations $\dot{z} = Lz$,[5] then the x vector can be augmented to include z; the solution of this augmented homogeneous system only involves the first terms on the r.h.s. of (11) or (11′) and (12) (or (12′)). For many purposes, and especially for optimal policy design, it is however very informative to keep the explicit dependence of x and y on actual and anticipated future values of z.

III **Three problems**

Three issues arise in connection with the solution method outlined in Section II. They are: (1) the rather minor problem of ensuring that the eigenvalues are 'assigned to' the proper state variables where such an unambiguous assignment is dictated by the structure of the model; (2) the existence of solutions other than the minimal state solution involving only fundamentals; and (3) the problem of zero eigenvalues or eigenvalues with zero real parts.

The right root in the right place

Consider the simple two-variable homogeneous system given in equation (14).

$$\begin{bmatrix} \dot{x}(t) \\ E_t\dot{y}(t) \end{bmatrix} = \begin{bmatrix} \alpha_{11} & \alpha_{12} \\ \alpha_{21} & \alpha_{22} \end{bmatrix} \begin{bmatrix} x(t) \\ y(t) \end{bmatrix} \tag{14}$$

Let $\alpha_{12} = 0$. The eigenvalues are $\lambda_1 = \alpha_{11}$ and $\lambda_2 = \alpha_{22}$. $x(t)$ is predetermined, with $x(t_0) = \bar{x}(t_0)$ and $y(t)$ is non-predetermined. The solution is given by:

$$x(t) = [\exp\lambda_1(t - t_0)]\bar{x}(t_0) = [\exp\alpha_{11}(t - t_0)]\,\bar{x}(t_0)$$

$$y(t) = \frac{\alpha_{21}}{\lambda_1 - \alpha_{22}}[\exp\lambda_1(t - t_0)]\bar{x}(t_0) + K[\exp\lambda_2 t] = \frac{\alpha_{21}}{\lambda_1 - \alpha_{22}}x(t)$$

$$+ K[\exp\lambda_2(t)] = \frac{\alpha_{21}}{\alpha_{11} - \alpha_{22}}x(t) + K[\exp\alpha_{22}t]$$

K is to be determined by a boundary condition for y.

Let $\alpha_{11} > 0$ and $\alpha_{22} < 0$. Clearly we have the right number of stable and unstable eigenvalues (one of each) but unfortunately the unstable root is unambiguously attached to the predetermined variable. Also, since $\alpha_{22} < 0$, we cannot use the convergence criterion to set $K = 0$. This problem will of course be revealed if the system is solved correctly. The purpose of pointing it out here is merely to remind the reader that equality between the number of stable eigenvalues and the number of predetermined state variables and between the number of unstable eigenvalues and the number of non-predetermined variables is not strictly sufficient for the applicability of the solution methods of Section II.

Sunspots and other forms of non-uniqueness

The solution for the non-predetermined variables given in (11) in terms of the current values of the predetermined variables and the current and anticipated future values of the forcing variables is what McCallum has called the 'minimal state' solution (McCallum [1983]). It involves only the fundamentals (i.e. the forcing variables actually appearing in the equations of the model) and a minimal representation of the state variables.

A simple scalar example will illustrate the wealth of alternative solutions that satisfy the equations of motion of these rational expectations models:

$$E_t\dot{y}(t) = \alpha y(t) + \beta z(t) \qquad \alpha > 0 \tag{15}$$

The minimal state solution for the non-predetermined variable y is:

$$y(t) = -\beta\int_t^{\infty}[\exp - \alpha(s - t)E_t z(s)ds \tag{16}$$

It is easily checked that any variable $u(t)$ can be added to this solution, provided that $u(t)$ satisfies the homogeneous equation of (15), i.e. provided that:

$$E_t \dot{u}(t) = \alpha u(t) \tag{17}$$

For instance, $u(t) = y(t_0)\exp \alpha(t - t_0)$ satisfies (15) as would $u(t) = z(t_0)$ $\exp \alpha(t - t_0)$. $u(t)$, however, need not involve y or z and could involve processes that are completely extraneous to the model under consideration (see e.g. Buiter 1981b). It is easily checked that $u(t)$ can be written as:

$$u(t) = \lim_{\tau \to \infty} E_t \left[\exp - \alpha(\tau - t)\right] y(\tau)$$

The extraneous element in the solution of (15) is generally ruled out on the grounds that, unless $u(t) = 0$ for all t, an explosive process will be added to the behaviour of the system and this would cause the system to violate (implicit) physical boundaries or other plausible constraints in finite time. Boundary condition (2b) is the expression of this view.

The same kind of nuisance process cannot be added to the solution of a boundary value problem involving an ordinary differential equation for a predetermined variable such as x in equation (18) because it would violate the initial condition:

$$\dot{x}(t) = \gamma x(t) + \delta z(t) \tag{18a}$$

$$x(t_0) = \bar{x}(t_0) \tag{18b}$$

The minimal state solution for x, given the initial boundary condition, is:

$$x(t) = [\exp\gamma(t - t_0)]\bar{x}(t_0) + \delta \int_{t_0}^{t} [\exp\gamma(t - s)]z(s)ds \tag{19}$$

We cannot add to this solution any non-zero term $u(t)$ because, although any $u(t)$ satisfying the homogeneous equation $\dot{u}(t) = \gamma u(t)$ would satisfy the equation of motion (18a), it would violate the condition $x(t_0) = \bar{x}(t_0)$ unless $u(t_0)$, and therefore $u(t)$, $t \geq t_0$, is equal to zero. The reason for the non-uniqueness in the solution for (15) and its absence in (18) is therefore not, as was pointed out by Shiller [1978], that (15) is a partial differential equation involving time in two ways: calendar time and the expectations or forecast horizon. At each instant, t, a boundary condition must therefore be given for $\lim_{\tau \to \infty} [\exp - \alpha(\tau - t)] E_t y(\tau)$. These boundary conditions cannot, however, be set completely independently of each other, as reflected in the constraint that $u(t)$ must satisfy (17). Without the expectation operator in (15) we would have to select a single boundary condition to determine $u(t) = \lim_{\tau \to \infty} [\exp - \alpha(\tau - t)]\, y(\tau)$. It is the lack of compelling economic arguments for choosing $u(t) = 0$ that is the fundamental reason for the indeterminacy, not the presence of the expectation operator.

In terms of the general model of Section II, we can add to the fundamental solution for the canonical forward-looking variables q, given in (10′), any $n - n_1$ vector process u (deterministic or stochastic) which satisfies the homogeneous system $E_t\dot{u}(t) = \Lambda_2 u(t)$. Through $q = V_{21}x + V_{22}y$ this non-uniqueness of q can be translated into non-uniqueness for y and x.

In what follows, the analysis will be restricted to the minimal state solution, for convenience rather than out of a deep conviction that any properly specified macroeconomic model would generate the right set of boundary conditions to puncture any extraneous bubbles at their inception.

Zero roots and the hysteresis phenomenon

There is nothing in the analysis thus far to rule out zero roots in Λ_1, the set of eigenvalues governing the behaviour of the homogeneous solution for x.[6] From (12) it can be seen that a zero root in Λ_1 means that, for one or more of the predetermined variables,[7] the influence of the initial conditions does not wear off, even asymptotically, and that the contribution of the exogenous variables is similarly undamped. The model will exhibit *hysteresis*: if the forcing variables become constant after some point in time and if the system converges to a stationary or steady state equilibrium, the stationary equilibrium values of one or more of the state variables will be functions of the initial conditions and of the values of the exogenous variables along the adjustment path to the stationary equilibrium; the steady state conditions alone do not suffice to determine unique steady state values for x and y (see e.g. Buiter and Gersovitz [1981] and Buiter and Miller [1983b]). A general algebraic treatment of the case where Λ_1 contains a zero root can be found in Giavazzi and Wyplosz [1983]. The main points can be brought out quite simply with the example given below, which also has some intrinsic economic interest. We also use this example to consider the case where a zero root is contained in Λ_2, i.e. where the non-predetermined variables (or q) are governed by a zero root.

The example is a contract model of the inflation-unemployment trade-off due to Marcus Miller. This is discussed in Buiter and Miller [1983b]. The basic version is represented in the following equations:

$$\dot{p}(t) = \Psi[y(t) - \bar{y}(t)] + \pi(t) \qquad \Psi > 0 \tag{20}$$

$$\pi(t) = \pi(t_0)\exp[-\zeta_1(t - t_0)] + \zeta_1 \int_{t_0}^{t} c(s)[\exp - \zeta_1(t - s)]ds$$
$$\zeta_1 > 0 \tag{21}$$

$$c(t) = \zeta_2 \int_t^{\infty} E_t \dot{p}(\tau)[\exp - \zeta_2(\tau - t)]d\tau \qquad \zeta_2 > 0 \tag{22}$$

p is the logarithm of the general price level, π the 'core' rate of inflation, c the current rate of contract inflation, y actual output and $\bar{y}$ the exogenous natural level of output.

Equation (20) is the familiar core inflation-augmented Phillips curve. Core inflation, in (21), is a backward-looking exponentially declining moving average of past contract inflation. Current contract inflation, in (22), is a forward-looking exponentially declining moving average of future expected inflation. Both the price level, p, and core inflation, π, are treated as predetermined. Current contract inflation, c, however, is non-predetermined and can move discontinuously at a point in time in response to 'news'. The model can be viewed as a modification of Calvo's [1983] continuous time contract model of the inflation process. Calvo specified the current general price *level* as a backward-looking function of past contract prices, and the current contract price *level* as a forward-looking function of expected future general price levels and excess demands. Inertia or sluggishness therefore characterises only the price level in Calvo's model, not both the price level and the core rate of inflation as in equations (20–22).

We can represent the model in state-space form as in equations (23a,b), treating the output gap $y - \bar{y}$ as exogenous:

$$\begin{bmatrix} \dot{\pi}(t) \\ E_t\dot{c}(t) \end{bmatrix} = \begin{bmatrix} -\zeta_1 & \zeta_1 \\ -\zeta_2 & \zeta_2 \end{bmatrix} \begin{bmatrix} \pi(t) \\ c(t) \end{bmatrix} + \begin{bmatrix} 0 \\ -\zeta_2\Psi \end{bmatrix} [y(t) - \bar{y}(t)] \tag{23a}$$

$$\dot{p}(t) = [1 \; 0] \begin{bmatrix} \pi(t) \\ c(t) \end{bmatrix} + \Psi \, [y(t) - \bar{y}(t)] \tag{23b}$$

The two characteristic roots of the state equation system (23a) are $\lambda_1 = 0$ and $\lambda_2 = \zeta_2 - \zeta_1$. The solutions for π, c and $\dot{p}$ are therefore given by:[8]

$$\pi(t) = \pi(t_0) + \zeta_1\zeta_2\Psi \int_{t_0}^{t} \int_{s}^{\infty} [\exp(\zeta_2 - \zeta_1)(s - \tau)] E_s[y(\tau) - \bar{y}(\tau)] d\tau ds \tag{24a}$$

$$c(t) = \pi(t) + \zeta_2\Psi \int_t^{\infty} [\exp(\zeta_2 - \zeta_1)(t - \tau)] E_t[y(\tau) - \bar{y}(\tau)] d\tau \tag{24b}$$

$$\dot{p}(t) = \pi(t) + \Psi[y(t) - \bar{y}(t)] \tag{24c}$$

The fact that $\lambda_1 = 0$ creates no problems whatsoever. Core inflation, $\pi(t)$, can be reduced below its initial value, $\pi(t_0)$, only through past expectations (formed between t_0 and t) of future recessions (negative values of $E_s[y(\tau) - \bar{y}(\tau)]$). Current contract inflation, $c(t)$, differs from current core inflation, $\pi(t)$, if the 'present value' of currently anticipated future booms or recessions differs from zero. Note that a sustained and sustainable reduction (e.g. a steady state reduction) in inflation, $\dot{p}(t)$, requires an actual reduction in core inflation, $\pi(t)$.

Consider an aggregate demand policy which keeps constant the output gap after some time $t_1 \geqslant t$ at $y(t_1) - \bar{y}(t_1)$. The only value of this permanent output gap for which a stationary equilibrium exists is of course zero. In that case the steady state conditions of (23b) only give us $\pi = c = \dot{p}$. The common stationary equilibrium value of core inflation, contract inflation and actual inflation cannot be determined from the steady state conditions alone. It is, from (24a), a function of the initial value of π and of the entire sequence of expectations of future values of the output gap. The rank deficiency of the state matrix in (23a) produces this 'hysteresis'. If the zero output gap for $t \geqslant t_1$ has been anticipated correctly from t_0 onwards, i.e. if $E_s[y(\tau) - \bar{y}(\tau)] = 0$, $\tau \geqslant t_1$; $s \geqslant t_0$, then:

$$\lim_{t\to\infty} \pi(t) = \lim_{t\to\infty} c(t) = \lim_{t\to\infty} \dot{p}(t) = \pi(t_0) \tag{25}$$

$$+ \zeta_1\zeta_2\Psi \int_{t_0}^{t_1}\int_{s}^{t_1} [\exp(\zeta_2 - \zeta_1)(s - \tau)]\, E_s[y(\tau) - \bar{y}(\tau)] d\tau ds$$

It will be apparent from equations (24a,b,c) that even if $\lambda_2 = \zeta_2 - \zeta_1 = 0$ (if there is no discounting of expected future inflation in the contract inflation equation) the model is still well-behaved, i.e. $c(t)$ is finite, if the undiscounted expected cumulative net output gap $\int_t^\infty E_t[y(\tau) - \bar{y}(\tau)]$ $d\tau$ is finite. If we again make the stronger assumption that the output gap expected after some time t_1 is zero, then this is sufficient (but not necessary) for π_t to remain bounded for all time with its steady-state value given by (25) with $\zeta_1 = \zeta_2$. A zero root in Λ_2 therefore merely puts tighter constraints on the permissible forcing processes to ensure bounded values for the non-predetermined variables; it does not invalidate the general solution procedure of Section II.

IV **Optimal and time-consistent policy design**

In this section we consider the optimal control of the model given in equation (1). The vector of forcing variables is divided into two components, u and z. u is an l vector of policy instruments and z a k vector of exogenous variables. The model is rewritten in (26a,b,c,d). For simplicity, the boundary conditions for the predetermined variables are assumed to take the form of n_1 initial values at t_0. Without significant loss of generality the non-explosiveness condition for the exogenous variables and the convergence condition for the non-predetermined variables given in (2b) are expressed as (26c) and (26d) respectively:

$$\begin{bmatrix} \dot{x}(t) \\ E_t\dot{y}(t) \end{bmatrix} = A\begin{bmatrix} x(t) \\ y(t) \end{bmatrix} + Bu(t) + Fz(t) \tag{26a}$$

$$x(t_0) = \bar{x}(t_0) \tag{26b}$$

$$\lim_{s\to\infty} [\exp - \beta sI]\ E_t z(s) = 0 \qquad \forall\beta > 0 \qquad \forall t \geqslant t_0 \tag{26c}$$

$$\lim_{s\to\infty} [\exp - \beta sI]\ E_t y(s) = 0 \qquad \forall\beta > 0 \qquad \forall t \geqslant t_0 \tag{26d}$$

The objective functional to be minimised is the familiar quadratic:

$$\min_{[u(t)]} J(t_0) \equiv \min_{[u(t)]} E_{t_0}\int_{t_0}^{\infty} [\tfrac{1}{2}\ [x(t)^T y(t)^T u(t)^T z(t)^T]\Omega \begin{bmatrix} x(t) \\ y(t) \\ u(t) \\ z(t) \end{bmatrix} + \omega^T \begin{bmatrix} x(t) \\ y(t) \\ u(t) \\ z(t) \end{bmatrix}][\exp - \zeta(t - t_0)]dt \tag{27}$$

where

$$\Omega = \begin{bmatrix} \Omega_{xx} & \Omega_{xy} & \Omega_{xu} & \Omega_{xz} \\ \Omega_{xy}^T & \Omega_{yy} & \Omega_{yu} & \Omega_{yz} \\ \Omega_{xu}^T & \Omega_{yu}^T & \Omega_{uu} & \Omega_{uz} \\ \Omega_{xz}^T & \Omega_{yz}^T & \Omega_{uz}^T & \Omega_{zz} \end{bmatrix}$$

$\omega^T = [\omega_x^T\ \omega_y^T\ \omega_u^T\ \omega_z^T]$

$\zeta \geqslant 0$ is the discount rate.

Ω is a symmetric positive semi-definite matrix. Like the vector ω^T it is partitioned conformably with x, y, u and z.

Ω_{uu} is a symmetric, positive definite matrix.

A, B and F are also partitioned conformably with x and y.

The objective function (27) is sufficiently general to include the case where the state equation (26a) is supplemented by an output equation

$$v(t) = G_1\begin{bmatrix} x(t) \\ y(t) \end{bmatrix} + G_2u(t) + G_3z(t)$$

and the integrand in the objective functional is specified in terms of the output vector as $v^T(t)\tilde{\Omega}v(t) + \tilde{w}^Tv(t)$.

Optimal policies

The natural interpretation of this optimal control problem is that of a non-cooperative Stackelberg leader – follower game. Equation (26a) represents the 'reaction function' of the follower (the economic system) who takes as given the current and anticipated future actions of the controller, who is the leader. To derive the optimal policy we define the Hamiltonian H:

$$\begin{aligned} H(t) = {} & \{\tfrac{1}{2}[x(t)^T\Omega_{xx}x(t) + 2y(t)^T\Omega_{xy}x(t) + y(t)^T\Omega_{yy}y(t) \\ & + 2x(t)^T\Omega_{xu}\, u(t) + 2y(t)^T\Omega_{yu}u(t) + 2x(t)^T\Omega_{xz}z(t) \\ & + 2y(t)^T\Omega_{yz}z(t) + u(t)^T\Omega_{uu}u(t) + 2u^T(t)\Omega_{uz}z(t) \\ & + z(t)^T\Omega_{zz}z(t)] + \omega_x^T x(t) + \omega_y^T y(t) + \omega_u^T u(t) \\ & + \omega_z^T z(t)\}\exp[-\zeta(t - t_0)] + \lambda_x^T(t)[A_{11}x(t) + A_{12}y(t) \\ & + B_1u(t) \\ & + F_1z(t)] + \lambda_y^T(t)[A_{21}x(t) + A_{22}y(t) + B_2u(t) + F_2z(t)] \end{aligned} \quad (28)$$

$\lambda_x(t)$ is the n_1 vector of co-state variables corresponding to the predetermined state variables $x(t)$ while $\lambda_y(t)$ is the $n - n_1$ vector of co-state variables corresponding to the non-predetermined state variables $y(t)$.

The first-order conditions for an optimum are given by the equations of motion (26a) and (29a,b,c):

$$\frac{\partial H(t)}{\partial u(t)} = 0 \qquad \forall t \quad (29a)$$

$$\frac{-\partial H(t)}{\partial x(t)} = E_t\dot{\lambda}_x^T(t) \qquad \forall t \quad (29b)$$

$$\frac{-\partial H(t)}{\partial y(t)} = \dot{\lambda}_y^T(t) \qquad \forall t \quad (29c)$$

Defining the current value co-state variables (shadow prices):

$$\mu_x(t) \equiv [\exp\zeta(t - t_0)I]\ \lambda_x(t) \quad (30a)$$

$$\mu_y(t) \equiv [\exp\zeta(t - t_0)I]\ \lambda_y(t) \quad (30b)$$

we can solve (29a) for the optimum instrument values as in (31):

$$\begin{aligned} u(t) = {} & -\Omega_{uu}^{-1}\Omega_{xu}^T x(t) - \Omega_{uu}^{-1}\Omega_{yu}^T y(t) - \Omega_{uu}^{-1}B_1^T\mu_x(t) \\ & -\Omega_{uu}^{-1}B_2^T\mu_y(t) - \Omega_{uu}^{-1}\Omega_{uz}z(t) - \Omega_{uu}^{-1}\omega_u \end{aligned} \quad (31)$$

Substituting for $u(t)$ from (31) into (26a) and into (29b,c), the behaviour of the state variables and the co-state variables under optimal control is given in (32):

$$
\begin{bmatrix} \dot{x}(t) \\ E_t\dot{y}(t) \\ E_t\dot{\mu}_x(t) \\ \dot{\mu}_y(t) \end{bmatrix}
=
\begin{bmatrix}
A_{11} - B_1\Omega_{uu}^{-1}\Omega_{xu}^T & A_{12} - B_1\Omega_{uu}^{-1}\Omega_{yu}^T \\
A_{21} - B_2\Omega_{uu}^{-1}\Omega_{xu}^T & A_{22} - B_2\Omega_{uu}^{-1}\Omega_{yu}^T \\
-[\Omega_{xx} - \Omega_{xu}\Omega_{uu}^{-1}\Omega_{xu}^T] & -[\Omega_{xy}^T - \Omega_{xu}\Omega_{uu}^{-1}\Omega_{yu}^T] \\
-[\Omega_{xy} - \Omega_{yu}\Omega_{uu}{}^{-1}\Omega_{xu}^T] & -[\Omega_{yy} - \Omega_{yu}\Omega_{uu}^{-1}\Omega_{yu}^T]
\end{bmatrix}
$$

$$
\begin{matrix}
-B_1\Omega_{uu}^{-1}B_1^T & -B_1\Omega_{uu}^{-1}B_2^T \\
-B_2\Omega_{uu}^{-1}B_1^T & -B_2\Omega_{uu}^{-1}B_2^T \\
-[A_{11}^T - \Omega_{xu}\Omega_{uu}B_1^T - \zeta I_{n_1}] & -[A_{21}^T - \Omega_{xu}\Omega_{uu}^{-1}B_2^T] \\
-[A_{12}^T - \Omega_{yu}\Omega_{uu}^{-1}B_1^T] & -[A_{22}^T - \Omega_{yu}\Omega_{uu}^{-1}B_2^T - \zeta I_{n-n_1}]
\end{matrix}
\Bigg]
\begin{bmatrix} x(t) \\ y(t) \\ \mu_x(t) \\ \mu_y(t) \end{bmatrix}
$$

$$
+\begin{bmatrix}
F_1 - B_1\Omega_{uu}^{-1}\Omega_{uz} \\
F_2 - B_2\Omega_{uu}^{-1}\Omega_{uz} \\
-(\Omega_{xz}\Omega_{xu}\Omega_{uu}^{-1}\Omega_{uz}) \\
-(\Omega_{yz} - \Omega_{yu}\Omega_{uu}^{-1}\Omega_{uz})
\end{bmatrix} z(t) +
\begin{bmatrix}
-B_1\Omega_{uu}^{-1}\omega_u \\
-B_2\Omega_{uu}^{-1}\omega_u \\
\Omega_{xu}\Omega_{uu}^{-1}\omega_u - \omega_x \\
\Omega_{yu}\Omega_{uu}^{-1}\omega_u - \omega_y
\end{bmatrix} \qquad (32)^9
$$

The $2n$ boundary conditions for the economy under the optimal policy take the form:

$$x(t_0) = \overline{x(t_0)} \qquad (33a)$$

$$\lim_{t\to\infty} [\exp - \beta(t - s)I]E_s y(t) = 0 \qquad \beta > 0,\ s \geqslant t_0 \qquad (33b)$$

$$\lim_{t\to\infty} [\exp - \zeta(t - s)]\ E_s\mu_x^T(t)x(t) = 0 \qquad (33c)$$

$$\mu_y(t_0) = 0 \qquad (33d)$$

The crucial boundary condition is the one relating to the initial values of the co-state variables corresponding to the non-predetermined state variables given in (33d). Since $y(t_0)$ is free, it will be set optimally, i.e. the values of the co-state variables μ_y at the initial date, t_0 which measure the marginal contribution of $y(t_0)$ to the objective functional, will be zero (see Bryson and Ho [1975, pp. 55–59], Calvo [1978]).[10]

The dynamic system under optimal control, given in (32), therefore contains n predetermined variables (x, the predetermined state variables and μ_y, the shadow prices of the non-predetermined state variables) and n non-predetermined variables (y, the non-predetermined state variables and μ_x, the shadow prices of the predetermined state variables). Following Miller and Salmon [1982, 1983], we rearrange (32) by grouping together the predetermined and non-predetermined variables and by subsuming the constant vector (the last term on the r.h.s. of equation (32)) under the exogenous variables. Letting$\bar{z}^T \equiv [z^T\ 1]$, we obtain:

$$\begin{bmatrix} \dot{x}(t) \\ \dot{\mu}_y(t) \\ E_t\dot{\mu}_x(t) \\ E_t\dot{y}(t) \end{bmatrix} = \bar{A} \begin{bmatrix} x(t) \\ \mu_y(t) \\ \mu_x(t) \\ y(t) \end{bmatrix} + \bar{B}\bar{z}(t) \quad (34)$$

and from (31):

$$u(t) = \bar{C} \begin{bmatrix} x(t) \\ \mu_y(t) \\ \mu_x(t) \\ y(t) \end{bmatrix} + \bar{D}\bar{z}(t) \quad (35)$$

If $\bar{A}$ can be diagonalised and if it has n stable and n unstable characteristic roots, the solution method of Section II can be applied to (34) and the optimal policy as well as the behaviour of the economy under optimal policy can easily be computed.

Time-consistent rational expectations solutions

It is obvious from the boundary condition (33d) and the equations of motion under optimal control (32) that in general, if the controller reoptimises at $t = t_1 > t_0$, his optimal plan from time $t_1 > t_0$ onwards will not be the continuation for $t \geqslant t_1$ of the optimal plan derived at time t_0, even if no new information about the exogenous variables has accrued between t_0 and t_1. The optimal plan is not in general *time-consistent* (see Kydland and Prescott [1977]). The reason is that while $\mu_y = 0$ at $t = t_0$, it will, in general, be different from zero for $t > t_0$, given the dynamics of equation (32). Reoptimising at $t = t_1 > t_0$, the controller will, taking $x(t_1)$ as given, be tempted to adopt a plan for $t \geqslant t_1$ that will set $\mu_y(t_1) = 0$.

Unless, under the optimal plan adopted at $t = t_0$, the value of μ_y at $t = t_1$ would have been equal to zero anyway, the reoptimisation at $t = t_1$ would falsify the expectations held between t_0 and t_1 by the agents represented in the model of equation (26a). It is these expectations that will have brought the system to $x(t_1)$[11] in the first place. Past expectations of future policy actions would have been used as an additional policy instrument, unconstrained by the requirement that they be equal to actual, realised policy actions (except for unforeseen exogenous shocks).

If the agents in the model anticipate that the controller will reoptimise at t_1, taking as given their past expectations of his future actions, embodied in $x(t_1)$, they will expect $\mu_y\ (t_1) = 0$. If the controller can reoptimise at each and every instant, they will anticipate $\mu_y(t) = 0 \ \forall \ t \geqslant t_0$. The characterisation of a time-consistent rational expectations solution is then straightforward.

A time-consistent rational expectations solution is characterised by zero values at each instant of the co-state variables corresponding to the non-predetermined state variables, i.e. by $\mu_y(t) \equiv 0,\ t \geqslant t_0$. The optimality condition $-\partial H/\partial y = \dot{\lambda}_y^T$ no longer applies as the controller is effectively forced to treat $y(t)$ as exogenous rather than as driven by the equations of motion of the system.

The equations of motion under time-consistent control are therefore obtained by omitting the rows corresponding to $\dot{\mu}_y(t)$ and the columns corresponding to $\mu_y(t)$ in (32). The behaviour of the system under time-consistent control is given by (33a,b,c) and:

$$\begin{bmatrix} \dot{x}(t) \\ E_t\dot{y}(t) \\ E_t\dot{\mu}x(t) \end{bmatrix} =$$

$$\begin{bmatrix} A_{11} - B_1\Omega_{uu}^{-1}\Omega_{xu}^T & A_{12} - B_1\Omega_{uu}^{-1}\Omega_{yu}^T & -B_1\Omega_{uu}^{-1}B_1^T \\ A_{21} - B_2\Omega_{uu}^{-1}\Omega_{xu}^T & A_{22} - B_2\Omega_{uu}^{-1}\Omega_{yu}^T & -B_2\Omega_{uu}^{-1}B_1^T \\ -(\Omega_{xx} - \Omega_{xu}\Omega_{uu}^{-1}\Omega_{xu}^T) & -(\Omega_{xy}^T - \Omega_{xu}\Omega_{uu}^{-1}\Omega_{yu}^T) & -(A_{11}^T - \Omega_{xu}\Omega_{uu}^{-1}B_1^T - \zeta I_{n_1}) \end{bmatrix} \begin{bmatrix} x(t) \\ y(t) \\ \mu_x(t) \end{bmatrix}$$

$$+ \begin{bmatrix} F_1 - B_1\Omega_{uu}^{-1}\Omega_{uz} \\ F_2 - B_2\Omega_{uu}^{-1}\Omega_{uz} \\ -(\Omega_{xz} - \Omega_{xu}\Omega_{uu}^{-1}\Omega_{uz}) \end{bmatrix} z(t) + \begin{bmatrix} -B_1\Omega_{uu}^{-1}\omega_u \\ -B_2\Omega_{uu}^{-1}\omega_u \\ \Omega_{xu}\Omega_{uu}^{-1}\omega_u - \omega_x \end{bmatrix} \tag{36}$$

$$u_t = -\Omega_{uu}^{-1}\Omega_{xu}^T x(t) - \Omega_{uu}^{-1}\Omega_{yu}^T y(t) - \Omega_{uu}^{-1}B_1^T\mu_x(t) - \Omega_{uu}^{-1}\Omega_{uz}z(t) - \Omega_{uu}^{-1}\omega_u \tag{37}$$

Note that, while the time-consistent solution is a product of the realisation (*ex ante*) by the agents in the model (the followers) that the controller (the leader) will cheat if he has an incentive to do so (if $\mu_y(t) \neq 0$), there is no cheating (*ex post*) along the time-consistent path because the incentive to cheat has been eliminated; the leader has lost his leadership. Obviously, the optimal policy will be time-consistent i.f.f. under the optimal policy, $\mu_y(t) \equiv 0,\ t \geqslant t_0$. If this is not the case, precommitment is necessary for the controller to implement the optimal solution.

Two comments on this time-consistent solution are pertinent. First, the 'loss of leadership' solution characterised in (36) and (37) does not *solve* the time-inconsistency problem associated with optimal policy in rational expectations models. It is merely an alternative solution that may be relevant when precommitment is impossible. Miller and Salmon [1982, 1983] have shown that the time-consistent solution is equivalent to the open-loop Nash equilibrium in a two-player linear-quadratic differential game. This sheds further light on the 'loss of leadership' interpretation of the time-consistent solution.

Second, the analysis of Section IV brings out the incompleteness of the standard specification of the optimal control problem. As pointed out by

Reinganum and Stokey [1981], the period of commitment is a crucial parameter of the optimisation problem. Treating the period of commitment as exogenous, we can interpret the optimal policy as the equilibrium policy when credibility is complete and the period over which the leader can make binding commitments is infinite. The time-consistent solution represents the other extreme when the period of commitment has shrunk to zero and no credible announcements of future policy actions are possible at all. Clearly, one could plausibly think of intermediate cases in which the period of commitment is positive but finite. Even more interesting would be an endogenous determination of the period of commitment or a theory of precommitment. Reputation effects, threats and sanctions, voluntary or self-imposed constraints on future freedom of action, etc. all would come into play. We are unfortunately still far removed from such a positive theory of constitutions.

V An example of optimal and time-consistent policies: Anti-inflationary policy in a contract model

As an example of optimal and time-consistent policy design we shall consider anti-inflationary policy in the model given by equations (20) to (22), whose state-space representation is in (23a,b). The level of demand y is treated as the control variable and the objective functional is given in (38):

$$\min_{[y(s)]} E_t \int_t^{\infty} \tfrac{1}{2}\{[y(s) - y^*]^2 + \gamma[\dot{p}(s)]^2\}\,[\exp - \rho(s - t)]ds$$
$$\gamma, \rho \geqslant 0 \tag{38}$$

Deviations of output from its target level y^* are penalised, as are deviations of the inflation rate from zero. y^* need not equal the natural level of output.

The equations of motion for the state variables π, c and their current value co-state variables μ_π and μ_c and the optimal path of demand are given in equations (39a,b):

$$\begin{bmatrix} \dot{\pi}(t) \\ \dot{\mu}_c(t) \\ E_t\dot{\mu}_\pi(t) \\ E_t\dot{c}(t) \end{bmatrix} = \begin{bmatrix} \zeta_1 & 0 & 0 & \zeta_1 \\ 0 & (\rho - \zeta_2) & -\zeta_1 & 0 \\ \dfrac{-\gamma}{1 + \gamma\Psi^2} & \dfrac{\zeta_2}{1 + \gamma\Psi^2} & \rho + \zeta_1 & 0 \\ \dfrac{-\zeta_2}{1 + \gamma\Psi^2} & \dfrac{-(\zeta_2\Psi)^2}{1 + \gamma\Psi^2} & 0 & \zeta_2 \end{bmatrix} \begin{bmatrix} \pi(t) \\ \mu_c(t) \\ \mu_\pi(t) \\ c(t) \end{bmatrix} + \begin{bmatrix} 0 \\ 0 \\ \dfrac{-\gamma\Psi}{1 + \gamma\Psi^2}(y^* - \bar{y}) \\ \dfrac{-\zeta_2\Psi}{1 + \gamma\Psi^2}(y^* - \bar{y}) \end{bmatrix} \tag{39a}$$

$$y(t) = \frac{-\gamma\Psi}{1 + \gamma\Psi^2}\pi(t) + \frac{\zeta_2\Psi}{1 + \gamma\Psi^2}\mu_c(t) + \bar{y} + \frac{y^* - \bar{y}}{1 + \gamma\Psi^2} \tag{39b}$$

with

$$\pi(t_0) = \overline{\pi(t_0)}$$

and

$$\mu_c(t_0) = 0$$

Note from (39b) that the optimal policy does not feed back directly from μ_π, the shadow price of core inflation. In (39a), $\dot{\pi}$ and $E_t\dot{c}$ similarly do not feed back from μ_π directly, but only indirectly through the effect of μ_π on $\dot{\mu}_c$. This is a reflection of our assumption that core inflation is simply an exponentially deciding moving average of past contract inflation. The shadow price of contract inflation therefore contains the relevant information about the shadow price of core inflation. The optimal policy has the sensible property that, if we start off with the 'bliss' rate of core inflation ($\pi = 0$) and if the target and natural levels of output coincide, demand will be kept at the natural level and full employment with zero inflation endures. *Cet. par.* a higher value of y^* relative to $\bar{y}$ means a higher optimal level of demand; also, a higher inherited value of core inflation implies a lower optimal level of demand. If $\mu_c > 0$, i.e. if current contract inflation makes a positive marginal contribution to the minimised value of the loss function, then current demand is high relative to its long-run value.

The steady state equilibrium under optimal policy is characterised by:

$$\pi = c = \dot{p} = \left[\frac{\rho^2 + (\zeta_1 - \zeta_2)\rho}{\gamma\Psi(\rho + \zeta_1)(\rho - \zeta_2)}\right](y^* - \bar{y})$$

$$\mu_c = \frac{\zeta_1}{\Psi(\rho + \zeta_1)(\rho - \zeta_2)}(y^* - \bar{y})$$

$$\mu_\pi = \frac{1}{\Psi(\rho + \xi_1)}(y^* - \bar{y})$$

$$y = \bar{y}$$

Thus, the system under optimal policy always converges towards the natural level of output. If the target level of output coincides with the natural level of output, steady state inflation will be zero.[12] For there to be a unique convergent saddlepoint equilibrium, the model should possess two stable and two unstable roots; the state matrix in (39a) should therefore have a positive determinant. This requires $\zeta_2 > \rho$. The shadow price of core inflation is always positive (negative) in long-run equilibrium if $y^* > \bar{y}$ ($y^* < \bar{y}$); the determinant condition for saddlepoint stability implies that the opposite holds for the shadow price of contract inflation. This reflects the backward-looking nature of π and the forward-looking nature of c.

In the numerical example given below,

$$\rho^2 + (\zeta_1 - \zeta_2)\rho < 0$$

so the long-run rate of inflation will be positive (negative) if $y^* > \bar{y}(y^* < \bar{y})$. I have not been able to establish whether or not this is a necessary condition for saddlepoint stability in general.

Following Section IV, a time-consistent policy is obtained by deleting the rows and columns corresponding to μ_c in (39a,b). The behaviour of the state variables, the remaining co-state variable and the policy instrument y is given in equations (40a,b):

$$\begin{bmatrix} \dot{\pi}(t) \\ E_t\dot{c}(t) \end{bmatrix} = \begin{bmatrix} -\zeta_1 & \zeta_1 \\ \dfrac{-\zeta_2}{1 + \gamma\Psi^2} & \zeta_2 \end{bmatrix} \begin{bmatrix} \pi(t) \\ c(t) \end{bmatrix} + \begin{bmatrix} 0 \\ \dfrac{-\zeta_2\Psi}{1 + \gamma\Psi^2}(y^* - \bar{y}) \end{bmatrix} \tag{40a}$$

$$y(t) = -\frac{\gamma\Psi}{1 + \gamma\Psi^2}\pi(t) + \bar{y} + \frac{1}{1 + \gamma\Psi^2}(y^* - \bar{y}) \tag{40b}$$

$$\pi(t_0) = \overline{\pi(t_0)}$$

The shadow price of core-inflation, μ_π, is determined recursively, given the solution for (40a), by (41), but policy has become completely 'backward-looking' and y no longer 'feeds back' from any shadow price:

$$E_t\dot{\mu}_\pi(t) = -\frac{\gamma}{1 + \gamma\Psi^2}\pi(t) + (\rho + \zeta_1)\mu_\pi - \frac{\gamma\Psi}{1 + \gamma\Psi^2}(y^* - \bar{y}) \tag{41}$$

The steady state conditions are:

$$\pi = c = \dot{p} = \frac{1}{\gamma\Psi}(y^* - \bar{y})$$

$$\mu_\pi = \frac{1}{\Psi(\rho + \zeta_1)}(y^* - \bar{y})$$

$$y = \bar{y}$$

Again, $y^* = \bar{y}$ implies zero inflation in the long run. Long-run inflation will be positive (negative) if $y^* > \bar{y}(y^* < \bar{y})$. Note that, if $\rho^2 + (\zeta_1 - \zeta_2)\rho < 0$, inflation will be higher in the long run under the time-consistent policy than under the optimal policy, where $y^* > \bar{y}$.

Figures 1 and 2 depict the behaviour of some of the variables of interest under optimal and time-consistent policy for the following values of the parameters: $\zeta_1 = 0.5$; $\zeta_2 = 0.6$; $\Psi = 0.5$; $\gamma = 1$ and $\rho = 0.03$. In Figure 1, $y^* = 0.02$ and $\bar{y} = 0$. In Figure 2, both y^* and $\bar{y}$ equal zero. The initial rate of core inflation at $t = 0$ is 10 percent.

In Figure 1, under optimal policy, inflation remains slightly above zero (at 0.028 per cent) even in the long run. There is a fairly sharp initial

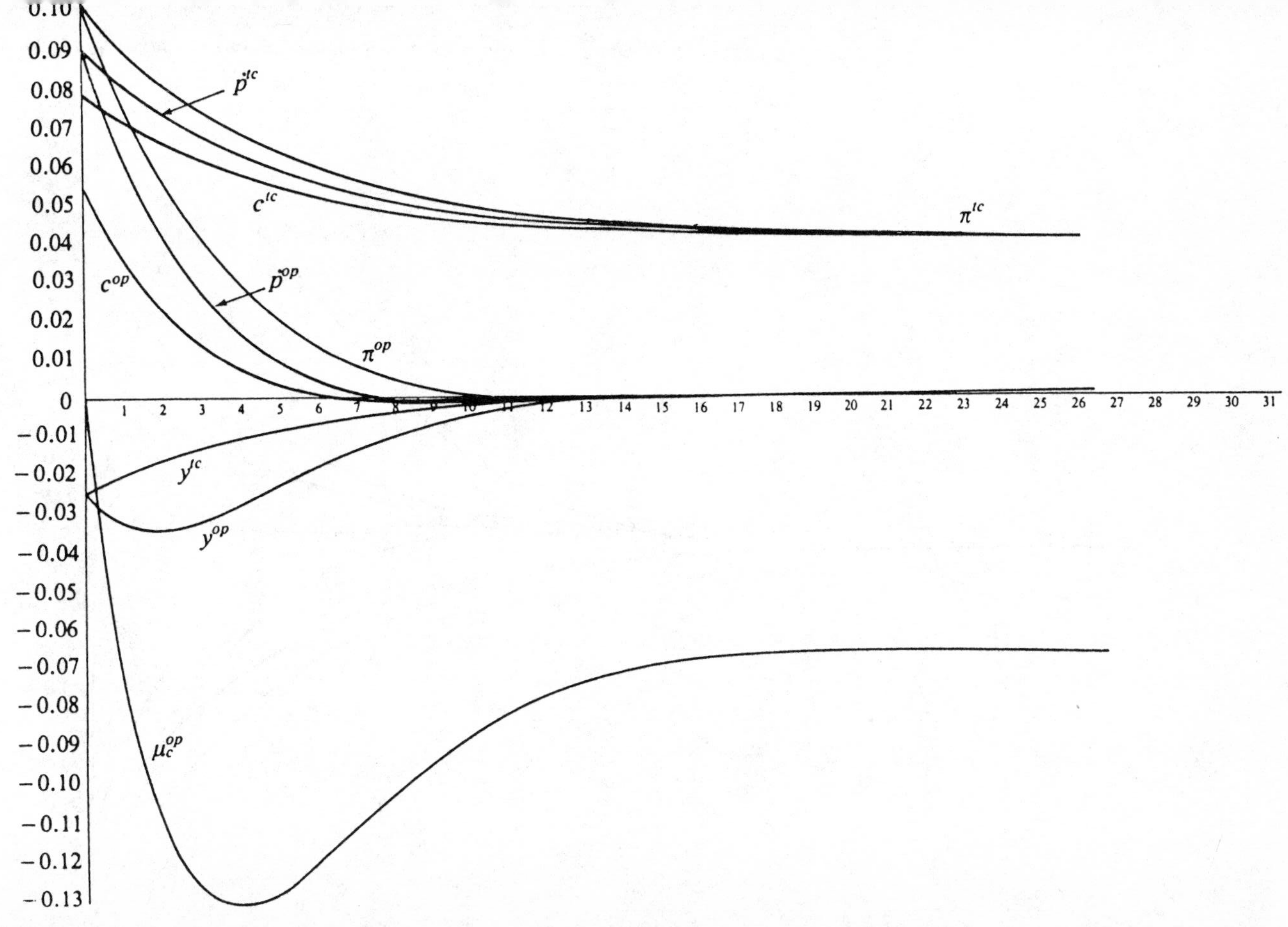

Figure 1 *Optimal (op) and time consistent (tc) anti-inflationary policies when* $y^* > \bar{y}$

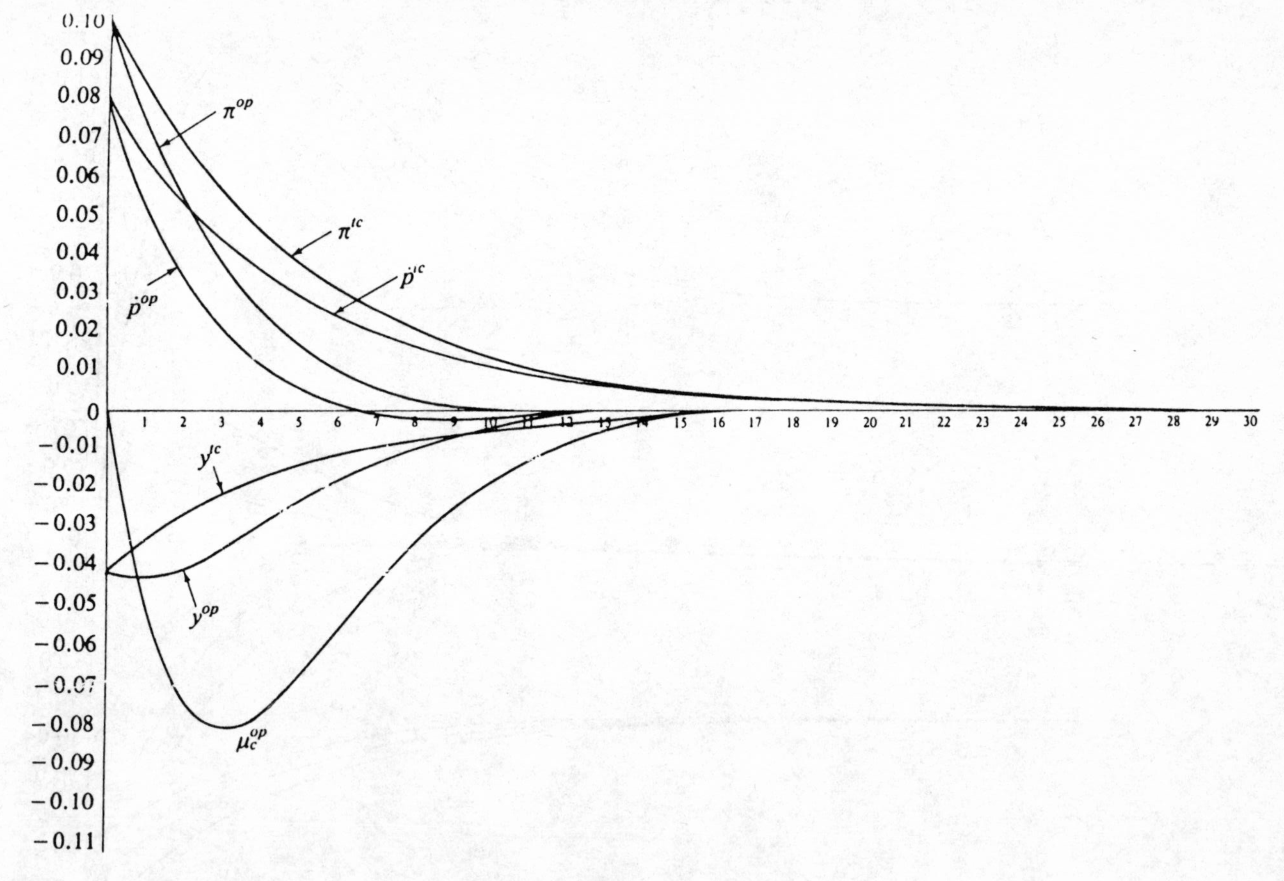

Figure 2 *Optimal (op) and time-consistent (tc) anti-inflationary policy when $y* = \bar{y}$*

recession. The shadow price of contract inflation starts at zero but becomes sharply negative and converges to a negative long-run value. The shadow price of core inflation (not drawn) jumps to 0.19 at $t = 0$ and converges to 0.075. The negative values of μ_c under the optimal policy signal the time inconsistency problem. The time-consistent policy has a small recession throughout. The authorities cannot credibly announce a path of deep recession, as they would be tempted not to have a fierce recession once the announcement effect of that recession had succeeded in bringing down core inflation. When the target level of output exceeds the natural level, the cost of not having credibility is a long-run rate of inflation which in the numerical example is four per cent – well above the optimal long-run inflation rate.

In Figure 2, $y^* = \bar{y}$ and the long-run conflict between output target and output constraint is absent. Both time-consistent and optimal policies yield zero long-run inflation. Inflation is, however, brought down more rapidly under the optimal policy. This is reflected in a deeper initial recession under the optimal policy. After period 9, however, the recession is slightly more severe under the time-consistent policy.

VI Conclusion

The solution method discussed in this paper can be used to study the behaviour of continuous time linear rational expectations models under exogenous policy, under ad hoc linear policy feedback rules, under optimal policy and under time-consistent policy. The consequences of any combination and sequence of anticipated or unanticipated, current or future and permanent or transitory shocks can be evaluated. The great virtue of the method is its analytical simplicity and computational efficiency, even for fairly large dynamic systems. As was indicated in Section II, the explicit consideration of uncertainty in the form of additive white noise is, because of certainty equivalence, a very simple matter. A more general specification of uncertainty (e.g. random parameters) very soon leads to awesome complications. Deterministic non-linear systems can be tackled on a 'try-it-and-see-if-it-works' basis with a wide variety of existing non-linear two-point boundary value problem solution algorithms. Successful applications of the technique of 'multiple shooting' in economics can be found, for instance, in the work of Bruno and Sachs [1982]; see also Lipton, Poterba, Sachs and Summers [1982].

Decentralised, non-cooperative policy design in continuous time linear rational expectations models has been pioneered by Miller and Salmon [1982, 1983] using a linear-quadratic differential game approach. As with the 'single player' optimal control problem of Section IV, the behaviour of the system under various kinds of decentralised control can be reduced to the standard format of equation (1). It appears safe to predict continued growth in the range of applications of these methods in the fields of macroeconomics and international finance.

Notes

Originally published in M. H. Peston and R. E. Quandt (eds.) (1986), *Prices, Competition and Equilibrium*, Barnes & Noble Books, pp. 84–108.

1 The first edition of this book appeared as early as 1951.
2 Note that, through the presence of the conditional expectations operator E_t, equation (1) strictly speaking represents a partial differential equation system. The solution chosen here is the 'minimal state' solution (see McCallum [1983]) involving only 'fundamentals'. Rational expectations and weak consistency ensure that the additional degrees of freedom introduced through the presence of the expectation operator are actually very limited.
3 And, if $F_2 \neq 0$, in x.
4 m^T denotes the transpose of m.
5 Or, in the stochastic case, $dz = Lzdt + dw$ where w is a stationary, zero-mean stochastic process with independent increments and is independent of the state vector $(x\ y)^T$.
6 Multiple zero roots will complicate the solution method somewhat, but the Jordan canonical form representation of the system can always be used even when A cannot be diagonalised as in (5).
7 And through them possibly also for one or more of the non-predetermined variables (see equation (11)).
8 Note that, in terms of the solution method of Section II,

$$V = \begin{bmatrix} 1 & 1 \\ 1 & -1 \end{bmatrix} \text{ and } W = \begin{bmatrix} 0.5 & 0.5 \\ 0.5 & -0.5 \end{bmatrix}$$

There are two linearly independent eigenvectors even though at least one and possibly both eigenvalues are zero.
9 I_k is the $k \times k$ identity matrix.
10 For (33d) to hold, a controllability condition for y must be satisfied: there must exist at t_0 a path of expected future policy $[E_{t_0}u(s); s \geq t_0]$ such that $y(t_0)$ can be set at the value required to make $\mu_y(t_0)$ equal to zero. See Bryson and Ho [1975, p. 58, p. 164 and Appendix B, pp. 455–457].
11 Note that the 'followers' whose behaviour is given by (26) form expectations not only of future values of $\bar{z}$ but also of future values of u. This is clear from equation (12), if we interpret z as containing both policy instruments and variables exogenous to the system and to the controller. The followers (the agents forming expectations in equation 26) take an open-loop view (in stochastic models an 'innovation-contingent' open-loop view (see Buiter [1981b])) of future policy.
12 If there is no discounting, the steady state value of the loss function is unbounded (unless $\bar{y} = y^*$) and no solution exists.

References

Austin, G. and Buiter, W. H. (1982), 'Saddlepoint: a programme for solving continuous time linear rational expectations models', SSRC LSE Econometrics Programme, Discussion Paper A.37, November.
Baumol, W. J. (1970), *Economic Dynamics*, 3rd edn, Macmillan.

Blanchard, O. J. (1983), 'Methods of solution and simulation for dynamic rational expectations models', National Bureau of Economic Research, Technical Working Paper No. 28, March.
—— and Kahn, M. (1980), 'The solution of linear difference models under rational expectations', *Econometrica*, Vol. 48, pp. 1305–11.
Bruno, M. and Sachs, J. (1982), 'Input price shocks and the slowdown in economic growth: the case of UK manufacturing', *Review of Economic Studies*, Vol. 49 (5), No. 159, Special Issue, pp. 675–705.
Bryson, A. E. and Ho, Y. C. (1975), *Applied Optimal Control*, Revised Printing, John Wiley.
Buiter, W. H. (1981a), 'A note on the solution of a two-point boundary value problem frequently encountered in rational expectations models', National Bureau of Economic Research, Technical Paper No. 12, June.
—— (1981b), 'The role of economic policy after the new classical macroeconomics', in D. Currie, R. Nobay and D. Peel (eds.), *Macroeconomic Analysis; Essays in Macroeconomics and Econometrics*, Croom Helm, pp. 233–79.
—— (1982), 'Saddlepoint problems in continuous time rational expectations models: a general method and some macroeconomic examples', National Bureau of Economic Research, Technical Paper No. 20 in *Econometrica*, 1984, pp. 665–80.
—— (1983), 'Optimal and time-consistent policies in continuous time rational expectations models', SSRC LSE Econometrics Programme, Discussion Paper No. A39, June.
—— and Gersovitz, M. (1981), 'Issues in controllability and the theory of economic policy', *Journal of Public Economics*, Vol. 15, February, pp. 33–43.
—— and Miller, M. H. (1982), 'Real exchange rate overshooting and the output cost of bringing down inflation', *European Economic Review*, Vol. 18, May/June, pp. 85–123.
—— and —— (1983a), 'Real exchange rate overshooting and the output cost of bringing down inflation: some further results', in J. A. Frenkel (ed.), *Exchange Rates and International Macroeconomics*, University of Chicago Press, pp. 317–58.
—— and —— (1983b), 'Costs and benefits of an anti-inflationary policy: questions and issues', *National Bureau of Economic Research*, Working Paper No. 1252, December.
Calvo, G. A. (1978), 'On the time consistency of optimal policy in a monetary economy', *Econometrica*, Vol. 46, pp. 1411–28.
—— (1983), 'Staggered contracts and exchange rate policy', in J. A. Frenkel (ed.), *Exchange Rates and International Macroeconomics*, University of Chicago Press, pp. 235–52.
Currie, D. and Levine, P. (1982), 'A solution technique for discrete continuous time stochastic dynamic models under rational expectations with full and partial information sets', Queen Mary College, Department of Economics, Programme of Research into Small Macromodels; Research Paper No. 1, April.
Dixit, A. (1980), 'A solution technique for rational expectations models with applications to exchange rate and interest rate determination', mimeo. University of Warwick.
Driffill, E. J. (1982), 'Optimal money and exchange rate policies', mimeo, Southampton University.
Giavazzi, F. and Wyplosz, C. (1983), 'The zero root problem: dynamic determination of the stationary equilibrium in linear models', mimeo, July.
Kydland, F. E. and Prescott, E. E. (1977), 'Rules rather than discretion: the

time-inconsistency of optimal plans', *Journal of Political Economy*, Vol. 85, pp. 473–91.

Lipton, D., Poterba, J. M., Sachs, J. and Summers, L. H. (1982), 'Multiple shooting in rational expectations models', *Econometrica*, Vol. 50, September, pp. 1329–33.

McCallum, B. T. (1983), 'On non-uniqueness in rational expectations models: an attempt at perspective', *Journal of Monetary Economics*, Vol. 11, March, pp. 139–68.

Miller, M. H. and Salmon, M. (1982), 'Optimal control and economic dynamics: an investigation of co-ordinated and decentralised policy formation in a multi-country setting with flexible exchange rates', mimeo, University of Warwick.

—— and Salmon, M. (1983), 'Dynamic games and the time inconsistency of optimal policies in open economics', mimeo, University of Warwick.

Reinganum, J. F. and Stokey, N. L. (1981), 'The period of commitment in dynamic games', Northwestern University, The Center for Mathematical Studies in Economics and Management Science, Discussion Paper No. 508 RR.

Shiller, R. J. (1978), 'Rational expectations and the dynamic structure of macroeconomic models: a critical review', *Journal of Monetary Economics*, Vol. 4, January, pp. 1–44.

Turnovsky, S. J. and Burmeister, E. (1977), 'Perfect foresight, expectational consistency and macroeconomic equilibrium, *Journal of Political Economy*, 85, April, pp. 379–93.

Whiteman, C. H. (1983), *Linear Rational Expectations Models; A User's Guide*, University of Minnesota Press.

Part 4

Debt neutrality and financial crowding out

Chapter 11

'Crowding' out of private capital formation by government borrowing in the presence of intergenerational gifts and bequests

I Introduction

In two recent studies (Buiter and Tobin [1979], Tobin and Buiter [1980]), James Tobin and I concluded that debt neutrality – the property that the real trajectory of the economic system is invariant under changes in the financing mix, for a given level and composition of real government spending – is a theoretical curiosum. The assumptions required for it to be valid can easily be shown to be contradicted by practical experience. In this paper, I provide a detailed statement of the case against debt neutrality in the context of a model constructed expressly to be as favorable as possible to classical invariance theorems. The model is a generalization of Diamond's version of Samuelson's overlapping generations model (Diamond [1965]), and allows for voluntary intergenerational gifts and bequests. (See Barro [1974], and Buiter [1979]). A comprehensive treatment of the subject can be found in Carmichael [1979]. Except for one significant simplification, the treatment of the case of agents with 'two-sided intergenerational caring' replicates the original work of Carmichael.

The overlapping generations model used to develop the non-neutrality theories is 'classical' in the sense that private actions are derived from explicit optimizing behavior, perfect foresight prevails and all markets are in equilibrium all of the time. All private agents act as price takers. I shall study the behavior of this decentralized, competitive economy when a given government spending program is financed by different combinations of lump-sum taxation or current borrowing. Without loss of generality the level of government spending is assumed to equal zero, which allows us to rephrase the argument in terms of the real effects of alternative debt issue-taxation programs. The restriction to lump-sum taxes is necessary to give the neutrality proposition a chance. Non-lump-sum taxes on labor income, profits, wealth or any other base, will introduce real distortions, impose excess burdens and, except in uninteresting special cases, have real effects.

Private, voluntary intergenerational gifts – from parents to children (bequests) or from children to parents – are essential for the debt neutrality property to prevail. Briefly, the argument for neutrality goes as follows. The stock of real government interest-bearing debt has no effect on private behavior because corresponding to every pound's worth of income on these bonds is a pound's worth of tax payments to finance the bond income. The value of the government bonds on the asset side of private portfolios is the present discounted value of these future income payments. The value of these bonds is therefore exactly matched by the present discounted value of the future tax payments required to service them. Even if we grant that the future payments stream and the future tax payments stream are identical and that both are discounted in the same manner, a shift from tax financing to borrowing could cause non-neutrality because of an intergenerational redistribution of resources. If the bonds are one-period bonds and each individual is supposed to live for two periods, the intergenerational redistribution that can be associated with such issues is immediately apparent. Let an extra pound's worth of bonds be issued in period t. It is bought by the then young members of generation t. Next period interest and repayment of principal occur. The tax revenue required for the debt servicing could be levied on the then young members of generation $t+1$. In that case, real resources have been redistributed from the young to the old. Consumption and capital formation will be affected. An unfunded social security program will have broadly similar effects. Longer maturity bonds can be incorporated in the analysis without materially altering it. Voluntary intergenerational gifts can remove the real consequences of involuntary intergenerational redistribution through the borrowing-taxation mechanism. Provided the taxes are lump-sum, such private intergenerational transfers will restore the original consumption-investment equilibrium as long as such private actions do not violate the non-negativity constraints on these voluntary intergenerational transfers. If, before the extra pound's worth of public debt is issued the members of the older generation were all leaving positive bequests to their descendants, the option of redistributing resources from the young to the old through a cut in bequests was already open to the older generation. Their decision not to exercise this option reflects that, at the margin, they receive greater utility from the well-being of their heirs than from their own consumption. The government's attempt to redistribute 'gross resources' from the young to the old will in that case be met be increased bequests from the old to the young, leaving the 'net resources' available to each generation unchanged. If, on the other hand, the older generations were initially at a 'zero bequest corner', i.e., if in order to increase their own life-time resources they would gladly have left their children a negative legacy, had this not been ruled out by law, the involuntary intergenerational redistribution would not have been neutralized by an exactly matching voluntary transfer in the opposite direction.

Within the bounds set by the non-negativity constraints on gifts and bequests, lump-sum redistribution through borrowing or unfunded social security schemes will be neutralized by voluntary intergenerational transfers, if bequest or gift motives are present. Private non-market transactions are required to neutralize public non-market transactions. A formal analysis follows below.

Notation

c_t^1 : consumption while young by a member of generation t

c_t^2 : consumption while old by a member of generation t

K_t : capital stock in existence at the beginning of period t

L_t : size of generation t

k_t : K_t/L_t

B_t : saving of a member of generation t while old (i.e., his bequest to young members of generation $t + 1$)

G_t : gift by a young member of generation t to old members of generation $t - 1$

D_t : stock of real one-period government debt in existence at the beginning of period t

$d_t \equiv D_t/L_t$

T_t : lump-sum tax levied on members of generation t while young

$\tau_t \equiv T_t/L_t$

r_t : interest rate on savings carried from period $t - 1$ into period t

n : one-period proportional rate of growth of population

δ : one-period discount rate applied to the utility of one's immediate descendant

ϱ : one-period discount rate applied to the utility of one's immediate forebear

II Government financing in an overlapping generations model without gifts or bequests

Each generation consists of identical households that live for two periods. During the first period of their lives each household works a fixed amount, 1. Income earned in the first period is either consumed or saved.

These savings, plus accumulated interest, are the only source of income in the second period of a household's life when it is retired. Households are also identical across generations. Initially there is no government borrowing or lending and no taxation. On the output side, the model has a single commodity that can either be consumed or used as a capital good. Until government bonds are introduced, real capital is the only store of value. The model is 'real': there are no money balances. The dual role to be performed by durable output – that of being an input in the production function and of being the only store of value may lead to inefficiencies in a decentralized, competitive economy. (See Diamond [1965], Buiter [1979] and Carmichael [1979]).

A competitive economy without government debt

In the absence of government borrowing and lending, the utility maximization program faced by a representative household of generation t is given by:

$$\max_{c_t^1,\, c_t^2} u(c_t^1, c_t^2)$$[1]

subject to

$$c_t^1 + \frac{c_t^2}{1 + r_{t+1}} \leqq w_t$$

$$c_t^1, c_t^2 \geqq 0 \tag{1}$$

Equation (1) states that the present discounted value of lifetime consumption cannot exceed that of labor income. Given our assumptions about the utility function, u, the budget constaint will hold with equality and all solutions for c_t^1 and c_t^2 will be interior. Utility is a function of own lifetime consumption only. There is no gift or bequest motive. The model is completed by adding the economy-wide constraints, (2), (3), and (4).

$$w_t = f(k_t) - k_t f'(k_t) \tag{2}$$

$$r_t = f'(k_t) \tag{3}$$

$$w_t - c_t^1 = k_{t+1}(1 + n) \tag{4}$$

Output is produced by a well-behaved neoclassical production function which is linear homogeneous in capital and labor. In intensive form it can be written as $f(k_t)$ with $f(0) = 0; f' > 0; f'' < 0$.[2] Equation (2) states that the labor market clears and is competitive. The real wage w equals the marginal product of labor. Equation (3) states that the capital rental market clears and is competitive with the rental rate (which in the one-commodity model also equals the interest rate) equal to the marginal product of capital. Equation (4) is the economy-wide capital market equilibrium condition. The stock of capital in existence at the beginning of period t, K_t, is equal to the savings of the previous period. Only the young save in this model without bequests, so saving in $t-1$ is given by $(w_{t-1} - c^1_{t-1})\, L_{t-1}$. Our conditions on the production function imply $k_t > 0$.

The interior first-order condition for an optimum is:

$$\frac{u_1(c_t^1, c_t^2)}{u_2(c_t^1, c_t^2)} = (1 + r_{t+1}) \tag{5}$$

Its interpretation in terms of a tangency between an indifference curve in c_t^1, c_t^2 space and the intertemporal budget constraint is familiar. From the first-order condition and the budget constraint, (1), we can solve for c_t^1 (and c_t^2) as a function of w_t and r_{t+1}. Substituting the solution for c_t^1 into the capital market equilibrium condition (4) and using (2) and (3) to substitute for w_t and r_{t+1} we obtain a first-order difference equation in k_t describing the evolution over time of this economy from any arbitrary set of initial conditions.[3]

$$f(k_t) - k_t f'(k_t) - c^1(f(k_t) - k_t f'(k_t), f'(k_{t+1})) = k_{t+1}(1 + n). \tag{6}$$

This system will be locally stable and converge to a steady state equilibrium

i.f.f. $\left|\dfrac{\partial k_{t+1}}{\partial k_t}\right| < 1$, i.e., when

$$\left| \frac{\left(\dfrac{\partial c^1}{\partial w} - 1\right) kf''}{1 + n + \dfrac{\partial c^1}{\partial r} f''} \right| < 1.$$

In what follows we shall assume existence, uniqueness and stability and proceed to analyze steady-state equilibria only.

In steady-state equilibrium, the capital – labor ratio and through that all real stock-stock and stock-flow ratios are constant. We solve for it by setting $k_t = k_{t+1}$ in equations (1) through (5). By substituting the marginal productivity conditions (2) and (3) into (1) and (4) we obtain equations (7) and (8), the stationary private budget constraint and aggregate capital market equilibrium condition.

$$c^1 + \frac{c^2}{1 + f'(k)} = f(k) - kf'(k) \tag{7}$$

$$f(k) - (k)f'(k) - c^1 = k(1 + n). \tag{8}$$

From (7) and (8) we can solve for the stationary decentralized consumption possibility locus, as in (9a) and (9b).

$$c^2 = \Psi(c^1) \tag{9a}$$

$$\Psi' = -(1 + f')\left[[1 + \frac{k(n - f')}{1 + f'}f''(1 + n + kf'')^{-1}]\right]. \tag{9b}$$

If the production function is Cobb-Douglas, with $f(k) = k^\alpha$, $0 < \alpha < 1$,

$$\Psi' = \frac{(1 + n)(1 + \alpha^2 k^{(\alpha-1)})}{(1 - \alpha)\alpha k^{(\alpha-1)} - (1 + n)}.$$

The stationary decentralized consumption possibility locus for the Cobb-Douglas case is graphed in Figure 1. At the origin its slope is $\frac{\alpha}{1 - \alpha}(1 + n)$. k increases monotonically as we move up from 0 towards A. As k approaches infinity (which would be beyond A in the infeasible region) the slope of the consumption possibility locus becomes -1. The locus is strictly concave towards the origin. For large k and more general constant returns production functions than the Cobb-Douglas, $\frac{\partial c^2}{\partial c^1}$ can even become positive again, a case of extreme overaccumulation. With the Cobb-Douglas this is not possible. At the golden rule capital-labor ratio:

$$f'(k) = n, \ \Psi' = -\frac{\partial c^2}{\partial c^1} = -(1 + f') = -(1 + n)$$

The steady-state equilibrium of a decentralized competitive economy could be achieved anywhere on this locus. Steady-state equilibria like E_3, corresponding to a capital-labor ratio below the golden rule capital-labor ratio k^*, defined by $f'(k^*) = n$, are possible as are those like E_2 corresponding to a capital-labor ratio in excess of k^*. The golden rule capital-labor ratio k^* could be achieved by a competitive equilibrium at E_1, but this is not more likely than any other point on the locus. A competitive stationary equilibrium satisfies two criteria: it lies on the stationary consumption possibility locus and it has a tangency between an indifference curve and a private budget constraint with slope $-(1 + r) = -(1 + f'(k))$. The private budget constraint will always cut the stationary consumption possibility locus in the manner indicated at E_3 and E_2. Only at the golden rule (E_1) will the private budget constraint be tangent to the locus.

It is instructive to contrast the private decentralized solution with the solution achieved by an omnipotent social planner. The latter is only subject to the aggregate resource constraint:

$$c_t^1 L_t + c_{t-1}^2 L_{t-1} = L_t f(k_t) - L_t(k_{t+1}(1 + n) - k_t) \quad \text{or}$$

$$c_t^1 + \frac{c_{t-1}^2}{1 + n} = f(k_t) - k_{t+1}(1 + n) + k_t \tag{10}$$

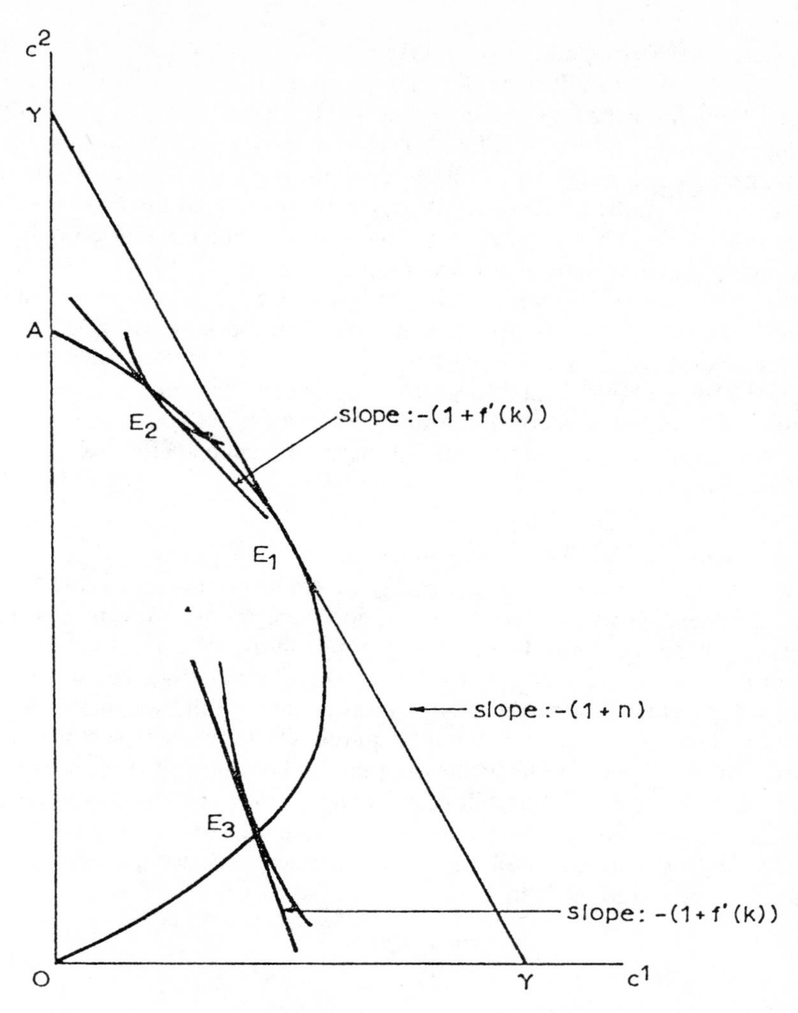

Figure 1 The Stationary Competitive Consumption Possibility Locus

The stationary aggregate resource constraint is

$$c^1 + \frac{c^2}{1 + n} = f(k) - nk \tag{11}$$

In order to maximize the stationary per capita amount of resources available for consumption, the social planner selects the golden rule capital-labor ratio k^*. The stationary social consumption possibility locus is the straight line $\gamma\gamma$ with slope $-(1 + n)$. By distribution through administrative fiat, any point on this $\gamma\gamma$ locus is available to the social planner.

A decentralized competitive equilibrium with a capital-labor ratio below k^*, as at E_3, is not inefficient. During any transition from E_3 to E_1, say, capital deepening has to occur, requiring the sacrifice of consumption during the transition in exchange for a permanently higher consumption path after E_1 has been achieved. A capital-labor ratio in excess of the golden rule is inefficient because it is possible to reduce the capital-labor ratio and thus to have a temporary consumption binge while enjoying a permanently higher path of consumption after k^* has been achieved. This inefficiency is due to capital's dual role as a store of value and a factor of production. In an attempt to shift consumption towards retirement, private agents save by accumulating capital. This depresses the rate of interest. By making available a store of value that has no additional intrinsic use, either as a consumption good or a capital good, government borrowing can alleviate and even eliminate any such inefficiency due to overaccumulation.

A competitive economy with government debt

Now consider the case in which the government issues real-valued one-period bonds. Bonds floated during period t are repaid with interest at a rate r_{t+1} in period $t+1$. Government bonds and real capital are perfect substitutes in private sector portfolios. D_t can be negative, in which case the public sector lends to the private sector. Such public sector lending to the private sector consists of public purchases of private sector bonds (which are also perfect substitutes for public bonds), not of real capital. T_t is the total lump-sum tax bill paid by the younger generation in period t. It can be negative in which case it constitutes transfer payments to the young. With government debt and taxes the economy we are considering can be represented as follows:

$$\max_{c_t^1,\, c_t^2} u(c_t^1, c_t^2)$$

subject to

$$c_t^1, c_t^2 \geqq 0$$

$$(w_t - c_t^1 - \tau_t)(1 + r_{t+1}) = c_t^2 \tag{12}$$

$$(1 + r_t)\, D_{t-1} = D_t + T_t \tag{13}$$

$$(w_t - c_t^1 - \tau_t)L_t = D_t + K_{t+1} \tag{14}$$

$$w_t = f(k_t) - k_t f'(k_t)$$

$$r_{t+1} = f'(k_{t+1})$$

$$k_t \geqq 0$$

Equation (12) is the modified household budget constraint, allowing for taxes while young. (13) is the government budget constraint. (14) is the modified capital market equilibrium condition. Total saving has to be equal to the total stock of assets consisting of government bonds and real capital. Private life-cycle optimizing behavior yields a consumption function $c_t^1 = c^1(w_t - \tau_t, r_{t+1})$. We again assume $o < c_1^1(\cdot) < 1$ and $c_2^1(\cdot) \leq 0$. The complete solution of the model is:

$$c_t^1 = c^1(w_t - \tau_t, r_{t+1}) \tag{15}$$

$$(w_t - c_t^1 - \tau_t)(1 + r_{t+1}) = c_t^2 \tag{12}$$

$$w_t - c_t^1 - \tau_t = d_t + k_{t+1}(1 + n) \tag{16}$$

$$(1 + r_t)d_{t-1} = d_t\,(1 + n) + \tau_t(1 + n) \tag{17}$$

$$w_t = f(k_t) - k_t f'(k_t) \tag{2}$$

$$r_{t+1} = f'(k_{t+1}) \tag{3}$$

$$c_t^1,\ c_t^2,\ k_t \geqq 0$$

At each point in time, t, this system of six equations determines the values of c_t^1, c_t^2, w_t, k_{t+1} and two of the three government instruments τ_t, d_t and r_{t+1}, given the value assigned to the remaining government instrument and the values of the predetermined variables r_t, d_{t-1} and k_t. I shall, through the rest of this section on debt neutrality, consider the case in which d_t, the per capita stock of real government debt is kept at a constant value $d_t = d$. In that case (17) simplifies to:

$$\tau_t = \frac{(r_t - n)d}{1 + n}. \tag{17'}$$

The model is stable *if* $\left|\frac{\partial k_{t+1}}{\partial k_t}\right| < 1$ in equation (18).

$$f(k_t) - k_t f'(k_t) - c^1\left(f(k_t) - k_t f'(k_t) - \frac{(f'(k_t) - n)d}{1 + n}, f'(k_{t+1})\right) - \frac{(1 + f'(k_t))d}{1 + n} = k_{t+1}(1 + n). \tag{18}$$

Stability requires

$$\left|\frac{(c_1^1 - 1)f''\left(k + \frac{d}{1 + n}\right)}{1 + n + c_2^1 f''}\right| < 1. \tag{19}$$

Since $k + \frac{d}{1 + n}$ is non-negative (because c^2 is non-negative), this stability condition is qualitatively the same as that for the model without government debt, given in (6).

The steady state equilibrium of the model with public debt is given in equations (20)–(23).

$$c^1 = c^1\left(f(k) - kf'(k) - \frac{(f'(k) - n)d}{1 + n}, f'(k)\right) \tag{20}$$

$$\left(f(k) - kf'(k) - \frac{(f'(k) - n)d}{1 + n} - c^1\right)(1 + f'(k)) = c^2 \tag{21}$$

$$f(k) - kf'(k) - \left(\frac{1 + f'(k)}{1 + n}\right)d - c^1 = k(1 + n) \tag{22}$$

$$\tau = \frac{(f'(k) - n)d}{1 + n}. \tag{23}$$

By substituting (20) into (22) we can derive the steady state effect of an increase in the per capita stock of public debt on the capital-labor ratio:

$$\frac{\partial k}{\partial d} = \frac{(1 + c_1^1 n + (1 - c_1^1)f')(1 + n)^{-1}}{(c_1^1 - 1)f''\left(k + \frac{d}{1 + n}\right) - [1 + n + c_2^1 f'']}. \tag{24}$$

If the model is stable (equation (19)) and if $c_2^1 \leqq 0$ and $0 < c_1^1 < 1$ the denominator of (24) is negative. The numerator is positive. We therefore obtain the familiar result that, comparing steady states, government debt issues reduce the capital-labor ratio, i.e., crowd out real capital. This 'crowding out' result also obtains in the short run, as can be checked from equation (18). Given k_t, the effect on k_{t+1} of an increase in d is

$$\frac{\partial k_{t+1}}{\partial d} = \frac{(1 + c_1^1 n + (1 - c_1^1)f')(1 + n)^{-1}}{-[1 + n + c_2^1 f'']}. \tag{25}$$

This is negative if $c_2^1 \leqq 0$.

Note that the steady-state value of d can be chosen to be negative or positive. Irrespective of d, if the economy is at the golden rule, no net taxes or transfers are required (23). The growth in the total demand for debt required to keep the per capita stock of debt constant just suffices to repay the debt held by the old generation, plus interest at the rate of population growth. Positive d requires positive τ at capital-labor ratios below the golden rule ratio k^* (at interest rates above n), negative τ in the inefficient region when $f'(k) < n$.

The steady-state effect of government debt issue can be illustrated using a generalization of the stationary competitive consumption possibility locus of Figure 1. The effect of an increase in d on the stationary competitive consumption possibility locus is to shift it up at a rate $-(1 + n)$. From (21) and (22) it is easily seen that, at any given k, $\frac{\partial c^1}{\partial d} =$

$-\dfrac{(1+f')}{(1+n)}$, while $\dfrac{\partial c^2}{\partial d} = 1 + f'$. Thus the rate at which, for any given k, c_2 is traded off for c_1 when d increases is $-(1+n)$. Figure 2 shows the general nature of the shift in the locus while Figure 3 focuses on a particular capital-labor ratio, $\bar{k}$ below the golden rule ratio k^*. A budget line with a common slope $-(1+f'(\bar{k}))$ passes through E_1 and E_2 in Figure 3.

Bequests
With bequests, the utility function, the budget constraint and the capital market equilibrium condition are altered. B_t is the bequest left in the second period of his life by a member of generation t to the members of generation $t+1$. The bequests are received by members of generation $t+1$ at the end of the first period of their lives. The value of the bequest to members of generation $t+1$ at the beginning of their second period is $B_t(1 + r_{t+2})$. When the rate of population growth is nonzero bequests are shared equally among all descendants. Note that bequests must be non-negative, a useful institutional constraint.

$$B_t \geqq 0 \qquad \text{for all } t. \tag{26}$$

The utility function of a member of generation t is $W_t = v(c_t^1, c_t^2, W_{t+1}^*)$. The utility of a member of generation t depends on his own life-time consumption, c_t^1, c_t^2 and on the maximum utility level attainable by a member of the next generation. For simplicity I shall consider the additively separable function:

$$W_t = u(c_t^1, c_t^2) + (1+\delta)^{-1} W_{t+1}^*. \tag{27}$$

u has all the properties attributed to the utility function of the household without a bequest motive. This ensures interior solutions for c_t^1 and c_t^2 and strict satisfaction of the household budget constraint. δ is the 'generational' discount rate; it is not to be confused with the individual's pure rate of time preference. Convergence, i.e., boundedness of W_t requires $\delta > 0$. The optimization problem solved by a representative member of generation t is given in equations (28) and (29). The new economy-wide capital market equilibrium condition is given in equation (30).

$$W_t^* = \max_{c_t^1, c_t^2, B_t} W = \max_{c_t^1, c_t^2, B_t} [u(c_t^1, c_t^2) + (1+\delta)^{-1} W_{t+1}^*];\; c_t^1, c_t^2, B_t \geqq 0. \tag{28}$$

subject to

$$B_t \leqq \frac{B_{t-1}(1 + r_{t+1})}{1+n} + (w_t - c_t^1)(1 + r_{t+1}) - c_t^2 \tag{29}$$

$$w_t - c_t^1 + \frac{B_{t-1}}{1+n} = (1+n)k_{t+1}. \tag{30}$$

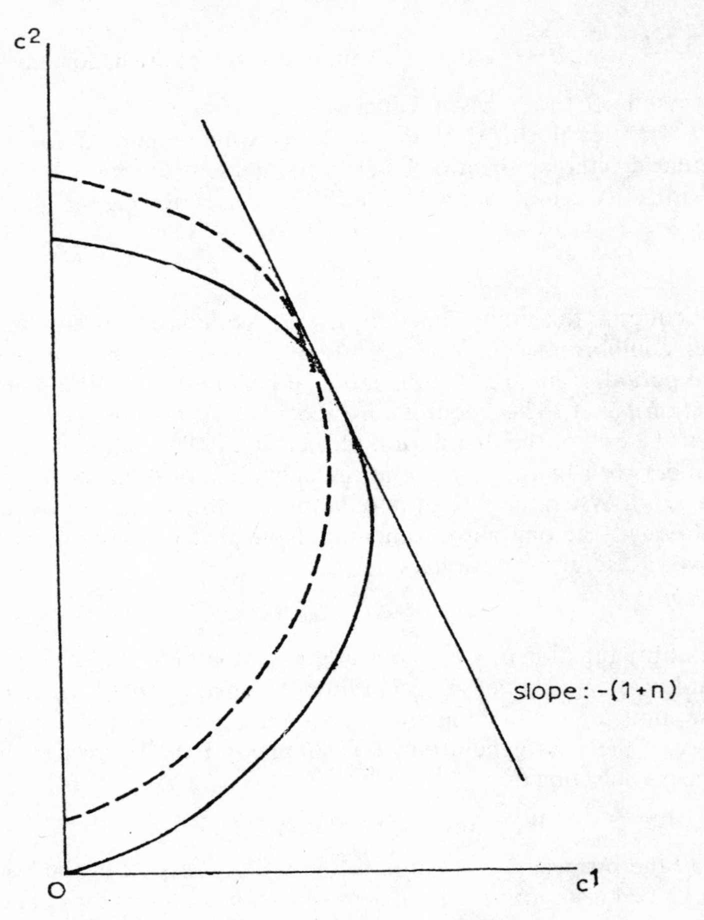

Figure 2 *Stationary competitive consumption possibility loci with low d (solid line) and with high d (dashed line)*

The individual's budget constraint now contains the bequest he receives and the bequest he leaves. The capital market equilibrium condition recognizes that now both the young and the old generation can save. As before we have $r_t = f'(k_t)$ and $w_t = f(k_t) - k_t f'(k_t)$

The first order conditions for an optimum are:

$$u_1(c_t^1, c_t^2) = (1 + r_{t+1})u_2(c_t^1, c_t^2) \tag{31a}$$

$$u_2(c_t^1, c_t^2) \geqq \frac{(1 + r_{t+2})u_2(c_{t+1}^1, c_{t+1}^2)}{(1 + n)(1 + \delta)}. \tag{31b}$$

If $B_t > 0$, i.e., if there is an interior solution for bequests, (31b) holds with equality. If there is a corner solution for bequests, i.e., if $B = 0$ is a

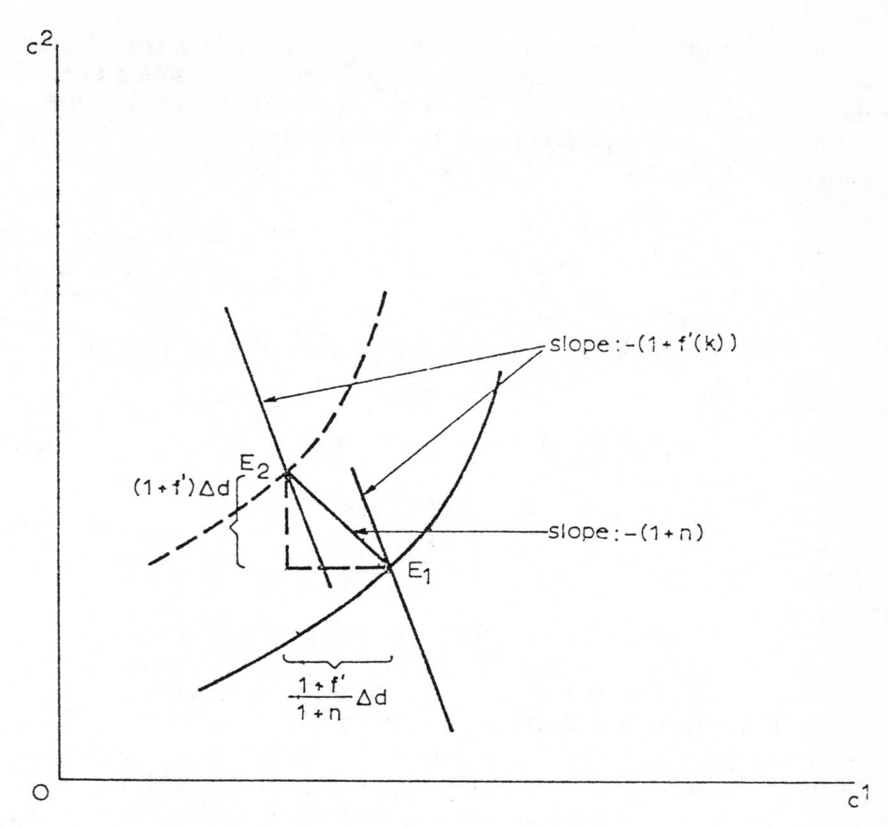

Figure 3 Shift of the stationary competitive consumption possibility locus when d increases, for a given capital-labor ratio $k < k^*$

binding constraint, (31b) holds with strict inequality. The interpretation of these first order conditions is straightforward. (31a) says that the discounted marginal utility of consumption in the second period of one's life should equal the marginal utility of consumption in the first period of one's life. (31b) states that if bequests are positive, the marginal utility of own consumption should equal the marginal utility of leaving a bequest. A marginal unit of income saved by an old member of generation t yields resources $(1 + r_{t+2})$ times larger to generation $t + 1$. The marginal utility to a member of generation t of bequests can be expressed as the discounted value of the marginal utility of consumption of a member of generation $t + 1$. The appropriate discount rate is the generational discount rate δ. Finally, since it is the utility of a representative member of generation $t + 1$ that was assumed to enter into the utility function of generation t, rather than the utility of all $1 + n$ descendants, the population growth factor $1 + n$ also discounts the marginal utility of consumption of generation $t + 1$. If the marginal utility of own consumption exceeds the marginal utility of bequests, here will be a corner solution with $B = 0$.

The steady state equilibrium of the model with bequests is given in equations (32a)–(32d).

$$u_1(c^1, c^2) = (1 + r)u_2(c^1, c^2) \tag{32a}$$

$$(1 + n)(1 + \delta) \geqq 1 + r \tag{32b}$$

if $B > 0$, $(1 + n)(1 + \delta) = 1 + r$
if $B = 0$ and the zero bequest constraint is binding, $(1 + n)(1 + \delta) > 1 + r$

$$\left(\frac{n - r}{1 + n}\right)B = (w - c^1)(1 + r) - c^2 \tag{32c}$$

$$(1 + n)k = \frac{B}{1 + n} + w - c^1 \tag{32d}$$

$$r = f'(k)$$

$$w = f(k) - kf'(k).$$

The stationary competitive consumption possibility locus with bequests is drawn in Figure 4. OA_2A_1 is the no bequest locus. At capital-labor ratios so high that $(1 + n)(1 + \delta) > 1 + f'(k)$, $B = 0$ and the no-bequest locus is again the relevant one. This critical capital-labor ratio, $\bar{k}$ *is at* A_2. Since $\delta > 0$, $\bar{k} < k^*$, the golden rule capital-labor ratio. Considering equations (32c) and (32d), we can draw a consumption possibility locus for each value of B. A higher value of B shifts the locus down and to the right at a rate $-(1 + n)$. Thus all steady-state equilibria with interior (positive) solutions for bequests lie on the line segment $A_2A_3A_4$. All interior bequest solutions have the same capital-labor ratio, defined by $f'(\bar{k}) = (1 + n)(1 + \delta)$ which is below the golden rule capital-labor ratio. One such interior solution for bequests is drawn at A_3, where an indifference curve is tangent to a budget constraint with slope $-(1 + f'(\bar{k}))$ on the line segment $A_2A_3A_4$. The stationary consumption possibility locus for the appropriate positive value of B is represented by the dashed curve through A_3. The complete stationary locus with bequests is given by the no-bequest locus above A_2 and the line segment $A_2A_3A_4$. If the stationary competitive equilibrium is on A_1A_2, i.e., if there is a corner solution for bequests, the effect of government lending and borrowing is as in the no-bequest model. If the model is stable, the introduction of government borrowing ($d > 0$) will reduce the equilibrium capital labor-ratio, while the introduction of government lending ($d < 0$) will increase it. However, government borrowing can never reduce the capital-labor ratio below $\bar{k}$.

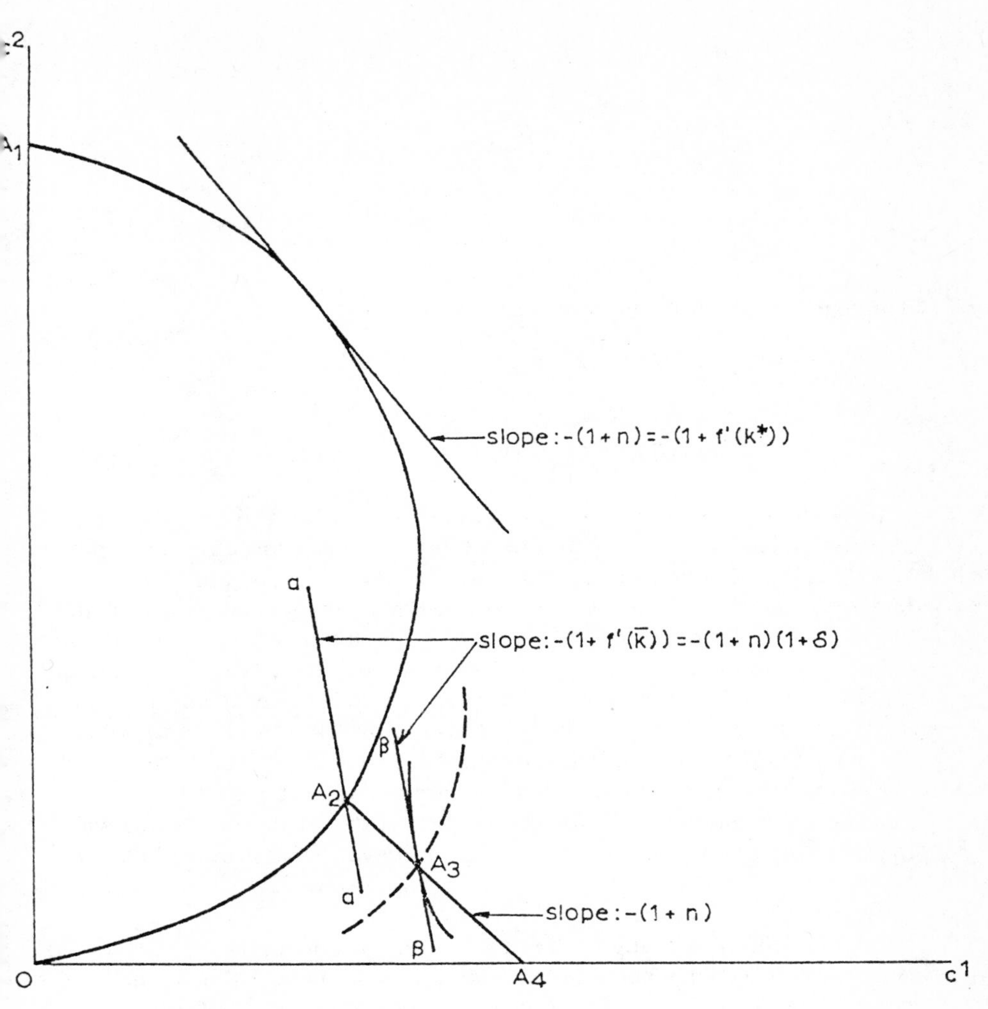

Figure 4 *An interior solution with bequests*

Once k falls to $\bar{k}$, any further increase in government borrowing (which represents an involuntary redistribution of income from the young to the old) will be matched by exactly offsetting bequests, voluntary transfers from the old to the young. This is most easily appreciated if we consider the effect of government lending. Start from an initial equilibrium, without government lending, with positive bequests as at A_3. With bequests, bonds and taxes the private budget constraint (29) and the capital market equilibrium condition (30) are replaced by (29′) and (30′) respectively.

$$B_t = \frac{B_{t-1}(1 + r_{t+1})}{1 + n} + (w_t - c_t^1 - \tau_t)(1 + r_{t+1}) - c_t^2 \qquad (29')$$

$$w_t - c_t^1 - \tau_t + \frac{B_{t-1}}{1 + n} = d + k_{t+1}(1 + n). \qquad (30')$$

We also have the budget constraint

$$(r - n)d = \tau_t(1 + n). \qquad (17')$$

The stationary constraints are:

$$\frac{(n - r)}{1 + n}(B - d(1 + r)) = (w - c^1)(1 + r) - c^2 \qquad (33a)$$

$$\frac{1}{1 + n}(B - d(1 + r)) + w - c^1 = k(1 + n). \qquad (33b)$$

If, with $d = 0$, a stationary solution obtains with $\mathrm{B} = \mathrm{B}^0 > 0$, a negative value of $d = d^0$ will still permit the same consumption-capital stock equilibrium to obtain as long as $B^0 \geqq |d^0(1 + r)|$, i.e., as long as bequests can be reduced by an amount equal, in present value, to the amount of government lending. Then the involuntary government redistribution from the old to the young will be neutralized as regards its effect on the life-time resources of the two generations alive at any one moment, by the reduction in voluntary private redistribution from the old to the young. Given any initial value of bequests, however, there always exists a volume of government lending large enough to put private agents in a zero-bequest corner. Thus, with bequests, the government can always raise the capital-labor ratio above $\bar{k}$. It can never bring it down below $\bar{k}$.

Gifts from the young to the old
With gifts from the young to the old, the utility function is $W_t = v(c_t^1, c_t^2, W_{t-1}^*)$. W_{t-1}^* is the maximum level of utility attained by a member of generation $t - 1$. We again adopt the additively separable form:

$$W_t = u(c_t^1, c_t^2) + (1 + \varrho)^{-1} W_{t-1}^*$$

We note that unlike standard time discounting, the utility of a member of the earlier generation is not compounded, but discounted. Convergence requires that the discount rate applied to parents' utility be positive, $\varrho > 0$. Gifts of course cannot be negative. $G_t \geqq 0$. The behavior of the competitive economy with gifts is summarized below

$$W_t^* = \max_{c_t^1,\, c_t^2,\, G_t} [u(c_t^1, c_t^2) + (1 + \varrho)^{-1} W_{t-1}^*];\ c_t^1, c_t^2, G_t \geqq 0. \qquad (34)$$

subject to

$$G_{t+1}(1 + n) + w_t(1 + r_{t+1}) \geqq (c_t^1 + G_t)(1 + r_{t+1}) + c_t^2 \qquad (35)$$

with

$$w_t - c_t^1 - G_t = k_{t+1}(1 + n) \tag{36}$$

and, as before

$$r_t = f'(k_t)$$
$$w_t = f(k_t) - k_t f'(k_t).$$

The private budget constraint allows for gifts handed out and received. The capital market equilibrium condition reflects the fact that resources given by the young to the old, who do not save, are no longer available for capital formation.

The first order conditions of the private optimization problem are:

$$u_1(c_t^1, c_t^2) = (1 + r_{t+1})\, u_2\,(c_t^1, c_t^2) \tag{37a}$$

$$\frac{u_2(c_{t-1}^1, c_{t-1}^2)}{(1 + \varrho)(1 + r_{t+1})}(1 + n) \leqq u_2\,(c_t^1, c_t^2). \tag{37b}$$

If $G_t > 0$, i.e., if there is an interior solution for gifts, (37b) holds with equality. If there is a corner solution for gifts, i.e., if $G = 0$ is a binding constraint, (37b) holds with strict inequality. Equation (37a) is the condition for the optimal allocation of consumption for a member of generation t between the two periods of his life. (37b) states that if gifts are given from generation t to generation $t - 1$, the marginal utility of own consumption should equal the marginal utility of gifts. The marginal utility of gifts is then expressed in terms of the marginal utility of own consumption of a member of generation $t - 1$. This marginal utility of own consumption of generation $t - 1$ is discounted at the generational discount factor $(1 + \varrho)$. Second-period consumption of members of generation $t - 1$ takes place one period before second-period consumption of members of generation t, so interest is foregone and further discounting by $(1 + r_{t+1})$ is required. Finally, there are more members of generation t than of generation $t - 1$. A member of generation $t - 1$ therefore receives $G_t(1 + n)$ for G_t given up by a member of generation t. If the marginal utility of own consumption exceeds the marginal utility of gifts, $G_t = 0$. The stationary solution with gifts is given by:

$$u_1(c^1, c^2) = u_2(c^1, c^2)(1 + r) \tag{38a}$$

$$\frac{1 + n}{1 + \varrho} \leqslant 1 + r \tag{38b}$$

$G > 0$ implies that (38b) holds with equality. A corner solution with $G = 0$ binding implies that (38b) holds with strict inequality. Stationary equilibrium is further characterized by:

$$G(r - n) = (w - c^1)(1 + r) - c^2 \tag{38c}$$

$$k(1 + n) + G = w - c^1 \tag{38d}$$

$$r = f'(k)$$

$$w = f(k) - kf'(k)$$

The interesting equation is (38b). Since ϱ is positive, $G > 0$ implies $r < n$. An interior solution for gifts implies that the economy is dynamically inefficient, at a capital-labor ratio k above the golden rule capital-labor ratio k^*. In models with inifite-lived households with a constant pure rate of time preference Ω, such an inefficiency can never arise. Steady state equilibrium is characterized by $(1 + n)(1 + \Omega) = 1 + r$. With $\Omega > 0$ this implies $r > n$. Earlier consumption is *cet. par.* valued more than later consumption. This is not true when we have a child-parent gift motive. Own earlier consumption may well be valued more than own later consumption. The pure rate of time preference for own consumption, $\Omega(c) = u_1(c, c)/u_2(c, c) - 1$, may well be positive. Earlier consumption by parents, however, is *cet. par.* valued less than later consumption by oneself. Parental utility is discounted, even though it 'accrues' earlier. Thus child-parent gifts do not make a private decentralized economy with finite-lived agents equivalent to an economy with infinite-lived agents. It also does not rule out the possibility of dynamic inefficiency through overaccumulation. Quite the contrary, if gifts are positive in the steady state, the steady state is necessarily inefficient. An operative gift motive is indeed a reflection of a very strong desire to shift resources away from early consumption towards later consumption.

The effect of gifts on the steady state consumption possibility locus is indicated in Figure 5. OA_2A_1 is the locus without gifts. For capital-labor ratios below $\bar{\bar{k}}$, defined by $f'(\bar{\bar{k}}) = \frac{1 + n}{1 + \varrho}$, the locus with gifts is identical with the locus without gifts because the equilibrium solution for G is zero. The stationary capital-labor ratio can never be above $\bar{\bar{k}}$ when there is a gift motive. All solutions with $G > 0$ lie on the line segment $A_4A_3A_2$ with slope $-(1 + n)$. Starting at A_2 where $G = 0$ and $k = \bar{\bar{k}}$, an increase in G shifts the stationary consumption possibility locus up and to the left at a rate $-(1 + n)$. A typical interior solution for G is drawn at A_3. An indifference curve is tangent to a budget constraint with slope $-(1 + f'(\bar{\bar{k}}))$ on the line segment $A_4A_3A_2$. The stationary consumption possibility locus for the appropriate positive value of G is represented by the dashed curve through A_3. The entire stationary consumption possibility locus with gifts is given by the segment of the no-gift locus OA_2 and the straight line $A_4A_3A_2$.

The effect of government borrowing and lending in the presence of a

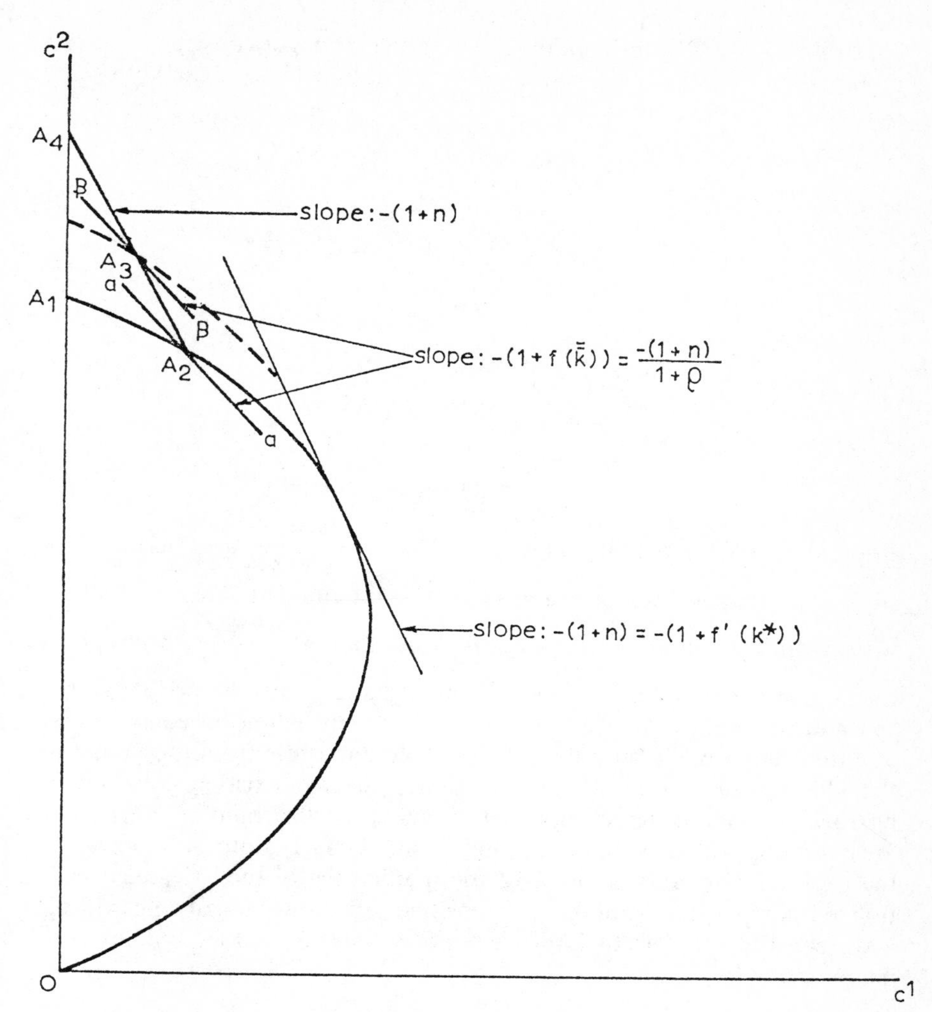

Figure 5 An interior solution for child-parent gifts

gift motive is easily analyzed. As long as the economy stays in the range of capital-labor ratios below $\bar{\bar{k}}$, government lending and borrowing will have the same effect as in the model without gifts and bequests. If $k = \bar{\bar{k}}$ initially (with $d = 0$), government lending ($d < 0$) will not have any effect on the steady-state consumption path and capital-labor ratio. Involuntary government redistribution from the old to the young will be neutralized immediately by matching voluntary gifts from the young to the old. Government borrowing, $d > 0$, will also be neutralized by matching reductions in gifts from the young to the old, up to the point that the constraint $G \geqq 0$ becomes binding. The private budget constraint, capital market equilibrium condition and government budget contraint with gifts, borrowing and taxes are

$$G_{t+1}(1 + n) + (w_t - \tau_t)(1 + r_{t+1}) = (c_t^1 + G_t)(1 + r_{t+1}) + c_t^2$$

and

$$w_t - \tau_t - c_t^1 - G_t = d + k_{t+1}(1 + n)$$

$$(r_t - n)\, d = \tau_t(1 + n)$$

The stationary equations are:

$$(n - r)(G + \frac{d(1 + r)}{1 + n}) + (w - c^1)(1 + r) - c^2 = 0 \qquad (39a)$$

$$G + \frac{d(1 + r)}{1 + n} + k(1 + n) = w - c^1 \qquad (39b)$$

Equations (33a) and (33b) show that G and $\frac{d(1 + r)}{1 + n}$ are 'perfect substitutes' as long as the constraint $G \geqq 0$ is not violated. Thus as long as, with $d = 0$, the initial G, (G^0, say) is larger than $d^0 \frac{(1 + r)}{1 + n}$, where d^0 *is* the size of the real per capita government bond issue, the private sector can and will undo the effects of the government action on consumption and the capital-labor ratio by reducing voluntary gifts from the young to the old. For any initial G, however, there always exists a government borrowing program large enough to make $G \geqq 0$ a binding constraint. Such actions will move the economy from $A_4A_3A_2$ onto A_20, lowering the capital-labor ratio. In view of the inefficiency of the private, decentralized competitive solution with positive gifts, such borrowing will always constitute a Pareto improvement as long as it does not lower k below k^*.

Gifts and bequests

I now consider the case of 'two-sided caring'. Each generation cares about the welfare of its immediate ancestors and its immediate descendants. The utility function is:

$$W_t = v(c_t^1, c_t^2, W_{t-1}^*, W_{t+1}^*).$$

The special case of the additively separable function is again considered:

$$W_t = u(c_t^1, c_t^2) + (1 + \delta)^{-1}W_{t+1}^* + (1 + \varrho)^{-1}W_{t-1}^*.$$

Convergence now requries not only $\delta > 0$ and $\delta > 0$ but $\delta\varrho > 1$.

It might be thought that the solution to the problem with both gifts and bequests is in some way a simple combination of the solutions to the cases with just gifts and just bequests. This is not so. With 'one-sided caring' (either gift or bequest motives but not both) the private agent's optimization problem is a standard problem in dynamic programming. With a bequest motive, each agent in generation t cares potentially for all his descendants. *Directly* as regards his immediate heir, *indirectly* through the dependence of the utility of his immediate descendant on the utility of generation $t + 2$, etc. In the same way, with a gift motive, each agent potentially cares for all his ancestors. In either case utility chains stretch out in one direction only. With both gift and bequest motives, this unidirectional simplicity no longer applies. An agent in generation t cares directly about generations $t - 1$ and $t + 1$. These generations both care directly about generation t. Generation $t - 1$ also cares directly about $t - 2$ and generation $t + 1$ about $t + 2$. Immediately, utility chains can be seen to be running in both directions. These issues were discussed for the first time in Carmichael [1979]. A particularly simple solution emerges when the following assumptions are made about the 'game' played by a member of generation t with past and future generations:

1. A member of generation t acts competitively in his labor and capital markets, i.e. he takes w_t and r_{t+1} as parametric. He also assumes that all past and future generations have acted or will act competitively in their factor markets.

2. A member of generation t, in formulating his consumption-gift-bequest plan, knows the utility levels and actions of all past generations and correctly anticipates utility levels and actions of all future generations (rational expectations or perfect foresight).

3. A member of generation t plays a *non-cooperative gift* and bequest game with past and future generations. He rationally believes that all past and future generations play the same game. This strategy is *closed-loop* as regards the utility and actions of the two generations with which he overlaps (generations $t - 1$ and $t + 1$). This means that when evaluating the alternative actions open to him at the beginning of period t, he believes that he can affect the total utility and the actions of his immediate descendants and his immediate forebears.

His strategy is *open-loop* as regards the utility and actions of all other generations ($t - i$, $t \geqq 2$ and $t + j$, $j \geqq 2$). Thus, when evaluating the effects of marginal changes in his actions, he ignores the impact on the actions and utility of generations that are already dead when he is born or that are born after his lifetime.[4]

4. When formulating his closed-loop strategy *vis-à-vis* generations $t - 1$ and $t + 1$, he believes that he can alter the behavior of these generations (i.e. their consumption, gift and bequest choices) only by altering the total resources available to them, i.e., only through direct transfers.

5. Each generation acts so as to maximize its utility.

6. Each generation views the world and plays the game in the same way as the member of generation t just described.

The resulting equilibrium in this differential game is a Nash equilibrium.

The behavior of this economy can be summarized as follows:

$$W_t^* = \max_{c_t^1,\, c_t^2,\, B_t,\, G_t} W_t = \max_{c_t^1,\, c_t^2,\, B_t,\, G_t} [u(c_t^1, c_t^2) + (1 + \delta)^{-1} W_{t+1}^* + (1 + \varrho)^{-1} W_{t-1}^*] \tag{40}$$

subject to:

$$B_t - G_{t+1}(1 + n) \leqq \left(\frac{B_{t-1}}{1 + n} - G_t\right)(1 + r_{t+1}) + (w_t - c_t^1)(1 + r_{t+1}) - c_t^2$$
$$B_t,\, G_t,\, c_t^1,\, c_t^2 \geqq 0, \tag{41}$$

with economy-wide constraints:

$$w_t - c_t^1 + \frac{B_{t+1}}{1 + n} - G_t = k_{t+1}(1 + n) \tag{42}$$

and

$$r_{t+1} = f'(k_{t+1})$$
$$w_t = f(k_t) - k_t f'(k_t)$$

The first order conditions are:

$$\frac{\partial W_t^*}{\partial c_t^1} = (1 + r_{t+1})\frac{\partial W_t^*}{\partial c_t^2} \tag{43a}$$

$$\frac{\partial W_t^*}{\partial B_t} \leqq \frac{\partial W_t^*}{\partial c_t^2} \tag{43b}$$

If $B_t > 0$, (43b) holds with strict equality. If $B_t = 0$ is a binding constraint, (43b) holds with strict inequality.

$$\frac{\partial W_t^*}{\partial G_t} \leqq \frac{\partial W_t^*}{\partial c_t^1} \tag{43c}$$

If $G_t > 0$, (43c) holds with strict equality. If $G_t = 0$ is a binding constraint, (43c) holds with strict inequality. Using assumptions (1) through (6), the first order conditions and the private budget constraints of current, past and future generations, we can express generation t's marginal utility from bequests in terms of the marginal utility of own consumption of generation $t + 1$.

$$\frac{\partial W_t^*}{\partial B_t} = \frac{(1 + \varrho)(1 + r_{t+2})}{[(1 + \varrho)(1 + \delta) - 1](1 + n)} \frac{\partial W_{t+1}^*}{\partial c_{t+1}^2}. \tag{44}$$

Combining (44) and (43b) we get

$$\frac{(1 + \varrho)(1 + r_{t+2})}{[(1 + \varrho)(1 + \delta) - 1](1 + n)} \frac{\partial W^*_{t+1}}{\partial c^2_{t+1}} \leqq \frac{\partial W^*_t}{\partial c^2_t} \tag{45}$$

If $B_t > 0$, then (45) holds with strict equality. If $B_t = 0$ is a binding constraint, (45) holds with strict inequality.

In an exactly analogous manner we can express generation t's marginal utility from gifts in terms of the marginal utility of own consumption of generation $t - 1$.

$$\frac{\partial W^*_t}{\partial G_t} = \frac{(1 + n)(1 + \delta)}{(1 + \varrho)(1 + \delta) - 1} \frac{\partial W^*_{t-1}}{\partial c^2_{t-1}} \tag{46}$$

Combining (46) and (43c) and using (43a), we obtain:

$$\frac{(1 + n)(1 + \delta)}{[(1 + \varrho)(1 + \delta) - 1]} \frac{\partial W^*_{t-1}}{\partial c^2_{t-1}} \leqq \frac{\partial W^*_t}{\partial c^2_{t-1}} (1 + r_{t+1}). \tag{47}$$

If $G_t > 0$, then (47) holds with strict equality. If $G_t = 0$ is a binding constraint, (47) holds with strict inequality.

The steady state conditions are:

$$u_1(c^1, c^2) = (1 + r)u_2(c^1, c^2)^5 \tag{48a}$$

$$1 + r \leqq \left[\frac{[(1 + \varrho)(1 + \delta) - 1]}{1 + \varrho}\right](1 + n) \tag{48b}$$

If $B > 0$ then (48b) holds with equality. If $B = 0$ is a binding constraint then (48b) holds with strict inequality.

$$1 + r \geqslant \frac{(1 + \delta)(1 + n)}{(1 + \varrho)(1 + \delta) - 1} \tag{48c}$$

If $G > 0$ then (48c) holds with equality. If $G = 0$ is a binding constraint then (48c) holds with strict inequality.

$$\left(\frac{n - r}{1 + n}\right)B + (r - n)\,G = (w - c^1)(1 + r) - c^2 \tag{48d}$$

$$k(1 + n) = \frac{B}{1 + n} - G + w - c^1. \tag{48e}$$

and

$$r = f'(k)$$
$$w = f(k) - kf'(k)$$

With n, ϱ and δ strictly positive, (48b) and (48c) cannot both hold with equality. This is the common sense result that there will not be both gifts and bequests in the steady state. Thus, if $B > 0$, then $G = 0$, and if $G > 0$ then $B = 0$. However, it is possible for (48b) and (48c) to both hold with strict inequality, i.e., for both gifts and bequests to be zero.

Note that if (48b) holds with equality, i.e., if there is an interior solution for bequests, we have $r > n$: the capital-labor ratio is below the golden rule capital-labor ratio.[6] Also, if (48c) holds with equality, i.e., if there is an interior solution with gifts, we have $r < n$: the capital-labor ratio is above its golden level. Figure 6 illustrates the stationary consumption possibility locus when there is both a bequest and a gift motive. For capital labor ratios below that defined by $(1 + f'(k)) = \dfrac{(1 + \delta)(1 + n)}{(1 + \varrho)(1 + \delta) - 1}$ but above that defined by $(1 + f'(k)) = \dfrac{[(1 + \varrho)(1 + \delta) - 1](1 + n)}{1 + \varrho}$, the stationary consumption possibility locus is the same as it is without gifts and bequests. On the curve segment A_2A_5, there are corner solutions for gifts and bequests: $G = B = 0$. When there is an interior solution for gifts the equilibrium is on the line segment A_1A_2 with slope $-(1 + n)$. A_2 is defined by $-(1 + f'(k)) = \dfrac{(1 + \delta)(1 + n)}{1 - (1 + \varrho)(1 + \delta)}$. As in the gifts only case, large positive values of G shift the locus up and to the left at a rate $-(1 + n)$. Note that the degree of overaccumulation relative to the golden rule is less when $G > 0$, if there is both a gift and a bequest motive than if there is only a gift motive.[7] The tendency to 'oversave', represented by the gift motive is partly, but not completely, neutralized by the presence of a bequest motive. A_3A_4 would be the locus of interior solutions for G if there were only a gift motive. If the bequest motive is operative, i.e., if $B > 0$, all stationary solutions lie on the line segment A_5A_6 with slope $-(1 + n)$. A_5 is defined by $(1 + f'(k)) = \dfrac{[(1 + \varrho)(1 + \delta) - 1]}{1 + \varrho}(1 + n)$. As in the case of bequests only, larger positive values of B shift the locus down and to the right at a rate $-(1 + n)$. A_7A_8 would be the locus of interior solutions for B if there were just a bequest motive. The degree of underaccumulation, relative to the golden rule, is less if there is both a bequest and a gift motive than if there is only a gift motive.[8]

The effects of government lending and borrowing on the steady-state capital-labor ratio are a straightforward combination of the effects of such policies when there was either a gift or a bequested motive but not both. Consider an initial equilibrium without government debt: $d = 0$. If the initial equilibrium is in the range of k for which there is a corner solution for both B and G, i.e, on A_2A_5, government borrowing ($d > 0$) cannot lower k below the value defined by $1 + f'(k) = \dfrac{[(1 + \varrho)(1 + \delta) - 1]}{1 + \varrho}(1 + n)$

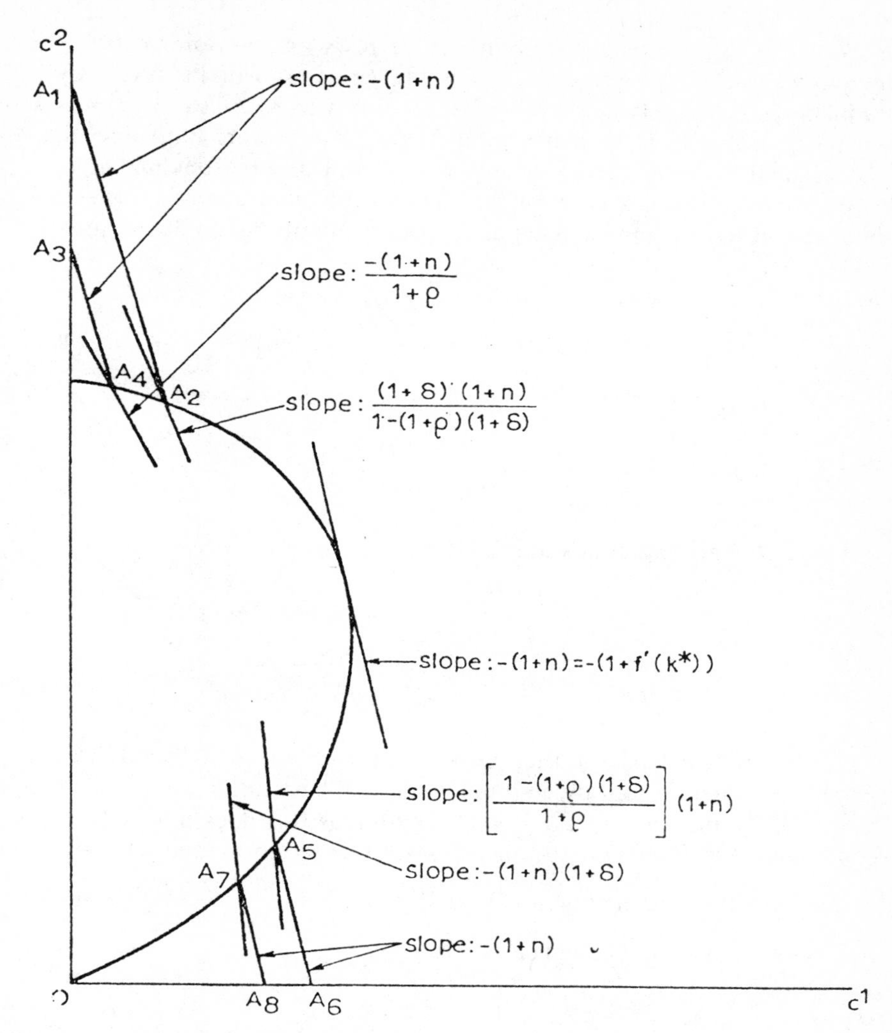

Figure 6 *Stationary consumption possibility loci, without gifts and bequests with either gifts or bequests and with both gifts and bequests*

nor can government lending ($d < 0$) raise k above the value defined by $1 + f'(k) = \dfrac{(1 + \delta)(1 + n)}{(1 + \varrho)(1 + \delta) - 1)}$ If there is an interior solution for gifts, on A_1A_2, government borrowing will be offset by a reduction in gifts of equal present value, thus leaving c^1, c^2 and k unchanged, unless the increase in d is larger, in present value, than the original value of G. In other words, there is always a positive value of d large enough to make $G \geqq 0$ a binding constraint. If there is an interior solution for bequests, on A_5A_6, government lending ($d < 0$) will be offset by a reduction in bequests of equal present value which leaves c^1, c^2 and k unchanged. Again, if the value of lending is larger, in present value, than the original bequest, the constraint $B \geqslant O$ will become binding.

With gifts, bequests, borrowing and taxes the private and public sector budget constraints and the capital market equilibrium conditions are:

$$B_t - \frac{B_{t-1}(1 + r_{t+1})}{1 + n} G_{t+1}(1 + n) + G_t(1 + r_{t+1}) - (w_t - c_t^1 - \tau_t)(1 + r_{t+1}) + c_t^2 = 0 \tag{49a}$$

$$w_t - c_t^1 - \tau_t + \frac{B_{t-1}}{1 + n} - G_t = d + k_{t+1}(1 + n). \tag{49b}$$

and

$$(r_t - n)d = \tau_t(1 + n).$$

The stationary equations are:

$$(n - r)\left[\frac{B}{1 + n} - G - \frac{d(1 + r)}{1 + n}\right] = (w - c^1)(1 + r) - c^2 \tag{50a}$$

$$\frac{B}{1 + n} - G - \frac{d(1 + r)}{1 + n} = k(1 + n) - w + c^1 \tag{50b}$$

We know that if $B > 0$, then $G = 0$ and if $G > 0$ then $B = 0$. Thus if $B > 0$, a reduction in d by an amount Δd will be neutralized by a reduction in B by the amount $\Delta d(1 + r)$, as long as this does not violate the constraint $B \geqslant 0$. If $G > 0$, an increase in d by an amount Δd will be neutralized by a reduction in G by the amount $\frac{\Delta d(1 + r)}{1 + n}$, as long as this does not violate the constraint $G \geqslant 0$.

III Conclusion

The policy conclusions of this theoretical investigation of debt neutrality are straightforward. While operative intergenerational gift and bequest motives turn finite-lived households into infinite-lived households in a certain sense, there remain essential differences. In particular, if the child-parent gift motive is operative, the decentralized, competitive equilibrium is socially inefficient because it is characterized by a capital-labor ratio above the golden rule. There is therefore a prima facie case for government intervention in the saving-investment process. The second conclusion concerns debt neutrality. Here every neutrality theorem is matched by a non-neutrality theorem. If neither bequests nor gifts are operative, government borrowing 'crowds out' capital formation. If child-parent gifts are operative, small increases in government borrowing are neutralized by reductions in gifts. If bequests are operative, small reductions in government borrowing (or increases in lending) are neutralized by reductions in bequests. There always exists an increase in lending or borrowing that will make $B = 0$, respectively $G = 0$ a binding constraint. There always is a government financial strategy that puts the private sector in a zero gift and zero bequest corner solution, where financial policy will affect the capital-labor ratio. In our simple model, all agents are identical, so either everyone is at a corner or no one is. If instead we visualize a distribution of agents, by δ, by ϱ, and by the other parameters of their utility functions and the constraints they face, increasing government borrowing can be expected to make the zero gift constraint binding for an increasing number of agents. The same analysis can be applied to the study of the effects of the introduction of an unfunded social security retirement scheme in a world where previously only private saving provided for retirement. Subject to the qualifications mentioned earlier, such a scheme will reduce private saving in the short run and the capital-labor ratio in the long run.

Even in this most classical of models, the conclusion emerges inexorably that the way in which the government finances its real spending program can have major consequences for saving and capital formation. Debt neutrality is not a plausible theoretical proposition. Future research should concentrate on empirical assessments of the extent and nature of non-neutrality.

Notes

Originally published in *Greek Economic Review*, 2, 1980, pp. 111–42.

1 u is assumed to be strictly quasiconcave and increasing in c^1 and c^2. $u_1(0, c^2) = u_2(c^1, 0) = +\infty$, $u_1(\infty, c^2) = u_2(c^1, \infty) = 0$.
2 We also assume $f'(0) = +\infty$; $f'(\infty) = 0$.
3 A solution will exist if c^1 and c^2 are both normal goods and if c^1 does not increase when r_{t+1} increases. It will be unique if the utility function is homothetic. See Carmichael [1979].
4 This is different from Carmichael [1979] who considers the case where an individual only ignores the impact of marginal changes in his actions on generations that are already dead, i.e. Carmichael uses a closed-loop strategy *vis-à-vis* all later generations. The symmetry imposed in my specification considerably simplifies the analysis.
5 From 43a we have, in the steady state, $\frac{\partial W}{\partial c^1} = (1 + r)\frac{\partial W}{\partial c^2}$

$$W = \frac{u(c^1, c^2)}{1 - (1 + \delta)^{-1} - (1 + \varrho)^{-1}}$$

6 We use the condition $\varrho\delta > 1$, for the stationary utility function to be bounded.
7 We assume ϱ to be the same in both cases.
8 We assume δ to be the same in both cases.

References

Barro, R. J. (1974) 'Are Government Bonds Net Wealth?', *Journal of Political Economy*, Vol. 82, pp. 1095–117.

Buiter, W. H. (1979), 'Government Finance in an Overlapping Generations Model With Gifts and Bequests', in G. M. von Furstenberg, (ed.), *Social Security Versus Private Saving*, Ballinger.

—— and Tobin, J. (1979), 'Debt Neutrality: A Brief Review of Doctrine and Evidence', in G. M. von Furstenberg (ed.), *Social Security Versus Private Saving*, Ballinger.

Carmichael, J. (1979), *The Role of Government Financial Policy in Economic Growth*, unpublished PhD Thesis, Princeton University.

Diamond, P. A. (1965), 'National Debt in a Neo-Classical Growth Model', *American Economic Review*, Vol. 55, pp. 1126–50.

Tobin, J. and Buiter, W. H. (1980), 'Fiscal and Monetary Policies, Capital Formation and Economic Activity', in G. N. von Furstenberg (ed.), *The Government and Capital Formation*, Ballinger, forthcoming.

Chapter 12

Government debt: comment

Written with Jeffrey Carmichael

In a recent article in this *Review*, John Burbidge [1983] argues that our analyses of overlapping-generations models with intergenerational gifts and bequests (Buiter [1979; 1980], and Carmichael [1982]) are logically faulty. On the basis of this assertion he goes on to argue that the real issue in the debate over debt neutrality is the nature of individual preferences. This comment argues that neither his criticism of our analyses nor his ultimate conclusion is valid.

I Specification of the utility function

Burbidge's criticism of *our* treatment of intergenerational transfers centers on our specification of the individual's utility function. We assume that population grows at the rate n and that bequests (gifts) are shared equally among immediate descendants (ancestors). Logic then requires that $1 + n$ enters the budget constraint in a perfectly obvious manner.

Nothing is implied by this about the relative merits of making my welfare an increasing function of the welfare of my *representative* descendant or ancestor (our specification), or of $(1 + n)$ times the welfare of my representative descendant of $1/(1 + n)$ times the welfare of my representative ancestor. It is an old and familiar issue in the optimal growth literature whether the utility of the representative individual should be optimized, or whether a 'the more the merrier' approach should be adopted as in Burbidge. This is not an issue of logical consistency but of tastes. I might care about the welfare of my representative descendant raised to an exponent equal to the logarithm of the cube root of $1 + n$. *De gustibus non est disputandum*.

This, of course, is not the end of the story. The ultimate analytic results derived by ourselves and Burbidge depend not so much on the specification of the utility function per se as on the restrictions imposed on the parameters of the chosen utility functions. It is here that the real difference between ourselves and Burbidge lies.

Consider the case under contention, in which the individual cares only about his parents. Using Burbidge's notation, we can write the individual's utility, v_t, as a function of his own consumption in periods 1 and 2 (c^1 and c^2) and of the per capita utility of his parents, v_{t-1}. Under the 'de gustibus...' principle, we can think of this latter relationship as some general function $F(\cdot)$ of v_{t-1}. In our earlier papers, we write the utility function in the form:

$$v_t = u(c_t^1, c_t^2) + (1 + \delta)v_{t-1}, \tag{1}$$

where $(1 + \delta)$ is the interpersonal discount factor applied to the *per capita* utility of the individual's parents. We will come back to the interpretation of this discount factor shortly.

Burbidge argues that, since each generation is $1 + n$ times larger than the previous generation, parental welfare should be weighted by the factor $1/(1 + n)$ in the descendant's utility function. Thus, he writes the utility function (his equation (3′)) as

$$v_t = u(c_t^1, c_t^2) + \left(\frac{1 + \rho}{1 + n}\right)v_{t-1}, \tag{2}$$

where ρ is again an interpersonal discount rate.

Equations (1) and (2) are a subset of the many acceptable utility functions in which v_t is a general function $F(\cdot)$ of v_{t-1}. What matters is the set of restrictions imposed on the derivative of this function, $\partial F/\partial v_{t-1}$. Clearly, any sensible restrictions on the interpersonal discount factor in equation (2) will have counterpart restrictions on the discount factor in equation (1).[1] For this reason we will work with Burbidge's specification from here on.

Burbidge argues that $\rho > n$ in equation (2) is a necessary condition for sensible results. If he is correct, a steady state with gifts will have the property that $\rho = r > n$ (from the first-order condition for operative gifts). Such a steady state is necessarily undercapitalized, thereby ruling out the case in which bonds are an unambiguous addition to net wealth and, with it, the proof in Carmichael's 1982 paper that bonds can be neutral even when they are an unambiguous addition to net wealth. Burbidge's restriction, however, has some bizarre implications.

II **Restrictions on the utility function**

There are two possible reasons for restricting the range of sensible values for ρ.[2] The first and most important source of restriction on ρ comes from the steady-state utility function, which from (2) is

$$v = \left(\frac{1 + n}{n - \varrho}\right) u(c^1, c^2).$$

A sensible model would have steady-state utility both bounded and of the same sign as $u(\cdot)$. Burbidge's condition, that $\rho > n$, however, does not yield a sensible steady state. If we assume a stationary consumption sequence $\{c_t^1, c_t^2\}$, utility defined by (2) with $\rho > n$, does not converge at all. Alternatively, if we assume that utility is stationary, the model has the peculiar characteristic that the steady-state utility function $v(\cdot)$ has the opposite properties to consumption utility $u(\cdot)$; for example, if $u(\cdot)$ is positive and increasing in c^1 and c^2, $v(\cdot)$ is negative and *decreasing* in c^1 and c^2.

Our specification of the utility function, which discounts parental welfare (i.e., $\rho < n$), is convergent for constant $\{c_t^1, c_t^2\}$ and the stationary utility level is, sensibly, increasing in c^1 and c^2. In terms of equation (1), (our specification) our restriction would be $\delta < 0$. The equivalent (sensible) restriction in Burbidge's formulation (equation (2)) is $\rho < n$.

The second potential source of restriction on ρ comes from consistency of the family's consumption plan; it is on this argument that Burbidge relies for his result. He asserts that consistency of the family's consumption plan requires that if the utility of heirs is discounted at ρ, the utility of parents must be 'reverse discounted' at ρ. To establish this claim, he proposes a utility function (his equation (4)) which avoids the unpalatable implications of reverse discounting in his equation (3′) (equation (2) herein) by including concern for ancestors and descendants, but truncating direct and indirect concern about ancestral utility after the first generation:

$$v_t = \sum_{i=-1}^{\infty} \left(\frac{1 + n}{1 + \rho}\right)^i u(c_{t+i}^1, c_{t+i}^2) \quad \rho > 0. \tag{3}$$

While, under the de gustibus ... principle, Burbidge is entitled to choose any utility function he likes, the asymmetry of equation (3) seems arbitrary. His justification for this truncation is unconvincing. Referring to equation (3) he argues, correctly, that 'Since someone born at time t can affect only the utility level of his or her parents, v_{t-2} is exogenous at time t'. (p. 223). However, the mere fact that I cannot affect something doesn't mean it cannot affect my utility. I may not be able to do anything about my toothache, or my father's toothache, or indeed a toothache suffered by my now deceased grandfather, but these events may well affect my utility. It is obviously correct that the optimal decision rule is independent of any additive term in the objective function which the decision maker takes as parametric. However, while exogenous to the individual, such terms are endogenous to the system as a whole and should not be dropped, as Burbidge proposes, when evaluating the long-run properties of the model.[3]

These objections notwithstanding, we can still evaluate Burbidge's claim about the discount rate using his formulation. Suppose, as Burbidge does, that individuals apply the discount rates $(1 + \rho^-)$ to ancestors and $(1 + \rho^+)$ to descendants. His 'two-sided' utility function becomes

$$v_t = \left(\frac{1 + \rho^-}{1 + n}\right)u_{t-1} + u_t + \sum_{i=1}^{\infty}\left(\frac{1 + n}{1 + \rho^+}\right)^i u_{t+i}. \tag{4}$$

So long as we assume that the individual takes the actions of others as given (i.e., a Nash concept of behavior), the relevant first-order conditions from maximizing (4) are

$$\frac{\partial u_{t-1}/\partial c_{t-1}^2}{\partial u_t/\partial c_t^2} \leq \frac{1 + r_{t+1}}{1 + \rho^-} \tag{5}$$

$$\frac{\partial u_t/\partial c_t^2}{\partial u_{t+1}/\partial c_{t+1}^2} \geq \frac{1 + r_{t+2}}{1 + \rho^+} \tag{6}$$

Burbidge argues that, in a steady state, an individual contemplating a gift to his parent will equate $(\partial u/\partial c_{t-1}^1)/(\partial u/\partial c_t^1)$ to $(1 + r)/(1 + \rho^-)$ while his parent, contemplating a gift to the individual will equate the same ratio of marginal utilities to $(1 + r)/(1 + \rho^+)$. Consistency of the family plan, he asserts, requires that these two ratios be equal; that is,[4] that $\rho^+ = \rho^-$. Since $\rho^+ > n$ is a necessary condition for (4) to converge to a sensible steady state, he also gets $\rho^- > n$.

Burbidge's conclusion, however, only holds if there are stationary equilibria in which both gifts and bequests are strictly positive. If this is the case, it should occur as a natural result of the model; it is not a condition that can sensibly be imposed. In this respect, the inequalities in (5) and (6) are crucial since they allow for corner solutions in gifts and/or bequests. If we impose the more plausible restrictions that $\rho^+ > n$ and $\rho^- < n$, the steady state has the characteristics that: if $r = \rho^- < n$, gifts are operative while bequests are zero; if $\rho^- < n < r = \rho^+$, bequests are operative, while gifts are zero; and if $\rho^- < r < \rho^+$ both gifts and bequests are at zero corner solutions. The actual steady-state configuration depends on tastes and technology.

Once the corner solution properties of intergenerational transfers are accounted for, it is no longer necessary for $\rho^- = \rho^+$, since it is no longer necessary for the two inequalities mentioned by Burbidge to hold with equality simultaneously. His is a special (we believe not very plausible) case.

It is worth emphasizing that, interpreted correctly, this model does allow for 'dynamically inefficient' steady states, in which the marginal product of capital is below the population growth rate. This occurs if the stationary equilibrium has positive gifts from children to parents. The reasons that inefficient steady states can exist are that: (a) parental consumption and utility, even though it accrues earlier in time, is *discounted* by moderately selfish descendants; (b) agents act competitively in all markets; and (c) successive generations play a noncooperative game with each other. If binding commitments could be entered into between generations, a cooperative solution could be achieved that would rule out inefficient equilibria. That this does not occur is a fundamental difference between overlapping generations models (even with interdependent preferences) and models with a single, infinitely-lived individual.

III Debt neutrality: the real issue

On the basis of his claim that $\rho^{-} > n$, Burbidge argues that inefficient steady-state equilibria ($r < n$) are ruled out, thereby strengthening Robert Barro's [1974] debt-neutrality theorem. He argues that the essence of debt neutrality is therefore in the specification of the utility function. Apart from being incorrect in asserting the ρ^{-} must be less than n, we believe that Burbidge's conclusion misses the point of our contributions.

The objective of Carmichael [1982] was to establish that the literature was focussing attention on the wrong questions. As shown in that paper, whether or not individuals perceive government debt as a contribution to net wealth is irrelevant to the question of debt neutrality. Neutrality or nonneutrality is entirely a consequence of budgetary substitutability between debt and intergenerational transfers. The proof of that proposition consisted of showing that an under-capitalized equilibrium *could* exist and that, in this equilibrium, under suitable (restrictive) conditions government debt was still neutral, despite the fact that it was an unambiguous contribution to net wealth.[5] To refute this proposition, Burbidge would need to have shown that $\rho^{-} < n$ is *never* possible – which he has failed to do.

IV Conclusion

Specification of utility functions is a matter of taste, not of logic. Analytic conclusions about steady-state behavior with intergenerational transfers, however, depend not so much on specification of the utility function as on restrictions imposed on the parameters of any given utility function; this is a matter of logic, not of tastes.

We see two main grounds on which to restrict interpersonal discount rates in Burbidge's (or any other) specification of the utility functions; the desirability of a sensible steady state; and consistency of the family consumption plan. Neither of these approaches leads to Burbidge's restriction that the utility of ancestors must be reverse discounted. Indeed they lead to the opposite conclusion.

Even allowing Burbidge's restriction as a possible (though not very plausible) case, his conclusion that debt neutrality revolves around the specification of the utility function is still a red herring. The essence of debt neutrality is budgetary substitutability between intergenerational transfers and government debt.

Notes

Originally published in the *American Economic Review*, 74, 1984, pp. 762–5.

1 Indeed, if one had a preference for Burbidge's formulation, the discount factor in equation (1) could be interpreted as a weighted discount factor such that $(1 + \delta) = (1 + \rho)/(1 + n)$. In fact, we see little to recommend Burbidge's formulation, since each individual always has one set of parents (not $1/(1 + n)$) regardless of the population growth rate. However, since utility functions are a matter of taste, we see no reason to reject his specification out of hand.
2 A third reason is intuitive. Since $1 + \rho$ is an interpersonal discount rate it should conform to reasonable priors about interpersonal preferences. A value of ρ greater than zero implies that the individual 'cares' more *per capita* for his parents than he does for himself. If, as in equation (2), the per capita utility of his parents is weighted by the factor $1/(1 + n)$ he will care more *absolutely* (i.e., in total) for his parents than for himself if $\rho > n$. Under normal (selfish) preference theory we would expect the individual to apply a positive discount factor to the utility of others, suggesting the minimal restriction that $\rho < n$.
3 These issues and the nature of the 'two-sided' utility function are considered in detail in Carmichael [1979].
4 Our notation here varies slightly from Burbidge's. In his fn. 4, he uses $1/(1 + \rho^-)$ instead of $(1 + \rho^-)$ which, apart from being confusing, leads him to the incorrect (given his definition) restriction that $\rho^- = \rho^+$.
5 Burbidge does point out, correctly, that the suitable conditions are even more restrictive than suggested by Carmichael, in that his Propositions 1 and 2 should be amended to include the proviso that the *same* transfer mechanism must be operative both before and after the policy action.

References

Barro, R. J., 'Are Government Bonds Net Wealth?', *Journal of Political Economy*, November–December 1974, 82, 1095–117.

Buiter, Willem H., 'Government Finance in an Overlapping-Generations Model with Gifts and Bequests', in G. M. von Furstenberg (ed.) *Social Security Versus Private Saving*, Cambridge: Ballinger, 1979.

——, '"Crowding Out" of Private Capital Formation by Government Borrowing in the Presence of Intergenerational Gifts and Bequests', *Greek Economic Review*, August 1980, 2, 111–42.

Burbidge, J. B., 'Government Debt in an Overlapping-Generations Model with Bequests and Gifts', *American Economic Review*, March 1983, 73, 222–7.

Carmichael, J., 'Economic Equilibrium and Steady-State Growth with Intergenerationally-Dependent Preferences', ERP Memo. No. 245, Princeton University, 1979.

——, 'On Barro's Theorem of Debt Neutrality: The Irrelevance of Net Wealth', *American Economic Review*, March 1982, 72, 202–13.

Chapter 13

The theory of optimum deficits and debt

I Introduction

This paper deals with some of the issues that arise in connection with the optimal financing of a given program of 'exhaustive' public spending on goods and services. The determination of the size and composition of this real spending program is not considered. A more general view would encompass the optimal joint determination of the public sector's consumption and investment program and its method of financing, but even the less ambitious approach adopted here raises a very wide range of issues and considerations.

Government financial policy is about the management of the public sector balance sheet, broadly defined. It includes the choice of taxation versus borrowing. It also concerns the composition or structure of taxes (lump sum, direct, indirect, degree of progression, etc.) and the characteristics of the debt instruments issued by the government (interest-bearing or noninterest-bearing, legal tender, maturity, degree of indexing, etc.). Monetary policy, exchange rate management and foreign exchange market intervention therefore belong to financial policy as much as open market operations or bond issues 'to finance the deficit'. It should be obvious that questions concerning the distribution of income (intragenerational as well as intergenerational) are inextricably intertwined with questions relating to the financing of a given real spending program. Stiglitz [1983a,b] has emphasized the inevitable intertemporal and intergenerational risk-sharing attributes of financial policy, something I shall return to in Section II.

Like any other kind of government intervention in the economy, government financial policy can be rationalized in one of two ways. The first is intervention for purely distributional reasons. While they are of major importance, I shall not pay much attention in what follows to the distributional objectives of the government. The distributional consequences of alternative financing rules will, however, be central. Indeed financial policy influences real economic variables largely by affecting the intertemporal and interpersonal (including intergenerational) distribution of income and wealth. The second justification for financial policy is the identification of instance(s) of market failure together with the attribution to the government of the ability to undertake remedial welfare-improving actions that private agents either cannot undertake or do not find in their own perceived self-interest to undertake.

The market 'imperfections' central to an appreciation of the potential welfare-improving role of financial policy are capital market imperfections. Included in this are any restrictions on the ability of private agents to effect intertemporal transfers of purchasing power in either direction at social intertemporal terms of trade. In the overlapping generations model with finite lives and without operative intergenerational gifts and bequests, the incompleteness of the set of forward markets (or the absence of a full set of Arrow-Debreu securities) is due to the 'technological' constraint that the dead cannot consume goods and services and the legal constraint that private agents cannot impose binding financial obligations on the unborn. In real life this nonexistence of certain forward markets is augmented by a wide array of capital market imperfections. Private agents are constrained in their spending plans by the illiquidity and nonmarketability of certain assets such as pension rights and human capital (including expected future income tax cuts). Collateral requirements limit access to credit. These cash flow constraints, liquidity constraints, lack of suitable collateral, nonmarketability of certain assets and a host of similar capital market imperfections need not take the form of strict credit rationing but may instead merely be reflected in a market price of credit that is in excess of its shadow price.

My inability to borrow on the same terms as the UK government is of course not in and of itself evidence of market failure. Recent applications of the theory of market equilibrium under asymmetric information to credit markets (see, for example, Webb [1981], Stiglitz and Weiss [1981, 1983]), however, have shown how adverse selection or moral hazard can generate privately rational but socially inefficient equilibria that may be characterized by credit rationing, excessive spreads between lending and borrowing rates, and so forth.

Granted the existence of significant and persistent capital market imperfections, does the 'opportunity set' of the government differ from and in certain respects dominate that of private agents? In the overlapping generations model already referred to, there are two features that differentiate private and public possibility sets. First, the institution of government is longer-lived than the individual private agents. Frequently endowed with eternal life, governments can, in these models, enter into contracts that extend beyond the life-span of any given generation. In this way governments can be a substitute for some of the nonexistent forward markets. Second, the authorities have the power to tax, that is the power to impose unrequited charges or payments on individuals. For good reasons, governments are exceedingly jealous of this power and discourage private agents from assuming this prerogative which is classified as theft when exercised on private initiative.

The power to tax enables the government to redistribute income between members of the same generation at a point in time, over time for an (a group of) individual(s) and between generations. This power to tax is also the reason why, in an uncertain world, governments can borrow on terms that that are superior to those faced by private agents.[1] Total current and future national income is, subject to political constraints on the tax burden, the collateral for government borrowing. The risk of default through insolvency (but not of discretionary or dishonest default) is therefore less for government bonds than for private debt. Most governments also have the power to determine what shall be legal tender. Almost all have opted for a government monopoly of legal tender, thus adding directly to the attractiveness of those of their liabilities designated to be legal tender (their monetary liabilities) and improving indirectly the quality of all public debt. Most of the other differences between private and public opportunity sets referred to in the literature derive from the greater longevity of the institution of government and the government's power to tax.[2] The view of government financial policy I am advocating has governments acting as a superior financial intermediary, changing the composition of private sector portfolios over time and altering private disposable income flows. Well-designed policy interventions of this kind exploit the government's 'comparative advantage' in borrowing to smooth out income streams and facilitate risk sharing. By exploiting its position as the 'natural borrower', or borrower of first resort, governments can minimize the extent to which disposable income, current cash flow and the portfolio of liquid, marketable or realizable assets become binding constraints on private consumption, investment, production and portfolio allocation decisions.

This view of financial policy is at the opposite end of the spectrum from the ancient 'debt neutrality' position as restated by Barro [1974], (see also Buiter [1979, 1980a] and Carmichael, [1982]). Debt neutrality, that is invariance of the real solution trajectories of the economy under changes in the borrowing-taxation mix prevails if financial policy cannot affect the intertemporal (including the intergenerational) distribution of income and terms of trade. With infinite-lived households or, equivalently, finite-lived households characterized by an operative chain of intergenerational gift and bequest motives, with private access to capital markets on the same terms as the government and with unrestricted lump-sum taxes and transfers, public sector financial policy is irrelevant. Relaxing any or all of these exceedingly restrictive assumptions causes this Modigliani-Miller theorem for the public sector to break down and a potential welfare-improving role for active financial policy to emerge.

Active financial policy is most easily defined as the orthogonal complement of passive financial policy. Passive financial policy I define as balanced budget financial policy, that is a continuous or period-by-period matching of receipts and expenditures. Weakly passive financial policy permits balanced budget redistribution; strictly passive financial policy compels taxes and taxes net of transfers and subsidies to be the same. It is well-known that, for example in the overlapping generations model of Diamond [1965], a balanced budget social security scheme implemented through lump sum taxes on the young and lump-sum transfer payments to the old will depress capital formation. Most balanced budget intertemporal or intergenerational redistribution schemes can be reproduced in terms of their effects on all real endogenous variables by unbalanced budget policies involving public sector borrowing or lending. For example, the social security scheme just mentioned is isomorphic to government borrowing with debt service financed by new debt issues and by lump sum taxes on the young. Without risk of ambiguity I shall therefore identify active financial policies with policies that permit, under specified conditions, systematic and predictable departures from budget balance.

Active financial policy, as just defined, has a wide range of functions and consequences, only a few of which can be considered here. By influencing the interpersonal, intertemporal and intergenerational distribution of income it will affect risk sharing, the extent to which households can smooth consumption over the life cycle, and capital formation. All this can occur in models in which current goods and labor markets clear continuously. I shall discuss this briefly in Section II. If lump sum taxes are not feasible, the timing of distortionary taxes will influence the total excess burden or deadweight loss imposed on the economy. The same will hold if tax collection costs in any given period are a more than linearly increasing function of the marginal or average tax rate in that period. This is considered in Section III. Again this applies in labor and output market clearing models.

For models with a strong new classical flavour, it has been established that various contingent or conditional financial rules (monetary or fiscal feedback rules) which are, in general, inconsistent with continuous budget balance, will alter the joint distribution function of real economic variables by changing the information content of currently observed prices when there is incomplete information about the current state (Weiss [1980], Turnovsky [1980], Buiter [1980b, 1981]). While of some theoretical interest, this financial stabilization channel appears to be of secondary practical importance and I shall not consider it any further here.

In a world with persistent labor market and/or output market disequilibrium, the capital market imperfections that are the *sine qua non* of financial policy spill over into the markets for output and labor. For example, the existence of the multiplier, which is due to the inclusion of current disposable income as an argument in the private consumption function, over and above its contribution to permanent income, reflects a capital market imperfection – the difficulty of borrowing against the security of anticipated future labor income. In a fixed price model the operation of the multiplier amplifies the effect of demand shocks on output and employment. Financial policy entailing temporary deficits may be the appropriate government response.[3] The balanced budget multiplier theorem would appear to suggest that any desired response to demand shocks can be achieved without deficits by varying both exhaustive public spending and taxes net of transfers. I would argue that, to a first order approximation, optimal budgetary stabilization policy of this kind would involve varying taxes and transfers in response to demand shocks while leaving the path of public consumption and investment spending unchanged. The intuitive reasons for this are that if public sector consumption spending is worthwhile, it is worthwhile regardless of the aggregate demand shocks that afflict the economy and that the time profile of public sector capital formation is dictated within rather narrow limits by the time profile of future planned public sector production. The government's spending program on goods and services should be designed to achieve the best feasible public-private consumption mix out of permanent national income. The tax-transfer-borrowing and money creation rules should be aimed at optimizing national permanent income, keeping private disposable income in line with private permanent income and ensuring an adequate share of disposable, realizable (financial) private wealth in total or comprehensive private wealth, which includes such illiquid assets as human capital.

The above applies to the *optimal* design of exhaustive spending policies and financing policies. If, as in the United Kingdom today, certain categories of public spending (especially public sector capital formation) have been cut to levels that are well below most reasonable notions of optimality and if at the same time a 'Keynesian' fiscal boost to aggregate demand is desirable, both structural (or allocative) and stabilization purposes can be served by a larger volume of spending on goods and services (social overhead capital formation and investment in some of the nationalized industries in the United Kingdom). In Section IV I review briefly some of the well-known arguments about the role of deficits and debt in short-run stabilization policy when there is disequilibrium in labor and product markets.

Concern about debt and deficits on the part of the authorities tends to derive from two alleged consequences of public sector deficits. First, to the extent that deficits are monetized they are feared to lead to inflation.

Second, to the extent that they are not monetized but financed by issuing interest-bearing debt, they are feared to 'crowd out' interest-sensitive private spending, especially private capital formation. This 'crowding out' can occur either through upward pressure on real interest rates caused by additional borrowing or by displacing private capital formation at given real interest rates, as in Sargent and Wallace [1981] (see also Buiter [1981a,b; 1983]). Section V considers in some depth the 'eventual monetization' implied by the government's fiscal and financial plans and the long-term financial crowding out[4] implications of the government's budgetary and monetary policy. While these issues belong to the domain of positive rather than normative fiscal and financial policy, they are of considerable practical interest. On the principle that feasibility is a prerequisite for optimality Section V therefore analyzes the sustainability, consistency and credibility of fiscal, financial and monetary policy. The comprehensive net worth and the permanent income of the public sector are two central concepts in this analysis.

II **Financial policy with lump-sum taxes and transfers when goods markets and factor markets clear**

Using the analytical framework of the simple overlapping generations model without intergenerational gift and bequest motives, Stiglitz [1983a,b] establishes the following propositions for the case where unrestricted lump sum taxes and transfers are possible and output and factor markets clear.

Proposition I (Stiglitz 1983a)
An increase in the government deficit has neither real nor inflationary effects so long as the associated changes in (lump sum) taxes are distribution neutral and so long as the debt will eventually be reduced to its original level.

Proposition II (Stiglitz 1983b)
A temporary change in the structure (maturity composition, nature and degree of index linking, etc.) of the public debt has no real or price level effects provided it is accompanied by the appropriate lump sum taxes/subsidies to avoid any distributive effects.

Proposition III (Stiglitz 1983a,b)
A change in the interest rate paid on (unindexed) government debt financed by a change in the supply of such debt has price level effects but no real effects.

Note that all these propositions apply to an economy in which there is no explicit or implicit transactions technology. Government debt has a store of value function only; there is no special medium of exchange or means of payment function for a subset of the public sector's financial liabilities, that is, there are no monetary assets. 'Inflation' in Stiglitz's models is a decline in the price of public debt in terms of real output. The first two propositions give the conditions under which the Modigliani-Miller theorem for the public sector holds in this economy. The third proposition is the familiar classical dichotomy.

The interest of Propositions I–III lies in the extreme restrictiveness of the conditions under which financial policy will be neutral.

Proposition IV (Stiglitz 1983a)
Stiglitz goes on to show that any anticipated changes in financial policy other than those described in propositions I, II and III have both real and price level effects on the economy. Any unanticipated change has no real effects on the economy only if it doesn't change individuals' subjective probability distributions concerning future government financial policy and if all changes in debt are accompanied by changes in lump-sum taxes and subsidies to neutralize any distributional consequences.

Having established the nonneutrality of 'almost all' financial policy actions or rules, the design of optimal financial policy can be tackled. Since the class of models under consideration is rather far removed from practical applications, I shall limit the discussion to two aspects of optimal financial policy.

Government debt and private capital formation
In the Diamond [1965], version of the overlapping generations model, debt issues involve redistribution from the young to the old. This depresses saving and capital formation in the short run and lowers the steady-state capital-labor ratio. In such economies private decentralized decision making can result in equilibria in which the real interest rate is below the natural growth rate. This dynamic inefficiency can be eliminated by issuing government debt to absorb excessive private saving. If the real interest rate exceeds the growth rate, such Pareto-improving financial policies are not feasible. Given the government's social welfare function (which would typically be strictly increasing in the welfare of each generation), social welfare improving financial policy actions may still exist. For example, budget surpluses and government lending can boost capital formation. The welfare loss this imposes on those currently old may be more than compensated for by the welfare gains of the young and of future generations.

Optimal intertemporal risk distribution schemes
The effects of financial policy on private capital formation occur even without uncertainty. In a stochastic environment, government financial

policy can generate changes in the intertemporal (and specifically the intergenerational) distribution of risk. In the two-period overlapping generations model, individuals of different generations cannot trade risks in the market place. The longevity of the institution of government permits intergenerational risk sharing through the public debt-tax-transfer mechanism. A detailed analysis can be found in Stiglitz [1983a,b] who shows that the optimal (in terms of an individualistic social welfare function)[5] intertemporal distribution of wealth and risk can be implemented, at a constant price level, through financial policy involving only a single financial instrument provided the government can impose age-differentiated lump-sum taxes and transfers. When lump-sum taxes and transfers cannot be fully adapted to individual characteristics, the existence of a variety of public sector debt instruments is potentially welfare-improving.

The time profile of debt and deficits under the optimal financial policy will be a function of all taste and technology parameters in the economy, of the stochastic shocks disturbing it, and of the authorities' objective functional. Generalizations are impossible other than the rather self-evident one that a policy of continuous budget balance is likely to be optimal under a set of conditions of measure zero.

III Financial policy with distortionary taxes and transfers when goods markets and factor markets clear

Recently Barro [1979, 1981] and Kydland and Prescott [1980] have applied a well-known 'uniform taxation' theorem in public finance to the macroeconomic problem of optimal public sector debt and deficits in an economy with continuous full employment. In the absence of uncertainty and given suitable symmetry, homogeneity and separability assumptions, it is optimal to levy wage taxes at a constant proportional rate throughout an individual's lifetime. (See Sandmo [1974, 1976], Sadka [1977] and Atkinson and Stiglitz [1980].) The argument assumes the nonavailability of lump-sum taxes and subsidies. The original public finance literature was formulated in terms of the deadweight loss or excess burden of fiscal programs involving distortionary taxes, whose minimization (under fairly strict conditions) required the equalization of planned tax rates over the present and the future. Barro's papers consider the possibility of tax collection costs being an increasing and strictly convex function of the ratio of the net total tax take to the tax base.[6] Even in nonstochastic models, a rigorous statement has not been given of the conditions under which the result holds true that the optimal total tax take as a proportion of GDP (or of labor income?) is constant over time, for an economy with the real-world plethora of direct and indirect taxes, taxes on labor and capital income and taxes on wealth. For a stochastic environment, Barro

[1981] has argued that the deterministic constant planned tax rate solution translates approximately into a Martingale process for the tax rate τ, i.e.

$$E(\tau_{t+i} \mid \Omega_t) = \tau_t \qquad i \geq 0 \tag{1}$$

E is the conditional expectation operator and Ω_t the information set conditioning expectations formed at time t (assumed to include τ_t).

Equation (1) follows from its deterministic counterpart only by abuse of certainty equivalence. For (1) to be strictly correct, a LQG (linear-quadratic-Gaussian) model structure is required. Given quadratic deadweight losses, linear constraints and additive white noise disturbances, equation (1) follows. An important (and implausible) restriction this imposes is that of nonstochastic discount rates.[7]

Many empirical as well as conceptual problems stand in the way of a direct application of (1) to normative or positive policy design. How does one approximate the 'average marginal tax rate' that belongs in equation (1)? What is the proper tax base to relate the tax rate to? Should one use taxes or taxes net of transfers and subsidies, as the theory suggests?

In spite of these and other objections to the strict 'uniform expected tax rates over time' proposition, the notion that it is optimal to smooth planned tax rates relative to planned exhaustive public spending because collection costs and/or excess burdens increase more than linearly with the tax rate, is likely to be robust.[8] In the strict version of equation (1) the theory implies that a temporary increase in public spending unaccompanied by a matching increase in real output (the tax base) should be financed at least in part by borrowing. A transitory increase in real output will, given public spending, be associated with a budget surplus. The 'countercyclical' behavior of the deficit that will characterize the economy if the exogenous level of output follows a regular cyclical pattern and public spending is constant[9] has nothing to do with Keynesian fiscal stabilization policy or the operation of the automatic stabilizers, however. These are considered in the next section.

IV **Optimal debt and deficits when labor and output markets do not clear**

The Keynesian arguments for running larger deficits (smaller surpluses) when effective demand is depressed and smaller deficits (larger surpluses) when effective demand is buoyant are familiar. Tax cuts in the face of negative demand shocks (or the 'automatic' decline of taxes and rise in transfer payments when economic activity falls, that are written into most existing tax and benefit laws) help maintain disposable income. To the extent that disposable income rather than permanent income is the binding constraint on private demand, such active financial policy helps dampen fluctuations in output and employment. In Keynesian models, with workers off their notional labor supply schedules and possibly firms off their notional demand curves for labor as well, avoiding demand-induced swings in real activity is sensible policy.

By reducing taxes (net of transfers) and increasing borrowing during the downswing, exhaustive public spending during the downswing will be financed to a larger extent by private agents who are not constrained by current disposable income – the purchasers of the bonds. Total consumption demand will therefore decline by less than if taxes, which I assume to fall equally on disposable-income-constrained and permanent-income-constrained private agents, had been kept constant during the downswing. When the economy recovers, the additional debt incurred during the downswing can be repaid out of higher than normal taxes. The demand effects of cyclical tax cuts during the downswing and tax increases during the upswing may not be symmetric if, as seems likely, more private agents are constrained in their spending by current disposable income during the downswing than during the upswing.

The smoothing out of consumption over the cycle permitted by countercyclical financial policy would be desirable because of its intertemporal allocative effects even if product and factor markets cleared. Its virtues are enhanced by the initial demand-disturbance-amplifying presence of labor and output market disequilibrium.

When used for cyclical stabilization, successful financial policy should not imply any trend increase in the real stock of debt or in the debt-output ratio. If real interest rates are increasing functions of current and anticipated future deficits, the transitory and reversible deficits that are associated with countercyclical policy should have but minor effects on real interest rates. Thus, by raising the level of activity, countercyclical deficits absorb private saving in the short run without lowering the capital stock in the long run. If real interest rate determination is more myopic, even short run and reversible increases in deficits and debt may lead to significant crowding out of interest-sensitive private spending. In most existing macromodels such crowding out can be avoided by monetizing part of the deficit. Provided this monetization is reversed (and is *expected* to be reversed) in proper countercyclical fashion during the upswing, it should have no effect on trend monetary growth and thus on inflationary expectations.

For the sake of completeness, I will conclude this section with the familiar reminder that there are no 'model-free' measures of the short-run effect of fiscal or financial policy on aggregate demand. Neither the uncorrected or raw deficit, nor the cyclically corrected deficit, nor the cyclically and inflation-corrected deficit, nor the permanent deficit of Section V are proper measures of fiscal impact. The 'demand-weighted' (that is, adjusted for the marginal propensity to spend on domestic output), cyclically corrected deficit calculated, for example, in the United Kingdom by the National Institute of Economic and Social Research, as well as the 'demand-weighted', cyclically adjusted and inflation corrected deficit calculated for the United Kingdom by Buiter and Miller, [1983], are appropriate indices of the short-run demand effect of fiscal policy only in a static, rather old-Keynesian and expectations-innocent model.[10] The first best approach would be to simulate one's preferred model of the economy under different values of fiscal and financial policy parameters and to call the difference between the solution trajectories (or the statistics describing them) the measure of fiscal impact. These fiscal stance measures will therefore a) be model-specific, b) have time subscripts attached to them and c) be functions of when a particular fiscal or financial action (or rule change) was first anticipated, of its anticipated degree of permanence, and of the degree of confidence with which these expectations are held.

V Longer-run aspects of the fiscal and monetary stance: Sustainability, consistency and credibility

Preoccupation with the current budget deficit or public sector borrowing requirement (PSBR) can be criticized for a variety of reasons. First, the budget deficit is likely to be a poor or even perverse indicator of the short-run cyclical demand effects of spending and taxation policy. Second, the size or change of the deficit bears no straightforward relation to the allocative or structural effects of government spending and tax programs. A third major reason for not paying too much attention to the PSBR is that it conveys little or no information on the *sustainability* of the fiscal stance, that is, on the *consistency* of long-term budgetary spending-taxation plans, monetary targets and financial crowding out objectives. The level or change in the current deficit is uninformative as to the *credibility* of the government's budgetary, debt and monetary policy.

In what follows I combine the comprehensive accounting framework developed in Buiter [1983] with the permanent cost of debt service approach of Miller (Miller [1982], Miller and Babbs [1983]). With this apparatus one can address the following issues. First, can previously planned spending programs be financed, given projected real output growth, without raising explicit tax rates or increasing seigniorage (the inflation tax)? Second, what is the 'eventual monetization' implied by the fiscal stance; is the government's anti-inflationary monetary stance fiscally compatible and credible? Third, given the spending and taxation plans and the monetary target, is there likely to be financial 'crowding in' or 'crowding out', that is, is there a tendency for the real stock of interest bearing debt to fall or to rise (relative to trend output)?

To evaluate sustainability and consistency we complement the government budget constraint given in (2) by a comprehensive public sector balance sheet in (3):

$$g + \dot{K} - \tau + i\frac{B}{p} + \frac{C}{p} - i^*\frac{\epsilon F^*}{p} - \rho_K K - \rho_R R + p_R\dot{R} \equiv \frac{\dot{M} + \dot{B} + p_c\dot{C} - \epsilon\dot{F}^*}{p} \equiv P.S.B.R. \qquad (2)$$

$$W \equiv p_K K + p_R R + T + \Pi - \frac{(M + B + p_c C)}{p} + \frac{\epsilon F^*}{p} + Z \qquad (3)$$

where g is public sector consumption spending; K the public sector capital stock; τ taxes net of transfers; i the short nominal interest rate; B the stock of short nominal bonds; p the general price level; C the number of consols paying \$1 each period; i^* the foreign nominal interest rate; F^* the net foreign currency denominated assets of the public sector; ϵ the foreign exchange rate; ρ_K the rental on public sector capital; ρ_R the return to a unit of publicly owned natural resource rights; R the stock of publicly owned natural resource property rights; p_R the price of R; M the nominal stock of high-powered money; p_c the money price of a consol; W real public sector net worth; p_K the value of a unit of public sector capital in the public sector; T the present discounted value of future expected taxes net of transfers τ; Π the real capital value of the state's note issue monopoly and r the short real rate of interest. Public sector net worth is made up of tangible real assets, K and R, financial liabilities M, B, C and $-F^*$ and intangible assets T and Π. The capital value of the note issue monopoly Π is found by discounting the future income derived from the assets that are held to 'back' the note circulation.

The public sector capital stock is valued not at replacement cost but as the present value of its future returns on the assumption that it remains in the public sector. The value of a publicly owned unit of capital (p_K) need therefore not be the same as its value in alternative (private) use or replacement cost which is set equal to 1. (See equation (2).) Indeed p_K could be negative. $Z(t)$ is the present discounted value of the revenue gains associated with the government's future capital formation program if $p_K \neq 1$. Without loss of generality the total (public + private) stock of natural resource property rights is treated as constant. $\dot{R} \gtreqless O$ therefore means public sector acquisitions (sales) of natural resource rights. Oil discoveries as well as changes in the price of oil are represented by changes in p_R. For simplicity expected rates of return on all assets are assumed to be equalized.[11] This heroic use of certainty equivalence is a serious limitation of the current presentation of the comprehensive wealth and permanent income approach. Index-linked bonds (short and/or long) could be added to the framework without complications. For expositional simplicity the entire maturity distribution of the public debt is represented by the shortest and longest maturities.

The PSBR in Britain is measured by the right-hand side of (2). Sales of existing public sector assets (natural resource rights and public sector capital) are put 'above the line' and *ceteris paribus* reduce the PSBR where they involve the ending of majority public ownership. The public sector financial deficit on a national accounts basis places all sales of existing assets 'below the line' with conventional borrowing and money creation.

Provided the present discounted value of 'terminal' government net worth equals zero, the present discounted value of government consumption must equal public sector net worth.

The rate of change of public sector net worth $\dot{W}(t)$ can be decomposed into an anticipated part, $W_1(t, t)$, and an unanticipated part, $W_2(t, t)$. It is easily checked that the anticipated change in W is given by:

$$\begin{aligned} W_1(t, t) &= r(t)W(t) - g(t) \\ &= -\left\{g(t) - r(t)\left[\frac{B(t) + p_c(t)C(t) - \epsilon(t)F^*(t)}{p(t)} \right.\right. \\ &\qquad \left.\left. - p_R(t)R(t) - p_K(t)K(t) - T(t) - S(t) - Z(t)\right]\right\} \end{aligned} \tag{4}$$

where the present value of future seignorage $S(t)$ is given by:

$$S(t) \equiv \int_t^{\infty} \frac{M_1(s, t)}{p(s, t)} e^{-\int_t^s r(u, t)du} ds \tag{5}$$

For *ex ante* or planning purposes only the expected change in $W(t)$ is relevant and we shall focus on this.

Public sector net worth decreases if and only if there is a 'real' deficit, that is, if public sector consumption expenditure exceeds the instantaneous (short run) real return on comprehensive public sector net worth, $r(t)\,W(t)$. Public sector capital formation does not affect public sector net worth if the shadow price of capital in the public sector, p_K, equals its opportunity cost, 1, but will raise (reduce) net worth if $p_K > 1$ (<1).

One characterization of a sustainable fiscal plan requires public sector net worth to grow at the natural rate of growth of output, n. That is:

$$W_1(t, t) = n\,W \tag{6}$$

or

$$\begin{aligned} &g(t) = \tilde{r}(t)\,W(t) \\ &\text{where } \tilde{r} = r - n. \\ &\text{and} \quad n = \dot{\bar{y}}/\bar{y} \end{aligned} \tag{6'}$$

If $g(t)$ were to exceed (fall short) of the right-hand side of (6′), public sector comprehensive net worth would be falling (rising) *ex ante* relative to trend GNP, $\bar{y}$. If $p_K K$, $p_R R$, T, Z, S and $\frac{\epsilon F^*}{p}$ all grew at the natural rate, the entire decline (increase) in the public sector net worth – GDP ratio would come about through an increase (reduction) in the interest-bearing debt-GNP ratio. In most models not exhibiting debt neutrality, such an increase (decrease) in the 'debt burden' causes financial crowding out (crowding in). The degree and time pattern of this financial crowding out (in) will of course be model specific. A simple model with full crowding out is given in Sargent and Wallace [1981]. (See also Buiter [1982a,b and 1983].)

A program satisfying (6′), which would keep the expected public sector net worth-trend GDP ratio constant, implies *anticipated* variations in the share of public consumption in trend net output, if the short real interest rate varies over time. An alternative and more desirable approach, following Hicksian permanent income notions, starts from the constraint (assumed to hold with strict equality) that the present value of public consumption must not exceed $W(t)$. That is:

$$G(t) = W(t) \equiv p_K K + p_R R + T + S - \left(\frac{B + p_c C}{p}\right) + \frac{\epsilon F^*}{p} + Z \qquad (7)$$

where

$$G(t) \equiv \int_t^\infty g(s, t) e^{-\int_t^s r(u, t) du} ds. \qquad (8)$$

Given the value of tangible assets and liabilities, $p_K K + p_R R - \frac{B + p_c C}{p} + \frac{\epsilon F^*}{p}$, and given Z, an increase in the public consumption spending program requires an increase in the present value of future explicit taxes-net-of-transfers (T) and/or in the present value of future seigniorage, S. An increase in S is commonly assumed to require an increase in the (average) future rate of monetary growth and thus in the rate of inflation.[13]

Other ways of raising public sector net worth discontinuously, at a point in time, to finance a costlier public consumption program are by improving the productivity of public sector capital (an increase in p_K) or, if $p_K < 1$, by a sale of public sector capital (at its replacement value) to the private sector, using the proceeds to reduce $\frac{B + p_c C}{p}$, say. Finally, default is an option, either *de jure*, by formally repudiating debt, or *de facto*, by engineering an upward jump in the price level (which is a possibility in most New Classical models), a downward jump in the price of long-dated bonds or, if $F^* > 0$, a real depreciation of the currency.

Note that there are certain to be mechanisms at work in the economy that link the various items in (7) together. For example, in a Keynesian world, a cut in the spending program ($G(t)$) may lower the tax base and thus $T(t)$ even at given tax rates. If the economy exhibits financial crowding out (the displacement of private capital by public sector interest-bearing debt) a larger value of $\frac{B(t) + p_c(t)C(t)}{p(t)}$ might reduce $T(t)$, and so on.

We can rewrite (8) as

$$\int_t^{\infty} \frac{g(s, t)}{\bar{y}(s, t)} e^{-\int_t^S [r(u, t) - n]\, du} ds = \frac{W(t)}{\bar{y}(t)}$$

The constant, indefinitely sustainable, share of public sector consumption in trend GNP, $\left[\frac{g}{\bar{y}}\right]^p$, is given by

$$\left[\frac{g(t)}{\bar{y}(t)}\right]^p = \bar{R}(t) \frac{W(t)}{\bar{y}(t)} \tag{9}$$

where

$$\bar{R}(t) = \left[\int_t^{\infty} e^{-\int_t^S [r(u, t) - n] du} ds\right]^{-1} \tag{10}$$

$\bar{R}(t)$ is the coupon yield on a real consol, when the instantaneous real rate of return is $r(t) - n$ and the strict expectations hypothesis holds, that is investors equate anticipated real rates of return.

Thus a share of public sector consumption in trend GDP in excess of $\left(\frac{g(t)}{\bar{y}(t)}\right)^p$ is unsustainable: it would lower permanent income. One way in which this unsustainability could show up would be through a steady rise in the real costs of narrowly defined debt service $\bar{R}\left(\frac{p_cC + B}{p}\right)$, that is through increasing financial crowding out pressure. Two useful indicators of the (un)sustainability of the current fiscal stance are therefore the excess of current consumption over the value consistent with a constant ratio of net worth to trend output or 'constant net worth deficit'

$$D^W(t) \equiv g(t) - \bar{r}(t)\, W(t) \tag{11a}$$

and the excess of current consumption over 'permanent income' (that value of consumption consistent with a permanently constant share of public consumption in trend output or 'permanent deficit').[14]

$$D^{P}(t) \equiv g(t) - \bar{R}(t)\, W(t) \tag{11b}$$

The two indices coincide when the real rate of return is expected to be constant ($\bar{r}(t) = \bar{R}(t)$).

The direct approach to evaluating D^W *or* D^P is, from (11a,b), by the construction of an empirical proxy for W. For $D^W(t)$ we multiply this by the short real rate of interest net of the natural rate of growth; for $D^P(t)$ the real consol coupon yield net of the natural rate of growth must be estimated. Even more informative would be a complete calculation of both sides of (7). As this involves projecting the entire course of future public consumption spending, it is also more difficult in practice. Recent government pronouncements in the United Kingdom about the need for medium and long-term cuts in spending programs to stop the tax burden from rising, can be evaluated using this framework, however.

At this stage, a piecemeal approach to the calculation of D^P and D^W involving a series of 'corrections' to the conventionally measured PSBR seems convenient. The various corrections required to go from the PSBR to the permanent and constant net worth deficits are summarized in equations (12a,b).

$$\begin{aligned} D^{P}(t) = {} & PSBR(t) - p_R(t)\dot{R}(t) - \dot{K}(t) + [\bar{R}(t) - i(t)]\frac{B(t)}{p(t)} \\ & + \left[\bar{R}(t) - \frac{1}{p_c(t)}\right]\frac{p_c(t)C(t)}{p(t)} - (\bar{R}(t) - i^*(t))\frac{\epsilon(t)F^*(t)}{p(t)} \\ & - \left(\bar{R}(t) - \frac{\rho_K(t)}{p_K(t)}\right) p_K(t)K(t) \\ & - \left(\bar{R}(t) - \frac{\rho_R(t)}{p_R(t)}\right) p_R(t)R(t) - (\bar{R}(t)T(t) - \tau(t)) \\ & - \bar{R}(t)S(t) - \bar{R}(t)\bar{Z}(t) \end{aligned} \tag{12a}$$

$$\begin{aligned} D^{W}(t) = {} & PSBR(t) - p_R(t)\dot{R}(t) - \dot{K}(t) - \left(\frac{p_1(t,\, t)}{p(t)} + n\right)\frac{B(t)}{p(t)} \\ & + \left(\bar{r}(t) - \frac{1}{p_c(t)}\right)\frac{p_c(t)C(t)}{p(t)} \\ & + \left[\left(n + \frac{p_1(t,\, t)}{p(t)}\right) - \frac{\epsilon_1(t,\, t)}{\epsilon(t)}\right]\frac{\epsilon(t)F^*(t)}{p(t)} \\ & - \left(\bar{r}(t) - \frac{\rho_K(t)}{p_K(t)}\right) p_K(t)K(t) \\ & - \left(\bar{r}(t) - \frac{\rho_R(t)}{p_R(t)}\right) p_R(t)R(t) \\ & - (\bar{r}(t)\, T(t) - \tau(t)) - \bar{r}(t)S(t) - \bar{r}(t)Z(t) \end{aligned} \tag{12b}$$

Since $D^p(t)$ is probably the more interesting of the two measures, we shall concentrate on it. Taking the corrections to the PSBR in (12a) in turn:

$-p_R\dot{R}(t)$: This is a proxy for those net sales of existing public sector assets that should be added to the PSBR to get the public sector financial deficit (PSFD) on a national accounts basis.

$-\dot{K}$: $g(t)$ in (12a,b) is public sector consumption spending. Many categories of exhaustive public spending possess characteristics both of consumption and capital formation. In the illustrative figures for the United Kingdom given in Table 1 I finesse these problems by following standard national income accounting conventions. On this basis, estimates of public sector net capital formation (at replacement cost) which should be subtracted from the PSBR and PSFD as one of the steps to get to D^p, are available in the United Kingdom.

$+(\bar{R} - i)\frac{B}{p} + \left(\bar{R} - \frac{1}{p_c}\right)\frac{p_c C}{p}$: this is not merely an inflation and real growth correction but also involves the permanent income smoothing reflected in the use of the long real interest rate.[15] (This last step is omitted in (12b).) In public sector permanent income, debt service on the bond debt should be evaluated by multiplying the real long run (consol) rate of interest net of the natural growth rate, $\bar{R}(t)$, into the market value of all bonds. Estimates for this correction for the United Kingdom and a discussion of its methodological foundations are given in Miller [1982] and in Miller and Babbs [1983]. They are reproduced here in Table 1.

$-(\bar{R} - i^*)\frac{\epsilon F^*}{p}$: This corrects for changes in the domestic currency value of foreign currency denominated assets and liabilities as well as for domestic inflation, real growth and permanent income smoothing. It is very important for a number of LDCs which have borrowed externally in dollars or other hard currencies. (See Buiter [1983].) Its significance for the United Kingdom and the United States is likely to be quite minor.

$-\left(\bar{R} - \frac{\rho_K}{p_K}\right)p_K K$: It is difficult to assess the size and magnitude of the excess of current income from public capital over permanent income and I do not attempt to do so. It is likely to be strongly procyclical.

$-\left(\bar{R} - \frac{\rho_R}{p_R}\right)p_R R$: North Sea oil revenues are currently at or near their expected peak value. While in the mid- and late seventies current oil revenue fell short of its permanent value (as perceived at the time) this

Table 1 Calculation of the permanent deficit

	PSBR	PSFD	Net Public Sector Capital Formation Correction $\dot{K}$	Permanent Debt Service and Exchange Rate Correction $+ [\bar{R} - i] \frac{B}{p} + \left[\bar{R} - \frac{\dot{I}}{p_c}\right] \frac{p_c C}{p} - [\bar{R} - i^*] \frac{\epsilon F^*}{p}$	North Sea Oil Correction $-\left(\bar{R} - \frac{\dot{p}_R}{p_R}\right) p_R R$	Cyclical Correction $-(\bar{R}T - \tau)$	Structural and Demographic Tax-Transfer Correction	Permanent Seignorage Correction $-\bar{R}S$	Permanent Deficit	% of GDP
1978	8354	7949	−2844	−5017	−1700	+4700		−187	2901	1.8
1979	12636	8271	−3006	−6461	−1400	+3900		−210	1040	.6
1980	12180	9869	−2625	−8215	− 900	+2700		−227	602	.3
1981	10583	8023	− 883	−9653	900	−2100		−240	−3953	−1.7
1982	5419	6734	0[a]	−9851	1900	−5000		−283	−6500	−2.5

[a]estimate

Sources:

- PSBR, PSFD: ET May 1983, 56.
- $\dot{K}$: Blue Book 1982 ed: 1.7 for 1978–1981.
  1982 own estimate.
- Permanent Debt Service Correction: Miller and Babbs, 1983.
- North Sea Oil Correction: Own calculations based on NIER, May 1983, F. J. Atkinson, S. J. Brook and S. G. F. Hall, 'The Economic Effects of North Sea Oil,' pp. 38–44: IFS, John Kay ed. *The Economy and the 1983 Budget*: M.P. Devereux, 'Changes in the Taxation of North Sea Oil,' pp. 75–79.
- Cyclical Correction: IMF World Economic Outlook, 1982. Table 49, p. 187.
- Permanent Seigniorage Correction: Monetary base × long-run real rate: Miller & Babbs, 1983.

situation is now reversed. The figures in Table 1 are merely illustrative but are quite conservative, in the sense that they are more likely to understate permanent oil revenue.

$-(\bar{R}T - \tau)$: It should be clear that *current* taxes net of transfers $\tau(t)$ is likely to be a poor proxy for $\bar{R}(t)\ T(t)$. The most important 'corrections' to $\tau(t)$ required to obtain a better approximation to $\bar{R}(t)\ T(t)$ are the following:

(a) 'Cyclical' corrections to tax receipts and transfer payments. The yield from several major taxes (income taxes, national insurance contributions, VAT, corporation tax) varies inversely with cyclical deviations of economic activity from its full employment, trend or natural level. The opposite correlation holds for such transfer payments as unemployment benefits. Cyclical corrections to the conventionally measured deficit are, from this perspective, desirable not because they provide a better approximation to the short-run demand effect of the budget, but as one step towards the calculation of public sector permanent income or of the permanent deficit.

In Table 1 I use the IMFs estimates of the cyclical correction.[16] These are very conservative in that they do not assign a zero cyclical correction to 1979 but instead assume the cyclically corrected deficit to be 2.3 per cent of GDP larger than the actual deficit in 1979 and 1.4 per cent of GDP in 1980.

This seems to indicate an expectation of a normal unemployment rate in the United Kingdom of 8 or 9 percent. The Institute of Fiscal Studies,[17] on the other hand, while coming up with very similar year-to-year changes in the cyclical correction, puts its level 2 to 2.5 percentage points of GDP higher. What matters for the sustainability calculation is that a reasonable proxy for the expected average future levels of capacity utilization and unemployment be used. These levels may well be functions of the fiscal policies adopted by the authorities and need not be equal to any 'natural' or 'full employment' values.

(b) There may be planned, projected or expected changes in the scale and scope of certain tax and benefit programs. For example, under existing legislation governing contributions and benefits, the greying of the United Kingdom population implies a growing excess of pension payments over contributions. Similar concerns have been voiced in the United States. While one could try to make some further rough structural or demographic corrections to the 'cyclically corrected' tax and transfer total, I have not done so in Table 1.

$-\bar{R}S$: The perpetuity value of future seigniorage revenue is not so easily determined. Following the definition of $S(t)$ given in (7), one must estimate future government plans for monetary base growth $\frac{\dot{M}}{M}$ and future demands for real high-powered money balances $\frac{M}{p}$

Note that

$$\bar{R}(t)\frac{S(t)}{\bar{y}(t)} = \bar{R}(t)\int_t^{\infty}\frac{M_1(s, t)}{M(s, t)}\frac{M(s, t)}{p(s, t)\bar{y}(s, t)}e^{-\int_t^s [r(u, t) - n]du}ds.$$

If both the rate of monetary growth and the income velocity of circulation of money are expected to be constant, then $\bar{R}(t)\ S(t) \equiv \bar{R}(t)\left(\Pi(t) - \frac{M(t)}{p(t)}\right) = \frac{\dot{M}(t)}{p(t)}$. Permanent seigniorage income relative to trend output equals its current value. I will make this assumption, but the overall outcome is not very dependent on it as the amounts involved are fairly small.

I have no means for attempting an estimate of $\bar{R}Z$

Adopting the IFS cyclical correction instead of the one calculated by the IMF would lower the permanent deficit by 2 to 2.5 per cent of GDP compared to the figures in the last column of Table 1. Together with a slightly more generous estimate of the permanent income from North Sea oil this would generate a 5 or 6 per cent of GDP permanent surplus in 1982. This would leave room for a sizable sustainable increase in the share of public consumption spending in trend GDP over is current level and/or a cut in taxes or increase in transfer payments. Alternatively the government could choose to indulge in a bout of financial 'crowding in', using its 'permanent' surplus to reduce the real stock of interest-bearing debt. The UK economy, unlike that of the US, would appear to have lots of fiscal elbow room.

Eventual monetization

The apparatus developed here can be applied to the calculation of the 'long-run' monetary growth rate implied by the fiscal stance.

From (5) and (7) it follows that

$$\int_t^{\infty}\frac{M_1(s, t)}{M(s, t)}\frac{M(s, t)}{p(s, t)}e^{-\int_t^s r(u, t)du}ds = G(t)$$

$$-\Bigg[p_K(t)K(t) + p_R(t)R(t) + T(t)$$

$$-\frac{(B(t) + p_c(t)C(t) - \epsilon(t)F^*(t))}{p(t)} + Z\Bigg]$$

This tells us what the amount of revenue to be raised through the inflation tax is (in present value terms) *given* the spending program and the government's tangible and intangible nonmonetary assets and liabilities. Solving this for a constant rate of monetary growth $\frac{\dot{M}}{M}$ and a constant income velocity of circulation $V \equiv \frac{p\bar{y}}{M}$ yields

$$\frac{\dot{M}}{M} = V\bar{R}(t)\left[\frac{G(t) - T(t)}{\bar{y}(t)} - \left(\frac{p_K(t)K(t) + p_R(t)R(t)}{\bar{y}(t)}\right) - Z(t) + \frac{B(t) + p_c(t)C(t) - \epsilon(t)F^*(t)}{p(t)\bar{y}(t)}\right] \tag{13}$$

If the long-run inflation rate is governed by the rate of growth of the money supply, say $\frac{\dot{p}}{p} = \frac{\dot{M}}{M} - n$, and if the inflation elasticity of velocity is less than unity, a higher monetary growth rate and a higher rate of inflation are implied by a higher present value of public spending relative to nonmonetary assets and liabilities. Only if the public sector's consumption and tax programs together with its nonmonetary assets and liabilities imply a high value of $\frac{\dot{M}}{M}$, is a fiscal correction a necessary condition for achieving credibility for an anti-inflationary policy. If we consider only stationary long-run equilibria, (13) becomes (assuming $Z = 0$):

$$\frac{\dot{M}}{M} = V\left[\frac{g - \tau}{\bar{y}} - \bar{R}\left(\frac{p_K K + p_R R}{\bar{y}}\right) - \frac{(B + p_c C - \epsilon F^*)}{p\bar{y}}\right] \tag{13'}$$

Eventual monetary growth is governed in steady state by the trend public sector current account (or consumption account) deficit, with debt service evaluated at the real interest rate net of the natural rate of growth. This deficit measure can differ dramatically from the conventionally measured public sector financial deficit or PSBR, which is often and erroneously taken as an indicator of eventual monetization. (See Sargent [1981], Sargent and Wallace [1981], and Buiter, [1982a,b] and Buiter [1983].)

VI **Conclusion**

Bringing together in an integrated analytical framework the many heterogeneous perspectives on debt and deficits that were touched upon in this paper is left as an exercise for the reader. What is apparent even now is that the theory of macroeconomic policy design, as it relates to public spending, taxation, debt management, social security, and monetary and exchange rate policy, is a branch of the theory of public finance, albeit a rather underdeveloped branch. Most traditional public finance theory has been restricted to the case of Walrasian, market-clearing economies with a complete set of markets. Most macroeconomic analysis, except for some simple supply-side economics, ignores the efficiency aspects of fiscal and financial policy. The arbitrary and indeed very harmful dichotomy between 'macroeconomic' stabilization policy – using fiscal and financial instruments to minimize deviations from full employment equilibrium – and 'public finance' allocative or structural policy – altering the full employment equilibrium – can no longer be justified.

Both the 'classical' and the 'Keynesian' approaches to financial policy reviewed in this paper force one to conclude that a balanced budget policy is very likely to be harmful in a wide range of circumstances. While mere sound economic analysis is unlikely to convince those who are firmly committed to a balanced budget, it may help persuade a sufficient number of uncommitted citizens of the need to ban this spectre of false fiscal responsibility.

Notes

First published in Federal Research Bank of Boston, Conference Series No. 27, *The Economics of Large Government Deficits*, October 1983, pp. 4–69.

1 Clearly IBM borrows on better terms than the state of Grenada. The insertion of the word 'most' before 'governments' and 'private agents' would, however, merely clutter up the text.
2 For example Webb [1981] shows how government financial policy will be nonneutral in a world with asymmetric information, if it is less costly for the government to extract taxes from reluctant taxpayers than it is for private lenders to compel performance by dishonest borrowers.
3 First best policy would eliminate the market imperfections. The discussion assumes that this has been pursued as far as is possible.
4 I only consider the familiar financial crowding out issue. Other forms of 'direct' crowding out due to complementarity or substitutability between private and public consumption and investment etc. are not dealt with (see Buiter [1977]).
5 Stiglitz [1983a] uses a social welfare function that is the discounted sum of each generation's utility. The proposition about optimal intergenerational risk-sharing transcends this specific parameterization.
6 A nonfatal flaw in his analysis is the absence of collection costs in the government budget constraint and the independence of the tax base from collection costs and the time path of taxes. (See Kremers [1983].)
7 The same assumptions have to be made to obtain the Martingale property for the stochastic process governing consumption. See Hall [1978].
8 The crucial constraint in the derivation of the uniform intertemporal pattern of tax rates in Barro [1979] is the government's balance sheet constraint.

$$\text{(i)} \quad \sum_{i=1}^{\infty} \frac{G_{t+i|t}}{(1+r)^i} + b_t = \sum_{i=1}^{\infty} \frac{T_{t+i|t}}{(1+r)^i}$$

$G_{t+i|t}$ is exhaustive public spending planned, at time t, for time $t+i$.
$T_{t+i|t}$ is taxes net of transfers planned at time t for time $t+i$.
For simplicity the real interest rate, r, is assumed constant, b_t is the total

stock of real valued single-period bonds in period t. Equation (i) follows from the budget constraint given in (ii) only if the real interest rate exceeds the real growth rate of the tax base.

(ii) $G_t + rb_{t-1} = T_t + b_t - b_{t-1}$.

From (ii) it follows that

$$\text{(iiia)} \quad \sum_{i=1}^{\infty} \frac{G_{t+i|t}}{(1+r)^i} + b_t = \sum_{i=1}^{\infty} \frac{T_{t+i|t}}{(1+r)^i} + \lim_{N\to\infty} \frac{b_{t+N|t}}{(1+r)^N}$$

or

$$\text{(iiib)} \quad \sum_{t=1}^{\infty} \frac{G_{t+i|t}}{Y_{t+i|t}} \left(\frac{1+n}{1+r}\right)^i + \frac{b_t}{Y_t} = \sum_{i=1}^{\infty} \frac{T_{t+i|t}}{Y_{t+i|t}} \left(\frac{1+n}{1+r}\right)^i + \lim_{N\to\infty} \left\{ \left(\frac{1+n}{1+r}\right)^N \frac{b_{t+N|t}}{Y_{t+N|t}} \right\}$$

Y_t is real output and n its proportional rate of growth.

Sensible solutions require that the debt-output ratio remains bounded forever. This would cause the last term on the right-hand side of (iii a,b) to vanish if $n < r$. If $n > r$, however, Ponzi games can work forever. Governments can forever service their debt by further borrowing without any risk of debt service requirements outstripping the government's collateral. A competitive, decentralized overlapping generations economy can have temporary and stationary solutions with $n > r$. Indeed, Carmichael [1982] and Buiter [1980a] show that if there are intergenerational gift and bequest motives and if there is a stationary equilibrium in which the child-to-parent gift motive is operative, then such an equilibrium is necessarily dynamically inefficient with $n > r$. Like Barro, I make use of a government wealth constraint such as (i) in Section V. This means that unless $n < r$, the 'no Ponzi game' restriction is imposed in an ad hoc manner.

9 This can be taken relative to trend output.

10 In the case of Buiter and Miller [1983] the 'inflation correction', or more appropriately, the debt service correction, presupposes that private financial intermediaries transform current interest payments from governments into permanent (disposable) real interest income flows to households.

11 We therefore assume that:

$$p_K(t) = \int_t^{\infty} \rho_K(s, t)\, e^{-\int_t^S r(u, t)du} ds$$

$$p_R(t) = \int_t^{\infty} \rho_R(s, t)\, e^{-\int_t^S r(u, t)du} ds$$

$$T(t) = \int_t^{\infty} \tau(s, t)\, e^{-\int_t^S r(u, t)du} ds$$

$$\Pi(t) = \int_t^{\infty} i(s, t) \frac{M(s, t)}{p(s, t)}\, e^{-\int_t^S r(u, t)du} ds$$

$$= \frac{1}{p(t)} \int_t^{\infty} i(s, t)\, M(s, t)\, e^{-\int_t^S i(u, t) du} ds$$

$$p_c(t) = \int_t^{\infty} e^{-\int_t^S i(u, t) du} ds.$$

$$Z(t) = \int_t^{\infty} (p_K(s, t) - 1)\dot{K}(s, t)\, e^{-\int_t^S r(u, t) du} ds$$

$$i^*(t) = i(t) - \varepsilon_1(t, t)$$
$$r(t) = i(t) - p_1(t, t)$$

For any variable, x, $x(s, t)$ is the value of x expected, at time t, to prevail at time s. $x_1(t, t) \equiv \lim_{\substack{h \to O \\ h > O}} \left(\frac{x(t + h, t) - x(t, t)}{h} \right)$ is the expected instantaneous rate of change of x. $x_2(t, t) \equiv \lim_{\substack{h \to O \\ h > O}} \frac{x(t + h, t + h) - x(t + h, t)}{h}$ is the unexpected rate of change of x. It is assumed that $x(s, t) = x(s)$ for $s \leqslant t$. Given some minor regularity conditions it then follows that $\dot{x}(t) = x_1(t, t) + x_2(t, t)$.

12 Unanticipated changes in W are due to unexpected changes in p_K, p_R, T, Π, p_c, ε and p. For example, the unexpected change in T is given by

$$T_2(t, t) = \int_t^{\infty} e^{-\int_t^S r(u, t) du} [\tau_2(s, t) - \tau(s, t) \int_t^S r_2(u, t)\, du]\, ds.$$

The present value of future taxes net of transfers increases if there is an unexpected increase in future values of τ and if there is an unexpected reduction in future discount rates (if $\tau(s, t) > O$).

13 This will not be so if the inflation elasticity of the demand for real high-powered money is negative and greater than unity in absolute value.

14 This is by abuse of language, since this deficit can by construction not be permanent.

15 For conventional inflation corrections see Siegel [1979], Taylor and Threadgold [1979] and Cukierman and Mortensen [1983].

16 IMF World Economic Outlook.

17 John Kay [1983].

Reference

Atkinson, A. B. and Stiglitz, J. E. (1980), *Lectures on Public Economics*. New York: McGraw-Hill.

Barro, R. J. (1974), 'Are Government Bonds Net Wealth?' *Journal of Political Economy*, 82, pp. 1095–117.

——. (1979), 'On the Determination of the Public Debt'. *Journal of Political Economy*, 87, pp. 940–71.

——. (1981), 'On the Predictability of Tax Rate Changes', NBER Working Paper No. 636, February 1981.

Buiter, W. H. (1977), 'Crowding Out and the Effectiveness of Fiscal Policy', *Journal of Public Economics*, 7.

——. (1979), 'Government Finance in an Overlapping Generations Model with Gifts and Bequests', in G. van Furstenberg, ed., *Social Security versus Private Saving*. Cambridge: Ballinger.

——. (1980a), 'Crowding Out' of Private Capital Formation by Government Borrowing in the Presence of Intergenerational Gifts and Bequests', *Greek Economic Review*, 2, pp. 111–42.

——. (1980b), 'Monetary, Financial and Fiscal Policy Under Rational Expectations', *IMF Staff Papers*, 27, pp. 758–813.

——. (1981), 'The Superiority of Contingent Rules over Fixed Rules in Models with Rational Expectations', *Economic Journal*, 91, pp. 647–70.

——. (1982a), 'Comment on T. J. Sargent and N. Wallace: Some Unpleasant Monetarist Arithmetic', NBER Working Paper No. 867.

——. (1982b), 'Deficits, Crowding Out and Inflation: The Simple Analytics', Centre for Labour Economics, London School of Economics, Discussion Paper No. 143.

——. (1983), 'The Measurement of Public Sector Deficits and Its Implications for Policy Evaluation and Design', *IMF Staff Papers*.

—— and M. H. Miller. (1983), 'The Economic Consequences of Mrs Thatcher', Unpublished.

Carmichael, J. (1982), 'On Barro's Theorem of Debt Neutrality: The Irrelevance of Net Wealth', *American Economic Review*, 72, pp. 202–13.

Cukierman, A. and J. Mortensen. (1983), 'Monetary assets and inflation-induced distortions of the national accounts–conceptual issues and the correction of sector income flows in 5 EEC countries', Commission of the European Communities, Directorate General for Economic and Financial Affairs, Economic Papers, No. 15.

Diamond, P. A. (1965), 'National Debt in a Neoclassical Growth Model', *American Economic Review*, 55, pp. 1125–58.

Hall, R. E. (1978), 'Stochastic Implications of the Life Cycle-Permanent Income Hypothesis: Theory and Evidence', *Journal of Political Economy*, 86, December, pp. 971–87.

Kay, J. ed. (1983), *The Economy and the 1983 Budget*, London: Basil Blackwell, p. 45.

Kremers, J. J. M. (1983), 'Public Debt Neutrality, Tax Collection Costs, and Optimal Public Financing', Nuffield College, University of Oxford, unpublished.

Kydland, F. and Prescott, E. C. (1980), 'A Competitive Theory of Fluctuations and the Feasibility and Desirability of Stabilization Policy', in S. Fischer, ed. *Rational Expectations and Economic Policy*, Chicago: University of Chicago Press, pp. 169–87.

Miller, M. H. (1982), 'Inflation-Adjusting the Public Sector Financial Deficit', in J. Kay, ed. *The 1982 Budget*, Oxford.

—— and S. Babbs. (1983), 'The True Cost of Debt Service and the Public Sector Financial Deficit', mimeo.

Sadka, E. (1977), 'A Theorem on Uniform Taxation', *Journal of Public Economics*, 7, pp. 387–91.

Sandmo, A. (1974), 'A Note on the Structure of Optimal Taxation', *American Economic Review*, 64, pp. 701–6.

——. (1976), 'Optimal Taxation: An Introduction to the Literature', *Journal of Public Economics*, Vol. 6, pp. 37–54.

Sargent, T. J. (1981), 'Stopping Moderate Inflations: The Methods of Poincare and Thatcher', unpublished.

—— and Wallace N. (1981), 'Some Unpleasant Monetarist Arithmetic', unpublished.

Siegel, J. (1979), 'Inflation-Induced Distortions in Government and Private Saving Statistics', *Review of Economics and Statistics*, pp. 83–90.

Stiglitz, J. E. (1983a), 'On the Relevance or Irrelevance of Public Financial Policy', NBER Working Paper No. 1057.

——. (1983b), 'On the relevance or irrelevance of public financial policy: Indexation, price rigidities and optimal monetary policy', NBER Working Paper No. 1106.

—— and Weiss, A. (1981), 'Credit Rationing in Markets with Imperfect Information', *American Economic Review*, 71, pp. 393–410.

—— and —— (1983), 'Cutting Off Credit: An Application of Constraints as Incentive Devices', *American Economic Review*, forthcoming.

Taylor, C. T. and Threadgold, A. R. (1979), '"Real" National Saving and Its Sectoral Composition', Bank of England, Discussion Paper No. 6.

Turnovsky, S. J. (1980), 'The Choice of Monetary Instruments under Alternative Forms of Price Expectations', *Manchester School*, pp. 39–62.

Webb, D. C. (1981), 'The Net Wealth Effect of Government Bonds when Credit Markets Are Imperfect', *Economic Journal*, 91, pp. 405–14.

Weiss, L. (1980), 'The Role for Active Monetary Policy in a Rational Expectations Model', *Journal of Political Economy*, 88, pp. 221–33.

Chapter 14

Death, birth, productivity growth and debt neutrality

This paper reconsiders the necessary and sufficient conditions for debt neutrality. There is debt neutrality if, given a programme for public expenditure on current goods and services over time, the real equilibrium of the economy is not affected by a change in the pattern over time of lump-sum taxes. If there is debt neutrality for instance, the substitution of borrowing today for lump-sum taxation today (followed by such further changes in the time path of future lump-sum taxes as are required for maintaining government solvency) does not affect the current and future behaviour of private consumption and capital formation.

I consider this issue in a simple model of a closed economy. The production side of the economy is that of a 'fruit tree' or endowment economy.[1] The exogenous labour endowment, which is perishable, is transformed one-for-one into current output which can either be consumed privately or publicly. Population and labour supply in physical units grow at the constant exogenous instantaneous proportional rate n. Labour-augmenting technical change occurs at the constant exogenous instantaneous proportional rate π. Full employment prevails throughout.

Private consumption behaviour is modelled following the Yaari-Blanchard uncertain lifetimes approach (Yaari [1965], Blanchard [1984, 1985]). The constant instantaneous probability of death of each individual is $\lambda \geq 0$.

The chapter combines the results of Blanchard [1984, 1985] about debt neutrality and uncertain lifetimes and of Weil [1985] about debt neutrality and population growth, and completes the triad by considering the implications of productivity growth for debt neutrality.

Blanchard showed in a model with a constant population ($n = 0$), with zero productivity growth ($\pi = 0$) and without an operative intergenerational bequest motive that uncertain lifetimes (i.e. a positive probability of death, $\lambda > 0$) implied absence of debt neutrality.

Weil showed that, in a model without productivity growth, without an operative intergenerational bequest motive and without uncertain lifetimes, a positive birth rate alone ($\beta > 0$) would destroy debt neutrality. For debt neutrality, intergenerational linkages are necessary (say through an operative bequest motive). Infinite horizons for 'isolated' individual consumers are insufficient if $\beta > 0$.

In this chapter I show that $\beta \equiv \lambda + n = 0$ is necessary and sufficient in the Yaari–Blanchard–Weil model for debt neutrality in the absence of operative intergenerational bequests. It follows that, as long as $\beta = 0$, a positive probability of death or non-zero productivity growth do not destroy neutrality. The intuition of this result is that the future flow of resources expected to be available to those private agents currently alive grows at the exponential rate $\pi - \lambda$. Governments can tax the resources not only of those private agents currently alive, but also of those yet to be born. Their resource base grows at the exponential rate $\pi + n$. Since $n \equiv \beta - \lambda$, the excess of the growth rate of government resources over the growth rate of the resources of those currently alive is β. In other words, private agents alive today are constrained in their consumption spending by their non-human resources and by their own human capital. The government has access to all of this and to the human capital of those yet to be born. Postponing taxes means shifting them (in part) to the 'new entrants'. In the simple models considered here this difference between aggregate private and public opportunity sets shows up as a higher effective private discount rate on aggregate human capital income which exceeds the public sector discount rate by β.

Section I develops the model. Section II gives the conditions for debt neutrality in a rather general way, for any pattern of lump-sum taxation over time that is consistent with government solvency. Under more restrictive assumptions concerning the pattern of taxation over time, a strong presumption in favour of financial crowding out is established. Section III illustrates the different effects of changes in λ, β and π on the behaviour of the economic system under two simple tax rules.

I The model

The individual's consumption behaviour

I shall use the simplest version of the Yaari–Blanchard model of consumer behaviour (Yaari [1985], Blanchard [1984, 1985]). The only novelties are the separating out of the contributions of birth and death rates to debt neutrality and the consideration of productivity growth in the subsection on aggregation.

At each instant t, a consumer born at time $s \leq t$ solves the following problem.

$$\max_{\{\bar{c}(s,\,v)\}} W(s,\,t) = \max_{\{\bar{c}(s,\,v)\}} E_t \int_t^{\infty} e^{-\delta(v-t)} \ln \bar{c}(s,\,v)\, dv \qquad (\delta > 0)^2 \tag{1}$$

E_t is the expectation operator conditional on period t information; $\bar{c}$ is individual consumption of the single good; δ is the pure rate of time preference. During his or her lifetime each consumer faces a common and constant instantaneous probability of death (or probability of dynastic extinction through childlessness) $\lambda \geqslant 0$. The probability at time t of surviving until time $v \geqslant t$ is therefore given by $e^{-\lambda(v-t)}$. Equation (1) can therefore be rewritten as

$$\max_{\{\bar{c}(s,\,v)\}} \int_t^{\infty} e^{-(\delta+\lambda)(v-t)} \ln \bar{c}(s,\,v)\, dv. \tag{2}$$

The consumer's instantaneous flow budget identity is given by

$$\frac{d}{dt}\,\bar{a}(s,\,t) \equiv [r(t) + \lambda]\,\bar{a}(s,\,t) + \bar{w}(s,\,t) - \bar{\tau}(s,\,t) - \bar{c}(s,\,t). \tag{3}$$

$\bar{a}$ is the consumer's financial or non-human wealth. r is the instantaneous real interest rate, $\bar{w}$ real wage income and $\bar{\tau}$ lump-sum taxes net of transfers.[3]

The term $\lambda\bar{a}$ on the right hand side of (3) reflects the operation of efficient life insurance or annuities markets. Consumers make the following contract with an insurance company: as long as they live, they receive a rate of return ρ on their total financial asset holdings at each instant. When they die, the entire estate accrues to the insurance company. (If $\bar{a}$ is negative, consumers pay the insurance company a premium rate ρ, with their debt cancelled when they die). The insurance industry is competitive with free entry. There is a large number of people (or 'cohort') born at each instant, and λ is both the instantaneous probability of death for an individual and the fraction of each cohort (and therefore of the total population) which dies at each instant. The competitive (zero expected profit) rate of return paid by or to the insurance company is therefore $\rho = \lambda$. (Note, *not* $\rho = n + \lambda$. A fraction λ of each cohort dies each instant, so a fraction λ of the economy's non-human wealth accrues to the insurance companies each instant. It is this that gets paid out by the insurance companies to the surviving agents.)

Integrating (3) forward in time and imposing the terminal boundary condition (4), we obtain the individual household's intertemporal budget constraint or solvency constraint given in (5a,b). The non-trivial technical and conceptual problems associated with (4) have been discussed in a very illuminating manner by Arrow and Kurz [1969].

$$\lim_{l \to \infty} \bar{a}(s, l) \exp \left\{ -\int_t^l [r(u) + \lambda] du \right\} = 0, \tag{4}$$

$$\int_t^\infty \bar{c}(s, v) \exp \left\{ -\int_t^v [r(u) + \lambda] du \right\} dv \equiv \bar{a}(s, t) + \bar{h}(s, t), \tag{5a}$$

$$\bar{h}(s, t) \equiv \int_t^\infty [\bar{w}(s, v) - \bar{\tau}(s, v)] \exp \left\{ -\int_t^v [r(u) + \lambda] du \right\} dv \tag{5b}$$

$\bar{h}$ is the consumer's human capital, the present discounted value (using the 'risk-adjusted' discount rate $r + \lambda$) of expected future after-tax labour income. Note that (5b) implies:

$$\frac{d}{dt} \bar{h}(s, t) \equiv [r(t) + \lambda]\bar{h}(s, t) - [\bar{w}(s, t) - \bar{\tau}(s, t)]. \tag{5b'}$$

The consumption function generated by this maximisation program is well-known to be:

$$\bar{c}(s, t) = (\delta + \lambda)[\bar{a}(s, t) + \bar{h}(s, t)]. \tag{6}$$

Equations (3), (5b′) and (6) imply

$$\frac{d}{dt} \bar{c}(s, t) = [r(t) - \delta]\bar{c}(c, t).^{4} \tag{6'}$$

Aggregation
Population at time 0 is $L(0) > 0$. Without loss of generality we set $L(0) = 1$. $\lambda \geq 0$, the constant instantaneous probability of death of an individual is also the fraction of each age cohort which dies at each instant. With a constant birth rate $\beta \geq 0$, the size of the cohort born at time t is $\beta L(t)$. The size of the surviving cohort at time t which was born at time $s \leq t$ is $\beta L(s)\, e^{-\lambda(t-s)} = \beta e^{-\lambda t}\, e^{\beta s}$. Except when the birth rate is zero, we can obtain the total population by integrating over the survivors of each cohort born to date:

$$\begin{aligned} L(t) &= e^{nt} \\ &= \beta e^{-\lambda t} \int_{-\infty}^{t} e^{\beta s}\, ds \qquad \text{if } \beta > 0 \\ &= e^{-\lambda t} \qquad\qquad\qquad\quad \text{if } \beta = 0. \end{aligned}$$

With a zero birth rate, now and at each instant in the past, it is hard to achieve a positive population at $t = 0$. In this case we do not worry about how the population of size $L(0) = 1$ at $t = 0$ came into existence.

Corresponding to any individual agent's stock or flow variable $\bar{v}(s, t)$ we define the corresponding population aggregate $V(t)$ to be

$$V(t) = \beta e^{-\lambda t} \int_{-\infty}^{t} \bar{v}(s, t)\, e^{\beta s} ds \qquad \text{if } \beta > 0$$
$$= \bar{v}(s, t) e^{-\lambda t} \qquad \text{if } \beta = 0. \tag{7}$$

Each agent, regardless of age, earns the same wage income and pays the same taxes, i.e.

$$\bar{w}(s, t) = \bar{w}(t), \tag{8a}$$

$$\bar{\tau}(s, t) = \bar{\tau}(t). \tag{8b}$$

It follows that each surviving agent has the same human capital.

$$\bar{h}(s, t) = \bar{h}(t). \tag{8c}$$

By straightforward direct computation, and using the notational convention given in (7), aggregate consumption is (for $\beta \geqslant 0$) given by:

$$C(t) = (\delta + \lambda)[A(t) + H(t)],\ ^{5} \tag{9a}$$

$$\dot{A}(t) \equiv r(t)\, A(t) + W(t) - T(t) - C(t),\ ^{6} \tag{9b}$$

$$\dot{H} \equiv (r + \lambda + n)\, H(t) + T(t) - W(t),\ ^{7}$$
$$\equiv (r + \beta)\, H(t) + T(t) - W(t). \tag{9c}$$

The absence of a λA term in (9b), unlike in (3), reflects the fact that the insurance companies' activities involve a transfer from those who die to those who survive, which does not alter the rate of return on aggregate non-human wealth. The presence of the βH term in (9c) reflects the fact that all surviving agents, even the newborn, have the same human capital.

There is a constant instantaneous proportional rate of growth of productivity π. Technical change is labour-augmenting or Harrod-neutral. By choice of units, the level of productivity at $t = 0$ is set equal to unity.

For each population aggregate stock or flow variable V, the corresponding quantity 'per unit of labour measured in efficiency units', v, is defined by:

$$v(t) \equiv V(t)\, e^{-(n+\pi)t}. \tag{10}$$

Using this notational convention, consumption per unit of efficiency labour is (again for $\beta \geqslant 0$) governed by:

$$c = (\delta + \lambda)(a + h),\ ^{8} \tag{11a}$$

$$\dot{a} \equiv [r - (n + \pi)]a + w - \tau - c, \tag{11b}$$

$$\dot{h} \equiv (r + \lambda - \pi)\, h + \tau - w. \tag{11c}$$

These last three equations imply:

$$\dot{c} \equiv [r - (\delta + \pi + \lambda)]\, c - (\delta + \lambda)na + (\delta + \lambda)\lambda h, \tag{12}$$

or

$$\dot{c} = [r - (\delta + \pi)]\, c - (\delta + \lambda)\beta a. \tag{12'}$$

Integrating (11c) forward in time and imposing the terminal boundary condition (13), we obtain human capital per unit of labour measured in efficiency units, h, as given in (14).

$$\lim_{l \to \infty} h(l) \exp\left\{-\int_t^l [r(u) + \lambda - \pi]du\right\} = 0, \tag{13}$$

$$h(t) = \int_t^\infty [w(v) - \tau(v)] \exp\left\{-\int_t^v [r(u) + \lambda - \pi]du\right\}dv. \tag{14}$$

Productivity growth expands the human capital base of those currently alive. The probability of death reduces their human capital base, and the birth rate does not expand it (given w and r) because there is no operative intergenerational gift motive.

Production, the public sector and market equilibrium
The production side of the economy consists of an exogenous perishable endowment of labour. One unit of labour produces one unit of perishable output. Output grows at the constant proportional rate $n + \pi$. Output per unit of efficiency labour y is constant and, through choice of units, equal to unity, i.e.

$$y = w = 1. \tag{15}$$

The government spends on goods and services g, levies lump-sum taxes τ and borrows by issuing government debt. (g, τ and b are per unit of efficiency labour.)[9]

The government's instantaneous budget identity is:

$$\dot{b} \equiv g - \tau + [r - (n + \pi)]b. \tag{16}$$

Integrating the government's budget identity forward in time and imposing the terminal boundary condition given in (17) we obtain the familiar government intertemporal or present value budget constraint, or government solvency constraint, given in (18).

$$\lim_{l \to \infty} b(l) \exp\left\{-\int_t^l [r(u) - (n + \pi)]du\right\} = 0, \tag{17}$$

$$b(t) \equiv \int_t^\infty [r(v) - g(v)] \exp\left\{-\int_t^v [r(u) - (n + \pi)]du\right\}dv. \tag{18}$$

Equilibrium in the goods market requires that:

$$c + g = 1. \tag{19}$$

Since there is only one non-human asset, government debt, it follows that:

$$a = b. \tag{20}$$

II Debt (non-) neutrality: a general statement

It is evident from equations (11a), (14), (18) and (20) that the conditions for debt neutrality are simply the conditions for $c(t)$ to be independent of $b(t)$ and of the current and future values of τ, as long as the path of g is left unchanged. Note that the conditions for debt neutrality are independent of the supply side of the economy. In what follows, the analysis is restricted to paths or rules for τ consistent with government solvency, as defined in (18): the present discounted value of future primary (i.e. net of interest) government surpluses should be equal to (and therefore sufficient to service) the initial debt. The relevant discount rate is the real interest rate net of the rate of growth of labour in efficiency units $r - (n + \pi)$. Population growth and productivity growth both expand the future resource base on which the government can levy taxes to service the debt.

Substitute for $h(t)$ in the consumption function (11a) using (14) and for $a(t)$ using (20). Then add and subtract the term

$$(\delta + \lambda) \int_t^\infty g(v) \exp\left\{-\int_t^v [r(u) + \lambda - \pi]du\right\}dv$$

and rearrange. This yields:

$$c(t) = (\delta + \lambda) \int_t^\infty [w(v) - g(v)] \exp\left\{-\int_t^v [r(u) + \lambda - \pi]du\right\}dv$$
$$+ (\delta + \lambda)\left(b(t) - \int_t^\infty [\tau(v) - g(v)] \exp\left\{-\int_t^v [r(u) + \lambda - \pi]du\right\}dv\right). \tag{21}$$

The second term on the r.h.s. of (21) is the crucial one for debt neutrality. Comparing it with the government solvency constraint (18) shows that this term will vanish if $\lambda + n \equiv \beta = 0$. If the birth rate is positive, debt neutrality will not hold. This is the most general statement of the conditions for debt neutrality. What follows becomes more specific by putting some restrictions on the paths of taxes.

Consider two economies identical in all respects except for the initial stock of debt, which is larger in economy I, and for current and future lump-sum taxes which differ between the two economies in such a way as to ensure government solvency for both economy I and economy II, in spite of the larger initial stock of debt in economy I. I.e. $\delta^{\mathrm{I}} = \delta^{\mathrm{II}} = \delta$; $\lambda^{\mathrm{I}} = \lambda^{\mathrm{II}} = \lambda$; $\pi^{\mathrm{I}} = \pi^{\mathrm{II}} = \pi$; $w^{\mathrm{I}}(v) = w^{\mathrm{II}}(v) = w(v)$; $r^{\mathrm{I}}(v) = r^{\mathrm{II}}(v) = r(v)$; $g^{\mathrm{I}}(v) = g^{\mathrm{II}}(v) = g(v)$ for all $v \geq t$. To maintain government solvency with $b^{\mathrm{I}}(t) > b^{\mathrm{II}}(t)$ we require, from (18) that

$$b^{\mathrm{I}}(t) - b^{\mathrm{II}}(t) = \int_t^{\infty} [\tau^{\mathrm{I}}(v) - \tau^{\mathrm{II}}(v)] \exp\left\{-\int_t^v [r(u) - (n + \pi)du\right\}dv > 0. \tag{22}$$

Adding and subtracting the term

$$\int_t^{\infty} [\tau^{\mathrm{I}}(v) - \tau^{\mathrm{II}}(v)] \exp\left\{-\int_t^v [r(u) + \lambda - \pi]du\right\}dv$$

in (22) and rearranging yields:

$$b^{\mathrm{I}}(t) - b^{\mathrm{II}}(t) = \int_t^{\infty} [\tau^{\mathrm{I}}(v) - \tau^{\mathrm{II}}(v)] \exp\left\{-\int_t^v [r(u) + \lambda - \pi]du\right\}dv$$
$$+ \int_t^{\infty} [\tau^{\mathrm{I}}(v) - \tau^{\mathrm{II}}(v)]\, exp\left\{-\int_t^v [r(u) - (n + \pi)]du\right\}[1 - e^{-\beta(v-t)}]dv. \tag{23}$$

It is clear that the higher initial debt in economy I could be serviced by tax policies that have $\tau^{\mathrm{I}}(v) \geq \tau^{\mathrm{II}}(v)$ for all $v \geq t$ and $\tau^{\mathrm{I}}(v) > \tau^{\mathrm{II}}(v)$ for at least one finite interval of time beyond t. For all such policies, the second term on the r.h.s. of (23) is strictly positive for $\beta > 0$. It equals zero for $\beta = 0$. Let us call this term $\Omega(t)$, i.e.

$$\Omega(t) = \int_t^{\infty} [\tau^{\mathrm{I}}(v) - \tau^{\mathrm{II}}(v)] \exp\left\{-\int_t^v [r(u) - (n + \pi)]du\right\}[1 - e^{-\beta(v-t)}]dv. \tag{24}$$

It is the excess of the present discounted value of the differences in future taxes using the government's effective discount rate $r - (n + \pi)$ over the present discounted value of the differences in future taxes using the private sector's effective discount rate $r + \lambda - \pi$.

The difference in private consumption between the two economies is given by

$$c^{\mathrm{I}}(t) - c^{\mathrm{II}}(t) = (\delta + \lambda)\, \Omega(t). \tag{25}$$

For the strictly higher path of taxes in economy I (i.e. with $\tau^{\mathrm{I}}(v) \geq \tau^{\mathrm{II}}(v)$ for all v and $\tau^{\mathrm{I}}(v) > \tau^{\mathrm{II}}(v)$ for some finite interval), $\Omega(t)$ is strictly positive if and only if $\beta > 0$, because in that case the household sector discounts a positive stream of differences using a higher effective discount rate than the government.[10]

To establish absence of debt neutrality, we only had to show that $c^{\mathrm{I}}(t)$

$\neq c^{II}(t)$ if $b^{I}(t) \neq b^{II}(t)$ and only lump-sum taxes differ between economies I and II to maintain government solvency. In fact we have shown more, by establishing a strong presumption of 'financial crowding out': $b^{I}(t) > b^{II}(t)$ was seen to imply $c^{I}(t) > c^{II}(t)$ if and only if $\beta \equiv \lambda + n > 0$ for the class of tax policies considered. How this incipient increase in private consumption is translated into actual behaviour is very model-specific, as it depends on the equilibrium behaviour of current and future expected interest rates and wage rates.

In the original version of this chapter (Buiter [1986a]) which had endogenous durable physical capital formation, early lump-sum tax cuts followed by later lump-sum tax increases raised consumption in the short run and reduced capital formation. The long-run capital stock and long-run private consumption level were reduced. In a small open economy with an exogenous real interest rate, the crowding out would take the form of public debt displacing net foreign assets rather than real capital (see Blanchard [1985] and Buiter [1986a]). In the endowment economy considered in the next section, an early tax cut followed by a tax increase will leave private consumption unchanged, both in the short run and in the long run. An increase in the real interest rate chokes off any incipient increase in consumption demand.

The findings of this section can be summarised as follows:

Proposition: $\beta \equiv \lambda + n = 0$ *is necessary and sufficient for debt neutrality in the Yaari-Blanchard-Weil model.*

Corollary: if $\beta = 0$, $\lambda >$ *or* $\pi \neq 0$ *do not invalidate debt neutrality.*

To appreciate why a positive death rate is irrelevant for debt neutrality, consider an economy with a zero birth rate ($\beta = 0$) and a positive death rate ($\lambda > 0$).[11] The 'good' news for those currently alive at time t is that they may not be around to pay future taxes. The probability that they will have to pay the per-capita tax bill at time $t' > t$ is only $e^{-\lambda(t'-t)}$. The 'bad' news is that the population is shrinking at a constant instantaneous proportional rate λ. A tax cut of one unit of output at time t therefore implies a per capita tax bill at t' equal to $e^{\lambda(t'-t)}$. With no new tax payers arriving, postponing taxes therefore does not relax the intertemporal budget constraint. In Blanchard's model (Blanchard [1984, 1985]) population growth was zero i.e. $\beta = \lambda$. A positive death rate implied a positive birth rate. It is the birth rate, however, that does the work (together with the absence of an operative intergenerational bequest motive) as regards the absence of debt neutrality.

Productivity growth, when $\beta = 0$, does not create any scope for expanding the private sector's intertemporal budget constraint by postponing taxes, even if $\lambda > 0$, as the benefits from productivity growth accrue only to those who are already alive.

Finally note that Blanchard's measure of fiscal stance $F(t)$ becomes (see Blanchard [1985])

$$F(t) \equiv g(t) - (\delta + \lambda) \int_t^{\infty} g(v) \exp \left\{ -\int_t^v [r(u) + \lambda - \pi] du \right\} dv$$
$$+ (\delta + \lambda)\left(b(t) - \int_t^{\infty} [\tau(v) - g(v)] \exp \left\{ -\int_t^v [r(u) + \lambda - \pi] du \right\} dv \right). \tag{26}$$

We have already discussed the third term on the r.h.s. of (26), the financing term. The first and second terms show the effect of public spending on aggregate (private plus public) consumption demand, at given current and expected future interest rates and wage rates. Demand is boosted by public consumption spending to the extent that its current value exceeds the 'permanent' value defined by the second term on the r.h.s. of (26).

III Financial crowding out and fiscal policy: an example

In this Section, I complete the model of Section I by adding a behavioural relationship for taxes which has the following properties: (*i*) it permits one to assign values to a single feedback parameter that will stabilise the public debt process; (*ii*) it pins down very transparently the change in the long-run level of taxes and (*iii*) it permits a convenient characterisation of a long-run increase in taxation preceded by a short-run cut in taxes and vice-versa. As shown in (27) τ feeds back from the deficit.

$$\tau = \tau_0 + \theta \dot{b}. \tag{27}$$

Under this rule, the debt dynamics are governed by:

$$\dot{b} = (1 + \theta)^{-1}(g - \tau_0) + (1 + \theta)^{-1}[r - (n + \pi)]b. \tag{28}$$

In the long run ($\dot{b} = 0$), taxes are given by τ_0. With $\theta = 0$ we have the case of exogenous lump-sum taxes. With $\theta < -1$, an increase in τ_0, however, implies in the short run a reduction in τ which disappears gradually and changes into an eventual increase (if the process converges).

$$\tau = \frac{1}{1 + \theta} \tau_0 + \frac{\theta}{1 + \theta} g + \frac{\theta}{1 + \theta} [r - (n + \pi)]b. \tag{29}$$

Assigning the value -2 to θ as was done in Buiter [1986a] results in the debt-deficit process becoming the exact mirror image of what it would be under exogenous taxes ($\theta = 0$) since with $\theta = -2$ we have

$$\tau = -\tau_0 + 2g + 2\,[r - (n + \pi)]b \tag{29'}$$

and

$$\dot{b} = -(g - \tau_0) - [r - (n + \pi)]b. \tag{28'}$$

The behaviour of the whole economy with the 'fruit tree' production sector is extremely simple and can be summarised in equations (30)–(32).

$$c = 1 - g \qquad (0 \leqslant g < 1), \tag{30}$$

$$r = \delta + \pi + \frac{(\delta + \lambda)\beta b}{1 - g}, \tag{31}$$

$$\dot{b} = (1 + \theta)^{-1}(g - \tau_0) + (1 + \theta)^{-1}(\delta - n)b + (1 + \theta)^{-1}\,\frac{(\delta + \lambda)}{1 - g}\beta b^2 = -\dot{h}. \tag{32}$$

Private consumption is what's left of the perishable endowment after the government has extracted its exhaustive spending share. The real interest rate is an increasing function of the stock of public debt if $\beta > 0$. It is dependent of the stock of debt if $\beta = 0$.

The determinants of the real interest rate are summarised in equations (33a–e). They are unsurprising and self explanatory.

$$\frac{\partial r}{\partial b} = \frac{(\delta + \lambda)\beta}{1 - g} > 0 \text{ iff } \beta > 0 \tag{33a}$$

$$\frac{\partial r}{\partial \pi} = 1, \tag{33b}$$

$$\frac{\partial r}{\partial \delta} = 1 + \frac{\beta b}{1 - g} > 0 \text{ iff } b > \frac{-(1 - g)}{\beta}, \tag{33c}$$

$$\frac{\partial r}{\partial \lambda} = \frac{\beta b}{1 - g} > 0 \text{ iff } \beta b > 0, \tag{33d}$$

$$\frac{\partial r}{\partial \beta} = \frac{(\delta + \lambda)b}{1 - g} > 0 \text{ iff } b > 0. \tag{33e}$$

Since private consumption is constant (barring changes in g or in the endowment) the change in human capital (reflecting changes in taxes and in interest rates) is equal and opposite to the change in the stock of public debt (non-human capital).

With $\beta = 0$ and exogenous taxes ($\theta = 0$) the debt process is linear:

$$\dot{b} = g - \tau_0 + (\delta - n)b.$$

It will be explosive if $\delta > n$, stable if $\delta < n$ (the case of the dynamically inefficient economy).

In the explosive case, assignment of the value -2 to θ will stabilise the debt process which becomes

$$\dot{b} = -(g - \tau_0) - (\delta - n)b.$$

With $\beta > 0$ and exogenous taxes ($\theta = 0$) the debt process is quadratic:

$$\dot{b} = g - \tau_0 + (\delta - n)b + \frac{(\delta + \lambda)\beta}{1 - g}\, b^2. \tag{34}$$

The steady state solutions for the government debt stock are:

$$b^*_{1,2} = \left\{ n - \delta \pm \left[(\delta - n)^2 - \frac{4(\delta + \lambda)\beta(g - \tau_0)}{1 - g} \right]^{\frac{1}{2}} \right\} \frac{(1 - g)}{2(\delta + \lambda)\beta}. \tag{35}$$

For this equation to have real solutions we require

$$(\delta - n)^2 \geqslant \frac{4(\delta + \lambda)\beta(g - \tau_0)}{1 - g},$$

i.e. the primary (non-interest) deficit should not be too large. For simplicity consider the case where $g = \tau_0$. In this case the two stationary solutions are

$$b^*_1 = 0, \tag{36a}$$

$$b^*_2 = \frac{(n - \delta)(1 - g)}{(\delta + \lambda)\beta}. \tag{36b}$$

When $\delta > n$, the solution trajectory is the $\dot{b}_0$ curve in Fig. 1*a*. Of the two stationary equilibria b^*_1 is locally unstable and b^*_2 is locally stable. A negative value for $g - \tau_0$ would shift the $\dot{b}$ curve downwards vertically, say to $\dot{b}_1$. Positive values for $g - \tau_0$ shift the $\dot{b} = 0$ curve upwards. There will be no stationary equilibrium if

$$g - \tau_0 > \frac{(1 - g)(\delta - n)^2}{4(\delta + \lambda)\beta}.$$

The minima on each $\dot{b}$ curve are at

$$\hat{b} = \frac{(n - \delta)(1 - g)}{2(\delta + \lambda)\beta}.$$

A tax cut from an initial equilibrium at b^*_1 will cause an explosive spiral of deficits leading to larger debt and (from equation (31)) to higher interest rates and thus to even larger deficits. A tax increase from b^*_1 will create a surplus which cumulates into a lower (in this case negative) public debt. The interest rate decines and, with the government now a net creditor to the private sector, this reduces and eventually eliminates the budget

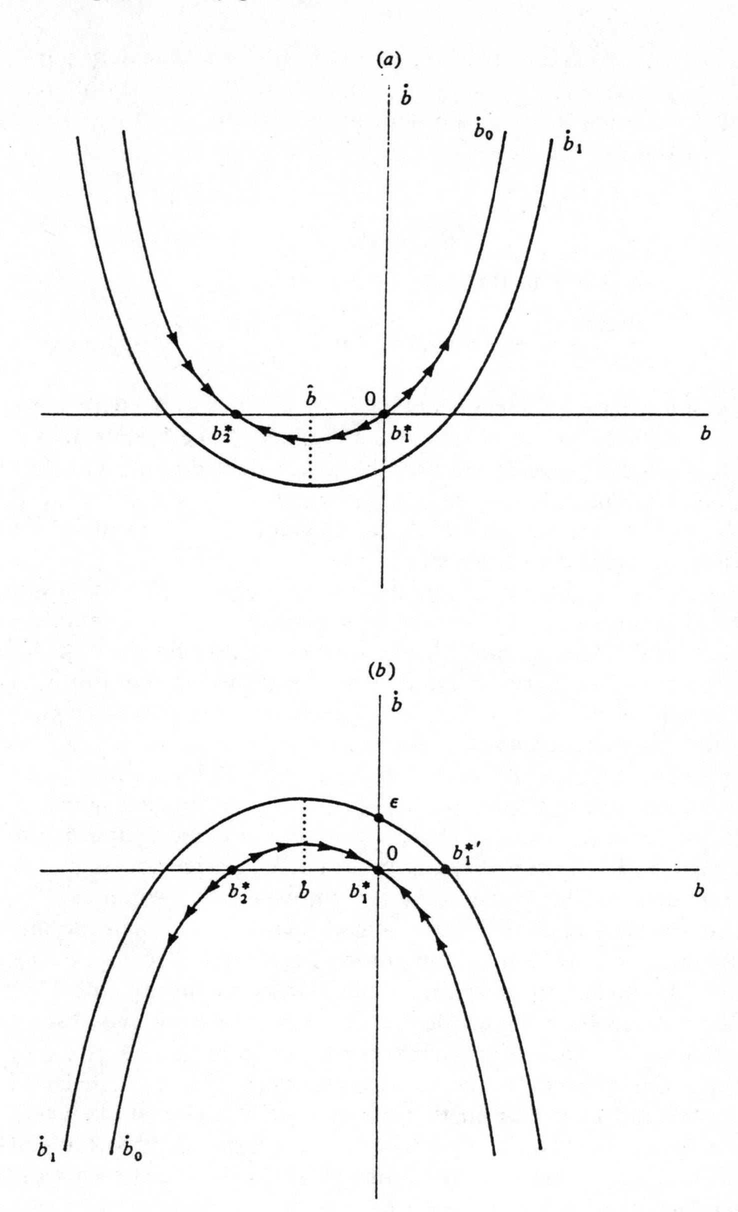
(a)
$\dot{b}$
$\dot{b}_0$
$\dot{b}_1$
$\hat{b}$
0
b_2^*
b_1^*
b
(b)
$\dot{b}$
ϵ
0
$b_1^{*\prime}$
b_2^*
$\hat{b}$
b_1^*
b
$\dot{b}_1$
$\dot{b}_0$

Figure 1

surplus. The consequences of a perturbation of the low debt equilibrium b_2^* can be derived easily and are omitted here for reasons of space.

With $\beta > 0$ and $\theta = -2$ the debt process is the exact negative of that given in (34), i.e. we have

$$\dot{b} = -(g - \tau_0) - (\delta - n)b - \frac{(\delta + \lambda)\beta}{1 - g} b^2. \tag{36}$$

Note that total taxes in this case are given by:

$$\tau = -\tau_0 + 2g + 2(\delta - n)b + \frac{2(\delta + \lambda)\beta}{1 - g} b^2. \tag{37}$$

The stationary equilibrium debt stocks are the same with $\theta = -2$ as with $\theta = 0$. When there are two such equilibria, the higher debt equilibrium is the locally stable one and the lower debt equilibrium the locally unstable one. The solution trajectories for this case are shown in Fig. 1*b*, again drawn for the $\delta > n$ case. A higher value of $\tau_0 - g$ shifts the $\dot{b}$ curve vertically upwards, say from $\dot{b}_0$ to $\dot{b}_1$.

An increase in τ_0 from an initial stationary equilibrium at b_1^* illustrates the implications of the absence of debt neutrality and the requirement of intertemporal solvency most clearly. From (37), an increase in τ_0 implies initially a tax *cut* equal in magnitude to the eventual long-run increase in taxes (given by the increase in τ_0). The economy moves from the origin, where the budget is balanced, to a position of budget deficit at ϵ. As debt accumulates, the tax cut is reversed. Even though the rising value of debt drives up the interest rate, the budget deficit is reduced and eventually eliminated as the economy moves from ϵ to $b_1^{*\prime}$ along the $\dot{b}_1$ curve. A higher level of long-run taxes is required to service the higher level of long-run debt at the higher long-run interest rate. When taxes are cut initially, human capital is unchanged. This is brought about partly through the anticipation of the future higher level of taxes and partly through the higher interest rate path that discounts all future after-tax endowment income.. While the interest rate does not rise discretely on impact, it is an increasing function of the level of the stock of debt. Except at the initial date, the interest rate path after an increase in τ_0 lies uniformly (and by a margin that grows until the new stationary equilibrium is reached) above the interest rate corresponding to the stationary equilibrium at b_1^*. Subsequent to the initial tax cut, debt rises and human capital decines with $\dot{b} + \dot{h} = 0$. The analysis of a perturbation of the low debt equilibrium at b_2^* is again left as an exercise.

IV Conclusions

The Yaari-Blanchard model of consumer behaviour has been generalised to allow for population growth and productivity growth. Blanchard's finding, in models without an operative intergenerational bequest motive, population growth or productivity growth, that uncertain lifetimes destroy debt neutrality (even with a perfect annuities market) and Weil's finding, in a model without an operative intergenerational bequest motive, uncertain lifetimes or productivity growth, that a positive birth rate alone destroys debt neutrality, are special cases of the general model.

The general conclusions of this paper are contained in the Proposition and its Corollary: debt neutrality requires $\beta = 0$; if $\beta = 0$, $\lambda > 0$ or $\pi \neq 0$ do not destroy debt neutrality. It is the difference between the public sector's future tax base (the resources of individuals alive today or yet to be born) and the future tax base of the individuals that are alive today (the resources owned by those individuals only, and not the resources of individuals yet to be born from whom they are separated by the absence of an operative intergenerational bequest motive in spite of potentially infinite individual horizons ($\lambda = 0$)), that accounts for the non-neutrality of variations over time in the pattern of lump-sum taxation. The individual's expected future flow of resources grows at a rate $\pi - \lambda$. The government's expected future flow of resources grows at a rate $\pi + \beta - \lambda$. Unless individuals are linked, through intergenerational gift and bequest motives to all those born after them, the resources of these future generations are not integrated into each person's intertemporal budget constraint. An infinite lifetime ($\lambda = 0$) is not the same as intergenerational concern, nor does it imply the ability to effect the desired intergenerational transfers of resources. Productivity growth, when $\beta = 0$, augments the individual's resources over time in the same way as it augments the government's tax base and does not destroy debt neutrality.

The analysis has been deliberately restricted to the case of lump-sum, non-distortionary taxes. Non lump-sum taxes have (dis)incentive effects that will destroy debt neutrality even when $\beta \equiv n + \lambda = 0$ and the government remains solvent. Here too, however, the Yaari-Blanchard-Weil model contributes something new. As shown in Engel and Kletzer [1985] and elaborated in Buiter [1986b], when there is a single 'conventional' distortion such as a non-lump-sum tax, changes in the distortionary tax rate may have first-order income effects even when they are evaluated at a zero value of the distortionary tax rate. This result occurs when $r \neq \delta + \pi$, which can be the case in well-behaved stationary equilibria of the Yaari-Blanchard-Weil model if $\beta \neq 0$. Different effective discount rates applied by the private sector (in the aggregate) to the income streams from human and non-human capital act like a second, 'intrinsic' distortion and land us in the realm of second-best even where there is but one conventional distortion.[12]

Finally, the Yaari-Blanchard-Weil model may well become the workhorse of the late eighties for analytical macroeconomic research and teaching, because of its simplicity and flexibility.

Notes

Originally published in the *Economic Journal*, 98, June 1988, pp. 279–93.

1 An earlier version of this paper. (Buiter [1986a]) considered a neoclassical production function with labour and durable capital as the two inputs.
2 This can without difficulty be generalised (as in Blanchard [1985] to the case of the instantaneous utility function which has constant elasticity of marginal utility, i.e.

$$W(s, t) = E_t \int_t^{\infty} e^{-\delta(v-t)} \frac{1}{\gamma} \bar{c}(s, v)^{\gamma} dv \qquad (\gamma < 1; \gamma \neq 0).$$

3 For simplicity labour supply is taken to be exogenous.
4 For the isoelastic instantaneous utility function of footnote 2, equation (6) would be replaced by:

$$\bar{c}(s, t) = \eta(t)[\bar{a}(s, t) + \bar{h}(s, t)],$$

where

$$\eta(t) = \left(\int_t^{\infty} \exp\left\{ -\left[\frac{\gamma}{\gamma - 1} \int_t^{v} r(u)du + (v - t)\left(\lambda + \frac{1}{1 - \gamma} \delta \right) \right] \right\} dv \right)^{-1}$$

so

$$\begin{aligned} \dot{\bar{c}} &= (r + \lambda - \eta)\bar{c} + (\bar{a} + \bar{h})\eta \left[\eta - \left(\frac{\gamma}{\gamma - 1} r + \lambda + \frac{1}{1 - \gamma} \delta \right) \right]. \\ &= \frac{(r - \delta)}{1 - \gamma} \bar{c} \end{aligned}$$

5 For the isoelastic instantaneous utility function we have:

$C = \eta(A + H)$ where η is defined in footnote 4.

6 We use the fact that $\bar{a}(t, t) = 0$, i.e. consumers are born without financial assets or liabilities.
7 We use $\bar{h}(t, t)e^{nt} = \bar{h}(t)e^{nt} = H(t)$.
8 For the isoelastic instantaneous utility function we have:

$c = \eta(a + h)$ where η is defined in footnote 4.

9 I am assuming that government spending on goods and services is neither useful as public sector capital formation nor as public consumption in the private utility function. g could be entered additively into the instantaneous private utility function without affecting any of the results (except of course the welfare economics of variations in g). For the issue of debt neutrality, the role of g is not relevant.
10 This result will also hold for many policies for which $\tau^{I}(v) < \tau^{II}(v)$ for some finite interval(s), but the proofs become very case-specific. The behaviour of taxes in the model studied in Section III with $\theta = -2$ is characterised by $\tau^{I}(v) < \tau^{II}(v)$ for small v and $\tau^{I}(v) > \tau^{II}(v)$ for large v.
11 I owe this example to P. Weil.
12 When $r = \delta + \pi$ in the initial stationary equilibrium, $a = 0$ in the model with $\beta > 0$ and the 'intrinsic distortion' is not binding.

References

Arrow, K. J. and Kurz, M. (1969), 'Optimal consumer allocation over an infinite horizon', *Journal of Economic Theory*, Vol. 11, pp. 68–91.
Blanchard, O. J. (1984), 'Current and anticipated deficits, interest rates and economic activity', *European Economic Review*, Vol. 25, No. 1, pp. 7–27.
—— (1985), 'Debt, deficits and finite horizons', *Journal of Political Economy*, Vol. 93 (April), pp. 223–47.
Buiter, W. H. (1986a), 'Death, population growth, productivity growth and debt neutrality', NBER Working Paper No. 2027 (September).
—— (1986b), 'Fiscal policy in open, interdependent economies', In *Economic Policy in Theory and Practice*, A. Razin and E. Sadka (eds.), London: Macmillan.
Engel, C. and Kletzer, K. (1985), 'Tariffs, saving and the current account', Mimeo.
Weil, P. (1985), 'Essays on the valuation of unbacked assets', Harvard PhD Thesis (May 1985).
Yaari, M. E. (1985), 'The uncertain lifetime, life insurance and the theory of the consumer', *Review of Economic Studies*, Vol. 32 (April), pp. 137–50.

Part 5
Exercises in macroeconomic theory

Chapter 15

Some unfamiliar properties of a familiar macroeconomic model

Written with H. Lorie

I Introduction

In recent contributions Barro and Grossman [1971, 1974] have argued that disequilibrium models involving trade at non-market clearing prices in product and factor markets yield a set of theoretical predictions considerably richer than those offered by the more traditional Keynesian approach. The latter views the product market as clearing instantaneously and limits disequilibrium to the labour market.[1] In particular, the Barro and Grossman model (a) no longer necessarily implies counter-cyclical variations of the real wage (which have received little empirical support)[2] and (b) permits levels of output and employment lower than those associated with the full employment Walrasian equilibrium to be generated by conditions of excess demand. This last result, referred to as 'suppressed inflation', is brought about by the functioning of the 'supply multiplier', the generalised excess demand analogue of the familiar demand multiplier.

Our first aim in this note is to show that both properties (a) and (b) can characterise the standard Keynesian model[3] (contrary to the impression conveyed by Barro and Grossman's work) provided we introduce one important modification. The standard Keynesian model (and Keynes') have *downward* rigidity of the money wage. Following Barro and Grossman we make this money wage rigidity symmetrical. The possibility of persistent excess demand for labour because of *upward* rigidity of the money wage is an essential feature of our model. A further attractive aspect of our model is that it offers a simple theory of product price and money wage determination. The flexible price, sticky wage assumption provides a fairly realistic account of the relative speeds of adjustment of the money wage and the product price. It also allows a simple and transparent analysis of the complete macrodynamics of quantity and price adjustments. Our second objective is to carry out this dynamic analysis.

The money wage adjustment equation is an expectations-augmented wage Phillips curve. The expected rate of inflation enters with a coefficient of unity. Two hypotheses concerning the generation of inflation expectations are considered. Adaptive expectations are treated in section III. This includes static expectations as a special case. With static expectations the money wage adjustment equation is equivalent to a 'naive' wage Phillips curve which does not allow for the expected rate of inflation. Section IV deals with the case of rational expectations (or perfect foresight). We show that under adaptive expectations even the local stability of the Walrasian full employment equilibrium is in question. With static expectations, instability problems only occur when the Keynesian model is extended to situations of excess demand for labour. Under perfect foresight, the Walrasian full employment equilibrium is (locally) stable.

II The model

The speeds of product price and interest rate adjustments are assumed to be infinite while the money wage is 'sluggish' (i.e. has a finite speed of adjustment). Disequilibrium trades can therefore occur only in the labour market. Given these assumptions the IS–LM model and the associated aggregate demand-aggregate supply apparatus are (when properly interpreted) quite consistent with the recent reappraisal of Keynesian economics.[4] With continuously clearing product and financial markets, the relevant labour demand and supply functions are in all circumstances the 'notional' ones derived respectively by equating the real wage with the marginal productivity and the marginal disutility of labour. There is no output sales (purchases) constraint to make the relevant labour market demand and supply signals different from those provided by the notional demand and supply schedules. A labour sales (purchases) constraint can feed back on the demand for (supply of) output and generate the Keynesian consumption function (or the 'labour supply constrained' output supply function). The relevant notional labour demand and supply functions $L^d(w/p)$ and $L^s(w/p)$ are illustrated in Fig. 1 where w denotes the money wage rate, p the price level and $L^{d'} < 0$, $L^{s'} > 0$.[5]

What we shall call the Walrasian full employment level L^* is associated with the real wage $(w/p)^*$. If exchange takes place in the labour market outside equilibrium, we assume that the short side of the market is realised. The thicker portions of L^d and L^s then represent the correspondence between *employment*, L, and the real wage: $L = \min[L^d(w/p), L^s(w/p)]$. Clearly, L^* constitutes an upper bound for employment. Given a short run production function $y = f(L)$ with $f' > 0$, $f'' < 0$, $y^* = f(L^*)$ is full employment real income and constitutes an upper bound for realised income: $y = \min\{f[L^d(w/p)], f[L^s(w/p)]\}$. More precisely, the 'regimes' for effective output or real income are $y = f[L^d(w/p)]$ if $w/p \geqslant (w/p)^*$ and $y = f[L^s(w/p)]$ if $w/p \leqslant (w/p)^*$.

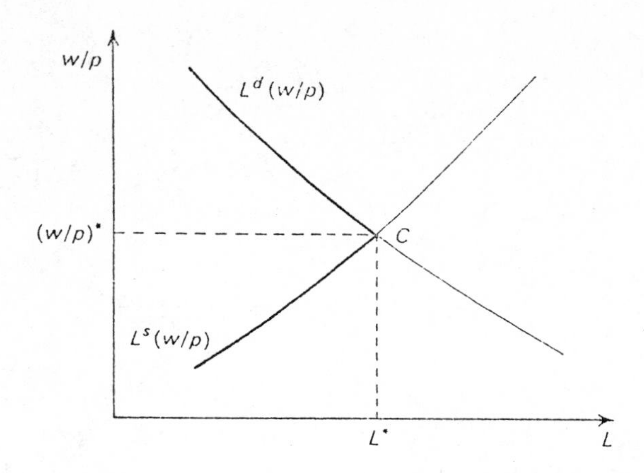

Figure 1

The following demands for consumption, investment and money are assumed to be derived from the optimisation of the consumers' and firms' objective functions:

$$c^d = c(y, M/p) \qquad (0 < c_1 < 1;\ c_2 > 0),$$
$$i^d = i(r - \pi) \qquad (i' < 0),$$
$$M^d/p = m(y, r) \qquad (m_1 > 0;\ m_2 < 0).$$

M is the nominal supply of outside money, r is the nominal rate of interest and π is the expected rate of inflation.

With $y = \min\{f[L^d(w/p)], f[L^s(w/p)]\}$, it should be stressed that c and m are only 'constrained' demands if $w/p > (w/p)^*$. Then indeed $y = f[L^d(w/p)]$ and output and employment are determined by the firms independently of the consumers' wishes. If $w/p \leqslant (w/p)^*$, $y = f[L^s(w/p)]$ and c and m are notional demand functions with w/p as one of their arguments.

Solving the financial market equilibrium condition $M/p = m(y, r)$ for the rate of interest, we obtain $r = g(y, M/p)$ with $g_1 > 0$ and $g_2 < 0$. Substituting this in the investment demand function we obtain the *demand price function* given in equation (1).

$$c(y, M/p) + i[g(y, M/p) - \pi] - y = 0. \qquad (1)$$

For a given nominal money supply and expected rate of inflation this defines the price level at which both the product and the financial markets are in equilibrium, for any given level of output y that firms may decide to produce (under whatever regime).[6] The interpretation of the demand price function as the locus of IS–LM equilibria for all possible values of the price level is of course familiar.

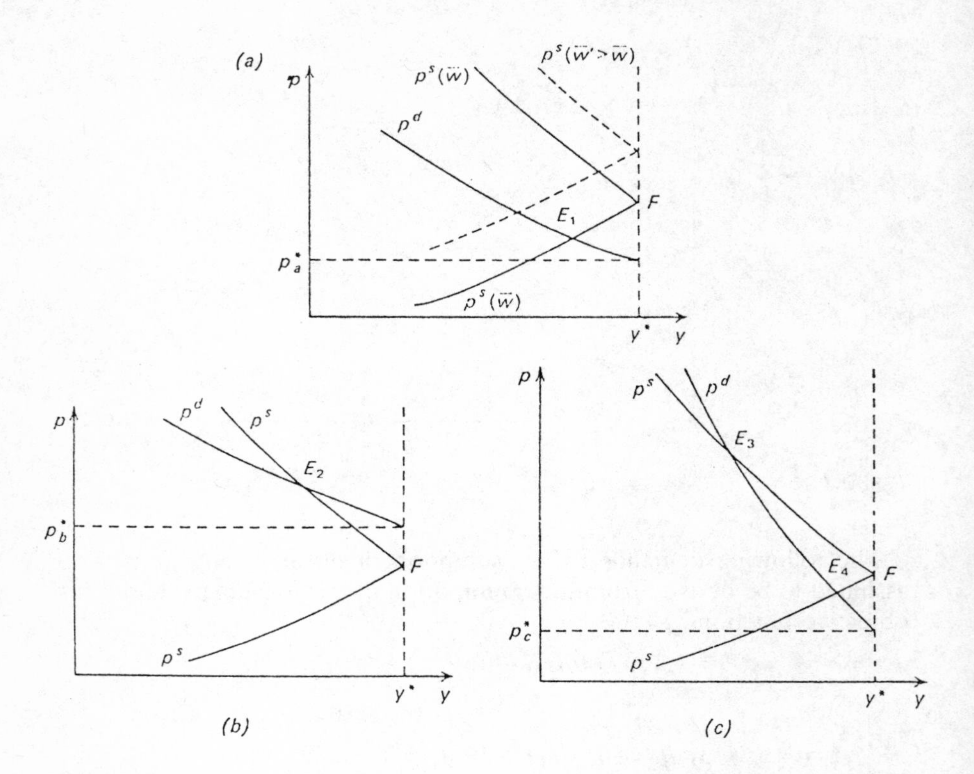

Figure 2

Solving (1) for p, as a function of y, π and M we obtain

$$p = p^d(y, \pi, M) \tag{2a}$$

with

$$p_1^d = \frac{c_1 + i'g_1 - 1}{(c_2 + i'g_2)(M/p^2)} < 0 \tag{2b}$$

and

$$p_2^d = \frac{-i'}{(c_2 + i'g_2)(M/p^2)} > 0. \tag{2c}$$

The demand price function p^d (illustrated in Fig. 2) is downward sloping because of the effect of changes in the price level on real money balances. This operates both through the financial market equilibrium condition and, via the Pigou effect, through the output market equilibrium condition. It should be noted that our interpretation of the demand price schedule as a function of the expected rate of inflation requires the expected rate of inflation to be parametric or predetermined in the short run (at a point in time). This is an appropriate assumption with adaptive (including static) expectations. With perfect foresight, considered in section IV below, both the price level and its expected rate of change are short run endogenous variables.

As firms may not be able to purchase their notional demand for labour services, the potentially 'constrained' profit maximisation leads them to produce and supply $y = f\{\min[L^d(w/p), L^s(\mathrm{w/p})]\}$ for a given w and p. Viewing p and y as the dependent and independent variables respectively, we can derive a *supply price correspondence* for any given money wage $\bar{w}$. This is illustrated in Fig. 2 with p^s. As the money wage increases (falls) the point F and the entire supply price correspondence shift upward (downward). The p^s curve corresponds to the left-hand side of Fig. 1 'inverted' i.e. E_1 and E_4 in Fig. 2 are on L^d in Fig. 1 while E_2 and E_3 are on L^s.[7]

Given the values assumed by the money wage rate, the expected rate of inflation and the nominal money stock at any particular instant, a short-run or temporary equilibrium is determined by the intersection(s) of the demand price function and the supply price correspondence. We shall concentrate on three typical cases illustrated in Fig. 2(a)–(c). The points E_1 and E_4 are short-run unemployment equilibria. p_a^*, p_b^* and p_c^* in Fig. 2(a)–(c) are the full employment product prices for a given value of π. E_2 and E_3 are unfilled vacancy equilibria characterised by a real wage below the one compatible with full employment. (Note that in Fig. 2(b) the money wage is 'too low' and the product price 'too high' at E_2, while in Fig. 2(c) both the money wage and product price are 'too high' at E_3).[8]

Barro and Grossman's account of the phenomenon of suppressed inflation can be illustrated by the following example. Assume that expansionary policies have disturbed an initial full employment equilibrium and created an excess demand for goods. With (short-run) rigidity of the price level and money wage, the consumers react to their frustrated demand for commodities not only by accumulating money balances but also by reducing their labour supply which becomes 'constrained'. An excess demand for labour develops while realised employment and output fall cumulatively until an unfilled vacancy and suppressed inflation equilibrium is reached. In our version of the Keynesian model on the other hand, increases of the product price immediately eliminate the excess demand for goods, but the reduction of employment and output still occurs because of the resulting fall of the real wage and the fact that supply is the short side of the labour market and is assumed to be responsive to changes in the real wage rate.[9] There is no shift of the labour supply function itself, but a downward movement along it. The differential speeds of wage and price adjustment are solely responsible for the fall in employment. This analysis therefore provides a theoretical justification for the view that slow wage adjustment, perhaps reinforced by a wages policy, will have very perverse effects on employment during inflationary periods if this inflation turns out to be demand and not supply or cost originated.[10]

One interesting implication of our model is that the real wage does not necessarily move in a direction opposite to the movement of employment and output, even though the product market clears instantaneously. Indeed, under conditions of excess demand in the labour market, any exogenous increase (decrease) of aggregate demand will, given a sticky money wage, be accompanied by a fall (increase) of real output and *pro-cyclical* fluctuations of the real wage. This is not to say that all pro-cyclical behaviour of the (de-trended) real wage must be due to some form of repressed inflation in the labour market (the 1932–3 experience in the USA is an obvious counter-example), but there have been times of obvious excess demand for labour during which the above formal model may help explain the apparent lack of systematic correlation between employment and the real wage. The available US data covering the 1946–7 period are perhaps best explained in the context of our model. While the wartime price and wage controls were removed by the beginning of 1946 (and employment had gone back very quickly to a more normal level after the end of hostilities) both the *absolute* level of employment and the real wage declined through 1946 and 1947 (which were also years of severe inflation). What the present model cannot explain, admittedly, is the pro-cyclical behaviour of real wages during periods of large scale involuntary unemployment. A positive relationship between the real wage and employment in our model implies a negative relationship between unemployment and the real wage only if we define unemployment as the difference between the Walrasian equilibrium level of employment and the actual level of employment. In our model, when output and employment move in the same direction as the real wage, actual employment equals the notional supply of labour and there is no involuntary unemployment. It should be observed, however, that the generalised disequilibrium model, as presented by Barro and Grossman, can explain this phenomenon only by postulating in effect that the speed of adjustment of the money wage is greater than that of the product price. This appears to be required if one is to make sense of their description of the cyclical pattern of employment and the real wage under conditions of excess supply in the product and labour markets: '. . . To the extent that real wages decline in response to this excess supply a fall in real wages . . . will accompany (follow upon) the decline in employment.'[11] This assumption about the relative stickiness of wages and prices is rather unappealing.[12]

III Dynamic adjustment with adaptative expectations

The money wage is assumed to be sticky although not completely unresponsive to excess demand for or supply of labour. Accordingly, the proportional rate of change of money wage is assumed to respond positively to the excess demand for labour, taking full account of the expected proportional rate of change of the price level.

$$\dot{w}/w = \mu[L^d(w/p) - L^s(w/p)] + \pi \qquad (\mu > 0). \tag{3a}$$

Equation (3b) represents the adaptative expectations process

$$\dot{\pi} = \beta[(\dot{p}/p) - \pi] \qquad (\beta \geqslant 0). \tag{3b}$$

Throughout this paper the nominal stock of money balances has been assumed constant. The economic system is therefore not subject to any intrinsic inflationary or deflationary bias. Static expectations (the special case of (3b) with $\beta = \pi = 0$) is therefore not too unreasonable an assumption. Under both expectations assumptions the unique long-run (or steady-state) equilibrium is the Walrasian full employment equilibrium with $w = w^*$, $p = p^*$ and $\pi = \pi^* = 0$. It is illustrated in Fig. 3 (see also the Appendix).

Under adaptative expectations, the Walrasian full employment equilibrium is locally stable if (a) β, the speed at which the expected rate of inflation adjusts to the actual rate, is not 'too large' (see the Appendix) and (b) the elasticity of the price level with respect to the money wage is less than unity.[13] This last condition is always fulfilled on the excess supply side of the Walrasian equilibrium, but not on the excess demand side.

With static expectations, a sufficient condition for local stability is that condition (b) holds. An equivalent condition is that, when the demand price schedule cuts the downward sloping part of the supply price correspondence, it cuts it from below (see the Appendix for a formal proof). A weak real balance effect on consumption and a high interest elasticity of demand for money lead to a relatively inelastic demand price function. This will make stability less likely. Hence, with static expectations a falling money wage in Fig. 2(a) will shift the supply correspondence down until the kink (F) occurs at p_a^*; a rising money wage in Fig. 2(b) will shift the supply correspondence up until it reaches the Walrasian equilibrium. In Fig. 2(c), however, the economic system will return to the Walrasian equilibrium if a fall in demand puts it in the unemployment regime (E_4),

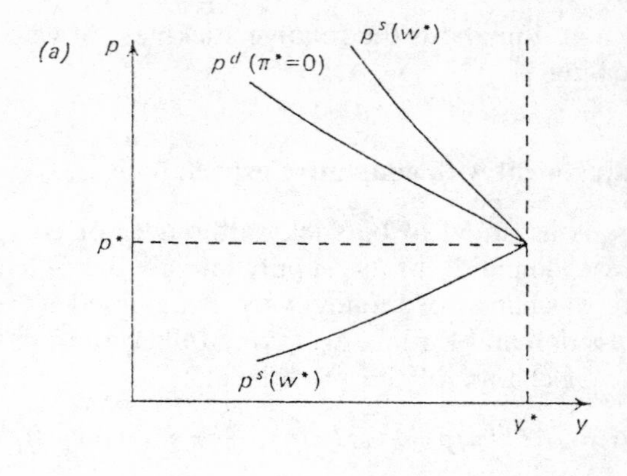

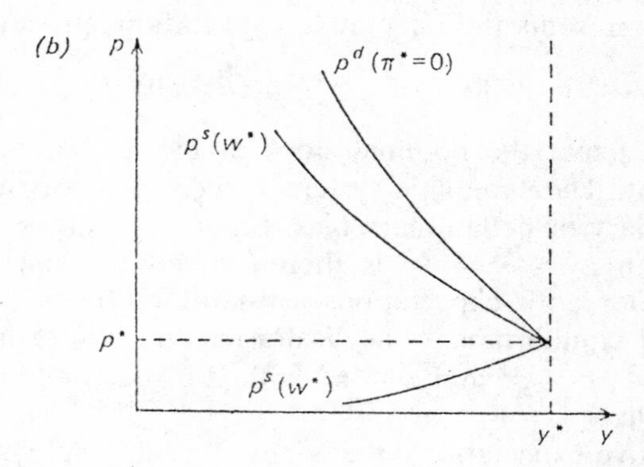

Figure 3

but will move progressively further away from the Walrasian equilibrium if an increase in demand puts it in the unfilled vacancy regime (E_3).

IV Dynamic adjustment with perfect foresight

Perfect foresight is defined as $\pi = \dot{p}/p$, where $\dot{p}$ denotes the *right-hand* time derivative of p. When we substitute this in the wage adjustment equation (3a), stability may appear to be trivial, because we can now rewrite (3a), in the most Classical form, as a real wage adjustment equation:

$$d/dt(w/p) = (w/p)\mu[L^d(w/p - L^s(w/p)]. \tag{4}$$

With $L^{d'} < 0$ and $L^{s'} > 0$, the stability of the long-run equilibrium real wage is assured. However, we do not just want the real wage to converge to its long-run equilibrium value $(w/p)^*$. Both the money wage and the price level must converge to their Walrasian equilibrium values, w^* and

p^*. To determine the movement over time of the price level we must consider (4) and (5).

$$\begin{aligned} &c(\min\{f[L^d(w/p)], f[L^s(w/p)]\}, M/p) \\ &\quad + i[g(\min\{f[L^d(w/p)], f[L^s(w/p)]\}, M/p) - \dot{p}/p] \\ &\quad - \min\{f[L^d(w/p)], f[L^s(w/p)]\} = 0. \end{aligned} \tag{5}$$

Note that with perfect foresight we cannot draw a demand price schedule for a given expected rate of inflation; p and $\dot{p}/p$ are not independent. In the Appendix we show that the Walrasian full employment equilibrium is locally stable under perfect foresight.

Our assumption that the expected rate of inflation is equal to the right-hand derivative of $p(t)$, which is the correct mathematical expression of the notion of perfect foresight, permits the price level to jump discontinuously at each moment in response to current or (expected) future disturbances. The steady state equilibrium which appears to be unstable when the price adjustment equation is solved 'backward' together with the wage adjustment equation from a given set of initial conditions for the money wage and the price level is stable when the price adjustment equation is solved 'forwards' with an initial condition for w and a terminal condition for p.[14] This solution method is the natural one with perfect foresight because in order to determine the expected rate of inflation at t we must 'determine the entire path of (expected) prices from t to forever'.[15]

V **Perspective**

Our main conclusions are stated in the introduction and show the possibility of short-run unfilled vacancy equilibria and pro-cyclical behaviour of the real wage in an economy where the product market clears instantaneously. The model generates such behaviour when shocks like an increase in the money supply or the expected rate of inflation perturb an initial full employment equilibrium. Some general comments on the dynamic properties of the class of disequilibrium models to which our model belongs may be appropriate.

Our model can be characterised as a sequential short-run monetary equilibrium model, provided we interpret equilibrium broadly so as to include quantity-constrained excess demand or excess supply equilibria. A specific ranking of speeds of adjustment of different *money* prices (the nominal wage and the product price) is postulated. Unless these independent adjustments of absolute *money* prices are effectively equivalent to a simple adjustment of *relative* prices (the real wage), the stability of the Walrasian equilibrium is in question. In our model, perfect foresight generates such an equivalence and stability holds unambiguously. But generally, whenever this equivalence is not complete, stability requires stronger conditions. When short-run price adjustment to a once and for all disturbance is allowed to generate expectations of sizeable further price changes (the case of adaptive expectations with $\beta \gg 0$), the model becomes inherently unstable.

Appendix

Analytically, given the money stock M and any money wage w, the product price associated with the short-run Keynesian equilibrium (under adaptative expectations) can be derived from (1) where y is replaced by

$$\min\{f[L^d(w/p)], f[L^s(w/p)]\};$$

i.e. from

$$\begin{aligned} &c(\min\{f[L^d(w/p)], f[L^s(w/p)]\}, M/p) \\ &\quad + i[g(\min\{f[L^d(w/p)], f[L^s(w/p)]\}, M/p) - \pi] \\ &\quad - \min\{f[L^d(w/p)], f[L^s(w/p)]\} = 0. \end{aligned} \tag{6}$$

For $L^d(w/p) \leqslant L^s(w/p)$, the solution of (6) for p is $p = \bar{n}(w, \pi; M)$ with

$$\frac{\partial p}{\partial w} = \bar{n}_1 = \frac{(c_1 + i'g_1 - 1)f'L^{d'}p}{w(c_1 + i'g_1 - 1)f'L^{d'} + (c_2 + i'g_2)M}, \tag{7a}$$

$$\frac{\partial p}{\partial \pi} = \bar{n}_2 = \frac{-i'p^2}{w(c_1 + i'g_1 - 1)f'L^{d'} + (c_2 + i'g_2)M}. \tag{7b}$$

Given the *a priori* restrictions we have imposed on the structural parameters it is clear that $0 < \bar{n}_1 < p/w$ and $\bar{n}_2 > 0$.

$\bar{n}_1 w/p$, the elasticity of the price level with respect to the money wage, will be denoted by $\bar{\varepsilon}(w, \pi; M)$. Therefore we have

$$0 < \bar{\varepsilon} < 1 \qquad (\bar{n}_2 > 0). \tag{8}$$

For $L^d(w/p) \geqslant L^s(w/p)$ the solution of (6) for p is $p = \tilde{n}(w, \pi; M)$ with

$$\frac{\partial p}{\partial w} = \tilde{n}_1 = \frac{(c_1 + i'g_1 - 1)f'L^{s'}p}{w(c_1 + i'g_1 - 1)f'L^{s'} + (c_2 + i'g_2)M}, \tag{9a}$$

$$\frac{\partial p}{\partial \pi} = \tilde{n}_2 = \frac{-i'p^2}{w(c_1 + i'g_1 - 1)f'L^{s'} + (c_2 + i'g_2)M}. \tag{9b}$$

As the numerator of (9a) is negative, the signs of $\tilde{n}_1$ and $\tilde{n}_2$ are ambiguous. Note however that $\tilde{n}_1$ and $\tilde{n}_2$ must always be of opposite sign. $\tilde{n}_1 w/p$, the elasticity of the price level with respect to the money wage in the excess demand for labour regime is denoted by $\tilde{\varepsilon}(w, \pi; M)$.

The p and $\dot{p}$ in equations (3a) and (3b) are eliminated using $p = n(w, \pi; M)$ (where $n(..;.) = \bar{n}(..;.)$ when $L^d \leqslant L^s$ and $n(..;.) = \tilde{n}(..;.)$ when $L^d \geqslant L^s$); one obtains after some manipulations:

$$\dot{w} = w\mu\{L^d[w/n(w,\ \pi;\ M)] - L^s[w/n(w,\ \pi;\ M)]\} + w\pi, \tag{10a}$$

$$\dot{\pi} = \frac{\beta}{n - \beta n_2}(n_1 w\mu\{L^d[w/n(w,\ \pi;\ M)] - L^s[w/n(w,\ \pi;\ M)]\} + n_1 w\pi - n\pi). \tag{10b}$$

The steady-state solution for (10a), (10b) is $w = w^*$, $\pi = \pi^* = 0$ and hence $p = p^*$. The local stability of this system of differential equations is analysed by taking the linear terms of a Taylor expansion around the steady state. Noting that at the long-run equilibrium $L^s = L^d$, we can reduce (10a) and (10b) to:

$$\begin{pmatrix} \dot{w} \\ \dot{\pi} \end{pmatrix} = \begin{bmatrix} A(p - wn_1)/p & w(1 - An_2/p) \\ \dfrac{\beta n_1}{p - \beta n_2} A(p - wn_1)/p & \dfrac{\beta}{p - \beta n_2}[-n_1 wAn_2/p - (p - n_1 w)] \end{bmatrix} \begin{bmatrix} w - w^* \\ \pi \end{bmatrix},$$

$$A = \frac{w}{p}\mu(L^{d'} - L^{s'}) < 0. \tag{11}$$

All the elements in the coefficient matrix (call it D) are evaluated at w^*, $\pi^* = 0$ and p^*. Local stability of the Walrasian equilibrium is guaranteed if the real parts of the characteristic roots of D are negative; i.e. if[16]

$$\text{trace of } D = A\,\frac{(p - wn_1)}{p} + \frac{\beta}{p - \beta n_2}\left[-n_1 wA\,\frac{n_2}{p} - (p - n_1 w)\right] < 0, \tag{12a}$$

$$|D| = \frac{-\beta}{p - \beta n_2}\,A(p - n_1 w)\,\frac{1}{p} > 0. \tag{12b}$$

For $L^d(w/p) < L^s(w/p)$, one has $0 < n_1 = \bar{n}_1 < p/w$ (or $0 < \bar{\varepsilon} < 1$) and $n_2 = \bar{n}_2 > 0$. Hence (12b) holds when $\beta < p/n_2$. (12a) will then be satisfied if the lower diagonal element of matrix D is negative or if β is sufficiently small.

For $L^d(w/p) > L^s(w/p)$ sufficient conditions for (12b) to be satisfied are $n_1 = \tilde{n}_1 < p/w$ or $\tilde{\varepsilon} < 1$ and $\beta < p/\tilde{n}_2$; those are also sufficient conditions for (12a) as $n_1 n_2 = \tilde{n}_1 \tilde{n}_2 < 0$.

In the particular case of static expectations where $\pi \equiv 0$ and $\beta = 0$, the stability conditions (12) are reduced to

$$p - wn_1 > 0. \tag{12'}$$

This is always satisfied when $L^d(w/p) < L^s(w/p)$ and will be satisfied when $L^d(w/p) > L^s(w/p)$ if $\tilde{\varepsilon} < 1$. The condition $\tilde{\varepsilon} < 1$ is equivalent to the condition that the downward sloping part of the supply price correspondence is steeper than the demand price curve where it intersects the latter. Indeed, the slope of p^d is given by (2); the downward sloping portion of the supply price function p^s is obtained by solving $f[L^s(w/p)] = y$ implicitly for p which gives $p = p^s(y,\ w)$ with

$$\frac{\partial p}{\partial y} = p_1^s = \frac{-1}{f'L^{s'}(w/p^2)} < 0. \tag{13}$$

Using (2), (7a) and (13) one verifies that $|p_1^s| > |p_1^d|$ if and only if $\bar{\varepsilon} < 1$.

With perfect foresight, the behaviour of the economic system is given by equations (4) and (5).

The linear approximation of (4) and (5) at the long-run equilibrium $(w/p)^*$, p^* is given by (14)

$$\begin{bmatrix} \frac{d}{dt}\left(\frac{w}{p}\right) \\ \dot{p} \end{bmatrix} = \begin{bmatrix} A & 0 \\ C & B \end{bmatrix} \begin{bmatrix} \frac{w}{p} - \left(\frac{w}{p}\right)^* \\ p - p^* \end{bmatrix}, \tag{14}$$

where

$$C = (c_1 + i'g_1 - 1)\frac{f'L^{d'}p}{i'} \text{ when } \frac{w}{p} > \left(\frac{w}{p}\right)^*,$$

and

$$C = (c_1 + i'g_1 - 1)\frac{f'L^{s'}p}{i'} \text{ when } \frac{w}{p} < \left(\frac{w}{p}\right)^*,$$

$$B = -(c_2 + i'g_2)\frac{M}{pi'} > 0.$$

The coefficient matrix of (14) is triangular. Its characteristic roots are therefore given by $A < 0$ and $B > 0$. For any initial value of the money wage, there exists a unique path converging to the long-run equilibrium because the coefficient matrix of (14) has one negative and one positive characteristic root.[17] Geometrically this unique path is a saddle path and the Walrasian full employment equilibrium is a saddle point. If we imposed initial conditions for both w and p the equilibrium would be unstable. The logic of our flexible price, sticky wage model under perfect foresight compels the imposition of an initial condition for w but not for p which is free to adjust instantaneously and discontinuously to any current or future disturbance. Instead of imposing an initial condition for the price level we follow Sargent and Wallace in imposing a terminal condition on the price process. While imposing such a terminal condition does not amount to assuming stability, it does impose some bounds on the behaviour of the expected price level. For our model Sargent and Wallace's terminal condition is sufficient. It can be interpreted as meaning that, if the supply of money is constant over time, people will not expect a process of forever accelerating inflation or deflation.[18] The prima facie unstable saddle point is then stable because we are solving for $p(t)$ going 'backwards' in time.

The solution for the real wage is given by

$$\frac{w(t)}{p(t)} = \left[\frac{w_0}{p(o)} - \left(\frac{w}{p}\right)^*\right] e^{At} + \left(\frac{w}{p}\right)^*,$$

where w_0 denotes the initial and predetermined value of money wage at $t = 0$. The price adjustment equation can now be written as:

$$\dot{p}(t) - Bp(t) = C\left[\frac{w_0}{p(o)} - \left(\frac{w}{p}\right)^*\right] e^{At} - Bp^*.$$

The 'forward' solution[19] of this equation is:

$$p(t) = p^* + ke^{Bt} - C\left\{\frac{[w_0/p(o)] - (w/p)^*}{B - A}\right\} e^{At}.$$

The terminal condition referred to above is $k = 0$ in which case $\lim_{t \to \infty} p(t) = p^*$.

Notes

Originally published in the *Economic Journal*, 87, December 1977, pp. 743–54.

1 There would seem to be little doubt that this is also Keynes' own apparatus. Chapter 2 of *The General Theory* seems quite unambiguous on that point.
2 See Bodkin [1969] for a survey of the econometric literature on this topic.
3 This is not to say that Barro and Grossman's framework does not provide new results. It can explain for instance why unemployment equilibrium (under a fixed price vector) can be associated with a real wage which is at or below the Walrasian one.
4 Cf. Clower [1965], Leijonhufvud [1968] and Barro and Grossman, *op. cit.*
5 We assume no real wealth effect in the labour supply function.
6 There is of course an associated equilibrium level for the interest rate.
7 Note that for any money wage $\bar{w}$, there exists a price $\bar{p}$ such that $\bar{w}/\bar{p} = (w/p)^*$ and the output supplied is y^*. The upward and downward sloping parts of the supply price correspondence are obtained respectively by solving for p as a function of y the equations $y = f[L^d(\bar{w}/p)]$ (for $(\bar{w}/p) > (w/p)^*$) and $y = f[L^s(\bar{w}/p)]$ for $(\bar{w}/p) < (w/p)^*$).
8 We rule out the cases of no short-run equilibria (the demand price schedule lies everywhere above the downward sloping part of the supply price correspondence) and of more than two equilibria (the demand price schedule intersects the downward sloping part of the supply price correspondence more than once).
9 If the supply of labour were inelastic with respect to the real wage (a vertical supply curve in Fig. 1) the downward sloping segment of the supply price correspondence would be replaced by a vertical segment above C.
10 Barro and Grossman's framework would of course better describe war-time periods characterised by strict wage and price controls and widespread rationing, and the suppressed inflation characteristic of centrally planned economies.
11 See Barro and Grossman [1971], p. 87.
12 For a more realistic account of this phenomenon see Lorie [1978].

13 Note that (a) and (b) are sufficient but not necessary conditions for local stability.
14 See Appendix.
15 See Sargent and Wallace [1973], p. 1045.
16 See Gantmacher [1959].
17 See Sargent and Wallace [1973] and Calvo [1975].
18 See Sargent and Wallace [1973], p. 1045.
19 The first-order linear differential equation: $\dot{y} + q(t)y = g(t)$ can be solved in two ways. The 'backward' solution is:

$$y(t) = \frac{1}{m(t)}\left[\int^{t} m(s)\, g(s)\, ds + c\right],$$

where

$$m(t) = \exp\left[\int^{t} q(z)\, dz\right]$$

and c is determined by an initial condition. The 'forward' solution is:

$$y(t) = -\frac{1}{m(t)}\left[\int_{t} m(s)\, g(s)\, ds + c\right],$$

where

$$m(t) = \exp\left[-\int_{t} q(z)\, dz\right]$$

and c is determined by a terminal condition.

References

Barro, R. J. and Grossman, H. I. (1971), 'A General Disequilibrium Model of Income and Employment.' *American Economic Review*, Vol. 61 (March), pp. 82–93.

—— and —— (1974), 'Suppressed Inflation and the Supply Multiplier.' *Review of Economic Studies*, Vol. 41 (January), pp. 87–104.

Bodkin, R. G. (1969), 'Real Wages and Cyclical Variations in Employment.' *Canadian Journal of Economics*, Vol. 2 (August), pp. 353–74.

Calvo, G. A. (1975), 'On Models of Money and Perfect Foresight.' The Economic Workshops Columbia University, no 75–7615.

Clower, R. W. (1965), The Keynesian Counter-revolution: A Theoretical Appraisal.' In *The Theory of Interest Rates* (ed. F. H. Hahn and F. Brechling). London: Macmillan.

Gantmacher, F. R. (1959), *The Theory of Matrices*, Vol. 11. New York: Chelsea Publishing Co.

Keynes, J. M. (1936), *The General Theory of Employment, Interest, and Money*. New York: Macmillan.

Leijonhufvud, A. (1968), *On Keynesian Economics and the Economic of Keynes*. New York: Oxford.

Lorie, H. (1978), 'Price-Quantity Adjustment in a Macro-Disequilibrium Model.' *Economic Inquiry* (forthcoming).

Sargent, T. J. and Wallace, N. (1973), 'The Stability of Money and Growth with Perfect Foresight.' *Eonometrica*, Vol. 41 (November), pp. 1043–8.

Chapter 16

Walras' law and all that: budget constraints and balance sheet constraints in period models and continuous time models

I Introduction

This paper aims to resolve two interrelated sets of problems in the modeling of dynamic economic systems: stock-flow problems and continuous time-discrete time problems. The main stock-flow problem concerns the choice between two specifications of asset market equilibrium in discrete-time or period models. The two contenders are beginning-of-period equilibrium, an instantaneous portfolio.equilibrium, and end-of-period equilibrium, which allows both initial stocks and current flows to contribute to current period market supply and views asset demand as planned carry-over to the next period.[1] Four aspects of this choice of specification are considered. When are the two equivalent? Is the beginning-of-period specification characterized both by a balance sheet constraint for the instantaneous stock excess demands in asset markets and by Walras' Law, a budget constraint that applies to (flow) excess demands in all markets? Can the saving and the portfolio allocation decision be separated and treated independently in the beginning-of-period model? What are the limiting properties of the two specifications as the length of the unit period goes to zero? This last question brings us to the second set of issues. A careful consideration of the 'time structure' of asset demand functions shows that there are many different 'unit-periods'. This chapter distinguishes three: the market period (the interval between successive market openings), the forecast interval and the delivery interval (the maturity of the forward contract). To these different unit periods correspond different ways of constructing limiting processes that turn the discrete-time model into a continuous-time model.

The chapter presents the correct financial constraints faced by different economic agents in sequential temporary or momentary equilibrium models. A novel interpretation of the distinction between beginning-of-period and end-of-period models in terms of incomplete spot and forward markets for assets is proposed. The correct derivation of continuous time – or more precisely, continuous decision-making – analogues of discrete time models is given. A new view is offered on the separation of the saving decision and the portfolio allocation decision in beginning-of-period models. The analysis also brings out an unfamiliar condition for Walras' Law of markets to be obtainable from the summation of individual budget constraints. A small macroeconomic model is used to illustrate the various points made in the paper. The analysis constitutes a natural extension of earlier work in this area by May [1970], Chand [1973], Foley [1975], Buiter [1975], Burmeister and Turnovsky [1976], Turnovsky [1977], Turnovsky and Burmeister [1977], and Buiter and Woglom [1977].

II The model

There is a uniform market period of length h for all goods, services and financial claims. The market period, or 'Hicksian week', is the time interval for which prices are constant. For simplicity this market period is also assumed to have the same length as the unit periods for all other economic activities (the period of production, the period for which expectations remain constant, etc.). At the beginning of each period, prices are determined that clear the markets for goods, services and financial claims during that period. In the end-of-period model, asset markets can be viewed as one-period forward markets. There exist no instantaneous spot markets for financial claims. Asset demands and supplies refer to stocks to be delivered at the end of the period (the beginning of the next period). In the beginning-of-period model, asset markets are instantaneous spot markets. There are no one-period forward markets. Asset demands and supplies refer to asset stocks to be delivered to and held by the buyer at the same moment that the exchange is agreed upon. Only initial asset holdings can be reallocated. Current income flows are not included in the resources that households can spend in beginning-of-period asset markets and current asset flows do not constitute part of market supply. Both can be viewed as special cases of a general model in which there exists, each period, a complete set of spot and forward markets. This interpretation is to some extent implicit in Foley [1975] but has not before been stated explicitly. There is one financial claim,[2] equity, the ownership claim to the residual income of corporations. There is one commodity which can be used as a private consumption good or as a private investment good. Finally there are labor services.

There are two sectors, the household sector and the business sector. Households own all financial claims. They do not hold real capital directly in their portfolios. They consume output bought from the business sector, sell labor services to the business sector and, as owners of the firms' equity, receive the excess of the value of current sales over wage outlays as dividends. There are no retained profits.[3] Firms organize production. They are the custodians of the stock of capital. They hire labor services and sell output to households (as private consumption), and to themselves (as investment). Any excess of current outlays over receipts from sales is financed by issuing equity.

Notation:

E^d	number of shares of equity demanded
E^s	number of shares of equity supplied
$E(t)$	number of shares of equity in existence at the beginning of period t
$N^d(h, t)$	demand for labour during period t
$N^s(h, t)$	supply of labour during period t
$N(h, t)$	amount of labour employed during period t
$C^d(h, t)$	consumption demand during period t
$C(h, t)$	actual consumption during period t
$Q^s(h, t)$	supply of output from new production during period t
$Q(h, t)$	actual production during period t
$\Pi^H(h, t)$	real value of dividends expected by households during period t
$\Pi^f(h, t)$	real value of dividends firms plan to pay out during period t
$\Pi(h, t)$	real value of dividends paid out during period t
$I^d(h, t)$	investment demand during period t
$I(d, t)$	actual investment during period t
p_E	price of equity in terms of output
p_E^*	expected price of equity
w	real product wage

Output is non-durable. The only capital is circulating capital with a period of circulation equal to h. All functions are assumed to be twice continuously differentiable.[4]

III The 'time structure' of asset demand functions, price functions and price expectations functions

In the literature on this subject, asset demand functions have been specified with one time argument (Foley [1975]) or two time arguments (Buiter and Woglom [1977], Turnovsky [1977], Burmeister and Turnovsky [1977]). It is argued here that time enters into fully specified asset demand functions (and supply functions) in four ways. The complete specification of the 'time structure' of the equity demand function, E^d is:

$$E^d = E^d(t - \Delta t_3, t, t + \Delta t_1, \Delta t_2) \qquad \Delta t_1, \Delta t_2, \Delta t_3 \geq 0. \tag{1}$$

Equation (1) describes the amount (number of shares) of equity an economic agent plans, at time $t - \Delta t_3$, to demand at time t (in the market that will open in period t), for delivery at time $t + \Delta t_1$, when the length of the interval between successive markets is Δt_2. Δt_1 will be a non-negative integer multiple of Δt_2. In the end-of-period model $\Delta t_1 = \Delta t_2 = h$, and we only need consider the case where $\Delta t_3 = 0$. Thus, end-of-period asset demand functions have the time structure of E^d in (2).

$$E^d(t, t, t + h, h). \tag{2}$$

In the beginning-of-period model, $\Delta t_1 = 0$ and $\Delta t_2 = h$. We need to consider both the case where $\Delta t_3 = 0$ and where $\Delta t_3 = h$. Thus end-of-period asset demand functions have the time structure of E^d in (3a) and (3b).

$$E^d(t, t, t, h) \tag{3a}$$

$$E^d(t, t + h, t + h, h). \tag{3b}$$

The distinction between planning time, $t - \Delta t_3$, and market time, t, is essential for the analysis of saving in the beginning-of-period model (Section 6). Δt_2 needs to be considered explicitly because a basic feature of the model is altered when markets open more frequently (Hellwig [1975]). A greater frequency of market openings means that new information can be incorporated into market prices sooner. Economic agents are committed to portfolio composition choices for a shorter period of time; they can implement changes in plans, due to changes in tastes, information or endowments, with less delay. Underlying a finite trading interval are transactions costs or indivisibilities of assets. Continuous trading in assets, i.e., the ability to reshuffle portfolios at any moment, only makes sense if transactions costs and indivisibilities are absent.

The time structure of actual asset prices requires three arguments. (4) gives the price at time t, for a share of equity to be delivered at time $t + \Delta t_1$ when the length of the interval between successive markets is Δt_2.

$$p_E(t, t + \Delta t_1, \Delta t_2) \tag{4}$$

In the end-of-period model (4) becomes:

$$p_E(t, t + h, h) \tag{5}$$

In the beginning-of-period model (4) reduces to:

$$p_E(t, t, h) \tag{6}$$

Anticipated prices have the same time structure as the asset demand functions.[5] The price expected, at time $t - \Delta t_3$, to prevail in the market at time t, for a share of equity to be delivered at time $t + \Delta t_1$, when the length of the market period is Δt_2.

$$p_E^*(t - \Delta t_3, t, t + \Delta t_1, \Delta t_2)^6 \tag{7}$$

The price expectations relevant to the end-of-period model are given in (8a) and (8b).

$$p_E^*(t, t, t + h, h) \quad (8a)$$

$$p_E^*(t, t + h, t + 2h, h) \quad (8b)$$

The beginning-of-period model's price expectations are given in (9a) and (9b).

$$p_E^*(t, t, t, h) \quad (9a)$$

$$p_E^*(t, t + h, t + h, h) \quad (9b)$$

In the simple model used in the rest of this paper, we assume that expectations about current prices are correct. Thus, in the end-of-period model:

$$p_E^*(t, t, t + h, h) = p_E(t, t + h, h) \quad (10a)$$

and in the beginning-of-period model:

$$p_E^*(t, t, t, h) = p_E(t, t, h) \quad (10b)$$

IV An end-of-period model

The discrete time version of the end-of-period model

The ex-ante budget constraint is the consistency requirement equating the value of all planned uses of funds with the value of all expected sources of funds. For the household sector this is:

$$\begin{aligned} &p_E(t, t + h, h)E(t) + w(t, t, h)N^s(h, t) + \Pi^H(h, t) \\ &\quad \equiv p_E(t, t + h, h)E^d(t, t, t + h, h) + C^d(h, t) \end{aligned} \quad (11)$$

Instead of assuming the income flow to be fixed and known, as in Turnovsky [1977], it is broken down into expected income from employment, wN^s, and expected dividend receipts, Π^H. The budget constraint should include the net planned purchases or sales of equity during period t, $E^d(t, t, t + h, h) - E(t)$ valued at the price that actually prevails during period t, i.e., $p_E(t, t + h, h)$. In Turnovsky's analysis, however, planned equity sales are not evaluated at the price at which the transactions are made, but the price expected at t, to prevail at $t + h$, $p_E^*(t, t + h, t + 2h, h)$.

Asset demands are *real* demands, i.e., demands for a certain amount of purchasing power over consumable commodities. The relevant prices for translating real end-of-period asset demands into nominal asset demands are next period's expected prices. Let $j(t, t, t + h, h)$ be the real end-of-period demand for equity. Then:

$$E^d(t, t, t+h, h) = \frac{j(t, t, t+h, h)}{p_E^*(t, t+h, t+2h, h)} \tag{12}$$

The ex-post household budget constraint or flow of funds identity is obtained by replacing all ex-ante (planned or expected) variables in (11) by their realized values.

$$\begin{aligned} &p_E(t, t+h, h)E(t) + w(t, t, h)N(h, t) + \Pi(h, t) \\ &\quad \equiv p_E(t, t+h, h)E(t+h) + C(h, t) \end{aligned} \tag{11'}$$

The ex-ante budget constraint of the business sector is:

$$\begin{aligned} &Q^s(h, t) + p_E(t, t+h, h)[E^s(t, t, t+h, h) - E(t)] \\ &\quad \equiv w(t, t, h)N^d(h, t) + \Pi^f(h, t) + I^d(h, t) \end{aligned} \tag{13}$$

The ex-post flow of funds identity of the business sector is:

$$\begin{aligned} &Q(h, t) + p_E(t, t+h, h)[E(t+h) - E(t)] \\ &\quad \equiv w(t, t, h)N(h, t) + \Pi(h, t) + I(h, t) \end{aligned}$$

Summing the ex-ante budget constraints of the two sectors and rearranging terms we obtain:

$$\begin{aligned} &p_E(t, t+h, h)[E^s(t, t, t+h, h) - E^d(t, t, t+h, h)] \\ &\quad + w(t, t, h)[N^s(h, t) - N^d(h, t)] + Q^s(h, t) - C^d(h, t) - I^d(h, t) \\ &\quad \equiv \Pi^f(h, t) - \Pi^H(h, t) \end{aligned} \tag{14}$$

The market equilibrium conditions for this three good economy are:

$$E^s(t, t, t+h, h) = E^d(t, t, t+h, h) \qquad (= E(t+h)) \tag{15a}$$

$$N^s(h, t) = N^d(h, t) \qquad (= N(h, t)) \tag{15b}$$

$$Q^s(h, t) = C^d(h, t) + I^d(h, t) \qquad (Q^s = Q,\ C^d = C,\ I^d = I). \tag{15c}$$

The sum of the values of the excess demands for all goods, $X(h, t)$ is

$$\begin{aligned} X(h, t) &\equiv p_E(t, t+h, h)[E^s(t, t, t+h, h) - E^d(t, t, t+h, h)] \\ &\quad + w(t, t, h)[N^s(h, t) - N^d(h, t)] + [Q^s(h, t) - C^d(h, t) - I^d(h, t)] \end{aligned} \tag{16}$$

Walras' Law of Markets is the proposition that $X(h, t) \equiv 0$. From (14) and (16) we see that this is only implied by the sectoral budget constraints if $\Pi^f - \Pi^H \equiv 0$. The dividends households expect to receive from firms must equal the dividends firms plan to pay out. Thus homogeneous expectations with respect to non-market variables entering the budget constraints of several economic agents during the current period, will in general be required to ensure that Walras' Law holds.[7] Because income is often treated as predetermined, this aspect of the relationship between ex-ante individual budget constraints and Walras' Law has not become evident in the rest of the literature (e.g., Turnovsky [1977]). In conventional Arrow-Debreu general equilibrium analysis identical profit terms are always entered into both household and firm budget constraints, without any justification.[8] Note that, for every market transaction, the price at which the buyer plans to purchase and the price at which the seller plans to sell should also be the same (after allowing for transactions costs and indirect taxes or subsidies). If this is not the case, excess demands and supplies for the same good can not be summed using a single price and Walras' Law has no meaning. Dividends extend to non-market transactions this requirement of homogeneous expectations of current period prices. In the rest of this paper all economic agents are assumed to have homogeneous expectations of both current and future variables.

The continuous trading version of the end-of-period model

The primitive flow variables of the model are N^d, N^s, N, C^d, C, Q^s, Q, Π^H, Π^f, Π, I^d and I. For any flow variable $Z(h, t)$ we define: $Z(h, t) \equiv \int_t^{t-h} z(\tau, h, t)d\tau$. From the fundamental theorem of the calculus we have: $\lim_{h\to 0} Z(h, t)/h = z(t, 0, t) = z(t)$. It is also clear that $\lim_{h\to 0} Z(h, t) = 0$.

When we let h go to zero, we obtain from the household budget constraint (11):

$$p_E(t, t, 0)E(t) \equiv p_E(t, t, 0)E^d(t, t, t, 0). \tag{17}$$

When the length of the delivery period is zero and successive market periods are arbitrarily close together, the value of the asset stocks one plans to carry over into the next period is constrained to be equal to the value of the endowment of assets at the beginning of the period. (17) is the household sector balance sheet constraint.[9] Combining (11) and (17), rearranging terms, dividing by h and taking the limit as $h \to 0$ yields:

$$\begin{aligned} &p_E(t, t, 0)[E_3^d(t, t, t, 0) + E_4^d(t, t, t, 0)] \\ &\quad + [p_{E,2}(t, t, 0) + p_{E,3}(t, t, 0)][E^d(t, t, t, 0) - E(t)] \\ &\quad \equiv w(t, t, 0)n^s(t) + \pi^H(t) - c^d(t) \end{aligned} \tag{18}$$

When h changes one effect is that the length of the delivery period changes. This is captured by the third partial derivative of the asset demand function E_3^d. The fourth partial derivative of an asset demand function shows how, keeping everything else constant, asset demand expressed at time t for the asset to be held at some fixed future date will vary when markets open more or less frequently. For any given frequency of market opening, including the limiting case when $\Delta t_2 = 0$ and markets open continuously, $E_4^d(t, t, t, \Delta t_2)$ measures how equity demand is altered when this frequency changes. Thus even $E_4^d(t, t, t, 0)$ (interpreted now as a *right-hand* partial derivative because $\Delta t_2 \geq 0$) is an integral part of a full description of asset accumulation behavior. The rate at which the demand for equity to be delivered at some given future date changes as one gets closer to that date is given by $E_1^d + E_2^d$. The rate of change of the demand for equity is given by $dE^d/dt = E_1^d + E_2^d + E_3^d$. Earlier studies have derived continuous time budget constraints from discrete end-of-period models that involved terms equivalent to our E_3^d. The fourth partial derivatives of the asset demand functions have been ignored uniformly. Similarly, no author has included terms like $[p_{E,2}(t, t, 0) + p_{E,3}(t, t, 0)][E^d(t, t, 0) - E(t)]$. The term $(p_{E,2} + p_{E,3})(E^d - E)$ will vanish if households are always in portfolio equilibrium. If that is not the case, and there are net instantaneous planned sales or purchases of equity, one has to allow in the budget constraint for the fact that the price of equity may vary when h varies. It should be noted that the single household budget constraint in the discrete time case (equation (11)) generates both a balance sheet constraint (17) and a flow budget constraint (18) in the continuous time case. This confirms earlier results by May [1970], and Chand [1973].

The ex-post flow of funds identity for the household sector in continuous time is: $p_E(t, t, 0)\dot{E}(t) \equiv w(t, t, 0)n(t) + \pi(t) - c(t)$. We also obtain a balance sheet constraint and a flow of funds constraint for the business sector (using (13)).

$$E^s(t, t, t, 0) = E(t) \tag{19}$$

$$\begin{aligned} -p_E(t, t, 0)[E_3^s(t, t, t, 0) + E_4^s(t, t, t, 0)] \\ \equiv -w(t, t, 0)n^d(t) - \pi^f(t) - i^d(t) + q^s(t) \end{aligned} \tag{20}$$

The ex-post flow of funds identity for the corporate sector is:

$$-p_E(t, t, 0)E(t) \equiv -w(t, t, 0)n(t) - \pi(t) - i(t) + q(t)$$

Aggregating over the two sectors we obtain the economy-wide balance sheet constraint and flow budget constraint.

$$p_E(t, t, t, 0)[E^s(t, t, t, 0) - E^d(t, t, t, 0)] \equiv 0 \tag{21}$$

$$\begin{aligned} p_E(t, t, 0)[E_3^d(t, t, t, 0) + E_4^d(t, t, t, 0) - E_3^s(t, t, t, 0) - E_4^s(t, t, t, 0)] \\ + [p_{E,2}(t, \mathrm{t}, 0) + p_{E,3}(t, t, 0)][E^d(t, t, t, 0) - E(t)] \\ + w(t, t, 0)[n^d(t) - n^s(t)] + c^d(t) + i^d(t) - q^s(t) \equiv \pi^H(t) - \pi^f(t) \end{aligned} \tag{22}$$

With homogeneous expectations, the r.h.s. of (22) is zero and the continuous time analogue of Walras' Law holds. The continuous time market clearing equations are:

$$E^s(t, t, t, 0) = E^d(t, t, t, 0) \qquad (= E(t)) \tag{23a}$$

$$n^s(t) = n^d(t) \qquad (= n(t)) \tag{23b}$$

$$q^s(t) = c^d(t) + i^d(t) \qquad (q^s = q,\ c^d = c,\ i^d = i). \tag{23c}$$

V Saving, wealth and disposable income

The preceding analysis did not make use of the concepts of saving, actual and target wealth (or net worth) and disposable income. It was conducted in terms of 'primitive' concepts such as asset demand and supply functions and asset endowments. 'Derived' concepts such as saving, net worth and disposable income are useful only to the extent that they permit the information contained in the balance sheet and flow of funds constraints to be presented in a more familiar or economical manner.

An implication of the end-of-period model is that the decision on how much additional wealth to carry over to the next period and the decision on how to allocate this planned increase in wealth over the entire menu of assets in the portfolio are inextricably intertwined.

Let $Y(h, t)$ denote expected real disposable income during period t, $\bar{Y}(h, t)$ realized real disposable income, $S(h, t)$ real planned personal saving during period t and $\bar{S}(h, t)$ real realized personal saving. Following the national income accounting conventions we have:

$$Y(h, t) \equiv C^d(h, t) + S(h, t) \tag{24}$$

$$\bar{Y}(h, t) \equiv C(h, t) + \bar{S}(h, t) \tag{25}$$

In our model, planned personal saving equals the real value of net planned purchases of financial claims, i.e., of equity.

$$S(h, t) \equiv p_E(t, t + h, h)[E^d(t, t, t + h, h) - E(t)] \tag{26}$$

or, using the real asset demand function (12):

$$S(h, t) \equiv p_E(t, t + h, h)\left[\frac{j(t, t, t + h, h)}{p_E^*(t, t + h, t + 2h, h)} - E(t)\right]. \tag{27}$$

From (24), (26) and (11) it then follows that

$$Y(h, t) \equiv w(t, t, h)N^s(h, t) + \Pi^H(h, t) \tag{28a}$$

Realized disposable income can then easily be seen to be:

$$\bar{Y}(h, t) \equiv w(t, t, h)N(h, t) + \Pi(h, t) \tag{28b}$$

Realized saving is: $\bar{S}(h, t) \equiv p_E(t, t + h, h)[E(t + h) - E(t)]$. The planned increase in real wealth is the sum of real planned saving and expected capital gains or losses on assets to be carried over to the next period, i.e., on $E^d(t, t, t + h, h)$. Capital gains or losses are incurred on initial stocks and on current asset flows. Let $A^d(t, t + h, h)$ denote the real wealth households, at time t, plan to hold at time $t + h$, when the length of the interval between market periods is h. $A(t)$ denotes real household wealth at the beginning of period t.

$$A(t) \equiv p_E(t, t + h, h)E(t) \tag{29}$$

$$A^d(t, t + h, h) \equiv j(t, t, t + h, h) \tag{30}$$

Thus the planned increase in real wealth is

$$A^d(t, t + h, h) - A(t) \equiv S(h, t) + \left[\frac{p_E^*(t, t + h, t + 2h, h) - p_E(t, t + h, h)}{p_E^*(t, t + h, t + 2h, h)}\right] j(t, t, t + h, h). \quad (31)$$

Ex-post the actual change in real wealth is given by:

$$A(t + h) - A(t) \equiv E(t + h)p_E(t + h, t + 2h, h) - E(t)p_E(t, t + h, h) \equiv \bar{S}(h, t) + [p_E(t + h, t + 2h, h) - p_E(t, t + h, h)]E(t + h)$$

We can obtain the continuous trading version of equations (24)–(31) through the same kind of limiting process used before. We now also require the assumption of equations (10a) and (10b) that the expectation of a current period price is the actual price. In the limit as $h \to 0$ we get:

$$y(t) \equiv c^d(t) + s(t) \quad (32)$$

$$\bar{y}(t) \equiv c(t) + \bar{s}(t) \quad (33)$$

$$s(t) \equiv j_3(t, t, t, 0) + j_4(t, t, t, 0) - [p_{E,2}^* + 2p_{E,3}^* + p_{E,4}^*] \frac{j(t, t, t, 0)}{p_E(t, t, 0)} + [p_{E,2}(t, t, 0) + p_{E,3}(t, t, 0)]\left[\frac{j(t, t, t, 0)}{p_E(t, t, 0)} - E(t)\right].^{10} \quad (34)$$

VI A beginning-of-period model

In the discrete time beginning-of-period model, contracts are made at time t for instantaneous delivery of asset stocks. This has been interpreted as implying that decisions on how much to add to one's wealth during period $t - t + h$, are taken without regard for the asset composition of this net increase or decrease in wealth. In this section I show that in the beginning-of-period model too, all sectors have to satisfy an ex-ante consistency requirement relating planned changes in asset holdings, expected income flows and planned consumption. The planned future holding of an asset is not represented by current-period market demand for future delivery, but by planned future spot asset demand. Rather than facing a *market* budget constraint, as in the end-of-period model, household current and planned future spot transactions have to satisfy an *internal* or 'psychological' consistency requirement. Earlier work in this area which did not differentiate between planning date and market date could not provide a satisfactory account of saving behavior in the beginning-of-period model.

The first consistency requirement for the household sector in the beginning-of-period model is that the balance sheet constraint be satisfied: current period flows of income and expenditure do not add to or diminish the asset stocks that are to be priced and allocated in the instantaneous asset markets.[11] With only one asset in the model, the balance sheet constraint is rather trivial:

$$p_E(t, t, h)E(t) \equiv p_E(t, t, h)E^d(t, t, t, h) \tag{35}$$

The 'psychological' budget constraint or consistent planning requirement is:

$$\begin{aligned} p_E^*(t, t+h, t+h, h)E^d(t, t, t, h) + w(t, t, h)N^s(h, t) + \Pi^H(h, t) \\ \equiv p_E^*(t, t+h, t+h, h)E^d(t, t+h, t+h, h) + C^d(h, t). \end{aligned} \tag{36}$$

Note that $E^d(t, t+h, t+h, h)$, etc., is not a *market* demand. It represents the plans at time t for purchases of equity in the spot market at $t+h$ at the spot price expected to rule at $t+h$. With perfect foresight we have $E^d(t, t+h, t+h, h) \equiv E^d(t+h, t+h, t+h, h)$. The ex-post budget constraint for the household sector is:

$$\begin{aligned} p_E(t+h, t+h, h)E(t) + w(t, t, h)N(h, t) + \Pi(h, t) \\ \equiv p_E(t+h, t+h, h)E(t+h) + C(h, t). \end{aligned} \tag{36'}$$

This is only the same as the ex-post budget constraint of the end-of-period (11′) model if $p_E(t+h, t+h, h) = p_E(t, t+h, h)$: today's one-period forward price of equity in the end-of-period model must equal the spot price of equity next period in the beginning-of-period model.

The ex-ante and ex-post balance sheet constraint and 'psychological' budget constraint for the business sector are given below, together with the economy-wide constraints.

The business sector:

$$E^s(t, t, t, h) - E(t) \equiv 0 \tag{37}$$

$$\begin{aligned} Q^s(h, t) + p_E^*(t, t+h, t+h, h)[E^s(t, t+h, t+h, h) - E^s(t, t, t, h)] \\ \equiv w(t, t, h)N^d(h, t) + \Pi^f(h, t) + I^d(h, t). \end{aligned} \tag{38}$$

$$\begin{aligned} Q(h, t) + p_E(t+h, t+h, h)[E(t+h) - E(t)] \\ \equiv w(t, t, h)N(h, t) + \Pi(h, t) + I(h, t). \end{aligned} \tag{38'}$$

The whole economy:

$$p_E(t, t, h)[E^s(t, t, t, h) - E^d(t, t, t, h)] \equiv 0 \tag{39}$$

$$\begin{aligned} p_E^*(t, t+h, t+h, h)(E^s(t, t+h, t+h, h) - E^s(t, t, t, h) \\ -[E^d(t, t+h, t+h, h) - E^d(t, t, t, h)]) + w(t, t, h)[N^s(h, t) \\ - N^d(h,t)] + Q^s(h,t) - C^d(h,t) - I^d(h,t) \equiv \Pi^f(h,t) - \Pi^H(h,t). \end{aligned} \tag{40}$$

Something fairly close to Walras' Law is implied by (40) and the assumption of homogeneous expectations about dividends. Defining planned household saving $\tilde{S}$ as in equation (41) below, we preserve the national income identity that $\tilde{S} \equiv Y - C^d$.

$$\tilde{S}(h, t) \equiv p_E^*(t, t + h, t + h, h)[E^d(t, t + h, t + h, h) - E^d(t, t, t, h)]. \tag{41}$$

This expression differs from the end-of-period version given in equation (26) in that non-existent forward contracts and forward prices have been replaced by planned future spot contracts and expected future spot prices. Thus in the beginning-of-period model too the saving decision is completely determined as soon as the full time structures of the asset demand functions and expectations functions are given.[12]

The continuous trading case of the beginning-of-period model
When we take the limit as $h \to 0$ of (35) we obtain:

$$p_E(t, t, 0)E(t) \equiv p_E(t, t, 0)E^d(t, t, t, 0). \tag{42}$$

Subtracting (42) from (35), dividing by h and taking the limit as $h \to 0$ yields

$$p_E(t, t, 0)E_4^d(t, t, t, 0) + p_{E,3}(t, t, 0)[E^d(t, t, t, 0) - E(t)] \equiv 0. \tag{43}$$

The rate at which household demand for equity changes when the length of the interval between markets increases ($E_4^d p_E$) must be zero when households are in instantaneous portfolio equilibrium $[E^d(t, t, t, 0) = E(t)]$. A change in the market frequency will not change the 'physical' endowment, $E(t)$, at a point in time. It will, however, by changing p_E, alter the value of the endowment. This has to be matched by $p_E E_4^d$, unless asset endowments and instantaneous asset demands coincide, in which case both would be equally affected by the change in p_E. No condition like (43) holds for the continuous time version of the end-of-period model. Putting (35) and (36) together we obtain in the limit as $h \to 0$:

$$\begin{aligned} &p_E(t, t, 0)[E_2^d(t, t, t, 0) + E_3^d(t, t, t, 0)] \\ &\quad \equiv w(t, t, 0)n^s(t) + \pi^H(t) - c^d(t).^{13} \end{aligned} \tag{44}$$

Balance sheet constraints and 'psychological' budget constraints for the business sector and the economy as a whole are omitted for reasons of space.

Compare the continuous trading balance sheet constraints and flow budget constraints of the end-of-period and the beginning-of-period model. (17) and (42) are the same. (18) and (44) are equivalent if markets clear i.e., $E^d(t, t, t, 0) = E(t)$ and if $p_E(t, t, 0)E_2^d(t, t, t, 0) \equiv 0$.[14] Asset demands for delivery at some fixed future date do not vary when the market date is varied. This 'irrelevance of the market date' requirement will be satisfied if transactions costs are not dependent on the market date and if there is perfect foresight. Together these two sufficient conditions for equivalence can be referred to as the *perfect foresight* and *perfect market requirement*. This analysis can be repeated for the other sectors and for the economy as a whole. Thus, when we consider only the physical but not the real asset demand functions, it would appear that the continuous trading versions of the beginning-of-period model and the end-of-period model are equivalent if markets clear and the market date is irrelevant, or more suggestively although rather less precisely, if there are perfect markets and perfect foresight. Under these conditions, the beginning-of-period continuous time saving rate $\tilde{s}(t)$ will also be equivalent to the end-of-period continuous time saving rate $s(t)$. This equivalence result applies not only in the limit, as $h \to 0$, but also for finite h.

What do these equivalence conditions imply for the real demand and supply functions? Equivalence of beginning- and end-of-period models requires in discrete time:

$$\begin{aligned} E^d(t, t, t + h, h) &= E^d(t, t + h, t + h, h) = E(t + h) \\ &= E^s(t, t, t + h, h) = E^s(t, t + h, t + h, h). \end{aligned} \tag{45}$$

Substituting in (45) the real end-of-period demand and supply functions given in (12) and the real beginning-of-period functions defined in (46a) and (46b) we obtain (47).

$$E^d(t, t, t, h) = \frac{j(t, t, t, h)}{p_E^*(t, t, t, h)} = \frac{j(t, t, t, h)}{p_E(t, t, h)} \tag{46a}$$

$$E^d(t, t + h, t + h, h) = \frac{j(t, t + h, t + h, h)}{p_E^*(t, t + h, t + h, h)} \tag{46b}$$

$$\frac{j(t, t, t + h, h)}{p_E^*(t, t + h, t + 2h, h)} = \frac{j(t, t + h, t + h, h)}{p_E^*(t, t + h, t + h, h)}. \tag{47}$$

Equation (47) suggests the following sufficient condition for equivalence. *Real* one-period forward demand equals real planned spot demand one period hence ($j(t, t, t + h, h) = j(t, t + h, t + h, h)$) and the one-period forward price of equity expected, at t, to prevail in the market at $t + h$, equals the spot price of equity expected, at t, to prevail in the market at $t + h$, ($p_E^*(t, t + h, t + 2h, h) = p_E^*(t, t + h, t + h, h)$). This second condition amounts to a high degree of stationarity in expectations and, if expectations are correct, also in the actual economy. In a stationary economy expected (and actual) spot prices are equal to expected (and actual) forward prices. Outside the stationary state, the beginning-of-period and end-of-period specifications will not in general be equivalent.

VII **Conclusion**

This chapter considers the many ways in which time enters into sequential temporary equilibrium models.[15] The minimal representation of the time structure of asset demand functions and price expectation functions requires four dimensions: the date at which plans are made (expectations are formed); the market date to which plans (expectations) refer; the maturity of the forward contracts concluded in the market, i.e., the 'delivery period' and the interval between market openings.

Beginning-of-period and end-of-period models make different assumptions about the existence of spot markets and forward markets for assets. They are not in general equivalent. A sufficient condition for equivalence is the existence of perfect markets in a stationary economy. The saving decision and the portfolio allocation decision cannot even conceptually be separated in the end-of-period model. In the beginning-of-period model, too, a complete specification of the time structure of asset demand and expectations functions fully determines the saving decision. In both models the standard national income and flow of funds accounting concepts of saving, wealth accumulation and disposable income can be identified naturally.[16]

By not treating income as predetermined, an unfamiliar necessary condition for the aggregation of ex-ante individual, or sectoral, budget constraints to imply Walras' Law is brought out: expectations concerning current period non-market transfers (such as the distribution of profits) must be identical for all agents involved in a given transaction.

The result of May [1970] that the single ex-ante budget constraint of the discrete time end-of-period model decomposes in continuous time into a balance sheet constraint and a flow budget constraint is confirmed. Both the end-of-period and the beginning-of-period model have well-defined limiting forms under fairly mild restrictions.

Further research is required into the role of the frequency of market openings. That frequency itself is to be viewed as the outcome of individual or collective optimizing behavior rather than as a non-economic institutional datum. When we considered the limiting properties of the end-of-period model as h went to zero, both the maturity of the forward contracts and the interval between market openings went to zero. Future research should consider the case in which continuous trading in spot and forward markets occurs but in which forward contracts retain a finite maturity.

Notes

Originally published in the *International Economic Review*, 21, February 1980, pp. 1–16.

1 The terminology is due to Foley [1975]. The substantive issue goes back at least to Keynes [1937] and Ohlin [1937] in the liquidity preference versus loanable funds debate.

2 An earlier draft of the chapter had three financial claims: equity, government fiat money and government bonds. To improve readability and simplify notation the public sector has been omitted altogether in this version.

3 If government bonds were held by the household sector, debt service income and taxes would constitute additional sources and uses of household income.
4 This is stronger than the minimum conditions required for the limiting processes in Sections IV, V and VI. It permits us to concentrate on the economic interpretation of our analysis rather than on mathematical niceties.
5 Price expectations are single-valued.
6 Δt_3 in (7) need not be the same as in (1). For simplicity this is ignored in what follows.
7 If there is a public sector and households anticipate net tax payments T^H while the government anticipates net tax receipts T^g, Walras' Law requires $\Pi^f - \Pi^H + T^H - T^g \equiv 0$. See Buiter [1977].
8 Taxes and transfers tend to be ignored altogether.
9 With only one asset in the model, the balance sheet constraint is rather trivial. For a treatment of a money-bond-equity model see Buiter [1977].
10 To derive (34) we use the continuous time balance sheet constraint. The term $2p^*_{E,3}$ comes from using the approximation:

$$p^*_E(t, t + h, t + 2h, h) \approx p^*_E(t, t + h, t + h, h) + p^*_{E,3}(t, t + h, t + h, h)h.$$

11 If income and expenditure flows between t and $t + h$ were to constitute sources and uses of funds that could be allocated to beginning-of-period asset stocks, at t, beginning-of-period and end-of-period models would be virtually identical. Beginning-of-period asset demands like $E^d(t, t, t, h)$ would be the asset stocks people plan to carry over to the next period, i.e., in equilibrium, $E^d(t, t, t, h) = E(t + h)$, etc. A single budget constraint would link beginning-of-period asset demands at t and other income and outlay flows from t to $t + h$. The only difference with the end-of-period model would be that in the end-of-period model asset sellers carry the asset stocks from the market date at t to the delivery date at $t + h$. In the beginning-of-period model asset purchases carry the asset stocks from one market date at t to the next market date at $t + h$.
12 This is not to say that the instaneous portfolio demand $E^d(t, t, t, h)$ cannot be 'independent' of the saving decision in the sense that the reallocation of existing net worth may depend only on current (spot) prices and on spot prices expected one period from now. By analogy with the theory of investment of firms (e.g., Gould [1968]), such 'independence' will prevail when portfolio readjustment is costless. It is the absence of transactions and adjustment costs that makes for such independence, not the beginning-of-period specification *per se*. There also is no logical requirement that a beginning-of-period model be characterized by complete absence of transactions costs. The amount of instantaneous portfolio rebalancing is admittedly likely to decrease as transactions costs increase.
13 Compare (44), the continuous version of Walras' Law in the beginning-of-period model, with (18) the continuous version of Walras' Law in the end-of-period model. The former requires the existence of continuous first order partial derivatives of physical asset demand functions such as E^d_3 and E^d_4 and the existence of first order partial derivatives of price functions such as $p_{E,2}$ and $P_{E,3}$. When we consider the real asset demand functions and the expectation functions underlying these physical demand functions, we find that the conditions for the existence of a continuous version of the end-of-period model are slightly stricter than those for the existence of a continuous version of the beginning-of-period model; the former requires there to be a continuous second-order partial derivative of the expectations function with respect to its third argument; *vide* $p^*_E(t, t + h, t + 2h, h)$ in (12).
14 Note that (43) is used to establish this equivalence.

15 'Equilibrium' can be interpreted broadly so as to include quantity-constrained excess supply or excess demand situations and other 'non-Walrasian' equilibria.
16 The consequences of confusing beginning-of-period and end-of-period specifications have been brought out in a recent discussion of the relationship between asset market equilibrium and balance of payments equilibrium. Both Kuska [1978] and Miller [1978] conclude, erroneously, that asset market equilibrium requires balance-of-payments equilibrium. (See also Buiter and Eaton [1978]).

References

Buiter, W. H., *Temporary Equilibrium and Long-Run Equilibrium*, Pt. I, Some Alternative Notions of Demand and Supply in Asset Markets, PhD Thesis, Yale University (1975), to be published by Garland Publishing, Inc., 1979.

——, 'Walras' Law and All That, Budget Constraints and Balance Sheet Constraints in Period Models and Continuous Time Models', Econometric Research Program Research Memorandum No. 221 (December 1977), revised June 1978.

—— and Eaton, J., 'On the Almost Total Adequacy of Keynesian Balance-of-Payments Theory', Princeton University Working Paper (September 1978).

—— and Woglom, G., 'On Two Specifications of Asset Equilibrium in Macroeconomic Models: A Note', *Journal of Political Economy*, 85 (April 1977), 395–400.

Burmeister, E. and Turnovsky, S. J., 'Specification of Adaptive Expectations in Continuous Time Dynamic Economic Models', *Econometrica*, 44 (September 1976), 879–905.

Chand, S., 'Period Analysis and Continuous Analysis in Patinkin's Macroeconomic Model – A Critical Note', *Journal of Economic Theory*, 6 (October, 1973), 520–4.

Foley, D. K., 'On Two Specifications of Asset Equilibrium in Macroeconomic Models', *Journal of Political Economy*, 83 (April, 1975), 305–24.

Gould, J. P., 'Adjustment Costs in the Theory of Investment of the Firm', *Review of Economic Studies*, 35 (1968), 47–55.

Hellwig, M., 'The Demand for Money and Bonds in Continuous Time Models', *Journal of Economic Theory*, 8 (December, 1975), 462–4.

Keynes, J. M., 'Alternative Theories of the Rate of Interest', *Economic Journal*, 47 (1937), 241–52.

Kuska, E. E., 'On the Almost Total Inadequacy of Keynesian Balance-of-Payments Theory', *American Economic Review*, 68 (September, 1978), 659–70.

May, J., 'Period Analysis and Continuous Analysis in Patinkin's Macroeconomic Model', *Journal of Economic Theory*, 2 (March, 1970), 1–9.

Miller, N. C., 'Monetary vs. Traditional Approaches to Balance of Payments Analysis', *American Economic Review*, 68 (May, 1978) 406–11.

Ohlin, B., 'Alternative Theories of the Rate of Interest', *Economic Journal*, 47 (1937), 241–52.

Turnovsky, S. J., 'On the Formulation of Continuous Time Macroeconomic Models with Asset Accumulation', *International Economic Review*, 18 (February, 1977), 1–27.

—— and Burmeister, E. 'Perfect Foresight, Expectational Consistency and Macroeconomic Equilibrium', *Journal of Political Economy*, 85 (April, 1977), 379–93.

Index

Note: References to authors who have been mentioned frequently have generally been subdivided according to chapter headings.